MEMORIES
& DREAMS

OFFICIAL PROGRAMME AND SPORTS MAGAZINE

MAPLE LEAF
Gardens

25¢

MAPLE LEAF GARDENS
MEMORIES
& DREAMS
1931-1999

Maple Leaf Sports and Entertainment, Ltd.

A
Dan Diamond and Associates
Mint Publishers
Book

Published by:
Maple Leaf Sports and Entertainment, Ltd.
Air Canada Centre
40 Bay Street, Suite 300
Toronto, Ontario M5J 2X2
Canada

Editor: David Kilgour
Design: Andrew Smith
Page composition: Andrew Smith Graphics Inc.

For Dan Diamond and Associates, Inc.
Managing editor: Eric Zweig
Contributing editors: Ralph Dinger, James Duplacey,
Ernie Fitzsimmons
Assistant editor: Paul Bontje
Project manager: Dan Diamond

ISBN 0-920445-61-6

Printed in Canada

10 9 8 7 6 5 4 3 2 1

A
Dan Diamond and Associates
Mint Publishers
Book

CONTENTS

Looking west on Carlton Street on June 26, 1931. Toronto Transit Commission workers tear up the intersection at Church Street. Fenced off behind the TTC crews is the Maple Leaf Gardens construction site.

Setting The Stage

The facade of the Gardens is festooned with Union Jacks, displaying Canada's—and Conn Smythe's—patriotism during the early years of World War II.

Though many mocked his plan to build a new arena during the Depression, Conn Smythe knew that people would come. Hockey fans flocked to the Gardens in record numbers from the very beginning. The banners mark the success of the Maple Leafs and other Toronto teams.

In the early days of the Gardens,
grey seats were benches rather than chairs.

INTRODUCTION

PAUL QUARRINGTON

THINGS CHANGE.

It's a glib statement, but hard to argue with. Things change.

There is no such thing as permanence. Even a huge physical object like the Sphinx is disappearing, eaten away, day by day, by wind and sand. Eventually it will be gone, and even though the change may stretch out over eons, there will be Gizans who stop one day, stare at the emptiness in the desert, and wonder aloud, "Didn't there used to be something sitting over there?" My point is two-fold: 1) people are always caught off-guard, no matter how inevitable the change, no matter how long coming, and 2) as Joni Mitchell put it, you don't know what you've got 'til it's gone.

I'm a Torontonian, by birth and constant residence, so instead of the Sphinx I have Maple Leaf Gardens. And I'm not just making the analogy to the Sphinx because of the building's illusory permanence. For me Maple Leaf Gardens also had an oracular function: the marquee overhanging Carlton Street answered a vital question: "Who are the Leafs playing next?" At least part of me expected the building to be there always, to be home to the Toronto Maple Leafs. Oh, certainly, I knew that all the other "original six" professional hockey arenas had disappeared, eroded by sand and time. And I'd read enough of the business section to know that the Gardens had become financially unfeasible. But I'd only glanced at the headlines as I tore the newspaper apart, eager to get to the Sports section, eager to see how my boys were doing, and it is that part of me—all right, I'll admit, the unsophisticated, the boyish part—that thought things at Carlton and Church would never change.

The fact that I am writing these words, that you are holding this beautiful book in your hands, is testament to the fact that I was wrong. The Maple Leafs are gone from the Gardens, and though the structure may remain standing, things have changed. If you, like me, were caught off-guard, perhaps you can find some solace in these pages. You can relive the past, you can take part in events that, unaccountably, were held in your absence. And if it's true that we don't know what we've got 'til it's gone, this book is an excellent way of reminding ourselves what we did have.

This isn't intended to be a linear history of the Gardens. It's a book of memories, and memories are anything but linear. You will find in these pages a jumble of facts and feelings, often contrasting, even contradictory. After all, everyone sees and remembers things differently. So think of these pages as a celebration.

My job in this introduction is to give a brief overview of the men who ran the building at 60 Carlton Street (into the ground, according to some) and also to serve as a guide, to remind you of Maple Leaf Gardens' significance and history, and then point you to places in the book where the significance is more eloquently expressed, the history more learnedly expounded. My credentials are, I admit, suspect. I am not an expert on any facet of the Gardens except what the building means to me.

I don't remember going to Maple Leaf Gardens for the first time, but I know who took me there: my father. He was a professor of psychology at the University of Toronto, and early into computers as a research tool. Computers then weren't as compact as they are today: the one my father worked on occupied most of a small brick building on College Street. He would work there on Saturday mornings, and my brother and I would often accompany him. When he was done, my father would take us somewhere by way of reward. Sometimes he would take us to Kensington Market, perhaps to make us more worldly and cosmopolitan. I was fascinated by the sight of the rabbis slaughtering chickens, a task they executed with a grim-faced propriety that seemed entirely out of keeping with what looked, to an eight-year-old boy, like a fairly keen activity. To make us more cultured, my father once or twice hauled us down to the O'Keefe Centre—the Hummingbird Centre now, I shall point out hastily if a little clumsily. Things change, after all. I remember seeing Humperdinck's Hansel and Gretel; I remember squirming around in my chair and thinking that the opera wasn't half as much fun as watching sombre men killing chickens.

But most often my father would lead us east along College Street, across Yonge, and into Maple Leaf Gardens.

It might seem most natural if I proceeded along lines that you may have

Piper Bain was a member of the Toronto Maple Leafs lacrosse team. Mann Cup championship games were played in the Gardens from 1932 to 1956.

Six-day bicycle races were a popular form of entertainment during the Depression. Though this event was staged at the Mutual Street Arena, six-day races were held at the Gardens in 1934, 1935, and 1936. Cyclists returned to the Gardens for a final time nearly thirty years later in 1965.

assumed, that my professorial father was mystified by the athletic proceedings inside the building, while his two youngest sons hollered support for the home team and abuse for the visitors. But my father, despite the requisite professorial spectacles, was tall, well-built, and much more sports-minded than either of his sons. He would sit down and watch the game—we're talking about the Marlies, mostly, although one or two Saturday afternoons ran us into the evening Leafs games—and my brother and I would go looking for something.

And what, exactly, were my brother and I looking for as we roamed that huge building? I'll tell you what was most easily found, what we saw on our adventures. I remember legs, flannelled, the shoes invariably shelled with wet galoshes. I remember a cloud of cigarette smoke so thick you could part it with the side of your hand. Gazing upwards through it, I could discern scarves and fedoras, although the men who wore them remained rather faceless. Everything is grey and blue in my memory, and they remain my favourite colours. I remember the long troughs inside the mens' washrooms, which suggested a kind of organized rowdiness—hey, everybody, let's all pee in here!—that I found very appealing.

What my brother and I sensed was history. It was the nearness of history that excited us and sent us running through the hallways, up and down the stairs. Because when you're a little kid, history is indistinguishable from haunting.

We were looking for ghosts.

(Below and opposite) The war years saw Maple Leaf Gardens stage many kinds of fundraisers, including bingo nights.

In 1931, Constantine Falkland Smythe, the young sand-and-gravel tycoon, was planning to build a new home for his hockey club, the Toronto Maple Leafs. He had considered various options. He'd first thought to build his arena near the waterfront. He'd considered a site just north of Wood Street (the northern limit of the actual building), which would have pleased young Smythe as it was less than a hundred yards from where he was born. And for a while there was a plan to build on Spadina, making room for the arena by knocking down Knox College. But Connie (early in life he campaigned for this version of his name) ultimately convinced Eaton's to sell him the land where the Gardens now stands, although the owners of the company, whose flagship department store was just a block away, were more than a little reluctant. "The people who attended sports events," explained Smythe's associate Frank Selke, "were hardly the type to whom Eaton's catered." The main attraction for Smythe was the existence of streetcar tracks.

Smythe was a young man with a vision of a grand construction, born (I'm conjecturing) during his brief employment at Madison Square Garden. By 1926, he had distinguished himself as a smart and savvy manager of amateur hockey teams (that spring he'd shepherded the Toronto Varsity Blues to the inter-collegiate championship), so, that year, Colonel John S. Hammond hired him to assemble a New York Rangers side. This Smythe did, although Hammond, upon learning that the more recognized Lester Patrick was available, ousted Smythe as general manager. The circumstances involving his dismissal have become part of hockey lore: Colonel Hammond shortchanged Smythe, paying him only $7,500 of an agreed-upon $10,000. Some time later, Madison Square Garden president Tex Rickard made good on the money; Smythe, betting on college football and hockey games, soon parlayed $2,500 into $10,000, and that was his nut. He used it to buy a thirty-day option to purchase the Toronto St. Patricks, bottom-dwellers in the still young National Hockey League. Conn Smythe knew the team was better than its record indicated. He had a keen eye for talent, and saw that the St. Pats had at least two outstanding players, Irvine "Ace" Bailey and Clarence "Happy" Day.

The first thing he did was change the name, which he considered a sop to the Toronto Irish population. He thought about what to put across their chests. Smythe had fought with great distinction in World War I, and remembered the Canadian insignia: a maple leaf. And the hockey sides he had managed in inter-varsity competition had worn the leaf as well. So he called his boys the Maple Leafs and they wore that emblem across their jerseys, although for the first year the name "St. Pats" was stitched on their arms, because a) being a savvy businessman, Smythe didn't want his boys to get the idea they were playing for an entirely new team and therefore not under contract; and b) a sop to Toronto's Irish population was a pretty good idea.

It was perhaps also as a sop to the Irish that Smythe then went about acquiring little Francis Michael Xavier Clancy from the Ottawa Senators. But I suppose more than that, Smythe perceived in the feisty little defenceman a spirit that would infuse his new team. The Ottawa franchise was experiencing financial woes at the time, and had let it be known that Clancy was available, but for a steep price: $35,000. The new Toronto Maple Leafs were cash-

Four hundred women line the floor at Maple Leaf Gardens for an exercise demonstration during a wartime rally.

strapped and out of the competition. But Conn Smythe owned a filly named Rare Jewel, and although her record was none too impressive, she had been posting progressively better times. Smythe bet on her; he actually bet more than he'd intended to, taking umbrage at a remark made by someone waiting at the wicket with him. And Rare Jewel won, of course, possibly because both the trainer and his partner fed her half a flask of whiskey. With the money won by Rare Jewel, Smythe acquired Clancy.

There are many, many stories concerning the rather impish "King"—a nickname he inherited, his father being King Clancy before him—but space allows me only one. So here's my favourite, featuring as antagonist (as many Clancy stories do) the dark spirit of hockey, defenceman Eddie Shore. A play ended with Shore down on hands and knees. Clancy saw him there and couldn't contain himself, skating by and pasting Shore one on the jaw. Shore shook it off and then lumbered upwards until he towered above his little rival. "Okay, Clancy," he said grimly, "try that again." "Sure thing, Eddie," answered King Clancy. "Get back down on your hands and knees."

It is possible that the explanation for a very sad mystery lies here. No one knows why, exactly, Eddie Shore charged Ace Bailey, sending him to the ice and causing such grievous injuries that Bailey lingered outside death's door for days and, when recovered, never played hockey again. The incident happened while play was at the other end of the ice and Bailey hunched over, drawing in breath. There are those who think that Shore mistook him for the King, who was also on the ice at the time.

It is interesting, too, to note this little bit of history: because he was busy transforming the lowly St. Pats into the formidable Toronto Maple Leafs, Conn Smythe had to beg off leading the Varsity Grads team to the 1928 Olympic Games in St. Moritz. That distinction went to W.A. Hewitt (whose son Foster was then a cub reporter who moonlighted as a radio broadcaster, calling hockey games out of the Mutual Street Arena). W.A. Hewitt was the sports editor of the *Toronto Star*, and secretary of the Ontario Hockey Association. He had with him, as an assistant (or oversized team mascot), a twenty-five-year-old man named Harold Edwin Ballard. Indeed, young Ballard carried the Canada banner in the opening ceremonies. What had he done to deserve this distinction? Absolutely nothing, other than being so well liked by the team that they insisted upon it.

The first game in Maple Leaf Gardens was played on November 12, 1931. The Leafs lost to Chicago, 2–1, which was not really a poor augury, since they

(Opposite) The war was over by the start of the 1945–46 hockey season and these soldiers were recognized for their valour as the Maple Leafs honoured Canada's Victoria Cross winners.

N·H·L ALL STAR GAME 1951

OFFICIAL PROGRAMME AND SPORTS MAGAZINE

MAPLE LEAF GARDENS 25¢
TORONTO   CANADA

went on to win the Stanley Cup that year. As the team and fans celebrated, Conn Smythe rushed to embrace the Maple Leafs stickboy, his young son Stafford. The two were probably never again so close.

Though Lord Stanley's Cup only graced Toronto once in the 1930s, the team was a perennial contender throughout the Depression, reaching the finals on seven occasions between 1931–32 and 1939–40. And the best was yet to come.

Those were the years when everything was running smoothly and the Toronto Maple Leafs were without question the finest hockey team on the planet. I know that such a statement makes Montrealers bristle, but hey, I've got the numbers on my side. While it is true today that the Canadiens have won more Stanley Cups than any other team, it certainly wasn't true for the first half of the century. The honour belonged to Toronto. The most glorious decade was the 1940s, when the Blue-and-White claimed five of the ten available Cups.

The pivotal point seems to have been Conn Smythe's decision to replace Dick Irvin with Hap Day as coach. Smythe had known Day for a long time as a player—Smythe had even employed Day in his gravel pits—and saw in the man the makings of a fine coach. Hap Day certainly seems to have known how to motivate. The most famous example, a story that seems to have sprung from some Hollywood screenwriter's clanky Underwood, involves Day walking into the dressing room clutching a crumpled piece of paper. He stared long and hard at his players, who looked at the ground and avoided his eyes. For the Toronto Maple Leafs were involved in a playoff round with the Detroit Red Wings, and they were down three games to none. So Hap Day stared at the players—Syl Apps, Wally Stanowski, Gord Drillon, Bingo Kampman, Bucko McDonald (I love those names), and the superlative goaler Walter "Turk" Broda—and began to read the letter he held in his hand, a letter from a young girl named Doris Klein. Doris's family had moved from Toronto to Detroit, and she was suffering pain and humiliation there because her beloved team was losing. The Maple Leafs left the dressing room and began winning games. Every year, it seems, in all sorts of different sports, a team will lose the first three games of a seven-round playoff and the colour commentator will glibly state that no team has ever rebounded. It's just not true—the Toronto Maple Leafs did, in 1942.

And the Toronto Maple Leafs continued their winning ways until 1951. After they won the Cup that year, the man who had scored the winning goal, "Hollywood" Billy Barilko, set off in an airplane for a late summer fishing trip. He disappeared and, eerily enough, the troubles started. The Leafs wouldn't win another Stanley Cup until 1962, the same year Bill Barilko's body was found.

During the winless '50s, Conn Smythe began to distance himself from the operations at Maple Leaf Gardens. He appointed a board to govern in his stead, an aggregation of men who took as their collective name "The Silver Seven," a nod both to the famous early Ottawa hockeyists and, presumably, to their collective eminence grise. I will name them out of historical duty: William Hatch, Jack Amall, George Mara, George Gardiner and (here's where the names get really interesting) John Bassett, Harold Ballard, and, tapped by his father to lead them all, Stafford Smythe.

Conn Smythe said of his son: "He was rarely good at choosing his friends. If there were two boys, one straight and good at everything and the other a born troublemaker, Stafford would hang out with the troublemaker every time." Perhaps Stafford did not pick his friends wisely even as an adult—his best friend was a man his father called "an old-fashioned buccaneer"—Harold Ballard, eighteen years Stafford's senior. Many have described Staff Smythe as a man with a keen eye for hockey talent, but those same people have added that this eye was too often trained at women. People mention that he drank quite a bit. I offer these observations not out of sanctimony—hey, my eye is often trained at women and I drink quite a bit, too—but to illustrate how Stafford

These fans (below and opposite) are following the action during a tennis match at Maple Leaf Gardens in January 1953. The two matches featured Frank Sedgman versus Jack Kramer and Pancho Segura versus Ken McGregor.

Smythe was regarded by the hockey community. By citing Staff's weaknesses, most people were simply saying, "He's not Connie."

There were machinations in the Gardens' boardroom; three of the Silver Seven had made a secret pact. And one morning in 1961, the president of the Bank of Nova Scotia arrived at work promptly at nine in the morning and found an impatient Harold Ballard waiting. When asked what he wanted, Ballard had a ready answer: two and-a-half million dollars. When it became clear that the banker was inclined to loan him this money, Ballard got on the telephone to Staff Smythe and told him gleefully, "We got the money we need to buy out your old man."

Ballard, Smythe, and John Bassett took over control of Maple Leaf Gardens that year, right around the time my brother and I were roaming through the building's hallways.

Ballard, who came to dominate the triumvirate, was, you'll recall, the young man who had carried the Canada banner in the 1928 Olympics. But he was young no more—never was young, in my memory. By the time he impressed himself upon the public imagination—which he did with a force and determination very rarely seen—he was comfortably into a florid, well-fed

middle age. Certainly he would tell stories of his own youth, many of which he told so often that reporters finally wearied of doubting them and set them down as truth. Ballard claimed to be a speed-skating champion; he claimed all sorts of national victories and a few world records. He claimed to have set any number of water-speed marks when he raced motorboats, an activity he pursued with passion in his twenties. The few unassailable facts about his youth are easily set forth: he was born in 1903, in Toronto. As a young man, he took over his father's company, the Ballard Machinery Company, and ran it with a good deal of vision and success. One triumph Ballard claimed was a machine he made for a local restaurateur. Ballard liked the smoked meat at this establishment, but felt its slicing machine was too slow and cumbersome. He built a new, far more efficient one, and Harry Shopsowitz was able to slice more meat and serve more customers. Today "Shopsy's" is one of the most famous restaurants both in the city and on the planet.

But the machinery business never occupied Harold's full attention; that honour was held by sports. Even if his claims of world records are suspect—let's just say "hard to verify"—there's no denying the energy he put into athletic activities. When Ballard found himself a little old to play, he thought about managing. He managed the Sea Fleas, an amateur hockey team named after the speedboats he used to race. ("Sea fleas," Ballard once said sneeringly. "It was like riding a f___ing plank with a motor attached.") In 1933, Ballard took the team to Europe for some exhibition and tournament games. His gang became known more for its off-ice antics and bench-clearing brawls than for on-ice talent. Indeed, the Sea Fleas club has the distinction of being the first Canadian side to lose an international title. At least, that's the somewhat snide little factoid that sportswriters like to bandy about, even though if Ballard hadn't been the first the next guy would have been, and we can't blame our subsequent long-lasting failures in international hockey on Harold Ballard.

Being a sport-minded Upper Canada College boy—a surprising number of the participants in our tale attended that academy—it was inevitable that Ballard should infiltrate Maple Leaf Gardens. He did so by working with, and ultimately overseeing, the team that I, having an early bedtime away back when, saw more often than the Maple Leafs, the junior Marlies. That team was started by Frank Selke, who was with Conn Smythe in the earliest days. (The two had a falling-out, which is why these days Selke's name is associated more with the Montreal Canadiens and their wonderfully deep farm system, which Selke organized.) Frank Selke was, apparently, a great fan of the Duke of Marlborough, and his intention in naming the junior team was to honour that man, although the word proved too long and cumbersome for the jerseys and was shortened officially to "Marlboros" and commonly to "Marlies." The team made an enormous contribution to the Toronto Maple Leafs. The Marlies alone produced such storied players as Carl Brewer, Bob Pulford, Bob Baun, Red Horner, and two-thirds of the famous "Kid Line," Charlie Conacher and Harvey Jackson.

Both the junior and senior Marlies won national championships in the 1950s under Ballard's stewardship. And, almost as if it was pre-ordained, Stanley Cup titles quickly followed for the Ballard—Smythe—Bassett Leafs teams of the 1960s.

These teams were moulded by George "Punch" Imlach, the small, bald man who led the Maple Leafs to four Stanley Cups. Imlach had coached in the minors and was serving as the Leafs' assistant general manager when he was named coach by Stafford Smythe in 1958. This was seen by many as an odd move because Imlach, unlike all previous Leafs coaches with the exception of Conn Smythe, had never played in the NHL. But Stafford hired him, which lends credence to the notion that the junior Smythe knew what he was doing. Imlach immediately started fashioning a very successful—although oddly dysfunctional—hockey team. He acquired Red Kelly, an all-star defenceman, moved him to centre, and solidified his credentials as a Hall of Famer. He brought a career minor-league goalie to the bigs and wound up with the legendary Johnny Bower. (And when Bower was incapacitated, as he was during the improbable drive in the 1967 playoffs, there was another hockey legend, Terry Sawchuk, waiting to pull himself together and save the day.) This is the era of Eddie "The Entertainer" Shack and George "Chief" Armstrong. But I will always associate Imlach with his troubled relationship with two players. There was Carl Brewer, the cerebral and brooding defenceman, who clashed with Imlach, largely over financial issues, although the clashes were of such ferocity that one wonders if there wasn't something much deeper, psychologically, at stake.

There are historical repercussions; Brewer found other malcontents and a champion in Alan Eagleson, and was to some degree responsible for the formation of the NHL Players' Association. And, of course, there was Frank Mahovlich, arguably the most talented hockey player to ever wear the maple leaf on his chest. Imlach tried to motivate Mahovlich through intimidation and when the sensitive man began to buckle, Imlach increased his efforts out of frustration. Mahovlich was actually hospitalized on a couple of occasions, and was finally, mercifully, traded. It says something about his stature that after the trade the Leafs were able to ice the "Wing Line" (Norm Ullman, Floyd Smith, Paul Henderson), all players received from Detroit as part of the deal that saw the Big M, Garry Unger, Pete Stemkowski, and the rights to Carl Brewer traded to the Red Wings.

Some might think that I'm being overly harsh in my assessment of Punch Imlach, and it is true that my opinion is shaded by the so-called "second coming" of the early '80s, which I shall discuss in a bit. So on the plus side, I should point out that Imlach played a very large role in 1967. That is the year that every Toronto youngster—even though we may be in our mid-'40s now—has tattooed on the heart. That is the year that Imlach took the Stanley Cup. In the year of our nation's centennial, a team of aging shinnymen managed to vanquish the opposition to win that most prized trophy. For me, the defining moment happened late in the seventh game, when the Montreal Canadiens pulled their goaltender. Imlach, responding with uncharacteristic sentimentality (although I'm sure it was in equal part stick-it-in-your-face pugnaciousness) put Kelly, Armstrong, Tim Horton—i.e., all of his "old" guys—on the ice to defend.

Behind even these happy scenes, there were endless skirmishes and uprisings. John Bassett tried to wrest control from his two partners in the early '70s. He thought, with some reason, that their position was tenuous, being as both Ballard and Stafford Smythe had been charged with tax evasion, theft, and fraud. But Ballard and Smythe still had allies and friends, and after much battling, Bassett finally ceded to them his portion of the shares. Stafford Smythe died before his trial began, ravaged by worry and alcohol. His last words to his father were, "See, Dad, I told you they wouldn't put a Smythe in jail."

Conn Smythe wrote afterwards, "The moment has been with me ever since. I have thought about it and thought about it. Sometimes I wonder if I didn't imagine those last words he said."

In 1972 Harold Ballard went to jail for tax evasion—he served a full year in the Bath Correctional Institute near Millhaven Penitentiary—but he returned as the undisputed czar of Maple Leaf Gardens.

It was during Ballard's reign that I became a rabid hockey fan. I can even recall the precise moment: I was sitting in a tavern, reading a book and nursing

a beer while my friends watched a game on television. Borje Salming, the supremely talented Swedish player, took the puck from behind his own blue line, up the entire length of the ice, and fired it into the enemy goal. By the end of that rush, I was up on my feet and hollering.

After that, when finances allowed, I would go down to the Gardens to watch a game. What I'll always remember is the eerie quiet in the building. The air itself had a heavy, oppressive quality, and no matter how much or how loudly the fans screamed, the noise would be swallowed up and enveloped in hush. Toronto fans long had a reputation for being staid, of course. This was to some extent the legacy of Conn Smythe, who insisted on civility and decorum inside the Gardens. Men would arrive in suits, heavy overcoats, and fedoras, women in tasteful headgear and stoles. Perhaps these people didn't scream as much as fanatics in other buildings, and perhaps it was a tradition that persevered because of our decorous Canadian natures, but it is my belief that the Leafs fans did hoot and holler only to have the noise dissipate in the cathedral-like acoustics.

Still, it is undeniable that the Toronto fans were more restrained than, say, American football enthusiasts. Although it has probably happened once or twice, it is hard to imagine a doughy young man entering the Gardens in bikini briefs, half his body painted blue and the other half painted white. And we weren't big on doing the Wave in the Gardens. I've seen a few attempts to start one rolling, but the wave would sputter at the north end and then fail to clear the little hop over the Zamboni bay. Some people cite this as evidence of the staid and Protestant Toronto character, of some inborn emotional chilliness. I say it was because we were busy watching the game. I would like at this point to make the claim that the fans inside Maple Leaf Gardens have been, historically, among the most knowledgeable hockey fans in the world. I put in that word "among" so that you can include, should you care to, fans inside other buildings in other cities, because I was asked to write an introduction to a book about Maple Leaf Gardens, not start fistfights with Montrealers, etc. But part of the reason for the staidness is that Torontonians were usually staring intently at the play, trying to discern trends and strategies. And if there were few huge huzzahs during a game, there were countless collective gasps and groans. If, during a Leafs power-play, the puck dribbled away from the pointman's stick, there would be a small groan from everyone the very instant that the puck cleared the blue line.

It is likewise undeniable that, should the team be playing badly, the Toronto fans would fall silent and brood. And since 1967, Maple Leaf fans

often had cause to do so.

Since 1967, to put it as gently as possible, the team has struggled. Toronto fans continued to come to the Gardens—indeed, even more came, because Harold Ballard managed to cram 3,000 more seats into the Gardens. He found other ways of making the building pay, like creating the Hot Stove Lounge, the private members' club. "Membership in the Hot Stove Lounge is so exclusive," Dick Beddoes wrote in his book Pal Hal, "that anyone listed in the Metro Toronto telephone directory can get in." It is certainly true that some of Ballard's actions were detrimental to the lore and legend of Maple Leaf Gardens. The transgression that stands out—symbolic in many ways of Ballard's reign—was when he ripped out and trashed Foster Hewitt's gondola, dismissing it as just so much lumber and nails. (A little point of information here, just in case anyone out there wonders about this, as I did for years: it was called the "gondola" not after a Venetian canal boat but after the undercarriage of a dirigible, which it resembled.)

Harold Ballard's actions directly relating to hockey were often no more thoughtful. He dismissed the threat of the World Hockey Association, refusing to take the upstart league seriously, and in doing so lost Bernie Parent, one of the premier goaltenders in the league. He hired Gerry McNamara as general manager in the early '70s after McNamara, working as a scout, had returned from Europe with two Swedish players in tow, the skilful Inge Hammarstrom and the virtually superhuman Borje Salming. As a general manager, however, McNamara would prove to be much less adept.

Ballard continued to muck about, directing the action like a bloated dauphin. He ran through general managers (Jim Gregory, Punch Imlach, McNamara, and Gord Stellick) with a tragic whimsy that was exceeded only by his succession of coaches: John McLellan, Red Kelly, Roger Neilson, Floyd Smith, Joe Crozier, Mike Nykoluk, Dan Maloney, John Brophy, George Armstrong. One story suffices to illustrate Ballard's antics: he was angry at Roger Neilson, "Captain Video," the former coach of the Peterborough Petes who coached the Leafs to their best finish in years, all the way to the 1978 semi-finals. Harold announced publicly, prior to a game against Montreal, that if the Leafs lost, Neilson would be fired. The Leafs did lose (achingly, 2–1) and Ballard told the television viewers that Neilson was out. But Ballard had no replacement, so he was forced to go with Captain Video for the next game. And as if he hadn't already humiliated Neilson enough, Ballard came up with the

Karen Magnussen headlined the Ice Capades during 1973. Here she poses with some figure-skating cowgirls backstage at the Gardens.

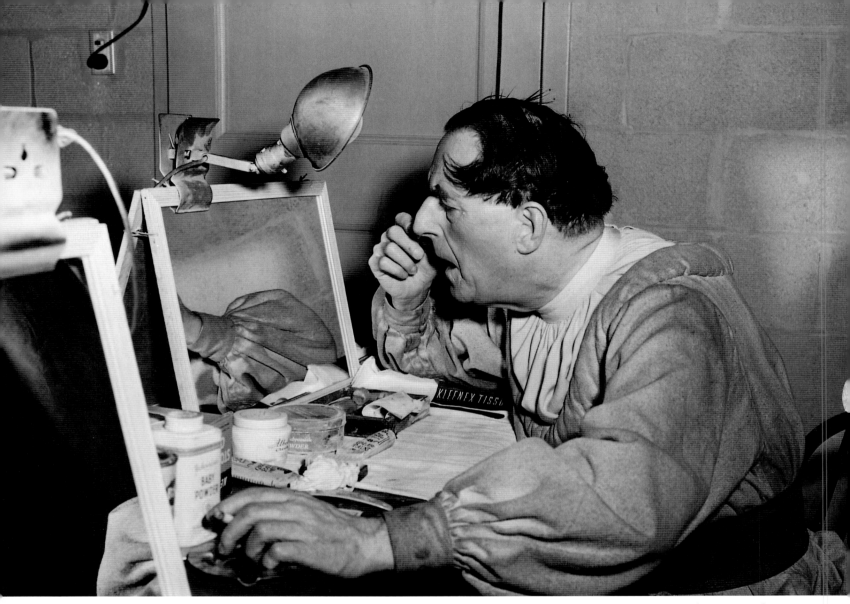

*Stanley Holloway applies his
make-up for The Old Vic
Company's presentation of
A Midsummer Night's Dream
in December 1954.*

idea of having the coach stand behind the bench with a paper bag over his head, to maximize mystery and delight the fans. Neilson refused.

The worst time came in 1979, when desperation combined with nostalgia convinced Ballard to rehire Punch Imlach. This time Imlach battled with Darryl Sittler, sensing that the popular Toronto captain had a firmer hold over the team than he. Darryl Sittler had both a fierce sense of loyalty and a no-trade clause in his contract, so Imlach, acting with all the logic and sagacity of the storm-addled King Lear, began to dismantle the team, trading away Sittler's linemates and friends, Lanny McDonald and Tiger Williams. Although not all of his trades were poor ones—Rick Vaive and Bill Derlago, acquired in the Williams trade, played with distinction—Imlach did destroy a truly competitive team. And because Ballard did nothing to stop Imlach—stood by his side out of a sort of twisted old-boy fraternity—Harold must shoulder much of the blame.

Ballard was cruel and capricious, no one could deny. But I will report this: I once met a Gardens employee, a man I will not name (not for legal reasons, only because I can't recall it). We got to talking about Harold Ballard, and this fellow had the requisite nasty things to say, how his boss was petulant, impulsive, bullying, cruel. But then he added, "But you know, if my son was sick and needed a really expensive operation, there's only one place I could go where I'd be sure to get the money... and that's to Ballard."

And I should say that whenever I was at a hockey game, I used to keep half an eye cocked at the northeast end, where there was a rectangle cut into the brickwork and deep shadows lying behind. This was the Bunker, and at some point during the game, Ballard would appear there to watch. He would rest his forearm on the ledge and banter with the fans nearby. There was always a grin stretching across his face, at least so I recall, even when the team was foundering. Ballard seemed to find endless amusement in the world, which I count as a trait too rarely seen. And when he appeared in the Bunker, King Clancy would be by his side, grinning as large (although the King would pay more attention to the game, and he would fashion his features into a rock of consternation and puzzlement when things were not proceeding well). Conn Smythe was indeed prescient when he thought to acquire Clancy from the Ottawa Senators—the little man's spirit did light up not just the glory team of yore, but the building itself. Clancy was associated with hockey for his entire life—as a player, a referee, a coach—and with the Toronto Maple Leafs for much of it. When he died, in 1986, I was one of several thousand Torontonians who marched solemnly down to Maple Leaf Gardens to pay last respects to the man who was the King of all the hockey players.

Ballard was, of course, himself an old man at this time, debilitated by diabetes and wearied by the internecine warfare being waged around him. The battle was fought chiefly between his children and Yolanda, his companion in the last years, a moderately attractive middle-aged woman who, the Ballard children were certain, was out to get the old man's money. Yolanda Babik MacMillan Ballard—she simply assumed the last name at some point—had been in prison for conspiracy to commit fraud and perjury relating to a forged signature on a phony will which related to a $3-million estate. A report for Correctional Services concluded, "The offender is a remarkable woman of determination and ambition. She is both manipulative and persistent and able to employ an assortment of tactics including domination and flattery." So the Ballard children were right to be worried. Harold himself seemed aware of Yolanda's less-than-noble motives, and often demanded that she be put out of the Gardens, or locked out of the apartment, but he always relented and let her back in, and they made up

Memoir of a Fan

In 1979, my father was able to buy gold tickets so I could watch my hero—Mike Palmateer—from rinkside at a Leafs-Canadiens exhibition game. I hoped to get his autograph during the pre-game skate and though I managed to get Walt McKechnie and Dave Burrows I was still disappointed when I returned to my seat. The game, however, took my mind off autographs.

Late in the third period, however, my appetite for autographs returned and I set out for Harold Ballard's Bunker to try and find King Clancy. As I approached, my path was blocked by a security guard. My mission appeared to be thwarted until I heard Ballard bark: "Touch that kid and you're fired!" He then gave me his autograph and engaged me in some friendly banter about hockey and that evening's game.

Although my opinion of Mr. Ballard has changed somewhat since that night, I still treasure that autograph and the moment in Maple Leaf Gardens when I chatted with one of the building's most notorious legends.

GLEN C. PHILLIPS
London, Ontario

with an enthusiasm that would be unseemly in teenagers.

Still, he usually had other things on his mind. When Clancy died, Ballard became fixated on giving his old friend a proper memorial, out of fidelity, certainly, perhaps as a kind of escape from the craziness that surrounded him (even though Ballard himself had created much of it). But most of his associates, spotting the emptiness near the old man, were too busy jockeying for position to do anything about it. The exception was Steve Stavro; he and his wife did much of the nuts-and-bolts planning, even to the extent of purchasing floral arrangements and laying them on each of the tables.

(Below) Fans enjoy the sights as they parade through the newly renovated Gardens on September 25, 1965.

As a boy, Monoli Stavroff Sholdas watched many, many hockey games at Maple Leaf Gardens—and whatever other type of game he could watch, wherever he could, because the lad was something of a fanatic. His family, who had emigrated from Gabresh in Greek Macedonia when Stavro was a young boy, owned a small grocery store on Toronto's Queen Street. And when he grew up, Stavro opened his own store, taking the name from a crate of produce he happened to notice—"Knob Hill Farms." Now the fact that you're all saying, "Oh, so that's where he got that name," tells us something, namely, that the store(s) grew very successful, and Stavro was able to indulge his passion. His first foray into the world of big-time sports ownership was as one of the creators of the Eastern Canadian Professional Soccer League. The newly formed board of governors felt that they needed some experience and visibility at the helm, so they asked Harold Ballard to serve as league president. He accepted, and soon Ballard and Stavro were close friends. More like father and son, many people have claimed. Ballard's own sons were busy enjoining Yolanda on legal matters, as was his daughter. Harold Ballard's relationship with his children was baffling, alternately coddling and standoffish. He was, it seemed, forever announcing that they were cut out of the will, that they would never inherit his kingdom. And, indeed, he did revise his will several times, so much so that upon his death, in

(Opposite) The March of Dimes and Easter Seals have long been a favourite charity at Maple Leaf Gardens. Here Easter Seals poster child Timmy stops by the "Hockey Night in Canada" TV studio for a chat with Jack Dennett and Ward Cornell on March 10, 1968.

1990, things became (improbably) even more confused at Maple Leaf Gardens.

Yolanda almost won the war, it appears. In Ballard's last days she spirited him out of his apartment at the Gardens and smuggled him to a tiny Caribbean island. There she found a justice-of-the-peace who agreed to perform the wedding—and agreed, moreover, to come to their hotel room because the bridegroom was not able to get around very well. As Yolanda preened, Ballard sat in a wheelchair, aged and addled. The justice made some idle comment about the upcoming marriage, whereupon Ballard summoned up enough wits to croak out, "I don't want to get married." The ceremony never took place, but it's good fun to imagine the chaos that might have ensued had Harold and Yolanda been legally wed when he died. As it was, Yolanda pressed on with her claim as his common-law wife and his children contested the will, which seemed to please no one. (Except, one suspects, Harold in the Afterworld, chuckling about the confusion he'd created.) Ballard left the bulk of his estate to charity; he also left a perplexing list of instructions for its dispersal. Various parties began to buy up stock, to seek to gain an upper hand. Harold's son Bill seemed ready to assume control at one point, and hockey executives Harry Ornest and Jim Devellano both owned sizeable amounts of Gardens stock. But ultimately it was Steve Stavro who survived the legal challenges and took over Maple Leaf Gardens.

Stavro has implemented some good changes, first bringing in Cliff Fletcher as general manager and then turning to an unlikely candidate as Leafs saviour, Ken Dryden, the brilliant and soft-spoken goaltender from the Montreal Canadiens (humph!) who stonewalled the Leafs many times during his stellar career. Things change. Things grow outward, don't they, from a small focal point, and maybe today we've grown beyond a petty rivalry with the Montreal Canadiens. Today, players don't come just from our frosty provinces, they come from all corners of the globe. And as people like to say so often, sport has become big business. (Although I think Constantine Falkland Smythe would have been mighty surprised to learn that it was ever anything but.) Salaries have grown to such an extent that the economics of the old arena are simply no longer viable. The Toronto Maple Leafs, and their fans, have outgrown the Gardens, even though the place once seemed so huge, almost endless, when I was boy of eight and roaming around inside it.

Speaking of that, I was lucky, wasn't I? I will write what some of you may have been thinking since the beginning of this introduction, that my father was foolish to let my brother and me wander alone through the Gardens. Even though he was a professor of psychology at the University of Toronto, it never occurred to my father that there might be men with a

Wrestling has a long history at Maple Leaf Gardens and all of the mat game's greatest stars have called the Gardens home at one time or another. For much of the 1970s, the Sheik, at left, seen here battling Chris Markoff, was the villain fans loved to hate. Note the toes of the Sheik's wrestling boots.

particular sickness lurking inside that building. But there were.

My instinct is to not name names. I want to protect the innocent, to cast the guilty into the realm of the forgotten. But it seems to me that the young man who first spoke of the child molestation going on inside Maple Leaf Gardens possessed considerable courage, so I will name him: Martin Kruze. And Kruze's suicide—which occurred just after one of the guilty parties, Gordon Stuckless, a longtime Gardens employee, was sentenced—serves to show how devastating these crimes are. And it was not just this isolated circumstance, although no one is certain how widespread, how pervasive, it all was. Basically, there were men who used the magic of the Gardens to lure young boys inside, there to commit crimes against them. It is always disheartening to find out just how inhuman human beings can be, although part of me—hardened by years of newspaper reading—is hardly surprised that a sports arena serves as a magnet both for young men and for the creatures that lust after them. It's ironic, too, to realize that this is a perverted aspect of Ballard's quirky, erratic philanthropy: he liked to give lonely men a place to be, not realizing that their loneliness often resulted from psychopathy.

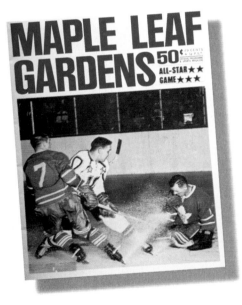

It's a shameful piece of history, but it's important to remember that it is that, history. Things change. With the Maple Leafs gone, Maple Leaf Gardens has ceased to function. It is no longer Maple Leaf Gardens. The structure will continue standing—for some length of time, at any rate—and the OHL Junior St. Michael's Majors will play home games there. But the ghosts—the ghosts of men who built the arena, the ghosts of men who played there, the ghosts of children, like my brother and I, who roamed Maple Leaf Gardens—will be set free.

That is the story of Maple Leaf Gardens in a nutshell, and although it is quite a large and cumbersome nutshell, there was much that was left out. Fortunately, the editors have assembled a stellar group of top-notch writers with nutshells of their own.

In Part I, "Setting the Stage," my friend Charlie Wilkins (Charles, I guess I should say, being as I'm mentioning Charlie in this handsome and elegant book) knows as much about the building of the Gardens as anyone and has written a wonderful essay entitled "Maple Leaf Gardens (and how it got that way)." Readers are fortunate to benefit from Charlie's meticulous research, although he stopped short (fearful of the boredom factor of lists, as any fine writer would be) in detailing the materials used in the building. I myself have no qualms: Maple Leaf Gardens consists of 750,000 bricks, 230,000 concrete blocks, 77,500 bags of

cement, 950,000 board-feet of lumber, 540 kegs of nails, and 14 miles of pipe.

Oh, yeah, I remember that last item from my childhood. It was often recited by my friends and myself. Although we had trouble remembering anything they taught us at school, we could all glibly chant that they needed 14 miles of pipe to carry the 16,000 gallons of brine needed to make the ice. We didn't understand how pipes full of brine would help in the making of ice, mostly because we had no clear idea what brine was. I didn't truly understand the process until my adulthood, when I saw an old film that explained how the brine wouldn't freeze at 0° C, how it would travel through the 14 miles of pipe and cool everything down. The film also contained a remarkable revelation—the ice surface was painted. I watched in amazement as a man standing beside a canister, clutching a hose, sprayed paint in a methodical manner. I had always assumed that the ice was white, like an ice-cube broken out of a tray.

Of course, as Wilkins's essay reminds us so trenchantly, Maple Leaf Gardens is more than just a glorified ice rink. Indeed, I was surprised to learn that in its earliest days the Gardens was a true entertainment centre; it housed a bowling alley, a billiards room, and a gymnasium. And the arena itself was used by the great speakers of the time, political leaders like Winston Churchill and R.B. Bennett (he was prime minister back then— don't worry, I didn't know either.) The popular preacher Denton Massey taught huge Bible classes in the hall. (My grandfather, an adherent of Massey's watered-down Christianity, attended these.) Maple Leaf Gardens has been used for all manner of sport (tennis, roller derby) and spectacle (the Buster Crabbe Water Follies, for example), and many, many circuses.

I suppose every event was a circus, in a way, and the Gardens a kind of brick big-top. For every event, excited crowds clogged the intersection of Yonge and College. (I know that the Gardens is technically at Church and Carlton, but I always think of it as being at Yonge and College. That's where people pop up from the subway to get swallowed by the river of humanity.) In the essay "In and Out of the Gardens," Rosie DiManno writes about how it felt to be there. Her writing instantly takes me back to my own childhood—my thoughts are claimed by memory, even though I don't think I saw a single act that DiManno describes, not the Stones, not Placido Domingo, certainly not Rita Pavone.

Part II, "Showtime," deals with the panoply of activities and spectacles the Gardens hosted. Hockey, of course, is the recurring theme. Three essays deal with different aspects of this most Canadian of sports. The venerable Milt Dunnell writes about the Leafs captains—as you'll learn, the honour of wearing the "C" comes with a certain amount of peril to one's career. Stephen Cole writes about Mr. Imlach in his essay "Punch." Stephen is one of those grown-up boys with the numbers "1967" inscribed on his heart, and his essay delightfully relives those heady days. "Senior and Junior Hockey, written by Eric Zweig and James Duplacey, deals with that level of the game that is the "starter" set for players and spectators alike.

Mind you, hockey—as wonderful as it is—is not the whole story. Interspersed are diversions into other facets of Gardens history. For me, the extra-hockey related activities are most easily divided neatly into two large

(Opposite) The 48th Highlanders, performing here in 1980, have been part of opening night at the Gardens since the beginning. (Above) Clarence Campbell drops the ceremonial face-off puck for Red Berenson and Dave Keon on opening night in 1970.

parts: entertainment and fighting.

I'm going to talk about the fighting first, wrestling and boxing (both of which are written about by Stephen Brunt). When I make those subdivisions, I'm not separating buffoonery from athleticism, because wrestling, as I first recall it, was a legitimate sport. Frank Tunney held many, many wrestling matches at the Gardens in the days of "scientifical" wrestling, of men with brushcuts, cauliflowered ears, and bulky, oddly soft-looking bodies. An exception there would be Lord Athol Layton, a tall, elegant English-born gentleman with a remarkable physique. He was a star when I was a lad, along with men like Bulldog Brower, Sweet Daddy Siki, Gene Kiniski and—most certainly— Whipper Billy Watson.

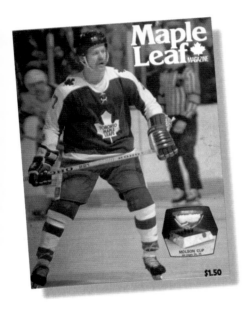

I was a huge Whipper Billy Watson fan, and apparently still am, because I think I can make a case that Watson embodied everything that was good about the Gardens, the city, the times. He was a smart brawler, for one thing—my mental image is not of the Whipper actually grappling with other wrestlers, but sidestepping about the ring, his hands cocked for action, his dark eyes looking for weakness and opportunity. Of course, when grappling came to be done, the beefy Watson was very effective. I suppose you don't earn the epithet "Whipper" for wussing around. But outside of the ring, Watson was a community-minded and generous man. I sometimes attended my grandparents' church, not out of some nascent Christianity, but because I might spot Watson sitting in one of the front pews. He devoted much of his time and energy to charity, particularly "The March of Dimes," which benefitted children. It is one of the saddest ironies I know of that a young boy died while trying to get Watson's autograph, backed up by the crowd into the street and into the path of a car. After that, Whipper Billy Watson seemed to redouble his charitable work.

I saw Watson fight on a number of occasions. My friends and I would purchase tickets in the greys, the cheapest seats, and we would stare down at the distant ring and scream support and abuse in equal measure. I remember sitting beside a woman, a perfervid but eerily elderly fan. While we hurled verbal abuse she tried to hurl the more physical variety—her program, popcorn bags, candy wrappers, and a few wads of kleenex that she scooped out of her handbag. But being elderly, the lady could never clear more than about two rows, and her garbage kept landing on a young thug who assumed that I had delivered it, because I looked like the type of kid who would.

I can't really remember how that situation unfolded, but I'll claim that just before the young thug was going to beat me up, our mutual hero Whipper Billy Watson entered the ring, and the thug and I were united in our cheering.

One important match happened before I was able to witness it: Whipper Billy Watson fought against Lou Thesz, hoping to wrest the world championship away from him. Thesz was the champion throughout most of his career, and today many speak of him as the best wrestler who ever lived. Those who think that all wrestling is rigged need, I think, only look at a photograph of Thesz— try telling that guy to do anything.

I'd like to take issue with one point Stephen Brunt makes in his essay on wrestling: he says that Watson beat Thesz. I say they battled to a draw which, following a complicated set of rules and regulations which I don't claim to understand, enabled Thesz to retain the crown. I have asked the editors not to clear up this disagreement, mostly because such squabbles are unavoidable as event becomes history. Anyway, Steve is probably right.

I remained a wrestling fan even as the spectacle became more and more outsized. I can remember attending, at the Gardens, something called a "Texas Death Match." I wasn't sure what exactly a Texas Death Match was, although I savoured the implication that the combatants would go at it until only one remained alive. The wrestlers were Bobo Brazil and the Sheik, another wrestler discussed in Mr. Brunt's essay. I suppose it is possible that the outcome was pre-arranged, although if memory serves, there was no "outcome" as such, things simply degenerated into total chaos. But it would be hard to apply the word "faked" to the proceedings. Bobo Brazil's trademark move was the "Cocobonk," wherein he would grab his opponent's head and then butt it with his own, usually producing a wooden sound that resonated even up into the greys.

I haven't been to a wrestling match in a while, although I see from

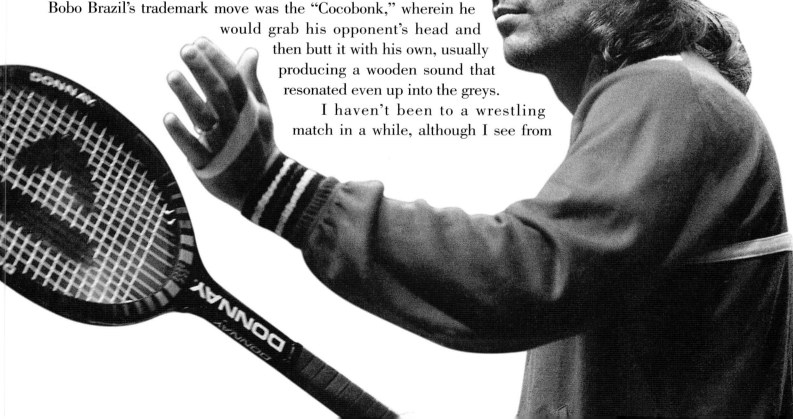

Bjorn Borg warms up for a Gardens match in February 1981.

the television that they are informed by melodrama and fairly obvious sleight-of-fist. Oh, well...

Things change.

As for wrestling's more legitimate brother, there have been many historic boxing matches at Maple Leaf Gardens. The most famous bout was held on March 29, 1966: Canada's own George Chuvalo went toe-to-toe with Muhammad Ali, then the undisputed heavyweight champ. The fight was mounted with much hoopla and excitement. Howard Cosell was there, but—according to an account written by Stan Obodiac, longtime Gardens publicist—seemed more interested in hockey-related stuff, asking people how Dave Keon was doing, etc. Chuvalo lost the fight, but impressed everyone (none more so than Ali) with his courage and determination. Stephen Brunt writes an exciting and detailed account in his essay on boxing.

There was one man who didn't think much of the proceedings. You'll recall that Muhammad Ali had refused induction into the U.S. Army, stating, famously, "I ain't got no quarrel with them Vietcong." This didn't sit well with Conn Smythe, who had fought in the First Great War and then, at the age of forty-four, had organized the so-called "Sportsmen's Battery" to fight in WWII. Indeed, Smythe had previously refused to let Ali fight in the Gardens, but by then there had been a changing of the guard at the arena. Conn Smythe no longer called the shots, and was told bluntly, by his son Stafford and Harold Ballard, that things would proceed as scheduled.

Ballard himself used to tell a story about Muhammad Ali—Ballard told stories all the time—that when the world champ was in the Gardens' private offices before the Chuvalo fight, he asked for a quiet place, facing east, where he could pray. Ballard mischievously directed him to the washroom, where Ali's humble supplication would bring his head near the toilet. Ballard would tell this story and then laugh, and his chubby face would explode with colour.

Another sport with a storied history is track and field, although I have to admit I always identified more with the pale, doughy wrestlers than with those lean, graceful athletes. (If you could see me, you'd understand why. I was just born looking this way.) But there are legions who watch these unadorned but thrilling contests, so Bruce Kidd has written about them. This is a remarkable instance of a writer describing with insight and eloquence a sporting scene in which he played a very important role.

As vital as sports has been to the Gardens, the building's reputation is also built on entertainment. Over the years Maple Leaf Gardens has featured all manner of spectacles, but it is best known as a venue for musical entertain-

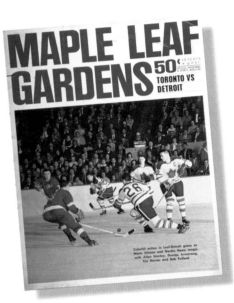

MAPLE LEAF GARDENS 50¢ TORONTO VS DETROIT

Colorful action in Leaf-Detroit game as Norm Ullman and Gordie Howe tangle with Allan Stanley, George Armstrong, Tim Horton and Bob Pulford.

ment. Here is but a very partial list of the artists who have played there: Duke Ellington, Bruce Springsteen, Elvis Presley, Elton John, Bob Dylan, Spike Jones, the Beatles, Bill Haley, the Paul Whiteman Orchestra, the Rolling Stones, Johnny Cash, Tommy Dorsey, James Brown, Paul Robeson, and the Village People. (I wrote those down in no particular order, although I did contrive to put Paul Robeson and the Village People together at the end.) To answer the query, trying to square the Gardens' musical reputation with its odd acoustics, let me assert quite bluntly that these artists sounded, to varying degrees, horrid. It's almost impossible for music to sound good in that arena. High notes get driven up into the high vaulted dome, there to flutter about like crazed pigeons. Bass notes and drum beats get driven to the back of the building; they bounce back and re-encounter the music half a second late.

But acoustic shortcomings notwithstanding, the history, as detailed by Richard Crouse in "Rock and Roll," is pretty damn impressive. Crouse, a diligent researcher, has dug up a fact or two about Elvis Presley's appearance there which will only add lustre to the Gardens' reputation as a musical venue.

Hundreds of fans take to the Gardens ice to raise money for charity at the Bobby Orr Easter Seals Skate-a-Thon for Timmy and Tammy on December 20, 1987.

Elvis Stojko's Tour of Champions has been making stops at Maple Leaf Gardens since 1994, bringing along such figure-skating stars as Nancy Kerrigan (opposite) to star with Richmond Hill's world champion.

Here's my first, and probably best, musical memory: when I was perhaps thirteen, a friend informed me that his mother could get tickets to see a concert by the Lovin' Spoonful. My friend's mother, who had hitherto seemed like just a normal mom, came up with seats on the ice level, second row, no less, and backstage passes. So we went into the bowels of the Gardens and hung about with the musicians—the Association were also on the bill, as well as the Canadian group, the Children, who I believe counted Bruce Cockburn among them—but I was distracted, still on the lookout for fourteen miles of brine-filled pipe.

Part III of the book is a section entitled "Memories" that features essays by three generations of Gardens-goers. There is the politician Dalton Camp (who rubbed elbows with the grand old man Connie Smythe), the author Rick Salutin (who became famous for a play entitled Les Canadiens but was ever a Maple Leafs fan) and Dave Bidini, who is, among other things, the rhythm guitarist for the Rheostatics. Bidini is also proving himself to be a writer of great style and originality—I was happy to include a piece he wrote in a little book I edited entitled *Original Six*. The book's launch party took place at the Gardens, in the visitors' dressing room. Bidini and I were very excited and attended the event with our skates smuggled in under our dress clothes. But—this is the startling information—we were shocked to discover that the visitors' dressing room is, well, not very nice. It's small and cramped, and has a tiny shower stall that looks like nothing so much as a high school vault of public humiliation, naked grey tiles garishly lit by a single light bulb.

I guess that the visitors' dressing

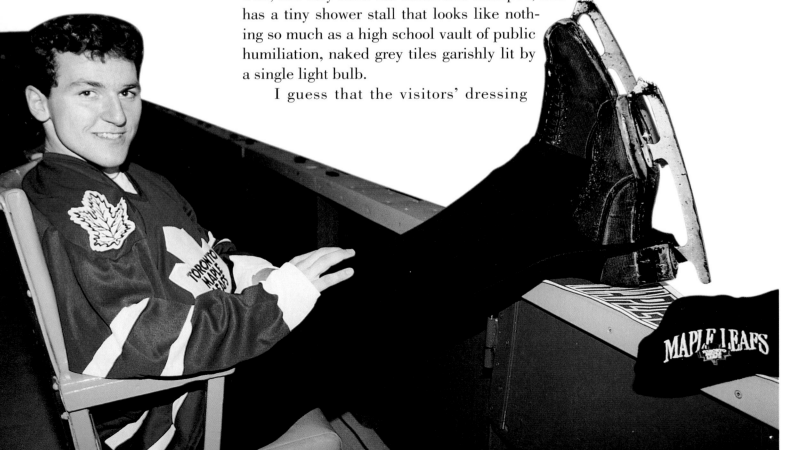

room isn't the only thing that's "wrong" with Maple Leaf Gardens. (My brother —the one I used to roam the hallways with—would assert that there is no problem with the visitors' quarters being shabby; indeed, he'd find impish delight in the fact.) The book's fourth section, "Post-Game," includes the essay "The Gardens: New Memories... New Dreams" by Ken Dryden, who first played on the arena's ice as a seven-year-old goaltending prodigy and is now president and general manager of the Maple Leafs. Dryden is aware of the building's physical shortcomings (tight seats, cramped concourses, etc.) but recognizes the importance of the special "feel" that the Gardens imparts to every event. The challenge, as Dryden sees it, is to build a new arena that feels as right as Maple Leaf Gardens.

The book you're holding in your hands also contains "100 Special Events," that is, a hundred occasions when the building sang a little more loudly with huzzahs than it did typically. And in the section "People of the Gardens" you will meet some of the men and women behind the scenes. There is also the Maple Leaf Gardens "Chronology," which lists thousands of contests, tournaments, pageants, spectacles, and extravaganzas held at 60 Carlton Street between November 12, 1931 (when the Leafs played Chicago), to February 13, 1999 (when the Leafs played Chicago).

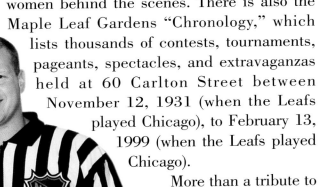

More than a tribute to Maple Leaf Gardens, this book is a tribute to memory. Anchoring the book are short pieces written by people of all ages and stations, beautiful little things that I would call "koans" or "poems" or "prayers" except that I might embarrass their composers. They are memories. Enjoy them.

Welcome your own.

MAPLE LEAF GARDENS

(and how it got that way)

CHARLES WILKINS

ON THE MORNING OF MAY 6, 1931, CONN SMYTHE CROSSED KING STREET in downtown Toronto, dodged a westbound Model T Ford, and pushed through the heavy glass doors of the Bank of Commerce (a building known then to every Canadian school kid as the tallest in the British Empire). Smythe had not had an easy winter or spring. As he once put it, "My leg ached constantly [from an old war wound], my head ached from financial pressures, and it hurt me inside to see the Depression gobble once-healthy businesses and send family after family into penury." But on this particular morning he looked none the worse for wear in his signature grey fedora and simple balmacaan topcoat. His chin was high, his moustache impeccable, his eyes as bright and hard as ball bearings.

He emerged from the elevator on the building's twenty-eighth floor and entered the thickly carpeted office of the bank's president, John Aird. Six other men had arrived before him, having gathered to assess tenders on the extraordinary contracting job that would have to begin within a month if Smythe's dream of a magnificent new home for his Toronto Maple Leafs was to be fulfilled in time for the 1931–32 hockey season.

Smythe was born in Toronto on February 1, 1895, and was raised by his father. (His alcoholic mother did not live with them.) He grew up in the city as a proud and loyal son of the British Empire—traits he would display for the rest

At the time of its completion Maple Leaf Gardens dominated the skyline around Carlton and Church. Gradually, the modest, tree-lined residential neighbourhood was transformed into a high-rise business district, including the Toronto Hydro building (seen here under construction in 1933), which still stands today at 14 Carlton Street.

of his life. He played hockey in school and first came to prominence as the captain of the University of Toronto team that won the Ontario junior championship in 1915 before he and most of his teammates answered Britain's call and enlisted in the army. Smythe returned to U of T after the Great War and graduated in 1920. Capitalizing on a postwar building boom, he went into business with a sand and gravel company which he would continue to run even after he became a hockey mogul.

Smythe kept his hand in hockey after graduation by coaching at his alma mater. His Varsity Grads won the Allan Cup as Canada's senior amateur champions in 1927 and added an Olympic gold medal in 1928. Smythe had been hired by the New York Rangers while still coaching at U of T, and his knowledge of the amateur ranks helped build a powerhouse in the Big Apple. That same skill as an evaluator of hockey talent would quickly transform the sad-sack Toronto St. Pats into the mighty Toronto Maple Leafs and his business savvy would result in fans flocking to the old arena on Mutual Street. By 1930, he was convinced that he needed a new place for his team to play.

For much of the next year, Smythe had conducted an exhausting, often futile campaign to find support for his arena among the nabobs of Toronto's business community. He had bruited and bullied and begged; had sent star hockey players to the offices of real estate tycoons; had dispatched his solicitous general manager, Frank Selke, to speak to any group that would listen to him; had mailed out 90,000 pamphlets describing the need for an arena. When all else failed, he invoked the Depression itself, arguing that the costs of labour, supplies, and land would never be cheaper. He pitched the grand new edifice as a kind of sporting Carnegie Hall, a place that would lift hockey forever out of the realm of cigar-chomping hustlers and back-alley knockabouts—a place, he promised, to which men could bring their wives or girlfriends, where dress suits and furs would be standard attire, as they were in the city's swankier restaurants and concert halls. Above all, he told potential investors, it would be a place that would seat enough fans, with enough money to spend, to balance the rocketing costs of running a big-league hockey franchise in a big-league century and society.

But at every turn, he had run smack into the Depression—into men who grumbled in his absence that it was preposterous to think any sane entrepreneur would attempt such a project when there was no money with which to build, and even less in the hands of those who would be expected to buy tickets.

But by sheer force of will, Smythe had won a modicum of backing from the likes of the Sun Life Insurance Company, the Bank of Commerce, and Toronto businessman Alf Rogers (who later claimed that he had been ordered by Smythe to put up $25,000).

In February, buoyed by the pledges in hand, Smythe had approached the T. Eaton Company, hoping to purchase a plot of land the firm owned on the northwest corner of Church and Carlton streets. Understandably, he felt that the Eaton name attached to his project would help dispel pro hockey's slightly unsavoury image. The Eatons, on the other hand, feared that a big-league rink would contaminate the atmosphere of their splashy new store just a block to the west, at Yonge Street. Smythe argued that the arena would not only equal the prestige of the store, but what's more would bring 2 million shoppers a year to within a block of the store's windows and doors.

It is a testimony to Smythe's tenacity and salesmanship that the Eatons not only sold him the $350,000 patch of land but also bought $35,000 worth of his stock.

In March, Smythe hired the Montreal architectural firm of Ross & MacDonald to give pattern to his vision, having been impressed by their work on Toronto's Union Station, Front Street Post Office, and Royal York Hotel. Meanwhile, like a plate spinner, he went from one backer to the next, reassuring, ministering, reinforcing, begging an extra $10,000 here, $20,000 there. When the Sun Life Insurance Company threatened to withdraw, claiming capital shortages (which Smythe interpreted as a shortage of faith in his dream), he went immediately to friends on the company's board of directors, who won the day by threatening to resign from Sun Life if it abandoned its commitment.

Conn Smythe (sporting a Leafs uniform) all but guaranteed a new arena would see the Stanley Cup return to Toronto. Coach Dick Irvin (left) guided a championship team in the very first season at Maple Leaf Gardens.

In early April, Smythe called for contracting tenders.

And, now, one by one, in the bank tower on King Street, these vital documents were being opened and read. And with each revelation of figures, Smythe's heart and mood darkened: $1.6 million; $1.7 million; $2 million.

In the end, even the lowest of the bids, Thompson Brothers' at $1.5 million, was some $300,000 higher than the sum Smythe had been able to raise. "A few hundred thousand wouldn't seem like much today," he said a few months before his death in 1980. "But in the early '30s it was a mountain. We had tapped everybody who had any money, not once but two or three times. There was no going back to them and nowhere else to go, either."

With the fateful evidence before him on the desk, Aird recommended to Smythe that he postpone his project until times were more prosperous.

Discouraged, Smythe emerged for a break and, in the hallway outside, spotted, Frank Selke, a man who, more than any other, had supported Smythe's vision for a new arena.

"It's over," Smythe told him quietly, "It isn't going to happen."

The two paced glumly in the corridor, attempting, as Smythe once put it, "to come up with one last rabbit" that they might pull from their hat.

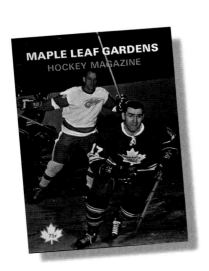

Selke ventured that if it was impossible to increase capital, they could perhaps reduce expenditures.

"Ya mean build it out of logs?" snapped Smythe, who had already pared expenses as close to the bone as he cared to.

"I was thinking of wages," muttered Selke. And in a moment of inspiration, he suggested that to get the working men paid, Smythe might consider substituting shares for cash. The boss looked at his manager, and two minutes later Selke was running up Yonge Street towards the Labour Temple, where, by coincidence, the business managers of Toronto's two dozen unions were holding their weekly conclave.

They had barely begun their meeting when Selke, who for years had been an agent for the International Brotherhood of Electrical Workers, lurched into their midst, begged their pardon, and breathlessly laid forth a scheme whereby union men who wanted work on the Gardens would receive 20 percent of their wages in shares—in other words, would assume some of the project's risk, but also the possibility of profit. Should the proposal be rejected, he advised the executives, 1,300 union men who could be employed at the site for the summer would most likely be splitting kindling or panhandling to keep their families fed. Selke's revelation that he had staked everything he owned on the project, including mortgaging his house, convinced them he meant business, and, though at first they balked, they agreed in the end to recommend the plan to their membership.

Selke sprinted back to the bank, summoned his boss from the meeting, which by this time had dragged into its third hour, and informed him of the officials' decision.

"Gentlemen," Smythe said as he slipped back into Aird's office, "I have news." And he described Selke's visit to the union hall. "We're not there yet," he told his investors, "but with the unions onside, I believe we can get the job done."

"If the labourers are convinced," Aird responded, "so am I. Our bank will make up any shortfall."

Smythe would eventually claim that the making of the Gardens had been sealed and delivered in that hour of inventive manoeuvering. And for years afterwards, he took pride in recounting how a number of the working men had held onto their shares, and had seen them multiply a hundred times—generally neglecting to mention that many labourers sold the stock immediately to their unions, or back to Gardens officials, who are said to have paid for the shares with a commodity far more attractive than printed paper to construction workers of the day: cartons of cigarettes.

Smythe was a hard-headed businessman. But he was also a visionary and a gambler (he had purchased the Leafs with money won on bets). And the

Unions representing workmen like this one agreed to their members receiving 20 percent of their wages in Gardens shares. The decision allowed construction to be carried out on time and on budget.

Gardens was both his greatest vision and his greatest gamble. His promises to those who backed him were extravagant: the arena would put hockey on the map, make heroes of its denizens, and put money in its shareholders' pockets.

Even Smythe, however, would not have tried to convince his investors that by backing his scheme they would be contributing to an institution that would imprint itself on the better part of a century of Canadian history and culture—and would eventually represent that culture in a way that no other building or fixture had done before, or has done since.

But that is what happened.

Sportswriter Frank Orr wrote in 1994, "Hockey is the national pastime, Canada's grassroots theatre, and since the day it opened Maple Leaf Gardens has been its main stage."

David Wise, a past chairman of the Ontario Heritage Foundation, told a Conservation Assessment Review in 1989 that events that had taken place at the Gardens "had not only given us many of our heroes but had helped to define us as a people. An important part of our history is contained in the bricks and mortar of Conn Smythe's monument on Carlton Street."

One need look no further than the nicknames that have been applied to the Gardens over the years to get a glimpse, however brash, of the building's legendary stature: "The Taj Ma-Hockey," "Make Believe Gardens," "Puckingham Palace."

Other dubs, such as "The Maple Leaf Mint," and "Carlton Street Cashbox," hint at the financial prosperity that Smythe promised.

On the morning of May 16, 1931, a little less than six months before the facility would be needed for the first game of the upcoming season, the demolition of buildings on the Gardens site began. So obsessive was Smythe about every detail of the endeavour that, even before the piles of old bricks were removed, he assigned one of his hard-nosed young hockey players, Buzz Boll, to round-the-clock security duty at Carlton and Church.

Judging by the evidence, journalists of the day were unable to envision the breadth or potential of Smythe's dream as it evolved from smoke and mirrors and decimal points into brick and steel and glass. And, given the Depression, they were as uncertain as anyone else of its advisability as a business venture. They gloried, rather, in the obvious, writing paeans to the building's physical dimensions—to the 750,000 bricks, the 230,000 cinder blocks, the 1,200 tons of gravel, and so on, that would be the substance of the capacious arena. Years after the fact, King Clancy, one of the Leafs' brightest stars of the '30s, recalled being "overwhelmed" on visiting the half-finished building "because it was so much bigger than anything I'd ever seen. I wondered where they'd ever find people to fill all those seats."

No less impressive was the almost miraculous speed at which the building went up. "Looking back," Smythe said later, "I don't know how we did it. I do know that part of it was accomplished because the men who built it believed in what they were doing. After all, they were going to be shareholders in it, weren't they? I was down there day and night that summer. I had to scrounge, beg, and borrow, everything but steal, in order to keep it all moving. And I did a lot of praying."

Which evidently did some good. For on November 12, 1931, with the paint still wet on its interior walls, the Gardens welcomed 13,233 fans (many of them attired in tuxes and gowns) to its premiere event, the year's home opener between the Chicago Black Hawks and Toronto Maple Leafs.

From the start, the Gardens and its contests were an unparalleled suc-

cess—in Toronto and across the country. It might be argued that what went on at the arena in those years was an easy sell to Canadians, who, under the stress and deprivation of the Depression, were hungry for the diversion that professional sport could provide. Certainly, if any sport could be sold to them it was their own sport, hockey, and if any team it was the Maple Leafs, who wore one of the most enduring symbols of the country on their chests at a time when patriotism was an almost obligatory badge of citizenship.

But if the "sell" was a natural, so was the chief salesman—a round-faced broadcaster with a theatrical style and a religious fervency to his voice. Foster Hewitt chose the location of his broadcast booth in the Gardens by going from floor to floor of a downtown Toronto building, and looking out onto the street at each level to see which prospect gave the best view of the people below. He chose a site fifty-four feet above ice level, and it was in that precarious location,

Memoir of a Fan

This (below) is a picture of my father Fred W. Norton welding the pipes at Maple Leaf Gardens with an oxy-acetylene torch. Ideal Welding Company Limited in Toronto had the contract. When my father was informed that part of his pay would be made up in shares he refused the offer and left the job. In 1931, in the Depression years and with a young family, he needed cash in his pocket. It would be interesting to know the value of the shares at the time of issue and what the return on the investment has been through the years.

ROY T. NORTON
Wasaga Beach, Ontario

More than any player, or even Conn Smythe himself, the man who came to represent Maple Leaf Gardens in the minds of Canadians was Foster Hewitt. In the 1930s, when Canada's population totalled only 10 million people, it was estimated that as many as 1 million would tune in to hear Hewitt on Saturday nights.

beneath an unadorned girder, that his simple box-like booth—"the gondola" as it was called—became the most famous broadcast site in Canada.

On Saturdays during the '40s and '50s, Hewitt had millions of listeners and received 90,000 fan letters a year. In a survey during the war, his name was recognized by more Canadians than that of the prime minister, Mackenzie King.

In 1993, a retired Saskatchewan wheat farmer named Jack Warner recalled that during the Depression, he and his family had "gathered around the radio every Saturday night to hear Hewitt's broadcast. Even though we couldn't see what he was talking about, we seemed to know what it all looked like: the game, the building, the gondola, the players."

"Our little world was brightened by those broadcasts," said journalist Dick Beddoes in 1981. "They were money from home at a time when there was no money at home or anywhere else. In retrospect, we didn't know how rich we were to be so well entertained on Saturday nights."

Punch Imlach once said that Hewitt "did more for hockey than any man alive." And when the broadcaster died in 1985, Trent Frayne wrote that he had brought together millions of Canadians "in living rooms and kitchens and bathtubs and cars and on lonely dark farms and in small snow-packed towns and in big brightly lit cities from one ocean to the other"—all of them united in a kind of Maple Leaf Gardens of the imagination.

Its growing fame notwithstanding, the building was never quite the architectural accomplishment Smythe had originally imagined it would be. For example, in order to save money, a pair of balconies on the east and west sides had been eliminated from the plans. The windows had been reduced in number and size, and cinder blocks had been used to line lobbies and entranceways which, in another decade, might well have been faced with polished marble or tile. There was a utilitarian plainness about the exposed steel beams and linoleum floors; and despite what was implied by the building's horticulturally suggestive name, there has never been a lawn or flower bed within sight of the place. (The term Garden or Gardens in connection with sports and entertainment venues dates back to the 1870s when the lavishly decorated Gilmore's Garden—later renamed Madison Square Garden—opened in New York.)

All of which is not to suggest that the Gardens was, or is, an aesthetic dud, as some observers have suggested. Its vast, lanterned dome (which give or take an angle or two shows the satisfying dimensions of an elephant's back) is one of the most pleasing architectural contours in Toronto; and the soft yellow brick of the walls throws a winter-long warmth. What's more, there are both drama and elegance in the building's steep windows and setbacks, and a sense of simple but stylish decorum in the art moderne embellishments beneath and around the Carlton and Church Street windows.

And there is a presence to the building, a sense of range and height and import that perhaps reveals itself best from the southeast corner of the Church-Carlton intersection.

More importantly, from the fans' point of view, the Gardens was a masterpiece of functionality, its interior space and unobstructed sight lines far surpassing those of, say, Madison Square Garden in New York or the Forum in Montreal. It was, in fact, the first big-league arena to be constructed without interior support pillars. For the convenience of its patrons, it was also the first to install a four-sided timing clock—the five-ton SporTimer, built in the Port Arthur Shipyards in 1932. (Port Arthur was one of Canada's foremost manufacturers of ships during the first half of the twentieth century, but the shipbuilders were also adept at constructing other industrial equipment and had first built a stadium clock for the Port Arthur Arena.) With the advent of television, Toronto's SporTimer would become the most famous timepiece in Canada.

The building's greatness was, of course, never primarily about bricks or accoutrements or functionality but about mystique, nostalgia, and heroics—about the transporting quality of what went on there: events that inspired memory and imagination, that became history, and in some cases literature or even legend.

Smythe himself was something of a legend—a war hero, a survivor of German prison camps, a man who said that he respected courage, honesty, and loyalty above all other character traits. And from the beginning it was all but impossible to separate Smythe's personal character and credo from the character and credo of the Gardens. There was a solidity and propriety to the place, an implied patriotism and ruggedness—all of it surmounted by a kind of abstract castellated flair.

The teams that inhabited the Gardens under Smythe were of the same irreducible stuff—as were the executives with whom Smythe surrounded himself. One of the early presidents, Bill Barker, for example, was a World War I flying ace, a Victoria Cross winner, who once single-handedly battled sixty German fighter planes, downed six of them, and eventually crash-landed, safe within Allied lines but severely wounded, his plane in tatters. Another employee was a First World War Russian officer named Logvinoff, who in 1918 was imprisoned with Smythe in Blankenburg, Germany, where he made a future for himself by giving Smythe a pair of fine leather boots when Smythe's own were falling apart. "After the war, he came to Toronto and knew only one man, me," Smythe recalled in 1980. "I remembered what he'd done for me, and, even though he spoke very little English, I happily gave him a job as a supplies keeper, which he kept until he died in the 1950s."

So impressive was the mystique of Conn Smythe's teams and organization that his arena came to be viewed as—in fact, became—a kind of shrine. Of some 40 million tickets sold for Maple Leaf hockey games during the Gardens' sixty-seven years of operation, hundreds of thousands have gone to people who travelled significant distances to be there. "For decades, even in the middle of summer, people have come from all over the country just to take a look at the place," says Don MacKenzie, a member of Smythe's Sportsmen's Battery during World War Two, and, from 1946 to 1990, the Gardens' building superintendent. "I used to show lots of them around inside, and as they'd get out into the seating area I'd notice that a kind of reverence would come over them, and they'd get quiet, and I'd see them staring up into the rafters as if they were in a cathedral or something."

Dr. Leith Douglas, who for three decades had been the Leafs' plastic surgeon, said in 1995 that in spite of his familiarity with the Gardens, it still felt "like a temple" to him. "I like to be there in the evenings when there's nothing going on, no one's around, and the lights are down," he said. "At times like that, I can hear all these voices from the past talking to me: Punch Imlach, Turk Broda, King Clancy, Foster Hewitt..."

The Gardens' reverential reputation has by no means been diminished or betrayed by the structure itself. In the days before the north windows were obscured by seating expansion, for example, the light that poured through them threw a decidedly spectral glow into the cavernous space above the ice. And photos and drawings of the building have as often as not shown it as a kind of canonical monster. Depicted from street level it hints at something on the order of the Mormon Tabernacle, while from above, the massive domed roof (once black, now white) suggests an ecclesiastical tradition about equal parts Muslim, Hebrew, and Christian.

And yet as fabled as the building became, there remained something pleasingly accessible about it. When travellers arrived, they could locate themselves not only in its myths and immensity but in the physical premises, the curious hominess that over the years has been such a notable part of its charm: the old-style ticket windows and panelled wood doors (some of which have been replaced); the old black and white photos, with their hand-lettered mattes and common framing; the '30s-style grab joint in the lower south corridor, where a passing visitor or player could until recently stop for a bump of caffeine or a fifty-cent order of raisin toast. To this day, the narrow flight of stairs up to the special tickets window suggests a staircase in some pokey dockside warehouse or tenement. And the metal shades on the twenty-four original floodlights above the ice are so crude in design and craftsmanship that they might well have been manufactured by a grade eight industrial arts class.

Nor are the myths exclusively the stuff of Parnassus. Building superintendent Wayne Gillespie recalls, for example, that the late Gardens president, Harold Ballard—whose niggardly habits were a manifest joke—inquired one day as to how many cucumbers would fit in the 30,000-gallon brine tank, a holding vessel for the salt water and chemicals that are pumped out at sub-zero temperatures through the refrigeration pipes beneath the ice. "He said he wanted to make dill pickles to sell at games."

The doors to the Gardens have been open to thousands of fans night after night and year after year, but only a select few can pass through the door to the Maple Leafs' dressing room. If the Gardens is indeed a shrine, then the Leafs' dressing room is its most sacred place.

While many features of the Gardens remain as Smythe built them, some have changed. The early analog SporTimer was replaced during the '60s by an enormous box-shaped digital clock, which was in turn replaced by the present computerized giant. Escalators have been added, offices and dressing rooms modernized. The seating capacity has been increased by some 3,000 (making for narrower if better padded seats). Since the '60s, the Hot Stove Lounge has existed on the Church Street side of the building, while a sporting goods store has operated on Carlton Street. The cigar store and the billiards and bowling parlour that originally occupied the Gardens' southeast and southwest corners are long gone.

For me, the Gardens was, and remains, a very personal piece of Canada's cultural landscape. As a boy, in Deep River, Ontario, on Saturday nights during the 1950s, I kept an ear pressed to the family's small Viking radio, to catch amidst the static whatever tidbits of Foster's broadcasts filtered through. I saw the Gardens for the first time in 1961, at a point when I was so addicted to the exploits of its inhabitants that, thinking back, I have no trouble transferring what I recall of that night to an approximation of what the Crusaders must have felt when, after a journey that had lasted months if not years, they laid eyes on the gates and towers of Jerusalem (whose walls, incidentally, are a similar shade of yellow as those of the Gardens).

Over the years, I have had several opportunities to write about the Gardens, and have always been somewhat frustrated in my attempts to state the essence of what the building has meant to me.

If the Gardens' appeal to me had dissipated over the years, I might find myself better able to reduce that appeal to words. But even today I cannot go into the place without feeling a pretty much undiminished version of the excitement and anticipation that I felt there as a child. And, in that, I can only assume that I am like hundreds of thousands of others with an emotional stake in the building.

When the building was recommended for heritage status by the Toronto Historical Society in 1991—a status it now holds—some of the most vehement arguments against its protection came, ironically, from its owner, the late Harold Ballard, who was terrified of being bound to the place, unable because of heritage restrictions to tear it down or to sell it if and when he moved the team. His agents argued, among other things:

• that the building was at best a lacklustre example of art moderne styling, an aesthetic lemon compared to the nearby Eaton's College Street building, which is also in the moderne style;

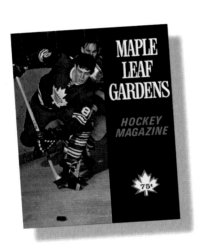

• that whatever architectural details were worth seeing on the Gardens were too high up to be visible from the street;

• that the glories of the past—indeed that hockey itself—had nothing to do with historical significance.

"The Gardens," said architectural historian Anne de Fort-Menares, "is just a decorated box."

In its incomplete way, her assessment takes the physical measure of the place but misses entirely its meaning.

Like any epic story, the story of the Gardens is a gathering of dramatic forces, the earliest embodied in Smythe's determination to see the place built—many more in the battles that ensued on the site.

Like any great story, it is also a flashpoint for the imagination, and is a reflection of the people and surroundings that imbued it with significance. In one way or another, it has always showed its widespread winter audience something about themselves—and in spirit at least has left them a little less widespread.

The Gardens is, in fact, not one story but many: of prime ministers and kings; wrestlers and rock stars. It is the story of Smythe's vision, of Hewitt's theatricality, of Ballard's bombast, of Imlach's cunning, of the brooding genius of Mahovlich, the hard-edged grace of Sittler, Salming, and Sundin.

It is the story, finally, of a country's fascination with a game and with a team.

A few years back, when the Leafs organization began contemplating its eventual move to a larger arena, Donald Crump, who was then the Gardens' comptroller, threw a wrench into the nostalgia mill by suggesting that Conn Smythe, being a consummate businessman, would probably have been quite enthused about abandoning the Gardens. "He always looked to the future," said Crump.

In 1931, Smythe invented the future for millions of North American hockey fans.

From today's perspective, he also invented a past—one well worth celebrating as his hockey team vacates the home he built for it, and moves on.

The man who built Maple Leaf Gardens preferred the view from the west greens above any other. Here Major Conn Smythe inspects his on-ice troops before departing with the 30th Sportsmen's Battery for overseas action during World War II. The woman seated in front of him is dressed to match the high standard Smythe demanded of Gardens patrons.

The birth of an icon

Blueprints for the new arena were drawn up in March 1931. Bids from contractors were accepted in April. The old buildings at the corner of Church and Carlton were demolished in May. By June, construction had begun in earnest.

In just 5 months and 26 days from the time the site was cleared, 10,000 cubic yards of concrete and 760 tons of structural steel were shaped into Maple Leaf Gardens, which opened in time to start the new NHL season on November 12, 1931.

June 19

THOMSON BROS. LIM
TORONTO

MAPLE LEAF GARDI
CARLTON & CHURCH S

NO.   DATE

July 6

July 18

THOMSON BROS. LIM
TORONTO
MAPLE LEAF GARDE
CARLTON & CHURCH ST
4   DATE *Jul*

THOMSON BROS. LIMITED
TORONTO
MAPLE LEAF GARDENS
CARLTON & CHURCH STS.
No. 6   DATE *July 18,*
ROSS & MacDONALD. ARCHITEC
JACK RYRIE &   ASSOCIATE

August 5

August 14

THOMSON BROS. L
TORONTO
MAPLE LEAF GAR
CARLTON & CHURCH
No 7 DATE A
ROSS & MacDONALD. A
JACK RYRIE &   ASS
MACKENZIE WATERS ARC

THOMSON BROS. LIMITED
TORONTO
MAPLE LEAF GARDENS
CARLTON & CHURCH STS
No 10 DATE AUG 14,
ROSS & MacDONALD. ARCHITECT
JACK RYRIE &   ASSOCIATE

August 28

September 11

THOMSON BROS. LIMITED
TORONTO
MAPLE LEAF GARDENS
CARLTON & CHURCH STS.
No 12 DATE AUG 29/3
ROSS & MacDONALD. ARCHITECTS
JACK RYRIE & ASSOCIATE

THOMSON BROS. LI
TORONTO
MAPLE LEAF GARD
CARLTON & CHURCH S

THOMSON BROS. LIMITED
TORONTO

MAPLE LEAF GARDENS
CARLTON & CHURCH STS

No *16*   DATE *Sep 2*

ROSS & MacDONALD, ARCHITEC

An Architectural Landmark

In addition to its significance as a hockey arena and concert venue, Maple Leaf Gardens is an important architectural landmark.

Stretching 106 metres along Carlton Street, the Gardens is a huge, reinforced-concrete box sheathed in buff brick with stone trim. Its architects, the Montreal firm of Ross & MacDonald with associates Jack Ryrie and Mackenzie Waters, drew upon two contemporary architectural styles to disguise the building's size and give it a strong but graceful exterior presence.

The first of these is Art Deco—the popular, jazz-age skyscraper style from the 1920s. The Gardens' façades are symmetrical, with subtle changes in wall plane and height to emphasize the central section. The windows are treated as vertical strips, adding a sense of height and rhythm when seen from a distance. Though built during the Depression, the design of the Gardens still includes subtle decorative elements, such as angled brickwork and flat stone panels with zig-zag patterns in the shape of an "M."

The second architectural style is known as "Streamlined Moderne." This sleek, horizontal style symbolized progress and the promise of a better future. On the Gardens, we see continuous horizontal bands of stone at the top and bottom, as well as "speed stripes"—stacked rows of slightly protruding bricks at the corners. Flagpoles at the roof line add a sense of ceremony.

Without doubt, Maple Leaf Gardens is an irreplaceable and sophisticated example of large-scale, Canadian 1930s architecture. It rewards those who stop to take a closer look.

TIM MORAWETZ

October 23

November 12

THOMSON BROS. LIMITE
TORONTO
MAPLE LEAF GARDENS
CARLTON & CHURCH STS.
NO. 19 DATE OCT 22
ROSS & MacDONALD. ARCHIT
JACK RYRIE & ASSOCIAT

THOMSON BROS. LIMITE
TORONTO
MAPLE LEAF GARDENS
CARLTON & CHURCH STS.
NO. 21 DATE NOV 12

The Gardens' changing face

The postwar world of the 1950s was a far cry from the depths of the Depression and Maple Leaf Gardens changed to reflect the differences. From the first facelift in 1955 to the new lobby of the 1990s, the Gardens continued to add modern innovations—from escalators to private boxes. Many of these changes are chronicled in the pages that follow.

Maple Leaf Gardens had been designed with the future in mind. Here, two construction workers knock a hole in the wall in the corner of a stairwell, revealing space for expansion during the building's first major renovation in 1955.

The Vezina Trophy winner in 1953–54 and runner-up to Terry Sawchuk in 1954–55, Harry Lumley shows off his locker following Gardens renovations in 1955. (Inset) The same renovations installed new concession stands in the hallways of the Gardens. Note the prices on the board behind these three attendants.

CARL

A Stanley Cup game? A championship fight? A concert? No! The attraction is the Gardens itself. Thousands of fans toured the building during an Open House to show off the renovations of 1955.

The great Maple Leafs teams of the 1930s and '40s established a winning tradition Toronto teams have always strived to live up to. Sid Smith and Harry Lumley's Leafs of the 1950s struggled to uphold the tradition, while the Leafs of the 1960s were proud winners of four Stanley Cup championships. Indeed, defeat did not rest lightly on their shoulders.

(Above) In September 1963, Harold Ballard and architect P. Allward examine the model of a proposed addition to Maple Leaf Gardens that would have extended the building over the sidewalks. City Council turned down the plan in February 1964.

(Left) The Hot Stove Lounge opened in 1963, giving the Gardens the first private club in the NHL. Here Turk Broda is the guest of honour at the weekly luncheon, which includes a question-and-answer session for Foster Hewitt's radio station, CKFH.

FRIDAY JAN. 24TH.
TELEGRAM-MAPLE LEAF TRACK MEET

7 P.M.
CANA

MAINLY BECAUSE OF THE MEAT!

Behind the scenes at the Gardens during the mid-1960s. (Above) The buffet in the Press Room was run by the mother of Leafs trainer Bob Haggert. Here she pours coffee for Gardens publicity director Stan Obodiac. Last in line is a young television personality named Brian McFarlane. (Left) The Zamboni is parked in the maintenance area, soon to clear the ice and promote Dominion grocery stores as well as an upcoming track meet.

Downstairs, a janitor mops the floor while in the executive offices (below) Harold Ballard holds court. The man in the hat is Dick Beddoes, who is questioning Ballard about the problems surrounding the upcoming heavyweight title fight scheduled at the Gardens in three weeks. Ernie Terrell was slated to face Muhammad Ali on March 29, 1966, but he pulled out three days after this picture was taken. George Chuvalo took his place and the fight would become a Canadian sports classic.

The neighbourhood would change—as would the car styles—and crowds would come and go. It might promote curling, wrestling, hockey or a concert—or pay tribute to the life of King Clancy—but whether it was the 1940s, the 1960s or the 1990s, the marquee outside Maple Leaf Gardens remained a constant source of information for Toronto sports fans. The canopy was refigured in the mid-1990s.

73

The march of progress has been reflected in the many renovations to the Gardens, but only three clocks have marked the time throughout the entire history of the building. (Left) The five-ton SporTimer, built in the shipyards of Port Arthur, was hung high over centre ice in time for the 1932–33 season, giving Toronto the NHL's first four-sided scoreboard. Here it indicates the dying seconds of a 3–3 tie between Toronto (T) and the Canadiens (C) on March 20, 1963. Known as the "Player's Please" clock for the advertisement it carried, the SporTimer lasted until 1967, when it was replaced by a new scoreboard designed by Gardens announcer Paul Morris. (Below) The "Dominion" clock could change the name for each visiting club and displayed time digitally rather than by clock hands. (Right) The current pixel-board clock was installed in 1982. Its display was upgraded in the summer of 1996.

(Above) The pipes beneath the Gardens were nearly fifty-two years old by the time they were finally replaced in the summer of 1983, when a new concrete floor was laid. (Left) An usher models the new "mod" outfit unveiled in 1971, while (right) a Gardens security guard displays the same lack of enthusiasm shared by most Toronto fans when Harold Ballard put the logo of his new football team—the Hamilton Tiger-Cats—on Gardens ice for the first time in March 1978.

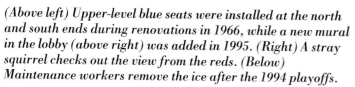

(Above left) Upper-level blue seats were installed at the north and south ends during renovations in 1966, while a new mural in the lobby (above right) was added in 1995. (Right) A stray squirrel checks out the view from the reds. (Below) Maintenance workers remove the ice after the 1994 playoffs.

CROWDS

Packing them in

ROSIE DiMANNO

MIDGET WRESTLERS AND MICK JAGGER, EVANGELISTS AND DIVAS, politicians and acrobats, royalty and scoundrels. But, most eternally and closest to the heart, the Toronto Maple Leafs.

Entertainers all, in their fashion. Whether they passed through Maple Leaf Gardens for but a day, or a night, or called this pile of yellow brick home; spent more hours within these hallowed and architecturally undistinguished walls than they did in the bosom of their own families.

This arena has been a sports and cultural epicentre over the past sixty-seven years, a Mecca for the most sparkling celebrities and those whose fame flashed and flared for only a matter of moments.

The crowds cheered their approval, occasionally hissed their displeasure, surged towards the stage and pressed their noses up against the glass. There was a time, in fact, when the venerable Gardens was the most notable Canadian stop on any whistle stop tour of international artists, all of them squeezed into those available dates when the heroes-in-residence were not occupying the premises. And on many of those occasions, these same Maple Leaf hockey players could be found among the spectators, clapping just as enthusiastically for a Bruce Springsteen encore or a Harlem Globetrotters exhibition or a Karen Magnussen lay-back spin.

Maple Leaf Gardens has been our Covent Garden or Hollywood Bowl, our

(Opposite) In 1960 teenage girls scream for their favourite singers at the "Biggest Show of Stars," which brought top rock and roll acts to the Gardens some two decades after a man in the stands at a hockey game (below) let 'em know who's a bum.

Greek amphitheatre, in fact, whether gussied up for the high-brow events or dressed down for the most populist of blue-collar affairs, bejewelled and wrapped in mink or slumming in jeans and toques.

There is no way of determining how many men, women, and children have spun through the turnstiles at Maple Leaf Gardens over the past seven decades. Millions, no doubt. Many of us came originally as wide-eyed kids, street scruffs, clambering up into the lofty greys. And we've grown old, aged along with the rink, wending our way down through the years and down through the greens, the blues, the reds, and the golds, as our economic fortunes improved or as we became more sophisticated in our ability to secure better tickets through friends and professional contacts and curbside entrepreneurs. Even as, over those years, the seats became narrower, the aisles shrank, and our knees were crunched up into our chests.

Some of us, a relative few, have been far more privileged than we could ever have imagined or probably deserved. Some of us were witnesses to history unfolding at Carlton and Church, without necessarily appreciating our - proximity to these events as they developed.

My first exposure to the Gardens came when I was seven or eight years old, in the company of my parents, when we attended a concert by a young tomboy Italian singing sensation called Rita Pavone—Italy's answer to Lulu, I think, or maybe Teresa Brewer. We took the College streetcar on a journey from the West End—just as future owner Steve Stavro approached on the TTC from the east— a trip that seemed so long and adventurous back then, stomping in out of the snow and blinded by the brilliant lights of the Gardens lobby, overwhelmed by the crush of bodies and the smell of wet mittens, feeding contentedly on rubbery hotdogs and syrupy pop and the warm chestnuts that street vendors sold out front.

We were from another culture, not the landed English, but we had ventured into what I then regarded as a Protestant shrine, a white people place, over-taken on this one evening by garlic-eaters, men with swarthy faces and women who wore their stockings rolled at the knee. And I didn't even know, back then,

In its own way, the history of Maple Leaf Gardens has provided a record of the changing face of Toronto. Whether it was Jewish political rallies, Ukrainian festivals, Italian concerts or Caribana, the Gardens has long catered to the needs of Toronto's ethnic communities. Here Italian Elvis look-a-like Little Tony performs for his fans.

how close to the truth I was; how much the Gardens was an embodiment of its original visionary, Conn Smythe, the proud patriot and sports entrepreneur who was ill-disposed towards francophone hockey players and who made the Maple Leafs very much an expression of Anglo Canada.

But a buck is a buck and the Gardens profitted mightily as host to a polyglot culture in sports, entertainment, politics, religion—every form of entertainment and diversion.

As an adolescent, I was among those who slept outside for several nights to secure Rolling Stones tickets when the world's best bar-band was touring stadium venues in its first hard-rock incarnation, long before Mick and Keith and the boys became the superannuated Peter Pans of contemporary music. And, like so many other singers who rumbled through town, the Stones donned

1960s Italian tomboy singing sensation Rita Pavone sports a Maple Leafs jacket and hat while posing with CHIN Radio's Johnny Lombardi and Harold Ballard.

Fedoras and furs were de rigeur *at the Gardens in the 1950s.*

Leafs jerseys at some point in their act, a gesture always guaranteed to elicit a ferocious roar of approval from the crowd. Then, just as predictably, would come a moment when the house would fade to black and thousands of us would flick our Bics, arms raised high, a thousand points of light, as if in a cathedral illuminated by votive candles. It was a rite of rock and roll passage and we were delighted with ourselves.

Protracted queues were a common occurrence outside the Gardens, twisting north on Church, then left on Wood Street, sometimes even extending up, up, up Yonge. There were never enough tickets to go 'round, never enough to meet demand, especially for hockey games. In the days when the Leafs usually played two home games a week, a small quantity of tickets would go on sale at 11:00 a.m., game-day, and many times I cut school to take my spot in the line-up at least three hours before the wickets opened, a long bus-subway ride from the 'burbs which would—if I was lucky—mean that I ended up in possession of a couple of greys, or a stray blue, but more often than not, nothing better than standing-room-only.

Knowing the Gardens primarily as a hockey venue, it was odd to come into the arena when it was being used for other purposes: the ice removed, folding chairs arranged in scores of rows on the floor of the bowl. The Gardens always looked denuded without ice. The acoustics were all off, the echoes unusual. It felt ... alien.

On many an evening, or an afternoon, it was alien. This was where the bible-thumpers for revivalist meetings screeched at us sinners, the preacher-men orating to the beat of the band and verily causing the rafters to quiver. Oh, the souls that must have been saved at Maple Leaf Gardens! Sweaty palms extended and waving to the ceiling, gospel music rolling over the stands; the devil was cast out and cast out again, exorcised from the premises with the same degree of revulsion more commonly reserved for the Montreal Canadiens.

All that fire and brimstone and piety. But it was an ecumenical cavalcade. Billy Graham sold out the joint on his crusade through Toronto, the Knights of Columbus presented a Living Rosary, the Hope United Church conducted widely attended Bible classes and Ukrainians celebrated 1,000 years of Christianity.

None of the churchy people found it unpalatable to share the space—though not at the same time—with the demonic messiahs of rock: The Who, who brought their twenty-fifth anniversary tour to the Gardens, or Alice Cooper in full satanic splendour on New Year's Eve, or the mop-head Beatles, who held a press conference in the venerated Hot Stove Lounge, or even the pelvic-thrusting King himself, Elvis Presley, who performed two shows in one night,

In the days before protective glass ringed hockey arenas, "railbirds" faced real dangers in the form of flying pucks, sticks, and elbows. These women cheerfully demonstrate their own personal solution.

These clean-cut kids were part of the audience for the Teen Towne Time show at Maple Leaf Gardens in April 1946. Simpson's department store sponsored several such shows, bringing in bandleaders who appealed to the youth audience in the days before rock and roll.

his first concert anywhere outside the United States.

On more swanky evenings, the likes of Placido Domingo drew opera devotees in satin and pearls, picking their way distastefully through rows of seats where the smell of popcorn still clung to the upholstery. Actually, what upholstery? There was no comfort or soft cushion to be found in the Gardens, most assuredly not before the advent of private boxes, which required whole chunks of public seating sections to be removed. Thus was the class system continued in the Gardens, though now the distinction between the have's and the have-not's was drawn along corporate lines.

The only vaguely plush environment within the Gardens was in the aforementioned Hot Stove Lounge, which has always felt to me like someone's drearily decorated rumpus room, with unimaginative cuisine to match. But the Hot Stove was a consecrated place, the doors firmly shut to non-members, and here the self-consciously privileged would convene, the matrons with their bouffant hairdos and their patent-leather snap-clasp purses. They verily reeked of status, if only the provincial backwater kind, in the days before Toronto became celebrity-mad and drop-dead cool, and when proper ladies saw their name in newspaper print only on the occasion of their birth, the marriage announcement, and their obituary.

I once interviewed wrestling impresario Jack Tunney in the Hot Stove. He shot his cuffs and told me, with a straight face, that the 'rassling was for real. Tunney disliked the subsequent story so much that he had my media pass withdrawn for the upcoming Wrestlemania spectacle. This was at the height of wrestling's mid-'80s renaissance as a broad-based phenomenon—not at all like the hardcore fanaticism of the traditional wrestling patrons from earlier decades, who never attempted to foist their bizarre culture on a mass market. I was reduced to buying scalper's tickets in order to cover the event but became so bored that I retired into the first-floor women's washroom, which boasts a comfortable outer lounge where at one time a constantly knitting, chain-smoking attendant always welcomed the company of idling visitors. Unfortunately, the crowd sounds are muffled in the lounge and, despite cocking my ear for what I presumed would be a thunderous welcome for the main event contestants, I completely missed the showdown between Hulk Hogan and Macho Man.

Few developments were as strongly resisted by the public as the smoking ban which was put into place, abruptly, in 1990, even before Toronto City Council passed its general butt-out by-law. Thick cigarette smoke was a feature of hockey intermissions, particularly in the stairwells, but political correctness was ushered into the Gardens with pro-active haste. On the first night the ban was in effect, I staged a one-woman protest and continued to puff in defiance, which brought first a warning from a member of the smoke police and then ejection from the premises by a real Metro cop. Generations of dead sports-writers must have been rolling over in their graves. They took away tobacco and

At an Open House to view renovations in September 1965, a brother and sister admire the sightlines from some of the new seats added to the Gardens.

gave us Sawmill Creek plonk in the press room.

At one time, the original press room—itself removed to accommodate private boxes about a decade ago—was little more than a gentlemen's lounge, drenched in the fumes of cheap cigars; the only other female in the room was usually the bar-tendress. There was always beer available in those days, despite owner Harold Ballard's well-chronicled parsimony. But after a female sportswriter—one of the first in Toronto, and long before the dressing room was open to women—wrote about sports scribes tippling on Ballard's dime, Pal Hal promptly withdrew all booze from the refreshments

What's new, pussycat? Some of Tom Jones's many female admirers look on longingly (while most of the men seem somewhat less interested) during a concert at the Gardens in June 1970.

menu. I think he welcomed the controversy because it gave him an excuse to slash costs in this previously sacred area.

The private apartment that Ballard maintained within the Gardens after the death of his wife—a place I remember for its dim lighting and bordello furnishings—has long since been converted into management office space. It's all quite unremarkable and conventional now. But once, once, that suite was the inner sanctum of Ballard's megalomaniacal reign.

It was from here, too, as Ballard went roaring ungently towards infirmity, that the unlovely Yolanda MacMillan—the crude yin to Ballard's vulgar yang—played chatelaine of the Gardens. Perfectly matched in their coarseness, alternately raging and cooing at each other, they provided far more entertainment, if often of a vaudevillian nature, than did the Leafs. They were a couple of grifters, really, who somehow made it to the top of the heap, scheming and chortling all the way. Yolanda, who ultimately took the name Ballard for herself—though she was thwarted in her attempts to marry the old coot—would play lady-to-the-manor-born as she commanded the household staff—the ancient retainers that Ballard kept on the payroll—to run her errands, walk her hideous little dog (after the cur dropped dead, she had its carcass stored in the freezer) and otherwise kowtow to her wishes.

Lordy, what a bizarre time it was; a circus at least as rivetting as the acrobats and dancing bears and trained tigers that also made regular incursions to the Gardens, though not during that period when Ballard decided the Moscow Circus, for one, was unwelcome, so he banned it too, as a nose-thumbing gesture aimed at the reviled Soviet Union. Just as well. The circus performers—presumably from the animal cast—were known to leave certain defecation calling cards behind. The hockey players would sometimes complain of "brown ice."

Maple Leaf Gardens has always emitted a corny and carny atmosphere. It's a building that cannot compete with the bells and whistles and technodazzle of modern NHL rinks where confections run to sushi and daiquiris, and patrons watch hockey games with cellphones attached to their ears. It has become an anachronism, no longer good enough for a generation raised on computer convenience and disposable everything.

So now the Gardens has become disposable too, all nostalgia and no currency. If the wrecker's ball does not claim it—the current laird assures us that won't be the case but we shall see—it has been fatally diminished all the same. The action that really counts, that's always counted the most, has been transferred to the Air Canada Centre, a modern construction that is only a distant cousin to the sweaty, smelly, grungy, wondrous arenas of the past.

Maple Leaf Gardens was the last of them. It's now a relic. A mausoleum of memories.

Bruce Springsteen and the E Street Band had the fans on their feet for most of two three-hour-long concerts on back-to-back nights in January 1981. Springsteen had failed to sell out his first Gardens appearance three years earlier, but this time Bruce was the Boss.

It's the opening night of the 1945–46 season and the Maple Leafs are honouring Victoria Cross winners from the recently concluded war. Private Ernest Alvia Smith, VC, of the Seaforth Highlanders drops the ceremonial face-off for Toronto's Billy Taylor and Boston's Milt Schmidt. Referee King Clancy looks on.

Showtime

LEAF CAPTAINS

Toronto's Sixteen C-Men

MILT DUNNELL

HALF OF THE GALLANT SIXTEEN WHO HAVE WORN THE COVETED "C" ON their chests during the sixty-seven seasons of sweat, blood, and toil at Maple Leaf Gardens have been traded, relieved of command or lost to draft or expansion procedures.

Shouldn't that be enough to make a likely suspect for the "C" yell, "Why me?" instead of gushing that it's an honour of which he has dreamt since the day he learned to say Zamboni?

"I'd be captain again and love it," assures Darryl Sittler, who hacked the "C" off his sweater and put it on the front pages of most Canadian journals.

"I enjoyed every minute," claims George Armstrong, who was a Leaf for his entire NHL career, a dozen years as captain.

That's dedication, folks, but what explains it, when you recall that loyalists such as Hap Day, the first captain in the Gardens, and Charlie Conacher, the legendary Blue Bomber who succeeded him, were traded while in office? Day was sentenced to the New York Americans. At the time, this was like being sent down to Peoria.

Slick centre Syl Apps (top right) alert for a rebound in front of the Detroit Red Wings goal, spent his entire career with the Maple Leafs and scored 201 goals in an era when the 200 mark was still a rare milestone. Apps became captain in 1940–41 and, except for the two years he missed due to military service, wore the "C" until he retired in 1948. Apps passed away on December 24, 1998.

And Conacher? He was traded to Detroit at a time long before the Red Wings had the kind of dough they lavished on Sergei Fedorov.

"Because it's for the team, man."

That's what they'll tell you—the survivors, that is—from Red Horner, who was born in 1909, the year Galt challenged for the Stanley Cup (you could look it up), to Mats Sundin, the Leafs' first European C-bearer.

Horner had put an exclamation mark—with his fist—behind that "It's for the team" edict well before he became captain. That was the night in 1933 at Boston Garden when he flattened Boston's Eddie Shore, an eventual Hall of Famer, who had just ended the hockey career of the Leafs' Ace Bailey with a check that is still recalled as one of hockey's ugliest moments.

"I had nothing personal against Shore," Horner maintains more than six decades later. "After Bailey recovered from his injuries, we had an all-star game at the Gardens. Shore was one of the stars. I went down to the railway station to meet him. We shook hands.

"We bore no grudges against each other. It was something different that night in Boston. What I did was for the team."

Conn Smythe, the alleged visionary who turned a struggling NHL franchise into one of the most profitable in sport and who quarter-backed the campaign to erect Maple Leaf Gardens during the century's worst economic depression, undoubtedly decided that very night who his next captain would be.

Smythe, rightly or wrongly, had been associated with a quote about not being able to lick 'em on the ice unless you could lick 'em in the alley, Maybe he didn't really say it, but his actions frequently indicated that he bought into the sentiment.

The politics of a modern NHL franchise can be labyrinthine: the agendas of club owner, general manager, coach, and players must all be balanced. And the role of the team captain in the balancing act has changed. Some argue that today's hockey captains are something like goal judges in that hardly anyone pays attention to either of them any more. They sit in their glass coops and flash their light when they think they see a goal scored, but everyone waits for the guys with the replay hardware upstairs to make it official.

Hockey players used to need the captain's advice in getting management to say why they were being demoted to the minors for less money. Was it because

Tough guy Red Horner epitomized the idea that you couldn't beat 'em on the ice if you couldn't beat 'em in the alley. A Leaf for all of his twelve seasons in the NHL and a Hockey Hall of Famer, Horner considers his two years as captain to be the highest honour of his career.

they hadn't been playing well? Or was it because management was still sour over the arguments that ensued before the last contract was signed?

Today, most players have agents to handle their off-ice problems. If they don't have agents, the NHL Players' Association goes to bat for them. The players' union has teeth and it has a collective bargaining agreement with the NHL's team owners.

Sure, a captain has the right to ask for an explanation if he thinks one of the striped shirts blew a call. But that's all he's likely to get: an explanation. Not even captains as articulate and respected as Syl Apps, Teeder Kennedy or Darryl Sittler expect a referee to reverse a decision.

But there still are many reasons for having a captain, Sittler maintains. He could be thinking of his own experiences, of course, during one of the Leafs' most troubled eras at the Gardens. It was a time when hockey was losing some of its old self-serving sanctions.

"Many of the players in any club's dressing room today are new to their

A worthy successor to Syl Apps when he assumed the Leafs captaincy in 1948–49, Teeder Kennedy excelled in the NHL through hard work and determination. Here he stands in front of the Detroit goal during the 1949 Stanley Cup Final that saw Toronto win for the third year in a row. "Come onnnnn, Teeder!"

Darryl Sittler is still a few years away from wearing the "C" as he fights off a check by Joe Watson behind the Flyers' net. On April 22, 1976, Sittler tied an NHL playoff record with five goals in Toronto's 8–5 victory over Philadelphia. He is the Leafs' all-time career leader in goals (389) and points (916).

clubs," Sittler argues. "A good number are from Europe and may not even speak the language. Roster changes are more numerous than they used to be. So you're talking about players who are looking for leadership."

Ironically, it was leadership—or perceived leadership—that contributed heavily to Sittler's unhappy captaincy. Club owner Harold Ballard and his general manager Punch Imlach interpreted leadership to mean unquestioned loyalty to management. Sittler was guilty of several sins, in the opinion of management. One of them was that he had a no-trade clause in his contract—something that Imlach, winner of four Stanley Cup titles during a previous term as manager and coach, found highly unorthodox. (Imlach had been rehired by Ballard in 1979 in a desperate attempt to restore the glory of the 1960s. It was in 1969, the tail-end of these good old days, that Ballard had concurred in the firing of Imlach by his partner Stafford Smythe only minutes after the Leafs had suffered an embarrassing defeat in a Stanley Cup playoff series against Boston.)

In 1979, both Ballard and Imlach used the press to make known their complaint that Alan Eagleson, then considered the most powerful figure in hockey, had too much influence in the Leafs' dressing room. Two of the top players on the club, Sittler and his close friend Lanny McDonald, were Eagleson clients. When McDonald was traded, Sittler resigned his captaincy.

Sittler is a member of the Leafs' front office think tank today, showing the flag from coast to coast on behalf of the club, but he hasn't changed his mind about the duties and responsibilities of a captain.

"I always respected Punch for what he had accomplished in hockey, but I couldn't accept his view that the captain had to represent management.

I regarded the captaincy as a symbol of the organization to the public. The captain must be for the players as well as for management. It's important that the captain make all the players feel that they are important to the team."

George Armstrong, who has been called the player's version of what the ideal captain should be, puts a slightly different spin on the Sittler philosophy. The Chief, as Armstrong was called, termed his approach the we-want-you principle.

"The idea that I was a better captain than guys like Syl Apps or Teeder Kennedy is crazy," Armstrong protests. "They were outstanding individuals. Me? I was from a mining town, the son of a miner. I was just one of the people.

"I was surprised when Mr. Smythe called me in at contract time and told me he wanted me to be captain. He added $1,000 to my salary for being captain.

"I considered myself the link between players and management. Maybe I did a few things that helped: I recall one time when [Bob] Pulford said he was going to quit and go back to school. He was having trouble with his contract.

We're on a bus trip and I sat down beside him. About all I told him was that I wasn't trying to dictate to him what to do with his life but, hey, if he wanted to know how the players felt, they wanted him [on the team]. I told him that we could win the Stanley Cup with him. I don't know how the contract dispute was settled, but Pulford stayed with the team and we did win the Stanley Cup."

Not only did Pulford remain with the team, he remained in hockey for his entire career: today he serves as senior vice-president of the Chicago Blackhawks.

"Another guy who was going to quit the club was Johnny Bower," the Chief recalls. "I went out to his house. All I said was: 'We need you. The players want you. Johnny came back.'"

Armstrong is still with the Leafs, of course. Asked for his official title, he replies: "The title is nothing. I do a little scouting of amateur

The longest-serving captain in Maple Leafs history (1957–58 to 1968–69), George Armstrong poses with Timmy, the Easter Seals poster child, in March 1967—two months before leading Toronto to its fourth Stanley Cup championship of the decade. The Chief played more games (1,187) than any other Leaf.

The Maple Leafs were Stanley Cup champions during five of Teeder Kennedy's first eight full seasons in Toronto. He captained the team to two of those championships. Here Teeder celebrates the first of those two titles with his arm around Turk Broda after defeating the Detroit Red Wings in 1949.

players when I feel like it." His wife, Betty, mentions that he seems to be in the scouting mood every day there's a game in the area.

Somewhere, out there, there could be another Bobby Orr, another Wayne Gretzky. Scouts have dreams, too, you know.

Armstrong might be surprised to know that Teeder Kennedy, whom he regarded as one of his choices as the ideal captain, considered the captaincy more honorary than practical.

"In [coach] Hap Day's dressing room, you didn't have anything to say during a game or between periods unless you were asked," Kennedy explains. "I don't think I felt any responsibilities except when I was on the ice where I might ask the referee to explain a call.

"Hap was a great coach and the players respected him. I remember the day [in 1948] I was named captain. We were in the dressing room waiting to go on the ice and Hap said: 'We need a captain. [Apps had retired.] Does anyone have a suggestion?' Turk Broda spoke up: 'I think Teeder should be captain.' There were no other nominations. That's how simple it was. And a great honour."

Kennedy was one of the fortunate ones who served in the days when the Leafs logo was a symbol of power equivalent to the Yankees pinstripes in baseball. It was an era in which the sentiment of doing it for the team was never stronger.

This sentiment prompted Kennedy into a brief comeback in 1956–57, but his loyalty to the club has been widely misunderstood. Most observers thought his return was dictated by Conn Smythe, who had two things in mind: a) he wanted to take the "C" away from Jim Thomson, who had been active in the first attempt to form an NHL players' union; and b) Smythe wanted a dressing room strong on leadership as he prepared to turn the club over to his son Stafford and his eventual partners.

"Actually, Conn Smythe had nothing to do with it," Kennedy advises. "My comeback was an attempt to help Hap Day, who had become the general manager, and Howie Meeker, who was the coach. They were in trouble with at least three guys [Armstrong, Rudy Migay, and Tim Horton] out with injuries. Howie and Hap both appealed to me for help.

"As for the idea that I wanted the "C" back from Thomson, nothing could be further from fact. I told Jimmy I would be back in retirement at the end of the season and that he should continue as captain. It was he who insisted on my accepting it.

"Incidentally, I never understood why Jimmy Thomson wasn't elected to the Hockey Hall of Fame. Especially in his own end of the rink, he was the most intelligent and effective defence player I ever saw."

Thomson never did get the "C" back. He was shipped to Chicago, a perennial NHL also-ran, as Smythe unloaded players who

Jim Thomson was a valuable stay-at-home defenceman who was twice named to the Second All-Star Team. He was captain of the Maple Leafs for part of the 1956–57 campaign, but his involvement in the fledgling players' union led Conn Smythe to sell him to Chicago after the season.

had been prominent in the move to form a union.

Sid Smith, who had preceded Thomson as captain in 1955–56 after Kennedy's first retirement, was in favour of the fledgling players' association too, but doubts that that was why his elevation lasted only a single season.

"Maybe I took the job too seriously," he jokes. "I know I had a terrible season. As for the players' association, it was simply an attempt to get more of a voice for the guys. What we had was a management-players committee composed of two owners, two players, and Mr. [Clarence] Campbell, who was paid by the owners. We seemed to lose all important decisions by a 3–2 margin. That's why [Ted] Lindsay and [Doug] Harvey wanted a players' association."

Smith doesn't say so, but it may have occurred to him that being captain of the Leafs never was much fun after Armstrong's long tenure. It wasn't that the Chief spoiled the job. More likely it was that professional hockey players were demanding the rewards that their exceptional skills deserved but management didn't seem to recognize what was happening.

If Ballard and Imlach had been right in their contention that Sittler's no-trade contract and his relationship with Eagleson were the reasons for the Leafs' failures, their fortunes should have improved drastically after Sittler finally got fed up and agreed to a trade to Philadelphia in 1982. Nothing so convincing occurred.

The Leafs' luck didn't change when they tried to win the Stanley Cup for the first time since 1967 without a team captain over three seasons, from 1986 to 1989.

How about trying a captain who had never played a game for the Leafs? That would be Rob Ramage, obtained in a trade with Calgary in 1989. He didn't get much of a chance to turn things around as the Leafs lost him in the NHL Expansion Draft in 1991. In Ramage's defence, he

Teeder Kennedy storms the Boston goal, where Sugar Jim Henry covers the puck. Bill Quackenbush, Leo Boivin, and ex-Leaf Gus Bodnar all try to muscle the Toronto captain out of the play.

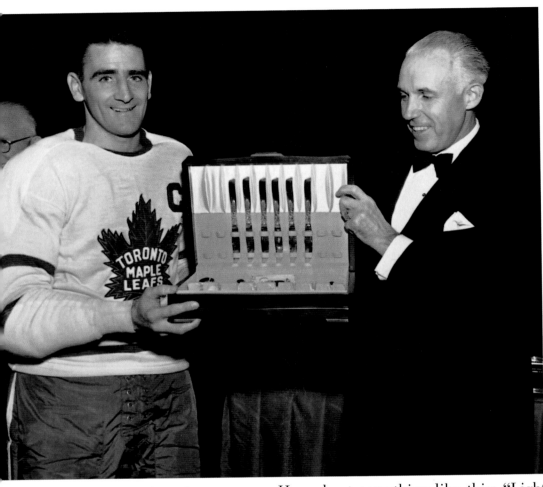

Sid Smith, who had won the Lady Byng Trophy and been named to the First All-Star Team the year before, accepts a silverware set from NHL president Clarence Campbell. Smith scored a career-high thirty-three goals in 1954–55, but struggled under the burden of wearing the "C." He slumped to just four goals and seventeen assists in his only season as captain of the Leafs in 1955–56.

didn't know he was going to be named captain until Ballard announced it, but he would have said what they all say: "Pin it on me and I'll wear it with pride."

Wendel Clark said as much. Traded. Doug Gilmour said it. He was traded, too. Dave Keon, the only Leaf ever to win the Conn Smythe Trophy as the most valuable man in the Stanley Cup playoffs, suffered an even stranger end to his captaincy. He jumped to the upstart World Hockey Association, returning to the NHL five years later when remnants of the rival league became part of the NHL.

So what can you tell Mats Sundin, whose sense of hockey history was acquired in Europe, where Anatoli Tarasov might have been a bigger name than Scotty Bowman?

How about something like this: "Lighten up. Remember, you're dealing with millionaires. Give them a few laughs. Ever hear of Frank Selke, Sr.? Get a copy of his book *Behind the Cheering* and read the chapter about some of the pranks that were orchestrated by Hap Day, the first captain at the Gardens."

Sure, when he became coach Day was a real disciplinarian and taskmaster, but while he was captain, he was a jokester and hell-raiser.

Selke tells how Day and Conacher, who would become the second captain at the Gardens, conspired to relieve the boredom of the University Club, where Conn Smythe dictated that the Leafs should stay when they played in Boston. Day had a suit that was ready for the cleaners. Conacher tricked Horner (the Leafs' captain after Conacher) into a $25 wager that he could induce Day to swim across the University Club's pool fully clothed, trailing his club bag behind him. To make the deal more attractive to Horner, Conacher agreed to collect $1 from each Leaf who attended the stunt. Horner would get the gate receipts.

Day made the swim, wearing the suit that was targetted for the cleaners anyway. Horner lost his bet, but when he asked for the gate receipts, Conacher said that he had been so excited he forgot to collect.

Pranks like this one from earlier eras might not fit with players today. How about making up a fake front page of the *Wall Street Journal* to make today's Leafs think they had lost their signing bonuses in a plunging stock market?

That would get everyone's attention, from the captain on down.

Dave Keon is shadowed by Gilles Tremblay of the Montreal Canadiens during the 1969–70 season, the year he became captain. The gentlemanly two-way centre wore the "C" in Toronto until jumping to the WHA after the 1974–75 campaign.

WRESTLING

Baby Faces and Heels

STEPHEN BRUNT

Andre the Giant (fighting Hulk Hogan, opposite) was already a Gardens mainstay when Eric the Animal fought Jack Brico (below) in September 1973. Wrestling prior to the 1980s lacked the Hollywood glamour Hogan would add, but none of the theatrics.

ON NOVEMBER 19, 1931, SEVEN DAYS AFTER THE GALA OPENING OF Maple Leaf Gardens featuring a game between the Toronto Maple Leafs and Chicago Black Hawks, the arena was packed once more for another sporting event. But this one would be a little different.

That night, Jimmy Londos, the "Golden Greek," one of the highest paid athletes of the decade, successfully defended his world professional wrestling title against Gino Garibaldi, to the delight of the Toronto fans. Londos, who had won the belt from the legendary Ed "Strangler" Lewis, was the first wrestler to exploit his charisma and his acting ability as much as his grappling skills. He was, in other words, the forefather of all that was to come, of Lou Thesz and Gorgeous George, of Whipper Billy Watson and the Sheik, of the Macho Man and Hulk Hogan.

And the Gardens would be a main stage for all of them. Over six decades, wrestling occupied more dates at the arena than anything other than hockey, and virtually all the sport's superstars passed through at one point or another.

Of course, that's "sport" in its loosest definition, since pro wrestling, from the turn of the century on, has been concerned more with entertaining the public than with staging a legitimate contest.

Thirty years before Londos, most of the big bouts were already "works"—as they're called in the trade—staged brawls in which the outcome was decided beforehand by the promoters, and at least some of the action choreographed.

Not that that seemed to bother the wrestling audience, which has always

Earl McCready was a much-decorated amateur who captained Canada's wrestling team to a sweep of the medals at the first British Empire Games (forerunner to the Commonwealth Games) in Hamilton in 1930. Later in the decade, he was grappling at the Gardens for fun and profit.

been more than willing to suspend disbelief in the interests of a good night out. The wrestling crowds at the Gardens were different than the hockey crowds, different than any other. Gone were the suits and ties, in came a broader-cross section of the city's population. The tuxedoed announcer—Jimmy Hill, for many years—would take the microphone and introduce the combatants. The fans dutifully cheered their heroes, heckled the bad guys, and were appalled by each breach of the rules. A villain entering or exiting the ring had to keep his wits about him, lest somebody's grandma stick him with a hatpin. Stylistically the wrestling of the 1930s bore very little resemblance to the wild spectacle so familiar today. The bouts were longer, most of the action took place on the mat, and there were no flying leaps off the top rope. In other words, it looked like "real" wrestling, even if the winner was predetermined.

The story of wrestling at Maple Leaf Gardens is in many ways the story of the Tunney family. That first card in 1931 was promoted under the banner of the Queensbury Athletic Club, founded and operated by Jack Corcoran. His secretary was a young man named Frank Tunney, who not long after would buy out his boss and take over the company. The Tunney name would continue to be associated with wrestling at the Gardens until 1995, when Frank's nephew Jack Tunney, who inherited the business after Frank's death in 1983, was squeezed out by the World Wrestling Federation.

What a run it was. From that very first card, all the greatest names in grappling took part in the "exhibition of skill and science" on Carlton Street. Primo Carnera wrestled there—the former carnival strongman and heavyweight boxing champion whose sad life story was the inspiration for the film *The Harder They Fall*. After the Second World War, he became a popular attraction on the wrestling circuit, more because of his sheer size than because of any appreciable wrestling skill.

Thesz, a protégé of Strangler Lewis, won a title for the first time in 1937 and was still going strong twenty years later, when he beat Buddy "Nature Boy" Rogers at the Gardens to capture the championship once again at age forty-seven. He would continue making occasional ring appearances into his '70s.

Television discovered wrestling in the late 1940s, and the big stars of the small screen found their way to the Gardens ring. Yukon Eric wrestled there, as did Killer Kowalski, the man who once tore off part of one of his ears during a bout.

So did one of the greatest stars wrestling ever produced, George Raymond Wagner, a Californian better known as Gorgeous George. His was among the most original and outrageous acts ever seen in the world of sport. With long, flowing blond hair held in place by "Georgie pins" (which could be used for nefarious purposes during the match should the occasion arise), and attended by a valet who sprayed the ring with perfume before he entered, George projected supreme arrogance, belittling his opponents and bragging of his own prowess. He enraged the wrestling fans, who pined for his defeat—and tuned in, or bought tickets every time he appeared, hoping to see it. A young boxer from Louisville, Kentucky, named Cassius Clay caught George's act on television, and incorporated some of it into the ring persona of Muhammad Ali.

Ever the good guy, Whipper Billy Watson (right) became the most famous, and most beloved, professional wrestler in the history of Toronto—not only due to his nearly perfect record in the ring, but also for his tireless devotion to children's charities.

Bruno Sammartino, Ric Flair, Harley Race—all of them were legendary champions, and all of them were featured performers at the Gardens. Because the Tunneys remained independent of any of the big wrestling organizations until 1984, it wasn't unusual to see different champions from different associations or federations wrestling on the same card.

But the two biggest attractions ever to grapple in the Gardens were local phenomena—one from Toronto, and one from just down the road in Detroit.

William John Potts was born in East York in 1916. He never knew his father, who was killed by a sniper's bullet in France two weeks before the armistice that ended the First World War.

A talented amateur wrestler, Potts left for

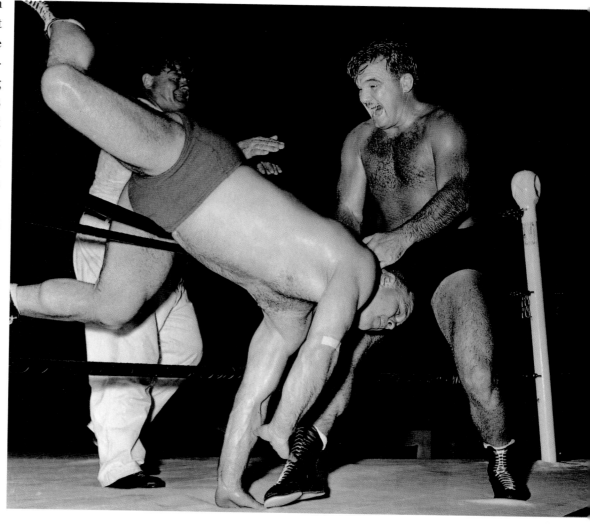

Wild-eyed local hero Bulldog Brower applies a headlock to legendary mat villain the Sheik at Maple Leaf Gardens in October 1974. The Sheik was in the midst of a 150-match Toronto winning streak that stretched from 1969 to 1976.

England at age twenty along with four friends (including future headliner Tiger Tasker), hoping to make a name for himself as a pro. One night, in London, he did just that—literally.

"I was wrestling a Scotsman named Tony Bear and I ended the match with the whip hold," he remembered many years later. "That is, I pulled him toward me, rammed my shoulder into his midsection and whipped him up over my shoulder about twelve feet in the air. As usual, it knocked the wind out of him long enough for me to get the pin. The next day in the newspaper, they were calling me Whipper Billy."

And a few days after that, a local promoter added the fictitious last name Watson. The newly christened Whipper Billy Watson would spend four years in England, learning the trade, building a following, and polishing his act. Preparing to head home in 1940, Watson sent a box of newspaper clippings in advance, addressed to Frank Tunney. Watson figured the local promoter would surely be thrilled to have a hometown headliner for his shows, but in fact Tunney wasn't so easily impressed. He didn't even bother to pick up the package of clippings at Canada Customs. Still, after Watson arrived Tunney agreed to book him, first as an undercard attraction, and soon, as his appeal grew, as a headliner. It was the beginning of a sixty-five-hundred-bout career that would see Whipper Billy become the most famous and most beloved professional wrestler in Toronto's history. Wrestling crowds, which had fallen below 1,000 before Watson's debut, soon climbed over 10,000. When Whipper Billy beat Gorgeous

George—and George was forced to cut his hair—it was an event splashed across the newspaper sports sections. When he beat Lou Thesz in St. Louis in 1947, winning the National Wrestling Association world championship for the second and final time, it was a big enough story for the front page of the *Toronto Star*.

Watson's ring character never changed. He was a good guy—a "baby face"—all the way, never a "heel"; he projected an unimpeachable character. As the great sportswriter Jim Coleman wrote in *Maclean's* magazine in 1944, "[Watson] is a paragon of virtue in the ring. If his opponent attempts to decapitate him with a tomahawk, misses and imbeds the tomahawk in one of the ring posts, Watson will help him to disengage the weapon. If his opponent strikes him illegally with a brass knuckle, Watson will smile a sad, brave smile and break his opponent in twain, like a stick of dry macaroni. Watson destroys his opponents with the air of Sir Galahad repelling scorpions, and the customers love him to pieces."

Watson met all the great wrestlers of his day, and maintained a long-running feud with an Englishman turned Australian who billed himself as Lord Athol Layton, and wrestled as a heel. In later years, the "Lord" would turn baby face and become a popular Toronto attraction in his own right, before heading for the announcing booth, where he would be a familiar figure on television for many years.

There were other heroes as well—Dick "the Bulldog" Brower and Sweet Daddy Siki, Tiger Jett Singh, and former football player Angelo Mosca, Billy "Red" Lyons, the Beast, Dewey Robertson (who also wrestled as the Missing Link), Haystack Calhoun, and Pampero Firpo. All of them enjoyed a loyal following at the Gardens.

But the biggest draw of them all from the mid-1960s well into the 1970s was the greatest heel of them all. His real name was Ed Farhat, and he hailed from the Motor City. But fans at the Gardens knew him—and hated him—as the Sheik, from parts unknown. The beginning of his great run in Toronto coincided with the last years of Whipper Billy Watson's career.

Rowdy Roddy Piper grew up in Toronto's Parkdale neighbourhood and became a popular attraction at the Gardens during the WWF's glory days of the 1980s and '90s.

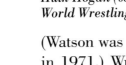

*After he was crowned heavyweight champion on January 24, 1984,
Hulk Hogan (seen here fighting the Ultimate Warrior) helped take the
World Wrestling Federation to unprecedented levels of popularity.*

(Watson was forced out of wrestling after his leg was shattered in a car accident in 1971.) Wrestling purists – yes, they really do exist—will tell you that the Sheik didn't have a whole lot of talent, that his matches were short and unremarkable and unusually bloody (an effect wrestlers achieve by cutting themselves across the forehead). He promoted his own shows in Detroit, a comfortable set-up since he ensured that he was always the featured wrestler in the main event, and that he never lost—even by disqualification.

In Toronto, the Sheik was nearly as successful, maintaining an undefeated streak that lasted for more than 150 cards over seven years. Managed by the evil Abdullah Farouk—a diminutive, fez-wearing fellow who tended towards the obnoxious, thus his nickname, "the Weasel"—the Sheik seemed to always find a way to get the better of his opponents. Sometimes, it would be the old foreign-object-in-the-trunks trick. Sometimes, he'd throw "salt" in their eyes to blind them. Sometimes Farouk would interfere. Somehow, a whole generation of referees, otherwise diligent enforcers of the rules, just couldn't seem to catch the Sheik in the act.

The end of the Sheik's glory years coincided with an overall decline in wrestling's popularity. Always a cyclical passion, it had fallen out of favour, in Toronto and elsewhere. During the early 1980s, crowds at the Gardens dwindled, forcing Jack Tunney to make what turned out to be a prescient decision. In 1984, he gave up the idea of independent promotion, and aligned himself with the World Wrestling Federation, a business based in suburban Connecticut, and headed by a promotional genius named Vince McMahon. It was McMahon's idea to sacrifice all pretense of "real" wrestling in favour of the show, to incorporate elements of rock concerts and comic books, to turn wrestlers (already a collection of tried-and-true stereotypes) into living, breathing superheroes and supervillains. Foremost among them was a bleached-blond giant from Florida named Terry Bollea, who had been rechristened Hulk Hogan.

Just as Toronto became part of the WWF empire, the WWF took off. In March 1985, McMahon staged the first Wrestlemania at Madison Square Garden, a kind of wrestling Super Bowl that would become as big an attraction as a heavyweight championship boxing match. Throughout the 1980s and into the 1990s, the stars of the WWF drew big crowds at the Gardens—Hogan, Macho Man Randy Savage, Rowdy Roddy Piper (who'd grown up in Toronto's Parkdale neighbourhood), and all the others. They were actors first, then acrobats—a far cry from the wrestlers of Jimmy Londos's era. But once again, wrestling was packing them in, to cheer the baby faces, to heckle the heels, to see the villain eventually get his due, and to celebrate the triumph of good over evil.

Toronto's George Chuvalo fought many times at Maple Leaf Gardens while posting a professional record of 80–15–2 with 68 knockouts from 1956 to 1979. He was ranked among the top ten in the world longer than any other heavyweight boxer.

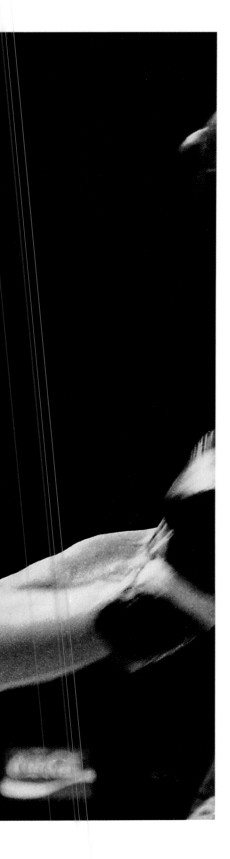

BOXING

In the ring

STEPHEN BRUNT

IT WAS NEVER MEANT TO HAVE BEEN. ONE OF THE MOST GLAMOROUS events ever held at Maple Leaf Gardens, and one of the pinnacles of Canadian sporting history, was a compromise, an afterthought. And the man who would become one of the most famous Canadian athletes of all time wasn't even supposed to be in the ring.

In 1966, the heavyweight champion of the world was known by two names. To most, he was still Cassius Clay, the brash, flashy young boxer from Louisville, Kentucky, who had won a gold medal at the 1960 Olympics, and then pulled off one of the greatest upsets in the history of the sport, beating Sonny Liston for the title in 1964. Since that night in Miami, using slick, dancing footwork and the fastest hands in the history of the division, he had beaten all comers to retain his crown.

Others had learned to call him Muhammad Ali, the name he had chosen after joining the Nation of Islam following his win over Liston. The sect, founded by Elijah Muhammad and popularized by Malcolm X, was considered by many to be a dangerous fringe group because of its black separatist dogma. Ali's popularity dropped dramatically after his conversion, and especially after he announced that, as a conscientious objector, he would refuse induction into the army of the United States, then deeply mired in Vietnam.

While that controversy raged, Ali was scheduled to defend his title against Ernie Terrell, a fighter from Chicago who was recognized as heavyweight champion by the splinter World Boxing Association. The fight was originally to be held in Chicago, then in Houston. In each jurisdiction, protests from local veterans' groups caused the boxing commission to refuse to sanction the bout.

Desperate for a site where he might escape the controversy, the fight's promoter looked to Canada, where he figured opposition might not be quite so strong. Ali and Terrell were set to meet at Maple Leaf Gardens on March 29, 1966.

Then Terrell, for one reason or another, got cold feet. The problem, according to his trainer, Sam Solomons, was that Terrell hadn't received his advance for training expenses. "We're not moving until we get some money," Solomons said. "I mean capital M-O-N-E-Y." Others figured Terrell simply didn't like his chances fighting outside of the United States—and perhaps didn't like his chances against Ali, period.

It was March 10, less than three weeks before the fight was scheduled to take place. The promoters desperately needed a substitute, a fighter who could offer a credible performance on short notice, not to mention sell a few tickets, fast. George Chuvalo was the only logical choice.

Chuvalo had made his professional debut ten years earlier at the Gardens, winning a Jack Dempsey Tournament for novice heavyweights in the spring of 1956. The son of Croatian immigrant parents, raised in Toronto's working-class Junction neighbourhood, Chuvalo soon became a favourite of local fight fans because of his straight-ahead aggressive style and his ability to take a punch. Rising through the professional ranks, toughness would be Chuvalo's calling card: though he had been beaten by top heavyweights, he had never, ever been knocked down. In November 1965, at the Gardens, he had failed in his only shot at the heavyweight title—or at least the fragment of the title claimed by Terrell—losing a unanimous fifteen-round decision.

So this was his chance of a lifetime, fighting for the real championship on his home turf, even if he barely had time to prepare properly. And this, for Toronto, was suddenly more than just another prize fight. It was the hometown boy trying to win the biggest single prize in all of sport. Not that that impressed outsiders much. Many American sportswriters, hostile to Ali in the first place, wrote off the fight as a terrible mismatch, and wrote off Chuvalo as simply a punching bag.

"The blindly stubborn promoters of the what-is-it involving Cassius Marcellus Clay and George Chuvalo at Maple Leaf Gardens tonight have the consummate gall to charge $100 for ringside tickets. The fight isn't worth thirty cents," Arthur Daley wrote in a pre-fight column in the *New York Times*. Daley suggested a boycott but it failed to materialize, though by fight night more than half of the theatres in the United States booked to show the fight via closed-circuit television had backed out because of the work of anti-Ali pressure groups. But in Toronto, fans were more than willing to ante up for tickets. A

Though battered for fifteen brutal rounds by Muhammad Ali on March 29, 1966, George Chuvalo could still boast that no one had ever knocked him off his feet. No one ever would. Chuvalo emerged from the most famous fight ever held at the Gardens with his face swollen and bloodied—and with the everlasting respect of the champion who beat him.

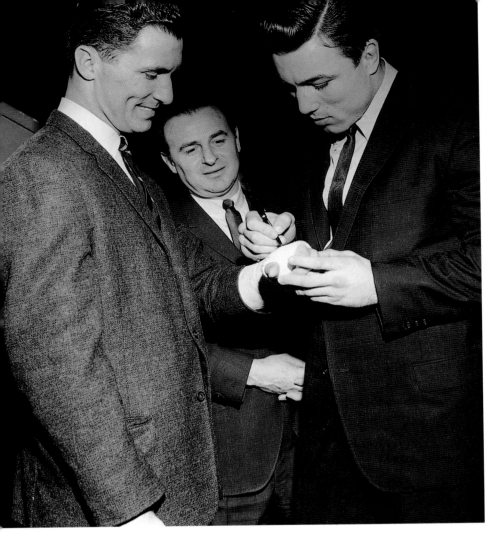

Three weeks before facing Floyd Patterson at Madison Square Garden in New York, George Chuvalo takes time out to sign an autograph on a cast on the wrist of the Toronto Maple Leafs' Andy Bathgate. Fight promoter Irving Ungerman looks on.

crowd sprinkled with local celebrities showed up to cheer on their hero, and to bask in the presence of the man who would become the most famous athlete—and arguably the most famous person—of his age.

The truth is, Chuvalo didn't have a hope. In 1966, the year in which most agree Ali was at his absolute peak, no one would have had a hope. Dancing left, flicking out his left jab, firing combinations at blinding speed, Ali dominated most of the fifteen-round match. Only in the second round did Chuvalo have the upper hand, and then only because—in a preview of the rope-a-dope maneouvre that would be used to bamboozle George Foreman ten years later – Ali seemed willing to stand still and let Chuvalo pound him. Chuvalo did just that, especially with blows to the body, and won the round on all three scorecards. It was the only frame he claimed convincingly, as Ali danced and fought his way to a unanimous decision.

Afterwards, as was often the case, Chuvalo's face was bloodied and swollen by the pounding Ali had applied. But throughout the course of the fight, he had never gone down, never taken a step backwards, winning praise for his heart and his courage.

Ali seemed to have enjoyed the experience of fighting in Toronto. "I might even give George a rematch here," he said after the fight. "I might even defend the next three times here." (A little more than a year later, following six more fights, including a win over Terrell, Ali was stripped of his title, and began three years in exile while facing draft evasion charges. He would return to boxing in 1970, and did indeed give Chuvalo a rematch in 1972, in Vancouver, with the same results.)

And even the doubters had been won over by Chuvalo's gritty performance.

"It had been written in advance here that the fight wasn't worth thirty cents," Daley wrote in an article published in the *Times* the day after the fight. "All eaters of crow agree it was worth a lot more."

From Maple Leaf Gardens' earliest days, boxing was a mainstay. During the 1930s, '40s, and '50s, the sport was far more of a mainstream interest than it is today, and cards were staged on a regular basis. The fans were loud and boisterous and partisan, cheering on the local heroes of the moment. They were also knowledgeable, as knowledgeable as Toronto's hockey fans, because in those days the city was a great boxing town.

Local promoters—most notably Frank Tunney and Jack "Deacon" Allen, Damon Runyon characters both of them—featured a succession of local stars on their rise towards a championship, as well as famous fighters from afar. All the way back in 1932, the Gardens hosted its first world title fight, featuring a pair of imports, as Panama Al Brown knocked out Emile "Spider" Pladner in the first round to retain his bantamweight title. The first real homegrown favourite at the Gardens was Sammy Luftspring, a tough, big-hearted lightweight from Toronto who enjoyed an outstanding amateur career. On May 18, 1936, he qualified for Canada's Olympic team, winning his weight class during trials held at the Gardens. But having heard of Nazi mistreatment of Jews, Luftspring and his teammate, Baby Yack, opted out of the Berlin Games. Instead, they went to the communist-sponsored Workers' Olympics in Barcelona, arriving in Spain just as civil war broke out. The games were cancelled.

Immediately after returning to Canada, Luftspring turned professional, winning the Canadian title at the Gardens on January 6, 1937, when he scored a technical knockout over Frank Genovese in the thirteenth round. Luftspring fought several times at the Gardens after that, and in the U.S. as well, moving up the rankings on his way to what seemed an inevitable world title shot. Then, on May 28, 1940, in a fight in New York against Steve Belloise, Luftspring was thumbed in the eye, suffering a torn retina. It was the end of his career as a boxer, though certainly not an end to his involvement with the sport. For many years afterwards, Luftspring served as Toronto's busiest and most popular referee, while other local fighters became the new heroes of the Gardens.

In the 1940s and through the 1950s, lightweight L'il Arthur King was probably the best of the lot. A wonderfully skilled boxer/puncher who never got his big break, King finally signed on with Frank "Blinky" Palermo, an organized crime figure from Philadelphia who managed several fighters, including the reigning lightweight champion Ike Williams. Williams was about to move up in weight, clearing the way for King. Unfortunately, Williams failed at the higher weights, and returned to lightweight, never granting King a shot— though for a three-year period ending in 1951, King was either the number-one or number-two contender for the crown. Still, he kept on fighting. He beat another Toronto favourite, Alan McFater, in 1953, at the Gardens. By 1957, King had moved up to middleweight, when he met world-ranked Ralph "Tiger" Jones—losing a tough ten-round decision in front of a crowd of 5,500. His Gardens swan song came later that year, when he won a ten-round split decision over ranked middleweight Yama Bahama, in front of only 2,000 fans.

There were other Gardens favourites as well, including heavyweights Earl Walls and James J. Parker. Chuvalo was, of course, a major presence. Other international stars also passed through: Joe Louis boxed four sparring partners in an exhibition on November 13, 1935—needless to say, beating them all. A year later, Max Baer, by then a former heavyweight champion, beat Dutch Weimer. In 1940, George Pace and Lou Salica battled to a fifteen-round draw for the NBA bantamweight championship. On December 4, 1961, the Gardens staged its first heavyweight title fight. The champ, Floyd Patterson, defended his title against Tom McNeeley, winning by KO in the fourth round. (McNeeley's son, Peter, would many years later be a comeback opponent for Mike Tyson.) In 1971, Jimmy Ellis, who once held a piece of the heavyweight championship, won a ten-round decision over Chuvalo, and in 1973, Ken Buchanan, by then the ex-lightweight champion, knocked out Frankie Otero in six rounds. But by the 1970s, the economics of professional boxing had changed dramatically.

Arenas were no longer able to compete with casinos (first in Las Vegas, and later in Atlantic City), which could offer better purses and recoup their investment at the gaming tables as well as the box office. For the most part, the grand arenas that had been the sites of so many great fights were relegated to serving as theatres, offering the latest super bout by way of the big screen. (The first at Maple Leaf Gardens was in 1961, the third fight between Floyd Patterson and Ingemar Johansson, with Patterson retaining his heavyweight title.)

It was during one of those closed-circuit nights that Clyde Gray, one of the world's best 147-pounders of the 1970s, made his debut, knocking out Luigi Colovita at Maple Leaf Gardens on February 16, 1970, a live feature before the showing of Joe Frazier's heavyweight title unification fight against Jimmy Ellis. The welterweight from Nova Scotia was shrewdly handled by Chuvalo's manager, Irving Ungerman, and continued as a featured attraction before televised fights until February 1973, when he was finally given a chance to headline on his own. That night, he beat Eddie Blay for the Commonwealth title.

Gray's big break came a few months later (the fight was staged during the day for ABC's "Wide World of Sports"), when he took on the great Jose Napoles,

regarded as one of the best pound-for-pound fighters of the time—the first title fight in the Gardens since Chuvalo and Ali, and the last to date. Gray was no match for the champion, losing a unanimous decision. In February 1974, Gray fought in the arena one last time, knocking out Bunny Grant to defend his Commonwealth crown.

That was almost the last live fight at the Gardens, though there was one more boxing event to come. On April 26, 1975, a few months after he'd lost the heavyweight championship to Muhammad Ali in Zaire, George Foreman took on five different journeyman heavyweights for three rounds each. "Foreman Fights Five" was a sad end to the days when boxing was a staple attraction at the Gardens, especially that one night in 1966 when the ring at centre ice was also the centre of the sporting world.

Solly Cantor (wearing the Jewish Star of David) jabs with a left at Dave Shad during a Gardens bout in April 1951. As with the Irish immigrants before them, and the blacks who would follow, boxing was seen as a way out of the inner city for many Jews during the 1930s and '40s.

PUNCH

The triumphs, the losses, and the legend

STEPHEN COLE

NHL ROSTERS WERE LADEN WITH STARS AND TALENTED JOURNEYMEN in the pre-expansion 1960s:

In Chicago, Bobby Hull could both skate and shoot at unprecedented speed, while the Scooter Line—Stan Mikita, Kenny Wharram, and Doug Mohns—were slick passers and scorers.

Detroit's Gordie Howe patrolled right wing with unrivalled economy of movement, scoring goals and meting out discipline with the barest flick of a stick.

Canadiens centres Jean Beliveau, Henri Richard, and Ralph Backstrom, and wingers Bobby Rousseau and Gilles Tremblay came at opponents in accelerating waves. "You'd hang on for two periods to keep them from running away with the whole dang thing," remembers Red Kelly. "Then if it was close at the end, you'd go for a tie."

And yet in the six seasons between 1962 and 1967, the team with the most championships was the Toronto Maple Leafs, with four Stanley Cups, including three in a row from 1962 to 1964. Those Leafs were a team of talented players that played unadorned solid hockey. Frank Mahovlich was a scorer with superstar potential before the phrase had been invented, but sometimes seemed uncomfortable in this role. His teammates, meanwhile, contributed in all of those large and small ways that together bear results.

Punch Imlach guided the Maple Leafs to four Stanley Cup titles in the 1960s, but his dictatorial ways did not sit well with players like Frank Mahovlich (opposite right).

It was easier to push a parked car uphill than move George Armstrong off the puck. Allan Stanley was as slow as church, but, as Scott Young observed, "played defence as if he had oncoming forwards on a string, drawn to him." Centres Kelly, Dave Keon, and Bob Pulford were relentless defenders; the trio, which combined the strategic, smart-passing, strong-willed playing of Kelly, the darting, ever-youthful exuberance of Keon, and the relentless competitiveness of Pulford, netted a mere thirty-four minutes in penalties one season.

Johnny Bower makes the save with Bobby Hull on his doorstep. Bower was a minor league veteran who enjoyed a "second" career in the NHL after Punch Imlach brought him to Toronto in 1958.

Yes, these were good players. Very good players. But other franchises, Chicago and Montreal in particular, were more talented, man for man. How was it, then, that Toronto most often won the Stanley Cup? The answer would have to be George "Punch" Imlach, the Maple Leafs coach and g.m., whose style and personality variously delighted and unsettled his players.

There were better coaches. "I never thought much of Punch as a strategist," remembers Boston's Harry Sinden. "He wasn't in the same class as Toe Blake. You could beat him with the same match-up all game... And he was a showboat."

The showboat turned into a destroyer when the Leafs faltered. "If we had a bad game we paid," recalls Ron Ellis. "Coming from Detroit, we might arrive in Toronto at two in the morning. Guys mightn't get home for another hour. Practice was nine. Which meant driving in rush hour. You'd get three hours sleep. Punch would call another practice for three... You were getting rush hour going home, too."

"No one ever died from hard work," comments teammate Brian Conacher. "But what Punch held wasn't practice, it was punishment...[He] skated us till we dropped."

If Imlach was often unpopular behind the bench, he was unquestionably resourceful as a general manager. He had to be. Chicago, Detroit and Montreal all iced strong teams in this era. Still, Punch got the players he needed. A look at how he secured the goalies who carried his team to the 1967 Stanley Cup reveals something of Imlach's character and nerve.

After a one full season and a handful of other games with the New York Rangers, Johnny Bower was settled in the minors, playing for the AHL Cleveland

The Maple Leafs claimed Terry Sawchuk on waivers in 1964. He and Johnny Bower shared the Vezina Trophy in 1964–65 and backstopped the Leafs to the Stanley Cup in 1967. Here Sawchuk makes the save while Carl Brewer moves in to cover New York's Don Marshall.

Barons, when Imlach convinced him to give the NHL another chance in 1958. Later Imlach grabbed Terry Sawchuk from Detroit in the 1964 Intra-League Draft. Sawchuk was a troubled man, and needed careful handling by Imlach to keep him involved and playing well through the 1966–67 campaign.

Punch's showy on-ice moves and curious off-ice behaviour, which ranged from baiting opponents ("Rangers win, I'll eat a horse's hat!") to vaudevillian dressing-room turns, as when he had himself introduced as the new coach,

On April 22, 1962, Don Simmons, Punch Imlach, Allan Stanley, Ed Litzenberger (in street clothes), Ron Stewart, and Dave Keon celebrated the Leafs' first Stanley Cup title in eleven years.

then waltzed into the players' room in a Beatles wig, were more than managerial eccentricities.

Born in 1918, Imlach was an only child who defined his life through playground and school sports in Toronto's east end. He played hockey for the Young Rangers, the Goodyears, and the Marlboros from 1935 to 1941, earning his nickname when he threw punches at the team trainer upon being revived after having been knocked out on the ice. He got into coaching while with the Quebec Aces, acting as a playing coach in 1949–50 and taking over behind the bench full-time the following season. When he arrived at Maple Leaf Gardens in 1958, after stints as both coach and general manager in Quebec City and Springfield, Imlach was dazzled by, then became addicted to, the spotlight.

It was more than his needing to win. In

George Armstrong and Eddie Shack (above) storm the Montreal Canadiens' goal, while (below) Paul Henderson and Tim Horton take care of the Leafs' end against Los Angeles. Henderson joined the Leafs on March 3, 1968, when Punch Imlach traded Frank Mahovlich to Detroit.

fact, Punch was sometimes churlish in victory. Writer Stan Fischler recalls Imlach in the dressing room after his Leafs took their first Cup, in Chicago, on Easter weekend 1962.

"I remember Carl Brewer on his hands and knees running around like a dog, and Billy Harris taking photographs, which I thought was touching... It was a warm scene. Then Imlach storms in. 'Cut out the bull, we got a plane to catch,' he screams. He was livid. Boy, I remember thinking, this guy is something else."

Imlach's proved to be a tough-minded antagonist, at various times harping on the flaws of his own players, opposing teams and the NHL. Nowhere was this more evident than in 1966–67, the last season season of the NHL's six-team era.

The campaign before, Toronto had been blown out in the first round of the playoffs by Montreal, four straight. Critics complained Imlach had painted the Leafs into a corner of the league basement by employing a team that could only possibly lead the league in birthday candles. They had a point, as seven Leafs—Bower (42), Stanley (40), Kelly (39), Armstrong (37), Sawchuk (37), Marcel Pronovost (36), Horton (36)—were high-mileage professional players.

Bob Baun shows off the Stanley Cup with wife Sally and their children after the Leafs defeated the Red Wings in 1963. Baun would be a hero one year later, scoring the winning goal in game six on a broken ankle, as the Leafs again beat the Red Wings in the Final.

In pre-season, the team seemed flat. Fifteen Leafs suffered injuries. And five players—defender Bob Baun, half the offence (Keon, Mahovlich, and Pulford) and two-thirds of the entertainment (Eddie Shack)—remained unsigned prior to opening night. The *Globe and Mail* and the *Telegram* picked Leafs to finish fifth in a six-team league. Which is where Toronto found itself two-thirds of the way through the season, having lost ten straight by a combined score of 47–15. In the wake of the sixth loss, Punch visited the players' dressing room and hissed, "Any you guys want to renegotiate contracts for next year, my office is open." After losing in Chicago the next night, Imlach turned torturer, putting his team through four marathon practices plus the grind of travel to and from Chicago within thirty-six hours.

In 1965, after spending thirteen seasons in Toronto, Ron Stewart was traded to Boston. Here he gains a small measure of revenge against Punch Imlach with a goal on Terry Sawchuk on January 29, 1966. Others on the ice include Bob Pulford, Eddie Shack, Larry Hillman, Marcel Pronovost, and Boston's Pit Martin. The Leafs won the game 6–3.

Paul Henderson is seen here creating traffic in front of Chicago's Denis DeJordy. The deal that Punch Imlach swung to bring him to Toronto was one of the biggest blockbusters in franchise history. The Leafs got Henderson from Detroit with Norm Ullman and Floyd Smith in exchange for Frank Mahovlich, Pete Stemkowski, Garry Unger, and the rights to Carl Brewer.

He was harder on himself. To cool his boiling stomach, Punch now took his scotch with milk. He forgot to eat. Went sleepless at night. All his waking hours were spent scheming. During the streak, Imlach shuffled lines. Shifted Tim Horton to forward. Benched Pulford. Demoted Jim Pappin. He even changed hats, going to a cream-coloured alpine yodeller's model against Boston one night. Nothing worked.

Not even working the phones. For suddenly every general manager in the league wanted to trade. Toronto needed help at left wing and defence, but had extra centres, with Pete Stemkowski and Mike Walton. Other teams expressed interest in Pulford and Pappin. Punch thought hard about a deal, then decided to hell with it, he'd go with what he had.

After the tenth loss, Punch came up with another typically gimmicky strategy. He'd move Pulford onto Stemkowski's left wing. Maybe two centres would ignite Pappin. And with his defence ailing, Imlach decided to give Larry Hillman a regular shift behind the blueline.

Finally, Punch rolled seven and eleven. Pulford, Stemkowski and Hillman began hitting opponents. Pappin hit the net. The revitalized Leafs tied Chicago, beat Boston, won in Montreal, and were suddenly, incredibly, in the middle of a ten-game undefeated streak.

Most of the wins were presided over by the affable King Clancy, a former Leafs star and NHL referee and who was already one of hockey's best-loved goodwill ambassadors. He was Toronto's assistant general manager when he took over the team from Imlach after Punch suffered a physical collapse and was forced to a bed at Toronto General Hospital. All the years of conniving and flim-flammery had finally taken their toll, explains former *Globe* reporter Louis Cauz.

"Though he swaggered around, Punch was never healthy," Cauz says. "He had stomach problems, heart problems, a hernia, gallstones. Hell, maybe that's why he swaggered, to fool everybody."

Clancy received credit for the team's rebound. And while it's true that with Imlach gone, players responded with some of their best hockey, there was no question who was responsible for the team's fortunes. "We knew we were always Punch's team," Stanley says. "We all knew he was coming back."

Punch returned from hospital for the challenge of his career. In the playoffs, the third-place Leafs would meet first-place Chicago, holders of 12 league scoring records. And if they slipped by the Hawks, Montreal would surely be waiting.

The Chief, George Armstrong, is the last Leafs captain to carry the Stanley Cup. Armstrong captained Stanley Cup winners in 1962, 1963, 1964, and 1967.

Imlach had been preparing for these teams since August. While diplomatic when discussing other squads, he wore a season-long sneer for Montreal and Chicago. Before the playoffs, he gave his rivals another well-placed needle, suggesting Hull's squad were shirkers and Beliveau's team lacked courage. "We can take Chicago in spades and Montreal in hearts," he told reporters. Then, referring to the once-famous vaudeville act that had, among other things, supplied many of the Munchkins for The Wizard of Oz, Imlach added: "Canadiens, ha! they're mostly a bunch of Singer's Midgets."

Punch wanted opponents to loathe him because he hoped they'd lose their cool, then the game. But it was due to some combination of genius and character flaw that he seemed content with the notion that his own players hated him too. Riling up his players surely had to be behind Imlach's 1967 playoff practice schedule. Finishing in Boston, the Leafs travelled to Trenton, Ontario, bussed to Peterborough for three days of gruelling work, flew to Chicago for game one, returned to Toronto for two quick practices, then grabbed another jet back to Chicago for game two.

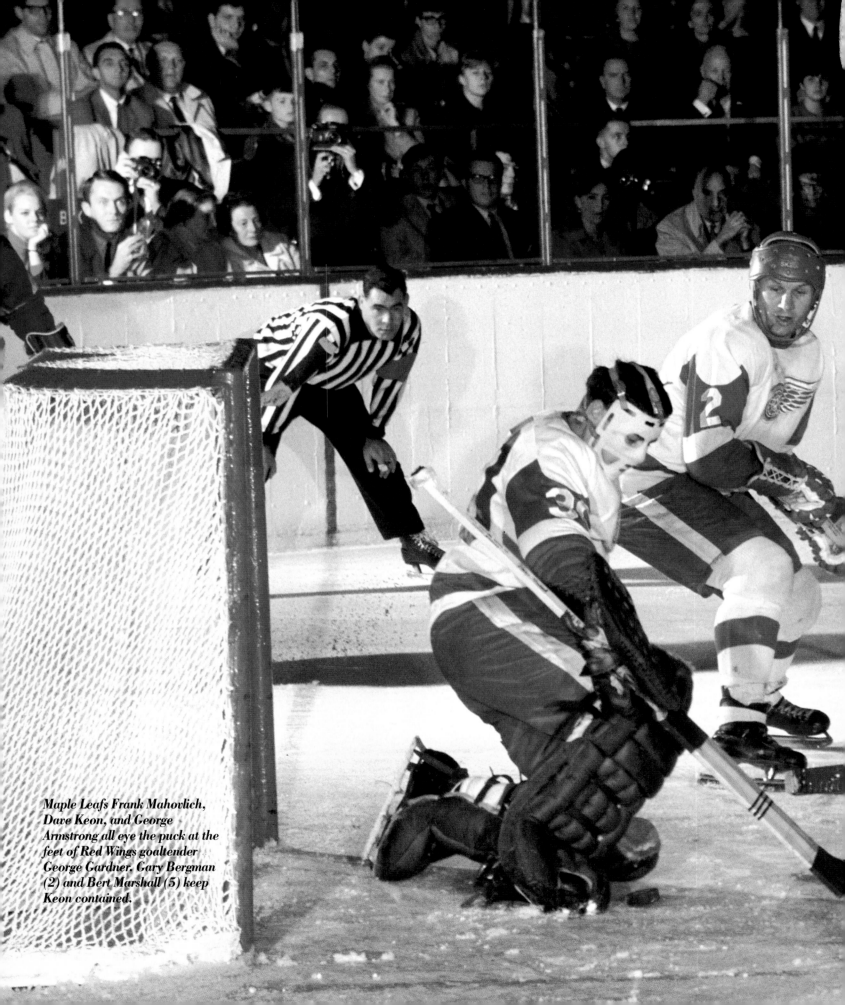

Maple Leafs Frank Mahovlich, Dave Keon, and George Armstrong all eye the puck at the feet of Red Wings goaltender George Gardner. Gary Bergman (2) and Bert Marshall (5) keep Keon contained.

*Leafs defencemen Allan
Stanley (26) and Tim
Horton (7) try to slow down
Montreal's Bobby Rousseau
(15) and Dick Duff (8)
during the 1967 Stanley Cup
Finals. Canadiens alternate
captain Henri Richard
moves in from the far side.*

Reporters covering the Leafs called Punch's playoff itinerary suicidal. But as the series unfolded, his perverse angle-playing began to pay off. After dropping the first match, the Leafs returned home for workouts, while the Hawks, because an ice show was in town, gathered rust on their skates. The Leafs started game two as if they'd never left the ice, coasting to a 3–1 victory. The team won by the same score in Maple Leaf Gardens in game three. In both wins, the Leafs outskated their younger opponents in the final minutes.

"Something Armstrong said in training camp came back to me then," Conacher recalls. "'You wonder why we're working so hard now?' he said, 'But come the sixth or seventh game of the playoffs no one will be able to keep up with us.'"

And that's exactly what happened as Toronto turned Chicago away in six compelling battles. Series heroes? Terry Sawchuk, the man Imlach talked out of quitting three times through the season, and who gave the Leafs solid goaltending against the Black Hawks—particularly in game five when he was supposed to be resting but took over from a shaky Johnny Bower, who was pulled after the first period. Punch's makeshift unit of Pulford—Stemkowski—Pappin was the series' best line. And Hillman was the top defender. For Imlach, the upset was so sweet that he refused to talk about the Leafs' final series opponent: "I don't want to talk about Montreal, I just want to enjoy this win."

It turned out Punch was saving his energy and when he did turn his attention to the Canadiens his taunting, as usual, had a design and purpose. Coaches remember goalies who've given them hard playoffs the way other men recall girls who've broken their hearts. Imlach remembered how the Habs' Gump Worsley had taken the superior Leafs to six games as a Ranger in 1962. He hoped Habs coach Toe Blake would play rookie Rogie Vachon, who was in just his first full season as a pro and had spent most of the previous year with the Thetford Mines Canadiens in a Quebec provincial league.

Which is why when Red Fisher of the *Montreal Star* phoned Imlach to talk

The Maple Leafs were given little chance of defeating Montreal in 1967, but Imlach's veteran squad rose to the occasion. Terry Sawchuk, seen here eluding the forechecking of Claude Provost while Allan Stanley trails, was brilliant during the series.

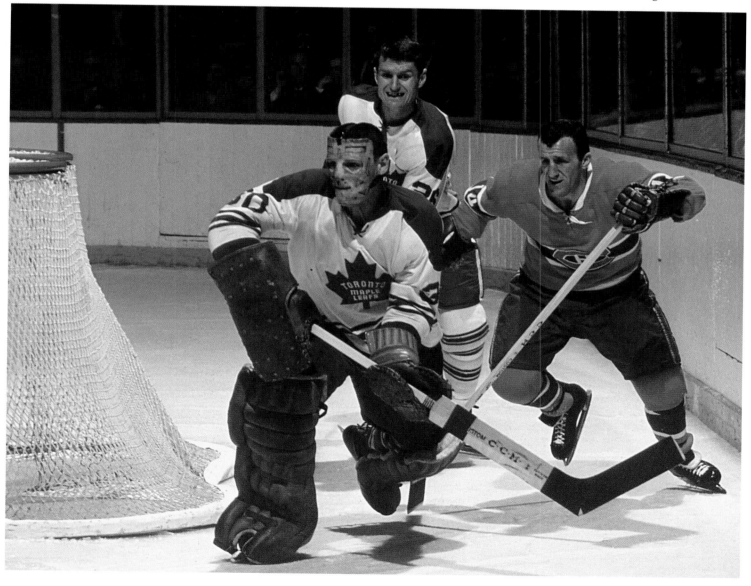

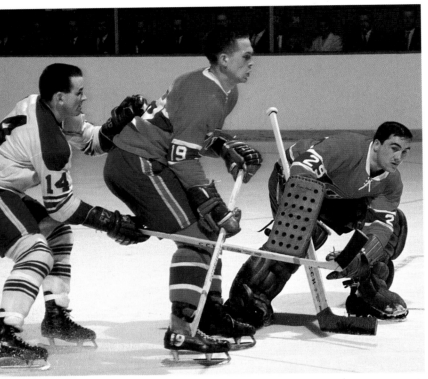

Terry Harper holds off Toronto's Dave Keon, while Rogie Vachon clears the puck into the corner. Punch Imlach ridiculed Vachon throughout the 1967 Stanley Cup Finals. Imlach's psychological games seemed to get the better of his Canadiens counterpart, Toe Blake.

about the upcoming series, Imlach gave Fisher a quote that he knew Blake would read. Using reverse psychology, Punch stated, "No way [the Habs] can beat us using a Junior B goalie."

Fisher pointed out that Vachon was riding a month-long unbeaten streak.

"He's been up against a bunch of pea-shooters," Imlach cried.

The Canadiens whipped the Leafs 6–2 in the opening game, prompting Blake to remark, "Vachon's got to be the only Junior B goalie to win five straight Stanley Cup playoff games."

Undaunted, Imlach embarked on a thirty-six-hour propaganda tour. "Come with me, we're going to show the flag," he told Clancy on the off day before game two. Britches hitched and fedoras lowered, the Leafs brass burst into the Montreal press club.

"They were something," recalls George Gross. "'Who's gonna win?' Punch would ask. If you said 'Montreal,' he'd shout, 'Ah, you're nuts,' then explain Toronto was going to win four straight... [He and Clancy] went from reporter to reporter, pointing and yelling, 'We're gonna win this thing, just watch.'"

Afterwards, Imlach hit Ste. Catherine Street and started jabbering at locals, telling everyone the Leafs were a cinch. Finally, he visited a clothing store for a suit. "Something special because I want to wear it the night we win the Stanley Cup," he advised the tailor. When the suit maker, a Habs fan, suggested that mightn't be any time soon, Punch snapped, "Just make me the suit!"

While Punch poked at the Canadiens in the press, his Leafs mapped out a plan to exploit what they felt was Montreal's secret weakness: Vachon. He could be beaten low, they figured. Sure enough, game two, three Leafs—Conacher, Walton, and Horton—rammed low whistlers past Vachon, and Bower was brilliant in a convincing 3–0 shutout.

After the game, Punch tweaked Vachon again and then demonstrated how his goalie should use his stick to skewer Montreal's overly attentive left winger, John Ferguson.

After game three in Toronto, a deliciously tense five-period affair that Montreal controlled but the Leafs won 3–2 by virtue of Bower's brilliant play and goals from Pappin, Stemkowski, and Pulford, Punch pounded away at the defeated Canadiens. "Ask [your team] if they want to be humiliated any more," he told a Montreal reporter. He also had a message for Blake. "Vachon's up to Junior A now."

The attacks on Vachon were getting to Blake, the Habs' Terry Harper says. "[Toe] was a genius," he says. "I never saw him outsmarted once in my whole career. Except for that Toronto series. Man, Imlach got to him with all that stuff with Vachon... Toe wanted to prove Imlach was wrong; that we could win with Rogie."

The only problem was that Montreal was playing nervous, tentative hockey with a rookie goalie. Vachon was good, one day he'd be great, Harper says, but "in a real old-fashioned playoff war, I think we would've been better with an old pro like Worsley."

Bower was injured during the warm-up for game four. Sawchuk started in his place and looked shaky in a 6–2 Habs win. Back in Montreal, game five, the Habs seemed about to put the Leafs away. Montreal scored first. But Pappin beat Vachon on a long, low shot. Conacher converted a fat rebound. Then, with

The Leafs and their fans behind the bench celebrate Toronto's 3–2 victory in game three of the Stanley Cup Final. Bob Pulford's goal in the second overtime period put the Leafs ahead two games to one in the series.

*"Terry Sawchuk was a loner,"
Johnny Bower once recalled.
"After a game, he'd go his own
way. He didn't mix too much
with the other players." Here,
however, Sawchuk shares a
rare light moment with his
goaltending partner during
the 1967 playoffs.*

Montreal on the power play, Marcel Pronovost broke up a pass, idled down left wing, killing time, and let a floater go that sailed past Vachon into the net. When the rookie netminder hopped up from his crouch, his eyes and mouth were three large Os. The Leafs won 4–1 and went home with a chance to win it all.

Punch wisely kept his trap shut before game six. Blake would play Worsley; besides, Montreal was the underdog now —there was no gain in provoking them. Imlach's pre-game speech was an appeal for sixty more minutes of hard work from a group that had given nine years of faithful toil: "It's been said I stuck with the old ones so long we couldn't possibly win the Stanley Cup. For some of you it's a farewell. Go out and ram that puck down their goddamn throats."

The game at the Gardens defined what was wonderful about these grand teams. The Canadiens were bold as Beliveau and his teammates executed four no-look passes in one swooping rush through the neutral zone.

In the face of all that grace and fury, the Leafs were imperturbable, cautious. This supremely co-ordinated defensive team felt ahead in a tie game. Montreal pressed. Sawchuk and teammates held. Then a blocked shot from Stanley sent Kelly and Ellis in two on one and the Leafs had a lead. Later, Pappin and Stemkowski responded to Habs pressure with a second scoring rush. This was Leafs hockey: twenty-five minutes of careful defence and then, with the opponent overextended, a stinging series of counter-punches.

Dick Duff rushed the puck to score for Montreal, making it close in the third. Then the agonizing countdown started. With a minute left and the score 2–1, Blake pulled Worsley for an extra attacker. Punch responded with a tribute to his old guard, sending out Horton, Stanley, Kelly, Armstrong, and Pulford. The average age was thirty-seven. Ha! Who said Toronto was too old? As his charges spilled over the boards, Punch couldn't resist a strategy that could be interpreted either as reckless or a smart hunch.

"Stanley, you take the face-off," he shouted. Number 26 was non-plussed, as he was rarely seen inside the face-off circle.

When the puck dropped, Stanley ignored it, lunging forward to tie up Montreal centre Jean Beliveau. The puck rolled to Kelly, who nudged it up to Pulford. He took three steps, then passed to Armstrong, who crossed the centre red line and slid a wrist shot one hundred feet into the empty Canadiens net.

In the dressing room after the Leafs collected their fourth Stanley Cup in six years, Imlach had an "I told you so" for everyone who'd listen. When a francophone reporter from Montreal commented that the Leafs coach had been right in sticking with his veterans, George "Punch" Imlach rose to his full height and shouted, "When was I ever wrong?" In his column, the scribe would suggest that the response was a joke.

He obviously didn't know Punch very well.

Punch puts his feet on the desk and relaxes with a glass of champagne. The job is done. The Stanley Cup is won.

MAPLE LEAF GARDENS

(Opposite) At one time during the mid-1960s, Toronto's Bill Crothers held every Canadian record from 440 yards to 1500 metres. His success, and that of teammate Bruce Kidd, brought about the return of track and field to Maple Leaf Gardens.

TRACK & FIELD

The *Grande Soirée*

BRUCE KIDD

ON THE COVER OF THE OFFICIAL PROGRAM FOR THE MAPLE LEAF GAMES, Friday, March 12, 1937, an unidentified artist has drawn the Gardens from above and across Carlton Street. It's a cold night, the sky clear but black. Men and women in hats and long coats press along the darkened sidewalks towards the entrances, eight deep. Another tide of people spills across the street from the south, bringing traffic to a halt.

The only significant light in the tableau comes from a row of spotlights which illuminate the upper reaches of the building from the overhang above the crowd. It draws the eye of the viewer and the imagination of the people below into the warmth and excitement inside. At the top of this light, as if it's an x-ray of what's inside, is a photograph of the American miler Glenn Cunningham, in summer shorts and singlet, outsprinting two rivals in a thrilling rush to the tape.

Although I ran there a generation later, my distilled memories of track and field at the Gardens turn on the same dynamic captured by the Depression artist: the dark cold of winter briefly transformed by the magic inside. There

Sprinter Harry Jerome competed at the Olympic Games in 1960, 1964, and 1968. He won a gold medal at the 1967 Pan-Am Games in Winnipeg. Champion distance runner Bruce Kidd (opposite) was Canada's Male Athlete of the Year in 1961–62.

was always a Cinderella quality to those magnificent meets. Track and field winters are long, hard, and lonely. It's the season of intense training, when runners, walkers, jumpers, and throwers prepare for the major summer championships through longer distances, heavier weights, and higher repetitions. The rush and sociability of competition are far and few between.

While hockey players play themselves into shape, competing as often as they practise, a track athlete may train as much as thirty or forty times for every winter race or time trial. In the days before modern indoor facilities and warm weather training, it was often outside, in the early morning and evening shadows, bundled up against the wind, pushing tight muscles and bruised feet over frozen concrete, slush, and snow. Jumpers and throwers lifted in cold, damp garages and practised on makeshift runways.

But once a year, the Gardens meet was a *grande soirée*, bringing members of a community isolated by winter and distance together for a night of adrenalin, artistry, and passion, amid elegance (the officials always wore tuxedos), warmth, glittering light, celebrity, and applause. While there were indoor competitions elsewhere—after Bill Crothers and I became headliners in Boston, New York, and Los Angeles, our coach Fred Foot persuaded Stafford Smythe to try a meet in Toronto—the Gardens was tops.

It was an extraordinary thrill to run against some of the best athletes in the world in front of hometown fans. The seating came right down to the edge of the track, and when the crowd got behind you in the later stages of a race, they could buoy you up with their energy so that you felt you were riding towards shore on the top of a gigantic wave.

The Gardens was one of the best designed and maintained arenas anywhere. I particularly appreciated its cleanliness. Sometimes I would get sick in places like Madison Square Garden, where the smoke from cigarettes and fried fat hung thickly over the infield, and Chicago's Stadium, where exuberant fans threw paper cups of beer onto the track.

There was conviviality, too. After the mile relay, the traditional last event, there was a party at the Westbury, a tradition started by Ken Twigg, who directed the first postwar meets. It was one of the very few events in the stiffly hierarchical world of amateurism where athletes and officials were ever invited to anything together, and it gave Toronto a cachet which ensured that most of the athletes in the world put it on their dance cards. During those early morning revels, winter seemed a million miles away.

While every year there were doubts that the show would continue, track and field found a home in the Gardens in two distinct periods, between 1935 and 1938, and 1963 and 1988. Over the years, six different organizations, including three daily newspapers, lent their support as sponsors. During those years, virtually all the best Canadians and many famous champions from around the world competed there, treating fans to a showcase of the sport at its best.

In the 1930s, while the remarkable Cunningham, who had overcome the loss of several toes in a childhood fire to become a world record holder, regularly won the featured mile, most of the events went to homegrown champions, like sprinters Johnny Loaring and Bill Fritz, hurdlers Larry O'Connor, Jim Worrall, and Roxy Atkins, jumpers Sam Richardson and Hal and Wally Brown, and walker Henry Cieman. After he came back from the 1936 Olympics with a bronze medal, O'Connor was untouchable; he set a world record for the sixty-yard hurdles in that 1937 meet.

Atkins enjoyed a wide following not only for her winning ways on the track. She was an articulate advocate for women in sports, taking on misogynist sportswriters like the *Toronto Star*'s Andy Lytle and the *Montreal Herald*'s Elmer Ferguson, who felt that sports made women unattractive to men. ("Elmer, you're goofy. You don't understand us girls and you don't even know your men," she once retorted in *Maclean's*.) While still an active athlete, she became a volunteer sports organizer as well, helping manage the extensive activities of the Women's Amateur Athletic Federation.

In reading through the programs from the 1930s, I realize that many of the athletes who competed then became the volunteer officials I knew later on.

The Gardens meet affirmed and stimulated the resurgence of Canadian track and field in the 1960s. Dave Bailey, Bill Crothers, Dave Ellis, Abby Hoffman,

Harry Jerome, Nancy McCredie, and Jenny Wingerson all won featured events there. Crothers, who won the silver medal in the eight hundred metres in the 1964 Olympics in Tokyo, Japan, was a superb tactician who could find his way through a crowded pack while running at full speed and seemed to know exactly the right time to strike. He was a master of the tight corner running required by the narrow, bouncing one hundred and sixty yard indoor board tracks, often passing other runners on the inside, like a nimble, charging deer. He won five consecutive races at the Gardens, and set meet records at both six hundred and one thousand yards.

Four-time Olympian Abby Hoffman was another perennial favourite, not only for her courageous running but her charismatic encouragement of girls and women in sports.

From the very first, the international character of the meet was provided by invited stars from not just the United States, but Europe, Australia, and New Zealand. In 1964, American Bob Schul (who won the Olympic five thousand metres in Tokyo) and I chased Aussie Albie Thomas to a world record in the three miles. But during the 1970s, in the buildup to the 1976 Olympics in Montreal, more and more of the top athletes from beyond the seas competed in Toronto.

The forerunners of the African running revolution—Mike Boit, Kipchoge Keino, Filbert Bayi, Henry Rono and Miruts Yifter—all competed here, as did their major New Zealand and European rivals, like John Walker, Dick Quax, Rod Dixon, Juha Vaatainen, and Henryk Szordykowski. The Gardens brought the first athletes from the "miracle" sports machine of the German Democratic Republic to Canada (persuading the Department of External Affairs to allow them to enter the country, because during those Cold War years, Canada did not recognize the communist regime), and other eastern European stars, like perennial sprint queen Irene Szewinska from Poland.

The meet became an indoor Olympics, with races and jumping contests as memorable as the Games themselves. No one who was there will ever forget the explosive kick of the diminutive Yifter at the end of three miles, the tragic duel

Canadians were among those who took part in track and field events when women were first allowed to compete at the Olympics in Amsterdam in 1928. By the 1960s Abby Hoffman (wearing #28, above), who had played pee-wee hockey with boys, was Canada's premier female athlete. Diane Jones Konihowski (opposite) ranked among the world's best in the 1970s.

The high jump competition produced plenty of drama at Maple Leaf Gardens over the years. Here Jacek Wszola, who would beat Greg Joy at the 1976 Montreal Olympics, clears the bar at the Toronto Star Indoor Games in 1974.

between Grant McLaren and Kipchoge Keino (when an official inadvertently blocked and stopped the Canadian champion just as he was about to overtake the Kenyan Olympic champion), the fingerbiting jumpoffs between Canadians Debbie Brill, Greg Joy, and Milt Ottey and Olympic champions Rosemarie Ackermann, Jacek Wszola, and Patrick Sjoberg.

It was an international athlete—Ireland's Eamon Coughlin—who became the most accomplished athlete in the meet's history, winning seven one-mile races between 1976 and 1985. The popular Coughlin was known as the "chairman of the boards" because he could lead from the gun, or sit back and kick. In most of his Toronto races, he brought the crowd to its feet with his last-lap heroics.

The Gardens boosted Canadian amateur sports and fitness in other ways as well. During the day, the track was made available to high schools, colleges, and universities so that hundreds of other athletes got the chance to compete. During the evening's gala, there were relay events for local teams so that fans got to see and encourage the best of the up-and-coming generation.

The Gardens also provided a window on the efforts of those other than able-bodied youth to enjoy the challenges of competition. Long before master's competition became popular, the Gardens offered a race for runners over forty. (The first, in 1967, was won by 1936 Olympian Milt Wallace, then fifty.)

Perhaps the most moving race I ever saw there was a sprint for blind runners, the first I'd ever witnessed. The crowd had to be totally silent, because the athletes ran to a helper's call at the end of the track. It seemed that no one took a breath as one by one the runners charged into what must have felt like nothingness. Each one earned a standing ovation. The message was that sport is for everyone.

The Gardens meets also provided a window on the changing demographics of Toronto and Toronto sports. During the 1980s, it was the brilliant sprinting of the young British and Caribbean black immigrants—Angela Bailey, Tony

Interest in amateur sports began to wane in Toronto during the 1980s, but track and field had still been able to draw huge crowds just a decade before. Here, 15,949 fans (then the largest crowd to witness an indoor meet in Canada) fill the Gardens for the 1973 Toronto Star Games.

Ben Johnson was still the darling of Canadian track and field when this picture was taken at the Sherbrooke Invitational in 1987. In January 1988 Ben shattered the world record over fifty metres at Maple Leaf Gardens. In October of that year the gold medal he won at the Seoul Olympics was stripped from him for steroid use.

Sharpe, Desai Williams, Angella Taylor, Mark McKoy, and Ben Johnson—which gave the crowd their most pleasurable memories. They even changed the patterns of attendance. The ritual of indoor track is that the sprints and hurdles are held first, when one end of the oval is removed to permit the longest possible straightaway. Then there is an intermission, to enable crews to assemble the circular track. When the featured events were the mile and three miles, many arrived late, even after the intermission, but Angella and Ben put everyone into their seats before the opening gun.

The last track and field meet in the Gardens was held in 1988. With the professionalization of the Olympic sports, in 1983, the costs of inviting so many athletes became too great. The tragic disqualification of Ben Johnson for using steroids at the 1988 Olympics in Seoul, and the damaging admission by so many admired athletes before the Dubin Commission that they, too, had resorted to performance-enhancing drugs, bewildered many traditional supporters of the sport.

At the same time, Toronto was becoming so preoccupied with the major continental professional leagues that there was less and less place for the made-in-Canada amateur sports. The one recent attempt at a major track meet—the World Indoor Championships at SkyDome—failed to draw decent crowds. Even in a highly marketable Olympic sport like figure skating, the major competitions are held in smaller centres like Hamilton, Halifax, and Kamloops.

Torontonians still excel in track and field, but they perform elsewhere. I hope the possible 2008 Olympics in Toronto will create new opportunities to showcase local talent—they're desperately needed.

But during its glory years, the fortunes of the Gardens and Toronto track and field converged.

We can always be grateful for that.

Angella Issajenko (formerly Angella Taylor) competes at the Toronto Sun Miller Lite Meet at Maple Leaf Gardens in 1988. Like Mazda Optimist Club teammate Ben Johnson and others, Issajenko raced to national champion status in Canada before being caught up in the Dubin Inquiry into steroid use.

JUNIORS & SENIORS

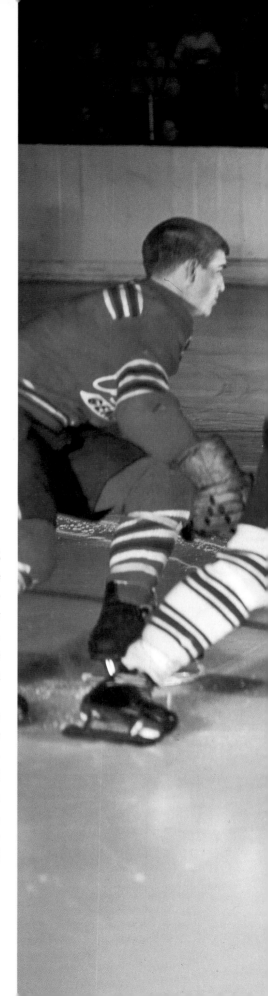

Senior hockey's past—Junior hockey's presence

ERIC ZWEIG,
WITH RESEARCH BY JAMES DUPLACEY

WHEN THE ST. MICHAEL'S MAJORS OF THE ONTARIO HOCKEY LEAGUE announced that they would be moving into Maple Leaf Gardens to play the home portion of their 1998–99 schedule, it was a double blessing for the building. First, it kept the doors to the Gardens open for fans to watch and enjoy competitive hockey. Second, it was a worthy tribute to hockey's grand old lady. After all, junior hockey has been as much a part of the rich history of the Gardens as the Toronto Maple Leaf teams that won seven Stanley Cup titles on her home ice and raised a total of eleven championship banners to her rafters.

The Toronto Marlboros were the first junior hockey club to call the Gardens home. Although St. Mike's, the earlier incarnation, would later play home games on Gardens ice as well, the Marlies were the building's longest-serving non-NHL tenant, from 1931 to 1989, when the franchise was sold and moved to Hamilton. In the end, the Marlies were pulling in fewer than seven hundred fans a game, a far cry from their glory days before NHL expansion, when they were a major part of the Maple Leafs' farm system and would regularly draw between six thousand and eight thousand fans for each contest. And

Brushcut Bobby Orr and goaltender Dennis Gibson defend against the Malboros.

This amateur playoff game in 1940 (above) lacked the star power featured in the 1942 Allan Cup Final (right), in which Boston's Milt Schmidt, left, and Woody Dumart, right, led the Royal Canadian Air Force team to Canada's senior amateur championship while doing their military duty. Veteran NHL coach and manager Tommy Gorman (in the fedora) headed up the RCAF team.

The 1932–33 Newmarket Redmen are welcomed home with flags, clowns, and music after beating the Regina Pats in the first Memorial Cup championship ever contested on Gardens ice.

if their opponent happened to be a cross-town rival like the St. Mike's Majors or the hated Oshawa Generals—especially come playoff time—tickets could become scarce indeed.

The Marlies were actually formed in 1926, a year before Connie Smythe purchased the floundering Toronto St. Pats franchise and remolded it into the Maple Leafs. The Dukes, as the Marlies were sometimes called, made their Gardens debut a memorable one. Just five days after the Leafs lost 2–1 to the Black Hawks, the Marlies shutout the Hamilton Tiger Cubs 6–0 on November 17, 1931.

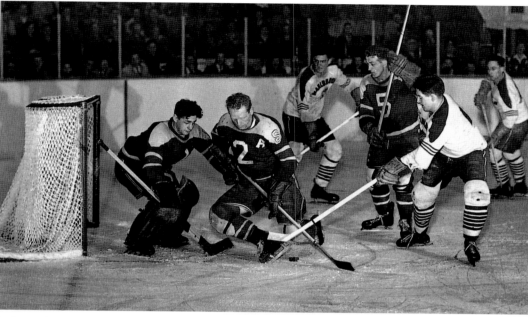

Over their 63-year history, the Marlies won the Memorial Cup seven times. The 1955–56 version of the club was extremely talented. Its defence included Carl Brewer, Bobby Baun, and Al MacNeil; among the forwards were Bob Pulford and Bob Nevin. Retired Maple Leaf goaltender Turk Broda coached. The Marlies easily handled the Regina Pats, going undefeated in the best-of-seven final, thanks to the goaltending of Len Broderick and the scoring touch of Pulford, who had ten goals in the series.

Although the Marlies would bring home four more Memorial Cup titles, only one—the 1964 showdown—was witnessed in the Gardens. Nine members of that club, who swept the Edmonton Oil Kings in four straight, would later join the Maple Leafs, as had players like Charlie Conacher, Red Horner, and Busher Jackson before them. Future Leafs in 1964 included Ron Ellis, Brit Selby, Pete Stemkowski, Jim McKenny, and Gary "Suitcase" Smith, who eventually would wear the colours of eight different NHL teams. The man who put these Marlie teams together was Jim Gregory, then in the early stages of a career that would lead him to becoming general manager of the Leafs during the 1970s and, later, vice-president of hockey operations for the NHL.

As a kid in the 1970s growing up in a Toronto suburb, the Marlies became my team. Leaf games were rare treats to be savoured, but the Marlies in their Leaf-like blue and white uniforms were mine to enjoy. My brothers and I could ride the subway for a dime and buy tickets to the game for a dollar. And what

With its east-west rivalry and strong community base, the Allan Cup senior amateur championship was once almost as important to Canadian hockey fans as the Stanley Cup. No Toronto team since the Varsity Grads in 1927 had won the Allan Cup when the Senior Marlboros claimed the championship in 1950. Here the Marlies face the Sherbrooke Saints in the Eastern Final before heading west to defeat the Calgary Stampeders.

The Whitby Dunlops helped crown the final golden age of senior hockey in Canada. The Dunnies won the Allan Cup in 1957, turning back the first American challenger when they defeated the Spokane Flyers in four straight games at Maple Leaf Gardens. They then returned the world championship to Canada with a victory in Oslo, Norway, in 1958. Here goalie Long John Henderson, captain Harry Sinden, veteran Sid Smith (far right), coach Wren Blair (kneeling, far right), and the rest of the Dunlops celebrate their second Allan Cup title in 1959.

players we could see at that price! Steve Shutt, Dave Gardiner and Billy Harris. Paulin Bordeleau and Wayne Dillon. Mark and Marty Howe. (Sometimes we would see Gordie in the stands watching his boys.) My favorite player was Bruce Boudreau.

NHL club sponsorship of junior farm teams was phased out and replaced by a Universal Draft of eligible players beginning in 1969. When I first attended Marlboros games at the Gardens, there was little chance that the players I was watching would be future Maple Leafs. Any NHL club—Leafs included—had an opportunity to select draft-eligible members of the Marlboros and give them a chance to play pro hockey. One Marlie who played his junior and NHL home games in the same building was goaltender Mike Palmateer, who was a hero in my household.

My brothers and I had a designated hockey room in our basement—we called it Make Belief Gardens—and on countless occassions in that arena of the imagination, we pretended to be Mike Palmateer in his first game with the Leafs. Palmateer was actually called up early in the 1976–77 season and did well. When he earned his first NHL shutout with a 1–0 win against the

JUNIOR & SENIOR

JUNIOR & SENIOR

Canadiens on November 17, 1976, it was a already old news to us. He'd blanked the Habs in our basement dozens of times!

Long before I ever began watching junior hockey, the Marlies' senior counterpart had been another prime-time resident of the Gardens. The Toronto senior Marlboros were established in 1903 and later became part of the Maple Leafs' farm system. Young players too old for junior but not ready to turn pro often refined their skills with the senior franchise. Hall of Fame defenceman Red Horner tells the story of playing a senior game for the Marlies in the afternoon, signing a pro contract in Conn Smythe's office after the match, and sticking around to make his NHL debut later that night.

The Marlboros only won the Allan Cup senior Canadian championship once. The 1949–50 club was described by the press as the "Dazzling Dukes," a team that featured a gangly centre by the name of Johnny "Goose" McCormack. A sensitive young man with a knack for making picture-perfect passes, Goose had actually retired in 1946 to enter the priesthood. However, after only one year of vespers and validation, he decided he enjoyed the atmosphere of the dressing room much more than the confessional. He returned to hockey and spent the next three seasons with the Marlies. In 1950–51, he finally earned a permanent spot with the Leafs. He was so excited by this amazing twist of fate that he quickly went out and married his sweetheart. However, by doing so, Goose broke one of Conn Smythe's ironclad rules: Never get married during the hockey season. Only moments after cutting the cake, Goose and his new bride were on their honeymoon, courtesy of a special wedding gift from Mr. Smythe: a one-way ticket to Pittsburgh, home of Toronto's AHL farm team. He never played for the Maple Leafs again.

In the days of NHL sponsorship of amateur clubs, the Toronto Marlboros groomed talent for the Maple Leafs while the Barrie Flyers were a starting point for future Boston Bruins. Both the Marlies and the Flyers fielded junior and senior teams. George Armstrong, seen at the far left, spent time with both Marlies clubs en route to the NHL.

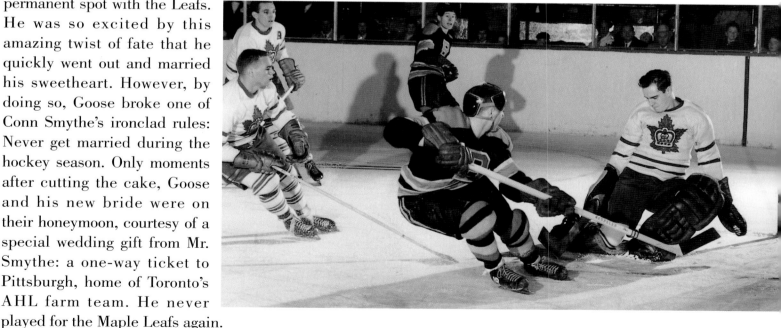

The Allan Cup was first contested at Maple Leaf Gardens in 1934 when the Moncton Hawks defeated the Fort William Thundering Herd. Two years later, many of those same Hawks players, including Jimmy Foster and Alex

Maple Leaf Gardens 1931–1999 **151**

The captain of the 1960–61 Malvern Collegiate hockey team poses with cheerleaders and the championship trophy after defeating Western Collegiate for the city high school championship at the Gardens on February 24, 1961.

Archer, played key roles in helping Great Britain pull off a stunning gold medal victory at the 1936 Winter Olympic Games. The final Allan Cup champions to be crowned on Gardens ice also featured ties to international hockey, as the Whitby Dunlops defeated the Verdun Flyers in 1959. Two years earlier, Whitby had put itself on the hockey map by capturing its first Allan Cup trophy. The Dunnies, as they were often called, cemented their claim to legendary status in November of that year when they defeated a Soviet all-star team 7–2 at Maple Leaf Gardens. The game marked the first time a Soviet team played in Canada, and the victory that night (followed by Whitby's World Championship victory in 1958) eased some of the sting of Canada's loss of the 1956 Olympic gold medal to the Russians.

The Soviet Nationals played an augmented Marlboros junior team in the Gardens in December 1965, winning 4–3. The best player on the ice was seventeen-year old Bobby Orr, who had been added to the Marlies from the Oshawa Generals.

More than nine years later, Central Red Army, the Soviet Union's top club team, defeated a reinforced Marlies team by a score of 7–6 in front of 16,284 fans at Maple Leaf Gardens on January 2, 1975. The Russian squad included Vladislav Tretiak, Valery Kharlamov, Vladimir Petrov, and others who had played against Team Canada in 1972 and against the WHA's best in 1974.

I attended one Marlboros game in the 1977–78 season. The attraction was Wayne Gretzky, then the best-known 17-year-old hockey player in the world and a member of the visiting Sault Ste. Marie Greyhounds. Four gold seats cost sixteen dollars, four times the cost of any of my previous junior tickets. Gretzky wasn't prominent that afternoon and I'd be lying if I said I saw the greatness there, but I do remember one goal he scored on a beautiful end-to-end rush. Sault Ste. Marie won the game. A year later, Gretzky turned pro. A year after that, he was the NHL's most valuable player.

His junior days were over.

So were mine.

With the Toronto Maple Leafs now playing in the new Air Canada Centre, junior hockey can play an important part in the ongoing operation of Maple Leaf Gardens.

All old arenas are said to have ghosts. I believe that the Gardens' will continue to tell their stories as long as there is hockey played in their presence.

I'll have to head down there and check it out.

The Toronto Marlboros won the Memorial Cup for the final time in franchise history in 1974–75 with one of the strongest junior teams of all time. Captain Bruce Boudreau and alternates Mark Napier and Mike Kitchen paced a high-powered offence that set an Ontario Hockey Association record with 469 goals in 70 games.

ROCK AND ROLL

Shaking the Rafters

RICHARD CROUSE

IN THE MID-1950S, WHEN ROCK AND ROLL WAS IN ITS INFANCY, a song called "Rock Around the Clock" hit Number One. Rock and roll had arrived, and nothing would be the same. Soon teenagers everywhere were transformed into finger-poppin' daddies and chicks, with their gobs of Brylcreem and their poodle skirts. On April 26, 1956, Bill Haley and His Comets swept into Maple Leaf Gardens for Toronto's first full-fledged rock and roll show.

The Gardens had long served as a concert venue. Eddie Duchin and his band began that tradition with an evening of music and dancing in September 1934. Musical presentations during the '30s, '40s, and '50s were diverse. The Canadian Opera Company opened their 1936 season with Aida. In 1938 bobby-soxers paid $1 to swing-and-sway with Paul Whiteman's Orchestra. Big bands dominated the '40s, with shows by Tommy Dorsey and Gene Krupa, but there were also appearances by others such as American baritone Paul Robeson. By the time Dean Martin and Jerry Lewis brought their variety show to Carlton Street in 1952, the Gardens had become Toronto's premier large entertainment venue.

(Opposite) Cyndi Lauper brought her "Girls Just Want to Have Fun" tour to the Gardens in November 1984. The man who started the whole "rock" ball rolling was Bill Haley, who blazed into town with his band, the Comets, on April 30, 1956.

The Gardens' ice surface was transformed into a giant ballroom on June 15, 1945, as hundreds of couples sashayed to the sounds of Charlie Spivak's Orchestra. Dances were a popular diversion during the war years, and the Gardens brought many of the top orchestras in the world to Toronto.

On that April evening in 1956, Bill Haley's Cadillac, followed by his band bus, drew up to the Gardens, riding a wave of controversy. Rock and roll was still new and dangerous. Parents wondered whether they should let their daughters go to the concert. Gardens officials expected a major flare-up, with one usherette admitting, "I'm scared to death."

Torontonians had little to be concerned about, however. Haley kept a tight rein on his band, forbidding alcohol during working hours, and even going so far as to conduct regular midnight bedchecks to insure his Comets hadn't tempted any local girls. As for the music, Haley often said that he avoided writing about anything suggestive, and took "a lot of care with the lyrics because we didn't want to offend anybody."

In an interview with Stan Rantin of the *Toronto Star*, Haley tried to interpret the rock and roll movement to the squares. Taking credit for inventing rock and roll by "combining Western music, Dixieland, popular music and old time rhythm and blues," Haley confessed that he didn't consider it "good music." He was a jazz fan, he said, and was just giving the kids "something they can dance to.

"The teenagers want a music of their own. This seems to be what they want."

In a press conference at the Gardens, Haley gave Toronto reporters a crash course in the origins of rock and roll. The early '50s had been a time of flux in the music business, he explained. Forward-thinking musicians, tiring of standard musical forms, had turned to progressive jazz. "But few people could understand it," he said, "and fewer musicians could play it. Rock and roll is basically easy to play and a lot of musicians are working today who otherwise would be out of a job."

Early rock and roll shows took the form of large touring ensembles. As many as seventeen acts would perform, each doing one or two songs, with the headliner playing for half-an-hour or more. "The Biggest Rock 'n' Roll Show of '56" included such musicians as Big Joe Turner, the Platters, the Drifters, Frankie Lymon and the Teenagers, the Teen Queens, the Flamingoes, the Colts, LaVern Baker, and Bo Diddley, all backed by a twelve-piece band. The house band's drummer earned special notice in the *Telegram* as the "unnamed, unsung hero" of the Red Prysocks band. "Anyone who can maintain the monotonous beat of rock and roll for two and a half solid hours...and I do mean solid,

(Opposite) Dean Martin and Jerry Lewis were at the height of their fame when they visited the Gardens in 1952. Pat Boone (seen here demonstrating his baseball skills) was a cool-crooning teen idol when he appeared on the Toronto stage in May 1957, while Woody Herman's classy clarinet stylings took the jazz world by storm during the 1940s. (Above) When New Orleans native Antoine "Fats" Domino arrived at the Gardens in 1958, he was riding high on the charts with his classic hit, "Blueberry Hill."

Elvis Presley, who would soon be crowned by his followers as the King of Rock and Roll, brought his entourage to Maple Leaf Gardens on April 2, 1957. The Gardens show was the opening date on Presley's brief tour of Canada that included shows in Ottawa and Vancouver. Those Canadian shows marked the only time in his career that Elvis performed outside the United States. Here he jokes with reporters backstage at the Gardens, giving the "thumbs down" to questions about marriage.

man! ... deserves a citation of honour."

The expected melee never materialized. "Nearly 13,000 teenagers almost went berserk in Maple Leaf Gardens last night in a fantastic rock 'n' roll orgy that resembled a wild west show, a jungle extravaganza and a revival meeting all rolled into one," wrote The *Toronto Star*. Despite the media's rabble-rousing, the show passed without incident. Gardens attendants, unused to dealing with rock and rollers, prowled the aisles, maintaining order, trying to prevent dancing by keeping patrons in their allocated seats. Several teeny-boppers jumped from their chairs during Big Joe Turner's "Flip, Flop and Fly," yelling, "Go, go, go!" but were soon returned to order by flashlight-wielding ushers. With official attendance counted at 12,764, it was the largest crowd Haley had performed to. "We never know what to expect," he said after the show, "But this was a reasonable, well-behaved crowd."

The evening's line-up, a Who's Who of '50s rock and roll, left most reviewers cold. But most of them were middle-aged reporters accustomed to covering opera and big band shows. The *Telegram*'s Helen McNamara slagged the artists, while also confessing, "At no time was it possible to hear just what the vocal groups, singers and musicians were playing ..."

If Bill Haley brought rock and roll to the Gardens, Elvis Presley's appearances there on April 2, 1957, proved it was here to stay. Arguably the most anticipated concert to date in Toronto's rock and roll history, his two-show stint was seen by 23,000, setting two milestones in his career. It was the first time he had performed outside the United States, and it was the largest crowd he had played to.

Taking the credit for bringing Elvis to Maple Leaf Gardens was Shirley Harris, a Presley super-fan who boasted of owning more than one thousand photos of her idol. While appearing on a radio show she asked Presley fans to write in if they wanted a Toronto concert. She got two thousand replies, and soon Elvis was on his way.

Toronto teenagers were mesmerized with Elvis fever. "I'm Elvisized," said one fan. "Such sex appeal," swooned a sixteen-year-old. But not all Torontonians were enthusiastic. "I'm a real Presley fan," said Joe Schulman, a taxi driver. "I'd like to fan him with a brick."

Bringing an act of the prominence of Elvis to Maple Leaf Gardens presented several logistical problems. District Chief George Elliott assigned eighty-nine policemen and six policewomen—far more officers than the normal detail assigned to a concert—to work the shows, some in uniform, some in plain-clothes. Their job was to make certain the crowd did not get out of hand. Elliott laid down strict rules—anyone who blocked aisles or left their seats was to be ousted. But the large force was also needed to accomplish another difficult goal—clearing the Gardens after the 6:00 show so that ticket holders for the 9:00 performance could get to their seats.

Before the first show Elvis met with a Bing Crosby and Glenn Miller-loving press at the Gardens. Wearing gold tasselled shoes, a silver silk shirt with ruffles, and a red jacket, he was the most flamboyant entertainer most of the reporters had ever seen. His southern charm disarmed everyone present, and he delivered what one scribe called an "impressive performance." Elvis admitted that he enjoyed the shrieks of the teenagers because, these musical purists were happy to note, they "cover up mistakes." On the subject of fan mail, Elvis revealed that he received more letters from Toronto and Winnipeg than from anywhere else in North America; whether or not it was true, the reporters made note of it.

Elvis made everyone laugh when asked—rather bizarrely—if he had ever considered becoming a doctor or psychiatrist. "I haven't thought about ever becoming a psychiatrist," he replied, "but I've often thought of going to one."

Then it was showtime. Elvis was whisked to the stage. According to the *Globe and Mail* the audience was comprised of "teenagers, some adults and a

(Clockwise from above) Some of the greatest rock, pop, and soul stars performed at the Gardens during the 1970s and '80s. Robert Plant and Led Zeppelin made their first Gardens appearance on September 4, 1971. When noted bad-boys the Rolling Stones appeared at the Gardens in 1972, a full complement of Toronto police were on hand. Lionel Ritchie and the Commodores brought their smooth R & B ballads to Toronto in 1982, while Welsh-born entertainer Tom Jones brought his gyrating hips and popular appeal to Toronto in 1970.

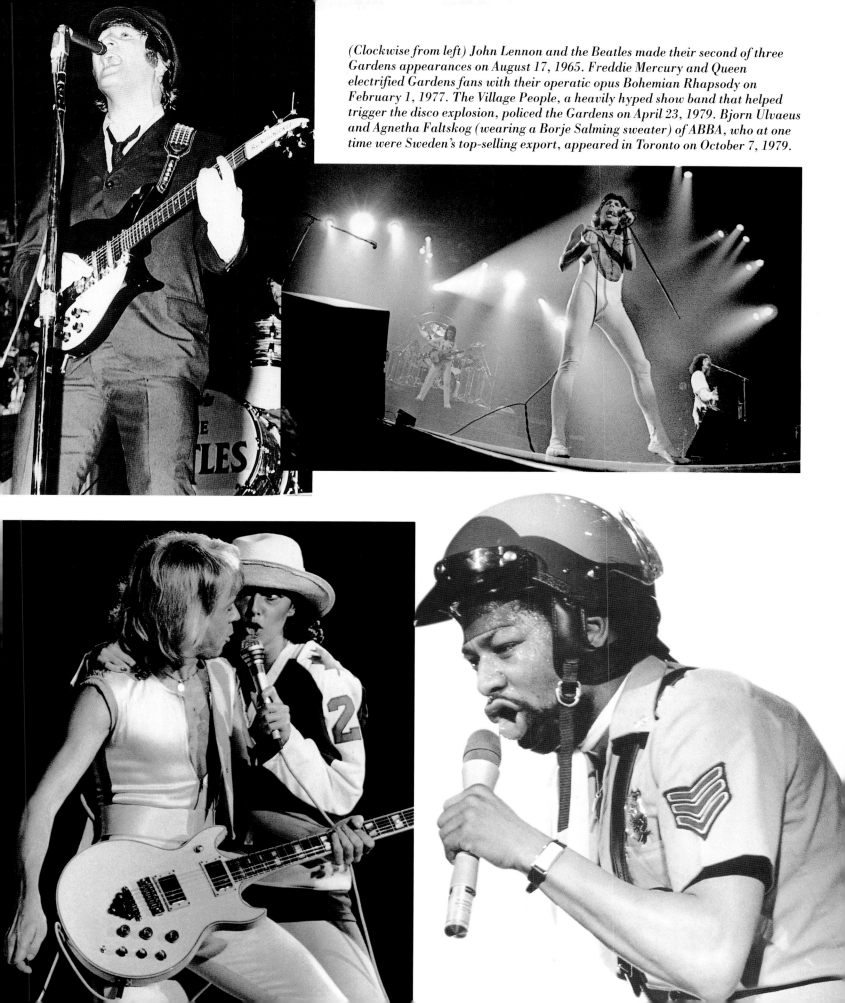

(Clockwise from left) John Lennon and the Beatles made their second of three Gardens appearances on August 17, 1965. Freddie Mercury and Queen electrified Gardens fans with their operatic opus Bohemian Rhapsody on February 1, 1977. The Village People, a heavily hyped show band that helped trigger the disco explosion, policed the Gardens on April 23, 1979. Bjorn Ulvaeus and Agnetha Faltskog (wearing a Borje Salming sweater) of ABBA, who at one time were Sweden's top-selling export, appeared in Toronto on October 7, 1979.

scattering of screwballs." The shrieks, handclapping, footstamping, and whistles from the audience were so intense, Elvis had to wait five minutes before starting to sing. He paced the stage and postured, at one point jabbing himself in the right eye with a microphone stand as he adjusted its height. For the rest of the concert he rubbed his eye, and by the second show it was noticeably inflamed.

Once under way, Elvis shook and shimmied in his $4,000 gold suit, every jiggle earning renewed howls of delight from the audience. Early in the show two teenaged girls were ejected from the Gardens when they tried to rush the stage. The pair were surrounded by twenty policemen and escorted out, the only casualties of George Elliott's stern policies.

It seems that many in the audience spent as much time snapping photos of Elvis as they did watching the show. "The show was lit by the chain lightning of amateur photographers flashbulbs," wrote The *Globe and Mail*. In fact, so many photos were snapped during the first show that Gardens clean-up crews filled

(Below) After going nearly a decade without a hit, Paul Simon re-emerged at the top of the charts with Graceland, an album that combined elements of jazz, folk, South African, and world beat rhythms. With South African singers, dancers, and musicians supporting him, Simon brought that record to life with a two-day appearance at the Gardens in June 1987.

(Above, clockwise) Androgynous pop vocalist Boy George greets the press on November 15, 1985. Elton John, the top-selling solo performer of the 1970s, made his first Gardens appearance of the 1980s on September 7, 1980. Former Max Webster frontman Kim Mitchell launched his solo career with a top-ten hit (Patio Lanterns) and an early New Year's Eve party on December 30, 1986. Frank Zappa, one of rock's most eccentric performers, gave a concert to remember on November 11, 1980.

three large boxes with used flashbulbs.

Perhaps the most enduring legacy of Elvis's brief Toronto stay came in the closing moments of the second show. With 15,000 teenagers howling for an encore, Elvis left the Gardens through a backstage exit and got into a waiting car which took him to Ottawa for another one-night stand. Concert organizers had to figure out how to clear the building. Thinking fast, someone stepped up to the microphone and made an announcement that would become a standard feature of every Elvis show for the rest of his career, and one of the most famous phrases in rock and roll history: "Elvis has left the building."

After that pair of shows the Gardens became a place of rock and roll dreams, a place that would represent the pinnacle of musical achievement in Canada, that would inspire countless kids to put down their hockey sticks and pick up guitars.

As a kid Neil Young had attended Maple Leafs games with his sportswriter father Scott. Watching the games, his mind would wander, picturing bringing his music to the arena some day. In 1973 he did it before a sold-out crowd.

While selling peanuts and potato chips in the stands, John Kay watched the acts come and go, and imagined life as a rock star. From his peanuts earnings he saved enough to buy his first guitar (a Harmony). As the leader of Steppenwolf, the ex-Gardens concessionaire earned his place in rock and roll history.

Although country music was a tough sell in Toronto during the 1980s, Kenny Rogers and Dolly Parton were able to sell out the arena when they appeared together at the Gardens on October 8, 1986.

Separating fact from fiction when it comes to the rock and roll shows at the Gardens could be a full-time job. The Beatles became the subject of several urban myths after their first visit to Toronto in September 1964. The best-known rumour involves their most celebrated album and a certain Toronto police sergeant. On the inside gatefold of Sgt. Pepper's Lonely Hearts Club Band, Paul McCartney is seen wearing an Ontario Provincial Police badge on his colourful uniform. "Ah ha!" said the amateur rock historians, uncovering what they assumed was a clue to the true identity of Sgt. Pepper. The story is that during the Beatles' 1964 visit to Toronto McCartney's bodyguard was a Toronto police officer name Sgt. Pepper.

The fierce heat in the Gardens during the Beatles' stint has also become the source of unsubstantiated rumour. Legend has it that Gardens vice-president Harold Ballard directed the heating system to be turned on to increase sales of soft drinks.

(Clockwise from left) Sting performed as a solo act at the Gardens on February 15, 1988, and was back in Toronto eight months later as a headliner in the Amnesty International Show. Canadian Bryan Adams rocked the Gardens on June 29, 1987. Paul McCartney made his first solo appearance in Toronto when he brought his "Wings Over America" tour to the Gardens on May 9, 1976.

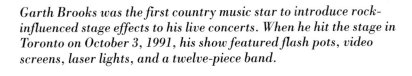

Garth Brooks was the first country music star to introduce rock-influenced stage effects to his live concerts. When he hit the stage in Toronto on October 3, 1991, his show featured flash pots, video screens, laser lights, and a twelve-piece band.

Are these rumours true? No. Does that matter? No.

The rumours have become part of the fabric of the legend of Maple Leaf Gardens. And our collective memories of the place—real or imagined—are now a part of our pop culture. While the building has always presented itself as a hockey rink, it is also a tangible monument to the rock and roll aspirations of anyone who ever bought a ticket for a show there. It is a place where anything is possible.

"Forget about what's happening today, tomorrow, or yesterday," said Jimi Hendrix during a 1969 show at the Gardens, just hours after being arrested for heroin possession at Toronto airport. "We'll build our own little world right here." With his future uncertain—Toronto police waiting backstage to detain him after the show—the guitarist delivered a blistering show, at times raucous, then subdued and introspective.

ROCK AND ROLL

Since Bill Haley's appearance, many of the greatest musicians and performers of our time—in rock and roll, rock, soul, and pop—have made the Gardens a regular stop on their tours: The Rolling Stones, James Brown, The Doors, Led Zeppelin, Elton John, Pink Floyd, Alice Cooper, and a whole grocery list more.

Venerable British rock legends the Who chose the Gardens as the site of their ìfarewell showî (the first of several) in 1982, a concert that was aired live on pay television all over North America.

For one instant in 1994, Canadian superstars The Tragically Hip focussed the Gardens' duality. As the band kicked into one of their best-known songs, they connected the rich hockey history of the building to its rock and roll legacy. "Fifty-Mission Cap" tells the story of Bill Barilko, a Maple Leafs defenceman who scored the Stanley Cup-winning goal in 1951, only to disappear while flying home from a fishing trip that summer. The Leafs didn't win another Stanley Cup until the police discovered Barilko's body a full eleven years later. In the moment the song faded into the darkness, it was as if the traditions of the Gardens had been encapsulated in a near-perfect, three-minute pop song. The Gardens with its long history—thousands of hockey games, hundreds of concerts—had inspired a fusion of rock and roll with Canada's favourite game. It's an unabashedly Canadian song, about a uniquely Canadian place.

(Opposite, left) Italian pop star Eros Ramazzotti poses with Toronto Sun *contest winners prior to his Gardens appearance on April 3, 1998. (Opposite, right) Julio Iglesias, a fixture on the "Adult Contemporary" charts, delivered a suave hit-filled performance at the Gardens on March 29, 1983. (Right) "The Chairman of the Board" gave his final concert in Toronto on November 12, 1991.*

Generations

Teenage Beatles fans screamed themselves into a frenzy during the Fab Four's first visit to the Gardens on September 7, 1964.

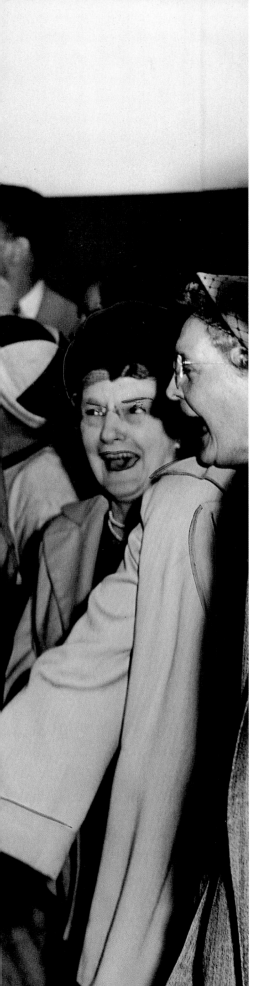

POWER-PLAYS

Politics
On Ice
and Off

DALTON CAMP

MY WRITING ABOUT MAPLE LEAF GARDENS SUGGESTS I KNOW something about hockey. The Gardens is many things to many people, but first and foremost it's a rink. So what do I know about hockey?

Not much. I jumped at the chance, however, to write about the old place, not as an expert on professional shinny, but because it has become special to me and it may soon be knocked down.

The Gardens, as a hockey rink, has become obsolescent. It happens. It happened to the railroad, the home boat that used to sail from Saint John's harbour, small-town armouries, and the militia. Still, I hope they won't be levelling Maple Leaf Gardens: they should bronze it. They should give it a 1-800 number that fans could dial to hear Foster Hewitt calling a Leafs-Canadiens game played forty years ago.

I suppose its time has come, though. Hard to make an honest dollar these days in a rink configured like the Gardens. The place lacks marketability; in the hockey business today you can't put a team on the ice until you've built and sold enough luxury boxes to underwrite the franchise. That's just being realistic.

As for me, the first seventeen years of my life were spent in the States, mostly in California, in the San Francisco Bay area. California was not exactly a hockey hotbed. I never owned a pair of skates and never learned to skate. In California, when it snowed in the foothills—which was not often—people would drive up to the hills and pack snow on the running boards of their cars, bring it back and put it on their lawns. No kidding.

I never even saw a hockey game until I was twelve. This is a rather

Two female admirers give Prime Minister Louis St. Laurent an affectionate pat on the behind as he leaves a Liberal rally at the Gardens in August 1953. The PM was astonished, the police perplexed, and the crowd amused by the unusual bit of political by-play.

R.B. Bennett was the millionaire prime minister who guided Canada through the Depression. Despite his expansive promises to Conservative supporters at Maple Leaf Gardens in October 1935, Bennett's party lost the election later that month.

advanced age to become a hockey fan and that first game—between two Pacific Coast league teams—didn't impress me much; I don't remember who won or even who played. What I do remember, vividly, is that after the game was over and the crowd emptied out onto the street, we heard newsboys crying, "Extra! Extra! Lindbergh baby kidnapped!" So I know where I was the day Lindbergh's child was stolen from its crib: I was at my first hockey game.

(Later on, my future father-in-law took me to a Rangers game at Madison Square Garden. He was a friend of Frank Boucher and the Cook brothers, Bill and Bun, all Rangers immortals. After the game, we went to a nearby hotel where some of the players were living and were seen sitting around their rooms in their underwear appearing decidedly unathletic and unglamorous with their pale white skin and gap-toothed smiles. I felt sorry for them. It did not appear to be much of a life, playing hockey in New York.)

My father died young and after that the family returned to New Brunswick where I was shipped off to Horton Academy, a private school on the campus of Acadia University in Wolfville, Nova Scotia. Horton was a hockey hotbed. I found myself in the company of peers whose consuming passion was hockey and whose emotional lives could turn on the result of a game between the Glace Bay Miners and the Sydney Millionaires. Each game carried in its wake scenes of wild jubilation, deep depression, and celebrations and humiliations as winners collected on their wagers and losers paid through the nose, literally. Classmate Ian MacNeill, who would later become a sportswriter, was once obliged to push a peanut by his nose from the gymnasium to the residence on a snow-packed sidewalk because the Millionaires lost.

I suffered acutely from culture shock, finding myself an immigrant in my own country. This was indeed an unknown land, so much of it invisible, incomprehensible, leaving so much to be imagined. Growing up Canadian proved not so much a deliberative effort as a process of acceptance. No one gave a damn who had won "the Big Game"—Harvard vs. Yale or Stanford vs. California—while baseball was entirely the Boston Red Sox, and then the Springhill Fence Busters, but then again, all that really mattered, the great common denominator, was the Toronto Maple Leafs.

Early on, I had once passed through Toronto, along its lakeshore, one Sunday morning during a thunderstorm. There did not appear to be anyone there. I later learned about Toronto as epicentre even before I had heard of Ottawa. Toronto was the site of the Canadian National Exhibition, the head office of the T. Eaton Co. Ltd., and of Maple Leaf Gardens, home ice for everyone's team at Horton Academy. In fact, at school, I enjoyed some small and vicarious measure of celebrity because my roommate's sister (he was from a Moncton family) had dated Gordie Drillon. Gordie Drillon!

At Horton, no one claimed to have ever been to Toronto. People knew people who had been to the CNE, encouraged by railway excursion fares. Still, it was a long way to travel; you wouldn't go there just for hockey, although some would kill for the chance. But during those years of a Canadian apprenticeship, I got to know Maple Leaf Gardens. It was, come to think of it, the first physical property in all the vast unseen Canada that I could imagine I knew, apart from Niagara Falls, which I had seen pictured on Shredded Wheat cereal boxes. I came to know the Gardens, in my mind's eye, as we all did, through the voice of Foster Hewitt and the rites and rituals of Hockey Night in Canada.

Hockey, as I've said, was not my game. But it was my introduction to the unknown country in

Prime Minister St. Laurent was heckled during a speech to Liberal supporters at Maple Leaf Gardens in June 1957. The rough treatment of the youthful dissident helped bring down the Liberal government.

The Liberal Party had formed the government of Canada for nearly twenty years at the time of this election rally in August 1953. Above the speakers and guests on the platform are larger-than-life photos of the Liberals' Big Three—Prime Minister St. Laurent, flanked by his predecessors, William Lyon Mackenzie King and Wilfrid Laurier.

which I had been born. It spoke to the sense of community, and of isolation, and of the frail strands of identity that held people together in a shared experience that bridged distances and darkness and the remoteness of the regions. I suppose some will think that corny or sentimental, but it is also very true.

Of course, the country has "filled in" some since Foster Hewitt first perched himself "high atop the gondola," as they said—whatever the hell that was—and gave us first the weather in Toronto (how very Canadian that was) before bringing us the game. Not that we're exactly crowded here, but we are now living closer together, see more of each other, and the silences are not so deep, nor are the sense of isolation and distance so awesome.

When Canada went to war, I enlisted in the army. As a young man with an identity crisis, I was lucky the army solved my problem: I no longer had an identity, but a khaki uniform, wool underwear, a pair of heavy boots, and a number—G1076. In the event I was captured by the enemy, according to the Geneva Convention, all I should tell my captors was my name, rank, and number. After six months in the army, that was all I could have told anyone anyway.

The war introduced new forms of isolation and loneliness. If hockey is Canada's game, isolation is its geography. Soldiers, in those days, didn't go out much and for good reason—they had little if any money and there was no place to go. For a time even the war was a long way off and someone else was doing whatever fighting there was.

With a "walking out" pass, a soldier could leave camp and wander aimlessly in the black night, in the general direction of town, without purpose or destination. I recall walking an empty street in a cold Canadian town on a Saturday night, in the sharp, biting cold, smoke rising from chimneys of huddled, shuttered houses, inside lights dimmed by drawn curtains, and then hearing the voice of Foster Hewitt celebrating the rites of Hockey Night in Canada, hearing the unseen but familiar rhythms of the game, the urgent voice, and the sound of the crowd rising and falling as a chorus as practised as any church choir. It was an epiphanous moment and, I have since thought, there has been nothing like it, nothing so unique, in all the entertainment arts in the national memory.

William Kilbourn, an ideal Torontonian, an alderman and an historian, once wrote: "If I were asked by some stranger to North American culture to show him the most important religious building in Canada, I would take him to Maple Leaf Gardens."

After the war, and some higher education, I reached the conclusion that the country was made up of two kinds of people—those who lived in Toronto and those who didn't. Travelling on borrowed money and with a new suit of clothes,

POWER-PLAYS

FOR THE BEST YEARS
OF YOUR LIFE VOTE **LIBERAL**

I arrived in Toronto, took a room in the King Edward Hotel, and walked up Yonge Street to College and Carlton. I turned right, and there was Maple Leaf Gardens. To tell the truth, it didn't look like all that much to me from the outside.

Not too long after, I went to a game in the Gardens and sat in the reds, nearest the ice and the action. I went with an ad agency friend whose father owned seasons tickets. In those days, all the men who came to the game were dressed in business suits and wore fedoras; their children wore flannels and blazers. Everyone in the reds, I guessed, had come from Upper Canada College or Havergal at one time or another.

Whenever I went to watch the Leafs play, I went on someone else's ticket and sat in the reds. I had not a minute of ice time to my name and hockey was still not my game, but I accepted the fact it was important to almost everyone I knew, both those who lived in Toronto and those who didn't. It was Canada's game.

The postwar years have been steeped in nostalgia; it had been a "good war" after all and it was followed by a lovely peace. Among the links and threads bridging the two was Hockey Night in Canada, Hewitt's descriptions of the game, and the roaring Toronto crowds in a rink where every seat was sold every night the Leafs took to the ice.

It was a special time in Canadian history, a very good time to live in Toronto, make a living, and raise a family. Everything worked. The city produced winners—E.P. Taylor and his racing stable, the Argos, the Maple Leafs, and the Marlboros, the best team in junior hockey, which played at the Gardens on Sunday afternoons. Life was just the way many had imagined it would be after the long, hard night of war.

Times change, are changing, and will always change. One thing about radio's version of hockey: the medium worked on the imagination and hockey became your own game in your own mind, and it is hard to be a critic of your own imagination. Later on, television made us experts, worse, made us critics. We could even referee the game. The Hot Stove League—Baldy Cotton, George Ferguson, and those guys – vanished. The place became a restaurant. Some vice-president of marketing at Imperial Oil fired Murray Westgate, everyone's favourite Esso dealer. The ads got slicker. The league had changed. The NHL now has a Pacific Division—Dallas, Phoenix, Los Angeles, San Jose, and Anaheim. Does this remind anyone else of Jack Benny?

Along the way, I came to know Conn Smythe, who was, for most of my years in Toronto, the president of Maple Leaf Gardens and the man who owned the team. I knew Smythe only through the Ontario Jockey Club, where he was a director and I a sometime consultant. Under Smythe, the Leafs had won seven

Ten years after John Diefenbaker became prime minister, the Gardens saw Dief's demise as the Tories turned their back on the Chief in favour of Dalton Camp's candidate for leadership, Robert Stanfield. Here Diefenbaker addresses the 1967 PC convention while being watched over by the likenesses of past prime ministers Sir John A. Macdonald and Sir Mackenzie Bowell.

One month after winning the Tory leadership, Robert Stanfield was back at the Gardens to help the Leafs open the 1967–68 season. Flanked by Maple Leaf Gardens board chairman John Bassett, Stanfield shakes hands with George Armstrong after having already greeted Black Hawks captain Pierre Pilote.

Stanley Cups and his racing stable produced two Queen's Plate winners. The Major had his own game with me. Whenever we would meet in the Directors' Lounge he would upbraid me for what he assumed was my part in electing Robert Stanfield as the leader of the federal Progressive Conservative party.

"Camp," he would say, "why would you pick a dull bastard like Stanfield to lead your party?" He would then offer his imitation of my friend, complete with the slow drawl and incoherent mumblings. I learned to take it in good form, but I didn't like it much, or him.

Willie O'Ree and I received honorary degrees together at Saint Thomas University in our native province. O'Ree was the first black to play for a National Hockey League team and often spoke with wry and gentle humour about encountering racism as a player, both from opposing teams and from his own, the Boston Bruins. Recently, he spoke about Herb Carnegie, a black player who, when he was in the Quebec Senior Hockey League (Jean Beliveau was a teammate), was once told by Conn Smythe that "if he could turn Herbie white he'd be in the National Hockey League."

What the hell, you can't expect a man like Smythe to be any more a visionary than he was. He built the Gardens and invented the Toronto Maple Leafs. The first Canadian I heard saying something had to be done to create more opportunities for blacks was Stanfield, which prompts memory to say he was, according to legend, a pretty fair hockey player himself as a schoolboy at Ashbury.

Among my first political memories of the Gardens was the Liberal rally at which Prime Minister Louis St. Laurent spoke, during the campaign in 1957. While the prime minister was speaking, a dissident youth mounted the platform and began hectoring. Someone shoved him and he fell backwards, striking his head on Smythe's own concrete floor, the sound heard by everyone in the audience and echoing throughout the country. The youth was carried from the rink to hospital, as I recall, taking with him the Liberal party's election prospects. It was, you could say, the loudest check ever delivered in the Gardens' history.

The party convention at which Robert Stanfield was chosen as Tory leader was held at the Gardens ten years later. In Canada, a hockey rink without the ice is useful to politics. A rink holds a political crowd comfortably, and, at the Gardens, people know it's hallowed ground whether they're from Toronto or Saskatchewan—especially if they're from Saskatchewan. And besides, politics is a game for so many people—a kind of non-contact sport.

A good place to watch hockey, the Gardens was also a good place to watch politics. If you sat up in the greys, the whole convention floor was before you and you could see who was wringing whose arm, who was romancing whom, and what candidate was walking where. I watched John Bassett and George Hees head out of the rink and sent someone down to see what was up: Hees, it was reported, was trying (unsuccessfully) to move Bassett from Stanfield. When the game was over, Stanfield had won. I sat in the empty rows, high over the floor, watching the crowd leave the building. I must have been the last one out.

In his acceptance speech, Stanfield had said he would "try to get along with that fellow Camp," a guy who couldn't skate and hardly knew a cross-check from a rent cheque. I heard my name resonate through Maple Leaf Gardens; not bad for someone who, thirty years before, had been a kid without a country.

Prime Minister Pierre Trudeau works the crowd outside the Gardens at a Liberal rally in May 1979. With a full house waiting for him, Trudeau spent some time with those stranded on the sidewalk before making his appearance inside the jammed arena.

FRONT-ROW GREENS

Observations From the Best Seats in the House

RICK SALUTIN

MY FIRST VISIT TO MAPLE LEAF GARDENS FOR A HOCKEY GAME WAS made under duress. Not my own, my father's.

One of the Clendenning twins next door—I think it was David, not Phil—had been taunting me all that Saturday because he was going to the Leafs game that night. The Black Hawks were playing. It was 1952 or '53 and there were only six teams. David (or Phil) and I were ten or eleven years old. We used to play board hockey together on the plywood games with the single sprung lever for all the men (except the goalie) and a ball bearing as the puck. The ones you got at Canadian Tire and can now find occasionally, if you look diligently, in antique stores along Queen Street West. That's where I got the one I have today. My mother gave my original away to the Hadassah Bazaar. She keeps everything but she gave that away. I have the new one mounted on the wall in my office. It's become an artifact.

But none of us had ever been to a real, live Leafs game. To tell the truth I don't know till this day whether David actually went that night or was simply, brilliantly using the claim to torture me. But it sent me—after I'd dispatched him from the front porch with the assurance I couldn't care less—into agonies of tears and recriminations. My mother finally broke and dialled the number for my father. It was a Saturday afternoon and he was playing cards at "the club" on Bathurst Street north of Harbord. She handed me the phone and I asked the barman to find my father. "Solly Salutin!" the barman yelled through the din and the cigar smoke. You could hear the smoke almost as clearly as the din. I told my

The Leafs' Harry Watson tries to split the Chicago tandem of Bill Mosienko and alternate captain Bep Guidolin. The Black Hawks were the NHL's worst team from 1944 to 1958, missing the playoffs for twelve of fourteen years and finishing in last place nine times.

father the problem and a few minutes later he called back to say he had a pair for that night and he'd come home to pick me up.

Looking back, I don't know if I took this as some kind of miracle that befell me and my dad, or as a sign that he was so untuned to my needs that it took crying to the verge of self-combustion to get him to score a couple of reds for us. It may not have been that much of a trick, in truth, since Chicago wasn't much of a team in those years. They had Bill Mosienko and they had Harry Lumley in goal, and that was about it. When I say reds, by the way, I mean your *vrai* reds. What are now called the golds and in years to come will again transform—into the implausible platinums. Rinkside. A mere six or seven rows above the Leafs' bench. Still, I felt there had to be something weird and significant for my dad to succeed in picking up seats that good, that easily, so close to game time. As you can tell, I still haven't worked it out—and my dad's been dead since 1995. He'll never tell.

The first thing I remember about that game was seeing Max Bentley on the far side of the ice, out to take a face-off. Wow. I had read a book about Max Bentley. I think it was called Dipsy Doodle Dandy. It had a little cartoon drawing of Bentley, in full hockey gear, sitting on a milking stool squeezing the udders of a cow. This illustrated how he'd strengthened his hands for his superb wrist shot by working on the farm when he was a kid.

Most of the book had been about Max and his brother Doug playing for Chicago together

Max Bentley, the Dipsy Doodle Dandy from Delisle, Saskatchewan, had twice won the NHL scoring title with the Black Hawks before the Maple Leafs sent five players to Chicago to acquire him in November 1947. Bentley helped Toronto win the Stanley Cup in 1948, 1949, and 1951.

in the 1940s, but he'd somehow materialized with the Leafs, in time for my first game.

Let me pause over the power of this moment. Bentley wasn't the first mythic sports hero to step off the pages of a book I'd read. My Big Baseball Book had a section showing the all-star team of all time, a full-page drawing for each player and a facing page of print; and on that team the only player still playing was Joe DiMaggio of the New York Yankees. (The other all-time outfielders were Babe Ruth and Ty Cobb.) One day—it may have been earlier that same fall, when the World Series was on—I came home from school and went upstairs to the Switzers', who had the only TV set in walking distance. As Shelley Switzer and I watched, someone from the National League team in the series lifted a fly ball into centre field, and down into the middle of the screen, as if descending from above, loped Joe DiMaggio to gather it in—more or less as I'd have pictured Jesus returning earthward through some nice clouds. It was stunning, in a way more so than seeing Bentley, because DiMaggio had already been apotheosized in my mind.

He was up there on Olympus with the great departed ones: Ruth, Gehrig, Bill Dickey, Honus Wagner and Walter Johnson, the Big Train. Maybe that's why I

Speedy Toronto forward Cal Gardner puts a move on future Maple Leafs goalie Harry Lumley while Chicago defenceman Lee Fogolin tries in vain to break up the play.

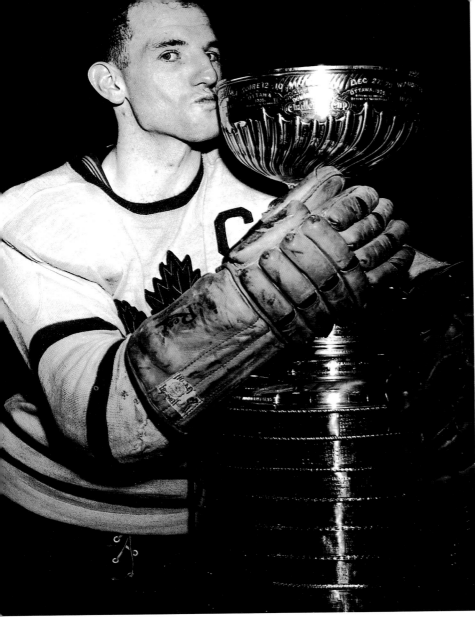

Captain Teeder Kennedy kisses the Stanley Cup after yet another successful Leafs season. The 1951 championship was the Maple Leafs' fifth title in seven years and the sixth in ten. Kennedy was a hero to a generation of Toronto hockey fans and the player Leaf teams would rally around.

experienced the shot, which was really just the function of camera placement and video limitations in the days before close-ups, as a supernatural moment. Bentley, though, was live before my eyes. He and I were existing in the same physical space. Wow.

The other thing I remember about that game is Teeder Kennedy. At some point he was suddenly there, as Bentley had been, for a face-off near one of the blue lines. I don't remember either of them taking the face-off for the start of the game or of a period. Maybe I had trouble focussing. Anyway at that moment, from the far upper corner of the Gardens to our left, came the legendary cry, a sort of equivalent to the call of the loon: "Come Onnnnnn, Teeder." I'd heard it on radio broadcasts of Leafs games, I suppose. Often I'd fall asleep part-way through a game, if my mother promised to listen to the end and leave me the final score, with the goals and assists and names of the three stars, on a little piece of paper for me to wake up to. The Come On Teeder cry had a special power, I now realize, since little else was distracting you during the games. There was no organ, the only music came from a live band, usually military, in the bandstand on one end, between periods. There was the SporTimer over centre ice, but all it gave you was the score and the time. Once, decades later, when I attended a game at Maple Leaf Gardens with Russian poet and hockey fan Yevgeny Yevtushenko, he expressed deep dismay, well on the way to disgust, with how many things were happening to distract from the play on the ice. Back then, at my first game, there was Come On Teeder and that was about it.

So I could see Kennedy, more or less facing us, over the shoulder of the Chicago centre, and the linesman dropped the puck. And very quickly it evolved into a scuffle between the two players, the linesman managing to intervene with them trying to get at each other, and I clearly saw, though I couldn't actually hear it over the roar of the crowd, Teeder Kennedy mouth,

"You son of a bitch!" It was the first time I had ever seen a grown-up swear. And it was Teeder Kennedy! The grown-up quality was probably heightened by the way Kennedy's hair was thinning and his hairline was receding, though for all I know he was still in his twenties. At any rate, he always looked to me like the paternal figure on that team. Later in my own adult life, I've generally had what actors and directors sometimes refer to as "ready access to anger." I don't think that's necessarily a bad thing, depending on what forces in society it's directed toward, and people without as ready an access to anger have sometimes expressed envy of it.

It makes me wonder whether Teeder Kennedy helped me out, in that impressionable moment, by legitimating it.

Over twenty years later—which included ten years in the U.S.; a marriage that ended in divorce and a relationship to God that ended when I left the seminary; various undergrad and graduate degrees and programs; getting arrested by New York police and rousted by right-wing construction workers in favour of the Vietnam war—in other words all the normal delights of the 1960s—I wound up back in Toronto and acquired (a share in) seats of my own

Teeder Kennedy bangs the puck past Terry Sawchuk while teammate Sid Smith tangles with a Red Wings defenceman during the 1953–54 season. Detroit would win the Stanley Cup that year and the next, giving Sawchuk three championships in four seasons. He would win his next Stanley Cup as a member of the Maple Leafs in 1967.

to the hockey games at Maple Leaf Gardens. In true Gardens tradition, they'd originally been acquired by Dr. Chalmers, father-in-law of my friend, John Saul, in 1936. They'd passed to John and Dr. Chalmers' daughter, Pat, who let me and several friends share in them. These seats were first-row greens, exactly halfway up the Gardens and an extra half-row or so above the last row of reds just below them, which meant we never had to cope with big heads or hats in the way.

They were also aisle seats, which helped, for instance, during the years when the seat next to us was occupied by a very large man (who actually caused his seat to bend back permanently, as can still be seen by siting down the row) and which meant we could only go to games during those years with a child or a very thin person. When neither was available, at least we had the aisle step to sit on. That seat next to us was a single and seemed to attract unusual occupants. There was the Old Ref, a gnarled, grizzled fellow who always came wearing an official's striped shirt, a whistle around his neck, kept a close record of all penalties, and assured us he was there in case one of the officials on the ice was injured. One night, finally, an official got hurt near the end of a period. The Old Ref left during the break and we never saw him again. Behind us sat Syd and Michel, a couple of buddies who worked in air traffic control at Toronto airport and were astute and acerbic commentators on the Leafs. After only nine or ten years, in the reticent Upper Canadian way, we began saying hello to each other and chatting between periods. Michel was transferred to Ottawa eventually and only made special appearances for the rare games when the Canadiens came to play. Now that the Leafs and Habs are in the same division, I wonder if he'll be down more often.

It was from those seats that I saw Darryl Sittler score his still-standing record of ten points in a single game. Since our seats were in the opposing team's end, which meant we saw the other side's goalie for both the first and third periods, we got to see Sittler score most of his record that night. At some point he seemed to tire of anything but goals and ended up with six of them, along with four assists. Mostly, though, the team wasn't very inspiring, which I suppose isn't a big revelation to anyone reading this. We held onto the seats largely because we held firm to a belief that one day Harold Ballard would die and then things would improve. Eventually Ballard died, and when things didn't turn around swiftly and permanently, it was of course a big disappointment.

Some of my worst moments in those seats, though, came when Ken Dryden was in goal for the Canadiens. I'd met Ken in 1976. I was writing plays at the

time and the Centaur Theatre, Montreal's biggest English-language company, had asked if I'd be interested in writing a play about their hockey team. I said no immediately: I was a lifelong Leafs fan, had either no or hostile feelings toward les Canadiens, and I felt it was important to be emotionally attached to the subject of your writing. But I started to think about what an honour it was to be asked to write a play on hockey in Canada; I did feel very involved with the history and politics of Quebec, and indeed had begun my career as a Canadian writer after returning from the States while I was living in Quebec City. I also knew the intense link between the hockey team and the history of Quebec—in short, I found reasons to say yes. Ken was a subscriber to the theatre's season and they'd asked if he'd be willing to meet me and consider helping with background material for the script. The collaboration went extremely well and when the Parti Quebecois won their first election on the night of a game at the Forum, we had the structure for the play's final act, along with its climax. I gave Ken an assist in the credits, which I felt would be appreciated by a goalie.

Bruins captain Milt Schmidt looks on anxiously as goaltender Sugar Jim Henry clears the puck into the corner in a 1954–55 game at the Gardens. Bill Quackenbush appears to trip Toronto's Ron Stewart as he tries to track down the rebound.

Toronto native and future Maple Leafs president Ken Dryden was a Montreal Canadien throughout his brief but stellar NHL career. Here he is down on one knee after making a save at the Gardens. Guy Lapointe (5) and Jacques Laperriere (2) watch closely as former Leafs great Frank Mahovlich clears the rebound from the clutches of captain Dave Keon.

Some time during that first year of knowing each other, perhaps after the season (hockey and theatre), the penny dropped for Ken. So did his jaw—or whatever his facial equivalent of astonishment is—and he said, "You really are a Leafs fan!" He'd grown up in Toronto but I guess he was so deeply involved in the Canadiens and the rich culture surrounding them that he was shocked I wasn't as fully in it myself. And I had written the damn play, which opened with a dying French-Canadian soldier on the Plains of Abraham, after the defeat by General Wolfe, throwing his rifle to his son with his last breath—and as his son catches it, it transforms into a hockey stick so he can carry on the battle in a different form. In fact in the play the opposing team was always the Maple Leafs. Maybe Ken also felt some pity for anyone trying to maintain the faith in the Leafs during those years (and many to follow). If you had a choice, who wouldn't stick with the Canadiens? I, at any rate, never felt I had a choice.

So during games when the Canadiens played in Maple Leaf Gardens in those years, on the rare occasions when the Leafs got a goal past Ken, and since our seats were almost level with the opposing team goal, and I'd leap to my feet with my arms over my head—as involuntarily as your knee goes up when the doctor taps it with his little hammer—then I'd break into a terrified sweat, fearing that Ken, who knew where our seats were, would dolefully gaze up to his right, through that familiar, mythic mask of his, and take in what a bad friend and collaborator I'd turned out to be. He never took well to goals that were scored on him anyway. He once told me he could remember every puck that ever went past him, and knew what he could and should have done to stop it. Every single one.

We still have those first-row greens, as the era of Maple Leaf Gardens draws to its conclusion. Or at least I still have my share. Another generation has moved up to take them over—John and Pat's son Nick, now in his early thirties, and his two cousins, Mike and Tim—and of the old bunch in section 74, row A, seats 3 and 4 (aisle seats nonetheless) I alone am left to tell the tale. For a long time I stuck with them in the vague, not really formulated thought that one day I too might have a kid to take to games and pass the tickets on to. I assumed it was a fantasy, a daydream.

Yet it turns out I really was waiting for Gideon Cole, who at age ten and-a-half days is bawling on the couch two floors below me as I write the concluding thoughts of this piece.

I'd like to think that sticking with the tickets till now and on into the millennium is another kind of affirmation too: affirming the value of live experiences of things like hockey over the mediated versions of them that you get through media like newspapers or TV. There's no doubt we live in an age in which representations of reality are taking over from reality itself.

Just 100 or 125 years ago, most Canadians might have seen an occasional newspaper with maybe the odd photograph. They had the Bible reading and sermon on Sundays. And perhaps a travelling theatre troupe that came through once a year. The rest of their experience of the world came direct from the world itself.

Today, on the other hand, we're inundated with endless images of reality: in papers, newscasts, ads, recorded music, videos, TV or the Internet. The range of experiences available through these media is far greater than the range of experience any of us will ever encounter directly. And for many people, these representations of reality seem more real than their direct experience. They talk as if they know Oprah and Princess Diana as well as or more intimately than they know their own families or friends. This goes for hockey too. Far more people follow the Leafs on TV than see them play at Maple Leaf Gardens. In fact many of them will never see a game live, and may well feel they're not missing anything serious. TV, they could say, is as good as or better than being there; you get all the close-ups and replays, not to mention the play-by-play and analysis. The strange thing is, it's not that easy pinning down the difference between the two kinds of experience.

You can try saying that we don't see a real hockey game on TV; we see 525 lines of shifting light created by an electronic beam scanning the back of a mosaic of photo-electric cells and we interpret this as a hockey game.

Lotsa luck with that one. Or you could say: when you're in the arena, you hear the skates cutting into the ice as the players swerve and corner. But now there are mikes set above the rink to pick up those very sounds. If your seats are close enough to ice level, you can get a feeling Bob Gainey once described: twelve big guys careening fast and without too much control on a small surface—but the cameras placed behind the net last season at Maple Leaf Gardens create a better sense of that crowding and how little time you have to do something with the puck than those centre-ice cameras we've been used to for so long. As I say, it isn't easy.

Personally, what I'd argue is that when I'm actually at a game, I get a sense that anything could happen and nothing is predetermined. Watching hockey on TV, even though I know it's coming to me live, always feels a bit like watching a movie. When you're there in the Gardens, you feel how utterly undetermined, contingent, random, and truly free the situation is. A player might stop the puck, or it might skip over his stick. If it happened one way, it could as easily have happened another. A play of great skill or finesse might as easily not quite have worked. It's all so damn... human. That's because a live hockey player in front of you is not the same as a set of electronic blips arranged to represent a live hockey player who's somewhere else. And the experience you have is never as powerful and... human, when you're not right there.

The great Canadian historian Harold Innis made his name by doing masterful studies of economic realities like the fur trade in Canada, the fisheries, and the railroads. Yet as he neared his death, in 1951, he became preoccupied not with those hard realities but with the different forms and technologies of communications through which they're depicted. He became a big fan of what he called the oral tradition, by which he really meant face-to-face communication as a way of dealing with each other, versus the written tradition: where media of communication like books or newspapers get in between the actual people who are trying to discuss things and make choices. In Innis's division between two traditions, TV really amounts to just an electronic version of the written tradition, it's something that comes in between

real human beings and their experiences of each other. By keeping on going to the games, whether they're at the Gardens or the new place, I'm trying, among other things, to strike a blow for live experience and the oral tradition, and keep faith with the Canadian vision of Harold Innis.

I know I've swept quite a few things into this short memoir about Maple Leaf Gardens, now that its career as a home for the Leafs is done. It feels a little like the case of the theological student at a seminary (which I once was) whose assignment in homiletics class was to give a sermon. When he finished, his teacher said: "This would be a good sermon if the preacher was about to leave his congregation the next day to move to Bolivia permanently and never return." That's more or less how I feel.

Darryl Sittler was the greatest Leaf of the 1970s, leading the team in scoring for eight straight seasons from 1972–73 to 1979–80. Though Rogie Vachon kept the puck out this time, Sittler collected four points in the game against Los Angeles on January 11, 1975. On February 7, 1976, Sittler set an NHL record with 10 points against the Boston Bruins.

FIRST PERSON

On Stage and Off

DAVE BIDINI

A product of the Toronto suburbs, Dave Bidini grew up watching concerts at the Gardens. He performed there with the Rheostatics in December of 1996.

"My stomach was twisted. Then the puck was dropped and the game was on. The clock of the game, and this part of my life, began to move."

SCOTT YOUNG AND GEORGE ROBERTSON,
"Face Off"

THE LAST TIME I VISITED MAPLE LEAF GARDENS WAS THE best. It was in early December 1997. The day was dark and wintry. Fat clouds hung above me like weightless grey zeppelins, their bellies forked by the tines of the city's towers. I pedalled my rusty old bicycle—a creaking blue racer with the silhouette of a riding child embossed in silver on the front—along Carlton Street, my pant bottoms splashed with road muck pinwheeling off cars and taxis and buses. The streets were thick with people, few of them smiling, their heads covered with parka hoods, ear-wraps, toques, mufflers, snoods, hunting caps, and fur-lined baseball caps.

On the north side of Carlton, a large sign hung above the street: COLORADO, 7:30 PM, TONIGHT.

Bands like the Beatles were long gone by the time that British acts ranging from Elvis Costello (opposite) to Ozzie Osbourne played Maple Leaf Gardens in the 1970s and '80s. The Gardens was the premier concert venue in Eastern Canada then, with every major North American tour making a stop. Neil Young was the first local musician to fill the seats when he appeared at the Gardens in 1973. Later in the decade Toronto bands Rush and Max Webster would pack the place. Rush's New Year's Eve concerts at the Gardens were a staple of the late '70s.

I read the words aloud. There was something about them that I couldn't quite put my finger on, something powerful and good and poetic. My mind was tweaked. I chained up my bicycle and set about my business.

As I left home that day, I had no intention of going to the Gardens. The Maple Leafs were mired—no, not mired, rather quicksanded, entrenched, grafted, smunched even—in another interminable losing season. This happened despite the fact that Hall of Famer (and noted Etobicokian) Ken Dryden had recently assumed leadership of the organization, a surprisingly wise and clear-headed move coming from the perennially unwise Leafs ownership. But even though they'd entrusted Ken with reviving their once-estimable team, his heroic deportment hadn't yet been assumed by his players. Glum and weak-spirited in their performances (save the tall Swede Mats Sundin, who was the stand-out in every game), the Leafs were bested nightly by teams from the American South, and their reputation as one of the original six's jewel franchises continued to be diminished by newer organizations steeped in as much tradition as yesterday's goulash.

So, COLORADO, 7:30 PM, TONIGHT didn't exactly evoke images of joyous athletic conquests. However, as I bounced those words around in my head, they began to resonate in the cavity of my memory. The sign was calling out to me like a lighthouse beacon, and then, right there, as I walked deep in thought across the snowy John Sheard parkette, I remembered the Gardens: the lambent glow of the ice, the taste of Fruitella and Coke and pink popcorn, the dirty tin roof, the Geigeresque steel ribbings, enormous television lamps, incandescent catwalks, and red velvet curtains, the cramped, cushioned seats, the hard, sticky benches of the end blues, the stiff-fingered organist, the white-haired ticket-takers and pimpled program sellers, the florescent wickets, the wood-panelled Will Call suite, the Ballard bunker, the photograph of handsome Teeder Kennedy meeting the Queen, the bustling of life outside the rink, and, ultimately, the shuffling of fans through the gates, their activities broadcast to a nation who had no choice but to watch a crummy hockey team representing Canada's richest city get their asses kicked by organizations with stupid nicknames who weren't fit to wipe the spit from Pug Saganiuk's chin strap.

COLORADO, 7:30 PM, TONIGHT

I needed a ticket, fast.

My memories of the Gardens, as they relate to hockey, are wonky. I'm sure that I visited there as a kid, but I couldn't give you the exact whos and whens of my first time in the rink. My impressions of it are much clearer when I think of watching games on television. I've recorded several unforgettable Gardens moments this way—Peter Mahovlich's short-handed goal in game two in '72; Sittler's 10-point night; Borje Salming, his long arms fanning out like the wings of a heron, swooping in on Bernie Parent and lifting the puck over the goaltender's orange and black shoulder. I was also at game two of the 1974 Summit Series, and while I retained a photograph that I snapped from my seat of Bobby Hull celebrating a goal, I still couldn't give you the score, even though it was probably the biggest sporting event I'd been to in my life.

Instead, since Maple Leaf tickets were (and continue to be) in short supply, I got to know the Gardens best back when it was the premier concert venue in Eastern Canada. In the 1970s, every North American touring act pencilled a date at the Gardens on their schedule. It was a classic rock barn. Critics like Peter Goddard of the *Toronto Star* used to complain about the lawlessness of its acoustics, but now that the SkyDome has usurped the Gardens' best bookings, I think that his complaints about bottomless bass rumbles and nrgggging electric guitars have been supplanted by a certain fondness for the simple purity of that noise. But any rock kids worth their stripes knew how to avoid these sonic trappings: by getting as close to the stage as possible and relying on amp sounds and stage monitors for a true impression of the music. This was easier at some gigs than at others. My friend Ozzie and I once did the old, run-for-it, Mark McKoy-style hurdle-hopping over chairs and barriers to get to the stage during The English Mugs Tour (featuring Elvis Costello and the Attractions and Squeeze), only to have our bodies pinned in a riot of flailing arms and metallic chairs. It was scary, but we eventually found our feet, not to mention a great spot right in front of bassist Bruce Thomas. That night, someone threw a towel at Costello and it hit him square in the face. It remained there for a few seconds, draping his head while the band played on. Slowly, it peeled off his face to reveal a broad smile, perhaps the first time anyone had seen old Elvis without the Scowl of Death pasted across his face. The Gardens had a powerful effect on everyone.

I saw the progressive rock band Yes twice at the Gardens. This is something I'm not used to admitting, but since their florid rock opuses have now faded into the discounted rock bins of most record stores (and now that I've said that, can a revival be far behind?), I'll come clean with the details. The first show was a real thrill. I believe it was my fourth concert experience, and it was memorable for several reasons, not the least being that I was offered marijuana for the first time. To evoke some uniquely '70s phraseology, this was a very heavy episode in my young life. Yes played in the round in the middle of the planked-off ice and their light show was loaded so that epileptics were warned to look away whenever a strobe was tripped. "Wow," I thought, "Real danger!" But it didn't end there. I saw drunks fighting in their seats and beer bottles plonking off the heads of stoned revellers. I saw firecrackers explode and lit cigarette butts land in the laps of teenage girls. I saw Rick Wakeman—his long silver hair sliding down the back of his white robe—press the flat of his forearm against one of his five keyboards, which created a thunderous noise that he sustained as he coaxed the shadows with the crook of his long-nailed finger. It was chilling, and not just because some hulking yeti on angel dust had stood up and was whirling his saddle-bag around his head like he was trying out for the hammer throw. The dope came my way and I felt my stomach tighten. I shook my head and looked down at the stage. From very early on, the Gardens was an illicit place; illicit, but way more exciting than anywhere I'd ever been.

I also saw Cheap Trick play with Graham Parker and the Rumour at the Gardens. Cheap Trick announced that it was drummer Bun E. Carlos's birthday, so the crowd gave him a standing O as he played a solo with thirty-inch novelty drumsticks. I later found out that they did this at every show. I saw Rush a few times, Max Webster too. Those shows were real cultural events, at least for teenagers from the suburbs. If you came from the 'burbs and you listened to CHUM FM, you were there, and you were psyched. Rush and Max were our hometown bands, and I'm sure that, for several thousand kids, they were the heroic templates from which many of our teenage dreams were designed (in fact, I once heard of a Scarberian teen who had plastic surgery to look more like Geddy Lee, but let's not think too hard about that). When Rush detonated their final blinding flashpot during the epic "Xanadu," it was one of the most exciting things I had ever witnessed in my life. To non-Rush fans, this may sound lamentable, but understand: there I was in the greatest rink in Canada watching the biggest band in the country and the lights were swirling and Alex had strapped on his white Gibson doubleneck and Geddy was furiously working up and down the neck of his Rickenbacker and Neil had just done his drum solo and the crowd was standing and cheering and there I was with my best friends and it all lined up so perfectly that I felt completely at home, even though I was forty minutes and fifteen subway stops from my house, a place whose warmth I never thought could be copied, certainly not inside a smoky rink crowded with wigged-out slags and loose-tongued girls in camel-toed jeans. Years later, I watched kids twenty years my junior holler and wave their fists as Kurt Cobain laid his guitar down and played a solo with his running shoe. I understood then that rock and roll at Maple Leaf Gardens was a continuum. One generation saw Bill Haley and Elvis play, the Beatles next, the Who after that, then Rush, then the Clash, Prince, Nirvana, and then, in December 1996, after sixteen years of rehearsals, bars, and clubs, I got to play there with the Rheostatics, opening for the Tragically Hip.

Our family and friends crowded the small dressing room, fathers slapping backs and clasping hands, young children pawing the old blue walls, mothers and sisters gnawing fingernails.

Our hearts were still as we marched along the back wall of the ancient building and climbed up there on the great stage of our youth. For the next forty-five minutes we felt as if we were being pulled through a strange and beautiful dream.

At the end of our set, I put down my guitar and walked away, my arms limp at my sides. We disappeared in a circus of colour and light. That was no dream at all.

That was us.

I was up there.

He was timid, this scalper. He stood alone on the south side of Carlton street like he'd been exiled from the regulars who patrolled closer to the building. He wore Coke bottle glasses and was unmenacing. As I passed, he smiled nervously and held out two tickets.

"Looking for tickets?" he asked.

"Ya, I am," I said, turning around. "Where're they?"

Gord Downie of the Tragically Hip performs in the building that helped inspire one of the group's hit songs. The Hip's "Fifty Mission Cap" tells the tragic tale of Bill Barilko who died in a plane crash the summer after the 1951 playoffs. "The last goal he ever scored won the Leafs the Cup."

The Rheostatics on stage at Maple Leaf Gardens. Don Kerr is on the drums while up front the band features, from left to right, Dave Bidini, Tim Vesely and Martin Tielli.

"Blues," he replied. "In the corner."

"Blues, eh? How much for one?" I asked.

"Hmmm," he mumbled, demonstrating a rather unsophisticated scalping technique.

"Well, they cost me forty," he said, deliberating aloud. "Let's see. How about fifty?" It was like he was asking me for a favour.

"Fifty? Well, okay," I said.

I pressed the money into his hand.

He pawed it over as I walked towards the rink.

I went early. You have to. The warm-up is like a private exhibition, a broad festival of skills which, when sped up at a hellion's pace, will later manifest into the most exciting sport in the world. Before the game, you can sit there and stretch out your legs and study your program like a horse player handicapping the ponies. You ask yourself: how's Jason Smith's hip doing? (sure looked okay on those two-on-one drills); will Steve Sullivan finally get a chance to play on the second line? (showed pretty good hustle on the shoot-in, shoot-out); and is Felix Potvin going to start, or will coach Murphy finally give Glenn Healy a shot? (geez, Healy took that Fred Modin bullet in the shoulder but, man, he didn't even flinch!). The warm-up is a lot more exciting than baseball's batting practice because it's faster and more varied, although it's basically the same idea. You get a feel, as the players do, for what may transpire over the next few hours (not to mention a rare chance to see the players without their helmets, which reminds one of Al Iafrate, the cueball-headed ex-Leaf, who refused to be seen au naturel, and for obvious reasons). The warm-up is also one of the few times at a hockey game when you can let your mind travel, and, if you're so inclined, write poetry or finish off that Master's thesis. Because of this, time tends to wander away and before you know it, the crowd has plugged their seats, the pucks have been swept into a bucket, and the busy-armed, blue-sweatered Gardens custodians have rolled out the carpet where the anthem singer stands, the microphone tilted in front of her face. Flags appear across the pixilated score clock as the singer sings, not forgetting that once upon a time, real flags descended from the bottom of the Gardens clock and were rippled by an automatic fan. After the anthem, coaches fill paper cups with crushed ice (the chewing tobacco of hockey), defencemen turn to the net to whack their goalies' pads, and the ref calls the starting centres to the red line, where they drift together, helmets lowered, not yet touching. The puck slaps flat against the rink. Wood spanks wood. Metal chisels snow.

The game begins.

Weirdly, I am surrounded by Colorado fans. I realize this after one of our guys takes a dumb penalty and no one within twenty feet of me groans. I actually find their behaviour remarkably un-American. I'm quite used to loutish Detroiters howling for blood over my shoulder, but these touring hock-eyists have their hands pressed tightly under their flanks and behave, well, Canadianly. Their only collective "Oooohhhh!!" comes after Patrick Roy makes an astounding save on a curvy screen-shot by Mike Johnson from the face-off circle. The first period, evenly played, ends up 1-1. At intermission, those around the Gardens wearing old Palmateer, Williams, Sittler, Clark and

A year after he performed at the Gardens, Dave Bidini returned to the arena to see the Leafs take on the Colorado Avalanche. Here Patrick Roy helps preserve a 2–2 tie with a stop on Fredrik Modin. Alexei Gusarov readies himself to clear the rebound.

Mahovlich jerseys stand up and look at each other and nod as if to say "Hey, pretty good period for the Leafs!", which tells you just how bad things have gotten around here.

The second period ends 2-1 for Colorado. By now, even I'm thinking, "Hey, pretty good period for the Leafs!" But it was. Domi and Kris King crashed the Avalanche's defence and caused havoc around the net; Jamie Macoun (Jamie Macoun!) rushed end-to-end and nearly tied the game; Russian defenceman Dmitri Yushkevich—who, as a teen, used to travel seven hours a day by train to play with his team—twice pasted Adam Deadmarsh against the boards with his hip; and Mats Sundin—the large, rare, beautifully skilled Sundin—passed the puck through a prone defenceman with all the steadiness of a man sliding a letter under a doorframe, pressing the dot on the black tape of Derek King's stick (whose shot missed the net by three yards, but you get the point). The Leafs matched Forsberg, Sakic, and Ozolinsh stride for stride and they out-shot them by four to one. It was a truly remarkable performance from a team whose system, until tonight, looked about as worked in as Preston Manning's copy of La Guerre, Yes Sir!

In the third period, we're all over them. We swarm the Avalanche, coming in waves, which is how Dan Kelly used to describe the Russians. Finally, at 5:49 of the third period, we tie the game. Tie Domi, the square-headed Albanian whose fan mail still gets sent to his mother, is the hero. But we don't stop there. Only the efforts of Patrick Roy thwart the Leafs' determined shooting men. Then, with just a few minutes left in the affair, the crowd does something that makes me realize why I've come here. Spontaneous. Huge. Fatter and louder and warmer and with more bombast than Joe Walsh's Marshall stack. Not prompted in the slightest by either a digital organ sample or an exploding sign or a rally towel or a clown on a moped or a shoot-out for a million dollars or a cheerleader or a dancing shark with its tail fin on fire. No. Born out of the ether, a torrent of voices washes over the rink, one voice made by thousands, a song, a chorus, a one-note tune that grabs at the fingers and hands of distant fans and hockey ghosts and reaches out across time and pulls together anyone who ever sat there and listened and spoke and sang and sopped it all in. Their hymn sounded, then wildly repeated, the mighty blue and white charge down the ice.

"GO LEAFS GO!!"

We are lifted out of our seats. Then, for the first time all night, a Colorado fan turns to me and speaks.

"Who are they saying sucks?"

Postscript

*The national anthem, last home opener
in the Gardens, October 10, 1998.*

The patterns in the play are clearly visible from the press box, but the sense of energy and emotion is missing. Up here you see everything, and feel nothing.

THE GARDENS

New Memories ...
New Dreams

KEN DRYDEN

I DON'T REMEMBER MY FIRST TIME IN THE GARDENS, BUT I DO REMEMBER the first time I skated on its ice. I was seven, goalie for the Humber Valley Hornets, one of only four teams in the Atom Division of the THL (Toronto Hockey League). It was 1954. We weren't a very good team, but we had connections. One of our right wingers was Tom Smythe, grandson of Leafs founder and owner Conn Smythe.

I remember this big, big dressing room, the white ice that stretched out forever, and me diving and sprawling, making every save against the hapless Redmen, the other Humber Valley team. The Redmen wore Canadiens uniforms; we wore Leafs. Several years ago, a researcher for a CBC series I was doing called *Ken Dryden's Home Game* came across film footage of that day and I made the mistake of watching it. I was much smaller than I wanted to be, and so was the dressing room. I didn't move at all like the adult-in-miniature I remembered myself being (after all, in the photos the *Globe and Mail* ran a few days later, hadn't the caption to mine read, "an embryo Broda"?). I looked like a kid! My thirty-year illusion had been much more fun. The best part was the morning the *Globe* ran the pictures. My grade 2 teacher, Miss Gordon, clipped my picture out and put it on the bulletin board. I learned I could be embarrassed and proud at the same time.

I would go to Leafs games about once a year. My father, a building materials salesman, had two season tickets which he gave out to his customers, except

Detroit's Steve Yzerman and Leafs captain Mats Sundin line up for the ceremonial face-off on opening night of the final season at Maple Leaf Gardens. The puck was dropped by longtime Gardens employee Bernie Fournier, along with Brian Young, whose grandfather was the first season ticket holder, Conn Smythe's grandson Tom Smythe, and Jim Thomson-Boulton, whose grandfather's company built the Gardens.

occasionally when someone not very good came to town, usually the Rangers or Bruins, and I might get a chance. The seats were in the greens, the best place to watch a game, my father told me. Up there you can see the patterns, he said, and patterns are what hockey is about.

Much more often I went to junior games. Before the NFL and shopping became Sunday afternoon rituals, and while junior teams were still farm teams of their NHL sponsor, junior hockey doubleheaders involving the Marlboros and St. Mike's would often attract 10,000 fans or more. I liked to watch the goalies. I imagined the excitement of being St. Mike's Gerry McNamara leading his team onto the ice to the galloping sound of "McNamara's Band." But the Marlboros' Johnny Albani was my favourite. He never made it to the NHL. I would learn later he was too small. But when he skated onto the ice, he would drop the puck his coach had entrusted to him, and shoot it off the glass. Only the Gardens had unbreakable glass. More than the huge, Big Ben-like SporTimer clock, more than the rows of brightly enamelled seats, more than Foster Hewitt's gondola, it was the glass that symbolized the Gardens. That unfathomable contradiction, glass that doesn't break, in that unfathomable place. As kids our biggest fear in neighbourhood games was that a misplaced shot would crash through someone's window. And here, Johnny Albani with his heavy, paddle-bladed, torqueless goalie stick was shooting a puck off the glass. Clink. It was those two things together—the glass and a goalie's shot—that more than anything emphasized the distance between my world and that one.

Johnny Albani and his shot would become my most enduring superstition. When I played with the Canadiens, I'd take the puck entrusted to me by my coach and fire the first shot of warm-up off the glass like Johnny Albani, and that would be a sign I would play a good game. When it became clear I couldn't do that with regularity, putting my whole night at risk, I lowered my sights. Thereafter, I had only to raise the puck off the ice and all would be well.

The first game I remember in the Gardens as an NHL player was Mike Palmateer's second home start for the Leafs. I was in the other net, in my fifth NHL season, and despite Toronto being outplayed and outshot, Palmateer shut us out 1–0. What I remember earlier and better was the constant ticket problem in Toronto. Each visiting team player was able to buy two tickets for a game, which in most cities was more than enough, which in Toronto never was. But try to explain that to family or friends who have been watching you all your life (and who now can't), who you haven't seen in six months though they have seen every other family member and friend (because weekends you work). When finally I had enough seniority with the team, and when finally I dared, I asked

Mike Palmateer's often spectacular play during his six years with the Leafs endeared him to Gardens fans. Knee injuries ended his career.

Scotty Bowman permission to fly to Toronto the day before, after practice, ahead of the team. I stayed at home; I slept in my old bed. I ate breakfast in the kitchen with my mom and dad. Then I took the subway to the Gardens and returned to the rhythm of every game-day.

I remember most in our games the great head-to-head match-up, Lanny McDonald and Bob Gainey, the scorer and the checker, proud, well-matched, running at each other like mountain sheep, shift after shift, loving it. I remember too 1979, the last time we played the Leafs in the play-offs. These were the McDonald, Sittler, Salming, Turnbull, Williams, and Palmateer years, the best the Leafs would have in more than two decades. The Leafs shut down Lafleur, Shutt, and Lemaire. In game three, Cam Connor, a seldom-used rookie in his only year with the Canadiens, scored in double overtime. In game four, the Leafs were down 4–0 but tied the game 4–4 before Larry Robinson scored in overtime with Tiger Williams in

The Maple Leafs signed Curtis Joseph as a free agent in the summer of 1998, hopeful the playoff heroics he had displayed for the Edmonton Oilers in previous years would help return Toronto to the top of the standings.

the penalty box. These are the improbable endings that are really destiny when one team is just a little too good.

But what I remember most about the Gardens in those years was a feeling of disappointment. The Leafs weren't just another team on the schedule, but they weren't *The Leafs*. The rivalry wasn't *The Rivalry*. The Gardens wasn't *The Gardens*. Whoever, whatever was responsible, things weren't what they should have been. Nothing, it turned out, could live up to a child's memory.

I didn't go to the Gardens much during the 1980s. The Leafs weren't very good. I had stopped playing and didn't want to risk getting close enough to miss what I could no longer do. It wasn't until the early 1990s that I really started coming again. The Leafs had improved. Pat Burns was the coach, Felix Potvin was a young goalie who stopped pucks and seemed entirely unimpressed with himself when he did. And Doug Gilmour, after Wayne Gretzky, may have been the most important player in the League.

The building was a lot noisier now. By the late 1950s, music had invaded sports arenas. Movies and TV shows had soundtracks to create mood, why not sports? We had become experts at excitement, taking the natural beat of the game and juicing it up—sound effects, lights, mascots, and just plain noise ("Let's Make Noise!"). And in the Gardens no sound mimicked the rhythm and joy of the game better than Stompin' Tom Connors's simple, toneless "The Hockey Song." (Late in his career, it was said of Frank Sinatra that he could hit only four notes, which may be three more than Stompin' Tom can, but as with Sinatra, it's not the number of notes, it's what you do with them.)

Some fans, having grown up with only the game's natural sounds, and with age having become sensitive to noise, found this all too much. Others, who had grown up with girder-rattling electronic sounds, and who had the present-day need not just to spectate but to participate, found it a bit tame. The unique ability of the Gardens to bring together those under eight and over eighty who had little in common but the Leafs and hockey had brought about the conflict. But the building, which visiting teams used to call "the library" because of its relatively quiet crowds, was never as solemn a place again.

For me, one more thing was different. I now had friends in high places. In the 1980s, when I went, I got tickets from former teammates who were still playing, or who had become coaches or managers, and the seats, near the top of the reds in the corner or on the end, weren't much different from my father's seats. In the 1990s, with a friend on the board of directors of the Leafs, and another who was an anthem singer, I got to sit down low. I discovered a game I had never seen before. The players were so big, so fast. There was no space or time to do what their skills allowed and their minds intended. Shift after shift, forty-five seconds at a time, the game was an immense, exhausting struggle. A few times I sat on the rails, right next to the glass. With nobody in front of me, it was as if the game was being played just for me. My father was wrong. Hockey isn't first of all a game of patterns, but one of blood-racing energy and emotion.

In the last two years, as president and general manager of the Leafs, I've moved my seats again. Upwards this time, just off the press box in the southeast corner of the building, above the highest seats, and I don't like it. Up there, the players are tiny, the white of the ice is immense. There is lots of space and time. Up there, everything is possible. Every mistake is avoidable. Every opportunity is visible to all but the blind. Up there, you see everything and feel nothing.

I look at the building differently now. Get close enough to it and it is just bricks and mortar. There's a lot wrong with it. In 1931, nobody thought much about office space in an arena. Today's offices had to be carved out of non-existent space, a little here, a little there, separating

With his offensive prowess and gritty defensive play, Doug Gilmour was the heart and soul of the Maple Leafs in the early 1990s. He won the Selke Trophy as the NHL's best defensive forward in 1992–93 and was also the runner-up to Mario Lemieux that year for the Hart Trophy as NHL MVP.

Doug Gilmour, Dave Ellett, and Felix Potvin shut down Steve Yzerman and the Detroit Red Wings during the 1993 playoffs. The Leafs rallied from a two-game deficit to win the series in seven.

people who need to be together. And who would have imagined corporate boxes sixty-seven years ago? So in the 1970s when someone did, the boxes were put in the only place there was room for them, along the roof of the building. Even the first of the NHL's new buildings, Detroit's Joe Louis Arena, which opened in 1979, was done in the old style with corporate boxes at the top, as if it had been reason not circumstance that had put them there.

The concourses are crowded; the washrooms are worse. Food tastes have changed. Once a shrivel-boiled hot dog in a soggy bun and an ice-watered Coke were all one expected from arena cuisine. Now deli sandwiches, pizza, even sushi and Mexican food are available in many arenas. Gardens food has improved, but not that much, and if you want french fries, forget it. There isn't the electrical capacity in the building to heat the oil for frying, nor the space for a hood over the grill for venting (eliminating hamburgers as well). And when laser shows are staged, pre-game is fine, but between periods when people

next split second a young man swung into the spotlight and caught her as she somersaulted through the air. My mouth hung open in awe and I can still remember when she missed grabbing her partner's wrists and fell through the darkness to the safety net. Some in the crowd screamed, but she bounced up from the net and flipped herself out and over the edge to land safely on her feet, taking a deep, graceful bow. The crowd went wild with applause.

EMILY BRADSHAW
Toronto

DURING THE 1945 NHL season my brother Herb and I went to Maple Leaf Gardens to watch our brother Elwyn play for the Leafs. We arrived early that day and were having sandwiches in Dowling's Grill when Lou Broda came in. Turk's brother was the Gardens plant manager and ice-maker and a friend of Herb's. I was introduced and after a short conversation Herb asked Lou if he would take me on a tour of the inner works of the Gardens.

Lou agreed and we went "underground," where I was shown the insides of the Gardens. Lou explained the ice-making technique he had developed over the years to give what many felt was the best ice in the NHL. Herb asked Lou to show me the log book he kept on ice-making procedures and that was how I discovered that Lou double-flooded the end of the rink the Leafs defended in the first and third periods: that meant Toronto was skating downhill for two out of three periods!

FRANK MORRIS
Edmonton, Alberta

Jack Tweddle *shared the following story when officiating at my father's funeral in July 1998:*

COUSINS BOB Lovell and Jack Tweddle were given hockey tickets by their beloved Uncle Rex in Toronto. They were fifteen and fourteen years old respectively. Without any means of transportation from Fergus, Ontario, the desperate duo hitchhiked to the Big City. Upon arriving on Saturday afternoon, the avid hockey fans headed straight to Maple Leaf Gardens to take in a junior game. The awestruck pair found themselves wandering the corridors of the Gardens, viewing the photographs and the memorabilia there. Soon they were approached by a gentleman who asked them if they'd be interested in seeing the Leafs dressing room. Thrilled beyond belief, the boys were then given a guided tour of Maple Leaf Gardens by none other than its founder—Conn Smythe. He also promised the keen and polite youngsters mini Leaf-autographed hockey sticks at a later date. True to his word, Smythe sent them shortly thereafter. Fifty-one years later that same memory-filled stick found its way to the hospital for the birth of Bob's first grandson, Conrad. Conn for short.

SANDY LOVELL
Waterloo, Ontario

MY MEMORIES of Maple Leaf Gardens date back to the late 1940s—1948 to be exact. I would line up for tickets at 5:00 in the morning. My parents would only let me go with my girl-friend's mother, who was also an avid hockey fan. We would

huddle outside, where the line-up would run all the way to Church Street before the box office opened at 8:30. When we finally reached the ticket wicket, we would buy two standing-room seats behind the greys. We did the same thing for St. Michael's games—especially the playoffs with the Winnipeg Monarchs. St. Mike's games were just as popular as the Maple Leafs.

I heard once that you could put down your name on a wait-ing list for purchasing season tickets so I decided to do that. Twelve years later I received a letter that said the Gardens was adding more seats and I could now become a subscription hold-er. By this time I was newly married, so my husband could help defray the cost—which was about four dollars per ticket. We have enjoyed having those seats over the years, as have our chil-dren and now our grandchildren.

NORAH MAUGERI
Willowdale, Ontario

ON SATURDAYS during the late 1940s and early '50s I would leave our home in Cabbagetown around 7:30 p.m. and run to the corner of River and Gerrard. There I would hop a streetcar heading west and disembark at the corner of Carlton and Church. I'd cross the street and get in line to buy a seventy-five-cent standing-room ticket behind the greys. Then I'd hustle to be among the first in line at the locked Church Street entrance to the Gardens. You see, standing-room ticket holders weren't allowed to enter the building until after the opening face-off at 8:30.

When they let us in, I would zip through the turnstile and sprint up the concrete stairs as fast as my little legs could take me. (My personal best time was twenty-nine seconds.) I'd take up a position behind the ledge of the last row of the greys. Many of the bigger and older out-of-shape brutes who came puffing up the stairs tried to muscle in on my territory, but this was where a five-foot-tall eleven-year-old learned to stick up for his rights!

RAYMOND HODOWANSKY
Thunder Bay, Ontario

IT WAS VERY early in the 1950s and I was only about four or five years old. I had fallen off my bike and suffered a black eye. I suppose Dad felt bad for me and to make up for my injury he decided to take me to work with him. My dad had an unusual job: he was a hockey player with the Maple Leafs. This was a very special thing in Toronto, but to me Howie Meeker was just my dad and playing hockey was just another job.

I remember walking along and holding his hand as we passed through the turnstiles and into the Gardens. First, we went to the dressing room. I remember how proud I was as he introduced me to the players because they were all very impressed with my "shiner" (which sounded much more excit-ing than a black eye!). They assured me it was every bit as good as any they had received.

When they were ready the players proceeded to the ice and I took my place in the stands. The empty Gardens was easily the most impressive sight I had ever seen in my short life. The seats seemed to disappear into the clouds and I thought that people who sat in them must be very brave indeed because I was afraid to climb up more than five or six rows.

Of course, I had been to the Gardens before. During a game I once asked my mother where Daddy was. She replied that he was in the penalty box and I started to cry. "Oh, Mommy," I said, "are they going to put the lid down on that box?"

After the practice, Dad took me to get something to eat with a few of the boys. It was just another day for him, but I have never forgotten it. In the busy and often absent life of a professional hockey player, Dad had given me something special—his time and attention and the feeling that he loved me.

JANE TUCKER
St. John's, Newfoundland

IT WAS EARLY IN Henri Richard's career, in the mid-1950s, and the Leafs' abrasive centre, Bob Bailey, welcomed him by working him over around the head when they both went for the puck. Big brother Maurice saw this and ran at Bailey, who sidestepped the check, making Rocket look foolish. I was standing by the Canadiens' bench, and I could see Rocket getting ready to explode. He and Bailey got into a fight, which ended with Rocket on the ice and Bailey's fingers in his eyes. When Rocket skated over to the bench, Habs coach Dick Irvin calmly said, "You're not going to let him get away with that, are you, Rock?" That set off Rocket even more, as Irvin knew it would, and Rocket and Bailey started swinging sticks at each other.

By this time, Conn Smythe had made his way down from his seats in the greens to the corridor by the bench, looking defiant in his trademark pearl-grey stetson and spats. Rocket went right after him. It looked like he was going to attack Smythe, and two big, burly Toronto policemen grabbed him. In his skates, the Rocket towered over Smythe, but Conn didn't flinch. He looked at Richard, then at the cops, and snarled, "Take your hands off the greatest hockey player in the world."

This seemed to bring Rocket to his senses, and Connie walked a much calmer Richard down the hall, patting him on the back as he directed him through he dressing-room door. It was an unforgettable moment for a young guy working game nights at the Gardens keeping track of out-of-town scores.

AL STEWART
Scarborough, Ontario

I GREW UP IN THE RADIO ERA, in a very small town in the interior of British Columbia. Listening to Foster Hewitt from the gondola and the studio in the Hot Stove Lounge was a sacred part of every winter Saturday night. My father was a rabid sports fan. When, years later, I went to Toronto to televise my first Grey Cup game in 1956, I was invited to join the Hot

Stovers on that Saturday night radio broadcast. My father, who had been pleased I was "doing so well" and televising the Grey Cup game, was absolutely thrilled that I was on the Hot Stove broadcast. To him, that, more than anything else, meant that I had made it! I felt pretty good about it too.

TED REYNOLDS
Vancouver

MAPLE LEAF GARDENS. To me, it was the smell. I could be blindfolded and driven around the city in circles for hours, but within seconds of walking through those doors I could tell you where I was. I have often wondered what made that aroma so recognizable. Was it the popcorn? The hot dogs? The frosty feeling of the ice?

Maybe it goes back to Sunday afternoons when I was five years old and watched my father's alma mater, St. Mike's, take on Rod Gilbert and the Guelph Biltmores or Bobby Hull and the St. Catharines Teepees. How my brother and I looked forward to those Sunday afternoon games, especially when St. Michael's played the Marlies. I remember it like it was yesterday. Especially that smell as you entered with the crowd from a blast of winter into pure excitement and anticipation. If someone could only bottle that fragrance I'd buy a case and pop one open at the start of every hockey season.

BOB PETRINEC
Thornhill, Ontario

WHEN THE Moscow Circus played the Gardens I decided to take my children—five of them at that time. We watched the dancing bears and then an act that involved a cat. I should mention, as

Back row, left to right: Tim Horton, Whipper Billy Watson, George Armstrong. Front row, left to right: John Watson, Doug Quinn, Richard Royds.

I GREW UP in East York, where my best friend was future NHL rookie of the year Brit Selby. Another chum was John Watson, the son of Whipper Billy Watson. Next door lived Scott Young and his son Neil. One day, three of us boys were told that "the Whip" needed some publicity for an upcoming wrestling match with "Hardboiled" Haggerty. We were asked if we would be interested in packing up our hockey gear and heading down to Maple Leaf Gardens to see something special. What a thrill, especially when we were joined on the ice by George Armstrong, Tim Horton, and Allan Stanley, who were recovering from injuries. Suddenly, Whipper appeared on the ice, wobbling somewhat in full goaltender's equipment. (He told us he had not skated as a boy.)

What memories I have of that day! Helping Whipper over to the crease; hoping he wouldn't fall and hurt himself; watching him try to keep a serious face and knowing that just one lapse in concentration could end in disaster. What a time the three of us had.

RICHARD ROYDS
Ancaster, Ontario

an aside, that this was at the very height of the Cold War. I told the children that it was very hard to train a cat to do anything — in contrast to a dog, who would lie down and play dead on an instant's command. But cats are ornery. "Leave it to the Russians to train a cat," I remarked, or something like that. Little Patsy, no more than eight years old, looked aghast, "The Russians!" she cried. "I'm gettin' outta here!" And with that she tried to climb over the seats to the aisle until forcibly restrained. Thus did the Cold War propaganda insinuate itself even into the heart of Maple Leaf Gardens.

PIERRE BERTON
Kleinberg, Ontario

MY FIRST VISIT to the Gardens was on a Thursday night in April 1963. I was part of a tired-out press corps following Lester Pearson during the closing day of the election campaign: too many late-night hospitality suites and early-morning wake-up calls. This night the final stop would be standing room only at the Gardens during a big game between Toronto and Montreal. A Toronto win would mean going on to meet Detroit for the Stanley Cup. The place was jammed.

Pearson was late getting to the game because of politicking, and we trooped in during the second period — the two teams in full flight with Toronto leading and the Habs trying desperately to catch up. I had never before been inside the Gardens for next to a playoff game. The place was electric! The energy! The noise—the sweat—the smells. I stood next to the ice surface, utterly transfixed. Mahovlich flashed by, looking gigantic. And Beliveau. I gaped like a school kid looking up at Foster's gondola and at those thousands of screaming fans. It was magic!

Toronto scored. The house trembled and then shook, thundering right up through the concrete. Politics and prime ministers paled, Pearson, the sports fan, was transported — his grin, literally from ear to ear, told everyone that the Commons and Diefenbaker and the campaign were the last things on his mind; this was Toronto and the Gardens and Hockey Night in Canada and the Leafs against Les Canadiens. It just didn't get any better.

Now if only that venerable old barn could play it all back to us. If only old Conn could somehow press the replay button. Then again—ah well, they play hockey in Florida now, don't they?

JOE MARIASH
Toronto

THE DATE was January 18, 1964. A game against the Boston Bruins. My father had taken me to the game for my eleventh birthday, which had been on the 16th. The final score was 11–0 for the Bruins, which was not a great highlight for us Leaf fans. At the end of the game I turned to my dad and

THANKS TO Maple Leaf Gardens, I had my fifteen minutes of fame on May 2, 1967.

A twenty-year-old from Prince Albert, Saskatchewan, I was at Maple Leaf Gardens to see the Leafs play the Canadiens for the Stanley Cup. As the final buzzer sounded, signaling the Leafs had won the Cup, I flashed my father's business card from CKBI radio in Prince Albert and ran out onto the ice. I jostled my way between the players and was on national television for over five minutes while the Stanley Cup was being presented.

My parents were watching back home and the phone started ringing off the hook. My father told me that his hand didn't leave the phone for over two hours, fielding what he estimated to be more than a hundred and fifty calls from friends who had seen me on TV. People didn't stop mentioning my moment at Maple Leaf Gardens for many, many years.

GORD RAWLINSON
Calgary, Alberta

said, "I'm just glad it wasn't my thirtieth birthday."

BILL MICHEA
Pickering, Ontario

"WHEN YOU get to the door, pretend you're with the guy behind you. Look like you belong. Be confident. The door guard will think you're somebody's kid."

We'd snuck into many games like this, but the biggest game of all was on May 2, 1967—the sixth game of the Stanley Cup Final. We snuck in through the Hot Stove Lounge. It was full of Toronto's blue bloods, so nobody was scrutinized very carefully—especially not two fifteen-year-olds wearing ties and blazers. Staring the usher in the eye, I pointed with my thumb to a man behind me. My friend Karl did the same. By the time the man handed over his tickets, we'd vanished into the crowd.

The game was exhilarating. This was my team in my city, and we were champions. I didn't want the celebration to end, but it seemed to have moved into the Leafs' dressing room. With the whirlwind of photographers, writers, shareholders, and others assaulting the dressing room, it was obvious the one doorman would be overwhelmed. I fell into the deluge and, before I knew it, I was swept into the inner sanctum. Dave Keon autographed the label of a champagne bottle for me. Later, Frank Mahovlich, Tim Horton, Jim Pappin, Red Kelly, and Mike Walton all added their signatures. I still have the bottle today.

RANDALL CRICKMORE
Niagara-on-the-Lake, Ontario

THE YEAR WAS 1967. I was a twenty-one-year-old disc jockey newly arrived in Toronto from the Prairies to work as a midmorning programming host at CKFH. The station owner—and my new employer—was Foster Hewitt. The station manager was his son Bill. I told them that I was a rabid hockey fan and asked if there was any way I could get access to the press box for games. I saw every one that season.

Harold Ballard held onto all the seats he could sell and complimentary tickets were hard to come by in those days, even for the likes of Foster Hewitt. The gondola was barely big enough to satisfy all the legitimate broadcasters, let alone some young rock and roll DJ. However, about halfway along the catwalk that led to the gondola was a small lighting platform. I called it "The Baby Gondola." The spotlights there were not needed for hockey so the Hewitts would let me in to watch the games from there.

One day my father was in town from Winnipeg and he asked me if I could get him tickets. "I'll do even better," I crowed. My father returned to Winnipeg with a story that must have seemed incredible to his colleagues and pals. "Not only did I see the game, but I went with Foster and Bill Hewitt and watched from my son's private box behind them."

The Baby Gondola.

CHUCK MCCOY
Vancouver

THE FIRST TIME Chicago came to Toronto, they came to the Gardens. I don't mean the Blackhawks. I mean the rock band. I was a big fan of their partly jazz, partly rock sound. And I made sure I got good seats down on what would be the centre-ice area of the arena for the show. About 8 o'clock, the warm-up band came out on stage and played a set. And then another. And another. When they had apparently exhausted their entire repertoire, they finally cleared off the stage and the concert promoter approached the mike. "Chicago's been held up at the border. But they're on their way." About 10 o'clock they arrived and bassist and lead vocalist Peter Cetera ran out on stage. He cussed the customs officials who'd held up the band and said, "We'll play on the warm-up band's instruments. Or you can wait 'til we set up our own stuff. It's up to you." We had come for the full effect of the Chicago sound, so shouted for them to set up their own gear.

It was about midnight when they launched into their opening number "Does Anybody Really Know What Time It Is?" It was the beginning of the best two-hour concert I'd ever experienced. Most of the thousands who stayed to hear them, hung in to the end—about 2 a.m.—and left the Gardens on a musical high. It had been a show to remember. However, the subways were now closed and it was a long walk home.

TED BARRIS
Uxbridge, Ontario

INCLUDED AMONG a treasure trove of souvenirs I obtained from the widow of former NHL player Normie Himes was a picture of King Clancy with the Ottawa Senators in 1926. I had copies of the picture made and sent two to Mr. Clancy at Maple Leaf Gardens, asking him if he could please sign one and send it back to me. I had trouble reaching him to see if he had received them until I finally spoke to him on the phone a few days before a game with the St. Louis Blues on November 5, 1986. Mr. Clancy invited me to come down and meet him near Harold Ballard's private box, where he always watched the games. It would be the last game he ever saw. He died on November 8.

I have met numerous hockey players and executives from the past and present, but no one was ever as friendly and warm as the King. This must be one of the last photos ever taken of this great man. It was taken in the Gardens, just behind "the Bunker."

RANDY FAIST
Cambridge, Ontario

IT WAS THE SUMMER of 1972. I was fifteen years old and the Canada–Russia Summit Series had just been announced. Game two of the series would be played at Maple Leaf Gardens on Monday, September 4. Labour Day.

I just had to get tickets.

Realizing that demand would be unprecedented, Hockey Canada decide to distribute all tickets by lottery. My cousin Bev and I made a pact. We would both mail in our lottery ballots and if one of us won we would take the other. Weeks later I received a letter in the mail. I had been awarded two seats in the front row of the blues, Section 48 (now the reds). Cost of the tickets? Seven dollars each.

The key moment in that game was Peter Mahovlich deking Vladislav Tretiak for a short-handed goal. We had a great view of it from our seats. That goal is forever etched in my memory.

RICK HENRY
Port Perry, Ontario

MY FIRST VISIT to Maple Leaf Gardens was in 1974, for a game versus Detroit, when I was eight years old. I don't recall much about the game except waiting for the replays of the goals, which, of course, never came. During intermission I was heading back to my seat with an ice-cream bar. Someone tapped me on the shoulder and said, "Hey kid, look into the camera and take a big bite." I didn't think much about it and sat down again. A few months later I was sitting in front of the TV on a Saturday night. There was a special on food during the intermission, and lo and behold, there was my face on the screen munching on an ice-cream bar!

WILLIAM PITMAN
Toronto

IT WAS EITHER 1974 or 1975. I was seventeen or eighteen years old and my two favourite things in life were the Toronto Maple Leafs and Elton John.

My sister and I were living in Toronto for a short time and a friend of hers gave us two tickets to a playoff game between the Maple Leafs and the Philadelphia Flyers. The seats were terrific, right at centre ice and about ten rows up. About ten minutes into the first period, four or five guys moved into the row in front of us and sat down. We didn't really notice anything because we were excited about the game. When the same thing happened in the second period I was curious, so I looked over their shoulders. Sitting right in front of my sister was Elton John! He was with four pretty big guys who looked like bodyguards. My sister said I was crazy. Elton John wouldn't be just sitting in the seats like that.

With five minutes to go in the second period they got up to go. I was torn between watching the game and following them. Just after that it was announced that the Leafs wanted to welcome Elton John to the game. During the second intermission, my sister and I agreed that as soon as they came back we would ask for an autograph—but they didn't come back for the third period.

That was the closest I have ever come to meeting a famous celebrity, but in those days hockey came first. The only problem is that I can't even remember who won the game!

DEBBIE ANDREWS
Oyama, British Columbia

THE FIRST TIME I went to Maple Leaf Gardens — my dad made it a point to take my two brothers and me individually to see a Leafs game — we sat in the greys and saw the Leafs play Chicago. What struck me was how bright the ice was, how white the Leafs' jerseys were, how red the Black Hawks' shirts were and how salty the Gardens popcorn was. My dad bought me popcorn and every time Mike Palmateer's name was mentioned I always pointed out that he used to eat a box of Maple Leaf Gardens popcorn before every game.

MIKE MYERS
Hollywood

FOR ME, THE most memorable experience of all at Maple Leaf Gardens was the time I took my wife on our very first date. It was a game against the Cleveland Barons on March 11, 1978. We sat midway up in the greens at centre ice and the ticket price was six dollars! My date was from Brockville, Ontario, and a Montreal Canadiens fan. This was her first NHL game. We have been together ever since and have been very happily married for eighteen and-a-half years. She's also been a die-hard Leafs fan ever since.

BILL MITCHELL
Brockville, Ontario

AS A YOUNGSTER I was fortunate enough to attend many games at Maple Leaf Gardens. My father had season's tickets in the corner golds. It was a hot spot for flying pucks and both my brother and I caught some over the years. There was one puck, however, that caught me.

It was a Saturday night in 1980. I was eleven years old. During the second period the Leafs were breaking out of their own

end when a bullet dump-in cleared the glass. I lost sight of the puck and leaned back to get a view past the lady sitting beside me. At that very instant the puck hit me just above my left eye. I could hear my brother asking if I was okay. Three ushers were also there to help, and all the players on the ice were looking up at me. Thank God I was in shock, so I couldn't think about crying.

I was hurried to the Leafs' training room, where I was given an ice pack and a quick inspection by the trainer. Tiger Williams came into the room during the second intermission and whether it was to see me or get a role of tape didn't really matter. I'd never been so close to a real hockey player before. I was given a puck and sent on my way. My brother and I went back to our seats, where I traded my new puck for the one that had hit me. From the first Monday back in the schoolyard with my shiner and my puck, I've had a story to tell for the rest of my life.

TODD FALLS
Toronto

MY MEMORIES of Maple Leaf Gardens go back to the late 1930s, when I would listen to Foster Hewitt's broadcasts on radio. To this lad living in the tiny hamlet of Armstrong (150 miles north of Thunder Bay), those games were the highlight of the week. The broadcasts began at 9:00—just about the start of the second period. The problem was that 8:00 was bedtime and my younger brothers insisted that if they had to go to bed I had to go too. Sometimes I would fall asleep with them only to be wakened by the gentle hand of my father on my shoulder while he whispered, "The game is on." I would sneak out of bed and listen with him. Turk Broda was my hero and there are still people today who call me Turk. I'm sure it was not because my goaltending skills were so great but because I was constantly talking about him.

As an adult, I lived in Toronto, where I would play intermediate hockey with my son Jim and his friends. During that time the Professional Prospectors and Miners held an annual convention in Toronto and rented Maple Leaf Gardens for an evening. In 1982, a fellow hockey player who worked at Teck Corp. asked me if I wanted to play in the game that year! I'm sure the other players thought I was the goalie's father bringing in his son's equipment.

I had not been so nervous since my wedding day when I skated out onto

OUR SON JEFFREY was four years old when we took him to his first Leafs game. He cried every time a goal was scored, and it was a high-scoring game that night! By the end of the second period he'd had enough. I took him with me into the ladies' washroom and he immediately relaxed and got comfy on a leather couch. I took this picture of him to remind us of his first Leafs game.

GRACE NIELSEN
London, Ontario

the Gardens ice. Tears streamed down my face when I stood at the blueline for "O Canada." I had to hide the tears from my teammates. They were so young; they wouldn't understand. With the help of God and Turk Broda (up there in Goalie Heaven), I overcame my nervousness and made some really good saves. We won the game 5–2.

LES LAIRD
Mactier, Ontario

FOR MY EIGHTH birthday, my brother, who is four years older, decided to take me to see the Maple Leafs. He saved the money from his paper route for weeks and weeks, but could only afford standing-room tickets. He asked me if I would like something else instead. "I wanna see the Leafs," was my only response.

Finally, the big day came and he, my dad, and I walked through the front gate. I took in everything, from the smell of the hot dogs to the sound of the staff selling programs. Every detail is etched in my mind.

The Leafs won 3–2, but on the way home my brother was unusually quiet. My dad asked him what was wrong and he explained that he was upset because our seats weren't very good. My dad pointed out that I hadn't stopped smiling since we had first entered the Gardens. Thirteen years later, I have never received a better birthday present.

JONATHAN STEWART
Brampton, Ontario

I'M NOT SURE what year it was. Perhaps ten years ago or so. I was a courier in Hamilton and often had a lot of deliveries to Toronto and area. One day I had a package for Bob Stellick. After I took it to his office I decided that I would sneak a look at the ice surface before I left. I went to one of the aisle entrances and as soon as I did Vincent Damphousse skated onto the ice. I had watched him shoot pucks for a few minutes when a voice to my left asked if he could help me. It was Gerry McNamara, the general manager. I said that I wanted to watch the practice and he told me it would be better if I did so from the lower level. Just then I heard a grunting sound to my right. When I looked over I saw Harold Ballard. So here I was, a guy from Cape Breton and a Leafs fan all my life, standing in the Gardens between the g.m. and the owner of the Toronto Maple Leafs!

RAY DOYLE
Stoney Creek, Ontario

MY DAD WAS a lifelong Leafs fan. I remember growing up watching "Hockey Night in Canada" with him and learning to hate the

From the *Canadian Statesman*, Bowmanville, Ontario, January 15, 1992:

IT'S 20 MINUTES before game time, and deep beneath the stands, a conversation between Bob Smith (Smitty) and the former NHLer with the hardest shot in hockey, Bobby Hull, is in progress. After 15 years of working security at Maple Leaf Gardens, it's just another night of Leafs hockey.

Being remembered by the retired players when they visit the Gardens is one of the most satisfying aspects of Smith's job. The other is watching players he has coached or been associated with in minor hockey over the years [Mike Veisor, Paul Lawless, Doug Dadswell, to name a few] emerge from the dressing room.

"Somewhere, along the line I like to think that something I did or said maybe helped them to get there."

ROBERT SMITH
Newcastle, Ontario

Canadiens. If you lived in Kingston, Ontario, it could only be one team or the other. My dad always talked about going to Toronto for a game, but my parents weren't very good with directions and those six-lane highways were just too much to think about.

In 1989 my dad was diagnosed with cancer and wasn't expected to live for another year. I decided it was finally time for him to go to the Gardens and I got tickets for a game against Vancouver in March. I told me parents I would leave work early and drive them, my wife, and my son to Toronto. What I didn't tell them was that I had actually rented a limousine for us.

My dad was thrilled. When we got to Maple Leaf Gardens he wanted to see everything, so we walked around the building some. My dad saw Darryl Sittler in the corridors and spoke to him. Our seats were in the greys, second row from the top, but for my dad it was as good as sitting right behind the Leafs' bench. He wasn't able to eat much then, but he did his best to finish a Gardens hot dog.

I can't recall if the Leafs won or lost, but it didn't matter. I'll always remember that night.

RON SEAMAN
Kingston, Ontario

I AM THIRTY-EIGHT years old and have been a Leafs fan since I was six and watched games with my grandmother. In 1991 I decided to realize a lifelong dream.

I was going to make the twenty-hour drive from Nova Scotia to Toronto with a one-night stop at my original home town, Iroquois, Ontario. My mother and younger brother talked me into taking them when I left Iroquois, so now three people—with no tickets—were heading to Toronto hoping to see our first hockey game there.

After getting lost several times, we arrived at Maple Leaf Gardens on a cold November afternoon. The scalpers were asking "a heart and a kidney" for tickets to the game, so I went into the box office to see if any seats were available. A middle-aged gentleman from the press box informed me that the game had been sold out for weeks, but after I told him how far we had come to get there he said a few seats had been broken at a Metallica concert the night before and if they became available he would let us know.

I was beginning to feel mighty empty as game time approached, but then the gentleman called me over. He had gotten us three tickets from a reporter friend of his! I was near tears and could not possibly give this man as much thanks as I should have.

The icing on the cake that night proved to be an event I had been total ignorant of. The Gardens was celebrating its sixtieth anniversary. The festivities and stars of yesteryear there that night helped me to fill one and-a-half rolls of film and gave me memories that I shall never forget.

TONY HALL
Fletcher's Lake, Nova Scotia

WHEN I WAS a boy growing up in Hamilton, watching the Leafs on TV on Saturday nights was a tradition. Little did I know that one day I would be a cameraman for "Hockey Night in Canada."

One of my earliest memories at the Gardens is of having to carry heavy camera equipment up the shaky stairs that led to the famous gondola. Even scarier was the climb to the rafters to lower microphones down to the ice.

For a while, one of my camera positions was in a little cubbyhole above the door at the south end of the building. Referred to as "the Bunker" by the crew, there is little room for movement in it once the swivel chair, camera, and operator are all crammed inside. It's also a bit hairy when flying pucks rattle around inside.

But with all my time spent at the Gardens the highlight for me is not a game, nor meeting famous celebrities, but skating on the ice with my nine-year-old daughter. Her skating class had performed at the Gardens and there was a free skate afterwards. As we made our way around the rink I thought back to that young boy in Hamilton who was just about her age, and I wondered if she knew what all this meant.

MICHAEL WALL
Toronto

I WAS NINE years old in 1992 when my hockey team was involved in the annual Timmy Tyke tournament. The winner would get to play at Maple Leaf Gardens. In the final game of the tournament, my team and the other were tied. We went to a shootout and I scored the goal that advanced our team to the Gardens. Unfortunately, I broke my wrist at school the next week and was not allowed to play hockey for six weeks. I was really upset.

The day of the game, my coach asked me to join the team and put on my sweater and skates. Before the playing of the national anthem they announced my name over the PA system and told what I had done and why I couldn't play. I skated out onto the ice and everyone clapped. I'll never forget how great that made me feel.

DAVID FANJOY
Markham, Ontario

I MADE MY first trip to Toronto during the Remembrance Day weekend in 1994. I hit all the big spots with a youth's excitement. There was a concert by Paul Simon at the SkyDome, a tour of the Hockey Hall of Fame, a visit to the CN Tower, and, most importantly, a trip to see Maple Leaf Gardens.

My brother, a friend, and I took some pictures out front, but we met with disappointment when we tried to get in. We were told that we could not go inside due to an ongoing Macedonian celebration. But I couldn't leave without an extra effort. I explained that we were all up from down east and just hoped for a small glimpse.

AS USUAL, I drove the car into the lot right across from Maple Leaf Gardens. But this time I was carrying my own equipment and here as a participant, not just a spectator. Walking into the Gardens, I recognized Vincent Damphousse, who was just leaving practice. After a lifetime of house league and adult pickup hockey, here I was standing next to the captain of the Montreal Canadiens, one hockey player to another—virtually peers!

The event was the first annual Hockey for the Homeless charity game in November of 1996. Just days from my fortieth birthday I pulled a sweater with my name on the back over my head and stepped onto the ice for the pre-game warm-up. The seats in the greys I purchased four times a year from my friend Tim Fujita seemed an awfully long way up.

We took some pictures and then the puck was dropped. The speed of the other players was greater than my usual opponents', but the real problem was keeping my awe in check. A silly tripping penalty got my name announced over the PA system—not by Paul Morris, mind you, but a thrill just the same. I'm a little fuzzy on the details, but I do remember that we won the game.

I returned for the second Homeless tournament in 1997. I was less nervous this time—until I saw Ken Dryden watching us from the stands. Here's a trivia question. Which Hall of Famer has seen Dave Lackey play at Maple Leaf Gardens, but not vice versa?

DAVID LACKEY
Scarborough, Ontario

HOCKEY IS A big part of my family. My grandfather plays, my father and brother play, and I play too. I live in Nova Scotia and I have never been to an NHL game. I had never even been to an NHL arena, so I was ecstatic when I found out that the 1997 OHL Entry Draft was going to be held at Maple Leaf Gardens.

My whole family was there and we were all nervous—but none more than my brother Colin. He had good reason to be, because he was the one who was going to be drafted. When they called out his name I was so happy that I forgot to clap. Instead, I just followed him down to the floor to try and get some pictures. To see his name up on the scoreboard above centre ice was a big thrill.

TRACY SCOTLAND
Cole Harbour, Nova Scotia

This comment drew the attention of the second doorman. Turned out the older, grey-haired man was from Glace Bay. I'm from Mabou. He was happy to see a fellow Cape Bretoner and let us in to wander on our own.

We had seen Maple Leaf Gardens and we wore grins from ear to ear as we exited to the street. Our benefactor had given us his name, but I am sad to say that I have forgotten it. Nonetheless, our thanks go out to the anonymous Cape Breton doorman.

DENNIS MACDONALD
Calgary, Alberta

I WAS SIX years old when I went to my first Leafs game in 1993. My dad bought tickets for a game against Calgary. When he went to work, he told a friend that he was going to be taking me to my first Leafs game. My dad's friend said his family had tickets right behind the Leafs' bench and offered my dad a trade. When we got to Maple Leaf Gardens I couldn't believe how close we were to the Leafs. I felt like I was part of the team!

In the second period, the Leafs cleared the puck out of their zone and it went into the Leaf bench. Wendel Clark caught the puck and gave it to the trainer. He cleaned it off, turned around, and, to my surprise, handed the puck right to me! I don't even remember who won the game, but I will remember that Saturday night for the rest of my life.

MATTHEW SIM
Mississauga, Ontario

MY PERSONAL high point at Maple Leaf Gardens occurred in 1992 when I was shooting the film *Gross Misconduct*, the story of

Brian "Spinner" Spencer, in the building. I still consider this to be my professional hockey debut at the Gardens because I actually got to skate around and play hockey during the breaks in shooting, which was an absolute thrill for me. And, of course, because the film was set in the 1970s, when Spinner Spencer played, all the ice markings and the team crests and everything were correct for that period. So I actually got to enjoy the ultimate fantasy of playing in Maple Leaf Gardens dressed as it was when I was a kid.

ATOM EGOYAN
Toronto

IN 1996 I WAS fortunate enough to attend a Tragically Hip concert at Maple Leaf Gardens. Although I had seen the band twice before at outdoor events, I could not wait to see the Hip—a truly Canadian band—at, as far as I am concerned, the home of Canadiana.

From my grey seats, the first hour of the show was everything that I could hope for. The Gardens was packed, the crowd was ecstatic, the sound was perfect, and, most importantly, the Hip were on! It was at this point that my moment happened. The Hip began to sing their song "Fifty Mission Cap," about the late Leafs great Bill Barilko. Hearing them sing this song in the home of the Maple Leafs was absolutely magical. With the lights down during the main verses, you could hear the crowd singing along. But when the chorus came, all the lights in the Gardens lit up and I saw thousands of Canadians singing as one, some waving flags, some arm in arm, some jumping up and down—all truly into the moment. It was one of the most awesome and inspiring sights I have ever seen.

DARRYL HUGHES
Toronto

WHEN I STARTED dating my husband Dean in 1982, it didn't take me very long to find out that he adored hockey. Dean wouldn't—and still doesn't—miss a game on TV. He always told me that it was his dream to see the Montreal Canadiens play Toronto at Maple Leaf Gardens. So for Christmas in 1997, I bought him an airline ticket for a flight to Toronto and arranged to get him a ticket for the game from my uncle, who works for UFCW union local 1252.

My husband flew to Toronto two days before the game on February 28, 1998, and stayed with his brother. Wayne Ralph, the president of the union, arrived the next day and my husband understood that he would leave the tickets for him at the Gardens box office. Come game time, my children and I as well as most of our small community turned on the TV to watch. Then the phone rang. It was my husband. He hadn't got his ticket; it wasn't at the box office. My husband had called Wayne on his cell phone and he explained that he had left the ticket in an envelope at his hotel. My husband then called the hotel, but there was no envelope for Dean Major.

The game was sold out and my husband tried to buy his way in but fifty dollars wasn't enough. My husband returned home, having missed the game and feeling terrible about the mix up.

A few days later we were talking to Wayne. He still had an envelope for my husband. Now we discovered what had caused the mix up: The envelope was addressed to Dean Sceviour. Wayne had assumed our family name was the same as my uncle's. Dean still has the unused ticket and we have a story to tell for the rest of our lives.

DONNA MAJOR
Burgoynes Cove, Newfoundland

IT WAS A Wednesday in February 1998 when the three of us had the opportunity to live out our dream of going to a game at Maple Leaf Gardens and meeting some players afterwards. From the small town of Blenheim, Ontario, we left work early and arrived in Toronto three hours later to find parking at a minimum. We finally found a spot but, as this was a residential area, we were worried about getting towed—until "Gouch" found a car that already had a parking ticket on it. We "borrowed" it and put it on our windshield, figuring this would make us less likely to get towed.

Three hours and a few beers later, the Rangers had beaten the Leafs 5–2. We headed down to the dressing room, where Blenheim native Todd Warriner had signed us in. We met Wendel Clark, Steve Sullivan, and Mats Sundin and got their autographs. At about 11:30 we decided we'd better leave because we had a three-hour drive ahead of us and work in the morning.

When we got outside our car wasn't there. After we'd spent two hours on pay phones bickering with towing companies, the police came down to meet us at the Gardens. It was about 2:15 in the morning when an officer got a call on his radio. A Toyota Celica had just dashed out of a gas station after being denied the use of Gouch's maxed-out MasterCard. Our vehicle was now in a high-speed chase across the city of Toronto! Five minutes later, another call informed us the car had been abandoned by the lake. It was approaching 3:00 a.m. when the officer took us to the location. In addition to our car, we found three cellular phones, two ladies' purses, two winter coats, and a couple of men's wallets, which we gave back to the police. It was 3:30 before the cops let us leave. We decided it was too late to drive home so we found a hotel and called in sick to work the next day.

Our most memorable moment at Maple Leaf Gardens was awesome, but not in the way we'd imagined!

RYAN GOULET, JASON TOLL,
and JOE LESSARD
Chatham, Ontario

I'M TWELVE years old, and I went to my first Toronto Maple Leafs game on March 11, 1998, with my dad. The Leafs were playing the Dallas Stars. When we got to the gate the man taking the tickets said, "By the time the game is over you are probably going to be very tired."

"No I won't," I assured him. "I'm so excited that I can't get tired tonight."

He asked me if I had school the next day. I told him I didn't because my March break had just started.

We went to our seats, which were close to the ice. That made me very happy. In the third period the Leafs tied the game at 2–2 and that was how it ended after overtime. Before we left to go home, that man who had taken our tickets saw me.

"I told you that you'd be tired by the end of the game," he said.

I told him he was right, and then I thanked him.

"For what?" he asked.

"For letting me into Maple Leaf Gardens and giving me a memory I will have for the rest of my life."

MARK RAZMOV
Thornhill, Ontario

IT WAS MY first visit to Maple Leaf Gardens and from the first time I saw it I knew it would be interesting. The lobby looked fancy, but once we got through the turnstiles I could tell that the building was really old. It reminded me of Bill Bolton Arena, where we go skating from school—only way bigger!

We rode up two escalators to get to the greens and when we walked up the tunnel to go out to the seats it made me feel dizzy because it's so steep. Sometimes I would look up at the stairs that lead to the roof and wonder who gets to go up there.

The ice show was lots of fun. Rudy Galindo and Philippe Candeloro—and, of course, Elvis Stojko—were my favourites. After, we went down by the stairs and we saw a maintenance room with lots of pipes. I wanted to see the pipes that go underneath to make the ice, but we couldn't go down there.

AMANDA HEHNER (age nine)
Toronto

MY FAVOURITE memory of Maple Leaf Gardens occurred during the 1998–99 pre-season. My newlywed Italian cousin Serena and her husband Roberto were honeymooning in Canada and topping their itinerary were three "Canadian" things they hoped to accomplish: 1) go salmon fishing; 2) ride The Maid of the Mist; 3) take in a hockey game.

The first task was impossible (Che cosa? It takes three days to drive out to British Columbia), but Serena's heart was in her throat as our tiny ship sailed into the thunderous mists of Niagara Falls. Fortunately, we were able to scare up four tickets to see the Leafs host the Buffalo Sabres. Greys. Row P. The uppermost row in the whole Gardens. I was not impressed, but Roberto took it in stride. "Non preoccupari. You can't even see the pitch from the worst soccer seats in Milano."

Whenever the Leafs scored on Dominik Hasek, Roberto and I would bellow "Goooaaaalll!" and thoroughly embarrass Serena and my fiancée Francesca. Unfortunately, Roberto also bellowed the battle cry when a shot got past Curtis Joseph. A few spectators glared at him. Then it happened. The one thing both Roberto and Serena were hoping for. Something that is legendary in Italy: a hockey fight broke out! Tie Domi was victorious.

The final score was 6–2 for the Leafs. And what did my cousins think of their first exposure to the great Canadian pastime? Buonissimo.

CATALDO BRUGNANO
Hamilton, Ontario

The Place and the People

November 12, 1931

LEAFS OPENING GAME

THROUGH A FRONT entrance festooned with ribbons and flags they came, 13,233 strong, paying prices ranging from 95 cents to $2.75 and enriching the coffers to the tune of $19,677.50. It was the largest crowd that had ever witnessed a sports event in Toronto. The 48th Highlanders and Royal Grenadiers entertained the crowd with a rendition of "Happy Days Are Here Again" and the Toronto players were presented with floral horseshoes. The formally attired men and women that evening were then subjected to a litany of speeches by provincial and municipal officials. Even team captains Hap Day of the Leafs and Cy Wentworth of the Chicago Black Hawks were called on to say a few words. Finally it was time to play hockey.

Though Busher Jackson would lead the NHL in scoring in 1931–32 and Charlie Conacher would top the league in goals, the honour of scoring the first goal at Maple Leaf Gardens on the night of November 12, 1931, fell upon a visiting player, Harold "Mush" March of the Black Hawks, who beat Lorne Chabot at 2:30 of the first period. The rest of the game was equally disappointing, as Chicago beat Toronto 2–1 in a lackluster affair.

There would be few disappointments at the Gardens this hockey season, however. In his attempt to rally support for the construction of a new hockey palace for the Maple Leafs, Conn Smythe had all but guaranteed that a new arena would bring the Stanley Cup back to Toronto, where it had not resided since the victory of the St. Pats in 1922. Perhaps even sooner than Smythe had thought, his hockey club would make good on the boast. On April 9, 1932, before a crowd of 14,366 at the Gardens, the Leafs beat the New York Rangers 6–4 to sweep the best-of-five Stanley Cup Final.

November 19, 1931

FIRST WRESTLING MATCH

BY THE MIDDLE of the 1920s, wrestling was clearly dividing into two separate categories. In one group were the amateurs, who continued to engage in one of the oldest and purest competitions of strength and skill ever devised. In the other were the professionals, who were already becoming more entertainers than sportsmen and would only continue to become more so with each passing decade.

Professional wrestling made its debut at Maple Leaf Gardens just one week after the official opening of the building when Frank Tunney's Queensbury Athletic Club staged a four-bout card on November 19, 1931. The top attraction of the evening was the meeting of heavyweight champion "handsome Jim Londos, Philadelphia Greek," and Italian champ Gino Garibaldi. The main bout was supposed to be the best two-out-of-three falls, but Londos retained his championship when Garibaldi was unable to continue after the first fall.

A crowd of 15,800 jammed the Gardens that night, making it the largest crowd to watch an indoor sporting event in Canada at the time. "The good old grappling game has gone high hat," reported the *Toronto Telegram*. "The folks sit in comfort with their coats off and the lighting is perfect, but the place is so big that the leather-lunged gents who used to tell us what was what from the ring in the old [Mutual Street] Arena have had to admit that they are licked. It is no longer necessary when applying for a job as announcer to show discharge papers from the army bearing the rank of regimental sergeant-major for the boys now croon their information into a pair of microphones. They do have to wear dinner jackets though, which just goes to show that this town is getting more and more like New York every day."

Soon Tunney was promoting weekly events at the Gardens that would regularly attract 8,000 to 14,000 fans. Television would further enhance wrestling's popularity. Though the weekly bouts were long gone by then, wrestling continued to attract huge crowds at the Gardens until 1995.

WINSTON CHURCHILL

DESPITE NEWSPAPER HYPE advertising it as "an unprecedented event, an unequaled opportunity to hear one of Britain's great men—good seats .50¢—$1.00," only 6,000 people turned out to hear Winston Churchill speak at Maple Leaf Gardens on March 3, 1932.

Churchill, who was on a speaking tour of the United States, spent forty-eight hours in Toronto, and in the process went down in Gardens history as the first politician of international renown to speak there. He would be followed over the intervening sixty-six years by a long line of dignitaries from local politicians to princesses.

The 48th Highlanders entertained the audience prior to Churchill's speech, while behind the curtain technical glitches were causing some awkward moments. Churchill had come to love the convenience of the lapel microphone which he had started using during his tour of the United States, but Foster Hewitt warned that using such a device with the Gardens' sound system would cause an echo. Churchill turned to Hewitt and said, "Young man, if I want your advice I will ask for it." The Gardens staff, fearing that Hewitt was right, provided a back-up microphone with a stand as well as the lapel microphone. When Churchill came on stage, he found that his lapel mike did cause a strange echo. After what a *Globe* writer described in the paper the next morning as a "brief tussle" with the microphone (but which was in fact Churchill kicking the stand-up mike off the stage), Churchill gave his speech without any microphone. Although a hush fell over the gathering, many could not hear the words of the great man that night.

In an almost prophetic way, Churchill spoke of the need for the strength of the British Empire in preserving world peace. But World War I had ended fourteen years before and this was a period when the famous white feather debate at Oxford University saw the student body vote overwhelmingly not to fight for King and Country. Perhaps because of the microphone trouble, but more likely due to the state of world affairs, Churchill's message was not heard that night.

April 3, 1933

THE GARDENS' LONGEST HOCKEY GAME

Toronto and Boston were the NHL's best teams in 1932-33, the Bruins at the head of the American Division with a record of 25–15–8, while the Leafs topped the Canadian Division at 24–18–6. Under the playoff system of the day, the two teams met in a best-of-five series to determine the NHL champion. The winner would then meet the survivor of the playoffs among the second- and third-place teams to determine the Stanley Cup champion.

The Leafs and Bruins alternated wins in the first four games, making them even going into game five on April 3. A crowd of 14,500 (1,000 above the listed seating capacity for hockey then) jammed Maple Leaf Gardens for a taut

TORONTO MAPLE LEAF HOCKEY CLUB, 1933-1934

thriller that remained scoreless until late in the third. With time running out, Boston's Alex Smith barged through for the apparent game-winner, but the play was ruled offside. For the fourth time in five games the teams headed into overtime, where the game remained tied through three more periods. Finally, in the fourth extra session, King Clancy put the puck past Boston's Tiny Thompson—but a whistle had sounded just before he shot.

After a fifth scoreless overtime session, NHL president Frank Calder suggested the teams toss a coin to determine a winner. The players were obviously struggling, but this idea (and another to play without goalies) was rejected. Finally, four and a half minutes into the sixth overtime session, Ken Doraty took a pass from Andy Blair, went wide around the Boston defence, and scored after 104:46 of overtime, ending what was then the longest (and is still the second-longest) game in NHL history.

Though the game ended at 1:55 am on the morning of April 4, the Leafs were required to be in New York that same night to open the Stanley Cup Final. Exhausted, they were beaten 5–1 by the Rangers, who went on to win the series three games to one.

February 14, 1934

ACE BAILEY ALL-STAR GAME

ON DECEMBER 12, 1933, the Toronto Maple Leafs visited Boston Garden. Toronto–Boston games of this era were often rough due to bad blood between Conn Smythe and Bruins general manager Art Ross, and tempers began to flare during the second period. At one point, Eddie Shore led a rush up ice and was checked heavily. By the time he got up, play had returned to the Boston end. Only Toronto forward Ace Bailey remained in the Leafs zone, covering for the defence. As Shore headed back, he ran Bailey from behind. The unsuspecting Toronto player fell over backwards, his head hitting the ice with a sickening thud.

Bailey was rushed to hospital, where he underwent two delicate operations for a fractured skull. Finally, in early January, his doctors predicted a complete recovery. Shore was suspended for sixteen games, but Conn Smythe demanded compensation for Bailey's medical treatment.

The NHL Board of Governors decided there should be a benefit game between Toronto and a team of NHL all-stars at Maple Leaf Gardens, the entire proceeds to be paid into the league, which would then cover Bailey's medical expenses and put any remaining funds into a trust for him.

Two players from each of the league's other eight teams were selected for the all-star team, including future Hockey Hall of Famers Shore, Howie Morenz, Aurel Joliat, Red Dutton, Nels Stewart, Lionel Conacher, Charlie Gardiner, Herbie Lewis, Hooley Smith, Bill Cook, and Ching Johnson. Bailey had already publicly stated that he accepted Shore's word that he had not deliberately attempted to injure him, but the two players had not seen each other until the night of the all-star game. As Foster Hewitt would later recall: "They looked at each other for a moment, then clasped hands and talked quietly." More than 14,000 fans roared a thunderous ovation. The Leafs won the game 7–3. Though Bailey did not play that night—and never would again—he worked as a penalty timekeeper at Maple Leaf Gardens and remained a fixture at the arena until his death in 1992.

These players wore special All-Star jerseys for the game, but wore their individual club uniforms for this photo. The little boy is Howie Morenz, Jr.

September 21, 1934

EDDIE DUCHIN

BORN IN 1910 in Cambridge, Massachusetts, and later trained as a pharmacist, Eddie Duchin chose the career of a musician instead. In the late 1920s he was featured as a piano player in Leo Reisman's Orchestra at New York's Central Park Casino. With his suave appearance and sophisticated, flashy piano style, Duchin quickly became the darling of New York City society. In 1931 he formed his own band, taking over residency at the Casino.

Presented by the Embassy and Music Corporation of America, Eddie Duchin and his Central Park Casino Orchestra became the first band to play Maple Leaf Gardens on September 21, 1934. Tickets were $1 plus an amusement tax of ten cents. There was no extra charge for the privilege of dancing on the Gardens floor. Three thousand fans danced the night away that evening at a show that almost didn't happen.

En route to Toronto from New York, Duchin and his bandmates were taken off the train at a Buffalo border crossing. Their entry permits into Canada had mistakenly been sent from Ottawa to Toronto instead of Fort Erie. Once the problem was taken care of, the orchestra boarded a bus, only to have it blow a tire. This was followed by a half-hour wait for a drawbridge in order to cross the Welland Canal. Still, Duchin and company made it to Toronto only forty minutes late for the show.

Duchin's star continued to rise after his Gardens appearance. He garnered recording contracts with Victor, Brunswick, and Columbia records and appeared in such movies as Coronado (1935) and The Hit Parade (1937). After the bombing of Pearl Harbor on December 7, 1941, Duchin joined the U.S. Navy, becoming a lieutenant. He returned to civilian life in 1945 but his popularity was never what it had been when he visited the Gardens. Soon his health began to decline and in February 1951 he died of leukemia. In 1956, he was immortalized by Tyrone Power in the film biography *The Eddie Duchin Story*.

October 21, 1934

SIX-DAY BICYCLE RACE

As THE TWENTY-FIRST century approaches, it is easy to forget how the invention of the modern two-wheeled "safety" bike transformed the way many of us got around, offering the working class, women, and children affordable transportation for the first time. But the bicycle also provided pleasure, exercise, and sport.

William John Peden was born in 1906. He left school at age fifteen to work in his father's grain and feed business, but was always encouraged by his parents to participate in sports. He proved to be best at cycling. After a fifteen-mile road race in his hometown of Victoria, British Columbia, in 1926, a sportswriter noted that "a flame-haired youth led the pack like a torch." William Peden was known as "Torchy" Peden from then on.

Peden competed in the 103-mile time trial at the 1928 Amsterdam Olympics, but two punctured tires cost him any hope of a medal. He spent the next three months winning

races all across Europe before returning to Canada. In 1929, he made a clean sweep of the Canadian indoor championships before embarking on a professional career. Professional cycling meant the marathon circuit of six-day races, which usually began at midnight Sunday with continuous racing until midnight the following Saturday. The area within the steeply banked track would be cluttered with double bunks, snack tables, and cycling equipment.

Maple Leaf Gardens staged its first six-day bicycle race from October 21 to October 27, 1934. Torchy Peden raced with England's Syd Cozens and Ireland's Polly Parrot on the British Empire team against seven other teams from around the world. Though clearly the fan favourite, Peden, along with his crew, finished second overall behind the Maple Leaf club, who were decked out in Toronto hockey sweaters although only Reggie Fielding of the three-man team called Toronto home.

Six-day bicycle events remained popular throughout the 1930s, with events held in Toronto until 1938. It would be another twenty-seven years after that before such an event was staged at the Gardens again, in 1965.

TIM BUCK

IN THE DEPTHS of the Depression, men rode the rails in search of work. Many of these same men had survived the blood and mud of World War I and helped forge the nation. Now left to the free hand of capitalism, this former army of soldiers who had once fought for King and Country had become an army of homeless and unemployed.

Communism seemed to offer them hope. The leader and spokesmen for communism in Canada was Tim Buck, who had been arrested in Toronto for his communist beliefs.

Communist leader Tim Buck, left, at the meeting of the Communist Labour and Total War Committee on October 13, 1942.

During his incarceration in Kingston, prison guards fired six bullets into his cell. Far from silencing him, the government had created a folk hero around whom the dispossessed could rally.

Buck was released from Kingston Penitentiary on December 2, 1934. That very night he took the stage at Maple Leaf Gardens, dwarfed by a red banner with a huge portrait of Stalin and a massive bust of Lenin. He was greeted by cheers from 17,000 people—many wearing red hats to symbolize their support of the Communist party. Another 2,000 who were turned away at the door stayed out front to show their allegiance.

To honour an agreement with Maple Leaf Gardens, "God Save the King" was played before the rally. Few in the audience stood, and as the national anthem played, the *Toronto Telegram* reported, "a sibilant hiss ran through the crowd and developed into a loud chorus of booing."

Tim Buck delivered his message in a forceful way, warning the government and in particular Toronto police chief Brigadier General Dennis Draper—who had authorized the harassment, beating, and hounding of the homeless for much of the 1930s—that they would no longer remain underground; that they were no longer afraid of either the chief or his "Cossacks"; that they would fight for the rights of a proletariat and the rights of the dispossessed.

That night in Maple Leaf Gardens, the Old Boy Order of the Orangemen came face-to-face with the colour red of communism and the anger of the dispossessed, who would no longer settle for the status quo.

March 22, 1935

FIRST TRACK MEET

On MARCH 22, 1935, a crowd of 13,569 jammed Maple Leaf Gardens for the first track meet to be held in the building. It was the largest crowd ever to attend such an event in Canada. "True," pointed out *Toronto Telegram* sports editor J.P. Fitzgerald, "the great part of this great crowd were there on 'booster' tickets at a quarter, but they were there and a rink packed at two bits is a lot better than empty seats at higher prices."

The Achilles Athletic Club, which organized the first Maple Leaf Gardens track meet, divided the events into open and invitation competitions. Among the stars of the day invited to attend were Glen Cunningham, the Kansas mile sensation, Chuck Hornbostel of Harvard and Indiana (who was considered the top half-miler in the U.S.), and sprinter Eulace Peacock of Temple University. But the surprise performance of the meet was turned in by sixteen-year-old Sammy Richardson of Toronto's Central Technical School. Richardson easily won the 60-yard dash in a time of 6.6 seconds, equalling the time posted by the flashy Peacock in the invitational race. The twelve-man team from the University of Toronto also fared well, with second-, third-, and fourth-place finishes in the 60 yards, a third place in the 60 invitational, third place in the 1,000 yards, third in both relays, two thirds in high jumping, and a first-place finish in the mile for those under nineteen.

As for the star attractions, according to the *Telegram*, "Cunningham clearly demonstrated his easy motion and style in defeating Gene Venzke, his persistent rival from Pennsylvania, in the mile, knocking off the distance in 4:17.2, five-tenths of a second slower than his time in Hamilton two nights before [which had set a new Canadian indoor record]." Hornbostel was an easy winner over 880 yards.

Despite the success of the first Maple Leaf Games and other events during the 1930s, track and field would not return to the Gardens until 1963.

RAMESES TEMPLE CIRCUS

THERE WERE LIONS and tigers and, yes, even bears, although there was no sign of Dorothy or Toto. There was no shortage of excitement, however, as the young and young-at-heart gathered under the "big top" at Maple Leaf Gardens for the first time.

Toronto's Mayor James Simpson and his wife officially opened the circus, which was sponsored by the Shriners. The Gardens was transformed into a place of wonders as a bear rode a bicycle around a track, elephants did a fan dance and then stood around smoking cigarettes. The wonders continued as the flying trapeze artists took to the air. Young ladies flew with the greatest of ease, doing amazing tricks including one in which what the newspapers described as a "hefty lady" dangled from the trapeze by her knees while holding onto three other young women who swung below her. At centre ice—now centre ring for the circus—the great lion trainer snapped his whip and forced a cage full of lions, pumas, and bears to perform amazing tricks.

Initially the mayor and his wife had planned to stay for only half an hour but two hours later they were still firmly in their seats, as enthralled by the circus as their young seatmates.

Towards the end of the night a great explosion brought everybody's shocked attention to the north end of the arena, where Wilmo the human bullet was about to be placed into a cannon. Wilmo got in, the fuse was lit, and he flew across the arena, landing in the net on the other side. The human bullet had done it again!

Finally at 11:30 the circus came to an end. It had been a great success and turned out to be just the beginning of a long association which would see the Rameses Shrine Circus return to the Gardens—much to the delight of generations of children—every year for twenty-five years.

DUKE ELLINGTON

On A DARK NOVEMBER night, with the world creeping closer to war, the air around Maple Leaf Gardens was filled not with the sound of political posturing, nor even the sound of pucks banging off the back boards. Rather, on November 23, 1938, the air was filled with shouts of glee as the young people of Toronto came to celebrate the swinging sounds of Duke Ellington and his orchestra.

Once the beat of the drums started up, the atmosphere inside the Gardens became electric as 7,000 young people took to the dance floor. Some were dancing, some were watching, and some were psyching themselves up as they got ready to take part in the first jitterbug jubilee ever held at Maple Leaf Gardens. Preparations seemed largely to involve shouting and squealing as Duke Ellington ran through his repertoire.

The young men in attendance that night were dressed in square jackets and baggy pants with long chains down the side, while the fashion of the day for the young women was a knee-length skirt, blouse and saddle shoes. It was soon obvious to even the most bashful observer what these young women were wearing under their skirts. The jitterbug involved a lot of quick steps and acrobatic moves with the young women being, as one observer described, "tossed around like a sack of flour, while the men shook and pulsated as if they were having a fit."

The jitterbug contest lasted for nearly an hour, with the main contestants continuing their dancing with quicker, more intricate steps as the contestants were whittled down to the three prize winners. It would be hard to imagine another event that generated such raw dancing excitement as the jitterbug did on that cold November night in 1938, with the war barely ten months away.

For at least one night, Swing was King at Maple Leaf Gardens.

SONJA HENIE AND HER HOLLYWOOD ICE REVUE

WHEN SONJA HENIE was a little girl in Norway, she had a love for skating. She described the feeling of freedom, speed and pushing through the air as more important to her then anything else.

Remaining true to her love of skating, Sonja Henie revolutionized the sport for women. Wearing a shorter skirt and more practical top, she was able to perform skating manoeuvres that the traditional women's skating gear made impossible. Combining her natural love for the sport with a determination and skill that made her the dominant woman figure skater in the world while she was still just a teenager, she went on to win ten world championships and two Olympic gold medals.

In 1937, Sonja capitalized on her incredible popularity as a skater with two Hollywood movie contracts. Her films were a great success and in 1938 she formed her own skating troupe, which would combine the grace of ballet, the speed of skating, and the magic of a Hollywood story and sets. She called her company Sonja Henie's Hollywood Ice Revue. In later years, she would admit that it was very difficult to find the sixty skaters she required for her revue in Hollywood, where ice skating still was not very popular. Once she exhausted the skating population, she started scouting ballet companies to make up the numbers.

After bringing her revue to the major cities of the United States, Sonja and company came to Toronto for performances on December 5 and 6, 1938. They performed before 13,000 people at Maple Leaf Gardens. An added bonus for the Toronto crowd was the fact that Henie's dance partner was a local boy, Stewart Raburn. The crowd went wild for the revue, which included scenes from Henie's latest movies. The costumes were spectacular, especially for film fans who until then had to conjure up the colours in their imaginations.

SAMMY LUFTSPRING

BORN IN TORONTO on March 14, 1916, Sammy Luftspring began boxing at age fourteen; six years later he qualified for the Canadian team at the 1936 Summer Olympics in Berlin. Being Jewish, Luftspring's parents feared for his safety in Nazi Germany and convinced him to boycott the Games. He went instead to Barcelona to participate in the counter-Olympics being staged in the Spanish city. Unfortunately, the Spanish Civil War broke out the day Luftspring arrived and the games were cancelled.

Already having fought 105 bouts as an amateur, Luftspring embarked on a professional career upon his return to Canada. In 1937, he defeated Frankie Genovese for the Canadian welterweight title in the first fifteen-round fight ever staged in Ontario. Two years later, the idol of Toronto's Jewish community took part in a five-bout card at Maple Leaf Gardens on February 27, 1939, staged to raise money for the Jewish Refugee Fund. "Every bout but one," reported the *Toronto Star* the next day, "was hammer-and-tongs, slam-bang and boom boom... If those were exhibitions we can't wait to see the real thing."

Luftspring fought Frankie Genovese again at the Gardens bout and though he had only had two rounds of training (due to a cut eye in his previous fight), the Canadian champ was confident he could beat his rival in five rounds. Genovese took a pounding, but he lasted the full ten rounds, re-opening the cut above Luftspring's eye and slicing his ear. Still, Luftspring won easily by decision.

By 1940, Luftspring was ranked third in the world, but he suffered a serious eye injury in a tune-up fight for a shot at Henry Armstrong's world title. Though he was only twenty-four years old, Luftspring was forced to retire. He remained in the fight game as a referee, eventually officiating at more than 2,000 fights.

Still a resident of Toronto, Sammy Luftspring is a member of Canada's Sports Hall of Fame.

242

January 10, 1941

WHIPPER BILLY WATSON'S FIRST MAJOR BOUT

By THE LATE 1940s, professional wrestling could be counted on to draw large crowds in Toronto and Montreal. Promoter Frank Tunney had several Canadians who attracted huge followings at Maple Leaf Gardens—including a local grappler known as Whipper Billy Watson.

In his youth, William John Potts (Whipper's given name) was a pitcher and second baseman in Legion softball, played defence in hockey, and played football with Eastside and Balmy Beach. He was also a marathon swimmer. His wrestling career began in England in 1930, and it was there that he earned the nickname he would be known by for the rest of his life.

Whipper Billy Watson became the European light heavyweight champion before returning to Canada. On January 10, 1941, he fought his first major bout at Maple Leaf Gardens on the under-card of a match pitting Frankie Taylor against Wild Bill Longson. According to the *Telegram*: "Whipper had no bargain in Jack Russell, the ruffian cowboy, but virtue will triumph and Billy, by blasting Russell with some flying tackles and a couple of Irish whips, pinned him in 12 minutes and 52 seconds."

Watson would become a household name in Canada during the 1940s and 1950s, twice holding the world championship and being the perennial Canadian and Commonwealth champ. His wrestling career continued until 1971, when he was forced to retire after a serious car accident. He wrestled in somewhere between 6,300 and 7,400 bouts in his career (sources differ)—and more of them at Maple Leaf Gardens than anywhere else.

As popular as he was as a wrestler, it was his dedication to charity that really made Whipper Billy Watson a hero. He formed the Whipper Safety Club, after a youngster being pushed and shoved in a crowd to get his autograph outside of the Gardens was knocked into the street and killed by an oncoming car. He later became a tireless campaigner on behalf of Easter Seals and did much to raise awareness of the plight of physically disabled children.

WATER FOLLIES

PERHAPS AS A WAY to keep up morale on the home front during the war, the early 1940s spawned a great many new forms of entertainment, including the Ice Follies, the Ice Capades, and the Roller Follies (an "ice show" on roller skates). Among the strangest new shows to debut at the Gardens during these years was the Water Follies.

Buster Crabbe and his bevy of bathing beauties.

The Water Follies of 1941 featured stars of the 1939-40 New York World's Fair Aquacade, including Buster Crabbe. By this time, the 1932 gold medal-winning swimmer was already a well-established celebrity, having starred in the movies as Tarzan, Flash Gordon, and Buck Rodgers. Crabbe brought the world's largest portable swimming pool (70' by 25' and 7' deep in the diving end) to Maple Leaf Gardens from May 27 to 31, 1941, and filled it with 80,000 gallons of water for a show that was billed as an "entertaining extravaganza of beauty, brawn, glamour and gaiety." It was essentially a demonstration of synchronized swimming, diving, and racing. Only 1,300 people attended on opening night, but crowds improved during the show's five-day run.

Crabbe and company were encouraged enough to return to the Gardens in 1942 for a second (and final) appearance. Perhaps the show was simply ahead of its time. In 1944, Esther Williams would turn synchronized swimming into a commercially acceptable (if somewhat bizarre) art form with the first of her underwater musicals, MGM's Bathing Beauty. Still, the Aqua Parade of 1949 marked the last time that water filled the Gardens floor in anything but its frozen form.

October 27, 1941

CAB CALLOWAY

BEFORE CAB CALLOWAY and his Cotton Club Orchestra took to the stage at Maple Leaf Gardens on October 27, 1941, it was obvious that there were some problems with the concert that were beyond the control of Cab Calloway and his band. When the fans were presenting their tickets to get into the concert, 300 were turned away. Their tickets were counterfeit. Police Inspector Robert Davie explained that they had been bought not from the Gardens box office but from somebody who was selling them for 25 cents less than the official price.

Cab Calloway and his band had worries of their own. Cab was backstage on the phone to a hospital in Youngstown, Ohio, checking on the health of one of the key instrumentalists of the Orchestra. Saxophonist Chu Barry had yet to regain consciousness after a car crash earlier that day which had involved Barry and two other members of the band. They had been en route to Toronto when their car skidded on the rain-slick pavement and crashed into a bridge abutment. The two others were all right but everyone waited to learn the fate of Chu Barry.

Despite the problems, the band was hot at the Gardens that night. It was not long before the thousands who had gathered to hear them play were caught up in the music and 100 couples took to the dance floor to show their latest moves. For the couple of hours the concert lasted, all in attendance—both on stage and on the floor—had put their cares and woes behind them.

FIRST ICE FOLLIES

FLAMBOYANT ICE SHOWS have been a part of Maple Leaf Gardens throughout most of its history. Though the Toronto Skating Club had previously performed at the Gardens, the forerunner of the modern ice extravaganza was Sonja Henie's Hollywood Ice Revue, which first played Toronto in December 1938. The Ice Follies made its Maple Leaf Gardens debut for a four-night run (November 18–21) in 1941 and was such a hit it would return every year for almost fifty years.

The enormous Shipstad and Johnson ice show ("It takes three baggage cars to carry the equipment," the *Toronto Telegram* informed its readers) had toured the United States for forty-nine straight weeks in 1940 and played to a total audience of more than 1.6 million people. In Toronto, the opening-night audience of 8,000 (which included many air force cadets) was quickly won over by the skaters and their fifty-piece orchestra.

Bess Erhardt, Roy Shipstad, and Oscar Johnson were the star attractions, but it was the novelty acts that attracted the most attention. Harris Legg was singled out for his loop-the-loop act of leaping through two flaming hoops revolving in opposite directions, while the Swiss comedy duo of Frick and Frack also earned raves ("They emulate any two of the Marx Brothers—including Groucho").

The success of the Ice Follies soon spawned the rival Ice Capades, which first appeared at Maple Leaf Gardens in 1943. It too, would return for decades to come, and the two shows together would bring such stars as Donald Jackson, Dick Button, Karen Magnussen, Jo Jo Starbuck, and dozens of others to Toronto audiences. Toller Cranston was among the first skaters to stage his own shows at the Gardens, appearing in 1975, 1976, and 1977. A decade later, the brilliant ice dancing team of Jane Torvill and Christopher Dean brought their own show to the Gardens for two appearances in 1986. Since 1994, Elvis Stojko has headlined the Tour of Champions at the Gardens.

January 30, 1942

MOOSE ECCLESTONE MEMORIAL GAMES

ROBERT "MOOSE" ECCLESTONE worked for the Goodyear Company and managed the Toronto Goodyears hockey team for Maple Leaf Gardens. Though only in his twenties when he took the job, Ecclestone built a powerhouse club during his eight-year tenure. The Goodyears were OHA Senior A champions from 1938 to 1940 and developed players such as George Parsons and Peanuts O'Flaherty for the NHL. Punch Imlach was also a member of the Goodyears. In an era when senior hockey rivalled the NHL for popularity, Ecclestone became a prominent member of the Toronto sports scene.

Early in the winter of 1941–42, Bob Ecclestone was killed in a car accident. On January 30, 1942, Maple Leaf Gardens staged the Moose Ecclestone Memorial to raise funds for his family. A crowd of 13,563 turned out in tribute.

The evening began with music from the Royal Regimental Band of Canada, followed by the St. Mary's Boys Band. Then the Toronto Marlboros and St. Catharines Saints faced off for a Senior A game. At the end of the first period there was an exhibition of figure skating by members of the Toronto Skating Club. Then came one of the two special highlights of the evening—a speed championship featuring stars of the NHL. Syl Apps, Doug Bentley, Lynn Patrick, Sid Abel, Tommy Anderson, Flash Hollett, and Jack Portland (one player from each of the NHL's seven teams) were all timed twice skating a lap around the Gardens ice with the puck. When the results produced a dead heat between Apps and Patrick, a final skate-off became necessary, with the Leafs captain edging the Rangers star in a time of 14.8 seconds to Patrick's 15 seconds flat.

Following the second period of the OHA game, a twenty-minute exhibition was played pitting the Maple Leafs against a team of NHL all-stars and oldtimers, including former Leafs Joe Primeau, Busher Jackson, Red Horner and Hap Day, plus Nels Stewart, Dit Clapper, and others. Some creative timekeeping allowed the friendly contest to end in a 3–3 tie. The evening was then capped off by the Marlies, who rallied for five goals in the final period to beat St. Catharines 7–3. In all, $9,800 was raised for Moose Ecclestone's family, with a promise that donations from other sources would swell the fund to $11,500.

King Clancy and Hap Day sport sweatshirts for the Moose Ecclestone Memorial.

LEAFS' 1942 RALLY

THE TORONTO MAPLE LEAFS of 1941–42 were one of the strongest hockey clubs in franchise history. The team featured four future Hockey Hall of Famers on the ice (Syl Apps, Sweeney Shriner, Gordie Drillon, and Turk Broda), one behind the bench (Hap Day), and two in the front office (Conn Smythe and Frank Selke). The star-studded team finished second to New York during the regular season, but eliminated the Rangers in the playoffs. They then finished the season with a historic come-from-behind victory over the Detroit Red Wings.

The 1942 Stanley Cup Finals opened on April 4, and though the Red Wings were underdogs they won the first three games. No team, before or since, has ever rebounded from a 3–0 deficit in the Stanley Cup Final. Facing instant elimination in game four, Conn Smythe and Hap Day decided to shake up the roster by benching Gordie Drillon and Bucko McDonald. Although replacements Don Metz and Hank Goldup did nothing out of the ordinary, the Leafs stayed alive with a 4–3 victory. Gaye Stewart was added to the line-up in game five and the Leafs showed they were back in the series for real by thumping the Red Wings 9–3. Toronto then forced a deciding game by shutting out Detroit 3–0 in game six.

The largest crowd ever to witness a hockey game in Canada at that time, 16,218, jammed Maple Leafs Gardens for the seventh game on April 18, 1942. The crowd was silenced when a slightly shaken Red Wings team settled down to score the game's first goal, but Turk Broda in the Leafs net would not be beaten again. Early in the third period, Sweeney Schriner scored a power-play goal to tie the game. A few minutes later, Pete Langelle put the Leafs ahead. The greatest comeback in hockey history was clinched when Schriner scored again late in the period. "We wouldn't be celebrating the championship if it hadn't been for Hap [Day] and his faith in us," said Leafs captain Syl Apps. "He won the Cup more than anybody."

Conn Smythe shakes hands with Stanley Cup hero Pete Langelle. Sweeney Schriner and Lorne Carr look on.

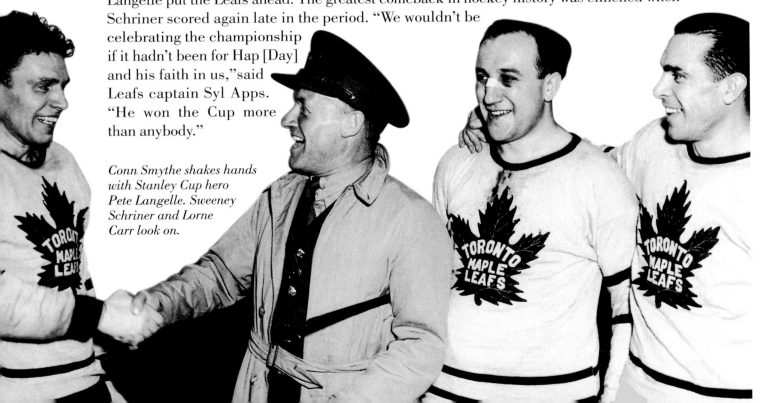

A SALUTE TO OUR RUSSIAN ALLY

IN THE EARLY years of the war, as long as Hitler and Stalin abided by their mutual non-aggression pact, the Soviets were viewed by the Allies as sinister, possibly dangerous—not exactly enemies, but certainly not friends.

It was, then, with a great sense of relief that, in 1941, the West watched the Nazis turn their attention eastward and break their own non-aggression treaty with the Soviet Union. Russia retaliated with the full might of her vast resources of people and materials. Two years later the tide of the war would begin to turn. Optimism prevailed, along with a much more positive attitude to the Soviets.

So the mood was buoyant as 17,000 people gathered in an almost unbearably hot Maple Leaf Gardens on June 22, 1943, waving their programs to cool off. The evening was billed as "A Salute to Our Russian Ally" and the speakers included such high-profile politicians as Prime Minister Mackenzie King, Russian ambassador to Canada Feodor Gousev, Joseph E. Davies (former United States ambassador to the Soviet Union), and Sir Ellsworth Flavelle, chairman of the Canadian–Soviet Friendship Council. The Master of Ceremonies was Raymond Massey.

The newspapers reported the next day that there was only one audible heckler during the ceremonies. He could be heard calling for a lift on the ban against the Communist party in Canada. The speakers, however, spoke only about the end of the distrust between East and West and about the new bond of friendship that had been forged to fight against the Nazi war machine. Propaganda, perhaps, but the high attendance in a sweltering sports arena on a June day indicated a genuine feeling of solidarity with a distant ally.

GUS BODNAR'S FIRST GOAL

AMONG THE MANY newcomers in training camp for the Toronto Maple Leafs in 1943 was Gus Bodnar. Originally from Fort William, Ontario, Bodnar was impressive enough to earn a spot on the Leafs roster and was on the ice to start the season when it opened at the Gardens on October 30, 1943.

A crowd of 11,654 witnessed opening festivities that included a ceremonial face-off between Toronto captain Bob Davidson and New York Rangers captain Ott Heller, the puck dropped by Ontario premier George Drew. When the puck was dropped for real, Davidson won the draw back to Moe Morris, who played the puck to Bodnar. At the fifteen-second mark of his first game, Bodnar put the puck past Rangers goalie Ken McAuley. More than fifty-five years later, Bodnar still holds the record for the quickest goal ever scored by a player in his first NHL game. The Leafs won 5–2 that night and Bodnar, who finished the game with two goals and an assist, went on to enjoy a brilliant rookie campaign. He would score twenty-two goals that season and register forty assists, easily winning the Calder

Trophy. His forty assists are still a Leafs rookie record and his sixty-two points were the first-year standard for almost forty years.

Though he would never again reach such lofty numbers, Bodnar helped the Maple Leafs win the Stanley Cup in 1945 and remained in Toronto until, on November 2, 1947, he was traded to the Chicago Black Hawks, along with line-mates Bud Poile and Gaye Stewart, plus Ernie Dickens and Bob Goldham, for Max Bentley and Cy Thomas. With

(Top) Gus Bodnar and Leafs alternate captain Nick Metz try to take the puck from a fallen Ted Lindsay. (Above) Bodnar receives the Calder Trophy from NHL president Red Dutton.

Chicago in 1951–52, Bodnar established another speed record setting up Bill Mosienko for three goals in twenty-one seconds. Bodnar finished his career with the Boston Bruins in 1954–55.

THE ANDREWS SISTERS

SOME AMERICAN ENTERTAINERS were famous for their part in the war effort, performing for the troops, appearing in uplifting patriotic movies, and singing songs that took the edge off the harsh realities of the times. Bob Hope, Bing Crosby, and Betty Grable come to mind. But they all also continued to perform for civilians.

Among the most popular were three sisters from Minneapolis—Patti, Maxine, and LaVerne. Bursting onto the scene in the late '30s, the Andrews Sisters had charmed the public with their harmonies and sense of humour for years.

So it was that thousands of fans showed up to enjoy a two-hour program on October 30, 1944, when the Andrews Sisters brought their show to Maple Leaf Gardens. They started their set with a beautifully harmonized version of one of their biggest wartime hits, "Boogie Woogie Bugle Boy."

While the fans of the Andrews Sisters enjoyed their singing, as the *Toronto Telegram* reported the next day, "to the full," they were further entertained by the blonde sister, Patti, who acted as Mistress of Ceremonies. Her sense of humour and timing made her the hit of the show. In addition to "Bugle Boy," the sisters sang what at the time was the new Cole Porter ballad, "Don't Fence Me In"—much to the delight of the audience. The song that brought tears to people's eyes, however, was introduced as an American ballad, "Down in the Valley."

Several piano players also performed on the bill that night. They played fast-paced and complicated piano pieces such as "Flight of the Bumble Bee" and "Ritual Fire Dance." At the end of the concert both the American and Canadian national anthems were played as a standard bearer fitted the flag.

December 19, 1944

TOMMY DORSEY

TOMMY DORSEY AND his brother Jimmy were groomed for the music business from childhood. Tommy became a respected soloist on both the trumpet and the trombone, while Jimmy played the sax and clarinet. It seemed natural that the brothers would form a band together, and they did in the early 1930s. It was during this period that the brothers recorded their first big hit, "I'm Getting Sentimental Over You." In 1935, however, sibling rivalry led the two brothers to go their separate ways. (They would not collaborate musically again until 1953.) Tommy formed the Tommy Dorsey Band.

Tommy Dorsey's skill on his chosen instrument earned him the nickname "Mr. Trombone" among his band, known as the "Hep Cats," but it was not until he hired "The Voice" that the band soared to new heights. Francis Albert Sinatra was the perfect complement to this collection of some of the best jazz musicians of the time—

An older Tommy Dorsey is surrounded by fellow musicians and club owners.

names such as Bunny Berigan, Pee Wee Erwin, Buddy Defranco, and Louis Bellson.

On December 19, 1944, Tommy Dorsey and his thirty-four-member orchestra held court at Maple Leaf Gardens. It had not been a great year for Tommy. Frank Sinatra had left the band to pursue a solo career. Freddie Stewart was now behind the microphone. His tenor voice sang through the repertoire of hits which included Torontonian Ruth Lowe's hit, "I'll Never Smile Again." Only 3,600 people saw the concert and fewer still got up to dance.

Adding to the general turmoil surrounding the band, Tommy had just gone through a very public and embarrassing trial in the United States after being charged with breaking the nose of actor Jon Hall. The charges were dismissed, but Tommy's reputation was damaged. However, the *Globe* reported following the concert that one need not worry about Tommy. He still made $1.25 million a year.

UNITED CHURCH TWENTIETH ANNIVERSARY

On JUNE 10, 1925, the inaugural service of the United Church of Canada was held inside Mutual Street Arena. On June 10, 1945, the United Church celebrated its twentieth anniversary at Maple Leaf Gardens. Almost 20,000 people filled the Gardens that evening, with an overflow crowd of some 1,200 meeting at the Carlton Street United Church.

Many church dignitaries spoke at the Gardens service, the theme of which was "Advancing for Christ and His Kingdom." A little more than a month after the war in Europe ended, the Right Reverend J.H. Arnup, moderator of the United Church, spoke of the huge social undertaking required for the "complete rehabilitation into civil life" of veterans and war workers. Bishop F.J. McConnell of New York spoke of the work being done in San Francisco (where the United Nations was being formed from the ashes of the League of Nations) as generating "a feeling of oneness among the people of the earth [and] thus making strides toward the Kingdom of God."

Music was an important part of the evening at Maple Leaf Gardens. A symphony orchestra and a huge choir of 1,200, including guest soloist Portia White, performed. "Had the mammoth choir in its massive chancel not been so accurate in tonal expression," noted the *Toronto Telegram*, "the audience never would have sung with such splendid sonority." As it was, nearly 20,000 strong, it participated in nine hymns, becoming "a gigantic choir of adoration and praise." The final Hallelujah chorus was reported as "a fitting and triumphant climax."

March 31, 1946

RECEPTION FOR CARDINAL McGUIGAN

On SUNDAY, MARCH 31, 1946, a crowd of 15,000 filled Maple Leaf Gardens for one of the largest public Roman Catholic celebrations in Toronto prior to the visit of Pope John Paul II in 1984. This was a welcome home for archbishop of Toronto James McGuigan, who had been elevated to cardinal in Rome just five weeks before, the first anglophone Canadian to be accorded the honour.

Cardinal McGuigan entered through the northwest door of the Gardens at 3:00 and proceeded to a scarlet-draped platform at the south end. "As he walked, flanked by purple-robed monsignors," reported the *Toronto Telegram*, "the cheering swelled until, in sheer volume, it surpassed the plaudits of the sports-maddened thousands who make Maple Leaf Gardens their cathedral." The cardinal removed his scarlet biretta and waved to the crowd. He waved again after he mounted the platform and the cheers continued until the 200-member choir, augmented by 500 schoolchildren, broke into song.

During his address Cardinal McGuigan warned that the evil which produced the Second World War was still present. "Our world is not only still bleeding from the terrible wounds inflicted in the recent war, but the evil principle which produced that war is still operative, still powerful, still menacing. That evil principle is the greed for totalitarian power." He further stated that there was no solution to the world's problems on the basis of power politics. "There will be no respect for the human person," he said, "if we do not recognize in every person the immortal soul made in God's image and likeness."

November 1, 1946

TORONTO HUSKIES DEBUT

IN DECEMBER 1891, at the YMCA training school in Springfield, Massachusetts, James Naismith of Almonte, Ontario, asked a custodian to nail two peach baskets to the gymnasium balcony. A new sport was born. It spread quickly, and several professional leagues came and went until, at a meeting in New York City on June 6, 1946, the Basketball Association of America—forerunner of the NBA—was formed. The first game in its history was played in Toronto on November 1, 1946.

"Professional basketball lays out its first line of samples at the Maple Leaf Gardens tonight," wrote the *Toronto Star*, "with the Toronto Huskies opposed to New York's Knickerbockers... For this latest addition to the Gardens sports roster the Gardens' technical staff has constructed a special wooden floor and a set of transparent backboards, the latter so the fans can follow the ball from any seat in the house." Any of those fans taller than Huskies centre George Norstrand (6'8") would be admitted free.

The Huskies appeared slower and out of shape when compared to the New Yorkers ("not having had the chance to go against top calibre teams such as [those] the Knicks [played] in the New York region") and the Knicks led in the first half. Playing coach Ed Sadowski was Toronto's best performer, pouring in 18 points before he fouled out early in the third quarter. He was replaced by George Norstrand, who scored 16 points of his own and pushed the Huskies into a 48–43 lead. In the end, it was the Knicks' better team speed that allowed them to prevail 68-66.

Season's end found Toronto tied with the Boston Celtics for last place in the Eastern Division with a record of 22–38. Only the Western Division's Detroit Falcons (20–40) and Pittsburgh Ironmen (15–45) had worse records among the league's eleven teams. Toronto, Detroit, Pittsburgh, and the Cleveland Rebels all folded after the 1946-47 season, leaving the fledgling Basketball Association of America with just seven teams.

(Above) Two Huskies players talk strategy with new coach Robert "Red" Rolfe. (Opposite) The Huskies in action at the Gardens during their one and only season.

MEEKER SCORES FIVE

"HOW MANY DID you actually get?" asked Vic Lynn of Howie Meeker last night in the Maple Leaf dressing room as the crew-cut young Leaf right winger tossed aside his hockey clothes and made for the shower.

"I got three that I put in and two others I steered in," replied Howie. And a broad grin spread over his face as he said it.

Bobby Hewitson's intro to his *Toronto Telegram* report of the game may well have confused many of the 12,059 who had been at the Gardens on the night of January 8, 1947. Most who had watched the home team fire fifty-one shots at Chicago's Paul Bibeault and beat the beleaguered Black Hawks 10–4 went home thinking Meeker had scored a hat trick. Very few were aware that he had set a new rookie record (and one that has been equalled only once, by Don Murdoch of the New York Rangers in 1976) by scoring five times.

Coach Hap Day and Meeker celebrate the rookie's big night.

"The goals came so thick and fast that even the official scorer didn't know where they were coming from," wrote Joe Perlove in the *Toronto Star*. In fact, goals credited to Wally Stanowski (and announced over the public address system as such) in each of the first two periods were later awarded to Meeker (who had, in fact, tipped them in). Halfway through the season, Meeker now ranked third in the league, behind Rocket Richard and Teeder Kennedy.

"Meeker has been more or less unofficially declared as the Leaf most likely to get the Calder Trophy this season," wrote Hewitson in the *Telegram*, and he was right. Meeker finished the season with twenty-seven goals, a rookie record that stood for thirty-six years.

That Howie Meeker could play at all in 1946-47, let alone become rookie of the year, was something of a miracle. His legs had been badly damaged by a grenade during World War II, and only lengthy and difficult rehabilitation had made his career possible.

April 29, 1947

ICE REVUE STARRING BARBARA ANN SCOTT

BARBARA ANN SCOTT received her first pair of skates from her parents when she was seven. Joining the Minto Skating Club in Ottawa, she won her first national (junior) title in 1939 at the age of eleven. She was Canadian champ by 1944 and North American champion the following year. In 1947 Barbara Ann Scott became the first non-European to win the World Figure Skating Championship, and suddenly she was "Canada's Sweetheart."

On April 29 and 30, 1947, Scott headlined an ice skating revue at Maple Leaf Gardens to raise money for British flood victims. She arrived in Toronto the day before the show and visited with youngsters at the Hospital for Sick Children. She also appeared before her fans in a display window at Eaton's downtown store. Her two Gardens shows were a huge success, but in order for more Torontonians to see her (and no doubt to increase the gate) she agreed to stay in town for two more days and greet fans at a Kiwanis Club presentation of Cleveland's Orpheus Male Chorus.

In 1948 Barbara Ann Scott won a gold medal at the Winter Olympics in St. Moritz, Switzerland, and she became even more popular back home. "Tourists were beginning to visit me as though I were one of Ottawa's institutions," she would later write in her autobiography Skate With Me. "They were likely to come at curious hours and it was not much good refusing to go to the door." Soon afterwards, Scott turned professional and moved to Toronto, where she made several more appearances at Maple Leaf Gardens, the first being in 1952, as the headliner of the Hollywood Ice Revue, which she had taken over from longtime star Sonja Henie. Barbara Ann's "Romantic Leading Man" in the show was Toronto's Mike Kirby, while hometown girls Betty Cornford and Inez Gates also appeared in the lavish production.

FIRST NHL ALL-STAR GAME

AT AN NHL BOARD of Governors meeting in 1946, a letter from John Carmichael of the *Chicago Daily News* was presented, asking permission to promote a charity game in Chicago between the NHL champions and a team of NHL all-stars. That permission was granted on condition that 25 percent of the game receipts would go to the Players' Emergency Fund. No game was played that year, but a year later the first official NHL All-Star Game (with proceeds going to the newly created Players' Pension Fund) was held at Maple Leaf Gardens on October 13, 1947.

Clarence Campbell drops the puck for Ted Lindsay and Syl Apps before the first NHL All-Star Game.

The defending Stanley Cup champion Maple Leafs took on the All-Stars in a game that proved anything but a tame exhibition contest. "The game had all the explosive qualities of a playoff and it didn't lag for action," wrote Red Burnett in the *Toronto Star*. "The way the boys went at each other they must have been trying to line up a few early prospects for that pension fund." There were twelve minor penalties and one major. The lone serious casualty was Chicago's Bill Mosienko, who suffered a fractured ankle when he fell awkwardly into the boards after a clean check by Jim Thomson. He would be out of action for two months.

For almost two periods the Leafs played like Stanley Cup champions. Syl Apps was Toronto's top performer, setting up goals by Harry Watson and Bill Ezinicki (though he only earned an assist for the second) and potting the third himself after stepping around Butch Bouchard and beating Bill Durnan. Boston's Frank Brimsek took over in the All-Star goal at that point, while Maurice Richard went about engineering a comeback.

With the score 3–2 entering the third period, the Rocket beat Turk Broda to tie the game after just twenty-eight seconds. One minute and twenty-seven seconds later, the All-Stars led 4–3 after Richard set up a play with Boston's Milt Schmidt that saw Doug Bentley of the Black Hawks score the go-ahead goal. Brimsek held off all Leafs attempts to rally, even after Turk Broda was pulled in the final minute, and the game ended 4–3.

May 16, 1948

RALLY FOR ISRAEL

WHEN THE MODERN STATE of Israel was proclaimed on May 14, 1948, Jews around the world rejoiced. Almost 2,000 years after Jerusalem had fallen to Roman soldiers in 66 A.D.—and just three years after six million perished in the Holocaust—the Jewish people finally had a homeland once again.

The following weekend, Toronto's Jewish community celebrated, decorating houses and shops with the distinctive Star of David from the flag of Israel, giving thanks and prayer in the synagogue, and taking to the streets in outbursts of joy. The weekend concluded with a mammoth parade from Bathurst and College streets to a historic rally at Maple Leaf Gardens.

Mira Koschitzky was a twelve-year-old girl in 1948, and a newcomer to Canada. "I remember marching along College Street as a proud member of the Jewish community celebrating the establishment of the state of Israel," she says in the anthology, Voices from the Heart. "After the horrors of the Holocaust, which my family was lucky to survive in Slovakia, to be able to march into Maple Leaf Gardens with thousands of fellow Jews, not because we had to but because we wanted to, was an unbelievable feeling. I'll never forget the wonder, excitement, and goodwill of that evening."

Long before the doors to Maple Leaf Gardens opened on the night of May 16, 1948, crowds of people seven and eight deep had already surrounded the building, and at 7:15 a swarm of 20,000 filled the arena from the seats on the floor to the uppermost row. The evening begin with an opening prayer and the singing of "Hatikvah" ("The Hope," the historic Jewish song that would become Israel's national anthem). A host of notables, Jews and non-Jews alike, addressed the crowd, including Sir Ellsworth Flavelle, Senator Arthur W. Roebuck, and Rabbi Abraham L. Feinberg of Toronto's Holy Blossom Temple. The rally urged the Canadian government to recognize Israel and to work towards admission of the new Jewish State into the United Nations.

Mass **RALLY**
MAPLE LEAF GARDENS
SUN., MAY 16th - 8.15 p.m.

● Come and proclaim your solidarity with the Provisional Jewish Government in Palestine!

We have waited for this day for 2,000 years

● Come early and participate in this event of historical importance!

Noted Speakers Will Address The Meeting

Doors open at **7.15 p.m.**   No solicitation for funds

Sponsored by the
United Zionist Council of Toronto

ONTARIO JEWISH ARCHIVES

MISS CANADA PAGEANT

ON AUGUST 18, 1949, Margaret Lynn Munn was crowned "Miss Canada" on the stage of Maple Leaf Gardens. It was the only time the event was ever held at the Gardens and it was not a success. Only about 1,500 people attended, and about one-third of them had been admitted free of charge.

"The result was a financial headache," reported the *Toronto Star*. But "none of the girls will be stranded away from home despite the failure of the enterprise. Their expenses to and from Toronto were provided by the local group or individual who sponsored the entry."

Prize money ($10,000 to be split among eleven women) had also been guaranteed by event sponsors. Miss Munn would also, for obscure reasons, receive a free trip to Peru courtesy of the Peruvian government. The small gate, however, meant there were concerns as to whether there would be funds to send her to Atlantic City to compete in the "Miss Universe" contest.

Miss Canada 1949 was a native of Vancouver who had come to Toronto to study at the Royal Conservatory of Music. "The new beauty queen plans to complete her training, which started when she was seven years old."

May 26, 1950

MANITOBA FLOOD RELIEF

THE 1950 RED RIVER VALLEY FLOOD devastated the area more than any other in this century. Though the volume of water was actually greater during the flood of 1995, modern technology was able to limit much of the damage. In the spring of 1950, 17,000 Manitoban homes were damaged or destroyed by the raging waters and a national Manitoba Flood Relief Fund set a goal of raising $10 million to aid the many victims.

On May 26, 1950, CBC Radio staged an entertainment extravaganza in aid of Red River Valley flood victims at Maple Leaf Gardens. It was attended by 14,907 people and broadcast live to 128 radio stations across Canada. Every English-language station in the country (both CBC stations and independents) cancelled its own programming in order to carry the special show. More than 600 stations in the United States carried the broadcast, either in full or in part, live or on tape.

The mammoth project was put together in a little over a week and featured almost 250 performers, including the Toronto Symphony Orchestra, the Leslie Bell singers, and the Fred Waring Glee Club. Actors included Beth Lockerbie and Jim McRae, as well as Hollywood comedian (and native of Carmen, Manitoba) Jack Carson, who flew in from a movie shoot in New York City. (While few of these names are remembered today, many were the biggest Canadian radio personalities of the time.) Announcers during the ninety-minute show were Foster Hewitt, Jack Scott, Jack Dennett, and John Fisher.

A check for $25,336 (representing the box office receipts for the evening) was presented to Manitoba deputy premier John S. McDiarmid during the show. The city of Toronto collection for the Manitoba Flood Relief Fund reached $46,563 that night, while the national total climbed to $1,709,000 as the many listeners were urged to donate as generously as possible.

GAME SEVEN, 1950 MANN CUP FINALS

THOUGH LACROSSE SHARES an official designation with hockey as Canada's national sport (hockey is the national winter game, lacrosse the national summer game) it has been many years since it has enjoyed hockey's huge following. Lacrosse had been the game of choice for athletes and fans at the turn of the century, reaching such popularity that religious leaders deemed it immoral. It had been Canada's game since the 1850s (of course, Native people had been playing it for centuries), but by the end of World War I its popularity had dwindled to the smaller cities and towns of south/central Ontario and British Columbia's lower mainland.

Until the 1930s, lacrosse had traditionally been a field game, but "we thought that lacrosse could keep the Gardens going in the summertime," Frank Selke once recalled and box lacrosse was born. On May 3, 1932, the Maple Leafs lacrosse team squared off against the Tecumsehs in the inaugural game of the International Lacrosse League. Though 8,000 fans attended the opener, the league was short-lived. Nonetheless, the Mann Cup Canadian senior lacrosse championship was held at the Gardens for the first time later that year, and would be every second year from 1936 to 1956.

Perhaps the best series was the 1950 final between the Owen Sound Crescents and the New Westminster Adanacs.

Owen Sound was leading the best-of-seven series three games to two when their brilliant goalie Moon Whootton was carried from his crease with a badly injured ankle during game six. He was replaced by Doug Favell (father of the future NHL netminder of the same name). Favell was brilliant in making twenty-six saves, but New Westminster tied the series with a 6–5 victory.

There were 6,588 fans on hand for game seven on October 22. Once again Favell sparkled, holding New Westminster to just one goal in the second half as Owen Sound broke a 6–6 tie en route to a 15–7 victory. Playing coach Doug Gillespie led the new Mann Cup champions with three goals and an assist, while captain Onions Smith collected three points. Following the game, Moon Whootton hobbled out on crutches to accept the Michael Kelley Medal as the series MVP.

Doug Favell of St. Catharines had been designated as the spare goaltender for the 1950 Mann Cup Finals. He came up big for Owen Sound in their seventh-game victory over New Westminster.

April 21, 1951

BILL BARILKO'S GOAL

IT IS ONE OF THE most famous images in hockey history: Bill Barilko soaring through the air, his body parallel to the ice. Gerry McNeil is down in the Canadiens goal. The puck sails above him. The Toronto Maple Leafs win the Stanley Cup.

Barilko's goal capped the most exciting game in one of the most exciting Stanley Cup series ever played. Every game went into overtime, including the fifth and final one on April 21, 1951. Rocket Richard gave the Montreal Canadiens a 1–0 lead that night, beating Al Rollins in the second period. Tod Sloan tied the game three minutes later, but a goal by Paul Meger in the third restored Montreal's advantage. The 2–1 lead held up late into the period until, with just thirty-two seconds remaining and Rollins on the bench for an extra attacker, Sloan scored again for the equalizer. Early in overtime, Harry Watson flattened a rolling puck and fed it to Howie Meeker, who circled behind the Canadiens goal. Meeker sent the puck out front for Barilko, whose goal at 2:53 of the extra session gave the Maple Leafs their fifth Stanley Cup victory in seven years.

(Above) Leaf teammates carry Bill Barilko off the ice after his goal against Montreal's Gerry McNeil (below) won the Leafs the Cup.

Though best known for his bashing bodychecks, Barilko loved to join the play in the offensive zone. It was a tactic that was not encouraged by Leafs coaches. But of course, it is not merely the fact that Barilko was an unlikely hero that has made his goal the most famous in Maple Leafs history. It is because Barilko's goal proved to be the last one he ever scored.

On August 26, 1951, Barilko was traveling to Timmins after a fishing trip when the light plane he was flying in went missing, presumed crashed. When Barilko had not been found by October 1, Conn Smythe offered a $10,000 reward. So reluctant were the Leafs to accept their hero's fate that his equipment was still laid out for him at his locker when the 1951–52 season opened on October 13. Bill Barilko's remains would not be discovered until 1962, the year the Leafs next won the Stanley Cup.

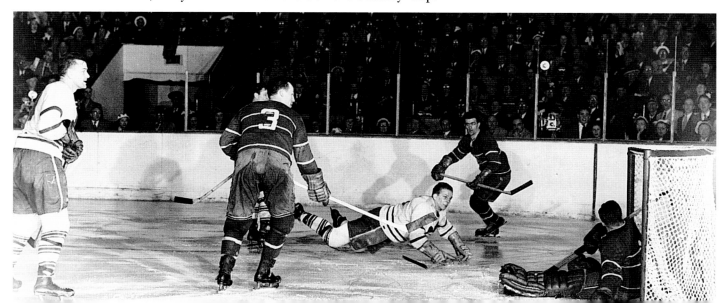

1951 ALL-STAR GAME

IN 1951 THE NHL changed the format of its All-Star Game. For the first four years of its existence, the pre-season classic had pitted the NHL All-Stars against the previous year's Stanley Cup champions. On October 11, 1951—two days before the start of the 1951–52 season—the NHL's First All-Star Team from the 1950–51 campaign faced the Second All-Star Team at Maple Leaf Gardens.

To bolster the two All-Star rosters First Team coach Joe Primeau made selections from the four American-based NHL teams. Dick Irvin of the Second Team chose from the Toronto Maple Leafs and Montreal Canadiens. Joining First Team All-Stars Terry Sawchuk (Detroit), Red Kelly (Detroit), Bill Quackenbush (Boston), Milt Schmidt (Boston), Gordie Howe (Detroit), and Ted Lindsay (Detroit) were: Harry Lumley (Chicago), Frank Eddols (New York), Lidio Fogolin (Chicago), Al Dewsbury (Chicago), Don Raleigh (New York), Ed Sanford (Boston,) Doug Bentley (Chicago), Johnny Peirson (Boston), Reg Sinclair (New York), and Gaye Stewart (New York). Second Team All-Stars Chuck Rayner (New York), Jim Thomson (Toronto), Leo Reise (Detroit), Teeder Kennedy (Toronto), Maurice Richard (Montreal), and Sid Smith (Toronto) were joined by Gerry McNeil (Montreal), Butch Bouchard (Montreal), Doug Harvey (Montreal), Gus Mortson (Toronto), Max Bentley (Toronto), Tod Sloan (Toronto), Harry Watson (Toronto), Kenny Mosdell (Montreal), Floyd Curry (Montreal) and Paul Meger (Montreal).

A crowd of 11,455 paid $25,259.75 (two-thirds of the amount going to the players' pension fund) to see the game, which ended in a 2–2 tie. "The results prove how evenly matched the top players in the NHL are," wrote *Toronto Star* columnist Red Burnett, adding, "they didn't loaf through a dull listless game."

Gordie Howe opened the scoring for the First Team All-Stars at 7:59 of the first period. Tod Sloan evened things for the Second Team early in the second before Johnny Peirson restored the one-goal lead. Kenny Mosdell's goal midway through the third period resulted in the final tie. The goaltending was superb. "But for the splendid work of Chuck Rayner and Gerry McNeil [the First Team would] likely have won. All four—Rayner, McNeil, Terry Sawchuk and Harry Lumley—shone."

Goaltender Gerry McNeil keeps an eye on teammate Doug Harvey in the corner while Bill Quackenbush patrols the front of the net. Ted Lindsay and Gordie Howe are in the dark sweaters.

October 13, 1951

ROYAL VISIT

ON OCTOBER 8, 1951, Princess Elizabeth and Prince Philip arrived in Canada to begin the first true royal visit since King George VI and Queen Elizabeth had toured the Dominion in 1939. Millions of Canadians turned out to see the future Queen in cities and towns across the country. On Saturday, October 13, 1951, Princess Elizabeth and Prince Philip greeted the citizens of Toronto at a series of events planned to the minute from 10:00 a.m. until 8:15 p.m., when they would attend a dinner hosted by the lieutenant-governor of Ontario at the Royal York Hotel.

Perhaps the highlight of their time in Toronto was a visit to Maple Leaf Gardens. The Toronto Maple Leafs and Chicago Black Hawks (who would open the NHL's regular season that evening) staged a fifteen-minute benefit game for the Princess with proceeds going to the crippled children of Ontario. Before the game, the Princess was presented with a bouquet of flowers by eleven-year-old Deanna Chartrand, one of 2,000 handicapped youngsters present.

Conn Smythe sat next to Princess Elizabeth during the game (which ended in a scoreless tie) and, according to a story he told the *Globe and Mail*'s Al Nickleson, both she and Prince Philip found the game most enjoyable. "That was apparent in the way Prince Philip roared with laughter at the upsetting bodychecks and the way the eyes of Princess Elizabeth glowed as they players shot by her at full speed... The Princess asked many technical questions, such as the speed attained by the players... During a goalmouth scramble [she] said she felt sorry for the goalies and didn't fancy playing that position in hockey... Once, when there was a particularly heavy crash of bodies on the ice, she asked: 'Isn't there going to be a penalty?'"

Leafs Captain Teeder Kennedy bows as he shakes hands with Princess Elizabeth. Prince Philip stands behind the future Queen while Conn Smythe is at her side.

As the Royal couple left the Gardens, Conn Smythe presented them with the puck used in the game. "I told the Princess it was for Bonnie Prince Charlie and that the Leafs were putting him on the negotiation list."

Bob "Showboat" Hall cradles the ball. Trotters teammate Jesse Arnelle is on the left, Andy Johnson on the right.

HARLEM GLOBE-TROTTERS' FIRST VISIT

AT ONLY 5'5", IT ISN'T surprising that Abe Saperstein made very little money as a professional basketball player. He earned just $5 per game. When he formed his own team in 1927, it earned just $75 in its first game and didn't begin to make money until 1940. But that team would go on to be the most famous in basketball history, for Abe Saperstein was the founder of the Harlem Globetrotters.

Born in London in 1903, Saperstein moved to Chicago with his nine brothers and sisters as a young boy. After his brief and unprofitable playing career, he became coach of an all-black team called the Savoy Big Five, named for the Savoy Ballroom in Harlem. In 1927, he changed the team's name to the Harlem Globetrotters, piled his five players into a Model T Ford, and took the show—"a blend... of vaudeville and solid basketball skills"—on the road.

In discussing the name many years later, Saperstein explained: "We chose Harlem because Harlem was to those fellows what Jerusalem is to [the Jews]. And Globetrotters? Well, we had big dreams. We hoped to travel. We made it all right." By the time of Saperstein's death in 1966, the team had traveled to eighty-seven countries, playing before kings and queens, a Soviet premier, and Pope Pius XII.

The Globetrotters first came to Maple Leaf Gardens on October 23, 1951. They played the Toledo Mercurys in the second game of a doubleheader that featured the Minneapolis Lakers against the Philadelphia Warriors in the opener. NBA superstar George Mikan disappointed the fans with his ordinary play in game one but, after the great sprinter Jesse Owens gave a motivational speech between games, the fans got what they had come to see. The showmanship of Goose Tatum and the brilliant dribbling of Marques Haynes had the fans hollering for more. And they got it. The Globetrotters would make annual visits to Maple Leaf Gardens for more than thirty years.

February 15, 1952

GEORGE VI MEMORIAL SERVICE

He WAS THE PEOPLE'S King, beloved in England and throughout the Commonwealth. George VI had not been born to the role of monarch, but had it thrust upon him with his brother's abdication for the woman he loved in 1937. Plagued with a speech impediment that made him uncomfortable in public, King George nonetheless handled himself with dignity and grace. Together, he and Queen Elizabeth would reign over a war-torn Britain with a common touch, refusing to leave London when the bombs began falling. Though his health had long been failing, his death on February 6, 1952, saddened the world. More than eight million people lined the funeral route from London to Windsor Castle.

The death of King George VI caused the Maple Leafs to cancel their game that night against the New York Rangers. It was only the second time in the club's history that a home game had been postponed. The first had been for the death of the King's father, George V, on January 21, 1936. (Only three other Leaf games at the Gardens have been postponed.)

The day of King George VI's funeral (February 15, 1952) was declared a national day of mourning in Canada, with state ceremonies in Ottawa and civic undertakings throughout the country. Memorial services for the King were held in Toronto at Maple Leaf Gardens and at Queen's Park, with thousands of people in attendance. The entire city also observed two minutes of silence. A similar Maple Leaf Gardens memorial and a citywide two-minute silence had previously been held for George V on January 28, 1936.

METROPOLITAN OPERA

"A FIRST-NIGHT CROWD of 11,500 saw a miracle come to pass last night at Maple Leaf Gardens. A whole grand opera, a grandiose opera, "Aida", came to life in the appropriately grand manner, on a huge stage. It was breathtaking."

Opera had first been staged at Maple Leaf Gardens on October 14, 1936. The production of Aida that night was plagued with acoustical problems caused by the vast size of the building. Opera would not return to the Gardens until May 26, 1952, when the Metropolitan Opera of New York staged its own production of Aida to open a four-night run. It was this show that prompted Rose MacDonald's rave review in the *Toronto Telegram*.

Extras from the production of Aida.

Much had been improved in terms of the sound at Maple Leaf Gardens between 1936 and 1952. The special microphone system that had been installed for the Met did produce some rough moments in the early going, but "everything came well into focus as the opera progressed: sound and lights were adjusted and as the stage became more populous, and the observer more accustomed to proportions, the feeling of small miniature figures on a giant stage disappeared."

Of course, it helped to be on the floor or in the box seats. Those in the blues, greens, and greys were an awfully long way away and many complained that Robert Merrill's voice wobbled. Be that as it may, the productions of "Aida", "La Boheme", "Carmen", and "Rigoletto" attracted 43,344 people over four nights.

Productions of the Metropolitan Opera of New York were staged annually at Maple Leaf Gardens until 1960, when the cost of such lavish tours became prohibitive. The events would prove the cultural highlight of every season and the city's newspapers were filled with stories about who was there and what they wore. But were these operas really art? Perhaps the best answer comes from Rudolf Bing, general manager of the Met. When asked what he thought of staging opera in sports venues, he replied: "Better than ice hockey at the Metropolitan."

December 14, 1954

A MIDSUMMER NIGHT'S DREAM

Maple Leaf Gardens has housed a staggering variety of entertainment. Up to now, however, never a comedy—legitimate comedy that is. After all—there's always wrestling.

TORONTO TELEGRAM, DECEMBER 14, 1954

FROM DECEMBER 14 TO 16, 1954, Maple Leaf Gardens was home to the Old Vic Company's presentation of *A Midsummer Night's Dream*, a lavish adaptation of the classic Shakespeare comedy featuring ballet and music. The London production was nearing the end of a North American tour, lugging around thirteen tons of scenery that filled an entire cargo plane. Opening night drew a black tie-only crowd of Toronto society and other curious theatre goers willing to shell out $6 for a top ticket. Moira Shearer as Titania was singled out for praise, as were male leads Robert Helpmann and Stanley Holloway. Still, the Gardens production was not without its problems.

"The first actors out on the stage showed signs of terror at the prospect before them and almost shouted lines across the vast spaces in front and around," reported Rose MacDonald in the *Telegram*. "Consequently, voices tangled with echoes that threatened to reverberate. But even that straightened itself out in time." Ultimately, however, the problems created by the sheer size of the Gardens proved insurmountable. "What may look impossibly exaggerated from the fifth row of the main floor," wrote Jack Karr in the *Toronto Star*, "may just possibly look like gross underplaying from the last row of the grays."

Moira Shearer as Titania.

The three-night run of *A Midsummer Night's Dream* proved to be the first and last theatre production to be staged at Maple Leaf Gardens, though to call it a failure would not be entirely accurate. "If the Gardens is not ideal for even such an extravaganza as *A Midsummer Night's Dream*," wrote Rose MacDonald, "it is well to remember that nowhere else in Toronto could an audience have the opportunity to see it." By 1960 such large-scale productions would be put on at the brand-new O'Keefe Centre, a venue that may well have been inspired by the success of the theatre, ballet, and opera at Maple Leaf Gardens throughout the 1950s.

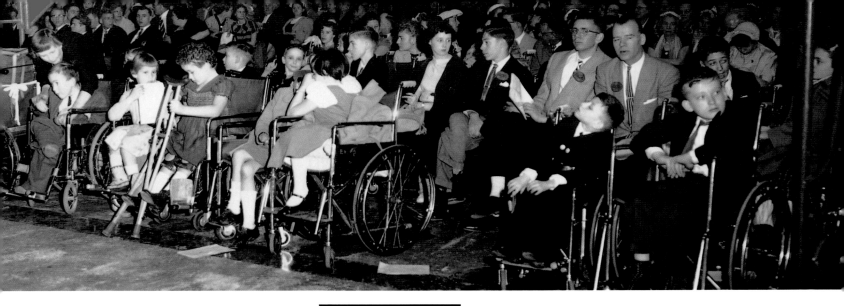

April 3, 1955

EASTER SEALS

Lɪᴛᴛʟᴇ ᴊᴏᴀɴ ꜰʀʏᴇʀ went to a show yesterday. It was the biggest show of its kind ever held, and Joan, five, was one of the smallest people there.

But that didn't bother Joan. She humped her small crutches at great speed, weaving through the 15,000 crowd in Maple Leaf Gardens.

She hobbled into the white TV glare and stared calmly at Byng Whitteker and Timmy (11-year-old Sandy McDonald), who introduced the 1955 Easter Seals show in aid of crippled children. The crowd contributed nearly $3,800. Last year $4,300 was raised from a capacity crowd.

"I can't make her sit still," said Joan's mother, Mrs. Jack Fryer, of Montcalm Ave., "but I don't know that I should try. She's had polio since she was 21 months old.

"You know," she added, watching the show, "you never appreciate what these crippled children's societies are doing until your family is hit."

The show, televised for the first time, was show business's big voluntary give to the Easter Seals campaign. Howard Caine was chairman of the radio an TV committee.

The vast audience sat motionless as Timmy, a solitary figure in a leg brace, sang "Can a Little Child Like Me?" in his clear soprano voice.

[Marathon swimmer] Marilyn Bell, demure in a dark blue dress, was there to make her appeal for the crippled children, many of whom she has taught to swim at the Lakeshore Swimming Club.

Joan, who swims at the club, made a bee-line for her as she waited to go on stage. She climbed up and sat on Marilyn's knee, swinging her iron-braced legs, and clapped delightedly.

— *TORONTO TELEGRAM*, ᴀᴘʀɪʟ 4, 1955

Easter Seals fundraisers at the Gardens were an annual occurrence for many years. (Below) Perry Como, with Whipper Billy Watson, appeared at the 1957 event.

BILLY GRAHAM

BILLY GRAHAM, THE most famous evangelist of our time, was just a young preacher when he made his first visit to Maple Leaf Gardens as part of a Youth for Christ rally in 1946. When he returned to Toronto on October 2, 1955, a crowd of nearly 17,000 turned out to see him. Another 4,000 who could not get seats inside the arena listened on special speakers set up behind the Gardens at the corner of Church and Wood streets. As the crowd swarmed over the road, police were needed to block off the intersection.

Graham spoke of Noah's belief in God. "If Noah was building his ark today," Graham said, "he would be surrounded by hot dog stands. The Americans would be there commercializing on it, setting up roller coasters and carnival booths. He would be a tourist attraction." Noah looked foolish building his ark," said Graham, "but he was a man of faith." The evangelist wondered how many shared that strong devotion this day, as the Cold War escalated and the end of the world was once again near.

"It is now possible for man to depopulate the whole world," Graham warned. "For the first time in history it is possible to destroy life on this planet. We are told that with the H-bomb it may be possible to drop twenty bombs and make this planet no longer inhabitable. The U.S. already has twenty bombs and they probably have twenty behind the Iron Curtain. We are just waiting for the moment of iniquity and madness to destroy the world…

"I came to tell you what the bible says. It says a day of judgement is coming." Graham then gazed upon his large audience. "I know that up in the stands today there are men and women who need God. You need God in your life and in your home. I beg you to give your life and heart to Him today. I beg you not to neglect it, to neglect it is the most dangerous thing of all."

BILL HALEY AND HIS COMETS

SOMETHING STRANGE BEGAN happening to the music industry in the early 1950s. It began with black rhythm and blues and jazz musicians, but as the power and passion of the music spread, white musicians started imitating the sound. Mainstream radio started playing the music. It was called rock and roll. Before long, it was claimed by teenagers as their own music with its own style of dance, its own language, and its own beat.

From the outset Maple Leaf Gardens was a barometer for change, attracting politicians, performers, and public speakers as well as hockey players. So it was natural that when rock and roll arrived in Toronto on April 30, 1956, in the form of Bill Haley and His Comets that the Gardens would be their stage. Bill Haley and the Comets had formed in 1954. By the time they arrived in Toronto, they had a string of hits with songs such as "Razzle Dazzle," "See You Later, Alligator" and, of course, "Rock around the Clock." The young in Toronto, like the young across most English-speaking countries, had fallen in love with the band and their music. They flocked to the Gardens to see Bill Haley and His Comets, as well as several other bands of this emerging style of music: the Platters, the Drifters, the Teenagers, the Teen Queens, the Flamingos, and the Colts.

As things heated up, the kids began dancing in the aisles and on their seats. Some even got up on stage. A few shocked parents watched 12,764 kids going crazy to tunes as incomprehensible as Haley's "Flip, Flop and Fly." Once the Comets launched into their big hits there was no stopping the crowd from surging towards the stage and the security people gave up. One commentator remarked the following day that "None of these musicians will ever make the music hall of fame—it really is doubtful that in fact it is music."

But the critics were wrong. Rock and roll was here to stay!

April 2, 1957

ELVIS PRESLEY

"THE MUCH PUBLICIZED pelvis was plainly in action..."
And before Elvis had left the building, 23,000 people had
jammed the Gardens to see him perform two shows, one
at 6:00 p.m., the other at 9:00. The late show alone drew
a crowd of 15,000 fans, making it the largest audience
Elvis Presley had ever played for.

"Elvis rocks his hips back and forth," wrote Joe
Scanlon in the *Toronto Telegram*. "He shakes his knees and
wobbles his legs and bumps like a fan dancer. He throws out one
arm and then the other and sometimes he even gets down on his
knees and leans forward at the audience. At times he even bal-
ances on both toes with his knees forward, hips wiggling and
chest thrown out." The teenage girls in the audience
screamed with delight, though "members of the troupe said
the whooping and hollering and shenanigans just didn't
compare to what they had seen in other cities." Toronto
the Good—though maybe the presence of some ninety
police officers had something to do with it. "Whenever a
youngster bounced up in his seat a policeman would
reach over and plunk him down again. Sometimes
this gave the Gardens the appearance of a large
jack-in-the-box."

The opening act was tap dancer Frankie Trent,
who claimed that he had heard a lot more heckling
in Toronto than was usual in most towns. Irish tenor
Frankie Connors was also booed. The Jordannaires
(who had backed up Elvis on his Peace in the Valley
album and would continue to do so for the rest of his
career) also performed on the bill, as did Pat Kelly,
"an attractive blonde," Jimmy James, and comic Rex
Marlowe (who got few laughs). When he finally took
the stage Elvis sang for an hour, though he didn't
perform Blue Suede Shoes.

"I have five pair of blue suede shoes at
home, but I never wear them," Elvis
said. "That kind of thing gets worn out
after a while."

April 30, 1957

WHITBY WINS ALLAN CUP

IN ITS HEYDAY, the Allan Cup was as important to many local hockey fans as the Stanley Cup. The NHL teams could only ever cover a handful of Canadian cities, but virtually every community of any size could ice a senior amateur team. The Allan Cup's East-West playoff format pushed the game's local rivalries across both regional and provincial boundaries and made senior amateur hockey a truly national spectacle. The added knowledge that the Allan Cup champion would almost always represent Canada at the Olympics and World Championships added further luster to the tall silver trophy.

One of the truly legendary teams of Canadian sports captured the Allan Cup for the first time in 1957. In fact, the victory by the Whitby Dunlops at Maple Leaf Gardens on April 30, 1957, encompassed a number of firsts: It was the first time that a team had leaped from Senior B status to become champions of Senior A hockey, and it marked the first time in the forty-nine-year history of the trophy that the Allan Cup finals ended in a four-game sweep. Urged on by a chant that had become a familiar part of the area's hockey arenas—"Go, Dunnies, Go"— Whitby completed the sweep with a 6–2 victory over the Spokane Flyers.

The game was much closer than the score would indicate. The Flyers led 1–0 in the second period before Bobby Attersley netted two goals in thirty-three seconds. Charlie Burns added two goals in the third period (the second after a great play by Harry Sinden), and goalie John Henderson held off a late Spokane charge before two more Dunlops goals iced the victory.

"We should go to the [World Championships]," hollered team manager Wren Blair in the victorious Whitby dressing room. And, indeed, a few weeks after their Allan Cup victory, the Canadian Amateur Hockey Association announced the Dunlops would compete at the 1958 World Championships. The Dunnies swept to the gold medal with a perfect 7–0 record after beating the Soviets 4–2 in the final game.

November 22, 1957

WHITBY vs. RUSSIA

AFTER LOSING THE World Championship to the Soviets in 1954 and the Olympic gold medal in 1956, Canadians would get their first chance to see the Russians close up in 1957. The Moscow Selects (an all-star squad that included most of the Soviet national team) played eight games against Senior A clubs across Ontario. The first was played against the Whitby Dunlops at Maple Leaf Gardens on November 22, 1957.

Since Whitby would be representing Canada at the 1958 World Championships, the game attracted much attention and was a sell-out. The day before the game, more than 200 hockey officials, NHL scouts, and members of the media had shown up to watch the Soviets practise at the Gardens.

"They started it by giving each player a puck," wrote Don Hunt in the *Toronto Telegram*, "and coach Anatoli Tarasov ordered them to go from one end to the other on one skate. While the goalie jumped about four feet in the air, walked on his ankles, did the bends and other forms of weird exercises, the rest of the team skated back and forth on one leg, shaking their wrists."

If Canadians found the Soviet warm-up amusing, they stopped laughing after Tarasov put the team through its paces. "They can really control the puck," marvelled Leafs scout Bob Davidson. Added the Montreal Canadiens' Ken Reardon: "Even our club, which is supposed to be the best in the NHL, can't pass like that."

On game night the Selects started out by scoring two goals back to back. "Then the Dunlops reverted to one aspect of Canadian hockey that brings out the best—and worst—in men," wrote the *Telegram*'s Hal Walker. "The solid teeth-rattling bodycheck." By the end of the first period, Whitby led 5–2. The final score was 7–2.

Though the Moscow Selects recovered to end their eight-game tour with a record of 5–2–1, the Whitby victory gave the Dunlops an added boost of confidence at the World Championships in Norway, where they returned the world title to Canada.

April 28, 1959

BENNY GOODMAN

WHEN SWING WAS the thing, from the mid-1930s to the late 1940s, Benny Goodman was one of the kings. Goodman would stand out in front of his orchestra playing solos on his clarinet—known to the followers of his big band with the strong jazz overtones as his "licorice stick"—and the crowds agreed that he was the best.

By the late 1950s, swing was no longer the thing. Rock and roll was beginning its reign and the orchestra, fronted by a soloist and a singer, seemed almost antiquated. So it was when Benny Goodman took to the stage of the Gardens on April 28, 1959. Far from the sellout crowds he had attracted in his glory days, the Gardens stood largely empty with a disappointing turnout of just 2,400. The former teenagers of the 1930s and '40s heard the music they loved, the sounds of the bygone age of jazz and blues filling the Gardens to the rafters, although very few of these aging swing kids jumped up to dance.

The concert included classic songs such as "My Funny Valentine" and "Ain't No Use" (made popular by Sarah Vaughan) played by a twelve-piece orchestra that accompanied the beautiful voice of Dakota Station. Along with Benny Goodman on the clarinet, there were a number of piano solos and a trumpet solo by Taft Jordon, who played a great rendition of "One O'clock Jump." Each artist was given a lot of leeway with regards to time—likely due to the variety of fans who were attracted to the concert through their shared love of jazz in all its different forms.

The concert may not have lived up to its billing as "America's Top Jazz Concert," but it was a good evening of entertainment.

June 11, 1959

BOLSHOI BALLET

ON OCTOBER 25, 1935, the Radio City Ballet opened a two-night performance at the Gardens, featuring a hundred-piece orchestra and dancers who performed selections from a number of famous ballets. The acoustics of the large arena proved difficult, as they did for the early productions of opera, and it would not be until October 1953 that ballet returned to the Gardens with the Sadler's Wells production of Tchaikovsky's *The Sleeping Beauty* and *Swan Lake*. The three-night run featuring prima ballerina Margot Fonteyn was a huge success and the company returned to the Gardens in 1955 and again in 1958 and 1965 after it had become the Royal Ballet. The 1965 performances featured Rudolf Nureyev.

Ballet at Maple Leaf Gardens had become a truly international spectacle during the 1950s. Visits from the London Ballet Festival in 1954, the Royal Danish Ballet in 1956 and the Moiseyev Dance Company from the Soviet Union in 1958, were all well-received, but the biggest ballet event was the three-night performance of Moscow's Bolshoi Ballet from June 11 to 13, 1959. Ticket requests came from all over North America to see only the second appearance of the famed dance troupe in the West.

The dancers arrived in Toronto on Tuesday, June 9, and spent Wednesday visiting Niagara Falls. On the night of their first performance, a handful of picketers protested Soviet foreign policy outside the Gardens while those inside were dazzled by what they saw. "This fantastic company did everything technical except take off into outer space," gushed the critic from the *New York Times*. "It is still difficult to believe," wrote Rose MacDonald in the *Toronto Telegram*, "that at last we have seen the nearly legendary Galina Ulanova her very self dance on a Canadian stage. Seeing her exquisite Giselle one could only wish that the experience had not been delayed so long." Ulanova was forty-nine.

Picketers protest the appearance of the Bolshoi Ballet at Maple Leaf Gardens.

The Bolshoi Ballet returned in 1967, and various Soviet and Polish dance companies continued to perform at the Gardens throughout the 1960s and into the 1970s.

December 4, 1961

FIRST HEAVYWEIGHT TITLE FIGHT
Floyd Patterson vs. Tom McNeeley

MORE WORLD CHAMPIONSHIPS have been contested at the Gardens in boxing than in any other sport. Champions have been crowned across every major category, with the first heavyweight championship fight taking place on December 4, 1961. Floyd Patterson defeated Tom McNeeley that night in his last successful championship defence.

Patterson was first declared heavyweight champion when he knocked out Archie Moore on November 30, 1956, and solidified his claim to the belt with a TKO over Tommy Jackson in July 1957. Patterson defeated three more challengers before being knocked out by Sweden's Ingemar Johansson in June of 1959. A year later, Patterson became the first man to regain boxing's heavyweight title when he defeated Johansson in a rematch. After beating Johansson again in March 1961, he made his seventh title defence against McNeeley.

The twenty-four-year-old McNeeley was a former football player from Boston. "Irish Tom," as the papers called him, proved no match for the champion in their Gardens bout as Patterson knocked him down nine times before he was counted out in the fourth round of a ferocious battle that lasted only twelve minutes. "He's a helluva puncher," admitted McNeeley after the bout. "Hits much harder than I expected. I don't remember anything that happened after the third round."

Patterson first floored McNeeley with a smashing left hook in the first round. After the mandatory eight-count, he subsequently slipped to the canvas but held Patterson around the body and pulled himself up. Patterson floored McNeeley four times in the third round and four more in the fourth before referee Jersey Joe Walcott counted him out at 2:51.

Earlier that evening, number-one contender Sonny Liston had KO'd Germany's Albert Westphal after just 1:58 of the first round of their fight in Philadelphia. After the Gardens fight, reporters wondered when the champion would face Liston. Ten months later Patterson did fight Liston and was knocked out in the first round. Liston confirmed he was truly the new world's champion when he KO'd Patterson again in the first in a rematch.

MOSCOW CIRCUS

AT THE HEIGHT OF the Cold War, every achievement of East and West—in sports, in space, in technology—was viewed as part of a contest, a battle of opposing ideologies and ambitions.

But all this was forgotten when the Moscow Circus arrived in Toronto to play the Gardens from September 4 to 14, 1962. The first European circus to perform in the city was unlike anything the Gardens crowd had witnessed before. North American circuses had remained basically unchanged since the days of Huckleberry Finn and Tom Sawyer, an array of lions and tigers and death-defying stunts with side shows featuring the rubberman, the fat lady, the bearded lady, and the tattooed man. The Moscow Circus was very different. It did not have the traditional three rings with different acts competing for the

audience's attention. Its performers were more like artists. The high wire act was, for the most part, only twelve feet off the ground. The idea was not to thrill the crowd by risking lives, but to awe the crowd with feats of skill and strength developed through years of practice. One man balancing another man on his head went down into the splits and then stood up again, all the time balancing on a thin wire. Following that, three men balancing on a wire on each other's shoulders caught a fourth man who was flying through the air. He landed upright on the third man's shoulders.

The company of the Moscow Circus was small, with only thirty-six performers. There was just one clown, but his skill with comedy brought a crowd that was separated by both language and culture into fits of laughter. The Gardens echoed with Russian words as the performers went through their routines. The crowds burst into laughter or spontaneous gasps of amazement, and for eleven days in the Gardens, there was no Iron Curtain. (see page 219)

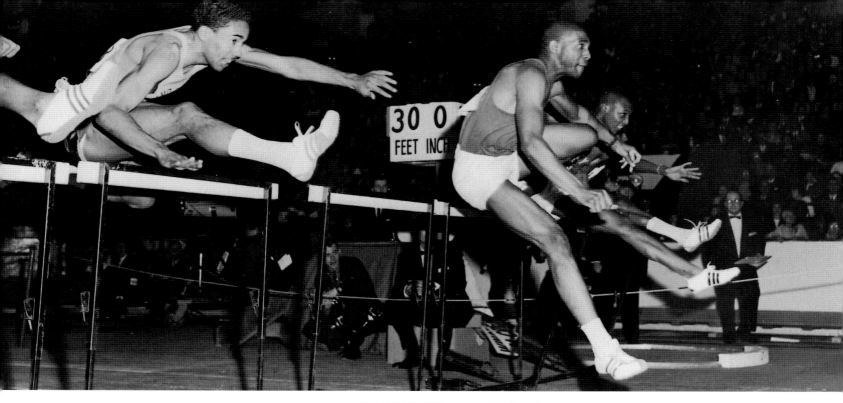

Hurdlers compete indoors at the Gardens.

January 25, 1963

TELEGRAM INDOOR GAMES

Indoor track and field, dormant and undisturbed for 27 years, vaulted and raced back to life in Toronto last night with a fervor that rocked Maple Leaf Gardens for five excited hours.

SO WROTE AL SOKOL in the *Toronto Telegram* on the morning after the first *Telegram*–Maple Leaf Indoor Games. The meet had begun just after 7:00 p.m. and most of the crowd were still in their seats just before midnight when the event concluded with Dave Tork of West Virginia setting a new world indoor mark in the pole vault at 16 feet, 2¼ inches. In between, the crowd had plenty more records to cheer for—including a new Canadian standard established by Bruce Kidd.

Kidd was a nineteen-year-old Toronto distance runner who had previously won a gold medal for Canada at the British Empire Games in Australia. At the Gardens event, running on a new track custom-built for $25,000, he cruised to victory in the three-mile race, lapping the field twice towards the finish. With only the clock as competition, Kidd sprinted the final quarter-mile while the crowd roared. He wound up setting a new Canadian record with a time of 13:34.6, only eight seconds off the world mark.

The Maple Leaf Indoor Games became an annual event, with Kidd, Bill Crothers, Harry Jerome, and Abby Hoffman among the many Canadians to star amid the international field. Sponsorship of the games was taken over by the *Toronto Star* in 1972 and the *Toronto Star* Indoor Games lasted until 1986, when Ben Johnson broke a world record with a time of 5.27 seconds in the 50-metre dash. In 1988, the *Toronto Sun* hosted the Miller Lite challenge. Once again Johnson starred in what proved to be the final track meet held at the Gardens. His time of 5.15 seconds shattered the world record. Johnson was reaching the height of his popularity. It would peak with his gold medal victory in the 100 metres at the Seoul Olympics, only to come crashing down a few days later when he tested positive for steroid use.

Goalie Seth Martin, seen here against the College All-Stars, starred internationally with the Trail Smoke Eaters and, later, Father David Bauer's national team.

February 11, 1963

TRAIL vs. COLLEGE ALL-STARS

As ALLAN CUP champions in 1962, the Trail Smoke Eaters had earned the right to represent Canada in the World Championships in 1963. The former World Champions of 1961 would be the last independent amateur club to play for its country.

The Smoke Eaters left British Columbia in early February and embarked on a cross-Canada tour before leaving for Europe. The results were disastrous. The team won only two of nine exhibition games. The low point came at Maple Leaf Gardens, when Trail played a team called the College All-Stars, assembled of players from the University of Toronto, the University of Montreal, McGill, Laval, McMaster, and Ryerson. A crowd of only 1,011 saw the All-Stars defeat the Smoke Eaters 3–1.

"These kids haven't even played together for three hours," said College All-Stars coach Joe Kane. "They were just playing their positions." Bill Mahoney of McMaster scored the only goal of the first period and Ward Passi of U of T made it 2–0 on a breakaway in the second. Howard Jones replied four minutes later, but another breakaway goal by Raymond Cadieux of Laval put the game away. It was Trail's fifth loss in a row.

"Without a doubt this is the worst we have played," said Smokies playing coach Bobby Kromm. "I don't know how we can play so badly."

The Smoke Eaters left for Switzerland a few nights later and redeemed themselves with seven wins in ten games in Europe en route to Stockholm for the World Championships. Once there, Trail rattled off three straight victories against East and West Germany and the United States. A heroic effort by goalie Seth Martin allowed the Smokies to tie Czechoslovakia despite being outshot 42–18, but any hopes of a gold medal ended with a 4–1 loss to Sweden. A silver medal was still within sight, but a 4–2 win by the Soviets meant Canada finished out of the medals for the first time in history.

August 13, 1963

ANGLICAN CONGRESS

THE LARGEST ANGLICAN conference held anywhere in the world in this century welcomed delegates from seventy-eight countries to Toronto during the summer of 1963.

Following afternoon receptions from civic, provincial, and federal officials, the World Anglican Congress opened with a service at Maple Leaf Gardens on the evening of August 13. The glittering multicultural rally attracted 17,000 people. Included among the scarlet-and-white gowned bishops of the world's eighteen autonomous Anglican churches was the Most Reverend Arthur Michael Ramsey, Archbishop of Canterbury.

Dressed in the traditional golden robe of his office, the archbishop gave voice to the emerging Anglican view that it was time to move forward towards a new sharing of missionary responsibilities. Emphasizing that it was time to stop equating the term missionary with colonialism, he called on African and Asian missionaries to come to England and "convert our English Church to a closer following of Christ." The Most Reverend Howard Clark, Archbishop of Rupert's Land and Primate of All Canada, called on Anglicans to take to heart the first petition of the Lord's Prayer: "Hallowed be Thy Name." Such honouring of

God, he said, must not be restricted to the church. "We must be ready, indeed eager, to see God's named being hallowed outside the church as well as inside."

CANADIAN CHAMPIONSHIP RODEO

BOTH ROY ROGERS AND Gene Autry had headlined rodeos at the Gardens in the 1940s, but the cowboys who called Toronto home from November 24 to 29, 1963, weren't the singing kind. These were the toughest rodeo riders of Canada's west, competing in the Canadian Championship Rodeo.

Dismissing detractors with a wave of his hand, Stafford Smythe had agreed to have the

foam chips, sawdust, and soil needed for the rodeo dumped directly onto the ice. He had been assured that there would be no problem cleaning up the mess. For five days the cowboys roped cows and rode bucking broncos, competing for a $13,000 purse as well as for charity, donating one day of events to the Ontario Society for Crippled Children and Bloorview Home. For five days the ice lay unprotected beneath the action. Unfortunately, the ice gradually heated up and bonded with the soil and animal urine.

After the rodeo ended on November 29, the Gardens clean-up crew went in to tackle the mess. It soon became apparent that the assurance had been false. As the layers of mud and foam were removed, the ice underneath came up in sheets. The crew worked through the night to try and repair the damage.

When the Red Wings arrived to play the Leafs the next night, the staff was still trying to patch up holes in the ice with snow. The patching continued as the fans started to arrive and take their seats. Toronto's Frank Mahovlich could be seen skating around the rink prior to the game, bouncing over the ruts. At first he had his usual serious expression, but the more he skated the wider the smile on his face. Finally he skated over to the bench and doubled over in laughter. The coaches from both teams met and an argument ensued about whether the game should be played. When it was decided that the game would go on, another argument followed about who would take the north side of the rink, where the damage was the worst.

In the end, the game started late. Fittingly, it ended in a tie.

TOURNAMENT OF CHAMPIONS

WITH THE LEAFS on the road following a 2–0 victory over the Boston Bruins on December 28, 1963, the ice at Maple Leaf Gardens was given over to another great Canadian winter sport for the first four days of 1964—curling. The Tournament of Champions Invitational Bonspiel featured eight of the top rinks in Canada playing a seven-game round-robin tournament to determine a winner. Ernie Richardson of Regina was the pre-spiel favorite, but the final match on Saturday morning, January 4, 1964 (the Leafs were back home for a game with Chicago that night), featured Ernie Houck's Winnipeg rink against Hec Gervais of Edmonton. Houck's foursome won 12–5.

With Jimmy Ursel at third, Ross Murdock at second, and Morely Handford at lead, Houck's foursome had played together for six years and had just missed winning the Brier at Kitchener the year before. But despite their win at Maple Leaf Gardens, they would not represent Manitoba at the Brier in 1964 because they had actually broken up already. "So," wrote Neil MacCarl in the *Toronto Star*, "although the Houck rink finally has mastered Richardson and Gervais, it may be a year too late for Manitoba, which has won the Brier only once in the last 10 years."

Total attendance for the four-day event was just under 10,000, "well below the break-even point and a big disappointment to the promoters." The Toronto Curling Association had been hoping to land the Brier for Maple Leaf Gardens in 1967 (they would not be successful). MacCarl wrote that at least they had learned one lesson from the failure of the Tournament of Champions: "In order to draw people to see curling, they've got to do a better selling job in advance."

The Gardens might have been one of Canada's grandest curling rinks, but a kettle of hot water was still required to get the ice around the hacks exactly right.

1964 STANLEY CUP FINALS, GAME SEVEN

FOR SIXTEEN YEARS Bob Baun was a hard-nosed defensive defenceman. In 964 regular-season NHL games, and 96 more in the playoffs, Baun totalled just 40 goals. Yet the rugged blueliner is best remembered for a goal he scored on April 23, 1964. He did it in overtime, playing on a broken ankle, and it helped bring the Toronto Maple Leafs their third consecutive Stanley Cup.

Though they had won the previous two seasons, the Leafs finished in third place in 1963–64. But Toronto knocked off first-place Montreal in the semifinals and advanced to face Detroit for the Cup.

Bob Baun's memorable goal came in game six with Toronto trailing the Red Wings 3–2 in games. At 13:14 of the third period, Baun was taken from the ice on a stretcher with an injury later diagnosed as a cracked fibula. Baun simply had his painful right ankle iced and taped and returned to the ice for overtime. After only 1:43 of the extra session, Baun's long shot deflected off the Red Wings' Bill Gadsby and past Terry Sawchuk.

Game seven proved to be no contest. Andy Bathgate opened the scoring after four minutes of play and Johnny Bower made it hold up until Dave Keon, Red Kelly, and George Armstrong tallied third-period goals to make the final score 4–0. "They showed all the signs of true champions tonight," reflected Punch Imlach after the game. "Baun, [Carl] Brewer, and Kelly all took needles to deaden the pain in their legs... boy were they up for it tonight." Perhaps no one savoured the victory more than Bathgate, the perennial star of the sad-sack New York Rangers who had been traded to Toronto midway through the season. "Not only is this the first time I've won the Cup," said Bathgate, "this is the first time I've even been in the finals."

Billy Harris, left, and Ron Stewart shower Stanley Cup hero Bob Baun with champagne (above) following a team celebration on the ice (opposite).

Edmonton defenceman Glen Sather can't prevent this Marlies goal during the 1964 Memorial Cup Final.

May 11, 1964

MARLIES WIN THE MEMORIAL CUP

ONLY ONCE IN HOCKEY history have the Memorial Cup and Stanley Cup champions been crowned in the same building in the same year. The year was 1964. The teams were the Toronto Maple Leafs and the Toronto Marlboros. The building, of course, was Maple Leaf Gardens.

The Leafs had defeated the Detroit Red Wings on April 25 to win the Stanley Cup. Eight days later, the Memorial Cup Finals opened in Toronto with the Marlboros hosting the Edmonton Oil Kings.

The Marlies had been everyone's pick to represent the East after posting a 40–9–7 record during the regular season. They swept the Niagara Falls Flyers, then the Montreal Junior Canadiens after a 5–5 tie in game one. Only a loss to Scotty Bowman's Notre Dame de Grace Monarchs of Montreal in the Eastern final spoiled the Marlies' undefeated run to the Memorial Cup championship round.

The 1964 Marlies were one of the greatest junior teams in history. Their offence was led by Pete Stemkowski, Ron Ellis, Mike Walton, Wayne Carelton, and Brit Selby. The defence featured Gary Smith in goal and Jim McKenny and Rod Seiling on the blueline. Most of these players (plus several others) as well as coach Jim Gregory had joined the Marlies from the Neil McNeil high school team that had been formed after St. Michael's disbanded.

"We won because we have more good players than any other team," said Gregory. Oil Kings coach Buster Brayshaw agreed. "They're just a superb hockey club," he said. "There's nothing they can't do."

Despite the team's prowess, and its strong local flavour, only 10,000 fans witnessed the Marlboros' four-game sweep of the Memorial Cup final. Only 2,811 spectators attended Toronto's 7–2 victory in the clinching game. "Increased ticket prices, the late date for staging the series and lack of series promotion hurt the gate," wrote Frank Orr in the *Toronto Star*.

September 8, 1964

THE BEATLES

BEATLEMANIA HIT TORONTO hard. Between the time Ray Sonin of CFRB first spun a Beatles record on his radio show "Calling All Britons" in 1963 and their first North American tour a year later, the city's Beatles fan club attracted 50,000 members, making it the largest in the world. Torontonians got their first chance to see the Fab Four in person when the group played to 35,522 fans in two Gardens concerts on September 8, 1964.

From their arrival at the airport, to the street outside their suite at the King Edward Hotel, to the Gardens itself, the Beatles drew crowds everywhere they went. Their first show began at 4:00 and featured the Bill Black Combo, the Exciters, Clarence "Frogman" Henry, and Jackie deShannon before CHUM's Jungle Jay Nelson introduced the Beatles shortly before 5:30. "For the next 30 minutes," wrote Jeremy Brown in the *Toronto Telegram*, "at least 5,000 girls were screaming in turn. Every movement, every caper, every bit of clowning raised the shriek-level to a point one didn't think possible... If one covered one's ears properly, one could hear some of the music... There were even times, and apparently this is a rarity at Beatles concerts, when Paul McCartney could actually be heard introducing a song." The Beatles played only twelve songs. Dozens of girls fainted. After a press conference (the biggest of their tour) and a photo session between shows, the second concert featured more of the same.

Capitalizing on the Beatles phenomenal success, Harold Ballard sold out two more concerts a year later on August 17, 1965. The Beatles had been booked for only one Toronto appearance, and Ballard all but dared manager Brian Epstein to walk away from the second full house. He didn't. The Gardens was roasting through a Toronto heat wave and Ballard instructed the concession stands to sell only large soft drinks. The *Telegram* reported that more than 200 gallons of pop were sold along with 900 pounds of ice cream.

THE SHEIK

THE SHEIK WAS GRAPPLING'S premier bad guy of the 1960s and '70s, voted "greatest mat heel of all time" by readers of *Wrestling Observer*. He specialized in the use of foreign objects to gouge his opponents during a long career of bloody battles and was the wrestler fans most loved to hate at the Sunday fights at Maple Leaf Gardens.

The Sheik made his first Gardens appearance on January 3, 1965, fighting Johnny Valentine in the main bout on a card that also featured four midget wrestlers and a 600-pound bear. (Terrible Ted, as the bear was known, pinned both Killer Conroy and Benny Lima.) The Sheik lost his match, but defeats would be rare during much of his career. He was undefeated in his hometown of Detroit from 1965 to 1971 and had a seven-year stretch of more than 150 fights without a loss in Toronto. The secret of his success was that he was also a booker and promoter, giving him his pick of opponents in many cities.

The Sheik uses the dreaded foreign object against Chris Markoff at the Gardens.

Among the most memorable of the Sheik's many Gardens fights was a bout with Haystack Calhoun on May 10, 1970.

According to the *Toronto Telegram*, "one might conclude that the last thing [Calhoun] would do would be to turn his back on The Sheik, the nastiest, meanest, baddest, most arrogant, blood-thirstiest wrestler in the history of Frank Tunney's wrestling cards at Maple Leaf Gardens.

"But he did it all right. Haystack turned to chase manager Abdullah (the Weasel) Farouk in last night's main card encounter before 13,300 Gardens wrestling fans, a witless move since The Sheik had time to crawl to a neutral corner, grab a chain with a horseshoe on the end and sneak up behind Balloon Calhoun.

"The Sheik lowered the boom and Haystack… flopped to that horizontal position from which he finds it so difficult to recover."

The Sheik's Gardens win streak ended in 1976. On August 8 of that year, he was disqualified by referee Andre the Giant for attempting to gouge his way to victory in a bout with Gene Kiniski.

March 29, 1966

ALI vs. CHUVALO

LOCAL FIGHTER GEORGE CHUVALO made his first professional appearance at Maple Leaf Gardens on April 23, 1956. By 1958, he was the Canadian heavyweight champion and was being touted as a possible world champion. In November 1959, Chuvalo fought and lost to former world champion Floyd Patterson in a Madison Square Garden bout that was broadcast by closed circuit back to the Gardens in Toronto.

Although Chuvalo's stock had fallen by 1966, he still had never been knocked off his feet. His next bout—a Gardens date with heavyweight champion Muhammad Ali—would put that distinction to the test. Top ticket prices that night were $100 (the highest for a Gardens event to that time). What the crowd witnessed was perhaps the most memorable boxing event in Toronto history.

"Chuvalo accepted Clay's [Ali's] best punches without flinching," wrote Jim Proudfoot in the *Toronto Star*, "and kept plodding straight ahead, stubbornly flailing away until it seemed impossible that he could go on. But his pace never slackened for 15 rounds. At the end, Chuvalo's face was red and lumpy. Clay's wasn't marked in the least. All he had was a bruised right hand, caused by repeated smashes against Chuvalo's head."

"He's the toughest I ever fought," Ali said after the fight. "I kept saying he was tough, tougher than Sonny Liston, tougher than Floyd Patterson, tougher than Ernie Terrell. People thought I was just trying to build up the gate. Now you know I was right."

His career revitalized, Chuvalo went on to hold the Canadian heavyweight title until his retirement in 1979, posting a career record of 80–15–2 with 68 knockouts, and was ranked among the top ten in the world longer than any other heavyweight boxer. "You people ought to be proud of this Chuvalo," said Ali's trainer Angelo Dundee after the 1966 Gardens bout. "I was proud and I was in the other guy's corner. If you care about boxing, you've got to admire a man like that."

May 16, 1966

EDMONTON WINS THE MEMORIAL CUP

THE EDMONTON OIL KINGS won the Abbott Cup as Western Canada's junior hockey champion every year from 1960 to 1966, but only once in their first six tries did they win the Memorial Cup, defeating Niagara Falls in 1963. Back for a seventh time in 1966, the Oil Kings took on Bobby Orr and the Oshawa Generals in a seven-game series at Maple Leaf Gardens.

Although only eighteen at the time, Bobby Orr had long been considered a can't-miss prospect. Still, there were detractors. "Of course [Edmonton manager Bill] Hunter jumped on the better-than-Orr bandwagon," wrote the *Toronto Star*'s Frank Orr of the pre-series hype. "Why, the Oil Kings have not one but two defencemen who are better than Oshawa's Bobby Orr. They are Al Hamilton... and Bob Falkenberg." Oil Kings coach Ray Kinasewich felt the Orr-Hamilton comparison would be interesting, but "there's much more to this series than that. I feel we have a good chance. Our team has a good defence and good balance on the forward line." Many of Edmonton's players would go on to careers in the NHL or the World Hockey Association, including Hamilton, Falkenberg, Ross Lonsberry, Jim Harrison, and goaltender "Smokey" McLeod. But, of course, none of them was Bobby Orr. In addition to Orr, Oshawa also had Wayne Cashman, plus Nick Beverley, Danny O'Shea, and others who went on to pro careers.

The Oil Kings tested Orr repeatedly in game one and romped to a 7–2 victory. Unfortunately, Orr aggravated a groin injury that hampered him for the rest of the series and though the Generals won games two and three, the Oil Kings won the Memorial Cup in six. Crowds ranging from 4,500 to 7,200 attended the games—good numbers for the times, but a far cry from the days of the 1930s and '40s when 12,000-plus had attended Memorial Cup games in Toronto. The 1966 Final was the last held at Maple Leaf Gardens.

Bobby Orr would move from Oshawa to the Boston Bruins, winning NHL rookie-of-the-year honours in 1966–67.

January 10, 1967

CANADIAN NATIONAL TEAM vs. SOVIETS

IN 1962, WITH THE Soviets beginning to dominate international hockey, Father David Bauer introduced the concept of a Canadian national amateur team. Father Bauer's "Nats" first represented Canada abroad at the 1964 Winter Olympics, where a technicality cheated them of a bronze medal. Following a bronze medal win at the World Championships in 1966, hopes were high that the Nats would win gold at Vienna in 1967.

Part of the optimism surrounding the Canadian team had to do with the addition of former NHL star Carl Brewer on defence. Hopes were also raised during a four-game visit by the Soviet national team in January 1967. The Nats looked impressive in beating the Russians 5–4 in Winnipeg in game one and were solid again in a 3–3 tie two nights later in Montreal. On January 10, 1967, the Nats faced the Soviet Union in Toronto and defeated them.

The Soviets took an early 1–0 lead in front of 15,878 fans, but

Canadian defenceman Terry O'Malley covers Soviet forward Vladimir Vikulov in front of goaltender Wayne Stephenson in action at Maple Leaf Gardens.

Fran Huck evened the score for Canada and Danny O'Shea put the Nats ahead 2–1 before the Soviets tied the game. Goals by Ted Hargreaves and Roger Bourbonnais put Canada ahead 4–2 in the third and the superb goaltending of Wayne Stephenson allowed the Nats to hold on for a 4–3 victory.

"Too good to be true? Too much too soon? A trap?" wrote Jim Proudfoot in the *Toronto Star*. Coach Jackie McLeod would have no part of it. "It's crazy to say the Russians are lying down," he argued. "We're making the Russians look bad by checking them closely and, for the first time in years, outskating them."

The first-string Soviet line-up ended the tour with a 5–3 win in Kitchener two nights later, but the Canadian team was confident they could win gold in Vienna in ten weeks' time. Despite a valiant effort, the Nats lost 2–1 to the Soviets in the key game at the World Championships. Unable to shake off its disappointment, Canada was defeated 6–0 by Sweden in the final game and had to settle for another bronze medal.

LEAFS vs. CANADIENS, 1967 STANLEY CUP FINALS

THEY MAY NOT HAVE had the most talent, but few teams ever gave more of what they did have than Punch Imlach's Toronto Maple Leafs. After eleven years without winning the Stanley Cup the Leafs finally emerged victorious again in 1962. "Bert Olmstead was so tired that he couldn't get off the bench," Imlach recalled of that victory. But the Leafs' blend of a few young pups with Punch's "old pappies" proved they possessed the stuff of champions again in 1963 and 1964. Still, few expected the Leafs could pull off a victory against Montreal in 1967.

With the "original six" era drawing to a close, the Canadiens had regained their status as the top team in hockey by winning the Stanley Cup in 1965 and 1966. So confident were they of another victory in Canada's centennial year that Montreal officials had already designated an area to display the Cup at Expo 67.

Two of hockey's strongest men: Tim Horton pursued by Jean Beliveau in the sixth and deciding game of the 1967 Stanley Cup Finals.

The Stanley Cup finals began the way most had expected: the Canadiens clobbered the Leafs 6–2. But the Leafs rallied to win three of the next four and took a 3–2 lead going into game six at the Gardens. Gump Worsley replaced Rogie Vachon (whom Punch Imlach had ridiculed as a Junior B goaltender) and he matched Sawchuk save for save in a scoreless first period. Second-period goals by Ron Ellis and Jim Pappin had Leafs fans in a frenzy. Former Leaf Dick Duff scored for Montreal and the Leafs headed into the final minutes nursing a 2–1 lead.

"There was an underlying knowledge for some of the guys that there won't be many more for us to win," admitted Red Kelly after the series, and Punch Imlach turned to those veterans in the clutch. With Worsley on the bench for an extra attacker and a face-off deep in the Leafs' end, Imlach sent out Kelly, Tim Horton, George Armstrong, Bob Pulford, and Allan Stanley. Stanley beat Jean Beliveau to the draw and slid the puck to Kelly, who kicked it to Pulford. Pulford then fed Armstrong, who carried the puck to centre and fired it into the empty net. The Leafs were Stanley Cup champions.

September 9, 1967

STANFIELD ELECTED TORY LEADER

THE 1967 PROGRESSIVE Conservative leadership convention marked the end of an era in Canadian politics. John Diefenbaker, party leader since 1956 and prime minister from 1957 to 1963, was voted out by the party faithful. Nova Scotia premier Robert Stanfield was elected to replace "the Chief" in a five-ballot vote that ended a twelve-hour day at Maple Leaf Gardens.

The leadership hopefuls all delivered their final speeches on Friday night before voting took place on Saturday. Prior to the scheduled starting time of noon, Diefenbaker addressed the Tories' contentious Deux Nations policy by announcing that he could not stand as a candidate for leadership of a two-nation party. Though he was unable to force a final debate on the subject, Diefenbaker staged an impromptu press conference to announce that his candidacy would serve as a referendum on the issue.

New Tory leader Robert Stanfield is framed by bagpipes as he celebrates his victory at the Gardens.

Diefenbaker's handlers talked bravely about scoring 700 to 1,000 votes (approximately 1,200 votes were needed to win), but the former prime minister received only 271. Stanfield supporters had hoped for 600 votes; his 519 still put him in first place. As expected, Manitoba premier Duff Roblin and former Justice minister Davie Fulton were his closest competition.

When asked about the first ballot, Diefenbaker issued no comment except to say that he had no intention of withdrawing. But his hopes were dead. He garnered only 172 votes on the second ballot and withdrew after receiving only 114 on the third. Diefenbaker left the convention floor for his suite at the Royal York Hotel, giving his support to Roblin. It wasn't enough for the Manitoba premier and when Fulton gave his support to Stanfield after the fourth ballot (though he insisted that Stanfield come to him to shake his hand), the Nova Scotian finally had the backing he needed to win.

Pipers led Stanfield to the stage, where he was joined by the men he had defeated. John Diefenbaker received a thunderous ovation when he greeted his successor. Speaking from bitter experience, he appealed to Conservatives to give their new leader their undivided and unconditional loyalty.

1968 NHL ALL-STAR GAME

THE 1968 ALL-STAR GAME at Maple Leaf Gardens marked just the second time the exhibition contest was played during the course of the regular season after nineteen years as a pre-season game. It also marked the final time that a team of NHL selects took on the defending Stanley Cup champions. The freewheeling game was highlighted by outstanding goaltending, which wasn't surprising considering that All-Stars coach Toe Blake employed Ed Giacomin, Terry Sawchuk, and Glenn Hall. What was surprising was that the best goaltending came from a Toronto Maple Leafs team that was without Johnny Bower, who was resting a shoulder injury. Bruce Gamble stopped eighteen of nineteen All-Stars shots in the first period (robbing Jean Beliveau for his best save) and turned back ten of eleven in the second period before giving way to Al Smith, who preserved Toronto's 4–3 victory with a glove save on Bobby Hull late in the third period.

Stan Mikita tries to elude the checking of Marcel Pronovost as he stands in front of Leafs goalie Al Smith during the 1968 All-Star Game.

Smith had only two games of NHL experience before playing in the All-Star Game on January 16, 1968, but Leafs coach Punch Imlach wasn't surprised when he met the challenge. "Remember," said Imlach, "he's the same kid I brought up from the Marlboros juniors when they weren't using him three years ago and he won a big game for us in Chicago."

And how did Smith feel about facing the All-Stars?

"You forget I had the Stanley Cup champions in front of me. They put down quite a checking blanket in the third period."

Toe Blake figured the game should have been over long before then. "It was Gamble who killed us," he said from the All-Stars dressing room. "We should have had three or four in that first period alone. But I can't fault any of my team. They all played well, especially Bobby Orr." Blake thought Ron Ellis and Tim Horton were the best for the Leafs. Foster Hewitt selected Gamble, Stan Mikita, and Orr as the three stars. Punch Imlach called the 1968 All-Star Game a great one. "The only flaw is we don't get two points."

CARIBANA EXTRAVANGZA '70

TORONTO'S ANNUAL CARIBANA Festival has become the largest celebration of West Indies culture in the world. Back in 1970, Caribana was only in its third year, but it was already attracting a large international following. The week of festivities on Toronto Island was preceded that year by an evening of dancing and singing at Maple Leaf Gardens on July 31. One of the highlights of the evening was the crowning of Miss Caribana '70. The honour went to local girl Marianne Skanks, an eighteen-year-old part-time model and student at Vaughan Road Collegiate. The next day Miss Caribana rode in the parade of colourful floats and costumes, dancers, and steel bands that ran from Varsity Stadium to the Toronto lakefront and officially opened that year's festival.

Newly crowned as Miss Caribana, Marianne Skanks wears her tiara as she poses with a bouquet of roses.

TEAM CANADA SCRIMMAGE

FOR YEARS CANADIAN fans and hockey officials had been clamouring to pit the country's best against the best from the Soviet Union. Despite intense lobbying, the International Ice Hockey Federation refused to open its tournaments to Canada's top professionals. In retaliation, Canada withdrew from the IIHF in 1970. Finally, in April 1972, there was a breakthrough: the Soviets agreed to play a team of Canadian pros in an eight-game series in September.

On July 12, Harry Sinden met the press in the banquet room of a Toronto hotel. A few weeks earlier Sinden, who had been the captain of the Whitby Dunlops when they defeated the Soviets for the world title in 1958 and had coached the Boston Bruins to a Stanley Cup title in 1970, had been named the coach of Team Canada. This day, he would announce the thirty-five Canadian players who would come to training camp the following month. Harold Ballard had made Maple Leaf Gardens available to the team as a training site.

The players reported to the Gardens on August 14. After a week of workouts, the team made its public debut with the first of three intrasquad games on August 22—the only game action the team would see before the series. The surprise of the camp turned out to be the play of the forward line comprising Toronto wingers Paul Henderson and Ron Ellis and Philadelphia Flyers centre Bobby Clarke.

Soviet officials watched every Canadian workout with interest, though the Soviet team itself did not arrive in Canada until August 30. Canadians scouted only their final three workouts in Montreal. By September 1, the Canadian team had been working out for three weeks and many players were calling it the most rigorous training camp of their lives. The Soviets, of course, trained all year. "Until then," John Ferguson would later recall, "NHL players never worked on their upper-body strength and seldom used off-ice training. Sure, a few jogged in the summer but, mostly, players came to training camp and skated themselves into condition." In September 1972 it would require something more.

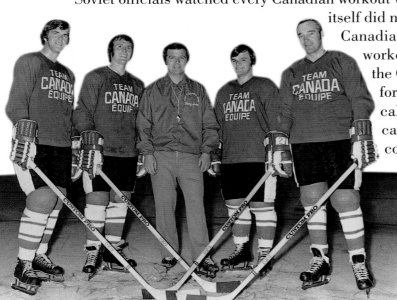

Team Canada hopefuls Dale Tallon, Paul Henderson, Marcel Dionne, and Frank Mahovlich surround coach Harry Sinden.

September 4, 1972

TEAM CANADA vs. SOVIETS

IT WAS GOING TO BE a rout. Canada's top professionals were finally playing the best from the Soviet Union. The historic series opened on September 2, 1972, in a muggy Montreal Forum. Phil Esposito scored after just thirty seconds. Six minutes later, Paul Henderson scored. It would be that easy.

But halfway through the second period something changed. The Soviets were taking over, making crisp passes, controlling the play, always in motion. It was 2–2 after twenty minutes and 4–2 Soviets after two periods. Bobby Clarke's goal at 8:22 of the third brought Canada within one, but the players were clearly tired. The Soviets showed no sign of fatigue. The final score was 7–3. A nation was stunned.

Coach Harry Sinden shook up his line-up for game two at Maple Leaf Gardens on September 4. In an attempt to bolster the team's toughness, Pat Stapleton, Wayne Cashman, Bill White, Bill Goldsworthy, J.P. Parise, Stan Mikita, and Serge Savard would join Gary Bergman, Brad Park, Ron Ellis, Phil Esposito, Yvan Cournoyer, Paul Henderson, Guy Lapointe, Bobby Clarke, and Frank and Peter Mahovlich on the Canadian roster. Tony Esposito replaced Ken Dryden in goal.

Peter Mahovlich scored the game's key goal while Canada was short-handed in the third period, beating Vladislav Tretiak with a shifty move.

Game two was much rougher than the first and Canada's aggression seemed to put off the Soviets. Still, it was scoreless after one period. Phil Esposito scored in the second, followed by Yvan Cournoyer early in the third. Alexander Yakushev responded at 5:53 and when Pat Stapleton was sent off for hooking twenty-one seconds later the Soviets had a chance to tie the game on the powerplay. While killing the penalty, Peter Mahovlich took a pass from Esposito, stepped around a defenseman and deked goalie Vladislav Tretiak to the ice, beating him at 6:47. Brother Frank's goal four minutes later pushed the final score to 4–1.

"The Canadians battled with the ferocity and intensity of a caged animal," Soviet hockey godfather Anatoli Tarasov would later say of the eight-game series, ultimately won on a goal by Paul Henderson with just thirty-four seconds remaining. "Our players were better conditioned physically and stronger in skills... but we could not match them in heart and desire."

NEIL YOUNG

NEIL YOUNG MAY have been ignored ten years earlier when he returned to Toronto by bus from Winnipeg. At the time he was an angry young man with a guitar, desperately seeking an audience to hear his message. Young, amongst his other gifts, could write songs, mainly auto-biographical, with a deeply personal message. In the early 1960s, he was an unknown, but after his stints with Buffalo Springfield and Crosby, Stills, Nash, and Young, people were now listening.

On January 15, 1973, Neil Young and his backup band performed at Maple Leaf Gardens as part of a North American tour. In the days leading up to the concert, the hype built until it became not just a rock concert but a social event—the welcoming home of a prodigal son. Chartered buses full of fans dressed like Young pulled up in front of the Gardens; they had come from Hamilton, Windsor, and even Ottawa.

When the concert finally got under way, the 18,300 in attendance rose to their feet to welcome Neil home. He was more talkative than usual that night, speaking about how wonderful it was to be playing at Maple Leaf Gardens. For the first half of his show, he sat on a stool centre stage, playing his guitar and singing his ballads—songs such as "Old Man" and "Heart of Gold"—his words and voice evoking bleak landscapes and profound sadness.

The concert lost some of its momentum in the second half when Young pulled back, allowing the spotlight to focus more on his band, which was, unfortunately, loose and sloppy. It sounded more like a rehearsal then a concert performance. Even the backup singers found it difficult to harmonize. In the end, the first sold-out performance by a Torontonian at the Gardens failed to live up to the hype. It was, however, a good concert and a great excuse for the crowd to celebrate one of their own.

February 12, 1973

CLYDE GRAY vs. EDDIE BLAY

CLYDE GRAY IS ONE of the top boxers Canada has ever produced, but for the Toronto resident it was a hard climb to the top. Because he was a supremely skilled fighter, other welterweights would often duck him rather than risk their own records. As a result, Gray was forced to make concession after concession to arrange bouts. In his first five years as a professional with a record of 35–2–1 he earned only $25,000 and had to work as a bricklayer to make ends meet.

Promoted by Irv Ungerman's All Canada Sports Promotions and Bobby Orr Enterprises, Gray fought Eddie Blay of Ghana for the British Commonwealth Welterweight Championship on February 12, 1973. The twenty-five-year-old Canadian prepared intensively for weeks and when he tipped the scales at 147¼ pounds at the official weigh-in he immediately popped two sticks of gum in his mouth and began the chew-and-spit process, which, coupled with a trip to the men's room, brought him to exactly the division limit.

Blay, a former Commonwealth Games gold medalist, got the better of Gray for the first two rounds, but the Canadian began to penetrate Blay's defences by the latter part of the third round. By the fifth, Gray had taken control of the fight and though Blay lasted the entire fifteen rounds, Gray was awarded a unanimous decision, earning $5,500 to Blay's $11,000. Attendance for the fight had been only 4,500. "I always get the short end of the stick," Gray growled. "I've been promised Napoles and I want him."

Seven months later, on September 22, Gray met Cuban-born Mexican José Napoles for the World Welterweight title at the Gardens. The bout was the first in the "Fight a Month" series at the Gardens that was also known as "Ali Presents" because the fights would be televised internationally with commentary by Muhammad Ali and Howard Cosell. Gray was beaten by Napoles, but would continue to fight until 1979, when he became the only fighter to retire while holding both the Canadian and Commonwealth titles.

After beating Eddie Blay, Clyde Gray lost this fight to José Napoles.

TEAM CANADA vs. SOVIETS

MOST CANADIANS KNEW little about the opposition when Team Canada faced the Soviet Union in 1972, but no one took the Russians lightly in 1974. Back were many of the familiar names that had so impressed Canadian fans two years earlier: Tretiak, Yakushev, Maltsev, Mikhailov, Petrov, and Kharlamov. Many in Canada knew these players better than the ones who would be representing them this time.

Team Canada 1974 was stocked with players from the World Hockey Association, the rival league which had sprung up to battle the NHL in 1972–73. Many had played in the NHL, but nobody was about to confuse Ralph Backstrom or Mike Walton with Phil Esposito. Bobby Hull—barred from playing for Canada in 1972 after his departure to the rival league—would be on hand this time, as would Gordie Howe, who had returned to hockey in the WHA in 1973 to play alongside sons Mark and Marty.

The series opened on September 17 in Quebec City, where Bobby Hull's late goal lifted Team Canada to a 3–3 tie. Two nights later, the series resumed at Maple Leaf Gardens.

A capacity crowd of 16,485 was on hand for a game that was fast and chippy from the start. A few minutes into the first period, Ralph Backstrom put the Canadians in front. Andre Lacroix beat Tretiak at 10:49 and the period ended 2–0. Bobby Hull and Alexander Yakushev traded goals in the second period. Two minutes into the third, Vladimir Petrov beat Gerry Cheevers with a shot that was ruled no goal by referee Tom Brown, although it appeared clear the puck had gone in to the top of the net. The Russians continued to press, but a late goal by J.C. Tremblay sealed a 4–1 victory.

Canada would not win again during the series, which ended 4–1–3 in favour of the Soviets.

J.C. Tremblay (3), Pat Stapleton, and goalie Gerry Cheevers try to fend off the Soviets' top line of Boris Mikhailov (13), Vladimir Petrov (16), and Valery Kharlamov.

HOUSTON AEROS vs. TORONTO TOROS

Having signed bobby hull away from the Chicago Black Hawks for its inaugural season of 1972–73, the World Hockey Association scored another coup prior to the 1973–74 campaign when the Houston Aeros drafted both Mark and Marty Howe and convinced Gordie Howe to come out of retirement and play with his sons. Though he was forty-five years old, Mr. Hockey's point total ranked third in the league behind Mike Walton and Andre Lacroix.

The 1973–74 season also marked the debut of the Toronto Toros, as John Bassett purchased the Ottawa Nationals and relocated the team. The Toros played out of Varsity Arena their first year before moving to Maple Leaf Gardens in 1974–75.

Howe was off his pace of the previous season when Houston arrived in Toronto on December 3, 1974. "I hurt my ribs and shoulder during the second game [of the 1974 Team Canada–Soviet] series here in Toronto and I'm still not right from that," Howe admitted. But even with Howe slumping and the Toros having lost four in a row at home, the chance to see Gordie and his boys in action attracted 14,020 people to the game. It was the Toros' second-highest draw of the season and would remain one of the largest crowds in the brief history of the franchise.

The Toros had an NHL legend of their own in the line-up, and two goals by Frank Mahovlich helped Toronto take a 3–1 lead after twenty minutes. The score was 4–1 Toros early in the second before the Aeros began a comeback. At 9:14 of the third period, a Gordie Howe blast was deflected in by Houston's Frank Hughes and the score was tied 4–4. Another goal 1:32 later put the Aeros ahead 5–4 and that was the way the game wound up. The score might have been 6–4 except that a goal set up by Howe early in the first period was disallowed by referee Bob Sloan.

"I told him he must have refereed in Russia," said Howe of his animated chat with the official. "I think he told me to show a little class," he added with a smile.

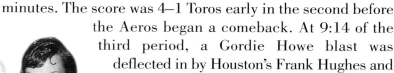

Sons Marty, left, and Mark flank father Gordie Howe.

January 2, 1975

MARLIES vs. RED ARMY

IN DECEMBER AND January 1974–75, the Moscow Central Red Army hockey team—bolstered by several other Soviet stars—played a seven-game set against teams from the Ontario Hockey Association. Though the Russians won all seven games, each of the contests was close.

On January 2, 1975, the Red Army played the Toronto Marlboros at the Gardens. The Marlies were the top team in the OHA at the time, but "we haven't had a workout with our full team since before Christmas," admitted coach George Armstrong. "We've had no opportunity to try to make special preparations for the Soviets."

The Marlies had bolstered their line-up to take on the Soviets. Former Toronto junior star and future Maple Leaf Mike Palmateer rejoined the team from Saginaw of the International Hockey League, while Tim Young and Peter Lee of the Ottawa 67s and player-coach Darryl Sly of the OHA Senior A Barrie Flyers were also added to the roster. Still, the Marlies were given little chance of defeating a Red Army team that featured stars like Vladislav Tretiak, Valery Kharlamov, Vladimir Petrov, Boris Mikhailov, and others who had given Team Canada so much trouble in 1972 and had beaten the WHA Team Canada squad just a few months before.

A near-capacity crowd of 16,284 was on hand for the game and loved every minute of the wide-open contest. John Tonelli

Mike Palmateer rejoined the Marlies from Saginaw of the IHL for the game against the Soviets.

started the scoring at 3:35 of the first period and the score seesawed back and forth to a 5–5 tie through forty minutes. A pair of third-period goals by Petrov put the Russians ahead before Mike McEwen responded. Though the Marlies had plenty more chances, the final score remained 7–6. After the game, George Armstrong was proud but realistic. "It was a one-game effort for these kids, don't forget. My gang was as high as a kite, and why not? This is the biggest game a lot of them will ever play."

May 10, 1975

FRANK SINATRA

THE LIGHTS WERE DIM, but the atmosphere electric. You could almost hear the clink of the martini glass as the cigarette smoke swirled overhead. The crooning sounds of a baritone's voice encompassed the room. No, this was not a trendy lounge off Broadway in the 1940s; it was Maple Leaf Gardens on May 10, 1975.

Frank Sinatra played two shows in Toronto that night, one at 8:00 p.m. and one at midnight. In total 36,000 people filled the Gardens, happily paying the $25 ticket price to hear the voice that many of them had danced their first dance to, kissed their first kiss to or fallen in love to. Thousands of cigarettes, martinis, and songs ago, when the world was at war and "Swing was King," Sinatra had been a young crooner with the Tommy Dorsey Band. His beautiful tenor voice, smooth style, and bright blue eyes caught the imagination and stole the hearts of a generation. But age had caught up with him by 1975. He was now a fifty-nine-year-old grandfather. The combination of hard living and the passage of time had taken its toll on his singing, which no longer had either the range or the grace that it had when Sinatra was known simply as "The Voice." But then with Frank Sinatra, musical accuracy was never his strong point. It was his ability to deliver a song, and it was obvious at the Gardens that he could still deliver in the distinct style which many have copied but none could perfect.

Sinatra stopped singing for a while during the evening and produced a copy of the *Toronto Star*. He stated that he never read newspapers, which he considered good for only two purposes—lining his bird cage or training a puppy— but he referred to a story in which a freelance photographer for the Star had accused one of his bodyguards of punching him. An outraged Sinatra declared that if the photographer could prove his case, he would personally give him $1 million. He then threw the paper down in disgust and resumed singing.

For Sinatra's fans, it was a swagger down memory lane.

February 7, 1976

SITTLER'S 10-POINT NIGHT

THE TORONTO MAPLE Leafs and the Boston Bruins were moving in very different directions at the midway point of the 1975–76 season. The Bruins were the hottest team in the league with a seven-game undefeated streak. The Leafs were slumping.

A day before Boston and Toronto met at the Gardens on February 7, 1976, owner Harold Ballard took a not-very-well-disguised verbal shot at captain Darryl Sittler, saying he was determined to find a sensational centre to play between Errol Thompson and Lanny McDonald—the team's top wingers. "We'd set off a time bomb if we had a hell of a centre in there," said Ballard. Sittler responded by setting a new NHL record with 10 points against the Bruins in an 11–4 Maple Leafs victory.

Sittler's record-breaking performance began with two assists in the first period, setting up Lanny McDonald with a long pass and combining with Errol Thompson to orchestrate a goal by Ian Turnbull. He set up goals by McDonald and Borje Salming in the second period, while also scoring three of his own. With seven points through forty minutes Sittler was just one behind the NHL record held jointly at the time by Rocket Richard and Bert Olmstead. He tied the mark early in the third period when he stuffed in a Salming pass, then broke the record with his fifth goal of the game on a forty-foot wrist shot that caught Bruins goalie Dave Reece off-balance. "My sixth was one of those 'when you're hot, you're hot' efforts," Sittler would later say. His attempted pass from the corner to Lanny McDonald out front bounced off a Boston defenceman and into the net off Reece's skate. Reece would never play another game in the NHL, and as for Harold Ballard: "He congratulated me very warmly and told me how great it was," Sittler said. In fact, Ballard claimed Sittler's feat "was a greater thing than what Paul Henderson did in Moscow" and later presented him with a silver tea service to commemorate the performance.

Darryl Sittler and his family accept a silver tea service from NHL president Clarence Campbell and Leafs owner Harold Ballard.

OLYMPIC BENEFIT CONCERT

The Olympic benefit show at Maple Leaf Gardens last night proves that Canadian performers are not merely self-indulgent artists thinking of themselves but individuals who are capable of setting aside everything to aid their fellow Canadians.

So reported the *Globe and Mail* the morning after Gordon Lightfoot, Murray McLauchlan, Sylvia Tyson, and Liona Boyd staged four concerts in one to raise money for the Canadian Track and Field Association and the Canadian Olympic Association one month before the Montreal Olympics.

The fundraiser was the brainchild of Gordon Lightfoot, who served as the show's emcee. He also performed as the opening act, kicking off the evening with the title track from his latest album, "Summertime Dream."

Next on the bill was Liona Boyd, who commented that "playing classical guitar in Maple Leaf Gardens was like playing hockey in the Central Library." She wondered aloud how the acoustics of the building might affect her music, but at least she didn't have to deal with the technical glitches that greeted Murray McLauchlan. His microphone failed on his opening number, "Little Dreamer," and later his guitar mike gave out. Still, his "intense delivery was enough to pick up any momentum that delay might have lost, and from then on he never lost the crowd." His performances of "The Farmer's Song," "Down by the Henry Moore," and "Honky Red" drew the most enthusias-

Sylvia Tyson, Murray McLauchlan, Liona Boyd, and Gordon Lightfoot after announcing details of their Olympic Benefit concert in a press conference at Lightfoot's home.

tic reception of the evening. Sylvia Tyson followed with a solid set before Lightfoot returned to close the evening with a medley of his greatest hits.

The goal of the Olympic benefit was to raise $200,000. Lightfoot had convinced Maple Leaf Gardens to donate the building for the evening so the gate receipts of $91,000 went entirely toward the Olympic fund. So too did the $100,000 Carling O'Keefe Breweries had paid for the broadcasting rights. At a reception for the performers in the Hot Stove Lounge after the show, Lightfoot quietly announced he was donating $10,000 out of his own pocket to push the proceeds over $200,000.

The Swedish team photo from the first Canada Cup. Toronto's Borje Salming is third from the left in the top row. Current Maple Leafs assistant gm Anders Hedberg is in the bottom row, fourth from the left.

September 7, 1976

CANADA vs. SWEDEN, 1976 CANADA CUP

THE INAUGURAL CANADA CUP tournament included Canada, the United States, and the top four European hockey nations (the USSR, Czechoslovakia, Finland, and Sweden) and gave NHL players a chance to represent their respective countries.

Team Canada's roster was built by Sam Pollock and coached by Scotty Bowman. It boasted one of the strongest line-ups ever assembled, including Bobby Orr and Bobby Hull. Canada opened the Canada Cup tournament on September 2 in Montreal with an easy 11–2 romp over Finland, then defeated the U.S. 4–2 before heading to Toronto to take on Sweden at Maple Leaf Gardens on September 7.

Sweden's Canada Cup team was led by Borje Salming, who, of course, starred with the Maple Leafs in the NHL. Several Canadian players were annoyed that Salming received a louder ovation than any of them during the pre-game introductions—but then Team Canada had singled out Salming for special attention too. "It's nothing new, eh?" Bobby Clarke said of Canada's strategy. "Just like playing the Leafs in the National Hockey League. Everyone knows you've got to shut down Salming or he'll murder you." Bobby Hull in particular did a fine job of stopping Salming, belting him with a pair of thunderous first-period bodychecks. The Swedish team also featured another pair of superstars who were familiar to Hull—Winnipeg Jets teammates Ulf Nilsson and Anders Hedberg.

In addition to his hits on Salming, Hull put Canada on the scoreboard with a first-period goal. Bob Gainey and Marcel Dionne scored in the second, with Gainey tallying again in the third to bring the final score to 4–0. Gainey, Darryl Sittler, and Lanny McDonald were teamed as a line to shut down the Swedish combination of Hedberg, Nilsson, and Roland Ericksson, and Gainey's solid two-way play earned him the selection as Canada's most valuable player of the game.

CANADA vs. SOVIETS, 1976 CANADA CUP

Having lost to Czechoslovakia at the 1976 World Championships in April, the Soviet nationals were a team in transition at the Canada Cup tournament in September. Gone were many of the names that had become familiar to Canadian fans since 1972. Nonetheless, the Soviets still iced a well-conditioned, experienced team and a win against Team Canada to close out the round-robin portion of the tournament would have knocked the Canadians out of first place.

Scotty Bowman made one key change to the Team Canada line-up prior to the September 11 game with the Soviets at the Gardens. He took Phil Esposito off the top line with Bobby Hull and Marcel Dionne and replaced him with Gilbert Perreault. "Taking Phil out was the toughest decision I've ever had to make," Bowman said. He would use Esposito for spot assignments during the game. Bowman also benched Richard Martin and replaced him with Steve Shutt, who would play alongside his Montreal linemates Guy Lafleur and Pete Mahovlich. The line-up changes paid big dividends, and as Frank Orr wrote in the *Toronto Star*: "The evolution of Team Canada's all-star players from strong individuals into a real team reached a pinnacle Saturday

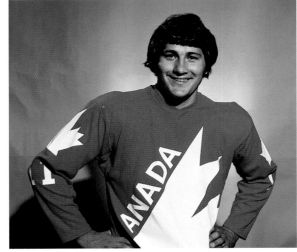

Gilbert Perreault was moved onto Team Canada's top line for the game with the Soviets.

night." The shots on goal were 43–28 in favour of Canada and only the brilliance of Vladislav Tretiak kept the game close.

Gil Perreault put Canada on top at 7:08 of the first period, then set up Bobby Hull for a second goal late in the frame after the Soviets had tied the game at 1–1. Bill Barber tipped in a Guy Lapointe drive late in the second to make it 3–1. Team Canada carried the play throughout the third period, though Tretiak held the Soviets in contention.

When asked about his reduced role after the game, Phil Esposito refused to complain. "The team won," he responded. "That's all that matters." Scotty Bowman announced that his line-up would remain the same when the best-of-three final between Team Canada and Czechoslovakia opened in Toronto two nights later.

Bobby Hull's goal broke a 1–1 tie as Canada went on to a 3–1 victory.

September 13, 1976

CANADA vs. CZECHOSLOVAKIA, 1976 CANADA CUP

THE BASIC ROSTER OF the Czechoslovakian national team that took part in the Canada Cup tournament in 1976 had been together for years. The majority of its players had helped to win the World Championship from the Soviets back in April, and many had been members of the 1972 World Championship team as well. Boasting stars like Milan Novy, Ivan Hlinka, Peter Stastny, and Jiri Bubla, the Czechs were the only team to defeat Team Canada during the round-robin portion of the Canada Cup tournament.

"The Soviets were very tough because of their consistency and the Czechs play the same way with great stamina," said Bobby Orr prior to the best-of-three Canada Cup final between the Canadians and Czechoslovakia. Coach Scotty Bowman said the Czechs "stick to their game plan, no matter what happens, with the confidence that eventually it will pay off. That's the patience we have to show against them."

Team Canada hero Darryl Sittler of the Maple Leafs shakes hands with Czech goalie Vladimir Dzurilla after the final game in Montreal. Rocket Richard looks on.

Extensive study of the films from their 1–0 loss and the scouting reports of assistant coach Al McNeil led to a solid game plan for game one at Maple Leaf Gardens on September 13. Executing the plan's hard-hitting and strong forechecking tactics to perfection, Canada was able to disrupt the Czechoslovakian team's well-practised plays and jump out to a 4–0 lead in the first period, and coasted to a 6–0 victory. The five-man defensive corps of Bobby Orr, Denis Potvin, Serge Savard, Guy Lapointe, and Larry Robinson was particularly effective in front of goalie Rogie Vachon, with Orr contributing two goals and an assist to the offence.

The second game of the Canada Cup final was played in Montreal two nights later, and Canada jumped out to an early 2-0 lead. The Czechoslovakian team quickly returned to form and the score was deadlocked at 4–4 after sixty minutes. At 11:03 of overtime, Darryl Sittler streaked down the left side of the Forum ice and, with a slight deke, slipped the puck past veteran goalie Vladimir Dzurilla for the Canada Cup-winning goal.

RUSH

"IMAGINE THE CHEER that would result," wrote Peter Goddard in the *Toronto Star* on December 29, 1978, "if Darryl Sittler scored the Stanley Cup-winning goal in the seventh game, in overtime, before a packed Maple Leaf Gardens against the dreaded Montreal Canadiens.

"Loud? Perhaps. But it would be a mere whisper compared to the roar produced by the 11,000 fans who turned up for the first of Rush's three homecoming concerts at the Gardens last night. This was the Titanic of hellos, the ultimate ho-ha complete with a standing ovation, hundreds of lit matches and a bevy of nervous ushers."

An appearance by Rush around New Year's Eve had become something of a tradition in Toronto during the late 1970s, "right up there with Gordon Lightfoot at Massey Hall, the Blue Jays finishing last, the Argos not finishing, and the annual clean-up of Yonge Street." The band might have become a big deal internationally, selling two million albums worldwide and grossing an estimated $18 million in 1978, "but in Toronto it's just three guys from Willowdale returning as your basic, paranormal superstars."

The three Rush performances on December 28, 29, and 31 featured hits from their "2112," "Farewell to Kings", and "Hemisphere" albums. The shows each lasted about two hours and the crowds "seemed to know more about the [music] than the band did." Before one piece was ended, everyone was cheering for the next. "It's important," Goddard joked, "to know how to anticipate a song so that when lead singer and bassist Geddy Lee raises his eyebrow in a certain way you'll know what's coming."

Rush had brought seven tons of equipment to the Gardens, including dry-ice machines and a giant screen that displayed space images throughout much of the show. But "the secret to Rush's success here," wrote Goddard, "is that every kid in town thinks he or she knows the band personally. Maybe the relationship is no closer than someone who knows someone who once in Dixie Plaza bumped into someone who looks like guitarist Alex Lifeson.

"No matter. Rush's local history is the stuff of legend."

(Left) Curly Neal was a magician with the ball.
(Below) The Globetrotters' water trick always got laughs.

HARLEM GLOBETROTTERS' RECORD VISIT

WHEN THE HARLEM Globetrotters first came to Maple Leaf Gardens on October 23, 1951, they attracted plenty of coverage from the city's three daily newspapers. The event was treated like a true sports spectacle. By the time of their visit on March 30, 1979, the Globetrotters were relegated to a tiny column in the *Toronto Sun*. But even if the media no longer treated their games like a sports event, the fans still flocked to see them.

"GLOBETROTTERS DRAW LARGEST CROWD EVER," read the *Sun* headline. "Curly Neal, Geese Ausbie, Nate Branch and the rest of the Harlem Globetrotters were the hit of the town Friday night at Maple Leaf Gardens.

"The Trotters, as usual, defeated the Washington Generals in their fun-filled performance before a record crowd for a basketball game in the city's history [16,700].

"All seats were sold for the event and numerous people were turned away. Ticket demand was heavy on the street prior to the game. The Trotters' previous best audience at the Gardens was 14,500."

The Globetrotters' crowd that night remained Toronto's biggest basketball audience for more than ten years until the yearly exhibition games at the SkyDome that predated the Raptors' admittance into the NBA.

BRUCE SPRINGSTEEN

Bruce SPRINGSTEEN AND his E Street Band may have been Born to Run, but at Maple Leaf Gardens on January 20, 1981, it was obvious that they were also born to rock and roll. It was the second time that Springsteen and his band had played the Gardens, the first time being in 1978. At that time, Bruce was still fairly unknown in Toronto and his shows were far from sold out.

By 1981 Toronto had come to know, love, and—in some cases, at least—worship Bruce Springsteen. His 1980 album The River had received a lot of attention and songs such as "Ramrod," "Wreck on the Highway," and "Sherry Darling" had quickly gained the status of rock classics.

The concert started with Springsteen entering the stage alone. The Gardens echoed as the fans chanted his name. As the music began and the rest of the E Street Band emerged, the concert looked like it was going to do the impossible and live up to the hype.

Fifteen minutes into the concert, the festive mood suddenly changed when Springsteen stopped singing and started speaking. His message was not about sex, drugs, and rock and roll, but about a childhood totally foreign to most in attendance, a childhood far from the excesses of wealth which he now enjoyed, one characterized by an unloving, distant father, lack of education, and lack of future. It was this dose of reality that brought the mood down in the Gardens on that cold January night. Over the course of the next three hours, the festive mood and hope could not be recaptured.

Many of his fans haven't noticed as they hum along, but Springsteen's songs speak of the underbelly of capitalism, the broken lives and hopes that litter former industrial towns. At the Gardens, he was caught in the trap of becoming an icon, formed not in his image but as a mirror reflecting back simply what the fans wanted to see.

RICK VAIVE SCORES 50

Rocket Richard's record of 50 goals (scored in 50 games back in 1944–45) had long been surpassed. Despite the fact that the NHL single-season record was in the process of being boosted to 92 by Wayne Gretzky, no Maple Leaf had been able to top Frank Mahovlich's total of 48 goals scored in 1960-61.

Late in the 1981–82 campaign, Leaf captain Rick Vaive began to believe he had a chance. Though the Leafs were suffering through one of the worst seasons in franchise history, the scoring combination of centre Bill Derlago and right winger Vaive gave fans something to cheer about—particularly on the night of March 21, 1982, when Vaive scored four times in an 8–5 win over the Chicago Black Hawks at the Gardens. The fourth goal went into an empty net at 18:59 of the third period to ice the Toronto victory. It was Vaive's forty-ninth of the season.

"About five games ago I started thinking about the record," Vaive admitted in the dressing room afterwards. "It still hasn't sunk in yet. I didn't expect it to happen this fast."

"It's nice that he got it," said Frank Mahovlich, whose team record had lasted for twenty-one years. "It's something the Leafs need to build around."

Two nights later when the Leafs hosted the St. Louis Blues, Vaive became the first player in Maple Leafs history to score fifty goals. The milestone came on a power-play goal late in the first period. The play was set up by Derlago, who stickhandled past two Blues before feeding the puck to Vaive on his opposite wing. He snapped it past Mike Liut before the St. Louis goalie had time to move. "Funny," said Vaive after the game, "but the goal didn't seem as big as I thought it would. Maybe it's because of all that happened last game."

Vaive also had two assists in the 4–3 win over the Blues that night, including one on Miroslav Frycer's winning goal at 19:48 of the third period. The win kept the Leafs' dim playoff hopes alive, though they would ultimately miss the post-season for the second time in three years.

THE WHO

THE WHO'S AGGRESSIVE style, noise level, and original sound and theatrics (including the smashing of their instruments after each concert) made them one of the most popular British hard-core rock bands of the 1970s. And Pete Townsend, the guitar player and creative genius behind the vast majority of Who songs, created a whole new art form with rock operas like "Tommy" and "Quadrophenia."

With the death of drummer Keith Moon in 1978, much of the original magic and energy of the band was lost. By 1982, with the youth and rebellious nature of the band replaced by middle age and prosperity, Pete Townsend proclaimed that the Who was dead; the band was merely a shadow of the boys who had originally formed it. It was this type of statement that led fans of the band to believe that the tour of 1982 would be the last time the Who would play together. Toronto fans had always been supportive of the Who—often to a greater extent than the fans in their native Britain—and the city had long been a favourite place of the band. After completing their lengthy 1982 tour (which had already included a stop in Toronto), the Who returned for two last performances at the Gardens on December 16 and 17.

It was with a sense that something historic was going to take place that fans flocked to Maple Leaf Gardens to witness a farewell concert that was to be broadcast internationally. The fans gathered, the Who took to the stage, and televisions were turned on all around the globe. It was a classic Who performance: Pete with his windmill guitar motion and lead singer Roger Daltrey throwing his microphone around by its extension cord. It would have been a great way to end a career... except that it wasn't the end. The Gardens concert proved to be only the first of several final Who concerts during the 1980s.

May 23, 1985

MADONNA

BY THE TIME SHE arrived in Toronto to play Maple Leaf Gardens on May 23, 1985, Madonna was already a huge star. Greeted wherever she turned by groups of screaming teens and pre-teens —many of whom were dressed to look like their idol— it was also apparent that the fans did not just love Madonna's music, they loved the package.

When Madonna finally took the stage for her first Canadian appearance, the 18,000 fans in attendance went wild. She ran through her repertoire of hits, including "Holiday," "Crazy for You," and "Material Girl." But as much as music, Madonna was about sex. She sold her sex appeal through her provocative costumes, her songs, and even her dance steps. It was, however, all in good fun, and her 1985 act more closely resembled that of a cheerleader than a stripper. For her encore, she came back on stage dressed in a bridal gown. When she called out to ask if anybody would marry her, thousands of voices answered a collective "I do." She then went into a wild, gyrating version of "Like a Virgin," much to the delight of the young crowd.

Many critics of Madonna picked on her singing, complaining that she had a tendency to sound metallic. To her legion of fans, however, Madonna seemed sexy, fashionable, and daring, pushing the limits of acceptability. Some compared Madonna on her 1985 tour to a combination of Marilyn Monroe and Doris Day. The review of the Maple Leaf Gardens concert which appeared in the *Toronto Sun* the following day compared Madonna's style of music and disco dance steps to another singing group—the Village People. But whatever she did, she was able to capture the attention of her fans, live up to the media hype, and leave town a little richer.

WRESTLEMANIA III ON CLOSED-CIRCUIT TV

Fʀᴏᴍ ᴛʜᴇ ᴛɪᴍᴇ it was first featured at the Gardens one week after the building opened in 1931 until the last World Wrestling Federation extravaganza on September 17, 1995, wrestling could always been counted on to draw large crowds. Generally, those crowds turned out to cheer for their heroes or heckle the villains live and in person. But not on March 29, 1987. The crowd was there (nearly 15,000 strong) but the wrestlers were not. They were at the Silverdome in Pontiac, Michigan, where the WWF was staging Wrestlemania III. Maple Leaf Gardens was one of 200 venues around the world that were carrying the event live on closed-circuit TV.

How big was Wrestlemania III? A total of 93,173 people turned out at the Silverdome. Another 10 million tuned in across North America. In Pittsburgh, a hockey game between the Penguins and the Canadiens had its start pushed back to 9:00 p.m. so that it wouldn't interfere with the wrestling. Both events had been sold out.

All the big stars of the wrestling world were on hand for Wrestlemania III, including Ricky "the Dragon" Steamboat, Jake "the Snake" Roberts, the Hart Foundation, the British Bulldogs, King Kong Bundy, and Koko B. Ware. At Maple Leaf Gardens, the loudest cheers were for local favourite Rowdy Roddy Piper and the lovely Elizabeth, manager of Randy "Macho Man" Savage. The biggest match on the card, however, pitted Hulk Hogan against Andre the Giant.

"For the uninitiated," wrote Frank Zicarelli in the *Toronto Sun*, "Hogan wrestled the title away from the Iron Sheik on January 24, 1984. From that day, the WWF has experienced unprecedented popularity, setting arena records in virtually every location the WWF stages a card. Hogan has been the kingpin."

Hogan could barely budge Andre for the first ten minutes of their match, but in the thirteenth minute he body-slammed the 7'4", 500-plus pound Giant. The Hulkster then administered his patented leg drop and pinned him.

As it usually does in the world of wrestling, good had once again triumphed over evil.

September 15, 1988

AMNESTY INTERNATIONAL CONCERT

Sting, Youssou N'Dour, Tracy Chapman, and Bruce Springsteen deliver Amnesty's message of "Human Rights Now."

ON SEPTEMBER 15, 1988, a crowd of 16,000 fans jammed Maple Leaf Gardens to see Bruce Springsteen, Sting, Traci Chapman, Peter Gabriel, and Senegalese singer Youssou N'Dour. They were also there to support a cause, as the stars on stage that night, as well as many others around the world, had spent the entire summer delivering the message of "Human Rights Now" in a global series of Amnesty International concerts. The long world tour would continue for another month before a final performance took place in Buenos Aires, Argentina, on October 15. Despite the rigorous schedule and rumours of ego problems, the Gardens show was a huge success.

The line-up for the Toronto stop included k.d. lang, who joined the others on stage to start things off shortly after 5:00 p.m. with a hand-clapping rendition of Bob Marley's "Get Up, Stand Up."

N'Dour opened the solo portion of the show and was followed by lang, who told the audience she was proud to represent Canada on the tour. ("Local" talent was included at all the Amnesty shows.) She delivered a cover of Roy Orbison's "Crying" that was one of the highlights of the show.

Other highlights from the Amnesty International concert included Traci Chapman's "Fast Car" and her appropriately titled song "Freedom Now." Sting included "They Dance Alone," his tribute to Chilean women mourning the disappearance of their loved ones, among his set, and Peter Gabriel was no less dramatic with his performance of "Biko." "Still," wrote Bob Thompson in the *Toronto Sun*, "Bruce Springsteen was the force [of the show] with his Born to Run power and his Promised Land insight into hope and glory."

The concert concluded with the entire cast back on stage together to sing Bob Dylan's "Chimes of Freedom."

k.d. lang provided Canadian content at the Amnesty concert.

PLACIDO DOMINGO

THE 1950s MARKED the height of cultured musical events at Maple Leaf Gardens, with opera and ballet taking regular places on the schedule alongside hockey and wrestling. By the 1960s, rock and roll dominated the Gardens music scene as it would for most of the next three decades. But from time to time, the Gardens would again be transformed into a classical music hall—albeit a somewhat acoustically challenged one.

"It's likely there was not a single person in Maple Leaf Gardens last night who wouldn't have rather heard the performance of the legendary tenor Placido Domingo in a hall more acoustically suited to the purpose," wrote John Coulbourn in the *Toronto Sun*. "But it's even more unlikely that any one of those thousands present would have foregone the opportunity to hear the great Domingo simply because of those regrettable acoustics."

As it was, 10,000 people were thoroughly enchanted by the magnificent voice of the Spanish tenor on January 19, 1993. Backed by a seventy-eight-piece orchestra and joined on stage by Gail Dobish of the New York City Opera, Domingo led his audience through an evening of classics including Verdi's "La Traviata" and Puccini's "Tosca."

"In the end, he scored more victories in a single evening than the Gardens has seen in too many years—for the simple reason that it's the voice of an angel you're hearing. Only a fool would stop to complain about something as inconsequential as acoustics."

February 13, 1993

DOUG GILMOUR'S SIX ASSISTS

IT WAS ONE OF THE greatest individual game efforts in the history of the Maple Leafs, likely ranking second all-time behind Darryl Sittler's ten-point night on February 7, 1976. It was also a game that symbolized the early 1990s rebirth of a hockey franchise that had floundered so badly for so many years, and showcased the skills of the one player most responsible for that dramatic turnaround.

Doug Gilmour had the season of a lifetime in 1992-93, establishing club records with 95 assists and 127 points. But team goals were what motivated Gilmour (he had refused to accept personal incentives when renegotiating his contract in 1992, insisting on team bonuses instead) and it was during February 1993 that Gilmour and the Leafs began a roll that would take them within one game of the Stanley Cup Final. Dave Andreychuk was traded from Buffalo to Toronto, and he was the perfect triggerman for Gilmour's pin-point passes.

In thirteen games after acquiring Andreychuk, the Leafs went 10–2–1, including a 6–1 victory over the Minnesota North Stars at Maple Leaf Gardens on February 13, 1993. Gilmour set up all six Toronto goals that night, tying Babe Pratt's forty-nine-year-old club record and finishing one short of the NHL record shared by Billy Taylor and Wayne Gretzky. Most amazing about Gilmour's performance was that he truly earned each of his six assists, making the key pass that resulted in every Leaf goal that night. He set up Mike Foligno and John Cullen in the first period, Andreychuk and Glenn Anderson in the second, and Andreychuk and Dave Ellett in the third. Coach Pat Burns left Gilmour on the ice for the final ninety seconds of the game, while the Leafs' fans roared their approval.

"When you have some success around here, you see the fans get louder and louder," said Gilmour in the dressing room after the game. "As we get closer to a playoff spot, the fans are getting excited. We're getting excited in this room too."

Gilmour's great play in the regular season carried over into the 1993 playoffs. Here he scores the winning goal in double overtime in game one against St. Louis.

UNIVERSITY CUP

WITH THE FORMATION of the Canadian Interuniversity Athletic Union as the governing body for intercollegiate sports in Canada in 1961, the concept of a true national championship game became a reality, and since the 1962–63 season the University Cup has been emblematic of CIAU hockey supremacy.

With a crowd of 7,842 in the stands when the national championship game was held in Maple Leaf Gardens for the first time on March 21, 1993, the University of Toronto Blues were left to chill on the Gardens ice for fifteen minutes after the Acadia Axemen returned to their dressing room before the opening face-off. The motor on their skate-sharpening machine had blown and the replacement sharpener they had found at the Eaton Centre left the players barely able to stand up, so the team had to scramble to gain access to the Gardens' pro shop. When the Axemen finally did hit the ice they scored twice in the first two minutes en route to a 4–0 lead after the first period.

"It's not right," complained Blues coach Paul Titanic. "We were already out there, then we're standing back in the hallway, waiting because we've got no key to the room. That killed us at the beginning. We were pumped up to go out and then they scored. It was a disaster. That start killed us."

Never able to play their tight-checking game, the Blues were crushed 12–1 as Acadia claimed its first national hockey championship.

One year later a new University Cup champion was crowned on Gardens ice. The University of Lethbridge had nearly cancelled its hockey program before the start of the 1993–94 season, but year's end saw the Pronghorns claim the national championship with a 5–2 victory over the Guelph Gryphons. Guelph was defeated again at the Gardens by the *Moncton Aigles Bleus* for the 1995 University Cup title, but after Acadia defeated the Waterloo Warriors in 1996, the Gryphons claimed their first national hockey crown the following year with a 4–3 win over the University of New Brunswick Varsity Reds.

(Top) Acadia fans celebrate in the stands after their team scores yet another goal (above) in a 12–1 romp over the University of Toronto.

May 15, 1993

LEAFS PLAYOFF RUN

THERE WAS A SENSE of optimism surrounding the Maple Leafs heading into the 1992-93 season. Cliff Fletcher's acquisition of Doug Gilmour in a blockbuster deal midway through the 1991-92 season had given Toronto its first star player in a decade. Felix Potvin was ready to emerge as a star, and the defensive crew of Dave Ellett, Jamie Macoun, and Todd Gill had been bolstered by the acquisition of Sylvain Lefebvre. The team also had a new bench boss in former Montreal Canadiens coach Pat Burns.

While employing Burns' system of defence first, the Leafs still received a record-breaking offensive season from Doug Gilmour, who established a new team high with 127 points. The Leafs set club records with 44 wins and 99 points, but they were still only third behind Chicago and Detroit in the tight Norris Division. The Leafs won the first round against Detroit in seven games. In the second-round playoff match-up with St. Louis (who had upset the Blackhawks), the teams split the first six games before returning to Toronto to decide the series on May 15, 1993.

A fired-up crowd of 15,720 fans turned out to witness the first game seven played at the Gardens since Toronto won the Stanley Cup in 1964. The team fed off the raw emotion coming from the stands and raced to a 4–0 lead after one period. When it was all over the Maple Leafs had a 6–0 victory and advanced to the Stanley Cup semifinals for the first time since 1978. Toronto faced the Los Angeles Kings in the semis and had a chance to end the series in six, but an overtime goal by Wayne Gretzky (after he was not penalized for cutting Doug Gilmour) sent the series back to Toronto for yet another seventh game. The Leafs were the first team to go to game seven in three straight series, and playing their twenty-first game in forty-two nights caught up with them. Los Angeles won the game 5–4 and the dream season came to an end.

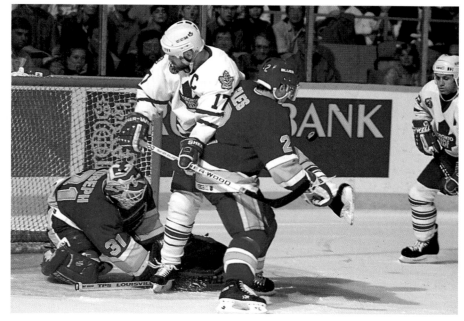

Captain Wendel Clark and top scorer Doug Gilmour spearheaded Toronto's 1993 playoff run, though they couldn't beat future Maple Leafs goalie Curtis Joseph on this play.

Dave Andreychuk comes out from behind the Dallas net and tries to jam the puck past goaltender Andy Moog on opening night in 1993.

October 7, 1993

LEAFS WIN TEN STRAIGHT

THE LEAFS OPENED the new season against the Dallas Stars at Maple Leaf Gardens on October 7, 1993. Dave Andreychuk put Toronto out front 1–0 on a Doug Gilmour feed late in the first period, then gave Toronto a 2–1 lead on another Gilmour setup in the second. Dallas tied matters again in the third period, but Toronto responded with four more goals and a 6–3 victory. Two nights later, Wendel Clark's third-period goal lifted Toronto past Chicago 2–1 in front of the home folks. When the Leafs beat the Flyers 5–4 in Philadelphia the next night, it marked the team's best start since opening the 1973–74 season 2–0–1. "I'm not getting excited about it," said coach Pat Burns of the winning streak. "Everybody wants to start this way."

The Leaf returned home on October 13 and ran their record to 4–0 with a 7–1 rout of Washington. A pair of wins over Detroit in home-and-home games pushed their mark to 6–0. A 7–2 romp over Hartford followed before the Leafs headed out on a three-game road trip one win short of the best start in NHL history.

The Toronto Maple Leafs of 1934–35 had opened that season with eight straight wins, establishing an NHL mark that had been equalled by the Buffalo Sabres in 1975. The 1993–94 Maple Leafs added their name to the record book with a 4–3 win over Florida on October 21, 1993. Two nights later they held the record alone after a 2–0 win in Tampa. The Leafs then improved to 10–0 with a 4–2 win in Chicago on October 28. The victory over the Black Hawks snapped a thirteen-game losing streak at the Chicago Stadium and also broke the franchise record of nine straight wins established back in 1924–25 when the club was still the Toronto St. Pats. The winning streak ended in Montreal two nights later when the Canadiens downed the Leafs 5–2.

November 4, 1993

NIRVANA

NIRVANA'S FIRST APPEARANCE in Toronto came on September 20, 1991. They kicked off a club tour that night at the 1,100-seat Opera House. The show didn't sell out. Four days later, the album Nevermind was released. By January 1992 it was the top album in North America. Seattle-based Nirvana had become the world's biggest alternative band and the single "Smells like Teen Spirit" had become a youth anthem.

Nirvana returned to Toronto on November 4, 1993. This time they sold out the concert bowl at Maple Leaf Gardens. "The band that spearheaded the grunge movement delivered a brilliant set that managed to satisfy the demands 9,000 fans bring with them any time they fill an arena and completely subvert them at the same time," wrote *Toronto Sun* music critic John Sakamoto. "Put Simply, Nirvana did not play The Hit." They did play eight other cuts from Nevermind and all but three tracks from their latest album, In Utero. The twenty-one-song set also featured "About a Girl" and "School" from their lesser-known debut album, "Bleach."

"If you don't have it, you should buy it," advised Kurt Cobain. It was one of few times he bothered to address the audience at all.

The hundred-minute concert ended with Cobain alone on stage throwing his guitar in the air and letting in crash on the ground. When he picked up the guitar for the last time, Cobain swung it over his head and then used the instrument to decapitate one of the life-sized anatomy dolls on stage. Then he turned to the crowd, smiled, and waved goodbye.

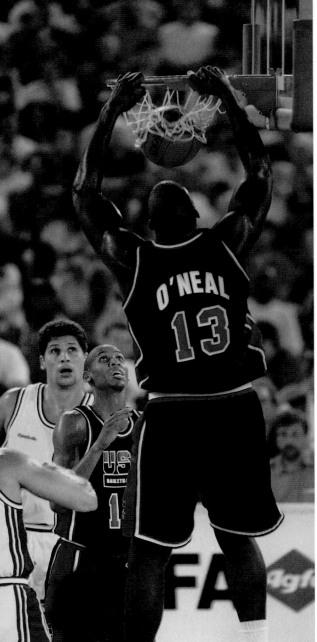

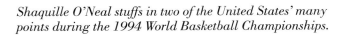

Shaquille O'Neal stuffs in two of the United States' many points during the 1994 World Basketball Championships.

August 4, 1994

WORLD BASKETBALL CHAMPIONSHIPS

AFTER THE TORONTO HUSKIES folded in 1947, it would be almost fifty years before the Raptors entered the National Basketball Association. In the intervening years, Toronto hoops fans had to content themselves with annual visits by the Harlem Globetrotters, a handful of experimental NBA games, and the occasional international event. The biggest of these international tournaments coincided with the birth of the Raptors when the cities of Toronto and Hamilton hosted the 12th World Basketball Championships in August 1994. Maple Leaf Gardens and Copps Coliseum co-hosted the first two rounds of the championship before the playoffs took place at SkyDome.

The 1994 World Basketball Championships marked the first time the event was held in North America and also the first time that NBA players were allowed to compete. Just two years earlier the NBA "Dream Team" (featuring Michael Jordan, Magic Johnson, and Larry Bird) had destroyed the competition when professionals had been allowed to compete at the Barcelona Olympics. Though a younger crop of superstars was featured on "Dream Team II," Shaquille O'Neal, Reggie Miller, Alonzo Mourning, and company were not expected to have much trouble taking the world title in 1994.

The tournament began on August 4 with four games each at Copps Coliseum and the Gardens. Canada closed out the Gardens schedule that day with an 83–52 win in front of 8,000 fans. Making his Gardens debut in the game was J.D. Jackson of Vancouver, whose great-uncle was Leafs legend Busher Jackson.

Canada played the majority of its World Championships games at the Gardens, but a 92–61 loss to Croatia in front of more than 16,000 fans on August 10 ended any hopes for a medal. The United States team made its Gardens debut that same night and a crowd of more than 16,000 watched them destroy Puerto Rico 134–83. Canada went on to record a disappointing seventh-place finish while the U.S. romped to their expected title, crushing Russia 137–91 in the championship game. A crowd of 32,616 witnessed the finale at the SkyDome, setting a record for the largest attendance at a basketball game in Canada.

February 15, 1996

TOP PROSPECTS GAME

IN THE EARLY DAYS of Maple Leaf Gardens, Toronto's junior teams regularly played to packed houses. The St. Michael's Majors could fill the Gardens while winning Memorial Cup titles in the 1940s, as could the Marlboros championship teams of the 1950s. Attendance began to decline during the 1960s, and though capacity crowds of 16,485 were occasionally on hand to watch the powerhouse Marlies teams of the early 1970s, the team played its final game in 1989. Junior hockey did not return to Maple Leaf Gardens until the inaugural Chrysler Cup Challenge on February 15, 1996.

The Chrysler Cup featured the top forty undrafted prospects from the Ontario Hockey League, the Quebec Major Junior Hockey League, and the Western Hockey League. Don Cherry and Bobby Orr were on hand as celebrity coaches and a crowd of 10,158—including some 200 scouts, 19 NHL general managers, and high-profile agents—saw Team Cherry defeat Team Orr 9–3. Among the stars of the game was Red Deer defenceman Chris Phillips, who picked up three assists and provided three crunching bodychecks for Team Cherry. Phillips was ranked number two by Central Scouting prior to the game, but would be selected first overall by the Ottawa Senators in the 1996 NHL Entry Draft. In total, thirteen of the forty players who took part in the prospects game that year were taken in the first round of the draft.

Captain Joe Thornton set up both goals for Team Cherry in a 7–2 loss at the 1997 game. Boston would select him first overall in the 1997 NHL Entry Draft.

The Chrysler Cup returned to Maple Leaf Gardens in both 1997 and 1998. Eight of the top ten players who would be selected in the 1997 Entry Draft had taken part in the Chrysler Cup. The game in 1998 featured fifteen future first-round draft choices, including number-one pick Vincent Lecavalier of Rimouski.

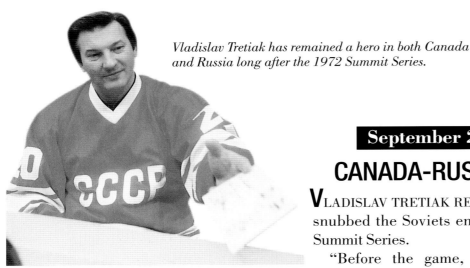

Vladislav Tretiak has remained a hero in both Canada and Russia long after the 1972 Summit Series.

CANADA-RUSSIA REUNION

Vladislav Tretiak remembers how the Canadians snubbed the Soviets entering game one of the 1972 Summit Series.

"Before the game, Team Canada didn't even acknowledge we were there," he told the *Toronto Sun*'s Mark Zeisberger on the twenty-fifth anniversary of Paul Henderson's historic goal. "They didn't say hello to us. They didn't even look at us. Each Canadian player thought, 'Oh, the Russians have no good players. There's no possible way they can play with us. Maybe we'll score 12 goals.'"

And what happened after the Soviets stunned Canada with a 7–3 victory?

"The next morning, Canadian players were coming up to us and saying, 'Oh, hello. Hello, buddy.'"

Even after Canada rallied to win the series, nobody ever again snubbed the great Soviet netminder. In 1989 Tretiak became the first player trained in the USSR to be inducted into the Hockey Hall of Fame, and to this day he remains a hero in both Canada and Russia. On September 28, 1997, he was invited to join members of Team Canada '72 at a twenty-fifth reunion at Maple Leaf Gardens.

A crowd of 7,000 fans showed up to watch many of the players from the Summit Series (augmented by a few extra NHL oldtimers including former Maple Leafs Darryl Sittler and Mike Palmateer) play an intrasquad game. Paul Henderson had a goal and an assist to lead Team Canada Red to a 4–1 victory over Team Canada White, but he was disappointed the whole team could not show up. "I guess everyone has their own personal reasons, but it would have been nice to have everyone here. We're not getting any younger."

Those who did take part in the game were caught up in the excitement once again. "When we took that skate around the ice at the end of the game, it was very emotional for all of us," Yvan Cournoyer admitted. "A lot of the guys had their heads down. I'm sure they were doing a lot of thinking."

"It was an emotional experience for me," said Ron Ellis, who cried when the national anthem was played after the game. "It's something I'll never forget."

The hero of 1972, Paul Henderson signs a youngster's helmet twenty-five years later.

March 31, 1998

RAPTORS vs. LAKERS

WITH THE EXCEPTION of a handful of Buffalo Braves games and special events, for almost fifty years there was no NBA basketball in Toronto until the Raptors began operation in 1995. They scheduled three games at the Gardens late in the 1996–97 season. No games were on the slate in 1997–98, but a conflict over dates at SkyDome forced two games to be moved that season. There were problems sorting out the ticket situation when the L.A. Lakers visited Maple Leaf Gardens on March 31, 1998, but, on the court at least, the game was a big success. Shaquille O'Neal was making his only visit of the season to

Toronto. He was, of course, the main attraction, but the game also featured some Canadian content in Shaq's teammate Rick Fox.

The Raptors had struggled throughout the entire 1997–98 season and there was every reason to suspect a blowout. However, the team played one of its best games of the year, though Toronto did come out on the wrong end of a 114–105 score. Still, "it was important for our confidence to compete against a very good team," said Chauncey Billups, who led the Raptors with 21 points.

It was stiflingly hot in the Gardens that night, but the Raptors seemed to feed off the steamy atmosphere and enjoyed playing in the smaller venue. "I can't say enough about playing here," coach Butch Carter enthused. "When you make a great play, there's instant gratification from the fans. The sound doesn't get lost in thirty storeys."

Three weeks later, on April 19, 1998, the Raptors hosted the Philadelphia 76ers in what is likely to be the last NBA game that will ever be played at Maple Leaf Gardens.

Indian superstar Shah-Rukh Khan.

SOUTH ASIAN CONCERTS

IN MANY WAYS, the history of Maple Leaf Gardens has provided a record of the changing face of Toronto. From Jewish political rallies, to Italian concerts, to Polish dance troupes, to Greek church services, the Gardens has always catered to the needs of Toronto's ethnic communities.

In the late 1970s, entertainers appealing to the South Asian population began to appear on the Gardens bill. Since then, southern Ontario's South Asian community has continued to fill the Gardens for musical extravaganzas featuring the stars of "Bollywood."

Movies from Bollywood—as the Indian film industry is known—dominate South Asian culture with an even more pervasive influence than Hollywood movies have in the Western world. As many as 900 movies are released annually in India (a total that surpasses Hollywood) and many of them succeed or fail based almost solely on the success of their songs. Two theatres in the Toronto area (one in Scarborough and one in Etobicoke) are devoted exclusively to the latest releases from Bollywood.

"Indian film stars are a sort of culturally unique hybrid," wrote *Toronto Star* diversity reporter Maureen Murray prior to a September 6, 1998 Maple Leaf Gardens stage performance. "[They're] part actor, part dancer, part acrobat, [and] part professional 'lip syncer.'"

The Toronto stop was part of a seventeen-city tour with dates in the United States and London, England. "It may be a different era and a different culture," Murray wrote, "but the hype surrounding the 'Awesome Foursome' has shades of Beatlemania." The top name on the Gardens bill was Indian superstar Shah-Rukh Khan, who was joined by female actors Juhi Chawla and Kajol. Completing the foursome was action star Akshay Kumar.

Tickets for the 1998 Bollywood show ranged from $25 to $100, with some of the proceeds going to the United Way of Greater Toronto. A crowd of 17,000 turned out to watch their favourite stars perform song and dance sequences from their movies. "It hardly seems to matter that the songs are actually sung by background singers, while the stars lip sync."

October 29, 1998

BOB DYLAN AND JONI MITCHELL

Bob DYLAN AND Joni Mitchell. Folk-rock icons of the 1960s and '70s. One (Mitchell) hadn't toured in sixteen years. The other (Dylan) had been on the road for much of the last decade and done much to rehabilitate his tarnished image. Both had performed at a select number of West Coast dates with Van Morrison in May 1998 before hitting the road together later in the year. On October 29, 1998, they arrived at Maple Leaf Gardens.

"It would be easy to characterize tonight's Bob Dylan/Joni Mitchell double bill... as an exercise in nostalgia," wrote Chris Dafoe in the *Globe and Mail*. "But it's clear that both Dylan and Mitchell have escaped the nostalgia trap... While the Rolling Stones have, since the late '70s, recorded dud after dud to justify lavish tours, both Dylan, 57, and Mitchell, 54, have recently released albums that can stand alongside their best work."

On the other hand, Peter Goddard wrote in the *Toronto Star* that he couldn't shake "the sensation that this is the full monty Las Vegas-ization of my culture, that the Bob and Joni show is my generation's version of that ultimate Vegas hubby-and-wife schmoozerino combo of Steve Lawrence and Edie Gorme."

The truth, of course, was somewhere in between.

Attendance for the concert was less than 10,000—something of a disappointment. Joni Mitchell was on stage first, opening her eighty-minute set with "Big Yellow Taxi" and performing a mix of classic songs and those from her new album Taming The Tiger.

"There was polite applause," wrote Jane Stevenson in the *Toronto Sun*, "but even when Mitchell returned for a one-song encore with 'Woodstock,' it seemed overwhelmingly obvious the crowd was ready for Dylan." The crowd leapt to its feet when he took the stage amid flashing lights and opened with "Serve Somebody."

Dylan, who had first performed at Maple Leaf Gardens with the Band in January 1974, played for one hour and five minutes. Like Mitchell, he mixed classics with cuts from his latest album (1997's triple Grammy-winner Time Out of Mind). He got the biggest reaction from "Masters of War," "Forever Young," "Tangled Up in Blue," and "Highway 61," all of which received standing ovations.

The Great One's last stand: Gretzky and the New York Rangers begin their last game at Maple Leaf Gardens.

GRETZKY'S LAST GAME IN THE GARDENS

WAYNE GRETZKY GREW UP just ninety-five kilometres southwest of Maple Leaf Gardens, saw his first NHL game there, and played a few minor-league hockey games in the arena. He made his own NHL Gardens debut on November 21, 1979, with a four-point night, beginning a string of impressive performances that parallelled his emergence as the game's greatest scorer.

En route to a record total of points for a visiting player at the Gardens (first as one of the Oilers, then as a King, finally as a Ranger), number 99 recorded three or more points on thirteen occasions, including four 4-point nights, three 5-point efforts, and two 6-point games.

The night of his last game there, the arena enjoyed a special buzz. As often throughout Gretzky's career, his father, Walter, was in attendance, as were his wife, Janet, and their three children. Late in the second period the Gardens' message board flashed "HAPPY 10TH BIRTHDAY PAULINA GRETZKY." Numerous number 99 jerseys could be spotted in the crowd.

The game proved somewhat anticlimactic for the Rangers, as the Leafs piled up a 4–0 lead before fifteen minutes had elapsed. The Rangers scored three late goals to make the tally respectable, but the Leafs controlled the game, which ended 7–4. Gretzky had assisted on the first and last Ranger goals.

His all-time league-leading totals for a visiting team player in Maple Leaf Gardens now stood at thirty goals and forty-seven assists — 77 points in thirty regular-season games, for an average of 2.56 points per game.

Throughout the contest, Toronto fans were generous with their applause for Gretzky. This was a change, because for much of his career he had been paid the ultimate hockey compliment when he played in Toronto: fans booed him whenever he touched the puck. This special treatment was reserved only for the game's greatest players. Bobby Orr, Maurice Richard, Bobby Hull, and Gordie Howe had received similar treatment in their prime years.

Gretzky's departure from the ice after his last game in the Gardens was a reminder that the building's days as a major-league hockey venue were indeed numbered.

PEOPLE OF THE GARDENS

From Accounts Payable to Zamboni Driver

PETER WILTON

CHRISTINE BUCHANAN,
SCOUTING CO-ORDINATOR
Joined Maple Leaf Gardens in 1992

CHRISTINE BUCHANAN has been told that at the age of three she was already able to recite the names of all the Toronto Maple Leafs. The Leafs were always an important part of her family, though her memories of the Gardens include not only the exploits of the hockey team and wrestlers like Hulk Hogan but her own athletic achievements as well. When she was in grades seven and eight, Christine took part in the Maple Leaf Junior Games. She still believes that she never ran better than she did on the old wooden, banked track.

Christine Buchanan

In 1992, Christine was one of the original beer servers hired when the building got its first liquor licence. She and the other servers had to follow strict rules, with the paramount responsibility being to ensure the safety of the fans and to see that people drank sensibly.

"One of the aspects that I loved about serving beer," recalls Christine, "was meeting celebrities. I remember Neil Young standing next to me waiting for his beer. I was thinking, 'I'm at the Gardens and Neil Young is standing next to me,' when suddenly Don Cherry walked by and I forgot everything except Don Cherry."

On the rare occasions when Christine forgets what a magical place the Gardens is to work in, she need only watch the faces of fans walking into the building for the first time—many of whom have had to wait years to make their first visit. Christine sometimes acts as a guide, taking people on official tours that include a walk out to centre ice. It is then that the magic returns for her. "Their faces just light up and they are in absolute awe of the place. And it's not just the fans. Young players' faces light up the same way when they first step onto the ice at Maple Leaf Gardens."

ANN CLARK,
EXECUTIVE ASSISTANT
to Leafs president and general manager Ken Dryden
Joined Maple Leaf Gardens in 1997

ANN HAS BEEN with the Maple Leafs since the spring of 1997. She remembers getting a call from her employment agency. "The girl on the phone said, 'You'll be working for Ken Dryden. I think he used to be a hockey player.' That night, I told my husband who I was going to work for. I think that if I had given him the chance, he would have taken the job!

"What I remember most about my first day is walking into the building. I had been to the Gardens before, always at an event. Even walking into the Gardens, when it was empty, there was still a feeling, an aura which encompassed the building. I was taken up the escalator. I thought to myself, 'Where are they taking me, to the reds?' Instead, we made a turn at the top of the escalator. Tucked away where thousands of fans pass after each game are the executive offices.

"On that first day I was shown to my work area, with its two little windows. I was shown a little door and told that this was the second entrance into Mr. Dryden's office."

For months Ann didn't use this door. "I always walked around to the main door into his office. Well, one day I thought that I would use the secret door. I opened it and Mr. Dryden almost had a heart attack. He was leaning back in his chair and when I opened the door he jumped out of his seat. He had never realized that the door existed. It had been blended into the moulding so

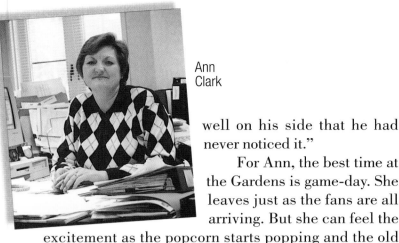
Ann
Clark

Sam
DeAngelis

well on his side that he had never noticed it."

For Ann, the best time at the Gardens is game-day. She leaves just as the fans are all arriving. But she can feel the excitement as the popcorn starts popping and the old building comes to life once again.

SAM DeANGELIS
ZAMBONI DRIVER
Joined Maple Leaf Gardens in the early 1960s

WHETHER YOU'VE watched the Maple Leafs on television or live at the Gardens, you've seen the familiar dark-haired man in the blue cardigan sweater who drives the Zamboni between periods. Since the early 1960s (he can't remember exactly which year), Sam has been that man.

In the old days, Sam and seven others would take the old ice-flooding machine out onto the playing surface between periods. The others would scrape the loose snow off the ice while Sam followed with the flooding machine, which had been invented by the father of long-time Leafs announcer Paul Morris. "We were told to march in step," recalls Sam, "which we did. At the time there was nothing going on between periods, so we were the only entertainment."

There is a certain pressure associated with driving a Zamboni in the NHL, but Sam says he tries not to think of it. He just concentrates on doing the job without sliding into the boards. Part of the fun of the job for Sam is being seen on TV by his family or friends. "They'll joke with me and say, 'I saw you last night. You missed a spot.'"

One of the challenges of driving the Zamboni at Maple Leaf Gardens used to be dealing with a dip at centre ice created by the hand- and footprints of Harold Ballard that are set in the concrete Hollywood-walk-of-fame style. What had not been anticipated when he placed his hands and feet in the wet concrete was that when it set, the ice above would settle into the dips

caused by the impressions. Sam had to go out after he flooded the ice with the Zamboni and fill in the dip by hand with a hose. "The players were always complaining about it," he says.

Ballard's hand- and footprints were filled in with fresh cement after his death, leading to the urban myth that he is buried under centre ice at Maple Leaf Gardens.

JEANNIE FERREIRA
RECEPTION, SWITCHBOARD
Joined Maple Leaf Gardens in 1974

WHEN JEANNIE started her job at the Gardens, she was working in the "nut house"—no, not a room in which overzealous fans were locked up, but the room used to package the nuts and popcorn that were sold during games.

Three years later, Jeannie began working at reception and switchboard. It's a front-line position, and Jeannie quickly learned how seriously the fans take their hockey. More than once, fans have called in during a game demanding to speak to the coach or complaining about what they felt was a bad call by the referee.

In order to survive at switchboard, it helps to be able to think on your feet.

"One night during the intermission a player was being interviewed," Jeannie recalls. "Apparently he was sweating very heavily and this lady phones in absolutely adamant that I should take a towel to this player right away so that he could wipe his face because the sight of all that sweat was making her sick. I said that I would take him a towel as soon as I hung up."

The demand for tickets is never-ending. Jeannie recalls one teenager in particular who continued to insist he needed tickets despite her repeatedly telling him the game was sold out. Exasperated, she finally said, "Well, I guess we could hang you from the rafters

Jeannie
Ferreira

Tony
Fertado

by your ankles." He phoned back later and wanted to know how much that would cost!

Like many of the long-time staff, Jeannie has fond memories of Harold Ballard and King Clancy. Clancy had an unusual gift of being able to make people laugh and feel good. He would always take time to visit the women at reception and Jeannie recalls his death as the saddest time at the Gardens. "It seemed like a part of the Gardens died with him. Everybody felt the loss."

TONY FERTADO
MAINTENANCE
Joined Maple Leaf Gardens in 1967

SIX MONTHS AFTER arriving in Toronto from his native Azores, Tony began working at Maple Leaf Gardens. He remembers his early days on the job, working on the cleaning crew at night while taking English lessons during the day. He also recalls how good people were to him —including Harold Ballard, whom, like other employees, Tony looked upon as a father figure. He also remembers the atmosphere of excitement around the Gardens, having started on the job shortly after the Leafs became Stanley Cup champions.

As it turns out, Tony would never see another championship banner raised to the rafters of the Gardens, but he remains a true fan of the Maple Leafs. "I like to watch all the Leaf games," he says. "But when they win, those games are the best." However, his greatest night at the Gardens was spent not at a hockey game but at a concert in May 1975. "I had been a fan of Frank Sinatra since 1951," recalls Tony. "I saw all of his movies and loved his records. I was cleaning up that night at the Gardens behind the stage when Mr. Sinatra walked by. I said hello to him and he said hello right back. He looked me right in the eye."

As a boy in the Azores, Tony played hockey on roller skates. The rules were a sort of hybrid of hockey and soccer with very strict regulations against touching the puck with your hands. Such a violation would result in a penalty shot. Although lots of people have offered to teach him, Tony has never skated on the ice at Maple Leaf Gardens. He has no desire to learn to skate or play hockey: "My old bones couldn't take the hits."

BERNIE FOURNIER
MAINTENANCE, SHIPPING AND RECEIVING, DRIVER
Joined Maple Leaf Gardens in 1952

THE FIRST THING that strikes you when you meet Bernie, one of the longest-serving employees of the Gardens, is his office: every inch of space is covered with memorabilia of the Maple Leafs and of all the owners whom Bernie has worked for over the past forty-six years.

The second thing is Bernie's accent, a rich French-Canadian. Bernie remembers, as a boy, lying in bed at night listening to the Montreal Canadiens on the radio: "They were usually playing either the Toronto Maple Leafs or the Detroit Red Wings, and in my mind's eye I would be at the game, either at the Forum or the Gardens, watching my beloved Montreal Canadiens playing with the great Rocket Richard leading the way."

Bernie finally saw his boyhood hero at the Gardens. "...I saw the Rocket! You know why they call that guy the Rocket? It was because he was lit up. He was electric, almost like he was plugged in. It was his eyes: I never have seen anything like it, they were on fire."

Bernie
Fournier

Sherry
McKeown

Bernie heard some interesting conversations when he chauffeured members of management. "I remember driving King Clancy and Harold Ballard around and King would say to Harold, 'You know Harold, we didn't have much money, but we sure had fun.'"

Today, according to Bernie, the business is so big and the money is so huge that the fun seems to have been forgotten. He thinks hockey has changed from being a game to being a business.

Bernie came forward into the spotlight in the fall of 1998, when, representing employees past and present, he was asked by Ken Dryden to drop the puck at the last opening game at the Gardens. "I was really nervous, I thought that I was going to faint as I stepped onto the red carpet." But he managed.

SHERRY McKEOWN
USHER (GOLDS)
Joined Maple Leaf Gardens in 1992

SHERRY HAS SPENT the last six years working in the golds in the southwest corner section of the Gardens. "I get the biggest kick out of the out-of-town visitors," she says. "They just can't believe how close they are to the ice and that they are watching a game at Maple Leaf Gardens—you can see them looking around in disbelief."

Sherry's section is next to the entrance and exit used by the opposing team, so it's a great place for the young fans to get a stick or an autograph from an NHL player. Sherry finds that the players are very generous in providing such souvenirs for the fans. She has also noticed that, in this last year at the Gardens, some visiting players are collecting souvenirs of their own, bringing their cameras and having their pictures taken as they play their last game in the building.

"A great thing about Maple Leaf Gardens and working the golds," explains Sherry, "is that you are a part of so many events which mean a great deal to people. A few things which come to mind are the Ice Capades, the circus, and corporate Christmas parties." Another part of Sherry's job is escorting people who are being honoured at the Gardens to centre ice. "I escorted an old gentlemen in his eighties who was one of the original season ticket holders, as well as past players such as Red Horner. These are long-time Maple Leafs supporters or past players who are legends and heroes to a lot of people. To be a part of their night is a big thrill for me as well.

"That's what's so great about the Gardens. A lot of events—not just hockey—mean so much to people that their enthusiasm is passed on to me. No matter how many games I work here, I still feel the magic."

MARGARET MAN
PAYROLL MANAGER
Joined Maple Leaf Gardens in 1975

UNTIL VERY RECENTLY, Margaret was the only person who worked in payroll, single-handedly preparing the cheques for the 2,000 employees of the Gardens, from players to ushers.

Margaret remembers that when she was growing up in her native Hong Kong, "I didn't even know that hockey existed," so it was not her love of the game that led to her employment at the Gardens. Margaret explains, "When I arrived in Toronto in 1972, I started working at the YMCA in payroll. Their main office was a very old building. I remember thinking one day, I am

Margaret Man

Paul Morris

young, I don't want to spend my youth working in an old building. So I put my name in at an [employment] agency. The next day, I received a call and the lady told me that there was a job at Maple Leaf Gardens. Well, I didn't know what the Gardens was, so I asked how old the building was. When she told me, I told her I wasn't interested in the job. The lady said to me, 'Are you crazy? The hours are 9:00 to 4:30, Monday to Friday.' I thought, well, maybe I should take the job after all. The building was fifty years younger than the old YMCA!

"I didn't know anything about hockey nor did I know any of the players. I think that this was an advantage because it meant that I treated everybody the same. I remember that somebody called me about his pay cheque. He told me his name and I said, 'Are you one of the ushers?' and he said, 'No, I am a player.'"

Margaret looks forward to the move to the Air Canada Centre. "After twenty-three years, I finally get to work in a new building!" She admits that she still does not watch much hockey, but unlike the young woman from Hong Kong who started at the Gardens, she now knows the players' names.

PAUL MORRIS
SOUND TECHNICIAN AND PUBLIC ADDRESS ANNOUNCER
Joined Maple Leaf Gardens full-time in 1952

PAUL MORRIS sits in his office in an upper corner of the Gardens looking out the window. Far below a practice is in progress. The players skate in circles and the sound of the puck resonates in the near-empty building. Paul has been an important part of the show at Maple Leafs' games for thirty-eight years, though few would recognize him. Until he speaks. Then the penny drops. That familiar tone. It has been announcing goal-scorers and penalties, contest winners, and three-star selections since 1960.

Members of the Morris family have been on the Gardens payroll from the beginning. Even before the first shovel broke ground, Paul's father, Doug, an electrician, was involved in the plans and construction of the building. But Doug's contributions to the Gardens go well beyond the wiring. He was an innovator. In fact, one of his inventions can still be seen in the Gardens lobby. It is the early ice-flooding machine — predecessor of the Zamboni.

During the war years, when no sports events were held in the building on Sundays, Doug Morris used to come in to check the power generators and work on various projects. He often brought young Paul, who would put on his skates and push a chair around the famous ice, learning to skate while his father worked. In 1952, fourteen-year-old Paul began to help out as a sound mixer for Bill Hewitt during junior games. He also helped the sound man with the mixing for the opera that year, taking over the job the following year, battling the difficult problem of reducing feedback.

In 1958, Paul started working as an announcer at junior games. He became the announcer for the Maple Leafs in 1960, and since then he has watched the concerts, rodeos, operas, dances, political rallies, track meets, and, of course, his beloved Maple Leafs.

Sometimes, though, when the light is just right and the rink is quiet, Paul Morris can almost make out the figure of a young boy pushing himself across the empty ice, determined to learn how to skate.

GEORGE SALAC
ACCOUNTS PAYABLE
Joined Maple Leaf Gardens in 1981

"IN THREE YEARS, I will have worked for Maple Leaf Gardens for half my life," George says. "I started as a data input clerk, just at the time when computers were

George
Salac

Mary
Speck

being introduced to the accounts department of the Gardens, so I started when accounts were still done by hand."

"You know, sometimes I just cross the street from 70 Carlton where the accounting office is housed and go into the Gardens and sit in the arena. I close my eyes, and although the arena is silent, the great games of the past are played in my head. I can hear the slap of long-silent pucks or the roar of the crowd. These memories are stored within the very walls of the building.

"One of the great aspects of working for the Gardens is meeting the alumni. Players such as George Armstrong or Johnny Bower will often come back to the Gardens and we will sometimes see each other in the halls. They will always say, 'How are you doing, George?' There is an unwritten rule at the Gardens that we are not to ask the players for autographs; to do so would break the spirit of us all working together...

"Every year Johnny Bower would play Santa Claus at the office Christmas skating party. One year he couldn't do it, so I donned the suit. Now when people see me they always ask me if I am going to be Santa again this year."

Staff members of the Gardens seem to have been pack-rats from the beginning: George even has the 1931-32 accounts payable ledger, neat little pencilled amounts paid out as the Gardens took shape.

George is a little sad about leaving a building that has been so much a part of his life, but he also looks on the move as a new beginning.

MARY SPECK
TRAVEL CO-ORDINATOR
Joined Maple Leaf Gardens in 1981

MARY WAS originally hired to work in the Gardens' accounts receivable department. She began to work part-time for the hockey office and three years later became Harold Ballard's secretary. Her fondest memories are reserved for Ballard and King Clancy. "You know, those two were so kind. They were both father figures to me."

"I remember that I had a bad habit of always leaving my desk drawer open. Whenever King would walk into the office he would always try to toss his cap into that drawer, or he would walk up to my desk and drop the change out of his pocket and say, 'If you can guess how much change was in my pocket you can have it!' They were silly games, I guess, but they were fun and it was this that made the people at the Gardens not just fellow employees, but friends as well."

Mary met her husband at the Gardens—he worked in the carpentry shop. She invited Ballard and Clancy to her wedding. "King attended but Ballard wasn't really too big on those sorts of events, so I didn't really expect him to come, but I remember that he came walking up the hall, sat down at the desk next to mine, pulled out a hundred-dollar bill, and said, 'There you go, buy yourself something nice.'"

Mary is now the travel co-ordinator for the Maple Leafs, responsible for ensuring that the chartered buses are on time, the chartered planes are ready for the team, the hotels are booked, pre-game meals and snacks are available for the players, and that everything runs smoothly on road trips.

"I'm going to miss the Gardens very much," Mary says, "It was my home away from home, but I'm also looking forward to our new arena. It will be an exciting change for everyone—fans, players and employees."

End Game

MAPLE LEAF GARDENS: A CHRONOLOGY

1931-1999

THIS LIST OF MORE THAN 9,500 EVENTS
at Maple Leaf Gardens was compiled using Gardens records, hockey archives,
and newspaper research. Not included are private functions—recreational ice rentals, corporate events,
and filming for movies, television programs or commercials.
Some scores could not be obtained for junior and senior hockey, basketball, and lacrosse.
For boxing and wrestling matches, winners' names are listed first.
Any additions to this list can be sent to the Toronto Maple Leafs, Public Relations Department,
Air Canada Centre, 40 Bay Street, Suite 300, Toronto, Ontario M5J 2X2.

1931 • Nov. 12–NHL: Chicago 2, Leafs 1 (opening night); Nov. 13–Sr. Hockey: National Sea Fleas 3, Sr. Marlboros 2; Nov. 14–NHL: Canadiens 1, Leafs 1; Nov. 16–Jr. Hockey: Toronto Canoe Club 10, U. of T. Schools 0; Nov. 16–Jr. Hockey: West Toronto 12, Aurora 2; Nov. 17–Jr. Hockey: Hamilton 2, Jr. Marlboros 3; Nov. 17–Jr. Hockey: Jr. Varsity 9, Danforth 0; Nov. 19–Wrestling: Jim Londos vs. Gino Garibaldi; Nov. 21–NHL: Rangers 5, Leafs 3; Nov. 23–Jr. Hockey: Newmarket 4, St. Michael's 2; Nov. 23–Jr. Hockey: Parkdale Canoe Club 12, St. Andrews 5; Nov. 24–Jr. Hockey: Toronto Lions 4, Upper Canada College 1; Nov. 24–Jr. Hockey: National Sea Fleas 2, Oshawa 0; Nov. 25–Sr. Hockey: National Sea Fleas 2, Hamilton 0; Nov. 26–Jr. Hockey: Stratford 5, Toronto Canoe Club 1; Nov. 26–Jr. Hockey: Kitchener-Waterloo 3, West Toronto 3; Nov. 27–Sr. Hockey: Niagara Falls 5, Sr. Marlboros 1; Nov. 28–NHL: Boston 5, Leafs 6; Nov. 30–Jr. Hockey: Newmarket vs. Parkdale Canoe Club; Nov. 30–Jr. Hockey: Stratford vs. West Toronto; Dec. 1–NHL: Americans 2, Leafs 2; Dec. 2–Sr. Hockey: National Sea Fleas 3, Sr. Marlboros 2; Dec. 3–Wrestling: Ray Steele vs. Jim Clinkstock; Dec. 4–Sr. Hockey: Hamilton 3, Sr. Marlboros 2; Dec. 6–NHL: Maroons 0, Leafs 4; Dec. 7–Jr. Hockey: West Toronto 2, Jr. Marlboros 3; Dec. 9–Jr. Hockey: Parkdale Canoe Club 6, West Toronto 13; Dec. 9–Jr. Hockey: Toronto Canoe Club 1, Jr. Marlboros 12; Dec. 10–Sr. Hockey: Kitchener-Waterloo 1, Sr. Marlboros 2; Dec. 12–NHL: Detroit 1, Leafs 3; Dec. 14–Jr. Hockey: Kitchener-Waterloo 1, National Sea Fleas 4; Dec. 16–Jr. Hockey: National Sea Fleas 4, West Toronto 6; Dec. 16–Jr. Hockey: Jr. Varsity 2, Toronto Canoe Club 3; Dec. 17–Wrestling: Ray Steele vs. John Paul Jones; Dec. 18–Jr. Hockey: Port Colborne 0, Sr. Marlboros 2; Dec. 19–NHL: Maroons 2, Leafs 4; Dec. 22–NHL: Americans 3, Leafs 9; Dec. 26–Jr. Hockey: West Toronto 2, Jr. Marlboros 3; Dec. 26–Jr. Hockey: Toronto Canoe Club 7, National Sea Fleas 5; Dec. 26–NHL: Canadiens 2, Leafs 0; Dec. 30–Jr. Hockey: West Toronto 2, Jr. Marlboros 3; Dec. 30–Jr. Hockey: Toronto Canoe Club vs. Parkdale Canoe Club; Dec. 31–NHL: Maroons 1, Leafs 3.

1932 • Jan. 1–Wrestling: George Zaharias vs. Gino Garibaldi; Jan. 2–Sr. Hockey: Port Colborne 0, National Sea Fleas 3; Jan. 4–Sr. Hockey: Niagara Falls 1, Sr. Marlboros 3; Jan. 6–Jr. Hockey: Parkdale Canoe Club 1, Jr. Marlboros 2; Jan. 6–Jr. Hockey: National Sea Fleas 2, Toronto Canoe Club 1; Jan. 9–Jr. Hockey: Varsity 2, Jr. Marlboros 3; Jan. 9–Jr. Hockey: West Toronto 2, National Sea Fleas 4; Jan. 11–Sr. Hockey: U. of T. Schools 1, St. Michael's 5; Jan. 12–NHL: Detroit 4, Leafs 7; Jan. 14–Jr. Hockey: Parkdale Canoe Club 2, West Toronto 1; Jan. 14–Jr. Hockey: Varsity 1, National Sea Fleas 2; Jan. 14–Wrestling: Condor vs. George Zaharias; Jan. 15–Jr. Hockey: St. Andrews 0, St. Michael's 5; Jan. 16–Jr. Hockey: National Sea Fleas, Jr. Marlboros (Postponed due to fire); Jan. 16–Jr. Hockey: Jr. Varsity, West Toronto (Postponed due to fire); Jan. 16–Sr. Hockey: Port Colborne 1, Sr. Marlboros 3; Jan. 19–NHL: Americans 3, Leafs 11; Jan. 20–Jr. Hockey: Upper Canada College 0, St. Michael's 3; Jan. 20–Jr. Hockey: West Toronto 3, Jr. Marlboros 2; Jan. 20–Sr. Hockey: Parkdale Canoe Club 1, Toronto Canoe Club 3; Jan. 22–Sr. Hockey: Sr. Varsity 4, National Sea Fleas 3; Jan. 23–NHL: Canadiens 0, Leafs 2; Jan. 25–Jr. Hockey: Upper Canada College 8, St. Andrews 1; Jan. 25–Jr. Hockey: Kitchener-Waterloo 2, Sr. Marlboros 7; Jan. 27–Jr. Hockey: National Sea Fleas 1, Toronto Canoe Club 1; Jan. 27–Jr. Hockey: Newmarket 0, West Toronto 1; Jan. 29–Jr. Hockey: Winnipeg 0, National Sea Fleas 1; Jan. 29–Jr. Hockey: National Sea Fleas 2, Toronto Canoe Club 1; Jan. 29–Jr. Hockey: St. Michael's 7, Jr. Marlboros 4; Jan. 30–NHL: Rangers 3, Leafs 6; Feb. 1–Jr. Hockey: U. of T. Schools 2, Upper Canada College 4; Feb. 1–Jr. Hockey: National Sea Fleas 0, West Toronto 3; Feb. 2–Sr. Hockey: Sr. Varsity 0, Sr. Marlboros 1; Feb. 3–Jr. Hockey: Toronto Lions 1, St. Michael's 5; Feb. 3–Jr. Hockey: National Sea Fleas 2, West Toronto 2; Feb. 6–NHL: Boston 0, Leafs 6; Feb. 6–Sr. Hockey: West Toronto 2, Sr. Marlboros 4; Feb. 8–Jr. Hockey: National Sea Fleas 1, Jr. Marlboros 6; Feb. 8–Jr. Hockey: Toronto Lions 4, North Toronto 3; Feb. 8–Jr. Hockey: Spring AC 4, Marlboro Midgets 5; Feb. 9–Sr. Hockey: Hamilton 0, Sr. Marlboros 1; Feb. 10–Jr. Hockey: West Toronto 1, Jr. Marlboros 0; Feb. 11–Wrestling: Ray Steele vs. Rick Daviscourt; Feb. 13–Jr. Hockey: Peterborough 0, St. Michael's 3; Feb. 13–NHL: Maroons 0, Leafs 6; Feb. 15–Jr. Hockey: West Toronto 1, Jr. Marlboros 1; Feb. 16–Jr. Hockey: Toronto Lions 3, North Toronto 4; Feb. 17–Sr. Hockey: National Sea Fleas 3, Sr. Marlboros 3; Feb. 18–Jr. Hockey: Trinity College 0, Upper Canada College 6; Feb. 18–NHL: Rangers 3, Leafs 5; Feb. 19–Jr. Hockey: West Toronto 0, Jr. Marlboros 3; Feb. 20–Jr. Hockey: Kingston 2, St. Michael's 3; Feb. 20–Jr. Hockey: Stayner 4, North Toronto 0; Feb. 20–Sr. Hockey: National Sea Fleas 4, Sr. Marlboros 1; Feb. 24–Jr. Hockey: Newmarket 5, North Toronto 0; Feb. 25–NHL: Detroit 5, Leafs 3; Feb. 27–NHL: Chicago 2, Leafs 4; Mar. 1–NHL: Americans 1, Leafs 3; Mar. 2–Sr. Hockey: Port Colborne 1, National Sea Fleas 2; Mar. 3–Winston Churchill Lecture; Mar. 4–Jr. Hockey: Newmarket 5, St. Michael's 2; Mar. 5–Jr. Hockey: Stratford 1, Jr. Marlboros 2 (OHA "A" Finals); Mar. 5–NHL: Canadiens 1, Leafs 1; Mar. 7–Jr. Hockey: Newmarket 1, St. Michael's 0; Mar. 9–Jr. Hockey: Newmarket 1, Jr. Marlboros 1; Mar. 10–Wrestling: Ray Steele vs. George Zaharias; Mar. 11–Sr. Hockey: Timmins 1, National Sea Fleas 5; Mar. 12–Jr. Hockey: Newmarket 0, Jr. Marlboros 3 (OHA "A" Finals); Mar. 12–NHL: Boston 3, Leafs 5; Mar. 14–Jr. Hockey: Sudbury 3, Jr. Marlboros 0; Mar. 15–Sr. Hockey: Timmins 0, National Sea Fleas 9; Mar. 15–Sr. Hockey: Doherty AC 2, Xebecs 1; Mar. 16–Sr. Hockey: Sudbury 2, Sr. Marlboros 4; Mar. 17–National Indoor Track Championships; Mar. 18–Jr. Hockey: Sudbury 2, Ottawa 0 (All-Ontario Jr. Finals); Mar. 19–NHL: Chicago 3, Leafs 11; Mar. 19–Sr. Hockey: Oshawa 1, Doherty AC 5 (City League Finals); Mar. 22–Boxing: Mel Glionna vs. Harvey Fleet; Mar. 23–Jr. Hockey: Ottawa 0, National Sea Fleas 3; Mar. 27–Easter Mass; Mar. 28–Jr. Hockey: Montreal AAA 0, Sudbury 3 (Memorial Cup Eastern Finals); Mar. 29–NHL: Chicago 1, Leafs 6; Mar. 30–Sr. Hockey: Windsor 3, Doherty AC 2; Mar. 31–Amateur Boxing; Apr. 2–NHL: Maroons 2, Leafs 3; Apr. 6–Wrestling: Ray Steele vs. Gino Garibaldi; Apr. 9–NHL: Rangers 4, Leafs 6 (Stanley Cup-winning game); Apr. 11–Boxing: Exhibition bouts featuring Max Schmelling; Apr. 12-13: Eastern Ontario Boxing Finals; Apr. 15–Music: The Spring Revue; Apr. 16–Annual Rodeo; May 1–Denton Massey York Bible Class; May 2–Lions Club Boxing Show; May 3–Lacrosse: Maple Leafs 12, Tecumsehs 5; May 4–Professional Badminton; May 12-13: Olympic Boxing Exhibition; May 19–Boxing: Panama Brown vs. Spider Pladner (Canadian Championship); Oct. 17–Lacrosse: Mimico 4, Fergus 3; Oct. 19–Lacrosse: Mimico 15, Montreal 3; Oct. 20–Wrestling: Earl McCready vs. Howard Cantonwine; Oct. 21–Lacrosse: Winnipeg 6, Mimico 16 (Mann Cup Finals); Oct. 22–Lacrosse: Buffalo 12, Toronto 6; Oct. 24–Lacrosse: Winnipeg 2, Mimico 4 (Mann Cup Finals); Oct. 24–Lacrosse: Leslie 8, Runnymede 6; Oct. 25–Lacrosse: St. Catharines 12, National Sea Fleas 6; Oct. 29–Lacrosse: Buffalo 11, Toronto 16; Oct. 31–Wrestling: Sammy Stein vs. Bibber McCoy; Nov. 3–Boxing: Lefty Gwynne vs. Marino Maurer; Nov. 4–Wrestling: Ed. Don George vs. Howard Cantonwire; Nov. 10–NHL: Boston 1, Leafs 1; Nov. 12–NHL: Rangers 2, Leafs 4; Nov. 15–Sr. Hockey: St. Catharines 1, National Sea Fleas 0; Nov. 16–Jr. Hockey: Danforth 2, Jr. Marlboros 6; Nov. 16–Jr. Hockey: Jr. Varsity 3, Toronto Lions 1; Nov. 17–Wrestling: Henri Deglane vs. Sammy Stein; Nov. 18–Jr. Hockey: Newmarket 8, Toronto Canoe Club 2; Nov. 18–Jr. Hockey: Parkdale Canoe Club 3, Toronto Native Sons 2; Nov. 19–Jr. Hockey: U. of T. Schools 3, National Sea Fleas 7; Nov. 19–Jr. Hockey: Galt 0, St. Michael's 10; Nov. 19–Sr. Hockey: National Sea Fleas 2, Sr. Marlboros 4; Nov. 21–Boxing: Frankie Petrolle vs. Billy Townsend; Nov. 22–Sr. Hockey: Niagara Falls 3, Sr. Marlboros 3; Nov. 23–Jr. Hockey: Barrie 2, Jr. Marlboros 10; Nov. 23–Jr. Hockey: Stratford 3, Jr. Varsity 1; Nov. 24–NHL: Canadiens 0, Leafs 2; Nov. 25–Jr. Hockey: Newmarket 5, National Sea Fleas 4; Nov. 25–Jr. Hockey: Parkdale Canoe Club 0, St. Michael's 5; Nov. 26–NHL: Maroons 2, Leafs 3; Nov. 28–Amateur Boxing Night; Nov. 29–Sr. Hockey: Sr. Varsity, Sr. Marlboros; Nov. 30–Jr. Hockey: Newmarket 0, Jr. Marlboros 2; Nov. 30–Jr. Hockey: Stratford 2, St. Michael's 1; Dec. 1–Wrestling: Ed Don George vs. Joe Malcewicz; Dec. 2–Sr. Hockey: Kitchener-Waterloo 1, National Sea Fleas 4; Dec. 3–Jr. Hockey: Stratford 1, Jr. Marlboros 3; Dec. 3–NHL: Ottawa 1, Leafs 4; Dec. 5–Sr. Hockey: Sudbury 0, Stratford 2; Dec. 6–Sr. Hockey: Hamilton 1, Sr. Marlboros 2; Dec. 7–Sr. Hockey: Sudbury 2, Stratford 1; Dec. 9–Sr. Hockey: Port Colborne 1, National Sea Fleas 1; Dec. 10–Jr. Hockey: St. Michael's 2, Jr. Marlboros 3; Dec. 10–Jr. Hockey: Parkdale Canoe Club 3, Toronto Canoe Club 1; Dec. 10–NHL: Americans 2, Leafs 2; Dec. 13–Sr. Hockey: National Sea Fleas 3, Sr. Marlboros 6; Dec. 14–Wrestling: Gus Sonnenberg vs. Joe Malcewicz; Dec. 15–NHL: Ottawa 1, Leafs 4; Dec. 16–Jr. Hockey: Danforth 2, Toronto Native Sons 9; Dec. 16–Jr. Hockey: Oshawa 4, Toronto Lions 2; Dec. 17–Jr. Hockey: Parkdale Canoe Club 0, Jr. Marlboros 3; Dec. 17–Jr. Hockey: Jr. Varsity 2, National Sea Fleas 3; Dec. 17–NHL: Detroit 0, Leafs 3; Dec. 19–Sr. Hockey: Port Colborne 0, Sr. Marlboros 1; Dec. 20–Jr. Hockey: Upper Canada College 4, U. of T. Old Boys 3; Dec. 21–Jr. Hockey: St. Michael's 4, Toronto Canoe Club 4; Dec. 21–Jr. Hockey: Jr. Varsity 0, Jr. Marlboros 4; Dec. 22–Jr. Hockey: Toronto Lions 1, Toronto Native Sons 2; Dec. 22–Jr. Hockey: Oshawa 2, Danforth 3; Dec. 23–Sr. Hockey: Kitchener-Waterloo 1, Sr. Marlboros 4; Dec. 24–NHL: Chicago 2, Leafs 1; Dec. 27–Sr. Hockey: Sr. Varsity 3, National Sea Fleas 1; Dec. 28–Jr. Hockey: Toronto Canoe Club 5, Jr. Marlboros 7; Dec. 28–Jr. Hockey: Parkdale Canoe Club 0, National Sea Fleas 1; Dec. 29–NHL: Maroons 0, Leafs 1; Dec. 30–Wrestling: Gus Sonnenberg vs. Ed Don George; Dec. 31–Jr. Hockey: Parkdale Canoe Club, Jr. Varsity; Dec. 31–Jr. Hockey: National Sea Fleas, St. Michael's; Dec. 31–Sr. Hockey: Hamilton, National Sea Fleas.

1933 • Jan. 2–Jr. Hockey: National Sea Fleas 2, Jr. Marlboros 3; Jan. 2–Jr. Hockey: Parkdale Canoe Club 3, St. Michael's 4; Jan. 3–Jr. Hockey: Danforth 1, Toronto Lions 5; Jan. 3–Jr. Hockey: Oshawa 0, Toronto Native Sons 1; Jan. 4–Jr. Hockey: Toronto Canoe Club 2, Jr. Varsity 1; Jan. 4–Jr. Hockey: St. Michael's 1, Jr. Marlboros 2; Jan. 5–Jr. Hockey: Oshawa 2, St. Michael's 1; Jan. 6–Sr. Hockey: Niagara Falls 3, National Sea Fleas 4; Jan. 7–Jr. Hockey: Jr. Varsity 1, St. Michael's 2; Jan. 7–NHL: Detroit 6, Leafs 1; Jan. 7–Sr. Hockey: Parkdale Canoe Club 4, Toronto Canoe Club 3; Jan. 9–Jr. Hockey: Danforth 4, Toronto Native Sons 11; Jan. 9–Jr. Hockey: Oshawa 4, Toronto Lions 5; Jan. 10–NHL: Rangers 2, Leafs 3; Jan. 11–Hockey: Lower Canada College, Jarvis Collegiate; Jan. 11–Jr. Hockey: Toronto Canoe Club 3, St. Michael's 4; Jan. 11–Jr. Hockey: Parkdale Canoe Club 1, Jr. Marlboros 2; Jan. 12–Wrestling: Nick Lutze vs. Joe Malcewicz; Jan. 13–Hockey: U. of T. Schools 1, St. Michael's "B" 1; Jan. 13–Sr. Hockey: Port Colborne 4, Sr. Marlboros 1; Jan. 14–Jr. Hockey: National Sea Fleas 3, Jr. Varsity 2; Jan. 14–Jr. Hockey: Toronto Canoe Club 1, Jr. Marlboros 4; Jan. 16–Amateur Boxing Night; Jan. 17–Jr. Hockey: Toronto Native Sons 7, Toronto Lions 4; Jan. 17–Jr. Hockey: Oshawa 7, Danforth 2; Jan. 18–Hockey: Upper Canada College 0, St. Michael's "B" 5; Jan. 18–Jr. Hockey: Parkdale Canoe Club 2, St. Michael's 2; Jan. 18–Jr. Hockey: National Sea Fleas 9, Jr. Marlboros 2; Jan. 19–NHL: Boston 0, Leafs 3; Jan. 20–Jr. Hockey: Parkdale Canoe Club 2, National Sea Fleas 1; Jan. 20–Jr. Hockey: Oshawa 3, St. Michael's 4; Jan. 21–Hockey: Maple Leafs vs. Four OHA Senior Teams (benefit game); Jan. 21–Sr. Hockey: Niagara Falls 3, Sr. Marlboros 1; Jan. 23–Hockey: Upper Canada College 5, Jarvis Collegiate 4; Jan. 23–Sr. Hockey: Port Colborne 0, National Sea Fleas 1; Jan. 24–Jr. Hockey: Danforth 2, Toronto Lions 6; Jan. 24–Jr. Hockey: Oshawa 5, Toronto Native Sons 4; Jan. 26–Wrestling: The Utica Panther vs. Dan Koloff; Jan. 27–Hockey: St. Michael's "B" 2, Jarvis Collegiate 1; Jan. 27–Sr. Hockey: National Sea Fleas 1, Sr. Marlboros 2; Jan. 28–Jr. Hockey: National Sea Fleas 1, St. Michael's 1; Jan. 28–NHL: Canadiens 2, Leafs 4; Jan. 30–Hockey: U. of T. Schools 5, Jarvis Collegiate 1; Jan. 30–Sr. Hockey: Hamilton 5, National Sea Fleas 1; Jan. 31–NHL: Americans 1, Leafs 7; Feb. 1–Hockey: Upper Canada College 0, St. Michael's "B"1; Feb. 1–Jr. Hockey: National Sea Fleas 5, Jr. Marlboros 2; Feb. 2–Sr. Hockey: Sr. Varsity 2, St. Michael's 1; Feb. 3–Hockey: Jarvis Collegiate 3, St. Michael's "B" 2; Feb. 3–Sr. Hockey: Kitchener-Waterloo 3, Sr. Marlboros 3; Feb. 4–Jr. Hockey: National Sea Fleas 0, Jr. Marlboros 1; Feb. 4–NHL: Chicago 2, Leafs 2; Feb. 6–Hockey: St. Columbia 3, Riverside Grads 4; Feb. 6–Jr. Hockey: Oshawa 2, Toronto Native Sons 4; Feb. 7–Hockey: U. of T. Schools 4, Upper Canada College 1; Feb. 8–Jr. Hockey: National Sea Fleas 1, Jr. Marlboros 0; Feb. 9–Wrestling: Harold Cantonwire vs. Count Zarynoff; Feb. 10–Jr. Hockey: St. Columbia 3, Riverside Grads 4; Feb. 10–Sr. Hockey: Hamilton 1, Sr. Marlboros 1; Feb. 11–Hockey: U. of T. Schools 1, St. Micahel's "B" 2; Feb. 11–Hockey: Sr. Varsity 1, St. Michael's 0; Feb. 11–NHL: Rangers 1, Leafs 2; Feb. 13–Amateur Boxing Night; Feb. 15–Hockey: Trinity College 2, Upper Canada College 3; Feb. 15–Hockey: Oshawa 8, U. of T. Schools 0; Feb. 16–Wrestling: Ed Don George vs. Joe Malcewicz; Feb. 17–Sr. Hockey: Niagara Falls 3, National Sea Fleas 2; Feb. 18–NHL: Detroit 1, Leafs 4; Feb. 21–Jr. Hockey: Owen Sound 0, National Sea Fleas 7; Feb. 23–Amateur Boxing Night; Feb. 25–NHL: Americans 1, Leafs 5; Feb. 28–NHL: Canadiens 2, Leafs 1; Mar. 1–Jr. Hockey: Newmarket 0, National Sea Fleas 0; Mar. 3–Sr. Hockey: Niagara Falls 3, Sr. Marlboros 1; Mar. 4–Jr. Hockey: Newmarket 3, National Sea Fleas 2; Mar. 4–NHL: Maroons 2, Leafs 4; Mar. 10–Jr. Hockey: Oakville 1, St. Columbia 0; Mar. 11–NHL: Boston 6, Leafs 2; Mar. 11–Sr. Hockey: Stratford 2, Newmarket 2; Mar. 13–Amateur Boxing Night; Mar. 14–Sr. Hockey: Stratford 2, Newmarket 3; Mar. 15–Jr. Hockey: Timmins 1, Hamilton 3; Mar. 16–Jr. Hockey: Stratford 1, Newmarket 3; Mar. 17–Sr. Hockey: Niagara Falls 1, Port Colborne 0; Mar. 18–Jr. Hockey: Newmarket 1, Sudbury 0 (All-Ontario Jr. Finals); Mar. 18–NHL: Ottawa 2, Leafs 6; Mar. 20–Jr. Hockey: Newmarket 2, Sudbury 1 (All-Ontario Jr. Finals); Mar. 21–Canadian National Track Championships; Mar. 22–Jr. Hockey: Newmarket 1, Sudbury 0 (All-Ontario Jr. Finals); Mar. 23–NHL: Chicago 2, Leafs 2; Mar. 24–Wrestling: Jim Browning vs. Sandor Szabo; Mar. 25–Jr. Hockey: Newmarket 1, Ottawa Shamrocks 0; Mar. 25–Jr. Hockey: Niagara Falls 2, Ottawa Rideaus 0; Mar. 27–Amateur Boxing Night; Mar. 29–Sr. Hockey: Niagara Falls 1, Moncton 0; Mar. 30–NHL: Boston 2, Leafs 1; Mar. 31–Sr. Hockey: Niagara Falls 1, Moncton 4; Apr. 1–Jr. Hockey: Montreal 0, Newmarket 1 (Memorial Cup Eastern Finals); Apr. 1–NHL: Boston 3, Leafs 5; Apr. 3–NHL: Boston 0, Leafs 1; Apr. 3–Tennis: Bill Tilden vs. Ellsworth Vines; Apr. 4–Jr. Hockey: Regina 1, Newmarket 2 (Memorial Cup Finals); Apr. 6–Jr. Hockey: Regina 1, Newmarket 2 (Memorial Cup Finals); Apr. 8–NHL: Rangers 3, Leafs 1 (Stanley Cup Finals); Apr. 11–NHL: Rangers 2, Leafs 3 (Stanley Cup Finals); Apr. 13–NHL: Rangers 1,

Leafs 0 (Stanley Cup-winning game); Apr. 18–Golden Gloves Tournament; Apr. 20–Wrestling: Joe Savoldi vs. Sammy Stein; May 5–Jehovah's Witnesses Convention; Oct. 2–Amateur Boxing Night; Oct. 5–Wrestling: Rudy Dusek vs. Mayes McLain; Oct. 12–Wrestling: Jim Browning vs. Jack Washburn; Oct. 16–Amateur Boxing Night; Oct. 19–Wrestling: The Utica Panther vs. Jack Washburn; Oct. 23–Amateur Boxing Night; Oct. 26–Wrestling: The Utica Panther vs. Jim Browning; Nov. 2–Wrestling: Joe Savoldi vs. Jim Browning; Nov. 6–NHL: Simon Pures 7, Newlyweds 4 (Maple Leafs' intrasquad game); Nov. 9–NHL: Boston 1, Leafs 6; Nov. 10–Wrestling: Ed Don George vs. Wee Willie Davis; Nov. 11–NHL: Rangers 3, Leafs 4; Nov. 13–Amateur Boxing Night; Nov. 14–Jr. Hockey: Niagara Falls 1, West Toronto 3; Nov. 15–Jr. Hockey: Toronto Young Rangers 15, Toronto Native Sons 5; Nov. 15–Jr. Hockey: Stratford 9, Toronto Canoe Club 4; Nov. 16–Jr. Hockey: St. Michael's Preps 6, U. of T. Schools 2; Nov. 16–Jr. Hockey: Toronto Lions 2, Preston 1; Nov. 17–Sr. Hockey: Port Colborne 0, Sr. Marlboros 7; Nov. 18–Jr. Hockey: Galt 6, U. of T. Schools 1; Nov. 18–Jr. Hockey: Oshawa 6, Parkdale Canoe Club 1; Nov. 18–NHL: Ottawa 1, Leafs 4; Nov. 20–Jr. Hockey: West Toronto 2, St. Michael's 3; Nov. 20–Jr. Hockey: Toronto Young Rangers 4, Stratford 2; Nov. 21–Sr. Hockey: Hamilton 1, Toronto Torontos 3; Nov. 22–Jr. Hockey: Toronto Lions 2, St. Michael's 6; Nov. 22–Jr. Hockey: Galt 1, Oshawa 2; Nov. 23–Wrestling: Rudy Dusek vs. Joe Malcewicz; Nov. 24–Amateur Boxing Night; Nov. 25–Jr. Hockey: St. Michael's Preps 2, Toronto Young Rangers 10; Nov. 25–Jr. Hockey: St. Michael's 4, Oshawa 4; Nov. 25–NHL: Canadiens 1, Leafs 0; Nov. 27–Sr. Hockey: Sr. Varsity 5, West Toronto 7; Nov. 28–NHL: Americans 3, Leafs 7; Nov. 29–Jr. Hockey: St. Michael's 6, Oshawa 6; Nov. 30–Wrestling: Rudy Dusek vs. Joe Malcewicz; Dec. 1–Sr. Hockey: Toronto Torontos 2, West Toronto 3; Dec. 2–Jr. Hockey: Oshawa 4, St. Michael's 10; Dec. 2–NHL: Maroons 3, Leafs 8; Dec. 4–Hockey: Cities Service 3, McColl Frontenacs 4; Dec. 4–Hockey: British Consols 3, Canada Cycle 2; Dec. 5–Sr. Hockey: Niagara Falls 5, Toronto Torontos 5; Dec. 6–Jr. Hockey: St. Michael's 4, Toronto Young Rangers 7; Dec. 7–Hockey: UCC Old Boys 11, UCC New Boys 8; Dec. 8–Sr. Hockey: Kitchener-Waterloo 3, Toronto Torontos 5; Dec. 9–Jr. Hockey: St. Michael's 13, Toronto Young Rangers 4; Dec. 9–NHL: Chicago 0, Leafs 1; Dec. 11–Hockey: Cities Service 8, Canada Cycle 4; Dec. 11–Hockey: McColl Frontenacs 1, British Consols 6; Dec. 12–Hockey: Sr. Varsity 1, Toronto Torontos 13; Dec. 13–Jr. Hockey: Toronto Canoe Club 1, Parkdale Canoe Club 10; Dec. 13–Jr. Hockey: Toronto Young Rangers 11, Jr. Varsity 6; Dec. 14–Wrestling: Jim Browning vs. Rudy Dusek; Dec. 15–Jr. Hockey: Port Colborne 1, West Toronto 1; Dec. 16–Jr. Hockey: Toronto Lions 6, Toronto Native Sons 1; Dec. 16–Jr. Hockey: West Toronto 2, St. Michael's 6; Dec. 16–NHL: Canadiens 1, Leafs 3; Dec. 18–Hockey: British Consols 6, Cities Service 1; Dec. 18–Hockey: McColl Frontenacs 1, Canada Cycle 4; Dec. 19–Jr. Hockey: Hamilton 3, West Toronto 3; Dec. 20–Jr. Hockey: Toronto Lions 3, West Toronto 2; Dec. 20–Jr. Hockey: Toronto Native Sons 3, St. Michael's 4; Dec. 21–Wrestling: Jim Browning vs. George Zaharias; Dec. 23–Jr. Hockey: Toronto Lions 5, Toronto Canoe Club 1; Dec. 23–Jr. Hockey: Oshawa 2, Parkdale Canoe Club 1; Dec. 23–NHL: Maroons 2, Leafs 8; Dec. 25–Hockey: Canada Cycle 1, British Consols 9; Dec. 25–Hockey: McColl Frontenacs 6, Cities Service 5; Dec. 26–Sr. Hockey: West Toronto 2, Toronto Torontos 0; Dec. 27–Jr. Hockey: Toronto Native Sons 1, Toronto Young Rangers 7; Dec. 27–Jr. Hockey: West Toronto 1, Parkdale Canoe Club 11; Dec. 29–Jr. Hockey: Kitchener-Waterloo 3, West Toronto 0; Dec. 30–Jr. Hockey: Toronto Native Sons 8, Toronto Canoe Club 6; Dec. 30–Jr. Hockey: Oshawa 9, West Toronto 2; Dec. 30–NHL: Detroit 1, Leafs 8.

1934 • Jan. 1–Hockey: Canada Cycle 1, Cities Service 2; Jan. 1–Hockey: British Consols 3, McColl Frontenacs 1; Jan. 2–Jr. Hockey: Hamilton 2, West Toronto 1; Jan. 3–Jr. Hockey: Toronto Native Sons 12, Jr. Varsity 4; Jan. 3–Jr. Hockey: St. Michael's 10, Toronto Young Rangers 5; Jan. 4–Wrestling: Rudy Dusek vs. Blue Sun Jennings; Jan. 5–Sr. Hockey: Niagara Falls 4, Toronto Torontos 3; Jan. 6–Jr. Hockey: Parkdale Canoe Club 2, Toronto Native Sons 2; Jan. 6–Jr. Hockey: Oshawa 7, Toronto Canoe Club 3; Jan. 6–NHL: Ottawa 3, Leafs 7; Jan. 8–Hockey: McColl Frontenacs, Canada Cycle; Jan. 8–Hockey: Cities Service, British Consols; Jan. 9–Sr. Hockey: Port Colborne 2, Toronto Torontos 0; Jan. 10–Hockey: Upper Canada College 4, St. Michael's Preps 8; Jan. 10–Jr. Hockey: Toronto Lions 4, St. Michael's 5; Jan. 10–Jr. Hockey: Toronto Native Sons 6, West Toronto 3; Jan. 11–Wrestling: Jim Londos vs. Rudy Dusek; Jan. 12–Hockey: U. of T. Schools 3, St. Michael's Preps 7; Jan. 13–Jr. Hockey: Toronto Young Rangers 14, West Toronto 3; Jan. 13–Jr. Hockey: Oshawa 6, Jr. Varsity 2; Jan. 13–NHL: Americans 2, Leafs 2; Jan. 15–Hockey: Jarvis Collegiate 2, Upper Canada College 2; Jan. 15–Hockey: Cities Service 2, McColl Frontenacs 1; Jan. 15–Hockey: British Consols 12, Canada Cycle 3; Jan. 16–Jr. Hockey: Kitchener-Waterloo 3, West Toronto 6; Jan. 17–Jr. Hockey: St. Michael's 11, Toronto Native Sons 5; Jan. 17–Jr. Hockey: West Toronto 1, Toronto Lions 0; Jan. 18–NHL: Boston 2, Leafs 6; Jan. 19–Hockey: St. Michael's Preps 3, Jarvis Collegiate 2; Jan. 19–Sr. Hockey: West Toronto 0, Toronto Torontos 8; Jan. 20–Jr. Hockey: West Toronto 6, Jr. Varsity 4; Jan. 20–Jr. Hockey: Oshawa 2, St. Michael's 4; Jan. 20–NHL: Chicago 2, Leafs 2; Jan. 22–Hockey: Cities Service 6, Canada Cycle 4; Jan. 22–Hockey: British Consols 5, McColl Frontenacs 3; Jan. 23–NHL: Maroons 4, Leafs 8; Jan. 24–Hockey: U. of T. Schools 3, Jarvis Collegiate 2; Jan. 24–Jr. Hockey: Toronto Native Sons 5, Toronto Lions 3; Jan. 24–Jr. Hockey: St. Michael's 6, West Toronto 2; Jan. 25–Wrestling: Rudy Dusek vs. George Zaharias; Jan. 26–Hockey: St. Michael's Preps 6, Upper Canada College 0; Jan. 26–Jr. Hockey: West Toronto 1, Niagara Falls 1; Jan. 27–Jr. Hockey: Jr. Varsity 2, St. Michael's 18; Jan. 27–Jr. Hockey: Oshawa 3, Toronto Young Rangers 2; Jan. 27–NHL: Detroit 2, Leafs 2; Jan. 29–Hockey: Jarvis Collegiate 1, St. Michael's Preps 9; Jan. 29–Hockey: British Consols 1, Cities Service 6; Jan. 29–Hockey: Canada Cycle 3, McColl Frontenacs 2; Jan. 30–Jr. Hockey: Port Colborne 1, West Toronto 2; Jan. 31–Hockey: U. of T. Schools 7, Upper Canada College 0; Jan. 31–Jr. Hockey: Toronto Lions 2, Toronto Young Rangers 7; Jan. 31–Jr. Hockey: West Toronto 1, Toronto Canoe Club 3; Feb. 1–Wrestling: Flying Tackle Night; Feb. 2–Hockey: Upper Canada College 8, Jarvis Collegiate 5; Feb. 2–Sr. Hockey: Hamilton 0, Toronto Torontos 2; Feb. 3–Jr. Hockey: Oshawa 15, Toronto Lions 0; Feb. 3–Jr. Hockey: St. Michael's 4, Toronto Canoe Club 1; Feb. 3–NHL: Ottawa 4, Leafs 8; Feb. 5–Hockey: Canada Cycle 1, British Consols 1; Feb. 5–Hockey: McColl Frontenacs 2, Cities Service 5; Feb. 6–North American Speedskating Championships; Feb. 7–Hockey: St. Michael's Preps 9, U. of T. Schools 1; Feb. 7–North American Speedskating Championships; Feb. 8–Jr. Hockey: St. Michael's 7, Toronto Lions 6; Feb. 8–Jr. Hockey: West Toronto 2, Toronto Native Sons 11; Feb. 9–Hockey: De La Salle 2, St. Michael's Preps 14; Feb. 9–Sr. Hockey: West Toronto 4, Toronto Torontos 1; Feb. 10–Jr. Hockey: Toronto Lions 6, Parkdale Canoe Club 2; Feb. 10–Jr. Hockey: Oshawa 7, Toronto Native Sons 3; Feb. 10–NHL: Canadiens 2, Leafs 4; Feb. 12–Hockey: De La Salle 2, St. Michael's Preps 11; Feb. 12–Hockey: Canada Cycle 4, Cities Service 5; Feb. 12–Hockey: British Consols 3, McColl Frontenacs 1; Feb. 13–Jr. Hockey: Toronto Young Rangers 4, Parkdale Canoe Club 2; Feb. 13–Jr. Hockey: Jr. Varsity 1, West Toronto 3; Feb. 14–NHL: Ace Team 7, NHL All-Stars 3 (Ace Bailey benefit game); Feb. 15–Wrestling: Jim Browning vs. George Zaharias; Feb. 16–Jr. Hockey: St. Michael's 10, Markham 5; Feb. 16–Sr. Hockey: Kitchener-Waterloo 0, Toronto Torontos 4; Feb. 17–Jr. Hockey: St. Michael's 8, Oshawa 2; Feb. 17–Jr. Hockey: Parkdale Canoe Club 1, Toronto Young Rangers 9; Feb. 17–NHL: Boston 4, Leafs 6; Feb. 19–Hockey: McColl Frontenacs 5, Canada Cycle 4; Feb. 19–Hockey: Cities Service 2, British Consols 7; Feb. 20–Hockey: St. Michael's Preps 6, Barrie 2; Feb. 20–Sr. Hockey: Sr. Varsity 3, Toronto Torontos 13; Feb. 21–Hockey: Upper Canada College 3, Pickering College 5; Feb. 21–Jr. Hockey: Oshawa 4, St. Michael's 10; Feb. 22–Wrestling: Jim Landos vs. Sandor Szabo; Feb. 23–Sr. Hockey: Hamilton 3, Toronto Torontos 3; Feb. 24–Jr. Hockey: St. Michael's 6, Toronto Young Rangers 0; Feb. 24–NHL: Rangers 3, Leafs 8; Feb. 26–Hockey: British Consols 6, Canada Cycle 4; Feb. 26–Hockey: Cities Service 9, McColl Frontenacs 2; Feb. 27–Jr. Hockey: Niagara Falls 2, West Toronto 2; Feb. 28–Hockey: Trinity College 2, Upper Canada College 4; Feb. 28–Hockey: St. Michael's 7, Toronto Young Rangers 3; Mar. 2–Hockey: St. Michael's Preps 2, Owen Sound 1; Mar. 2–Hockey: Ridley College 3, Upper Canada College 2; Mar. 3–Jr. Hockey: St. Michael's 7, Stratford 0; Mar. 3–NHL: Detroit 4, Leafs 6; Mar. 5–Hockey: Cities Service 5, Canada Cycle 4; Mar. 5–Hockey: McColl Frontenacs 0, British Consols 4; Mar. 6–Hockey: St. Michael's Preps 5, Peterbourgh 4; Mar. 10–Hockey: St. Michael's Preps 3, Preston 5; Mar. 10–NHL: Americans 5, Leafs 8; Mar. 12–Hockey: British Consols 5, Cities Service 2; Mar. 12–Hockey: Canada Cycle 6, McColl Frontenacs 2; Mar. 14–Wrestling: Jim Browning vs. Jim McMillan; Mar. 15–Hockey: St. Michael's Preps 3, St. Michael's 12; Mar. 15–NHL: Chicago 2, Leafs 1; Mar. 17–Jr. Hockey: St. Michael's 13, New Liskeard 3; Mar. 17–NHL: Rangers 3, Leafs 3; Mar. 19–Jr. Hockey: New Liskeard 3, St. Michael's 16; Mar. 21–Jr. Hockey: St. Michael's 8, Ottawa Shamrocks 2; Mar. 22–NHL: Detroit 2, Leafs 1; Mar. 23–Hockey: British Consols, Cities Service; Mar. 24–NHL: Detroit 6, Leafs 3; Mar. 24–Sr. Hockey: Ottawa New Edinburghs 3, Hamilton 3; Mar. 27–Jr. Hockey: St. Michael's 12, Charlottetown 2; Mar. 28–Sr. Hockey: Hamilton 2, Moncton 1; Mar. 29–Wrestling: Rudy Dusek vs. Henri Deglane; Mar. 30–Hockey: British Consols 2, Cities Service 2; Mar. 31–Jr. Hockey: St. Michael's 7, Charlottetown 2; Mar. 31–Sr. Hockey: Fort William 3, Moncton 2 (Allan Cup Finals); Apr. 2–Sr. Hockey: Fort William 2, Moncton 4 (Allan Cup Finals); Apr. 3–Hockey: British Consols 4, Cities Service 5; Apr. 4–Sr. Hockey: Fort William 1, Moncton 5 (Allan Cup Finals); Apr. 5–Hockey: British Consols 1, Cities Service 5; Apr. 8–Sr. Hockey: Moncton 1, Detroit White Stars 2; Apr. 9–Sr. Hockey: Moncton 4, Detroit White Stars 2; Apr. 10–Jr. Hockey: St. Michael's 5, Cities Service 5; Apr. 11–Sr. Hockey: Moncton 13, Detroit White Stars 3; Apr. 12–Jr. Hockey: St. Michael's 3, Cities Service 6; Apr. 14–Jr. Hockey: St. Michael's 4, Cities Service 5; Apr. 16–Amateur Boxing Night; Apr. 18–Hockey: Cities Service 5, Royal York 4; Apr. 19–Wrestling: Joe Savoldi vs. Rudy Dusek; Apr. 27–Independent Order of Foresters Pageant; Apr. 28–Toronto Girl Guides Rally; May 15-16–Catholic School Board Pageant; May 21-22: Dominion Boxing Championships; May 24–Boy Scouts Pageant; June 9–Wrestling: The Masked Marvel vs. Vic Christie; July 8–Jehovah's Witnesses Convention; Sept. 7–Aimee Semple McPherson Lecture; Sept. 21–Music: Eddie Duchin Orchestra; Oct. 4–Wrestling: Jim Browning vs. Hans Steinke; Oct. 11–Wrestling: Earl McCready vs. John Katan; Oct. 18–Wrestling: Earl McCready vs. Rudy Dusek; Oct. 21-27: Six-day Bicycle Race; Nov. 5–NHL: Leaf Regulars 4, Leaf Recruits 4 (Maple Leafs intrasquad game); Nov. 6–Boxing: Frankie Genovese vs. Eddie Dempsey; Nov. 7–Wrestling: Joe Savadoldi vs. Gino Garibaldi; Nov. 8–NHL: Boston 3, Leafs 5; Nov. 10–NHL: Canadiens 1, Leafs 2; Nov. 13–Amateur Boxing Night; Nov. 14–Wrestling: Ed Don George vs. Pat O'Shocker; Nov. 17–NHL: Maroons 1, Leafs 2; Nov. 19–Jr. Hockey: Galt 2, West Toronto 4; Nov. 19–Jr. Hockey: Markham 1, Young Rangers 6; Nov. 20–Jr. Hockey: Guelph 4, Native Sons 0; Nov. 20–Jr. Hockey: Barrie 3, St. Michael's 5; Nov. 21–Boxing: Premier Athletic Commisson Showdown; Nov. 22–Wrestling: Jim Landos vs. Joe Savoldi; Nov. 23–Sr. Hockey: Port Colborne 2, Sr. Marlboros 2; Nov. 24–NHL: Detroit 2, Leafs 3; Nov. 25–Jr. Hockey: Parkdale Canoe Club 2, Toronto Lions 7; Nov. 25–Jr. Hockey: Oshawa 8, U. of T. Schools 0; Nov. 26–Jr. Hockey: U. of T. Schools 3, Jr. Marlboros 2; Nov. 26–Jr. Hockey: Toronto Canoe Club 1, St. Michael's 1; Nov. 27–Jr. Hockey: West Toronto 3, Young Rangers 0; Nov. 27–Jr. Hockey: Guelph 8, St. Michael's "B" 2; Nov. 29–Jr. Hockey: Oshawa 5, Toronto Lions 1; Nov. 29–Jr. Hockey: U. of T. Schools 0, St. Michael's 10; Nov. 30–Sr. Hockey: Oakville 4, Sr. Marlboros 6; Dec. 1–Jr. Hockey: Oshawa 2, St. Michael's 4; Dec. 1–Jr. Hockey: Guelph 5, West Toronto 1; Dec. 1–NHL: St. Louis Eagles 3, Leafs 4; Dec. 2–Toronto District Labor Forum w/Tim Buck; Dec. 3–Hockey: McColl Frontenacs 3, Dominions 1; Dec. 3–Hockey: Cities Service 3, British Consols 0; Dec. 4–Jr. Hockey: Guelph 2, St. Michael's 9; Dec. 5–Hockey: UCC Old Boys, UCC New Boys; Dec. 6–Wrestling: Dick Shikat vs. Count George Zarynoff; Dec. 7–Sr. Hockey: Hamilton 3, Sr. Marlboros 6; Dec. 8–Jr. Hockey: Sudbury 3, St. Michael's 2; Dec. 8–NHL: Rangers 5, Leafs 2; Dec. 10–Hockey: Dominions 1, Cities Service 7; Dec. 10–Hockey: McColl Frontenacs 3, British Consols 8; Dec. 11–Jr. Hockey: Sudbury 4, St. Michael's 3; Dec. 12–Amateur Boxing Night; Dec. 13–Sr. Hockey: Hamilton 5, Sr. Marlboros 4; Dec. 14–Jr. Hockey: Toronto Native Sons 3, Toronto Lions 4; Dec. 14–Jr. Hockey: Oshawa 5, West Toronto 1; Dec. 15–NHL: Americans 3, Leafs 4; Dec. 16–Hockey: Cities Service 2, Dominions 5; Dec. 16–Hockey: Oshawa 1, McColl Frontenacs 4; Dec. 17–Jr. Hockey: Toronto Cubs 7, U. of T. Schools 1; Dec. 17–Jr. Hockey: Parkdale Canoe Club 3, Young Rangers 4; Dec. 19–Jr. Hockey: Toronto Lions 4, West Toronto 3; Dec. 19–Jr. Hockey: Toronto Native Sons 1, St. Michael's 5; Dec. 20–Sr. Hockey: Sr. Varsity 3, Sr. Marlboros 4; Dec. 21–Jr. Hockey: Toronto Lions 4, St. Michael's 6; Dec. 21–Jr. Hockey: Oshawa 8, Young Rangers 0; Dec. 22–NHL: Chicago 0, Leafs 1; Dec. 26–Hockey: Cities Service 5, Oshawa 4; Dec. 26–Hockey: McColl Frontenacs 2, Dominions 4; Dec. 27–Wrestling: Vic Christie vs. John Katam; Dec. 28–Sr. Hockey: Oakville 3, Sr. Marlboros 3; Dec. 29–Jr. Hockey: Oshawa 11, Toronto Lions 2; Dec. 29–Jr. Hockey: Toronto Native Sons 1, West Toronto 4; Dec. 29–NHL: Maroons 4, Leafs 2; Dec. 30–Music: Don Redman's Orchestra; Dec. 31–New Year's Eve Dance.

1935 • Jan. 1–NHL: Detroit 1, Leafs 0; Jan. 2–Jr. Hockey: Jr. Varsity 1, Young Rangers 5; Jan. 2–Jr. Hockey: Parkdale 3, Toronto Cubs 2; Jan. 3–Wrestling: Vic Christie vs. John Katam; Jan. 4–Sr. Hockey: Hamilton 6, Oakville 3; Jan. 5–Jr. Hockey: Toronto Native Sons 0, Toronto Lions 9; Jan. 5–Jr. Hockey: West Toronto 3, St. Michael's 3; Jan. 5–NHL: Canadiens 1, Leafs 3; Jan. 7–Hockey: Northern Vocational 6, Jarvis Collegiate 3; Jan. 7–Hockey: McColl Frontenacs 3, Cities Service 4; Jan. 7–Hockey: Dominions 4, British Consols 3; Jan. 8–Jr. Hockey: Young Rangers 3, Parkdale 5; Jan. 8–Jr. Hockey: Jr. Varsity 2, Toronto Cubs 2; Jan. 9–Jr. Hockey: Toronto Lions 9, West Toronto 3; Jan. 9–Jr. Hockey: Oshawa 6, St. Michael's 0; Jan. 10–Wrestling: George Zaharias vs. Jack Donovan; Jan. 11–Hockey: Northern Vocational 3, St. Michaels "B" 8; Jan. 11–Sr. Hockey: Oakville 1, Sr. Varsity 1; Jan. 12–Jr. Hockey: St. Michael's 1, Toronto Lions 3; Jan. 12–Jr. Hockey: Oshawa 3, West Toronto 1; Jan. 12–NHL: Chicago 1, Leafs 5; Jan.

14–Hockey: U. of T. Schools 3, Jarvis Collegiate 5; Jan. 14–Hockey: Dominions 2, Cities Service 5; Jan. 14–Hockey: McColl Frontenacs 2, British Consols 5; Jan. 15–Jr. Hockey: St. Michael's 10, Native Sons 5; Jan. 15–Jr. Hockey: West Toronto 3, Toronto Lions 5; Jan. 16–Hockey: Jarvis Collegiate, St. Michael's "B" 2; Jan. 16–Jr. Hockey: Jr. Varisty 3, Parkdale 4; Jan. 16–Jr. Hockey: Young Rangers 0, Toronto Cubs 1; Jan. 18–Hockey: U. of T. Schools 5, Upper Canada College 4; Jan. 18–Sr. Hockey: Port Colborne 3, Sr. Marlboros 5; Jan. 19–Jr. Hockey: Jr. Varsity 3, Young Rangers 4; Jan. 19–Jr. Hockey: Parkdale 3, Toronto Cubs 2; Jan. 19–NHL: St. Louis Eagles 2, Leafs 6; Jan. 21–Hockey: Upper Canada College 6, Jarvis Collegiate 6; Jan. 21–Hockey: McColl Frontenacs 3, Dominions 5; Jan. 21–Hockey: British Consols 2, Cities Service 4; Jan. 22–Hockey: U. of T. Schools 3, St. Michael's "B" 4; Jan. 22–Jr. Hockey: West Toronto 2, St. Michael's 4; Jan. 22–Jr. Hockey: Native Sons 4, Toronto Lions 12; Jan. 23–Amateur Boxing Night; Jan. 24–Wrestling: Vic Christie vs. George Zaharias; Jan. 25–Hockey: Jarvis Collegiate 6, St. Michael's "B" 9; Jan. 25–Sr. Hockey: Sr. Varsity 5, Sr. Marlboros 12; Jan. 26–Jr. Hockey: West Toronto 1, Toronto Lions 2; Jan. 26–Jr. Hockey: Native Sons 0, St. Michael's 7; Jan. 26–NHL: Detroit 0, Leafs 0; Jan. 28–Hockey: Northern Vocational 1, Upper Canada College 3; Jan. 28–Hockey: British Consols 4, Dominions 3; Jan. 28–Hockey: McColl Frontenacs 4, Cities Service 6; Jan. 29–Jr. Hockey: Young Rangers 4, Parkdale 4; Jan. 29–Jr. Hockey: Jr. Varsity 2, Toronto Cubs 4; Jan. 30–Wrestling: Rudy Dusek vs. Vic Christie; Jan. 31–NHL: Rangers 3, Leafs 2; Feb. 1–Hockey: Jarvis Collegiate 9, Upper Canada Collge 2; Feb. 1–Sr. Hockey: Hamilton 8, Sr. Marlboros 5; Feb. 2–Jr. Hockey: St. Michael's 4, West Toronto 1; Feb. 2–Jr. Hockey: Oshawa 1, Toronto Lions 5; Feb. 2–NHL: Americans 2, Leafs 1; Feb. 4–Hockey: McColl Frontenacs 5, Cities Service 1; Feb. 4–Hockey: Oshawa 2, British Consols 5; Feb. 5–Sr. Hockey: Port Colborne 2, Oakville 3; Feb. 6–Wrestling: Vic Christie vs. Ernie Dusek; Feb. 7–NHL: Boston 4, Leafs 2; Feb. 8–Jr. Hockey: Bradford 0, Jr. Marlboros 4; Feb. 8–Sr. Hockey: Oakville 3, Sr. Marlboros 5; Feb. 9–Jr. Hockey: Oshawa 5, St. Michael's 3; Feb. 9–NHL: Maroons 2, Leafs 4; Feb. 11–Hockey: Dominions 3, Oshawa 3; Feb. 11–Hockey: McColl Frontenacs 2, British Consols 3; Feb. 12–Jr. Hockey: Parkdale 2, Toronto Cubs 2; Feb. 12–Jr. Hockey: Jr. Varsity 3, Young Rangers 7; Feb. 13–Hockey: U. of T. Schools 1, St. Michael's "B" 2; Feb. 13–Jr. Hockey: St. Michael's 3, Toronto Lions 0; Feb. 14–Wrestling: Jim Londos vs. Vic Christie; Feb. 15–Sr. Hockey: Hamilton 6, Oakville 1; Feb. 16–Jr. Hockey: St. Michael's 2, Toronto Lions 5; Feb. 16–NHL: Rangers 1, Leafs 5; Feb. 18–Hockey: Oshawa 3, Cities Service 8; Feb. 18–Hockey: Dominions 3, British Consols 5; Feb. 19–Jr. Hockey: St. Michael's 2, Toronto Lions 3; Feb. 20–Sr. Hockey: Oakville 2, Sr. Marlboros 6; Feb. 21–Wrestling: Dan O'Mahony vs. Rudy Dusek; Feb. 22–Hockey: British Consols 1, Cities Service 0; Feb. 22–Hockey: McColl Frontenacs 3, Dominions 2; Feb. 22–Hockey: Milton 0, St. Michael's "B" 11; Feb. 23–Jr. Hockey: Oshawa 10, Toronto Lions 2; Feb. 23–NHL: Chicago 1, Leafs 4; Feb. 25–Hockey: British Consols 2, Dominions 4; Feb. 25–Hockey: McColl Frontenacs 5, Oshawa 4; Feb. 26–Jr. Hockey: Young Rangers 9, Parkdale 1; Feb. 27–Hockey: Upper Canada College 6, Trinity College; Feb. 27–Sr. Hockey: Oakville 0, Sr. Marlboros 2; Mar. 1–Sr. Hockey: Oakville 4, Sr. Marlboros 3; Mar. 2–Jr. Hockey: Oshawa 3, Young Rangers 4; Mar. 2–NHL: Americans 0, Leafs 6; Mar. 4–Hockey: Dominions 7, Cities Service 3; Mar. 4–Hockey: British Consols 8, McColl Frontenacs 2; Mar. 5–Toronto Inter-Religious Church Service; Mar. 6-8–Ice Show: Toronto Winter Carnival; Mar. 9–NHL: Boston 7, Leafs 4; Mar. 9–Sr. Hockey: Hamilton 1, Sr. Marlboros 12; Mar. 11–Hockey: Dominions 9, Oshawa 4; Mar. 11–Hockey: British Consols 6, Cities Service 3; Mar. 12–Jr. Hockey: Oshawa 3, Young Rangers 1; Mar. 13–Sr. Hockey: Hamilton 0, Sr. Marlboros 5; Mar. 14–Wrestling: Ernie Dusek vs. Vic Christie; Mar. 15–Sr. Hockey: Sudbury 4, Brockville 3; Mar. 16–Hockey: Niagara Falls 2, St. Michael's "B" 5; Mar. 16–NHL: Canadiens 3, Leafs 5; Mar. 18–Jr. Hockey: Oshawa 3, Kitchener 2; Mar. 19–NHL: St. Louis Eagles 3, Leafs 5; Mar. 20–Jr. Hockey: Sudbury 4, Oshawa 3; Mar. 20–Sr. Hockey: Sudbury 0, Sr. Marlboros 12; Mar. 22–Track and Field: Maple Leaf Athletic Games; Mar. 23–Jr. Hockey: Barrie 3, St. Michael's 5 (OHA "B" Finals); Mar. 23–Jr. Hockey: Sudbury 5, Oshawa 3 (OHA "A" Finals); Mar. 25–Hockey: McColl Frontenacs, Cities Service; Mar. 25–Hockey: British Consols, Oshawa; Mar. 27–Jr. Hockey: Sudbury 9, Verdun 4; Mar. 28–NHL: Boston 0, Leafs 3; Mar. 28–Sr. Hockey: Ottawa 0, Sr. Marlboros 11 (OHA Sr. Finals); Mar. 29–Jr. Hockey: Barrie 7, St. Michael's "B" 11 (OHA "B" Finals); Mar. 30–Jr. Hockey: Sudbury 3, Ottawa 0 (Memorial Cup East Finals); Mar. 30–NHL: Boston 1, Leafs 2; Apr. 1–Sr. Hockey: Montreal 2, Sr. Marlboros 5 (Allan Cup East Finals); Apr. 3–Wrestling: Dan O'Mahony vs. Ernie Dusek; Apr. 4–NHL: Maroons 3, Leafs 2 (Stanley Cup Finals); Apr. 5–Hockey: Cities Service 6, Dominions 4; Apr. 6–NHL: Maroons 3, Leafs 1 (Stanley Cup Finals); Apr. 8–Hockey: Cities Service 5, Dominions 2; Apr. 10–Hockey: Cities Service 12, Dominions 2; Apr. 11–Wrestling: George Zaharias vs. Little Beaver; Apr. 13–Hockey: Cities Service 1, British Consols 1 (Mercantile League Finals); Apr. 15–Hockey: British Consols 4, Cities Service 3 (Mercantile League Finals); Apr. 16–Ontario Amateur Boxing Championships; Apr. 17–Hockey: British Consols 3, Cities Service 2 (Mercantile League Finals); Apr. 18–Wrestling: Chief Little Wolf vs. Gino Gariboldi; Apr. 19–Tennis: Bill Tilden vs. Ellsworth Vines; Apr. 25–Wrestling: George Zaharias vs. Emil Dusek; Apr. 28–Boxing: Golden Gloves Tournament; Sept. 22-28: Six-day Bicycle Race; Oct. 5–Richard Byrd Lecture; Oct. 6–Salvation Army w/Evangeline Booth; Oct. 8–Liberal Party Rally w/Mackenzie King; Oct. 9–Conservative Election Rally w/R.B. Bennett; Oct. 11–Reconstructions Party Election Rally; Oct. 12–Public Meeting with Celebrities; Oct. 25-26–Music: Symphony and Radio City Ballet; Oct. 28–Nov. 2: Rameses Shrine Circus; Nov. 6–Amateur Boxing Night; Nov. 7–Wrestling: Lou Plummer vs. Vic Christie; Nov. 9–NHL: Americans 5, Leafs 5; Nov. 13–Boxing: Joe Louis Exhibition Bouts; Nov. 14–Wrestling: Lou Plummer vs. Ray Steele; Nov. 15–Sr. Hockey: Hamilton 1, Sr. Marlboros 4; Nov. 16–NHL: Rangers 2, Leafs 3; Nov. 18–Jr. Hockey: Jr. Marlboros 3, St. Michael's "B" 1; Nov. 18–Jr. Hockey: West Toronto 4, Young Rangers 1; Nov. 19–Jr. Hockey: Paris 2, Jr. Varsity 5; Nov. 19–Jr. Hockey: Stratford 0, Native Sons 1; Nov. 20–Amateur Boxing Night; Nov. 21–Jr. Hockey: Waterloo 0, Toronto Lions 1; Nov. 21–Jr. Hockey: Stayner 2, Scarboro 4; Nov. 22–Hockey: East York 0, Upper Canada College 11; Nov. 22–Sr. Hockey: Oakville 0, Sr. Marlboros 3; Nov. 23–Jr. Hockey: Jr. Varsity 1, St. Michael's "B" 8; Nov. 23–Jr. Hockey: Assumption College 7, Northern Vocational 1; Nov. 23–NHL: Maroons 5, Leafs 2; Nov. 25–Hockey: Toronto Goodyears 6, Dominions 1; Nov. 25–Hockey: McColl Frontenacs 1, British Consols 4; Nov. 26–Jr. Hockey: Stouffville 2, Jr. Marlboros 9; Nov. 26–Jr. Hockey: Barrie 2, West Toronto 9; Nov. 27–Music: Five-Piano Ensemble; Nov. 28–Wrestling: Dan O'Mahony vs. Lou Plummer; Nov. 29–Sr. Hockey: Port Colborne 2, Sr. Marlboros 3; Nov. 30–Jr. Hockey: Scarboro 1, Toronto Lions 2; Nov. 30–Jr. Hockey: Assumption College 4, Native Sons 4; Nov. 30–NHL: Canadiens 3, Leafs 8; Dec. 2–Hockey: Dominions 1, McColl Frontenacs 5; Dec. 2–Hockey: Toronto Goodyears 1, British Consols 3; Dec. 2–Jr. Hockey: Upper Canada College 2, Jr. Varsity 7; Dec. 3–Jr. Hockey: Assumption College 1, Native Sons 2; Dec. 3–Jr. Hockey: West Toronto 2, Toronto Lions 0; Dec. 4–Sr. Hockey: Port Colborne 1, Oakville 4; Dec. 5–Wrestling: George Zaharias vs. Vic Christie; Dec. 6–Amateur Boxing Night; Dec. 7–Jr. Hockey: Jr. Varsity 4, Jr. Marlboros 0; Dec. 7–NHL: Chicago 1, Leafs 2; Dec. 9–Hockey: Dominions 1, British Consols 6; Dec. 9–Hockey: Oshawa 10, McColl Frontenacs 3; Dec. 10–Hockey: UCC Old Boys, UCC New Boys; Dec. 11–Sr. Hockey: Hamilton 6, Oakville 1; Dec. 12–City of Toronto Boxing Championships; Dec. 13–Sr. Hockey: Oakville 4, Sr. Marlboros 4; Dec. 14–Jr. Hockey: Jr. Varsity, St. Michael's; Dec. 14–Jr. Hockey: West Toronto, Native Sons; Dec. 14–NHL: Detroit 4, Leafs 2; Dec. 16–Hockey: Dominions 5, McColl Frontenacs 5; Dec. 16–Hockey: British Consols 6, Goodyear Tires 5; Dec. 17–Jr. Hockey: West Toronto 4, St. Michael's 3; Dec. 18–Jr. Hockey: Jr. Varsity 2, Toronto Lions 3; Dec. 18–Jr. Hockey: Native Sons 4, Young Rangers 3; Dec. 19–NHL: Boston 0, Leafs 0; Dec. 19–Sr. Hockey: Oakville 4, Sr. Varsity 2; Dec. 20–Jr. Hockey: Toronto Lions 0, St. Michael's 5; Dec. 20–Jr. Hockey: Jr. Varsity 1, West Toronto 8; Dec. 21–NHL: Americans 3, Leafs 5; Dec. 22–Hockey: Dominions 4, Goodyear Tires 0; Dec. 22–Hockey: British Consols 3, McColl Frontenacs 1; Dec. 26–Wrestling: Don O'Mahony vs. Lou Plummer; Dec. 27–Jr. Hockey: Scarboro 1, Jr. Marlboros 7; Dec. 27–Sr. Hockey: Sr. Varsity 1, Sr. Marlboros 12; Dec. 28–Jr. Hockey: Young Rangers 2, Toronto Lions 0; Dec. 28–Jr. Hockey: Native Sons 3, West Toronto 2; Dec. 28–NHL: Rangers 3, Leafs 9; Dec. 30–Hockey: Dominions 7, Oshawa 1; Dec. 30–Hockey: McColls Frontenacs 5, Toronto Goodyears 4.

1936 • Jan. 1–Amateur Boxing Night; Jan. 2–Jr. Hockey: Toronto Lions 3, Native Sons 1; Jan. 2–Jr. Hockey: Young Rangers 0, West Toronto 2; Jan. 3–Sr. Hockey: Oakville 1, Sr. Marlboros 0; Jan. 4–Jr. Hockey: Toronto Lions 1, West Toronto 4; Jan. 4–Jr. Hockey: Native Sons 3, Young Rangers 1; Jan. 4–NHL: Maroons 1, Leafs 1; Jan. 6–Hockey: Oshawa 4, Toronto Goodyears 5; Jan. 6–Hockey: Dominions, British Consolls; Jan. 7–Sr. Hockey: Canadian Olympic Team 3, Sr. Marlboros 4; Jan. 8–Hockey: Upper Canada College 2, Northern Vocational 1; Jan. 8–Sr. Hockey: Hamilton 10, Oakville 2; Jan. 9–Wrestling: Joe Savoldi vs. Tom Alley; Jan. 10–Jr. Hockey: Upper Canada College 4, St. Michael's "B" 6; Jan. 10–Jr. Hockey: East York 1, Jr. Marlboros 11; Jan. 10–Sr. Hockey: Sr. Varsity 2, Sr. Marlboros 7; Jan. 11–Jr. Hockey: Jr. Varsity 0, Toronto Lions 3; Jan. 11–Jr. Hockey: Young Rangers 1, St. Michael's 5; Jan. 11–NHL: Canadiens 7, Leafs 3; Jan. 13–Hockey: Jarvis Collegiate 3, St. Michael's "B" 15; Jan. 13–Hockey: Oshawa 3, British Consols 4; Jan. 13–Hockey: McColls Frontenacs 2, Toronto Goodyears 4; Jan. 14–Jr. Hockey: Jr. Varsity 1, Native Sons 3; Jan. 14–Jr. Hockey: West Toronto 7, St. Michael's 3; Jan. 15–Amateur Boxing Night; Jan. 16–Wrestling: Ray Steele vs. Lou Plummer; Jan. 17–Jr. Hockey: U. of T. Schools, St. Michael's "B" 5; Jan. 17–Jr. Hockey: Stouffville 0, Jr. Marlboros 7; Jan. 17–Sr. Hockey: Oakville 1, Sr. Marlboros 2; Jan. 18–Jr. Hockey: Toronto Lions 2, St. Michael's 6; Jan. 18–Jr. Hockey: Native Sons 6, Jr. Varsity 0; Jan. 18–NHL: Boston 2, Leafs 5; Jan. 20–Hockey: Toronto Goodyears, Dominions; Jan. 20–Hockey: British Consols, McColls Frontenacs; Jan. 21–NHL: Canadiens, Leafs (Postponed due to death of King George V); Jan. 22–Hockey: U. of T. Schools 3, Upper Canada College 4; Jan. 22–Sr. Hockey: Hamilton 4, Sr. Marlboros 5; Jan. 23–Amateur Boxing Night; Jan. 24–Hockey: Upper Canada College 5, St. Michael's "B" 3; Jan. 24–Sr. Hockey: Oakville 6, Sr. Varsity 4; Jan. 25–Jr. Hockey: West Toronto 5, Young Rangers 1; Jan. 25–Jr. Hockey: Native Sons 1, St. Michael's 5; Jan. 25–NHL: Detroit 1, Leafs 6; Jan. 27–Hockey: Northern Vocational 5, Upper Canada College 8; Jan. 27–Sr. Hockey: McColls Frontenacs 3, Dominions 2; Jan. 27–Sr. Hockey: Toronto Goodyears 2, British Consols 4; Jan. 28–Memorial Service for King George V; Jan. 29–Jr. Hockey: U. Of T. Schools 2, Jarvis Collegiate 1; Jan. 29–Jr. Hockey: Aurora 1, Jr. Marlboros 2; Jan. 29–Sr. Hockey: Port Colborne 1, Sr. Marlboros 9; Jan. 31–Hockey: Upper Canada College 10, Jarvis Collegiate 1; Jan. 31–Sr. Hockey: Hamilton 2, Oakville 5; Feb. 1–Jr. Hockey: West Toronto 0, St. Michael's 2; Feb. 1–Jr. Hockey: Native Sons 4, Toronto Lions 2; Feb. 1–NHL: Chicago 2, Leafs 3; Feb. 3–Hockey: Northern Vocational 4, St. Michael's "B" 6; Feb. 3–Hockey: British Consols 5, Dominions 4; Feb. 3–Hockey: Oshawa 2, McColls Frontenacs 3; Feb. 4–Jr. Hockey: Young Rangers 1, St. Michael's 5; Feb. 4–Jr. Hockey: West Toronto 7, Native Sons 2; Feb. 5–Hockey: Upper Canada College 4, Jarvis Collegiate 5; Feb. 5–Jr. Hockey: U. of T. Schools 3, St. Michael's "B" 6; Feb. 6–Wrestling: Ray Steele vs. Dick Raines; Feb. 7–Sr. Hockey: Port Colborne 1, Oakville 5; Feb. 8–Jr. Hockey: Native Sons 1, St. Michael's 5; Feb. 8–Jr. Hockey: Young Rangers 6, Toronto Lions 4; Feb. 8–NHL: Americans 0, Leafs 3; Feb. 10–Hockey: Upper Canada College 2, St. Michael's "B" 3; Feb. 10–Hockey: Oshawa 3, Dominions 4; Feb. 10–Hockey: McColls Frontenacs 1, Toronto Goodyears 0; Feb. 11–Jr. Hockey: West Toronto 9, Toronto Lions 2; Feb. 11–Jr. Hockey: Jr. Varsity 2, St. Michael's 9; Feb. 12–Amateur Boxing Night; Feb. 13–Wrestling: Ray Steele vs. Dan O'Mahony; Feb. 14–Jr. Hockey: Jr. Varsity 4, Young Rangers 3; Feb. 14–Jr. Hockey: Aurora 2, Jr. Marlboros 9; Feb. 14–Sr. Hockey: Hamilton 5, Sr. Marlboros 4; Feb. 15–Jr. Hockey: Upper Canada College 2, St. Michael's "B" 8; Feb. 15–Jr. Hockey: Jr. Varsity 1, Young Rangers 5; Feb. 15–NHL: Detroit 2, Leafs 3; Feb. 17–Hockey: Toronto Goodyears 4, Dominions 3; Feb. 17–Hockey: British Consols 5, McColls Frontenacs 4; Feb. 18–Jr. Hockey: Native Sons 4, St. Michael's 3; Feb. 18–Jr. Hockey: Young Rangers 5, Toronto Lions 3; Feb. 19–Boxing: Jack Dempsey's White-Hope Tournament; Feb. 20–NHL: Canadiens 1, Leafs 2; Feb. 21–Sr. Hockey: Hamilton 3, Oakville 2; Feb. 22–Jr. Hockey: Native Sons 2, St. Michael's 6; Feb. 22–Jr. Hockey: Young Rangers 5, West Toronto 0; Feb. 22–NHL: Maroons 0, Leafs 1; Feb. 24–Hockey: McColls Frontenacs, Dominions; Feb. 24–Hockey: British Consols, Toronto Goodyears; Feb. 25–NHL: Rangers 2, Leafs 2; Feb. 26–Jr. Hockey: Young Rangers 3, West Toronto 1; Feb. 26–Sr. Hockey: Hamilton 7, Sr. Marlboros 2; Feb. 27–Wrestling: Ernie Dusek vs. Dick Raines; Feb. 28–Jr. Hockey: Bracebridge 1, St. Michael's "B" 8; Feb. 29–Jr. Hockey: West Toronto 1, St. Michael's 0; Feb. 29–Jr. Hockey: Brantford 3, Jr. Marlboros 4; Feb. 29–NHL: Chicago 2, Leafs 4; Mar. 2–Hockey: Lakefield 5, Upper Canada College 6; Mar. 2–Hockey: Oshawa 4, Toronto Goodyears 3; Mar. 2–Hockey: Dominions 4, British Consols 3; Mar. 3–Jr. Hockey: West Toronto 6, St. Michael's 1; Mar. 4–Sr. Hockey: Hamilton 10, Sr. Marlboros 2; Mar. 5–Wrestling: Dean Delton vs. Ernie Dusek; Mar. 6–Jr. Hockey: Barrie 3, St. Michael's "B" 6; Mar. 6–Jr. Hockey: Kingston 4, Jr. Marlboros 0; Mar. 7–Jr. Hockey: West Toronto 6, St. Michael's 5; Mar. 7–NHL: Canadiens 1, Leafs 8; Mar. 9–Jr. Hockey: Oshawa 2, West Toronto 5; Mar. 14–NHL: Maroons 1, Leafs 0; Mar. 14–Sr. Hockey: Sutton, Barrie; Mar. 17–Hockey: British Consols 5, Oshawa 2; Mar. 17–Hockey: McColls Frontenacs 5, Toronto Goodyears 2; Mar. 18–Jr. Hockey: Kingston 3, St. Michael's "B" 7; Mar. 19–NHL: Boston 2, Leafs 2; Mar. 19–Sr. Hockey: Sudbury 1, Hamilton 8; Mar. 20–Track and Field: Maple Leaf Athletic Games; Mar. 21–Jr. Hockey: Kitchener 3, West Toronto 6 (OHA "A" Finals); Mar. 21–NHL: Americans 1, Leafs 4; Mar. 23–Hockey: McColls Frontenacs 2, Toronto Goodyears 5; Mar. 24–Jr. Hockey: Guelph 6, St. Michael's "B" 7 (OHA "B" Finals); Mar. 25–Jr. Hockey: South Porcupine 3, West Toronto 6 (All-Ontario Jr. Finals); Mar. 26–NHL: Boston 3, Leafs 8; Mar. 27–Sr. Hockey: Sudbury 2, Montreal 1 (Allan Cup Eastern Finals); Mar. 28–Jr. Hockey: South Porcupine 2, West Toronto 7; Mar. 28–NHL: Americans 1, Leafs 3; Mar. 30–Hockey: Toronto Goodyears 7, McColls

Frontenacs 1; Mar. 31–Jr. Hockey: Quebec 4, West Toronto 16; Apr. 1–Sr. Hockey: Sudbury 5, Brockville 0 (Allan Cup Eastern Finals); Apr. 2–NHL: Americans 1, Leafs 3; Apr. 3–Jr. Hockey: Guelph 4, St. Michael's "B" 12 (OHA "B" Finals); Apr. 4–Hockey: Toronto Goodyears 2, McColls Frontenacs 5; Apr. 4–Sr. Hockey: Sudbury 6, Brockville 2 (Allan Cup Eastern Finals); Apr. 6–Hockey: Toronto Goodyears 3, McColls Frontenacs 0; Apr. 7–Jr. Hockey: Pembroke 3, West Toronto 4 (Memorial Cup Eastern Finals); Apr. 9–NHL: Detroit 3, Leafs 4 (Stanley Cup Finals); Apr. 10–Hockey: Post Office, Telegram; Apr. 10–Hockey: St. James, East Riverdale; Apr. 10–Hockey: Upper Canada College, Lito; Apr. 10–Jr. Hockey: Saskatoon 1, West Toronto 5 (Memorial Cup Finals); Apr. 11–Hockey: Toronto Goodyears 8, British Consols 2 (Mercantile League Finals); Apr. 11–NHL: Detroit 3, Leafs 2 (Stanley Cup-winning game); Apr. 13–Jr. Hockey: Saskatoon 2, West Toronto 4 (Memorial Cup Finals); Apr. 14–Hockey: Toronto Goodyears 0, British Consols 3 (Mercantile League Finals); Apr. 16–Wrestling: Dean Delton vs. Rudy Dusek; Apr. 17–Hockey: General Motors, R.H. Sloane; Apr. 18–Hockey: Toronto Goodyears 1, British Consols 7 (Mercantile League Finals); Apr. 21–Hockey: Toronto Goodyears 5, British Consols 1 (Mercantile League Finals); Apr. 22–Boxing: Jack Dempsey's White-Hope Tournament; Apr. 23–Hockey: Toronto Goodyears 2, British Consols 3 (Mercantile League Finals); Apr. 24–Independent Order of Foresters Pageant; Apr. 27–May 2: Six-day Bicycle Race; May 18–Boxing: Olympic Boxing Trials; May 22–Boxing: Jack Dempsey's White Hope Tournament; Aug. 2–National Model Aircraft Contest; Sept. 2–Lacrosse: Mimico 10, Orillia 8; Sept. 3–Wrestling: Dean Detton vs. Ray Steele; Sept. 4–Lacrosse: Mimico 2, Orillia 13; Sept. 10–Wrestling: Yvon Robert vs. Rudy Dusek; Sept. 11–Lacrosse: Hamilton 4, Orillia 9; Sept. 15–Amateur Boxing Night; Sept. 23–Pro Boxing Night; Sept. 24–Wrestling: Dean Detton vs. Mayes McLain; Sept. 28–Amateur Boxing Night; Oct. 1–Wrestling: Dean Detton vs. Lou Plummer; Oct. 2–Lacrosse: Orillia 10, Vancouver 8 (Mann Cup Finals); Oct. 5–Lacrosse: Orillia 6, Vancouver 8 (Mann Cup Finals); Oct. 7–Lacrosse: Orillia 11, Vancouver 9 (Mann Cup Finals); Oct. 9–Lacrosse: Orillia 20, Vancouver 9 (Mann Cup Finals); Oct. 14–Canadian Opera Company; Oct. 15–Wrestling: Dean Detton vs. Fred Grobmier; Oct. 18–Music: Toronto Symphony Orchestra w/Mendelssohn Choir; Oct. 19–Boxing: Max Baer vs. Dutch Weimer; Oct. 21–Canadian Grand Opera–Faust; Oct. 22–Wrestling: Dave Levin vs. Count Zarynoff; Oct. 26-31: Bob Morton's Rameses Shrine Circus; Nov. 2–NHL: Whites 4, Blues 2 (Maple Leafs intrasquad game); Nov. 5–NHL: Detroit 5, Leafs 1; Nov. 6–Wrestling: Lou Plummer vs. Ali Baba; Nov. 7–NHL: Americans 3, Leafs 2; Nov. 12–Wrestling: George Zaharias vs. Rudy Grobmier; Nov. 14–NHL: Chicago 2, Leafs 6; Nov. 17–Jr. Hockey: Galt 2, Upper Canada College 1; Nov. 17–Jr. Hockey: Young Rangers 6, Native Sons 3; Nov. 18–Reverand Hiram Hull; Nov. 19–Wrestling: Dean Detton vs. George Zaharias; Nov. 20–Jr. Hockey: Port Colborne 5, St. Michael's 6; Nov. 20–Jr. Hockey: Brantford 3, Northern Vocational 6; Nov. 21–Jr. Hockey: Paris 3, St. Michael's "B" 6; Nov. 21–Jr. Hockey: Stratford 2, Toronto Lions 1; Nov. 21–NHL: Boston 4, Leafs 3; Nov. 23–Hockey: Sr. Varsity, British Consols; Nov. 23–Jr. Hockey: Aurora vs. East York; Nov. 24–Jr. Hockey: Barrie 6, U. of T. Schools 1; Nov. 24–Jr. Hockey: Oshawa, Young Rangers; Nov. 26–Jr. Hockey: East Toronto 7, St. Michael's "B" 4; Nov. 26–Jr. Hockey: Galt 4, Aurora 0; Nov. 27–Jr. Hockey: Barrie 2, Northern Vocational 11; Nov. 28–Jr. Hockey: Galt 3, East Toronto 0; Nov. 28–Jr. Hockey: Stratford 8, British Consols 1; Nov. 28–NHL: Canadiens 2, Leafs 4; Nov. 30–Hockey: Toronto Goodyears 5, British Consols 2; Dec. 2–Jr. Hockey: Galt 4, Northern Vocational 7; Dec. 2–Jr. Hockey: Oshawa 2, St. Michael's 2; Dec. 3–Wrestling: Dean Detton vs. Ray Steele; Dec. 4–Jr. Hockey: Oshawa 1, St. Michael's 2; Dec. 4–Jr. Hockey: Northern Vocational 4, Stratford 1; Dec. 5–NHL: Maroons 3, Leafs 1; Dec. 7–Hockey: Oshawa 4, Dominions 2; Dec. 8–Jr. Hockey: St. Michael's 9, Northern Vocational 1; Dec. 9–Boxing: Baby Yack vs. Matt Ozanick; Dec. 10–Wrestling: Fred Grobmier vs. Ray Steele; Dec. 11–Hockey: UCC Old Boys, UCC New Boys; Dec. 12–Jr. Hockey: Young Rangers 2, St. Michael's 0; Dec. 12–Jr. Hockey: Jr. Varsity 5, Native Sons 0; Dec. 12–NHL: Rangers 5, Leafs 3; Dec. 13–Hockey: Dominions 0, Toronto Goodyears 2; Dec. 14–Jr. Hockey: Jr. Varsity 4, British Consols 7; Dec. 14–Jr. Hockey: Toronto Lions 1, St. Michael's 2; Dec. 19–Jr. Hockey: Native Sons 2, St. Michael's 6; Dec. 19–Jr. Hockey: Young Rangers 5, Jr. Varsity 1; Dec. 19–NHL: Americans 1, Leafs 3; Dec. 22–Jr. Hockey: Native Sons 4, Toronto Lions 3; Dec. 22–Jr. Hockey: Oshawa, Young Rangers; Dec. 26–Jr. Hockey: British Consols 6, Toronto Lions 2; Dec. 26–Jr. Hockey: Oshawa 3, Young Rangers 3; Dec. 26–NHL: Boston 2, Leafs 1; Dec. 28–Hockey: Dominions 2, British Consols 4; Dec. 29–Jr. Hockey: British Consols 6, Native Sons 2; Dec. 29–Jr. Hockey: Toronto Lions 1, Young Rangers 2.

1937 • Jan. 2–Jr. Hockey: Young Rangers 6, Native Sons 0; Jan. 2–Jr. Hockey: Oshawa 4, British Consols 4; Jan. 2–NHL: Maroons 0, Leafs 0; Jan. 5–Jr. Hockey: Native Sons 1, Toronto Lions 5; Jan. 5–Jr. Hockey: Young Rangers 6, British Consols 7; Jan. 6–Boxing: Sammy Luftspring vs. Frankie Genovese; Jan. 7–Hockey: Jarvis Collegiate 3, U. of T. Schools 5; Jan. 9–Jr. Hockey: Jr. Varsity 2, Toronto Lions 5; Jan. 9–Jr. Hockey: British Consols 3, St. Michael's 6; Jan. 9–NHL: Canadiens 1, Leafs 2; Jan. 11–Hockey: Oshawa 0, British Consols 1; Jan. 12–Jr. Hockey: British Consols 7, Native Sons 2; Jan. 12–Jr. Hockey: Oshawa 1, St. Michael's 2; Jan. 13–Hockey: Upper Canada College 6, Jarvis Collegiate 3; Jan. 14–Wrestling: Dan O'Mahony vs. Hardy Kruskamp; Jan. 15–Hockey: Upper Canada College 5, St. Michael's "B" 2; Jan. 16–Jr. Hockey: St. Michael's 6, Jr. Varsity 2; Jan. 16–Jr. Hockey: Young Rangers 8, Toronto Lions 2; Jan. 16–NHL: Chicago 2, Leafs 3; Jan. 18–Hockey: British Consols 3, Dominions 7; Jan. 19–Hockey: Upper Canada College 2, Northern Vocational 3; Jan. 19–Jr. Hockey: Young Rangers 1, St. Michael's 5; Jan. 20–Boxing: Jack Dempsey's White-Hope Tournament; Jan. 21–Wrestling: Dan O'Mahony vs. Jawbone Joe Cox; Jan. 22–Hockey: Northern Vocational 5, Jarvis Collegiate1; Jan. 23–Jr. Hockey: St. Michael's 8, Toronto Lions 1; Jan. 23–Jr. Hockey: Native Sons 2, Jr. Varsity 3; Jan. 23–NHL: Rangers 0, Leafs 4; Jan. 25–Hockey: British Consols 6, Toronto Goodyears 6; Jan. 25–Hockey: Jarvis Collegiate 2, Upper Canada College 6; Jan. 26–NHL: Canadiens 3, Leafs 1; Jan. 27–Jr. Hockey: Toronto Lions 3, Jr. Varsity 4; Jan. 27–Jr. Hockey: British Consols 3, St. Michael's 3; Jan. 29–Hockey: North Toronto, Northern Vocational; Jan. 29–Hockey: Northern Vocational 6, St. Michael's "B" 4; Jan. 30–Jr. Hockey: Jr. Varsity 3, St. Michael's 5; Jan. 30–Jr. Hockey: Oshawa 4, Native Sons 0; Jan. 30–NHL: Maroons 4, Leafs 7; Feb. 1–Hockey: Northern Vocational 5, Upper Canada College 4; Feb. 1–Hockey: Dominions 2, Toronto Goodyears 3; Feb. 2–Jr. Hockey: Jarvis Collegiate 2, St. Michael's "B" 8; Feb. 2–Jr. Hockey: Native Sons 1, St. Michael's 12; Feb. 2–Jr. Hockey: Oshawa 9, Toronto Lions 3; Feb. 3–Boxing: Sammy Luftspring vs. Johnny Jadick; Feb. 5–Hockey: Upper Canada College 6, St. Michael's "B" 3; Feb. 6–Jr. Hockey: Native Sons 1, Young Rangers 10; Feb. 6–Jr. Hockey: British Consols 9, Jr. Varsity 4; Feb. 6–NHL: Americans 0, Leafs 5; Feb. 8–Hockey: Northern Vocational 9, U. of T. Schools 3; Feb. 8–Hockey: Toronto Goodyears 2, British Consols 2; Feb. 9–Hockey: Upper Canada College 3, Northern Vocational 3; Feb. 9–Jr. Hockey: Oshawa 1, British Consols 4; Feb. 9–NHL: Rangers 5, Leafs 1; Feb. 11–Wrestling: Crusher Casey vs. Lord Albert Mills; Feb. 12–Hockey: Northern Vocational 6, Upper Canada College 8 (Schoolboy Finals); Feb. 13–Jr. Hockey: St. Michael's 7, Young Rangers 4; Feb. 13–NHL: Boston 3, Leafs 0; Feb. 15–Hockey: Dominions 3, British Consols 2; Feb. 16–Jr. Hockey: Young Rangers 4, St. Michael's 3; Feb. 17–Boxing: Baby Yack vs. Routier Parra; Feb. 18–NHL: Detroit 1, Leafs 3; Feb. 19–Jr. Hockey: Collingwood 5, East Toronto 8; Feb. 20–Jr. Hockey: Young Rangers 4, St. Michael's 12; Feb. 20–NHL: Americans 3, Leafs 4 (make-up of January 1 game); Feb. 22–Hockey: Oshawa 1, Toronto Goodyears 3; Feb. 23–Jr. Hockey: British Consols 3, St. Michael's 4; Feb. 24–Amateur Boxing Night; Feb. 25–Wrestling: Dan O'Mahony vs. Rudy Dusek; Feb. 26–Hockey: Dominions, British Consols; Feb. 27–Jr. Hockey: British Consols 3, St. Michael's 5; Feb. 27–NHL: Maroons 2, Leafs 3; Mar. 1–Hockey: Dominions 1, British Consols 0; Mar. 2–Jr. Hockey: British Consols 1, St. Michael's 3; Mar. 3–Boxing: Sammy Luftspring vs. Eddie Dempsey; Mar. 4–Wrestling: Crusher Casey vs. Wee Willie Davis; Mar. 5–Hockey: Dominions 3, British Consols 1; Mar. 6–Jr. Hockey: Stratford 2, St. Michael's 6; Mar. 6–NHL: Canadiens 1, Leafs 3; Mar. 8–Hockey: Dominions 6, Toronto Goodyears 0 (Mercantile League Finals); Mar. 9–Hockey: Northern Vocational 8, East Toronto 2; Mar. 10–Hockey: Dominions 1, Toronto Goodyears 3 (Mercantile League Finals); Mar. 11–Jr. Hockey: Northern Vocational 7, East Toronto 9; Mar. 11–Jr. Hockey: Stratford 5, St. Michael's 4; Mar. 12–Track and Field: Maple Leaf Athletic Games; Mar. 13–Hockey: Dominions 1, Toronto Goodyears 0 (Mercantile League Finals); Mar. 13–NHL: Chicago 2, Leafs 3; Mar. 15–Hockey: Dominions 1, Toronto Goodyears 6 (Mercantile League Finals); Mar. 20–Jr. Hockey: Stratford 3, St. Michael's 8; Mar. 20–NHL: Detroit 2, Leafs 3; Mar. 22–Hockey: Dominions 3, Toronto Goodyears 0 (Mercantile League Finals); Mar. 23–NHL: Rangers 3, Leafs 0; Mar. 24–Jr. Hockey: Copper Cliff 4, St. Michael's 3; Mar. 27–Jr. Hockey: Copper Cliff 4, St. Michael's 1; Mar. 29–Sr. Hockey: Sudbury 6, Dominions 1; Mar. 30–Jr. Hockey: Niagara Falls 4, Northern Vocational 10; Mar. 31–Jr. Hockey: Midland, Waterloo; Mar. 31–Jr. Hockey: Hamilton, Oshawa; Apr. 1–Wrestling: Dan O'Mahony vs. Chief Little Wolf; Apr. 2–Boxing: Gordon Wallace vs. Sammy Luftspring (Canadian Welterweight Championship); Apr. 3–Jr. Hockey: Iroquois Falls 3, Waterloo 1 (Juvenile Finals); Apr. 3–Jr. Hockey: Ottawa 1, Copper Cliff 12 (Memorial Cup Eastern Finals); Apr. 5–Sr. Hockey: Sudbury 14, Hull 2 (Allan Cup Eastern Finals); Apr. 7–Jr. Hockey: Barrie 8, Northern Vocational 3; Apr. 8–Wrestling: Ernie Dusek vs. Swede Olsen; Apr. 10–Jr. Hockey: Winnipeg 3, Copper Cliff 4 (Memorial Cup Finals); Apr. 12–Jr. Hockey: Winnipeg 6, Copper Cliff 5 (Memorial Cup Finals); Apr. 14–Jr. Hockey: Winnipeg 2, Copper Cliff 1 (Memorial Cup Finals); Apr. 16–Jr. Hockey: Barrie 6, Northern Vocational 4 (OHA "B" Finals); Apr. 17–Hockey: Hershey 3, Wembley 6 (World Amateur Championship); Apr. 17–Jr. Hockey: Copper Cliff 0, Winnipeg 7 (Memorial Cup Finals); Apr. 19–Int'l Hockey: Winnipeg 2, Wembley 4 (World Amateur Championship); Apr. 20–Int'l Hockey: Sudbury 5, Hershey 2 (World Amateur Championship); Apr. 21–Int'l Hockey: Winnipeg 4, Hershey 2 (World Amateur Championship); Apr. 22–Int'l Hockey: Sudbury 3, Wembley 3 (World Amateur Championship); Apr. 23–Tennis: Perry vs. Vines, Lott vs. Barnes; Apr. 24–Int'l Hockey: Sudbury 6, Wembley 1 (World Amateur Championship); Apr. 26–Int'l Hockey: Sudbury 1, Wembley 2 (World Amateur Championship); Apr. 29–Wrestling: Rudy Dusek vs. Swede Olson; Apr. 30–Independent Order of Foresters Pageant; May 1–May Day Labor Conference; May 8–Toronto Girl Guides Rally; May 19–Lacrosse: Orillia 22, Marlboros 16; June 1–Boxing: Sammy Luftspring vs. George Bland; Sept. 2–Lacrosse: St. Catharines 15, Jr. Marlboros 22; Sept. 7–Lacrosse: Mimico 18, Jr. Marlboros 19; Sept. 8–Boxing: Frankie Genovese vs. Harold Wallace; Sept. 20–Boxing: Henry Hook vs. Baby Yack; Sept. 27–Lacrosse: Cornwall 6, Orillia 25; Sept. 28–Lacrosse: Jr. Terriers 11, Jr. Marlboros 19; Oct. 6–Wrestling: Dan O'Mahony vs. Dazzler Clarke; Oct. 8–Boxing: Spider Armstrong vs. Henry Hook; Oct. 14–Wrestling: Yves Robert vs Dan O'Mahony; Oct. 22–Boxing: K.O. Morgan vs. Jackie Callura; Oct. 25-30: Bob Morton's Ramses Shrine Circus; Nov. 1–NHL: Eddie Power's Whites 5, Dick Irvin's Blues 3 (Maple Leafs' Intrasquad Game); Nov. 2–Lacrosse: Vancouver 9, Orillia 12 (Canadian Junior Championships); Nov. 3–Wrestling: Dan O'Mahony vs. Brusing Bob Wagner; Nov. 4–NHL: Detroit 2, Leafs 2; Nov. 6–NHL: Americans 3, Leafs 6; Nov. 13–NHL: Chicago 3, Leafs 7; Nov. 19–Jr. Hockey: Paris 0, Upper Canada College 6; Nov. 19–Jr. Hockey: Guelph 5, Native Sons 4; Nov. 20–NHL: Boston 3, Leafs 2; Nov. 22–Jr. Hockey: Aurora 1, Runnymede 6; Nov. 22–Jr. Hockey: Northern Vocational 2, U. of T. Schools 1; Nov. 23–Jr. Hockey: St. Michael's "B" 5, East Toronto 4; Nov. 23–Jr. Hockey: St. Michael's 6, Jr. Varsity 2; Nov. 24–Jr. Hockey: Galt 5, Barrie 4; Nov. 24–Jr. Hockey: Stratford 8, Oshawa 2; Nov. 26–Jr. Hockey: Guelph 9, Toronto Lions 5; Nov. 26–Jr. Hockey: Jr. Marlboros 6, Young Rangers 1; Nov. 27–NHL: Maroons 0, Leafs 4; Nov. 30–Jr. Hockey: Runnymede 2, St. Michael's "B" 4; Nov. 30–Jr. Hockey: Galt 4, Upper Canada College 3; Dec. 1–Jr. Hockey: Northern Vocational 1, St. Michael's 5; Dec. 1–Jr. Hockey: Stratford 2, Jr. Marlboros 3; Dec. 3–Jr. Hockey: St. Michael's 11, St. Michael's "B" 0; Dec. 3–Jr. Hockey: Galt 4, Guelph 8; Dec. 4–NHL: Canadiens 3, Leafs 3; Dec. 6–Jr. Hockey: Guelph 0, Jr. Marlboros 10; Dec. 8–Jr. Hockey: St. Michael's 4, Jr. Marlboros 1; Dec. 10–Sr. Hockey: Oshawa o, Toronto Goodyears 3; Dec. 11–NHL: Rangers 6, Leafs 3; Dec. 17–Sr. Hockey: Brantford 6, Toronto Goodyears 15; Dec. 18–Jr. Hockey: Jr. Varsity 5, Toronto Lions 1; Dec. 18–Jr. Hockey: Young Rangers 5, St. Michael's 4; Dec. 18–NHL: Americans 2, Leafs 3; Dec. 20–Jr. Hockey: St. Michael's 12, Toronto Lions 1; Dec. 20–Jr. Hockey: Native Sons 3, Jr. Marlboros 6; Dec. 21–Boxing: Frankie Genovese vs. George Salvadore; Dec. 22–Hockey: UCC Old Boys 5, UCC New Boys 2; Dec. 25–NHL: Detroit 1, Leafs 1; Dec. 28–Boxing: Mog Mason vs. Jimmy Chapman; Dec. 30–Jr. Hockey: Oshawa 5, Native Sons 4; Dec. 30–Jr. Hockey: Young Rangers 1, Jr. Marlboros 6.

1938 • Jan. 1–NHL: Canadiens 4, Leafs 6; Jan. 4–Jr. Hockey: Young Rangers 1, Native Sons 0; Jan. 4–Jr. Hockey: Toronto Lions 1, Jr. Marlboros 10; Jan. 5–Jr. Hockey: Northern Vocational 0, Runnymede 4; Jan. 7–Jr. Hockey: Upper Canada College 4, St. Michael's "B" 5; Jan. 7–Sr. Hockey: Kitchener 0, Toronto Goodyears 9; Jan. 8–NHL: Rangers 2, Leafs 3; Jan. 11–Jr. Hockey: Native Sons 5, Toronto Lions 2; Jan. 11–Jr. Hockey: St. Michael's 0, Jr. Marlborosrlboros 6; Jan. 11–Sr. Hockey: Toronto Goodyears 3, Brantford 3; Jan. 12–Jr. Hockey: U. of T. Schools 6, St. Michael's "B" 4; Jan. 12–Sr. Hockey: Port Colborne 3, Toronto Goodyears 5; Jan. 13–NHL: Maroons 2, Leafs 3; Jan. 14–Jr. Hockey: Upper Canada College 2, Northern Vocational 5; Jan. 15–NHL: Chicago 4, Leafs 4; Jan. 17–Boxing: Baby Yack vs. Mog Mason; Jan. 18–Jr. Hockey: St. Michael's "B" 2, Northern Vocational 5; Jan. 18–Jr. Hockey: St. Michael's 4, Oshawa 3; Jan. 19–Jr. Hockey: Runnymede 4, Upper Canada College 3; Jan. 21–Jr. Hockey: Northern Vocational 4, Upper Canada College 0; Jan. 21–Sr. Hockey: Toronto Goodyears 13, Kitchener 0; Jan. 22–Jr. Hockey: Native Sons 7, Toronto Lions 1; Jan. 22–Jr. Hockey: Jr. Varsity 3, Young Rangers 1; Jan. 22–NHL: Bruins 9, Leafs 1; Jan. 25–Jr. Hockey: St. Michael's "B" 5, Runnymede 1; Jan. 25–Jr. Hockey: Young Rangers 6, Native Sons 4; Jan. 25–Jr. Hockey: Toronto Lions 2, Jr. Marlboros 10; Jan.

27–Wrestling: Crusher Casey vs. Dan O'Mahoney; Jan. 28–Jr. Hockey: Runnymede 4, Northern Vocational 1; Jan. 28–Sr. Hockey: Port Colborne 5, Toronto Goodyears 2; Jan. 29–Jr. Hockey: Oshawa 2, Jr. Marlboros 9; Jan. 29–Jr. Hockey: St. Michael's 4, Jr. Varsity 3; Jan. 29–NHL: Detroit 1, Leafs 4; Jan. 31–Boxing: Baby Yack vs. Indian Quintana; Feb. 1–Hockey: U. of T. Schools 7, Upper Canada College 5; Feb. 1–Jr. Hockey: Toronto Lions 1, St. Michael's 5; Feb. 1–Jr. Hockey: Young Rangers 2, Oshawa 4; Feb. 3–NHL: Canadiens 0, Leafs 3; Feb. 4–Hockey: Northern Vocational 1, Northern Toronto Collegiate 0; Feb. 4–Jr. Hockey: U. of T. Schools 6, Runnymede 2; Feb. 4–Jr. Hockey: Northern Vocational "B" 3, St. Michael's "B" 1; Feb. 5–Jr. Hockey: Young Rangers 3, Toronto Lions 8; Feb. 5–Jr. Hockey: St. Michael's 0, Jr. Marlboros 2; Feb. 5–NHL: Boston 1, Leafs 3; Feb. 7–Boxing: Bobby Pacho vs. Sammy Luftspring; Feb. 8–Hockey: St. Michael's "B" 3, Upper Canada College 4; Feb. 8–Jr. Hockey: Oshawa 3, Toronto Lions 0; Feb. 8–Jr. Hockey: Young Rangers 3, Jr. Marlboros 5; Feb. 9–Hockey: U. of T. Schools 1, Northern Vocational 5; Feb. 10–NHL: Maroons 0, Leafs 3; Feb. 11–Jr. Hockey: Runnymede 3, St. Michael's "B" 5; Feb. 11–Jr. Hockey: East Toronto 9, Bowmanville 5; Feb. 11–Sr. Hockey: Brantford 0, Toronto Goodyears 8; Feb. 12–Jr. Hockey: Native Sons 5, St. Michael's 3; Feb. 12–Jr. Hockey: Jr. Varsity 4, Jr. Marlboros 5; Feb. 12–NHL: Chicago 2, Leafs 1; Feb. 15–Hockey: Runnymede 2, U. of T. Schools 2; Feb. 15–Jr. Hockey: Oshawa 8, Jr. Varsity 2; Feb. 15–Jr. Hockey: Young Rangers 4, St. Michael's 2; Feb. 17–Wrestling: Yves Robert vs Vic Christie; Feb. 18–Hockey: Runnymede 2, U. of T. Schools 3; Feb. 18–Jr. Hockey: St. Michael's 2, Jr. Marlboros 3; Feb. 19–Jr. Hockey: Oshawa 6, Young Rangers 7; Feb. 19–NHL: Americans 4, Leafs 0; Feb. 22–Jr. Hockey: St. Michael's 2, Jr. Marlboros 6; Feb. 23–Hockey: Northern Vocational 8, U. of T. Schools 5; Feb. 24–Wrestling: Strangler Wagner vs. Vic Christie; Feb. 25–Hockey: Runnymede 5, Sudbury "B" 3; Feb. 25–Sr. Hockey: Port Colborne 0, Toronto Goodyears 3; Feb. 26–NHL: Rangers 4, Leafs 2; Feb. 28–Boxing: Baby Yack vs. Spider Armstrong; Mar. 3–Wrestling: Vic Christie vs. Yves Robert; Mar. 4–Sr. Hockey: Port Colborne 1, Toronto Goodyears 15; Mar. 5–Jr. Hockey: Oshawa 1, Jr. Marlboros 7; Mar. 5–NHL: Maroons 0, Leafs 2; Mar. 12–NHL: Canadiens 3, Leafs 3; Mar. 12–Sr. Hockey: Port Colborne 1, Toronto Goodyears 2; Mar. 16–Jr. Hockey: Barrie 7, Northern Vocational 7; Mar. 17–Wrestling: Vic Christie vs. Dan O'Mahoney; Mar. 18–Hockey: Lawrence Park 2, Western Tech 2; Mar. 18–Hockey: Vocational 2, Parkdale 1; Mar. 18–Jr. Hockey: Northern Vocational 3, Kingston 8; Mar. 19–Jr. Hockey: Oshawa 3, Guelph 4; Mar. 19–NHL: Americans 5, Leafs 8; Mar. 21–Boxing: Johnny Gaudes vs. Baby Yack; Mar. 22–Sr. Hockey: Falconbridge 4, Toronto Goodyears 0; Mar. 23–Jr. Hockey: Brantford 2, Northern Vocational 3; Mar. 24–NHL: Boston 0, Leafs 1; Mar. 25–Jr. Hockey: Sudbury 3, Oshawa 2 (Memorial Cup Eastern Finals); Mar. 26–NHL: Boston 1, Leafs 2; Mar. 26–Sr. Hockey: Falconbridge 4, Toronto Goodyears 2; Mar. 28–Sr. Hockey: Falconbridge 1, Chatham 1; Mar. 29–Sr. Hockey: Falconbridge 5, Chatham 0; Mar. 30–Jr. Hockey: Oshawa 7, Sudbury 1 (Memorial Cup Eastern Finals); Mar. 31–Sr. Hockey: Falconbridge 1, Cornwall 5; Apr. 2–Jr. Hockey: Aurora 3, Orangeville 4 (OHA "C" Finals); Apr. 2–Jr. Hockey: Sudbury 2, Oshawa 4; Apr. 4–Jr. Hockey: Aurora 1, Orangeville 2 (OHA "C" Finals); Apr. 5–NHL: Chicago 3, Leafs 1 (Stanley Cup Finals); Apr. 7–NHL: Chicago 1, Leafs 5 (Stanley Cup Finals); Apr. 9–Jr. Hockey: St. Boniface 2, Oshawa 3 (Memorial Cup Finals); Apr. 12–Jr. Hockey: St. Boniface 4, Oshawa 0 (Memorial Cup Finals); Apr. 13–Hockey: Waterloo 3, Oshawa "B" 8; Apr. 14–Jr. Hockey: St. Boniface 2, Oshawa 4 (Memorial Cup Finals); Apr. 16–Hockey: Sudbury 2, Oshawa "B" 8 (OHA Juvenile Finals); Apr. 16–Jr. Hockey: St. Boniface 6, Oshawa 4 (Memorial Cup Finals); Apr. 18–Hockey: Post Office 6, Stockyard 2 (City League Finals); Apr. 19–Jr. Hockey: St. Boniface 7, Oshawa 1 (Memorial Cup Finals); Apr. 21–Wrestling: Vic Christie vs. Dan O'Mahoney; Apr. 25–Boxing: Indian Quintana vs. Johnny Gaudes; Apr. 28–Wrestling: Vic Christie vs. Lou Plummer; Apr. 30–Tennis: Ellsworth Vines and Fred Perry; May 2–Amateur Boxing Night; May 20-21: Toronto Kennel Club Dog Show; Sept. 15–Wrestling: Masked Marvel vs. Felix Miquet; Sept. 18–Jehovah's Witnesses Convention; Sept. 22–Wrestling: Masked Marvel vs. Mayes McLain; Sept. 23–Boxing: George Pace vs. Baby Yack; Sept. 28–Lacrosse: Mimico 32, Westmount 3; Sept. 29–Wrestling: Mayes McLain vs. Masked Marvel; Oct. 6–Wrestling: Mayes McLain vs. Killer Davis; Oct. 7–Lacrosse: St. Catharines 18, New Westminster 11 (Mann Cup Finals); Oct. 8–Music: Paul Whiteman's Orchestra; Oct. 10–Lacrosse: St. Catharines 22, New Westminster 11 (Mann Cup Finals); Oct. 12–Lacrosse: St. Catharines 10, New Westminster 8 (Mann Cup Finals); Oct. 13–Wrestling: Mayes McLain vs. Strangler Wagner; Oct. 20–Wrestling: Mayes McLain vs. King Kong Cox; Oct. 24-29: Bob Morton's Rameses Shrine Circus; Oct. 31–NHL: Blues 5, Whites 1 (Maple Leafs intrasquad game); Nov. 1–Boxing: Henry Hook vs. Sixto Escobar; Nov. 3–NHL: Boston 3, Leafs 2; Nov. 5–NHL: Chicago 2, Leafs 0; Nov. 7–Boxing: Johnny Gaudes vs. Baby Yack; Nov. 10–Wrestling: King Kong Cox vs. Mayes McLain; Nov. 12–NHL: Canadiens 1, Leafs 4; Nov. 17–Wrestling: King Kong Cox vs. Nick Lutze; Nov. 18–Sr. Hockey: Port Colborne 1, Toronto Goodyears 7; Nov. 19–Jr. Hockey: St. Michael's 4, Toronto Lions 1; Nov. 19–Jr. Hockey: Upper Canada College 7, St. Michael's "B" 1; Nov. 19–NHL: Americans 2, Leafs 1; Nov. 20–Canadian Jewish Congress Rally; Nov. 21–Boxing: George Pace vs. Henry Hook; Nov. 22–Jr. Hockey: Runnymede 11, East York 3; Nov. 22–Jr. Hockey: Guelph 4, Young Rangers 8; Nov. 23–Music: Duke Ellington and his Orchestra; Nov. 24–Wrestling: Crusher Davis vs. Dutch Heffner; Nov. 25–Jr. Hockey: St. Michael's "B" 1, Kingsway 5; Nov. 25–Jr. Hockey: Barrie 9, U. of T. Schools 0; Nov. 26–Jr. Hockey: Waterloo 3, Northern Vocational 4; Nov. 26–Jr. Hockey: Native Sons, Jr. Marlboros; Nov. 26–NHL: Detroit 0, Leafs 5; Nov. 28–Jr. Hockey: Woodstock 5, Aurora 4; Nov. 28–Jr. Hockey: Midland 9, Jr. Marlboros "B" 2; Nov. 29–Jr. Hockey: St. Michael's 3, Oshawa 1; Nov. 29–Jr. Hockey: De la Salle 9, Stouffville 2; Nov. 30–Jr. Hockey: Young Rangers 3, Jr. Marlboros 3; Nov. 30–Jr. Hockey: Runnymede 4, Upper Canada College 3; Dec. 1–Wrestling: Yvon Robert vs. Dan O'Mahony; Dec. 2–Sr. Hockey: Toronto Goodyears 3, Oshawa 0; Dec. 3–Jr. Hockey: De la Salle 6, Kingsway 1; Dec. 3–Jr. Hockey: Waterloo 5, Midland 5; Dec. 3–NHL: Canadiens 3, Leafs 1; Dec. 5-10–Ice Show: Sonja Henie and Company; Dec. 7–Jr. Hockey: St. Michael's 10, Jr. Marlboros 4; Dec. 8–Wrestling: King Kong Cox vs. Nick Lutze; Dec. 9–Sr. Hockey: Brantford 2, Toronto Goodyears 8; Dec. 10–Jr. Hockey: St. Michael's 6, Jr. Varsity 1; Dec. 10–Jr. Hockey: Native Sons 8, Toronto Lions 1; Dec. 10–NHL: Chicago 1, Leafs 4; Dec. 12–Boxing: Sammy Luftpsring vs. Tommy Bland (Canadian Welterweight Championship); Dec. 13–Jr. Hockey: Jr. Marlboros 3, Jr. Varsity 2; Dec. 13–Jr. Hockey: St. Michael's 4, Young Rangers 3; Dec. 14–Hockey: UCC Preps, UCC Pops; Dec. 14–Hockey: UCC Old Boys, UCC New Boys; Dec. 15–Wrestling: King Kong Cox vs. Crusher Davis; Dec. 16–Sr. Hockey: St. Catharines 1, Toronto Goodyears 5; Dec. 17–NHL: Rangers 3, Leafs 2; Dec. 19–Jr. Hockey: Oshawa 6, Young Rangers 2; Dec. 19–Jr. Hockey: De la Salle 1, Runnymede 6; Dec. 19–Jr. Hockey: Waterloo 13, Midland 3; Dec. 20–Jr. Hockey: Toronto Lions 2, Jr. Varsity 3; Dec. 20–Jr. Hockey: St. Michael's 4, Jr. Marlboros 1; Dec. 21–Jr. Hockey: Runnymede 4, Barrie 5; Dec. 21–Sr. Hockey: Niagara Falls 2, Toronto Goodyears 10; Dec. 23–Jr. Hockey: Barrie 4, Waterloo 3 (SPA "B" Finals); Dec. 23–Variety: Christmas Frolic; Dec. 24–NHL: Detroit 0, Leafs 2; Dec. 27–Jr. Hockey: Native Sons 3, Jr. Marlboros 2; Dec. 27–Jr. Hockey: Oshawa 7, Toronto Lions 1; Dec. 28–Sr. Hockey: Port Colborne 1, Toronto Goodyears 8; Dec. 31–NHL: Americans 3, Leafs 2.

1939 • Jan. 2–Jr. Hockey: Young Rangers 2, Native Sons 2; Jan. 2–Jr. Hockey: Oshawa 5, Jr. Marlboros 4; Jan. 3–NHL: Canadiens 2, Leafs 2; Jan. 6–Sr. Hockey: Oshawa 0, Toronto Goodyears 0; Jan. 7–Jr. Hockey: Toronto Lions 2, Native Sons 2; Jan. 7–Jr. Hockey: Guelph 4, St. Michael's 1; Jan. 7–NHL: Boston 0, Leafs 2; Jan. 10–Jr. Hockey: Toronto Lions 3, Jr. Marlboros 6; Jan. 10–Jr. Hockey: St. Michael's 9, Jr. Varsity 1; Jan. 11–Jr. Hockey: Upper Canada College 3, St. Michael's "B" 1; Jan. 11–Jr. Hockey: Oshawa 6, Young Rangers 1; Jan. 11–Jr. Hockey: Mimico 2, Kingsway 1; Jan. 13–Sr. Hockey: Brantford 4, Toronto Goodyears 9; Jan. 14–Jr. Hockey: Young Rangers 3, Jr. Varsity 2; Jan. 14–Jr. Hockey: St. Michael's 3, Toronto Lions 1; Jan. 14–NHL: Chicago 1, Leafs 3; Jan. 16–Boxing: Lefty Gwynne vs. Johnny Gaudes; Jan. 17–Jr. Hockey: Native Sons 4, Jr. Varsity 3; Jan. 17–Jr. Hockey: Young Rangers 4, Jr. Marlboros 2; Jan. 18–Jr. Hockey: De la Salle 2, Runnymede 7; Jan. 18–Jr. Hockey: Northern Vocational 14, St. Michael's "B" 2; Jan. 18–Jr. Hockey: Oshawa 2, St. Michael's 5; Jan. 19–Wrestling: Empire Title Elimination Tournament; Jan. 20–Jr. Hockey: Runnymede 3, Upper Canada College 2; Jan. 21–NHL: Americans 2, Leafs 7; Jan. 21–Sr. Hockey: St. Catharines 2, Toronto Goodyears 3; Jan. 22–Jr. Hockey: Young Rangers 0, St. Michael's 5; Jan. 22–Jr. Hockey: Guelph 0, Jr. Varsity 0; Jan. 24–Boxing: Dave Castilloux vs. Armanda Sicilia; Jan. 25–Hockey: Northern Vocational 5, St. Michael's "B" 3; Jan. 25–Jr. Hockey: Oshawa 4, Native Sons 1; Jan. 25–Jr. Hockey: Kingsway 5, North York 3; Jan. 26–Wrestling: Elimination Tournament; Jan. 27–Jr. Hockey: Upper Canada College 3, De la Salle 2; Jan. 27–Sr. Hockey: St. Catharines 0, Toronto Goodyears 0; Jan. 28–Jr. Hockey: Young Rangers 3, Jr. Varsity 1; Jan. 28–Jr. Hockey: Jr. Marlboros 4, Toronto Lions 2; Jan. 28–NHL: Detroit 0, Leafs 6; Jan. 30–Boxing: Lefty Gwynne vs. Johnny Gaudes; Jan. 31–Jr. Hockey: St. Michael's 6, Native Sons 3; Jan. 31–Jr. Hockey: Jr. Varsity 4, Toronto Lions 0; Feb. 1–Jr. Hockey: De la Salle 2, St. Michael's "B" 0; Feb. 2–NHL: Boston 2, Leafs 1; Feb. 3–Hockey: Western Tech 4, Northern Vocational "B" 1; Feb. 3–Jr. Hockey: Northern Vocational 6, Runnymede 2; Feb. 4–Jr. Hockey: Oshawa 7, Jr. Varsity 1; Feb. 4–Jr. Hockey: Guelph 1, Native Sons 4; Feb. 4–NHL: Rangers 4, Leafs 2; Feb. 7–Jr. Hockey: St. Michael's 10, Jr. Marlboros 3; Feb. 7–Jr. Hockey: Young Rangers 7, Toronto Lions 1; Feb. 8–Hockey: Toronto 4, Northern Vocational 1 (Hinder Cup Game); Feb. 8–Hockey: De la Salle 3, Northern Vocational "B" 4; Feb. 9–Wrestling: Joe Savoldi vs. Vic Christie; Feb. 11–Jr. Hockey: St. Michael's 5, Native Sons 4; Feb. 11–Jr. Hockey: Young Rangers 3, Jr. Marlboros 1; Feb. 11–NHL: Canadiens 3, Leafs 3; Feb. 13–Boxing: Dave Castilloux vs. Phil Zwick; Feb. 14–Jr. Hockey: Young Rangers 6, Native Sons 3; Feb. 14–Jr. Hockey: Runnymede 4, Upper Canada College 2; Feb. 15–Hockey: De la Salle 5, Upper Canada College 2; Feb. 15–Sr. Hockey: Port Colborne 1, Toronto Goodyears 7; Feb. 16–Wrestling: Jim Londos vs. Joe Savoldi; Feb. 17–Hockey: Runnymede 11, U. of T. Schools 3; Feb. 17–Jr. Hockey: Native Sons 4, Jr. Marlboros 2; Feb. 18–Jr. Hockey: Guelph 3, Young Rangers 4; Feb. 18–NHL: Rangers 1, Leafs 2; Feb. 21–Jr. Hockey: Native Sons 6, Jr. Marlboros 2; Feb. 22–Hockey: Northern Vocational 7, Runnymede 6; Feb. 22–Jr. Hockey: Oshawa 7, St. Catharines 2; Feb. 23–Wrestling: Jim Londos vs. Joe Savoldi; Feb. 24–Hockey: Runnymede 9, De la Salle 1; Feb. 24–Sr. Hockey: Oshawa 1, Toronto Goodyears 2 (OHA Senior Finals); Feb. 25–Jr. Hockey: Oshawa 1, St. Michael's 4; Feb. 25–NHL: Boston 0, Leafs 1; Feb. 27–Boxing: Sammy Luftspring vs. Frankie Genovese; Feb. 28–Jr. Hockey: Young Rangers 3, Native Sons 2; Mar. 2–Wrestling: Vic Christie vs. Chief Strongbow; Mar. 3–Hockey: Runnymede 6, Northern Vocational 3 (Schoolboy Finals); Mar. 3–Sr. Hockey: Oshawa 0, Toronto Goodyears 3 (OHA Senior Finals); Mar. 4–Jr. Hockey: Oshawa 8, St. Michael's 3; Mar. 4–NHL: Chicago 1, Leafs 1; Mar. 11–NHL: Detroit 1, Leafs 5; Mar. 11–Sr. Hockey: Lake Shore 3, Toronto Goodyears 4; Mar. 12–Tennis: Don Budge vs. Ellsworth Vines; Mar. 13–Sr. Hockey: Lake Shore 4, Toronto Goodyears 9; Mar. 14–Hockey: Northern Vocational 5, Runnymede 2 (Schoolboy Finals); Mar. 14–NHL: Americans 3, Leafs 7; Mar. 15–Leadership League Forum; Mar. 16–Wrestling: Jim Londos vs. Vic Christie; Mar. 17–Hockey: Runnymede 9, Northern Vocational 7 (Schoolboy Finals); Mar. 18–Jr. Hockey: Oshawa 6, Native Sons 3; Mar. 18–NHL: Rangers 1, Leafs 2; Mar. 20–Jr. Hockey: Kitchener 3, Runnymede 2 (OHA "B" Finals); Mar. 21–NHL: Americans 0, Leafs 4; Mar. 22–Jr. Hockey: Aurora 6, Milton 3 (OHA "C" Finals); Mar. 23–Wrestling: Jack Washburn vs. Joe Savoldi; Mar. 24–Jr. Hockey: Aurora 7, Milton 2 (OHA "C" Finals); Mar. 25–Jr. Hockey: Oshawa 7, North Bay 5 (OHA "A" Finals); Mar. 27–Jr. Hockey: Oshawa 5, North Bay 4 (OHA "A" Finals); Mar. 28–NHL: Detroit 1, Leafs 4; Mar. 28–Sr. Hockey: St. John 0, Toronto Goodyears 3; Apr. 1–Jr. Hockey: Oshawa "B" 3, Runnymede 3 (OHA "B" Finals); Apr. 1–NHL: Detroit 4, Leafs 5; Apr. 4–Sr. Hockey: Montreal 3, Toronto Goodyears 1 (Allan Cup Eastern Finals); Apr. 5–Jr. Hockey: Verdun 1, Oshawa 6 (Memorial Cup Eastern Finals); Apr. 6–Hockey: Niagara Falls 4, Runnymede 2 (OHA "B" Finals); Apr. 8–Sr. Hockey: Verdun 0, Toronto Goodyears 2 (Allan Cup Eastern Finals); Apr. 10–Jr. Hockey: Edmonton 4, Oshawa 9 (Memorial Cup Finals); Apr. 11–NHL: Boston 3, Leafs 1 (Stanley Cup Finals); Apr. 12–Jr. Hockey: Edmonton 4, Oshawa 12 (Memorial Cup Finals); Apr. 13–NHL: Boston 2, Leafs 0 (Stanley Cup Finals); Apr. 15–Jr. Hockey: Edmonton 4, Oshawa 1 (Memorial Cup Finals); Apr. 17–Jr. Hockey: Edmonton 2, Oshawa 4 (Memorial Cup Finals); Apr. 18–Hockey: Red Indians 2, Kodak 1 (City League Finals); Apr. 20-22: National Electric Show; Apr. 27–Wrestling: Joey Bagnato vs. Jackie Callura; Apr. 28–Independent Order of Foresters Pageant; May 2–Tennis: Don Budge vs. Fred Perry; Oct. 19–Wrestling: Everett Marshall vs. Crusher Casey; Oct. 24-29: Bob Morton's Rameses Shrine Circus; Nov. 2–NHL: Blues 6, Whites 4 (Maple Leafs intrasquad game); Nov. 4–NHL: Boston 0, Leafs 5; Nov. 9–Wrestling: Bronko Nagurski vs. Dan O'Mahony; Nov. 11–NHL: Rangers 1, Leafs 1; Nov. 15–Sr. Hockey: Galt 2, Toronto Goodyears 8; Nov. 16–Wrestling: Cy Williams vs. The Tallahasse Terror; Nov. 18–Jr. Hockey: Markham 5, Georgetown 4; Nov. 18–Jr. Hockey: Kingsway 5, Richmond Hill 0; Nov. 18–NHL: Detroit 0, Leafs 3; Nov. 20–Jr. Hockey: Oshawa 6, Guelph 3; Nov. 20–Jr. Hockey: Upper Canada College 9, Woodstock 1; Nov. 22–Sr. Hockey: Niagara Falls 2, Toronto Goodyears 14; Nov. 23–Wrestling: Crusher Casey vs. Wild Bill Longson; Nov. 24–Jr. Hockey: Barrie 1, Grimsby 1; Nov. 24–Jr. Hockey: Owen Sound 4, Niagara Falls 1; Nov. 25–Jr. Hockey: Waterloo 10, St. Michael's "B" 3; Nov. 25–Jr. Hockey: Hamilton 3, Newmarket 3; Nov. 25–NHL: Americans 3, Leafs 4; Nov. 27–Boxing: Dave Castilloux vs. Wally Hally; Nov. 28–Jr. Hockey: Markham 5, Milton 4; Nov. 28–Jr. Hockey: Native Sons 4, Jr. Marlboros 3; Nov. 29–Jr. Hockey: Barrie 3, Grimsby 1; Nov. 29–Jr. Hockey: Aurora 6, Kingsway 1; Nov. 29–Jr. Hockey: Brantford 7, Upper Canada College 2; Nov. 30–Wrestling: Bronko Nagurski vs. Ernie Dusek; Dec. 1–Jr. Hockey: Native Sons 4, Oshawa 3 (SPA Finals); Dec. 2–Jr. Hockey: Waterloo 5, Markham 1; Dec. 2–Jr. Hockey: Hamilton 6, Newmarket 1; Dec. 2–NHL: Chicago 3, Leafs 3; Dec. 4–Boxing: Lew Transparent vs. Baby Yack; Dec. 5–Jr. Hockey: Owen Sound 6, Hamilton 3; Dec. 5–Jr. Hockey: Aurora 2, Barrie 0; Dec.

6–Sr. Hockey: Hamilton 2, Toronto Goodyears 7; Dec. 7–Wrestling: Wild Bill Longson vs. Everett Marshall; Dec. 8–Sr. Hockey: St. Catharines 4, Toronto Goodyears 3; Dec. 9–Jr. Hockey: Waterloo 3, Aurora 1; Dec. 9–Jr. Hockey: Brantford 4, Owen Sound 1; Dec. 9–NHL: Canadiens 0, Leafs 3; Dec. 12–Jr. Hockey: Jr. Marlboros 4, Young Rangers 3; Dec. 12–Jr. Hockey: Native Sons 6, Jr. Varsity 4; Dec. 13–Sr. Hockey: Port Colborne 0, Toronto Goodyears 4; Dec. 14–Hockey: UCC Old Boys, UCC New Boys; Dec. 14–NHL: Boston 1, Leafs 1; Dec. 16–NHL: Americans 1, Leafs 5; Dec. 19–Jr. Hockey: Oshawa 7, Native Sons 1; Dec. 19–Jr. Hockey: Young Rangers 3, Jr. Varsity 2; Dec. 20–Sr. Hockey: Niagara Falls 1, Toronto Goodyears 10; Dec. 23–Jr. Hockey: Jr. Marlboros 9, Native Sons 0; Dec. 23–Jr. Hockey: Guelph 3, Young Rangers 2; Dec. 23–NHL: Detroit 1, Leafs 5; Dec. 26–Jr. Hockey: Jr. Marlboros 12, Young Rangers 2; Dec. 26–Jr. Hockey: Guelph 6, Native Sons 1; Dec. 27–Sr. Hockey: Galt 3, Toronto Goodyears 17; Dec. 28–Wrestling: Wild Bill Longson vs. Dan O'Mahony; Dec. 30–Jr. Hockey: Guelph 1, Jr. Marlboros 2; Dec. 30–Jr. Hockey: Oshawa 3, Young Rangers 1; Dec. 30–NHL: Chicago 2, Leafs 4.

1940 • Jan. 1–Sr. Hockey: Port Colborne 3, Toronto Goodyears 4; Jan. 2–Boxing: Dave Castilloux vs. Leo Rodak; Jan. 4–Wrestling: Wild Bill Longson vs. Dan O'Mahony; Jan. 5–Sr. Hockey: St. Catharines 5, Toronto Goodyears 8; Jan. 6–Jr. Hockey: Jr. Marlboros 13, Jr. Varsity 2; Jan. 6–Jr. Hockey: Young Rangers 4, Native Sons 1; Jan. 6–NHL: Canadiens 1, Leafs 3; Jan. 8–Amateur Boxing Night; Jan. 9–Jr. Hockey: Guelph 2, Jr. Varsity 1; Jan. 9–Jr. Hockey: Jr. Marlboros 5, Native Sons 1; Jan. 10–Hockey: U. of T. Schools 1, Upper Canada College 10; Jan. 10–Sr. Hockey: Hamilton 0, Toronto Goodyears 3; Jan. 11–NHL: Boston 5, Leafs 2; Jan. 12–Wrestling: Wild Bill Longson vs. Joe Savoldi; Jan. 13–Jr. Hockey: Jr. Marlboros 4, Jr. Varsity 1; Jan. 13–Jr. Hockey: Guelph 2, Young Rangers 5; Jan. 13–NHL: Rangers 4, Leafs 1; Jan. 15–Amateur Boxing Night; Jan. 16–Jr. Hockey: Jr. Varsity 7, Native Sons 3; Jan. 16–Jr. Hockey: Oshawa 5, Jr. Marlboros 4; Jan. 17–Hockey: Upper Canada College 3, St. Michael's "B" 0; Jan. 17–Sr. Hockey: Niagara Falls 3, Toronto Goodyears 7; Jan. 18–NHL: Detroit 2, Leafs 2; Jan. 19–Wrestling: Wild Bill Longson vs. Joe Savoldi; Jan. 20–Jr. Hockey: Guelph 6, Native Sons 3; Jan. 20–Jr. Hockey: Young Rangers 4, Jr. Varsity 3; Jan. 20–NHL: Americans 1, Leafs 5; Jan. 22–Amateur Boxing Night; Jan. 23–Jr. Hockey: Jr. Marlboros 8, Jr. Varsity 1; Jan. 23–Jr. Hockey: Young Rangers 7, Native Sons 4; Jan. 24–Hockey: St. Michael's "B" 7, U. of T. Schools 3; Jan. 24–Sr. Hockey: Port Colborne 2, Toronto Goodyears 4; Jan. 25–Hockey: St. Michael's "B" 4, Upper Canada College 4; Jan. 27–Jr. Hockey: Young Rangers 4, Native Sons 2; Jan. 27–Jr. Hockey: Guelph 6, Jr. Varsity 3; Jan. 27–NHL: Canadiens 1, Leafs 3; Jan. 29–Amateur Boxing Night; Jan. 30–Jr. Hockey: Native Sons 4, Jr. Marlboros 3; Jan. 30–Jr. Hockey: Young Rangers 4, Jr. Varsity 3; Jan. 31–Hockey: Upper Canada College 5, St. Michael's "B" 3; Jan. 31–Sr. Hockey: St. Catharines 1, Toronto Goodyears 5; Feb. 1–Wrestling: Bronko Nagurski vs. Wild Bill Longson; Feb. 2–Hockey: St. Michael's "B" 7, U. of T. Schools 6; Feb. 3–Jr. Hockey: Native Sons 6, Jr. Varsity 3; Feb. 3–Jr. Hockey: Guelph 1, Jr. Marlboros 6; Feb. 3–NHL: Chicago 3, Leafs 2; Feb. 5–Boxing: Dave Castilloux vs. Charley Gomer; Feb. 6–Jr. Hockey: Oshawa 11, Jr. Varsity 0; Feb. 6–Jr. Hockey: Jr. Marlboros 5, Young Rangers 0; Feb. 7–Hockey: Upper Canada College 6, St. Michael's "B" 1; Feb. 7–Sr. Hockey: Hamilton 4, Toronto Goodyears 6; Feb. 8–Wrestling: Wild Bill Longson vs. King Kong Cox; Feb. 10–Jr. Hockey: Young Rangers 7, Native Sons 1; Feb. 10–Jr. Hockey: Jr. Marlboros 4, Jr. Varsity 3; Feb. 10–NHL: Rangers 4, Leafs 4; Feb. 12–Amateur Boxing Night; Feb. 13–Jr. Hockey: Native Sons 4, Jr. Varsity 3; Feb. 13–Jr. Hockey: Oshawa 2, Young Rangers 5; Feb. 14–Hockey: Upper Canada College 4, St. Michael's "B" 4 (Prep School Finals); Feb. 14–Sr. Hockey: Galt 3, Toronto Goodyears 9; Feb. 15–Wrestling: Wild Bill Longson vs. King Kong Cox; Feb. 16–Hockey: Upper Canada College 6, St. Michael's "B" 1 (Prep School Finals); Feb. 17–Jr. Hockey: Oshawa 4, Jr. Marlboros 3; Feb. 17–NHL: Canadiens 1, Leafs 3; Feb. 19–Boxing: Steve Mamakos vs. Sammy Luftspring; Feb. 20–Jr. Hockey: Oshawa 4, Native Sons 4; Feb. 21–Sr. Hockey: Sr. Varsity 0, Toronto Goodyears 4 (benefit game for Finnish Relief Fund); Feb. 22–Wrestling: Eddie Eastup vs. Wild Bill Longsong; Feb. 23–Sr. Hockey: Port Colborne 0, Toronto Goodyears 3; Feb. 24–Jr. Hockey: Young Rangers 7, Jr. Marlboros 5; Feb. 24–NHL: Boston 1, Leafs 3; Feb. 26–Amateur Boxing Night; Feb. 27–Jr. Hockey: Young Rangers 3, Native Sons 2; Feb. 28–Sr. Hockey: Port Colborne 0, Toronto Goodyears 9; Feb. 29–NHL: Detroit 1, Leafs 3; Mar. 1–Wrestling: King King Cox vs. Eddie Eastup; Mar. 2–Jr. Hockey: Guelph 5, Jr. Marlboros 9; Mar. 2–NHL: Rangers 1, Leafs 1; Mar. 4–Boxing: George Pace vs. Lou Salica; Mar. 5–Jr. Hockey: Oshawa 4, Young Rangers 3; Mar. 6–Jr. Hockey: Upper Canada College 9, Aurora 5; Mar. 7–Wrestling: The Angel vs. Jerry Monohan; Mar. 8–Jr. Hockey: Aurora 5, Upper Canada College 3; Mar. 8–Sr. Hockey: St. Catharines 2, Toronto Goodyears 5; Mar. 9–Jr. Hockey: Jr. Marlboros 11, Guelph 4; Mar. 9–NHL: Chicago 2, Leafs 5; Mar. 16–NHL: Americans 6, Leafs 8; Mar. 16–Sr. Hockey: St. Catharines 0, Toronto Goodyears 3; Mar. 18–Ontario Conservative Party Rally; Mar. 19–NHL: Chicago 2, Leafs 3; Mar. 20–Sr. Hockey: Kirkland Lake 4, Toronto Goodyears 3 (OHA Senior Finals); Mar. 21–Wrestling: Wild Bill Longson vs. Ed Don George; Mar. 22–Jr. Hockey: Jr. Marlboros 4, Oshawa 3; Mar. 23–Sr. Hockey: Kirkland Lake 1, Toronto Goodyears 1 (OHA Senior Finals); Mar. 26–NHL: Detroit 1, Leafs 2; Mar. 27–Jr. Hockey: Oshawa 4, Jr. Marlboros 2; Mar. 28–Wrestling: Wild Bill Longson vs. Ed Don George; Mar. 29–Jr. Hockey: Markham 7, Grimsby 5 (OHA "C" Finals); Mar. 30–Sr. Hockey: Kirkland Lake 6, Sydney 1; Apr. 1–Boxing: Amateur Boxing Night; Apr. 3–Jr. Hockey: Oshawa 10, Dome Porkies 1 (All-Ontario Jr. Finals); Apr. 5–Jr. Hockey: Oshawa 6, Verdun 3 (Memorial Cup Eastern Finals); Apr. 6–NHL: Rangers 1, Leafs 2 (Stanley Cup Finals); Apr. 6–Sr. Hockey: Kirkland Lake 7, Sydney 0; Apr. 8–Sr. Hockey: Montreal 3, Kirkland Lake 1 (Allan Cup Eastern Finals); Apr. 9–NHL: Rangers 0, Leafs 3 (Stanley Cup Finals); Apr. 10–Jr. Hockey: Aurora 7, Waterloo 3; Apr. 11–Jr. Hockey: Markham 2, Grimsby 1 (OHA "C" Finals); Apr. 11–NHL: Rangers 2, Leafs 1 (Stanley Cup Finals); Apr. 12–Sr. Hockey: Kirkland Lake 6, Montreal 4; Apr. 13–NHL: Rangers 3, Leafs 2 (Stanley Cup-winning game); Apr. 15–Jr. Hockey: Waterloo 5, Grimsby "B" 1; Apr. 16–Hockey: Telegram 6, Donnell-Mudge 4 (Mercantile League Finals); Apr. 18–Wrestling: The Angel vs. Ivan Rasputin; Apr. 20–Sr. Hockey: Kirkland Lake 8, Calgary 5 (Allan Cup Finals); Apr. 22–Sr. Hockey: Kirkland Lake 9, Calgary 1 (Allan Cup Finals); Apr. 24–Sr. Hockey: Kirkland Lake 7, Calgary 1 (Allan Cup Finals); Apr. 25–Wrestling: Wild Bill Longson vs. Tor Johnson; Apr. 29–Boxing: Dave Castilloux vs. Billy Marquart; May 2–Wrestling: Wild Bill Longson vs. Tor Johnson; Oct. 4–Wrestling: Frank Taylor vs. Joe Cox; Oct. 7–Lacrosse: Vancouver 14, St. Catharines 9 (Mann Cup Finals); Oct. 9–Lacrosse: Vancouver 5, St. Catharines 15 (Mann Cup Finals); Oct. 10–Wrestling: Loan Wolf vs. Nanjo Singh; Oct. 11–Lacrosse: Vancouver 10, St. Catharines 17 (Mann Cup Finals); Oct. 14–Lacrosse: Vancouver 5, St. Catharines 18 (Mann Cup Finals); Oct. 17–Wrestling: Lone Wolf vs. Joe Savoldi; Oct. 18–Music: Toronto Star Coliseum Chorus w/Toronto Symphony Orchestra; Oct. 21-26: Bob Morton's Rameses Shrine Circus; Oct. 30–Wrestling: Golden Terror vs. Joe Cox; Oct. 31–Hockey: Whites 4, Blues 2 (Maple Leafs intrasquad game); Nov. 2–NHL: Rangers 4, Leafs 1; Nov. 6–Sr. Hockey: London 3, Sr. Marlboros 2; Nov. 8–Sports Service League Bingo; Nov. 8–Wrestling: Golden Terror vs. Frank Taylor; Nov. 9–NHL: Detroit 0, Leafs 3; Nov. 11–Boxing: Callura vs. Pace; Nov. 13–Sr. Hockey: Niagara Falls 4, Sr. Marlboros 4; Nov. 14–Wrestling: Golden Terror vs. King Kong Cox; Nov. 16–NHL: Canadiens 2, Leafs 4; Nov. 18–Jr. Hockey: St. Michael's "B" 11, Milton 1; Nov. 18–Jr. Hockey: Newmarket 6, Thorold 2; Nov. 19–Jr. Hockey: U. of T. Schools 6, Aurora 1; Nov. 19–Jr. Hockey: Etobicoke 6, Barrie 1; Nov. 20–Sr. Hockey: Oshawa 4, Sr. Marlboros 3; Nov. 21–Wrestling: Golden Terror vs. Ivan Rasputin; Nov. 22–Jr. Hockey: Young Rangers 2, Guelph 7; Nov. 23–Jr. Hockey: Upper Canada College 10, Markham 4; Nov. 23–Jr. Hockey: Weston 3, St. Catharines 5; Nov. 23–NHL: Chicago 1, Leafs 0; Nov. 26–Jr. Hockey: Waterloo 3, Burlington 1; Nov. 26–Jr. Hockey: St. Michael's "B" 11, Newmarket 1; Nov. 27–Sr. Hockey: Port Colborne 2, Sr. Marlboros 4; Nov. 28–Wrestling: Everett Marshall vs. Golden Terror; Nov. 29–Jr. Hockey: Jr. Marlboros "B" 9, Native Sons 4; Nov. 30–Jr. Hockey: U. of T. Schools 2, Etobicoke 4; Nov. 30–Jr. Hockey: Upper Canada College 9, St. Catharines 7; Nov. 30–NHL: Americans 1, Leafs 6; Dec. 2–Boxing: Salica vs. Montana; Dec. 3–Jr. Hockey: Oshawa 2, Guelph 4; Dec. 3–Jr. Hockey: St. Michael's "B" 5, Etobicoke 4; Dec. 4–Sr. Hockey: Hamilton 7, Sr. Marlboros 8; Dec. 5–Wrestling: Everett Marshall vs. King Kong Cox; Dec. 6–Canadian Seaman's Union Rally; Dec. 7–Jr. Hockey: Guelph 5, Jr. Marlboros 7; Dec. 7–NHL: Boston 2, Leafs 3; Dec. 9–Boxing: Spiegel vs. Castilloux; Dec. 10–Jr. Hockey: St. Michael's 5, Brantford 9; Dec. 10–Jr. Hockey: Upper Canada College 6, Waterloo 2; Dec. 12–NHL: Canadiens 3, Leafs 4; Dec. 13–Sr. Hockey: Sr. Marlboros 1, St. Catharines 2; Dec. 14–Jr. Hockey: Upper Canada College 3, Brantford 5; Dec. 14–NHL: Chicago 1, Leafs 2; Dec. 16–Boxing: Jack Armstrong vs. Ivy; Dec. 17–Jr. Hockey: Jr. Marlboros 4, Young Rangers 2; Dec. 17–Jr. Hockey: Guelph 9, Native Sons 6; Dec. 18–Jr. Hockey: UCC New Boys 8, UCC Old Boys 7; Dec. 20–Sr. Hockey: Sr. Marlboros 3, London 1; Dec. 21–NHL: Americans 2, Leafs 2; Dec. 23–Jr. Hockey: Jr. Marlboros 10, Native Sons 3; Dec. 25–Sr. Hockey: Sr. Marlboros 3, Niagara Falls 5; Dec. 26–Jr. Hockey: Young Rangers 11, Native Sons 5; Dec. 28–Jr. Hockey: Jr. Marlboros 7, Oshawa 7; Dec. 28–NHL: Rangers 2, Leafs 3; Dec. 30–Jr. Hockey: Guelph 6, Young Rangers 5.

1941 • Jan. 1–Sr. Hockey: Sr. Marlboros 2, Oshawa 0; Jan. 2–Wrestling: Jim Londos vs. K.O. Koverley; Jan. 4–Jr. Hockey: Jr. Marlboros 12, Guelph 4; Jan. 4–NHL: Detroit 3, Leafs 1; Jan. 7–Jr. Hockey: Jr. Marlboros 8, Young Rangers 3; Jan. 7–Jr. Hockey: Oshawa 13, Native Sons 0; Jan. 8–Sr. Hockey: Sr. Marlboros 3, St. Catharines 7; Jan. 9–NHL: Rangers 2, Leafs 3; Jan. 10–Wrestling: Whipper Billy Watson vs. Jack Russell; Jan. 11–NHL: Americans 0, Leafs 9; Jan. 12–Jr. Hockey: Jr. Marlboros 6, Native Sons 1; Jan. 14–Jr. Hockey: Oshawa 3, Young Rangers 3; Jan. 15–Jr. Hockey: Upper Canada College 2, St. Michael's "B" 0; Jan. 15–Sr. Hockey: Jr. Marlboros 5, Hamilton 4; Jan. 17–Wrestling: King Kong Cox vs. K.O. Koverley; Jan. 18–Jr. Hockey: Young Rangers 11, Native Sons 3; Jan. 18–NHL: Boston 1, Leafs 0; Jan. 21–Jr. Hockey: Young Rangers 2, Jr. Marlboros 7; Jan. 21–Jr. Hockey: Guelph 13, Native Sons 5; Jan. 23–Wrestling: Jim Londos vs. King Kong Cox; Jan. 24–Jr. Hockey: Upper Canada College 2, St. Michael's "B" 0; Jan. 24–Sr. Hockey: Port Colborne 2, Sr. Marlboros 2; Jan. 25–Jr. Hockey: Guelph 5, Jr. Marlboros 8; Jan. 25–NHL: Canadiens 2, Leafs 2; Jan. 27–Boxing: Castilloux vs. Spiegel; Jan. 28–Jr. Hockey: Jr. Marlboros 6, Native Sons 2; Jan. 28–Jr. Hockey: Oshawa 7, Young Rangers 6; Jan. 29–Sr. Hockey: Sr. Marlboros 1, Hamilton 4; Jan. 30–NHL: Detroit 1, Leafs 2; Feb. 1–Jr. Hockey: Jr. Marlboros 10, Young Rangers 4; Feb. 1–NHL: Chicago 1, Leafs 3; Feb. 3–Sr. Hockey: Sr. Marlboros 1, St. Catharines 3; Feb. 4–Jr. Hockey: Oshawa 12, Native Sons 4; Feb. 5–Sr. Hockey: Sr. Marlboros 4, Oshawa 1; Feb. 6–Wrestling: Masked Wolf vs. Wild Bill Longson; Feb. 8–Jr. Hockey: Jr. Marlboros 9, Oshawa 2; Feb. 8–NHL: Boston 3, Leafs 2; Feb. 11–Jr. Hockey: Young Rangers 8, Native Sons 4; Feb. 12–Jr. Hockey: St. Michael's "B" 4, Upper Canada College 3; Feb. 12–Sr. Hockey: Sr. Marlboros 5, Niagara Falls 2; Feb. 13–Toronto War Savings Committee Youth Rally; Feb. 13–Wrestling: Whipper Billy Watson vs. K.O. Koverley; Feb. 14–Jr. Hockey: St. Michael's "B" 4, Upper Canada College 3; Feb. 15–Jr. Hockey: Guelph 6, Young Rangers 4; Feb. 15–NHL: Rangers 3, Leafs 4; Feb. 17–Sr. Hockey: Guelph 4, Niagara Falls 1; Feb. 18–Boxing: Jack Armstrong vs. Pace; Feb. 19–Sr. Hockey: Sr. Marlboros 2, Niagara Falls 1; Feb. 20–NHL: Canadiens 1, Leafs 2; Feb. 21–Wrestling: Jim Londos vs. Wild Bill Longson; Feb. 22–Jr. Hockey: Jr. Marlboros 12, Native Sons 1; Feb. 22–NHL: Detroit 2, Leafs 6; Feb. 24–Sr. Hockey: Sr. Marlboros 2, Oshawa 1; Feb. 25–Boxing: Spiegel vs. Castilloux; Feb. 27–Wrestling: Masked Wolf vs. King Kong Cox; Feb. 28–Jr. Hockey: Young Rangers 5, Oshawa 4; Mar. 1–Jr. Hockey: Jr. Marlboros 4, Guelph 11; Mar. 1–NHL: Boston 0, Leafs 0; Mar. 3–Sr. Hockey: Sr. Marlboros 4, St. Catharines 1; Mar. 4–Jr. Hockey: Jr. Marlboros 14, Guelph 1; Mar. 5–Jr. Hockey: Young Rangers 6, Oshawa 1; Mar. 6–Wrestling: K.O. Koverley vs. Wild Bill Longson; Mar. 6–Wrestling: King Kong Cox vs. Masked Wolf; Mar. 7–Sr. Hockey: St. Catharines 1, Sr. Marlboros 0; Mar. 8–Jr. Hockey: Jr. Marlboros 9, Guelph 2; Mar. 8–NHL: Americans 1, Leafs 6; Mar. 15–NHL: Chicago 1, Leafs 7; Mar. 15–Sr. Hockey: Jr. Marlboros 3, St. Catharines 2; Mar. 17–Jr. Hockey: Jr. Marlboros 2, Oshawa 5 (OHA "A" Finals); Mar. 18–Boxing: Berger vs. Rinaldi; Mar. 19–Sr. Hockey: Timmins 1, Sr. Marlboros 2 (All-Ontario Sr. Finals); Mar. 20–Wrestling: Masked Wolf vs. Bill Hanson; Mar. 21–Sr. Hockey: Timmins 2, Sr. Marlboros 1 (All-Ontario Sr. Finals); Mar. 22–Sr. Hockey: Timmins 0, Sr. Marlboros 5 (All-Ontario Sr. Finals); Mar. 24–Canadian War Service Fund w/Wendell Wilkie; Mar. 25–NHL: Boston 2, Leafs 7 (Stanley Cup Finals); Mar. 26–Sr. Hockey: Montreal 3, Sr. Marlboros 2 (Allan Cup Finals); Mar. 27–NHL: Boston 2, Leafs 1 (Stanley Cup Finals); Mar. 28–Jr. Hockey: Jr. Marlboros 4, Oshawa 1 (OHA "A" Finals); Mar. 28–Sr. Hockey: Montreal 2, Sr. Marlboros 6 (Allan Cup Finals); Mar. 31–Sr. Hockey: Montreal 6, Sr. Marlboros 1 (Allan Cup Finals); Apr. 1–NHL: Boston 2, Leafs 1 (Stanley Cup Finals); Apr. 2–Jr. Hockey: Oshawa 8, Jr. Marlboros 4 (OHA "A" Finals); Apr. 3–Jr. Hockey: Markham 6, Bolton 4; Apr. 4–Wrestling: Masked Wolf vs. K.O. Koverley; Apr. 5–Jr. Hockey: Montreal Royals 7, Oshawa 4 (Memorial Cup Eastern Finals); Apr. 7–Jr. Hockey: Montreal Royals 2, Oshawa 10 (Memorial Cup Eastern Finals); Apr. 8–Jr. Hockey: Markham 10, Bolton 5; Apr. 9–Jr. Hockey: Montreal Royals 7, Oshawa 4 (Memorial Cup Eastern Finals); Apr. 11–Jr. Hockey: Markham 4, Bolton 2; Apr. 11–Wrestling: Whipper Billy Watson vs. King Kong Cox; Apr. 12–Hockey: Tip Tops 2, Telegram 4; Apr. 12–Jr. Hockey: Montreal Royals 1, Oshawa 7 (Memorial Cup Eastern Finals); Apr. 14–Boxing: Castilloux vs. Troisi; Apr. 16–Hockey: Donnell-Mudge 4, Telegram 2 (Mercantile League Finals); Apr. 17–Wrestling: Masked Wolf vs. Sammy Stein; Apr. 19–Hockey: Donnell-Mudge 1, Telegram 3 (Mercantile League Finals); Apr. 21–Jr. Hockey: Montreal Royals 2, Winnipeg 4 (Memorial Cup Finals); Apr. 22–Boxing: Perfetti vs. Pace; Blake vs. Spiegel; Berger vs. DeJesus; Apr. 23–Hockey: Donnell-Mudge 6, Telegram 4 (Mercantile League Finals); Apr. 24–Wrestling: Masked Wolf vs. Sammy Stein; Apr. 25–Tennis: Alice Marble vs. Mary Hardwick (first women athletes at Gardens); Apr. 26–Jr. Hockey: Montreal Royals 4, Winnipeg 6 (Memorial Cup Finals); Apr. 29–Hockey: Donnell-Mudge 8, Telegram 7 (Mercantile League

Finals); Apr. 30–Jr. Hockey: Montreal Royals 4, Winnipeg 7 (Memorial Cup Finals); May 10–Music: 48th Highlanders Bazaar; May 11–Boxing: Hurst vs. Bagnato; May 21–Toronto Board of Education Convention; May 27-31: Water Follies w/Buster Crabbe; June 3–Women's Victory Loan Rally; July 8–Canadian Tribune Forum; July 29–Canadian Corps Association Meeting; Oct. 2–Wrestling: Earl McCready vs. Roland Kirchmeyer; Oct. 9–Wrestling: Yvon Robert vs. Whipper Billy Watson; Oct. 16–Wrestling: Earl McCready vs. Wallace Muscovich; Oct. 17-18–Music: Toronto Star Coliseum Chorus/Toronto Symphony; Oct. 20-25: Bob Morton's Rameses Shrine Circus; Oct. 26–Canadian Tribune Convention; Oct. 27–Music: Cab Calloway w/Cotton Club Orchestra; Oct. 28–Boxing: Bob Pastor vs. Al Delaney; Oct. 30–Hockey: Whites 2, Blues 4 (Maple Leafs intrasquad game); Nov. 1–NHL: Rangers 4, Leafs 3; Nov. 6–Wrestling: Roland Kirchmeyer vs. Whipper Billy Watson; Nov. 8–NHL: Boston 0, Leafs 2; Nov. 11–Sr. Hockey: Sr. Marlboros 3, Niagara Falls 3; Nov. 12–Wrestling: Whipper Billy Watson vs. Roland Kirchmeyer; Nov. 13–NHL: Canadiens 2, Leafs 4; Nov. 15–NHL: Detroit 1, Leafs 2; Nov. 18-21: Ice Follies of 1941 (first Ice Follies show); Nov. 22–NHL: Chicago 0, Leafs 3; Nov. 24–Boxing: Dave Catilloux vs. Sonny Jones (Canadian Welterweight Title); Nov. 25–Jr. Hockey: St. Michael's 4, Native Sons 3; Nov. 25–Jr. Hockey: Jr. Marlboros 5, Young Rangers 3; Nov. 26–Sr. Hockey: Sr. Marlboros 0, Hamilton 3; Nov. 27–Wrestling: The Angel vs. Masked Wolf; Nov. 29–Jr. Hockey: Jr. Marlboros 6, Oshawa 7; Nov. 29–Jr. Hockey: St. Michael's 11, Brantford 6; Nov. 29–NHL: Americans 2, Leafs 8; Dec. 1–Jr. Hockey: Oshawa 8, Brantford 7; Dec. 2–Jr. Hockey: St. Michael's "B" 11, U. of T. Schools 3; Dec. 2–Jr. Hockey: Etobicoke 2, Markham 10; Dec. 3–Sr. Hockey: Sr. Marlboros 2, Port Colborne 1; Dec. 5–Jr. Hockey: Upper Canada College 6, De la Salle 5; Dec. 5–Jr. Hockey: Hamilton 5, St. Catharines 9; Dec. 6–Jr. Hockey: Oshawa 10, St. Michael's 4; Dec. 6–Jr. Hockey: Guelph 10, Native Sons 2; Dec. 6–NHL: Canadiens 1, Leafs 3; Dec. 8–Jr. Hockey: Milton 3, Oakville 1; Dec. 8–Jr. Hockey: Caledonia 5, Aurora 2; Dec. 9–Jr. Hockey: St. Michael's 4, Jr. Marlboros 2; Dec. 9–Jr. Hockey: Guelph 3, Young Rangers 2; Dec. 10–Sr. Hockey: Sr. Marlboros 1, St. Catharines 3; Dec. 12–Jr. Hockey: St. Catharines 4, Barrie 2; Dec. 12–Jr. Hockey: U. of T. Schools 3, Owen Sound 8; Dec. 13–Jr. Hockey: Oshawa 2, Young Rangers 6; Dec. 13–Jr. Hockey: Guelph 3, Jr. Marlboros 0; Dec. 13–NHL: Rangers 1, Leafs 2; Dec. 15–Jr. Hockey: Markham 9, Paris 0; Dec. 15–Jr. Hockey: Milton 4, Caledonia 1; Dec. 16–Jr. Hockey: Brantford 6, Young Rangers 3; Dec. 16–Jr. Hockey: St. Michael's 6, Guelph 4; Dec. 17–Sr. Hockey: Sr. Marlboros 7, Kingston 2; Dec. 18–Jr. Hockey: St. Catharines 5, Owen Sound 2; Dec. 18–Jr. Hockey: Markham 5, Milton 0; Dec. 19–Jr. Hockey: UCC New Boys 3, UCC Old Boys 6; Dec. 20–NHL: Chicago 2, Leafs 0; Dec. 20–Variety: Canada Starch Company Christmas Frolic; Dec. 22–Sr. Hockey: Sr. Marlboros 3, Niagara Falls 2; Dec. 23–Jr. Hockey: Jr. Marlboros 6, Native Sons 2; Dec. 23–Jr. Hockey: Markham 9, Upper Canada College 2; Dec. 25–NHL: Boston 0, Leafs 2; Dec. 26–Jr. Hockey: St. Catharines 12, Markham 6; Dec. 27–Jr. Hockey: Young Rangers 9, Native Sons 5; Dec. 27–NHL: Detroit 3, Leafs 5; Dec. 29–Jr. Hockey: Etobicoke 3, Milton 5; Dec. 29–Sr. Hockey: Sr. Marlboros 6, Hamilton 2.

1942 • Jan. 1–Jr. Hockey: Oshawa 5, Jr. Marlboros 3; Jan. 3–Jr. Hockey: St. Michael's 7, Brantford 6; Jan. 3–Jr. Hockey: Oshawa 12, Native Sons 3; Jan. 3–NHL: Americans 2, Leafs 4; Jan. 6–Jr. Hockey: Jr. Marlboros 4, Brantford 3; Jan. 6–Jr. Hockey: St. Michael's 5, Native Sons 0; Jan. 7–Sr. Hockey: Sr. Marlboros 6, Kingston 3; Jan. 10–Jr. Hockey: Young Rangers 4, Jr. Marlboros 5; Jan. 10–Jr. Hockey: Guelph 9, Native Sons 1; Jan. 10–NHL: Detroit 6, Leafs 4; Jan. 12–Jr. Hockey: De la Salle 3, St. Michael's "B" 1; Jan. 12–Sr. Hockey: Sr. Marlboros 6, Port Colborne 1; Jan. 13–Jr. Hockey: Oshawa 8, St. Michael's 5; Jan. 13–Jr. Hockey: Brantford 5, Native Sons 3; Jan. 14–Sr. Hockey: Sr. Marlboros 6, St. Catharines 3; Jan. 15–Jr. Hockey: De la Salle 8, St. Andrews 5; Jan. 15–Wrestling: Crusher Casey vs. Earl McCready; Jan. 16–Jr. Hockey: St. Michael's "B" 2, Upper Canada College 6; Jan. 17–Jr. Hockey: Young Rangers 11, St. Michael's 7; Jan. 17–NHL: Chicago 4, Leafs 2; Jan. 19–Jr. Hockey: U. of T. Schools 3, De la Salle 2; Jan. 20–Jr. Hockey: Guelph 3, St. Michael's 2; Jan. 20–Jr. Hockey: Young Rangers 5, Brantford 4; Jan. 21–Jr. Hockey: De la Salle 5, Upper Canada College 2; Jan. 21–Sr. Hockey: Sr. Marlboros 0, Niagara Falls 0; Jan. 22–Wrestling: Angel Tillet vs. Crusher Casey; Jan. 24–Jr. Hockey: Oshawa 5, Young Rangers 4; Jan. 24–Jr. Hockey: St. Michael's 3, Native Sons 2; Jan. 24–NHL: Americans 2, Leafs 3; Jan. 27–Jr. Hockey: St. Michael's 6, Young Rangers 3; Jan. 27–Jr. Hockey: St. Michael's "B" 4, U. of T. Schools 5; Jan. 28–Wrestling: Whipper Billy Watson vs. Nanjo Singh; Jan. 29–NHL: Canadiens 3, Leafs 7; Jan. 30–Hockey: Moose Ecclestone Night (benefit game); Jan. 30–Sr. Hockey: Sr. Marlboros 7, St. Catharines 3; Jan. 31–Jr. Hockey: Jr. Marlboros 4, Guelph 1; Jan. 31–NHL: Boston 3, Leafs 2; Feb. 3–Jr. Hockey: Guelph 3, Young Rangers 5; Feb. 3–Jr. Hockey: Jr. Marlboros 2, Brantford 5; Feb. 4–Hockey: De la Salle 6, St. Andrews 3; Feb. 4–Sr. Hockey: Sr. Marlboros 4, Hamilton 3; Feb. 6–Wrestling: Nanjo Singh vs. Whipper Billy Watson; Feb. 7–Jr. Hockey: Young Rangers 5, Jr. Marlboros 5; Feb. 7–NHL: Rangers 4, Leafs 6; Feb. 9–Hockey: St. Michael's "B" 9, St. Andrews 2; Feb. 9–Jr. Hockey: St. Michael's 2, Jr. Marlboros 3; Feb. 10–Hockey: Upper Canada College 4, De la Salle 4; Feb. 10–Sr. Hockey: Sr. Marlboros 10, Port Colborne 3; Feb. 12–Wrestling: Earl McCready vs. Nanjo Singh; Feb. 13–Hockey: De la Salle 6, U. of T. Schools 1; Feb. 14–Jr. Hockey: Brantford 7, St. Michael's 2; Feb. 14–Jr. Hockey: Young Rangers 8, Native Sons 4; Feb. 14–NHL: Detroit 2, Leafs 4; Feb. 16–Hockey: Upper Canada College 5, St. Andrews 4; Feb. 16–Sr. Hockey: Sr. Marlboros 3, Hamilton 2; Feb. 17–Jr. Hockey: Oshawa 6, Jr. Marlboros 3; Feb. 18–Hockey: U. of T. Schools 2, De la Salle 3; Feb. 18–Victory Loan Forum; Feb. 19–Wrestling: Nanjo Sinjh vs. Whipper Billy Watson; Feb. 20–Sr. Hockey: Sr. Marlboros 7, Hamilton 2; Feb. 21–NHL: Americans 3, Leafs 4; Feb. 23–Hockey: Military Hockey Tournament; Feb. 23–Jr. Hockey: Young Rangers 12, St. Michael's 3; Feb. 24–Hockey: De la Salle 1, U. of T. Schools 4; Feb. 25–Sr. Hockey: Sr. Marlboros 2, Hamilton 3; Feb. 26–Wrestling: Nanjo Sinjh vs. Roland Kirchmeyer; Feb. 28–Jr. Hockey: Young Rangers 3, St. Michael's 1; Feb. 28–NHL: Chicago 2, Leafs 8; Mar. 2–Victory Loan Forum; Mar. 3–Jr. Hockey: U. of T. Schools 10, Guelph "B" 1; Mar. 4–Jr. Hockey: Young Rangers 6, Guelph 4; Mar. 5–NHL: Canadiens 5, Leafs 2; Mar. 6–Wrestling: Don Louis Thesz vs. Nanjo Singh; Mar. 7–Sr. Hockey: Camp Borden 2, Ottawa RCAF 11 (Ontario Military Playoffs); Mar. 7–NHL: Rangers 2, Leafs 4; Mar. 14–NHL: Boston 4, Leafs 6; Mar. 16–Jr. Hockey: U. of T. Schools 3, Oshawa "B" 3; Mar. 17–Jr. Hockey: Milton 9, Oakville 4; Mar. 19–Wrestling: Angel Tillet vs. Strangler Lewis; Mar. 20–Sr. Hockey: Sutton 2, HMCS York 2; Mar. 21–Jr. Hockey: U. of T. Schools 7, Stratford 6; Mar. 21–NHL: Rangers 1, Leafs 3; Mar. 23–Jr. Hockey: Oshawa 6, Ottawa St. Pats 4; Mar. 24–Sr. Hockey: Peterborough Soldiers 6, Merritton 2; Mar. 25–Sr. Hockey: Ottawa RCAF 8, Hamilton 3 (OHA Sr. Finals); Mar. 26–Wrestling: Sinjh/Kirchmayer vs. Watson/Thesz; Mar. 27–Jr. Hockey: Ottawa St. Pats 5, Oshawa 11; Mar. 28–NHL: Rangers 1, Leafs 2; Mar. 28–Sr. Hockey: Paris 8, Markham 5; Mar. 31–NHL: Rangers 2, Leafs 3; Apr. 1–Jr. Hockey: Preston 1, Milton 10; Apr. 2–Wrestling: Nanjo Singh vs. Vic Christie; Apr. 3–Jr. Hockey: Montreal Royals 3, Oshawa 4 (Memorial Cup Eastern Final); Apr. 4–Hockey: Kirkland Lake 8, Owen Sound 3 (Juvenile Finals); Apr. 4–Hockey: Kingston 8, Ottawa 0 (Midget Finals); Apr. 4–NHL: Detroit 3, Leafs 2 (Stanley Cup Finals); Apr. 6–Sr. Hockey: Sutton 4, Fingal Bombers 3 (Intermediate "A" Playoffs); Apr. 7–NHL: Detroit 4, Leafs 2 (Stanley Cup Finals); Apr. 8–Jr. Hockey: Montreal Royals 4, Oshawa 6 (Memorial Cup Eastern Final); Apr. 9–Wrestling: Vic Christie vs. Nanjo Singh; Apr. 14–NHL: Detroit 3, Leafs 9 (Stanley Cup Finals); Apr. 16–Wrestling: Nanjo Singh vs. Vic Christie; Apr. 18–NHL: Detroit 1, Leafs 3 (Stanley Cup-winning game); Apr. 22–Sr. Hockey: Port Arthur 4, Ottawa RCAF 3 (Allan Cup Finals); Apr. 23–Wrestling: Angel Tillet vs. Nanjo Singh; Apr. 25–Sr. Hockey: Port Arthur 1, Ottawa RCAF 7 (Allan Cup Finals); May 9–Roller Skating Follies; May 16–Imperial Order of the Daughters of the Empire Convention; May 26-30: Water Follies with Buster Crabbe; June 13–Music: Dancing to the Modernaires; June 20-21–Music: Dancing to Ned Hamill; June 22-25: Rotary Club Convention; June 29–Music: Salute to Canada's Army w/Paul Robeson; July 2–Music: Dance and Vaudeville Show; July 17–Civil Liberties Union Convention; July 21–Lions Club Rally; Sept. 21–Public War Rally; Oct. 1–Wrestling: John Katan vs. Whipper Billy Watson; Oct. 7–Lacrosse: Mimico-Brampton 10, New Westminster 7 (Mann Cup Finals); Oct. 8–Wrestling: Wild Bill Longson vs. Nanjo Singh; Oct. 9–Lacrosse: Mimico-Brampton 15, New Westminster 9 (Mann Cup Finals); Oct. 12–Lacrosse: Mimico-Brampton 8, New Westminster 14 (Mann Cup Finals); Oct. 13–Citizen's Committee Forum; Oct. 14–Lacrosse: Mimico-Brampton 10, New Westminster 9 (Mann Cup Finals); Oct. 15–Wrestling: John Katan vs. Whipper Billy Watson; Oct. 19-24: Bob Morton's Rameses Shrine Circus; Oct. 26-28: Victory Loan Pageant w/Dionne Quintuplets; Oct. 29–NHL: Syl Apps' Blues 3, Nick Metz' Whites 2 (Maple Leafs intrasquad game); Oct. 31–NHL: Rangers 2, Leafs 7; Nov. 5–Wrestling: Whipper Billy Watson vs. Al Dunlop; Nov. 7–NHL: Detroit 2, Leafs 5; Nov. 11–Sr. Hockey: Air Force 5, Army 3; Nov. 11–Wrestling: Earl McCready vs. John Katan; Nov. 12–NHL: Boston 1, Leafs 3; Nov. 13–Sr. Hockey: Navy 8, Research Colonels 4; Nov. 14–NHL: Chicago 4, Leafs 3; Nov. 17-20: Ice Follies of 1942; Nov. 21–NHL: Canadiens 0, Leafs 8; Nov. 23–Sr. Hockey: Army 6, Research Colonels 5; Nov. 24–Sr. Hockey: Air Force 3, Navy 6; Nov. 25–Aid to Russia Forum w/Wendell Wilkie; Nov. 26–Wrestling: Whipper Billy Watson vs. Pedro Martinez; Nov. 28–Jr. Hockey: Oshawa 8, Young Rangers 0; Nov. 28–NHL: Rangers 6, Leafs 8; Dec. 1–Sr. Hockey: Army 6, Navy 8; Dec. 2–Jr. Hockey: St. Michael's 2, Young Rangers 4; Dec. 3–Wrestling: John Katan vs. Earl McCready; Dec. 4–Sr. Hockey: Air Force 7, Research Colonels 4; Dec. 5–Jr. Hockey: Stratford 4, St. Michael's 5; Dec. 5–NHL: Canadiens 1, Leafs 9; Dec. 7–Jr. Hockey: Hamilton 9, Jr. Marlboros 5; Dec. 8–Sr. Hockey: Army 3, Air Force 7; Dec. 9–Wrestling: Watson/McCready vs. Katan/Dunlop; Dec. 10–NHL: Chicago 2, Leafs 7; Dec. 11–Sr. Hockey: Navy 2, Research Colonels 5; Dec. 12–Jr. Hockey: Jr. Marlboros 4, Young Rangers 10; Dec. 12–NHL: Detroit 4, Leafs 5; Dec. 15–Jr. Hockey: Oshawa 7, St. Michael's 4; Dec. 16–Sr. Hockey: Army 7, Research Colonels 6; Dec. 17–Wrestling: Angel Tillet vs. Swedish Angel; Dec. 19–Jr. Hockey: Hamilton 4, St. Michael's 9; Dec. 19–NHL: Boston 3, Leafs 3; Dec. 22–Sr. Hockey: Air Force 4, Research Colonels 2; Dec. 23–Jr. Hockey: Young Rangers 5, Jr. Marlboros 6; Dec. 25–Sr. Hockey: Navy 8, Army 4; Dec. 26–Jr. Hockey: Stratford 7, Jr. Marlboros 3; Dec. 26–NHL: Boston 2, Leafs 7; Dec. 29–Sr. Hockey: Air Force 7, Navy 1; Dec. 30–Jr. Hockey: Jr. Marlboros 4, Young Rangers 6.

1943 • Jan. 1–Sr. Hockey: Research Colonels 2, Air Force 3; Jan. 2–Jr. Hockey: Brantford 3, St. Michael's 7; Jan. 2–NHL: Canadiens 3, Leafs 6; Jan. 5–Sr. Hockey: Army 3, Navy 5; Jan. 6–Jr. Hockey: Oshawa 3, St. Michael's 2; Jan. 7–Wrestling: Pat Fraley vs. John Katan; Jan. 8–Sr. Hockey: Army 5, Research Colonels 4; Jan. 9–Jr. Hockey: Young Rangers 5, St. Michael's 6; Jan. 9–NHL: Detroit 4, Leafs 0; Jan. 11–Jr. Hockey: St. Michael's "B" 6, Upper Canada College 1; Jan. 12–Sr. Hockey: Navy 8, Air Force 5; Jan. 13–Jr. Hockey: Oshawa 7, Young Rangers 4; Jan. 14–Wrestling: Pat Fraley vs. Nanjo Singh; Jan. 15–Sr. Hockey: Navy 4, Research Colonels 3; Jan. 16–Jr. Hockey: St. Michael's 8, Jr. Marlboros 5; Jan. 16–NHL: Canadiens 4, Leafs 8; Jan. 18–Jr. Hockey: Brantford 6, St. Michael's 4; Jan. 19–Jr. Hockey: De la Salle 8, Upper Canada College 3; Jan. 19–Sr. Hockey: Air Force 7, Army 6; Jan. 20–Wrestling: Whipper Billy Watson vs. Pat Fraley; Jan. 21–NHL: Rangers 4, Leafs 7; Jan. 22–Sr. Hockey: Research Colonels 10, Air Force 17; Jan. 23–Jr. Hockey: Jr. Marlboros 10, Hamilton 6; Jan. 23–NHL: Chicago 3, Leafs 5; Jan. 25–Jr. Hockey: St. Michael's 1, Jr. Marlboros 4; Jan. 25–Jr. Hockey: De la Salle 7, Upper Canada College 3; Jan. 26–Sr. Hockey: Navy 7, Army 7; Jan. 27–Jr. Hockey: Oshawa 4, Jr. Marlboros 5; Jan. 27–Jr. Hockey: U. of T. Schools 4, Upper Canada College; Jan. 28–Wrestling: Whipper Billy Watson vs. Nanjo Singh; Jan. 30–Jr. Hockey: St. Michael's 8, Young Rangers 1; Jan. 30–NHL: Boston 5, Leafs 3; Feb. 1–Jr. Hockey: Jr. Marlboros 9, Brantford 2; Feb. 1–Jr. Hockey: U. of T. Schools 8, Upper Canada College 0; Feb. 2–Sr. Hockey: Research Colonels 10, Navy 8; Feb. 2–Sr. Hockey: Army 4, Air Force 3; Feb. 3–Wrestling: Whipper Billy Watson vs. Nanjo Singh; Feb. 4–NHL: Detroit 3, Leafs 2; Feb. 5–Hockey: Aid to Russia Benefit Game w/RCAF and Sr. Marlboros; Feb. 5–Jr. Hockey: St. Michael's "B" 2, U. of T. Schools 6; Feb. 6–Jr. Hockey: Young Rangers 4, Jr. Marlboros 13; Feb. 6–Jr. Hockey: Hamilton 2, St. Michael's 2; Feb. 6–NHL: Rangers 2, Leafs 3; Feb. 8–Jr. Hockey: Upper Canada College 5, De la Salle 6; Feb. 8–Sr. Hockey: Research Colonels 12, Army 8; Feb. 10–Jr. Hockey: Oshawa 8, Jr. Marlboros 9; Feb. 10–Jr. Hockey: U. of T. Schools 4, De la Salle 3; Feb. 11–Wrestling: John Katan vs. Dan O'Mahony; Feb. 12–Jr. Hockey: St. Michael's "B" 9, Upper Canada College 3; Feb. 12–Sr. Hockey: Navy 8, Hamilton 3; Feb. 13–Jr. Hockey: St. Michael's 6, Jr. Marlboros 4; Feb. 13–NHL: Chicago 2, Leafs 3; Feb. 15–Jr. Hockey: De la Salle 4, St. Michael's 5; Feb. 15–Sr. Hockey: St. Catharines 2, Air Force 1; Feb. 16–Sr. Hockey: Niagara Falls 2, Army 9; Feb. 17–Jr. Hockey: St. Michael's "B" 6, U. of T. Schools 4; Feb. 17–Sr. Hockey: Hamilton 6, Navy 5; Feb. 18–Wrestling: Whipper Billy Watson vs. John Katan; Feb. 19–Jr. Hockey: De la Salle 17, Upper Canada College 7; Feb. 19–Sr. Hockey: St. Catharines 0, Air Force 3; Feb. 20–Jr. Hockey: Jr. Marlboros 11, St. Michael's 6; Feb. 20–NHL: Boston 2, Leafs 4; Feb. 22–Jr. Hockey: St. Michael's "B" 11, Upper Canada College 5; Feb. 22–Sr. Hockey: Air Force 7, Army 6; Feb. 23–Jr. Hockey: St. Michael's 6, Jr. Marlboros 2; Feb. 24–Sr. Hockey: Navy 4, Hamilton 3; Feb. 25–Wrestling: Whipper Billy Watson vs. John Katan; Feb. 26–Jr. Hockey: U. of T. Schools 9, St. Michael's "B" 3; Feb. 26–Sr. Hockey: Air Force 11, Army 1; Feb. 27–Jr. Hockey: St. Michael's 7, Jr. Marlboros 4; Feb. 27–NHL: Chicago 4, Leafs 1; Mar. 1–Jr. Hockey: U. of T. Schools 7, St. Michael's "B" 1; Mar. 1–Sr. Hockey: Air Force 4, Navy 5 (OHA "A" Finals); Mar. 2–NHL: Rangers 4, Leafs 0; Mar. 3–Sr. Hockey: Air Force 8, Navy 2 (OHA "A" Finals); Mar. 4–Wrestling: Watson/McCready vs. Katan/Dunlop; Mar. 6–NHL: Canadiens 2, Leafs 2; Mar. 6–Canadian Red Cross Youth Rally; Mar. 8-12: Ice Capades (first Ice Capades show); Mar. 13–NHL: Detroit 1, Leafs 3; Mar. 13–Sr. Hockey: Air Force 3, Navy 2 (OHA "A" Finals); Mar. 15–Sr. Hockey: Navy 5, Air Force 8 (OHA "A"

Finals); Mar. 17–Sr. Hockey: Air Force 6, Sudbury 0; Mar. 19–Hockey: Brampton Army 16, Nobel AC 4; Mar. 20–Jr. Hockey: U. of T. Schools 5, Kingston 4; Mar. 20–Sr. Hockey: Air Force, Sudbury 4; Mar. 22–Sr. Hockey: Air Force 3, Sudbury 2; Mar. 24–Sr. Hockey: Brampton Army 8, Peterborough Army 7; Mar. 25–NHL: Detroit 4, Leafs 2 (Stanley Cup Finals); Mar. 27–Jr. Hockey: Milton 8, U. of T. Schools 8; Mar. 27–NHL: Detroit 3, Leafs 6 (Stanley Cup Finals); Mar. 29–Sr. Hockey: Ottawa Commandos 6, Air Force 4; Mar. 30–NHL: Detroit 3, Leafs 2 (Stanley Cup Finals); Mar. 31–Jr. Hockey: Ottawa St. Pats 1, Oshawa 12; Apr. 1–Wrestling: Whipper Billy Watson vs. Jack Claybourne; Apr. 3–Sr. Hockey: Ottawa Commandos 1, Air Force 8; Apr. 5–Jr. Hockey: Milton 4, Port Colborne 7 (OHA "B" Finals); Apr. 6–Jr. Hockey: Montreal Canadiens 2, Oshawa 9 (Memorial Cup Eastern Final); Apr. 7–Sr. Hockey: Peterborough Army 5, Owen Sound 6; Apr. 10–Jr. Hockey: Montreal Canadiens 1, Oshawa 9 (Memorial Cup Eastern Final); Apr. 12–Sr. Hockey: Ottawa Commandos 5, Ottawa RCAF 1 (Allan Cup Eastern Final); Apr. 15–Wrestling: Whipper Billy Watson vs. Red Shadow; Apr. 16–Hockey: Windsor Colonial Tool 5, Aurora RCOC 15; Apr. 17–Jr. Hockey: Winnipeg Rangers 6, Oshawa 5 (Memorial Cup Finals); Apr. 19–Jr. Hockey: Winnipeg Rangers 2, Oshawa 6 (Memorial Cup Finals); Apr. 21–Jr. Hockey: Winnipeg Rangers 3, Oshawa 5 (Memorial Cup Finals); Apr. 24–Jr. Hockey: Winnipeg Rangers 7, Oshawa 4 (Memorial Cup Finals); Apr. 26–Jr. Hockey: Winnipeg Rangers 7, Oshawa 3 (Memorial Cup Finals); Apr. 28–Jr. Hockey: Winnipeg Rangers 6, Oshawa 3 (Memorial Cup Finals); Apr. 29–Wrestling: Whipper Billy Watson vs. John Katan; May 3–Victory Loan Rally; May 6-7: Roller Skating Follies; May 8–Roller Skating Follies; May 10–Canadian Women's Army Corps Graduation; May 11-12–Music: Sigmund Romberg and his Orchestra; May 15–Music: 48th Highlanders Carnival Night; June 22–A Salute to Our Russian Ally; Sept. 8–Canadian Jewish Congress; Sept. 12–Music: Guy Lombardo and his Royal Canadians; Sept. 30–Wrestling: Whipper Billy Watson vs. Tony Felice; Oct. 2–Lacrosse: Lachine RCAF 6, Mimico-Brampton 20 (Mann Cup Eastern Final); Oct. 4–Lacrosse: Lachine RCAF 13, Mimico-Brampton 15 (Mann Cup Eastern Final); Oct. 7–Wrestling: Whipper Billy Watson vs. Bill Longson; Oct. 14–Wrestling: Bill Longson vs. Whipper Billy Watson; Oct. 18-23: Shriners Charity Circus; Oct. 27–Wrestling: Whipper Billy Watson vs. Ralph Garibaldi; Oct. 28–NHL: Blues 12, Whites 9 (Maple Leafs intrasquad game); Oct. 29–Sports Service League Bingo; Oct. 30–NHL: Rangers 2, Leafs 5; Nov. 4–Wrestling: Whipper Billy Watson vs. Bill Longson; Nov. 6–NHL: Boston 5, Leafs 2; Nov. 11–NHL: Detroit 2, Leafs 2; Nov. 11–Wrestling: Vic Holbrook vs. John Katan; Nov. 12–Sr. Hockey: RCAF 3, Navy 8; Nov. 13–NHL: Chicago 4, Leafs 1; Nov. 14–Congress of Canadian-Soviet Friendship; Nov. 14–War Veterans Memorial Service; Nov. 15–Sr. Hockey: Hamilton 9, RCAF 2; Nov. 16–Jr. Hockey: St. Michael's 6, Jr. Marlboros 3; Nov. 16–Jr. Hockey: Brantford 2, Young Rangers 1; Nov. 17–Sr. Hockey: Navy 1, St. Catharines 7; Nov. 18–Wrestling: Whipper Billy Watson vs. Cowboy Graham; Nov. 20–Jr. Hockey: Jr. Marlboros 2, Galt 4; Nov. 20–Jr. Hockey: St. Michael's 7, Brantford 5; Nov. 20–NHL: Canadiens 7, Leafs 2; Nov. 22–Sr. Hockey: RCAF 8, Kingston 6; Nov. 23–Jr. Hockey: Young Rangers 1, Jr. Marlboros 2; Nov. 23–Jr. Hockey: Oshawa 3, St. Michael's 2; Nov. 24–Sr. Hockey: Hamilton 5, Navy 3; Nov. 25–Wrestling: Whipper Billy Watson vs. Cowboy Graham; Nov. 26–Kinsmen Bingo; Nov. 27–Jr. Hockey: Hamilton 2, Jr. Marlboros 4; Nov. 27–Jr. Hockey: St. Catharines 5, Young Rangers 2; Nov. 27–NHL: Boston 4, Leafs 7; Nov. 29–Sr. Hockey: St. Catharines 5, RCAF 4; Nov. 30–Jr. Hockey: Port Colborne 2, St. Michael's 6; Nov. 30–Jr. Hockey: Oshawa 5, Young Rangers 0; Dec. 2–NHL: Detroit 5, Leafs 6; Dec. 3–Sr. Hockey: Kingston 5, Navy 3; Dec. 4–Jr. Hockey: St. Michael's 12, Young Rangers 1; Dec. 4–Jr. Hockey: St. Catharines 7, Jr. Marlboros 1; Dec. 4–NHL: Rangers 4, Leafs 11; Dec. 6-10: Ice Capades; Dec. 11–NHL: Canadiens 2, Leafs 4; Dec. 13–Sr. Hockey: RCAF 4, Navy 3; Dec. 14–Jr. Hockey: Stratford 3, St. Michael's 8; Dec. 14–Jr. Hockey: Brantford 0, Jr. Marlboros 4; Dec. 15–Wrestling: Watson/DeGlane vs. Katan/Dunlop; Dec. 16–NHL: Detroit 4, Leafs 1; Dec. 18–Jr. Hockey: Young Rangers 0, St. Michael's 4; Dec. 18–Jr. Hockey: Port Colborne 1, Jr. Marlboros 2; Dec. 18–NHL: Chicago 4, Leafs 8; Dec. 20–Sr. Hockey: Hamilton 2, RCAF 6; Dec. 21–Jr. Hockey: Oshawa 7, Jr. Marlboros 4; Dec. 21–Jr. Hockey: Galt 0, Young Rangers 1; Dec. 25–NHL: Rangers 5, Leafs 3; Dec. 27–Sr. Hockey: St. Catharines 6, Navy 3; Dec. 29–Sr. Hockey: Kingston 4, RCAF 3; Dec. 30–Wrestling: Whipper Billy Watson vs. Al Dunlop; Dec. 31–Music: New Year's Eve Dance.

1944 • Jan. 1–Sr. Hockey: Navy 4, RCAF 6; Jan. 3–Sr. Hockey: RCAF 4, St. Catharines 3; Jan. 4–Jr. Hockey: Galt 4, St. Michael's 5; Jan. 4–Jr. Hockey: Hamilton 3, Young Rangers 2; Jan. 5–Wrestling: Whipper Billy Watson vs. Hardboiled Hannigan; Jan. 7–Hockey: UCC New Boys 4, UCC Old Boys 1; Jan. 7–NHL: Chicago 1, Leafs 6; Jan. 8–Jr. Hockey: St. Catharines 0, St. Michael's 8; Jan. 8–Jr. Hockey: Hamilton 8, Young Rangers 2; Jan. 8–NHL: Boston 3, Leafs 12; Jan. 10–Hockey: Upper Canada College 1, St. Michael's "C" 3; Jan. 10–Sr. Hockey: Kingston 7, Navy 6; Jan. 11–NHL: Canadiens 0, Leafs 5; Jan. 13–Wrestling: Bob Managoff vs. Hardboiled Hannigan; Jan. 15–Jr. Hockey: Stratford 2, Jr. Marlboros 1; Jan. 15–Jr. Hockey: Hamilton 4, St. Michael's 1; Jan. 15–NHL: Detroit 6, Leafs 4; Jan. 17–Jr. Hockey: De la Salle 7, Upper Canada College 4; Jan. 17–Sr. Hockey: Hamilton 2, Navy 3; Jan. 18–Jr. Hockey: Oshawa 5, Jr. Marlboros 2; Jan. 18–Jr. Hockey: Stratford 6, Young Rangers 4; Jan. 19–Jr. Hockey: U. of T. Schools 5, De la Salle 4; Jan. 19–Jr. Hockey: Victory Aircraft 3, Jr. Marlboros "B" 2; Jan. 20–Wrestling: Whipper Billy Watson vs. Hardboiled Hannigan; Jan. 21–Hockey: St. Michael's "C" 6, Upper Canada College 0; Jan. 22–Jr. Hockey: Jr. Marlboros 4, Hamilton 1; Jan. 22–Jr. Hockey: Young Rangers 3, Port Colborne 5; Jan. 22–NHL: Rangers 5, Leafs 1; Jan. 24–Jr. Hockey: U. of T. Schools 3, Upper Canada College 1; Jan. 24–Sr. Hockey: St. Catharines 11, Navy 7; Jan. 25–Jr. Hockey: De la Salle 3, St. Michael's "B" 3; Jan. 25–Jr. Hockey: Hamilton 2, St. Michael's 13; Jan. 26–Jr. Hockey: Jr. Marlboros 6, Young Rangers 5; Jan. 27–Wrestling: Bill Longson vs. Hardboiled Hannigan; Jan. 28–Jr. Hockey: De la Salle 5, St. Michael's "B" 4; Jan. 28–Jr. Hockey: Upper Canada College 2, U. of T. Schools 1; Jan. 29–Jr. Hockey: St. Michael's 11, Young Rangers 3; Jan. 29–NHL: Chicago 4, Leafs 3; Feb. 5–NHL: Detroit 1, Leafs 3; Feb. 7–Jr. Hockey: U. of T. Schools 3, St. Michael's "B" 1; Feb. 7–Sr. Hockey: St. Catharines 5, Navy 3; Feb. 8–Jr. Hockey: Oshawa 10, Young Rangers 2; Feb. 9–Jr. Hockey: Upper Canada College 4, De la Salle 5; Feb. 10–Wrestling: Hardboiled Hannigan vs. Whipper Billy Watson; Feb. 12–Jr. Hockey: St. Michael's 6, Young Rangers 0; Feb. 12–NHL: Canadiens 3, Leafs 2; Feb. 14–Jr. Hockey: De la Salle 7, U. of T. Schools 1; Feb. 14–Sr. Hockey: Hamilton 4, Navy 8; Feb. 15–Jr. Hockey: Oshawa 2, St. Michael's 5; Feb. 16–Jr. Hockey: St. Michael's "B" 5, Upper Canada College 3; Feb. 16–Jr. Hockey: Jr. Marlboros 2, Young Rangers 2; Feb. 17–Wrestling: Whipper Billy Watson vs. Hardboiled Hannigan; Feb. 18–Food Industry Stamp Drive; Feb. 19–Jr. Hockey: St. Michael's 4, Jr. Marlboros 3; Feb. 19–NHL: Boston 4, Leafs 10; Feb. 21–Jr. Hockey: U. of T. Schools 0, Upper Canada College 3; Feb. 21–Sr. Hockey: St. Catharines 3, Navy 4; Feb. 22–Jr. Hockey: St. Michael's 6, Jr. Marlboros 2; Feb. 23–Jr. Hockey: De la Salle 4, Upper Canada College 1; Feb. 26–Jr. Hockey: U. of T. Schools 2, St. Michael's "B" 3; Feb. 26–NHL: Chicago 3, Leafs 2; Feb. 28–Jr. Hockey: U. of T. Schools 0, De la Salle 2; Mar. 1–Jr. Hockey: Galt 4, St. Michael's 3; Mar. 1–Jr. Hockey: De la Salle 9, U. of T. Schools 1; Mar. 4–NHL: Canadiens 5, Leafs 2; Mar. 6–Jr. Hockey: Galt 2, St. Michael's 5; Mar. 7–Jr. Hockey: De la Salle 13, Niagara Falls 3; Mar. 7–Jr. Hockey: North Toronto 5, Northern Vocational 1 (Schoolboy Finals); Mar. 8–Jr. Hockey: Navy 4, Hamilton 6; Mar. 9–Wrestling: Bob Managoff vs. "Strangler" Warner; Mar. 10–Jr. Hockey: St. Michael's 5, Hamilton 2; Mar. 11–NHL: Rangers 0, Leafs 5; Mar. 13–Jr. Hockey: De la Salle 9, Kitchener 4; Mar. 15–Jr. Hockey: Hamilton 5, St. Michael's 11; Mar. 16–Wrestling: Bill Longson vs. Vic Holbrook; Mar. 17–Sr. Hockey: Hamilton 0, Sudbury 4 (All-Ontario Sr. Finals); Mar. 18–NHL: Boston 2, Leafs 10; Mar. 20–Jr. Hockey: Oshawa 5, St. Michael's 1 (OHA "A" Finals); Mar. 22–Sr. Hockey: Hamilton 2, Sudbury 7 (All-Ontario Sr. Finals); Mar. 23–Wrestling: Bill Longson vs. Vic Holbrook; Mar. 24–Jr. Hockey: Kingston 1, Barrie 4; Mar. 25–Jr. Hockey: Oshawa 2, St. Michael's 3 (OHA "A" Finals); Mar. 25–NHL: Canadiens 2, Leafs 1; Mar. 27–Jr. Hockey: De la Salle 4, Barrie 5; Mar. 28–NHL: Canadiens 4, Leafs 1; Mar. 29–Hockey: Toronto Young Leafs 5, Kitchener 3; Mar. 29–Jr. Hockey: Oshawa 10, Ottawa University 3 (All-Ontario Jr. Finals); Apr. 1–Sr. Hockey: Hull 0, Sudbury 7; Apr. 3–Jr. Hockey: Oshawa 6, Montreal 3 (Memorial Cup Eastern Finals); Apr. 4–Jr. Hockey: De la Salle 5, Barrie 3 (OHA "B" Finals); Apr. 5–Jr. Hockey: Oshawa 3, Montreal 2 (Memorial Cup Eastern Finals); Apr. 6–Wrestling: Tom Zaharias vs. Frank Sexton; Apr. 7–Hockey: Copper Cliff 4, Toronto Young Leafs 5; Apr. 8–Hockey: Gananoque 0, Toronto Young Leafs 17; Apr. 8–Sr. Hockey: Quebec Aces 6, Sudbury 2 (Allan Cup Eastern Finals); Apr. 10–Sr. Hockey: Quebec Aces 8, Sudbury 3 (Allan Cup Eastern Finals); Apr. 11–Hockey: Hanks Royals 6, Perpetual Help 5; Apr. 11–Hockey: Leaside 0, Toronto Young Leafs 4; Apr. 13–Wrestling: Whipper Billy Watson vs. Tom Zaharias; Apr. 15–Jr. Hockey: Oshawa 9, Trail 2 (Memorial Cup Finals); Apr. 17–Jr. Hockey: Oshawa 5, Trail 2 (Memorial Cup Finals); Apr. 18–Hockey: St. Michael's "C" 2, Toronto Young Leafs 5; Apr. 19–Jr. Hockey: Oshawa 15, Trail 4 (Memorial Cup Finals); Apr. 21–Wrestling: Frank Sexton vs. Bob Managoff; Apr. 22–Jr. Hockey: Oshawa 11, Trail 4 (Memorial Cup Finals); Apr. 27–Wrestling: Whipper Billy Watson vs. Krippler Davis; May 2-9: Texas Rodeo with Roy Rogers and Trigger; May 9–Victory Loan Rally; June 3–Music: 48th Highlanders Bazaar; June 23–National Council for Canadian-Soviet Friendship Rally; June 26–July 1: Garden Brothers Circus; Sept. 20–Comedy/Music: Bob Hope Show; Sept. 25-26–Music: Phil Spitalny and his "Hour of Charm"; Oct. 1–People's Church Forum; Oct. 5–Wrestling: Frank Sexton vs. Whipper Billy Watson; Oct. 6–Boxing: Joey Peralta vs. Dave Castilloux; Oct. 7–Lacrosse: St. Catharines 17, New Westminster 10 (Mann Cup Finals); Oct. 8–People's Church Forum; Oct. 9–Lacrosse: St. Catharines 4, New Westminster 13 (Mann Cup Finals); Oct. 10–Lacrosse: St. Catharines 11, New Westminster 10 (Mann Cup Finals); Oct. 10–Lacrosse: Camp Borden 12, #2 Armored 2; Oct. 12–Wrestling: Gino Garibaldi vs. "Strangler" Wagner; Oct. 14–Lacrosse: St. Catharines 8, New Westminster 11 (Mann Cup Finals); Oct. 25–NHL: Blues 8, Whites 2 (Maple Leafs intrasquad game); Oct. 26–Wrestling: Whipper Billy Watson vs. Frank Sexton; Oct. 28–NHL: Rangers 1, Leafs 2; Oct. 30–Music: The Andrews Sisters; Nov. 2–Wrestling: Whipper Billy Watson vs. Ivan Rasputin; Nov. 4–NHL: Boston 2, Leafs 7; Nov. 8–Wrestling: Gino Garibaldi vs. Frank Sexton; Nov. 11–NHL: Canadiens 1, Leafs 3; Nov. 12–Jehovah's Witnesses Convention; Nov. 15–NHL: Detroit 8, Leafs 4; Nov. 16–Wrestling: Ivan Rasputin vs. Whipper Billy Watson; Nov. 18–Jr. Hockey: Jr. Marlboros 1, St. Michael's 10; Nov. 18–NHL: Chicago 4, Leafs 5; Nov. 19–Navy League of Canada Convention; Nov. 20–Sr. Hockey: St. Catharines 3, Staffords 2; Nov. 21–Jr. Hockey: Oshawa 4, Jr. Marlboros 3; Nov. 23–Wrestling: Whipper Billy Watson vs. Ivan Rasputin; Nov. 25–Jr. Hockey: St. Michael's 10, Young Rangers 1; Nov. 25–Jr. Hockey: Galt 2, Jr. Marlboros 3; Nov. 25–NHL: Canadiens 0, Leafs 2; Nov. 27–Dec. 1: Ice Capades; Dec. 2–NHL: Rangers 3, Leafs 4; Dec. 4–Sr. Hockey: Hamilton 3, Staffords 3; Dec. 5–Jr. Hockey: Galt 5, Young Rangers 4; Dec. 5–Jr. Hockey: St. Michael's 15, Jr. Marlboros 1; Dec. 7–Wrestling: Whipper Billy Watson vs. Gino Garibaldi; Dec. 9–Jr. Hockey: Young Rangers 5, Port Colborne 1; Dec. 9–Jr. Hockey: St. Catharines 4, Jr. Marlboros 2; Dec. 9–NHL: Boston 5, Leafs 3; Dec. 11–Sr. Hockey: St. Catharines 0, Staffords 8; Dec. 12–Jr. Hockey: Oshawa, St. Michael's; Dec. 13–Jr. Hockey: Jr. Marlboros "B"3, Chewies Aces 2; Dec. 13–Jr. Hockey: Victory Aircraft 7, Etobicoke 4; Dec. 14–Wrestling: Whipper Billy Watson vs. Gino Garibaldi; Dec. 16–NHL: Detroit 1, Leafs 1; Dec. 18–Jr. Hockey: St. Michael's 9, St. Catharines 2; Dec. 19–Music: Tommy Dorsey and his Orchestra; Dec. 20–Jr. Hockey: Victory Aircraft 5, Jr. Marlboros "B" 4; Dec. 20–Jr. Hockey: Chewies Aces 9, Etobicoke 3; Dec. 21–Wrestling: Frank Sexton vs. Ivan Rasputin; Dec. 23–Jr. Hockey: Young Rangers 5, Jr. Marlboros 4; Dec. 23–NHL: Detroit 5, Leafs 4; Dec. 27–Jr. Hockey: Chewies Aces 5, Victory Aircraft 4; Dec. 27–Jr. Hockey: Etobicoke 7, Jr. Marlboros "B" 2; Dec. 28–Wrestling: McCready/Sexton vs. Wagner/Dunlop; Dec. 29–Jr. Hockey: Victory Aircraft 4, Etobicoke 4; Dec. 29–Jr. Hockey: Chewies Aces 2, Jr. Marlboros "B" 3; Dec. 30–Jr. Hockey: Oshawa 7, Young Rangers 4; Dec. 30–NHL: Chicago 0, Leafs 4.

1945 • Jan. 1–Sr. Hockey: Hamilton 3, Staffords 1; Jan. 4–NHL: Canadiens 2, Leafs 4; Jan. 5–Hockey: UCC New Boys 2, UCC Old Boys 1; Jan. 6–NHL: Detroit 5, Leafs 2; Jan. 6–Sr. Hockey: St. Michael's 18, Jr. Marlboros 2; Jan. 8–Hockey: St. Michael's "B" 12, Upper Canada College 2; Jan. 8–Jr. Hockey: Victory Aircraft 4, Jr. Marlboros "B" 2; Jan. 8–Jr. Hockey: Chewies Aces 5, Etobicoke 4; Jan. 9–Jr. Hockey: St. Catharines 4, St. Michael's 6; Jan. 9–NHL: Rangers 5, Leafs 4; Jan. 10–Jr. Hockey: Oshawa 5, Jr. Marlboros 2; Jan. 10–Jr. Hockey: St. Catharines 3, Young Rangers 4; Jan. 11–Hockey: U. of T. Schools 0, St. Michael's "C" 1; Jan. 11–Wrestling: Whipper Billy Watson vs. Vagone; Jan. 12–Hockey: U. of T. Schools 3, Upper Canada College 6; Jan. 13–Jr. Hockey: Young Rangers 3, Jr. Marlboros 6; Jan. 13–NHL: Boston 1, Leafs 2; Jan. 15–Hockey: De la Salle 7, Upper Canada College 4; Jan. 15–Sr. Hockey: St. Catharines 4, Staffords 2; Jan. 16–Hockey: U. of T. Schools 10, St. Michael's "B" 4; Jan. 16–Jr. Hockey: Oshawa 1, St. Michael's 3; Jan. 17–Hockey: St. Andrews 3, Upper Canada College 10; Jan. 17–Jr. Hockey: Victory Aircraft 1, Chewies Aces 2; Jan. 17–Jr. Hockey: Etobicoke 3, Jr. Marlboros "B" 6; Jan. 19–Hockey: Parkdale 1, Oakwood 7; Jan. 19–Hockey: Lawrence Park 4, Northern Vocational 1; Jan. 19–Hockey: Jarvis 1, Malvern 1; Jan. 19–Jr. Hockey: St. Michael's 7, De la Salle 3; Jan. 19–Wrestling: Wild Bill Longson vs. Gino Garibaldi; Jan. 20–Jr. Hockey: St. Catharines 8, St. Michael's 6; Jan. 20–NHL: Chicago 4, Leafs 8; Jan. 22–Hockey: U. of T. Schools 1, St. Michael's "C" 11; Jan. 22–Hockey: St. Andrews 11, St. Michael's "B" 0; Jan. 22–Jr. Hockey: Jr. Marlboros "B" 4, Chewies Aces 3; Jan. 22–Jr. Hockey: Etobicoke 1, Victory Aircraft 7; Jan. 23–Jr. Hockey: Young Rangers 6, Jr. Marlboros 3; Jan. 24–Hockey: Upper Canada College, De la Salle 3; Jan. 24–Jr. Hockey: Chewies Aces 2, Etobicoke 5; Jan. 24–Jr. Hockey: Victory Aircraft 9, Jr. Marlboros "B" 1; Jan. 25–Wrestling: Whipper Billy Watson vs. Dr. Len Hall; Jan. 26–Hockey: U. of T. Schools 2, De la Salle 4; Jan. 26–Hockey: Harbord 1, Riverdale 4; Jan. 26–Hockey: Central Tech 0, North Toronto 5; Jan. 26–Hockey: Western Tech 2,

Humberside 10; Jan. 26–Jr. Hockey: St. Andrews 2, De la Salle 10; Jan. 27–Jr. Hockey: Young Rangers 5, Jr. Marlboros 3; Jan. 27–NHL: Rangers 0, Leafs 3; Jan. 29–Jr. Hockey: Upper Canada College 2, St. Michael's "B" 13; Jan. 29–Sr. Hockey: Hamilton 3, Staffords 1; Jan. 30–Jr. Hockey: St. Michael's 5, Young Rangers 2; Jan. 30–Jr. Hockey: St. Catharines 7, Jr. Marlboros 5; Jan. 31–Hockey: U. of T. Schools 1, De la Salle 3; Jan. 31–Hockey: Jarvis 2, Northern Vocational 3; Jan. 31–Hockey: Lawrence Park 5, Malvern 2; Jan. 31–Hockey: Riverdale 2, North Toronto 3; Feb. 1–Wrestling: Whipper Billy Watson vs. Dr. Len Hall; Feb. 3–Jr. Hockey: Galt 2, St. Michael's 14; Feb. 3–NHL: Boston 4, Leafs 2; Feb. 5-9: Ice Follies of 1945; Feb. 10–NHL: Chicago 2, Leafs 1; Feb. 12–Hockey: Riverdale 2, Central Tech 2; Feb. 12–Hockey: Jarvis 1, Parkdale 6; Feb. 12–Hockey: Malvern 7, Northern Vocational 2; Feb. 12–Hockey: De la Salle "C" 2, St. Michael's "C" 2; Feb. 12–Hockey: De la Salle "B" 3, St. Michael's "B" 4; Feb. 13–Jr. Hockey: Oshawa 1, St. Michael's 8; Feb. 14–Hockey: Upper Canada College 1, De la Salle 1; Feb. 14–Hockey: Upper Canada College "B" 2, De la Salle "B" 3; Feb. 14–Hockey: Lawrence Park 4, Oakwood 6; Feb. 14–Hockey: Harbord 2, Western Tech 7; Feb. 14–Hockey: North Toronto 1, Humberside 2; Feb. 15–Wrestling: Whipper Billy Watson vs. K.O. Koverley; Feb. 16–Toronto Police Association Concert; Feb. 17–Jr. Hockey: Young Rangers 1, Oshawa 3; Feb. 17–Jr. Hockey: Galt 5, Jr. Marlboros 2; Feb. 17–NHL: Canadiens 4, Leafs 3; Feb. 19–Hockey: U. of T. Schools 0, De la Salle 4; Feb. 19–Hockey: U. of T. Schools "B" 3, De la Salle "B" 6; Feb. 19–Jr. Hockey: St. Catharines 2, Young Rangers 4; Feb. 20–Jr. Hockey: Chewies Aces 4, Victory Aircraft 10; Feb. 20–Jr. Hockey: Jr. Marlboros "B" 0, Etobicoke 3; Feb. 21–Hockey: 1935 Maroons 6, 1932 Leafs 3; Feb. 21–Hockey: St. Michael's 8, Toronto Navy 1; Feb. 22–Wrestling: Whipper Billy Watson vs. Cowboy Graham; Feb. 24–Jr. Hockey: Galt 5, Young Rangers 2; Feb. 24–Jr. Hockey: Chewies Aces 5, Jr. Marlboros "B" 1; Feb. 24–NHL: Rangers 4, Leafs 4; Feb. 26–Hockey: Upper Canada College 1, St. Michael's "C" 5; Feb. 26–Jr. Hockey: Upper Canada College 0, St. Michael's "B" 5; Feb. 26–Jr. Hockey: Jr. Marlboros 3, Young Rangers 4; Feb. 26–Jr. Hockey: Victory Aircraft 2, Chewies Aces 3; Feb. 27–Hockey: Jarvis, Riverdale; Feb. 27–Hockey: Sr. Marlboros, Malvern; Feb. 27–NHL: Chicago 3, Leafs 3; Feb. 28–Hockey: U. of T. Schools 0, Upper Canada College 5; Feb. 28–Jr. Hockey: U. of T. Schools 4, St. Michael's "B" 8; Feb. 28–Jr. Hockey: St. Catharines 1, St. Michael's 6; Mar. 1–Wrestling: Crusher Casey vs. Ivan Rasputin; Mar. 2–Hockey: Camp Borden 5, Centralia 3 (RCAF Final); Mar. 2–Hockey: Lawrence Park 2, North Toronto 6; Mar. 2–Hockey: Western Tech 4, Humberside 5; Mar. 3–Jr. Hockey: Young Rangers 2, Jr. Marlboros 0; Mar. 3–Jr. Hockey: Victory Aircraft 3, Chewies Aces 4; Mar. 3–NHL: Canadiens 2, Leafs 3; Mar. 5–Jr. Hockey: St. Michael's "B" 7, De la Salle 4; Mar. 5–Jr. Hockey: St. Catharines 3, St. Michael's 8; Mar. 6–Hockey: Toronto Young Leafs 6, Oshawa 1; Mar. 6–Hockey: Toronto Navy 7, Newmarket Army 5; Mar. 7–Jr. Hockey: St. Michael's "B" 5, De la Salle 1; Mar. 7–Jr. Hockey: Galt 6, Young Rangers 2; Mar. 8–Wrestling: Gino Garibaldi vs. Ivan Rasputin; Mar. 9–Hockey: Hughes 9, Fisher 4; Mar. 9–Hockey: Humberside 3, North Toronto 2 (Schoolboy Finals); Mar. 10–Jr. Hockey: St. Catharines 1, St. Michael's 14; Mar. 10–NHL: Boston 2, Leafs 9; Mar. 12–Jr. Hockey: Niagara Falls 5, Chewies Aces 3; Mar. 12–Jr. Hockey: St. Michael's 16, Toronto Mecca A.C. 5; Mar. 13–Hockey: Young Leafs 6, Windsor 4; Mar. 13–Hockey: Toronto Navy 6, Newmarket Army 5; Mar. 14–Jr. Hockey: St. Michael's 13, Galt 4; Mar. 15–Wrestling: Whipper Billy Watson vs. Gino Garibaldi; Mar. 17–NHL: Detroit 4, Leafs 3; Mar. 17–Sr. Hockey: Sudbury 3, Hamilton 4 (All-Ontario Sr. Finals); Mar. 19–Hockey: Sr. Marlboros 4, Oakwood 4; Mar. 19–Jr. Hockey: Galt 3, St. Michael's 8; Mar. 20–Hockey: Toronto Navy 7, Newmarket Army 10; Mar. 21–Sr. Hockey: Sudbury 4, Hamilton 3 (All-Ontario Sr. Finals); Mar. 22–Wrestling: Gino Garibaldi vs. Crusher Casey; Mar. 23–Jr. Hockey: Niagara Falls 4, St. Michael's "B" 22; Mar. 24–Jr. Hockey: St. Michael's 12, Porcupine Combines 3; Mar. 24–NHL: Canadiens 4, Leafs 1; Mar. 26–Jr. Hockey: St. Michael's 8, Porcupine Combines 6; Mar. 26–Sr. Hockey: Hamilton 2, Sudbury 0 (All-Ontario Sr. Finals); Mar. 27–NHL: Canadiens 3, Leafs 4; Mar. 28–Jr. Hockey: St. Michael's 12, Porcupine Combines 3 (All-Ontario Jr. Finals); Mar. 29–Wrestling: Whipper Billy Watson vs. Red Vagnone; Mar. 30–Hockey: Toronto Navy 5, Newmarket Army 10; Mar. 30–Hockey: Young Leafs 2, St. Catharines 5 (Juvenile Finals); Mar. 31–Jr. Hockey: St. Michael's 1, Montreal 3 (Memorial Cup Eastern Finals); Mar. 31–NHL: Canadiens 2, Leafs 3; Apr. 2–Jr. Hockey: St. Michael's 7, Montreal 1 (Memorial Cup Eastern Finals); Apr. 3–Hockey: Niagara Falls 4, Toronto St. John's 1 (Pee-Wee Finals); Apr. 3–Hockey: Blessed Sacrement 5, St. Catharines 1 (Bantam Finals); Apr. 3–Hockey: Holy Name 5, St. Catharines 5 (Bantam Finals); Apr. 3–Hockey: Niagara Falls 1, St. Brigid's 1 (Midget Finals); Apr. 3–Hockey: Niagara Falls 6, St. Brigid's 3 (Juvenile Finals); Apr. 4–Jr. Hockey: St. Michael's 3, Montreal 4 (Memorial Cup Eastern Final); Apr. 5–Wrestling: Nanjo Singh vs. Ivan Rasputin; Apr. 7–Hockey: Peoples 4, Bowser's 9 (Mercantile League Finals); Apr. 7–Jr. Hockey: St. Michael's "B" 9, Stratford 3 (OHA "B" Finals); Apr. 9–Hockey: Peoples 2, Bowser's 2 (Mercantile League Finals); Apr. 10–Jr. Hockey: St. Michael's "B" 9, Stratford 1 (OHA "B" Finals); Apr. 11–Jr. Hockey: St. Michael's 7, Montreal 4 (Memorial Cup Eastern Finals); Apr. 12–NHL: Detroit 0, Leafs 1 (Stanley Cup Finals); Apr. 14–Jr. Hockey: St. Michael's 8, Moose Jaw 5 (Memorial Cup Finals); Apr. 14–NHL: Detroit 5, Leafs 3 (Stanley Cup Finals); Apr. 16–Jr. Hockey: St. Michael's 3, Moose Jaw 5 (Memorial Cup Finals); Apr. 17–Wrestling: Nanjo Singh vs. Ivan Rasputin; Apr. 18–Jr. Hockey: St. Michael's 6, Moose Jaw 3 (Memorial Cup Finals); Apr. 19–Hockey: Toronto Religious Educational Council Finals; Apr. 20–Hockey: Peoples 2, Bowser's 4 (Mercantile League Finals); Apr. 21–Jr. Hockey: St. Michael's 4, Moose Jaw 3 (Memorial Cup Finals); Apr. 21–NHL: Detroit 1, Leafs 0 (Stanley Cup Finals); Apr. 23–Jr. Hockey: St. Michael's 7, Moose Jaw 2 (Memorial Cup Finals); Apr. 24–Hockey: Peoples 8, Bowser's 4 (Mercantile League Finals); Apr. 26–Wrestling: Whipper Billy Watson vs. Nanjo Singh; Apr. 30–Boxing: Joey Ferrier vs. Arthur King; May 1–Music: Gene Krupa and his Orchestra; May 23–Music: Tommy Dorsey Orchestra; June 10–United Church of Canada's 20th Anniversary Service; June 15–Music: Charlie Spivak Orchestra; June 16–Toronto Churches Youth Rally; June 23–Music: Ukranian Festival w/Woody Herman and his Orchestra; Sept. 11-15: Roller Skating Vanities; Oct. 3–Allied Aircraft Reconversion Forum; Oct. 4–Wrestling: Whipper Billy Watson vs. Frank Sexton; Oct. 5–Music: Tony Pastor and his Orchestra; Oct. 10–Wrestling: Vic Christie vs. Dr. Len Hall; Oct. 15-20: Bob Morton's Rameses Shrine Circus; Oct. 22–Music: Phil Spitalny and his All-Girl Orchestra; Oct. 24–Wrestling: Vic Christie vs. John Katan; Oct. 25–NHL: Blues 2, Whites 2 (Maple Leafs intrasquad game); Oct. 27–NHL: Boston 1, Leafs 1; Oct. 30–Victory Loan Rally with Fibber McGee and Molly; Nov. 1–Wrestling: Babe Sharkey vs. Vic Christie; Nov. 3–NHL: Rangers 4, Leafs 1; Nov. 7–NHL: Boston 4, Leafs 3; Nov. 8–Wrestling: Vic Christie vs. Bill Longson; Nov. 9–Ladies' Softball: New Orleans Jax 2, Simpson Sr. Ladies 1; Nov. 9–Ladies' Softball; New Orleans Jax 1, Sunday Morning Class 2; Nov. 10–NHL: Chicago 2, Leafs 3; Nov. 12–Jr. Hockey: St. Michael's 11, Jr. Marlboros 0; Nov. 12–Jr. Hockey: Barrie 5, Young Rangers 4; Nov. 14–NHL: Canadiens 6, Leafs 1; Nov. 15–Wrestling: Whipper Billy Watson vs. Sandy O'Donnell; Nov. 16–Hockey: Malvern 4, Lawrence Park 1; Nov. 16–Hockey: Jarvis 2, Parkdale 2; Nov. 16–Hockey: Humberside 6, Northern Vocational 3; Nov. 17–Jr. Hockey: Galt 1, St. Michael's 4; Nov. 17–NHL: Detroit 6, Leafs 5; Nov. 19–Jr. Hockey: Oshawa 6, Young Rangers 3; Nov. 19–Jr. Hockey: St. Catharines 3, Jr. Marlboros 1; Nov. 21–National Council for Canadian-Soviet Friendship; Nov. 22–Wrestling: Sandy O'Donnell vs. Whipper Billy Watson; Nov. 23–Hockey: North Toronto 5, Western Tech 4; Nov. 23–Hockey: Central Tech 1, Danforth Tech 2; Nov. 23–Hockey: Riverdale 0, Oakwood 1; Nov. 24–Jr. Hockey: Hamilton 1, St. Michael's 12; Nov. 24–NHL: Rangers 3, Leafs 4; Nov. 26-30: Ice Capades; Dec. 1–NHL: Chicago 8, Leafs 2; Dec. 3–Boxing: Pete Zaduk vs. Joey Ferrier; Dec. 4–Jr. Hockey: Barrie 2, St. Michael's 7; Dec. 4–Jr. Hockey: Oshawa 6, Jr. Marlboros 1; Dec. 5–Sr. Hockey: Hamilton 3, Staffords 8; Dec. 6–Wrestling: Whipper Billy Watson vs. Frank Sexton; Dec. 7–Hockey: Parkdale 2, Central Tech 4; Dec. 7–Hockey: Western Tech 3, Humberside 3; Dec. 7–Hockey: Danforth Tech 4, Riverdale 2; Dec. 8–Jr. Hockey: St. Michael's 6, Young Rangers 0; Dec. 8–NHL: Canadiens 1, Leafs 0; Dec. 10–Jr. Hockey: Barrie 1, Jr. Marlboros 6; Dec. 10–Jr. Hockey: Hamilton 3, Young Rangers 5; Dec. 12–Sr. Hockey: Staffords 6, Stratford 3; Dec. 13–Wrestling: Katan/O'Donnell vs. Christie/Bell; Dec. 14–Hockey: Northern Vocational 2, North Toronto 4; Dec. 14–Hockey: Jarvis 6, Malvern 5; Dec. 14–Hockey: Oakwood 3, Lawrence Park 3; Dec. 15–Jr. Hockey: Jr. Marlboros 2, St. Michael's 5; Dec. 15–Jr. Hockey: Galt 4, Young Rangers 0; Dec. 15–NHL: Detroit 1, Leafs 3; Dec. 17–Jr. Hockey: Oshawa 3, St. Michael's 6; Dec. 19–Sr. Hockey: Owen Sound 3, Staffords 7; Dec. 20–Wrestling: Taylor/Christie vs. Katan/Olson; Dec. 21–Hockey: Danforth Tech 2, Oakwood 1; Dec. 21–Hockey: Riverdale 1, Lawrence Park 1; Dec. 21–Hockey: Central Tech 1, Jarvis 1; Dec. 22–Jr. Hockey: Young Rangers 1, Jr. Marlboros 1; Dec. 22–Jr. Hockey: St. Catharines 2, St. Michael's 10; Dec. 22–NHL: Rangers 5, Leafs 5; Dec. 26–NHL: Canadiens 4, Leafs 2; Dec. 27–Wrestling: Wladyslaw Talun vs. Vic Christie; Dec. 28–Hockey: Humberside 7, Malvern 1; Dec. 28–Hockey: North Toronto 1, Parkdale 2; Dec. 28–Hockey: Western Tech 1, Northern Vocational 0; Dec. 29–Jr. Hockey: Galt 1, Jr. Marlboros 0; Dec. 29–Jr. Hockey: Barrie 0, Young Rangers 2; Dec. 29–NHL: Boston 4, Leafs 3; Dec. 31–Music: Ellis McLintock and his Orchestra.

1946 • Jan. 1–Jr. Hockey: St. Catharines 2, Young Rangers 4; Jan. 1–Jr. Hockey: Hamilton 1, Jr. Marlboros 7; Jan. 2–Sr. Hockey: Hamilton, Staffords; Jan. 3–Wrestling: Wladyslaw Talun vs. Swede Olson; Jan. 4–Hockey: Parkdale 2, Western Tech 2; Jan. 4–Hockey: Malvern 3, Danforth Tech 4; Jan. 4–Hockey: Oakwood 2, Central Tech 3; Jan. 5–Jr. Hockey: St. Catharines 1, St. Michael's 5; Jan. 5–NHL: Chicago 3, Leafs 0; Jan. 7–Jr. Hockey: St. Michael's "B" 27, Cantab 0; Jan. 7–Jr. Hockey: Young Rangers 6, Jr. Marlboros 1; Jan. 7–Jr. Hockey: Hamilton 2, St. Michael's 16; Jan. 9–Jr. Hockey: St. Michael's "B" 4, De la Salle 5; Jan. 9–Sr. Hockey: Owen Sound 5, Staffords 11; Jan. 10–Wrestling: Frank Sexton vs. Bill Longson; Jan. 11–Hockey: UCC New Boys 5, UCC Old Boys 1; Jan. 11–Jr. Hockey: U. of T. Schools 7, Cantab 1; Jan. 12–Jr. Hockey: St. Catharines 3, Young Rangers 2; Jan. 12–NHL: Detroit 3, Leafs 9; Jan. 14–Jr. Hockey: Upper Canada College "B" 1, St. Michael's "B" 7; Jan. 14–Jr. Hockey: Cantab 1, Upper Canada College 3; Jan. 14–Jr. Hockey: Galt 8, Jr. Marlboros 1; Jan. 14–Jr. Hockey: Hamilton 4, Young Rangers 7; Jan. 15–Hockey: U. of T. Schools 3, De la Salle 2; Jan. 15–Jr. Hockey: U. of T. Schools 5, De la Salle 11; Jan. 15–Sr. Hockey: Stratford 6, Staffords 7; Jan. 16–Basketball: Fort Wayne 47, Rochester 53; Jan. 16–Basketball: U. of T. Varsity 47, Western Ontario 46; Jan. 17–Wrestling: Wladyslaw Talun vs. John Katan; Jan. 18–Hockey: Jarvis 2, Northern Vocational 2; Jan. 18–Hockey: Lawrence Park 3, Humberside 3; Jan. 18–Hockey: North Toronto 0, Riverdale 4; Jan. 18–Jr. Hockey: De la Salle 9, Upper Canada College 3; Jan. 19–Jr. Hockey: Barrie 1, St. Michael's 16; Jan. 19–NHL: Rangers 1, Leafs 3; Jan. 21–Boxing: Arthur King vs. Jean Barriere; Jan. 22–Hockey: Upper Canada College 1, St. Michael's "C" 6; Jan. 22–Jr. Hockey: St. Michael's "B" 7, Upper Canada College 5; Jan. 22–Jr. Hockey: Galt 4, Young Rangers 1; Jan. 23–Hockey: De la Salle 1, St. Michael's "C" 8; Jan. 23–Jr. Hockey: De la Salle 16, Cantab 3; Jan. 23–Sr. Hockey: Hamilton 2, Staffords 1; Jan. 24–Wrestling: Wladyslaw Talun vs. Strangler Wagner; Jan. 25–Hockey: Humberside 2, Riverdale 3; Jan. 25–Hockey: Lawrence Park 6, Jarvis 1; Jan. 25–Hockey: Danforth Tech 1, Western Tech 0; Jan. 25–Jr. Hockey: U. of T. Schools 5, Upper Canada College 3; Jan. 26–Jr. Hockey: Young Rangers 1, St. Michael's 5; Jan. 26–Jr. Hockey: St. Catharines 6, Jr. Marlboros 2; Jan. 26–NHL: Chicago 5, Leafs 6; Jan. 28–Hockey: St. Michael's "C" 7, U. of T. Schools 0; Jan. 28–Jr. Hockey: St. Michael's "B" 10, Cantab 2; Jan. 28–Jr. Hockey: Galt 3, St. Michael's 5; Jan. 29–Music: Gyro Remembrance Night; Jan. 30–Hockey: St. Michael's "C" 4, De la Salle 0; Jan. 30–Jr. Hockey: St. Michael's "B" 4, De la Salle 3; Jan. 30–Sr. Hockey: Hamilton 3, Staffords 8; Jan. 31–Wrestling: Wladyslaw Talun vs. Chief Saunooke; Feb. 1–Hockey: De la Salle 3, Upper Canada College 1; Feb. 1–Hockey: Central Tech 3, North Toronto 3; Feb. 1–Hockey: Parkdale 6, Malvern 6; Feb. 1–Hockey: Northern Vocational 0, Oakwood 4; Feb. 1–Jr. Hockey: Upper Canada College 2, Cantab 0; Feb. 2–Jr. Hockey: Hamilton 5, Jr. Marlboros 12; Feb. 2–NHL: Boston 5, Leafs 3; Feb. 4-8: Ice Follies of 1946; Feb. 9–Jr. Hockey: Jr. Marlboros 4, Young Rangers 2; Feb. 9–NHL: Detroit 1, Leafs 4; Feb. 9–Sr. Hockey: Stratford 3, Staffords 6; Feb. 11–Hockey: Upper Canada College 2, De la Salle 1; Feb. 11–Jr. Hockey: Cantab 1, De la Salle 20; Feb. 11–Jr. Hockey: St. Michael's 7, Young Rangers 0; Feb. 11–Jr. Hockey: Oshawa 2, Jr. Marlboros 4; Feb. 12–Hockey: U. of T. Schools 0, St. Michael's "C" 7; Feb. 12–Hockey: St. Michael's New Boys 11, St. Michael's Old Boys 8; Feb. 12–Jr. Hockey: Upper Canada College 1, St. Michael's "B" 14; Feb. 13–Jr. Hockey: U. of Toronto Schools 3, St. Michael's "B" 14; Feb. 13–Sr. Hockey: Stratford 3, Staffords 5; Feb. 14–Wrestling: Whipper Billy Watson vs. Wladyslaw Talun; Feb. 15–Hockey: Central Tech 3, Humberside 4; Feb. 15–Hockey: Riverdale 5, Danforth Tech 3; Feb. 15–Jr. Hockey: St. Michael's 8, Jr. Marlboros 1; Feb. 16–Jr. Hockey: Oshawa 4, Young Rangers 3; Feb. 16–NHL: Canadiens 4, Leafs 2; Feb. 16–Sr. Hockey: Stratford 5, Staffords 8; Feb. 18–Jr. Hockey: De la Salle 5, Upper Canada College 1; Feb. 18–Jr. Hockey: Oshawa 2, St. Michael's 6; Feb. 21–Wrestling: Whipper Billy Watson vs. Wladyslaw Talun; Feb. 22–Basketball: Dow Athletics 48, Hayes Hellcats 46; Feb. 22–Basketball: Toronto Tip Tops 41, Windsor Assumption Coll. 46; Feb. 23–Jr. Hockey: Barrie 1, Jr. Marlboros 5; Feb. 23–NHL: Boston 2, Leafs 7; Feb. 23–Sr. Hockey: Hamilton 3, Staffords 2 (OHA Sr. Finals); Feb. 25–Jr. Hockey: De la Salle 7, U. of T. Schools 4; Feb. 25–Jr. Hockey: Jr. Marlboros 4, Young Rangers 3; Feb. 26–Jr. Hockey: Galt 3, St. Michael's 8; Feb. 27–Jr. Hockey: Jr. Marlboros 3, Young Rangers 2; Feb. 27–NHL: Rangers 6, Leafs 4; Feb. 28–Wrestling: Whipper Billy Watson vs. Wladyslaw Talun; Mar. 1–Jr. Hockey: St. Michael's "B" 4, De la Salle 5; Mar. 1–Sr. Hockey: Hamilton 2, Staffords 3 (OHA Sr. Finals); Mar. 2–Jr. Hockey: Galt 4, St. Michael's 5; Mar. 2–NHL: Chicago 4, Leafs 9; Mar. 4–Jr. Hockey: St. Michael's "B" 4, De la Salle 5 (Schoolboy Finals); Mar. 6–Jr. Hockey: Oshawa 6, Jr. Marlboros 4; Mar. 6–Jr. Hockey: Galt 1, St. Michael's 6; Mar. 7–Wrestling: Whipper Billy Watson vs. Chief Saunooke; Mar. 8–Hockey: East 4, West 1 (Schoolboy All-Star Game); Mar. 8–Hockey: Riverdale 7,

Humberside 5 (Schoolboy Finals); Mar. 9–Jr. Hockey: Barrie 2, De la Salle 6; Mar. 9–NHL: Canadiens 2, Leafs 1; Mar. 11–Jr. Hockey: Oshawa 7, St. Michael's 10 (OHA "A" Finals); Mar. 14–Wrestling: Whipper Billy Watson vs. Lee Henning; Mar. 15–Jr. Hockey: De la Salle 6, St. Catharines 3; Mar. 16–Jr. Hockey: Oshawa 7, St. Michael's 5 (OHA "A" Finals); Mar. 16–NHL: Detroit 3, Leafs 7; Mar. 20–Jr. Hockey: Oshawa 2, St. Michael's 4 (OHA "A" Finals); Mar. 21–Wrestling: Whipper Billy Watson vs. Lee Henning; Mar. 22–Hockey: Falconbridge 1, Weston 1 (Midget Tournament); Mar. 22–Hockey: Garson 3, Sudbury 6 (Midget Tournament); Mar. 22–Hockey: Copper Cliff 10, Georgetown 0 (Midget Tournament); Mar. 22–Hockey: Falconbridge, Sudbury (Midget Tournament); Mar. 22–Hockey: Weston, Copper Cliff (Midget Tournament); Mar. 22–Hockey: Georgetown, Garson (Midget Tournament); Mar. 22–Hockey: Copper Cliff 9, Sudbury 1 (Midget Tournament); Mar. 22–Hockey: Falconbridge 6, Georgetown 2 (Midget Tournament); Mar. 22–Hockey: Weston 3, Garson 0 (Midget Tournament); Mar. 26–Boxing: Arthur King vs. Juan Manuel; Mar. 27–Jr. Hockey: Copper Cliff 2, St. Michael's 13 (All-Ontario Jr. Finals); Mar. 28–Wrestling: Brother Jonathan vs. Wladyslaw Talun; Mar. 29–Jr. Hockey: De la Salle 2, Scarboro 4; Mar. 30–Jr. Hockey: Copper Cliff 10, St. Michael's 8 (All-Ontario Jr. Finals); Mar. 30–Sr. Hockey: Hamilton 9, Pembroke 1 (All-Ontario Jr. Finals); Mar. 31–Cardinal McGuigan Tribute; Apr. 1–Jr. Hockey: Scarboro 3, De la Salle 5; Apr. 3–Jr. Hockey: St. Michael's 8, Montreal 2 (Memorial Cup Eastern Finals); Apr. 4–Wrestling: Bill Longson vs. Fred Von Schact; Apr. 5–Jr. Hockey: De la Salle 7, Scarboro 1; Apr. 6–Jr. Hockey: St. Michael's 6, Montreal 5 (Memorial Cup Eastern Finals); Apr. 6–Sr. Hockey: Hamilton 5, Montreal 1 (Allan Cup Eastern Finals); Apr. 8–Jr. Hockey: Kitchener 1, De la Salle 2 (OHA "B" Finals); Apr. 10–Hockey: St. Catharines 1, St. Clare's 0 (Pee-Wee Finals); Apr. 10–Hockey: St. Catharines 4, St. Cecilias 5 (Bantam Finals); Apr. 10–Hockey: St. Catharines 4, Holy Name 4 (Midget Finals); Apr. 10–Hockey: Thorold 1, St. Brigid's 3 (Midget Finals); Apr. 10–Hockey: St. Catharines 6, Wexford 0 (Juvenile Finals); Apr. 11–Wrestling: Brother Jonathan vs. Fred Von Schact; Apr. 12–Hockey: St. Catharines 4, Etobicoke 10 (Bantam Finals); Apr. 12–Hockey: St. Catharines 2, St. Michael's "C" 1 (Midget Finals); Apr. 12–Hockey: St. Catharines 2, Young Leafs 2 (Juvenile Finals); Apr. 13–Jr. Hockey: Winnipeg Monarchs 3, St. Michael's 2 (Memorial Cup Finals); Apr. 15–Jr. Hockey: Winnipeg Monarchs 3, St. Michael's 5 (Memorial Cup Finals); Apr. 16–Boxing: Willie Joyce vs. Jimmy Hatcher; Apr. 17–Jr. Hockey: Kitchener 4, De la Salle 5 (OHA "B" Finals); Apr. 17–Jr. Hockey: Winnipeg Monarchs 3, St. Michael's 7 (Memorial Cup Finals); Apr. 18–Wrestling: Brother Jonathan vs. Fred Von Schact; Apr. 20–Jr. Hockey: Winnipeg Monarchs 4, St. Michael's 3 (Memorial Cup Finals); Apr. 22–Jr. Hockey: Winnipeg Monarchs 4, St. Michael's 7 (Memorial Cup Finals); Apr. 24–Jr. Hockey: Winnipeg Monarchs 4, St. Michael's 2 (Memorial Cup Finals); Apr. 25–Music: Simpson's Teen-Town Time Dance; Apr. 25–Wrestling: Whipper Billy Watson vs. Brother Jonathan; Apr. 27–Hockey: Sault Ste. Marie 2, St. Catharines 7; Apr. 27–Jr. Hockey: Winnipeg Monarchs 4, St. Michael's 2 (Memorial Cup Finals); Apr. 28–Canadian Council of Churches; Apr. 30–Boxing: Tommy Jonathan vs. Frankie Cordian; May 1–Tennis: Bobby Riggs vs. Don Budge; May 3–Music: 11th Annual Drummer's Ball; May 3–Wrestling: Whipper Billy Watson vs. Brother Jonathan; May 7–Board of Education Phys. Ed. Demonstration; May 13-18: S.Q. Ranch Rodeo with Gene Autry; June 14–National Council for Canadian-Soviet Friendship; June 15–Jehovah's Witnesses Convention; June 26–Canadian Legion Convention; Aug. 24–Ukranian Concert; Sept. 5–Wrestling: Whipper Billy Watson vs. Frank Sexton; Sept. 10-14: Roller Skating Vanities; Sept. 16–Boxing: Joey Bragnato vs. Arthur King; Sept. 19–Wrestling: Whipper Billy Watson vs. Krippler Davis; Sept. 26–Wrestling: Bill Longson vs. Wladyslaw Talun; Sept. 30–Lacrosse: St. Catharines 11, New Westminster 10 (Mann Cup Finals); Oct. 2–Lacrosse: St. Catharines 18, New Westminster 9 (Mann Cup Finals); Oct. 3–Wrestling: Bill Longson vs. Whipper Billy Watson World Title; Oct. 4–Lacrosse: St. Catharines 11, New Westminster 7 (Mann Cup Finals); Oct. 9-14: Bob Morton's Rameses Shrine Circus; Oct. 17–Wrestling: Frank Sexton vs. Ivan Rasputin; Oct. 19–NHL: Detroit 3, Leafs 6; Oct. 21–Boxing: Arthur King vs. Paul Frechette; Oct. 24–Wrestling: Whipper Billy Watson vs. Krippler Davis; Oct. 26–NHL: Chicago 1, Leafs 2; Oct. 30–Hadassah Bazaar; Oct. 31–Wrestling: Whipper Billy Watson vs. Sandy O'Donnell; Nov. 1–Basketball: NY Knicks 68, Toronto 66; Nov. 2–NHL: Boston 5, Leafs 0; Nov. 4–Sr. Hockey: Owen Sound 3, Staffords 6; Nov. 5–Fritz Kreisler Concert; Nov. 6–Jr. Hockey: St. Michael's 7, Stratford 1; Nov. 6–Jr. Hockey: Young Rangers 5, St. Catharines 0; Nov. 7–Wrestling: Kwarianni/Rasputin vs. Sharpe Brothers; Nov. 8–Basketball: Detroit 71, Toronto 73; Nov. 9–Jr. Hockey: Stratford 8, Jr. Marlboros 2; Nov. 9–Jr. Hockey: Barrie 8, Young Rangers 0; Nov. 9–NHL: Rangers 2, Leafs 4; Nov. 11–Sr. Hockey: Hamilton 5, Staffords 3; Nov. 13–Youth for Christ Rally; Nov. 14–Wrestling: Sharpe Brothers vs. Kwarianni/Rasputin; Nov. 15–Basketball: Providence 68, Toronto 85; Nov. 16–Jr. Hockey: Barrie 2, Jr. Marlboros 3; Nov. 16–Jr. Hockey: St. Catharines 0, St. Michael's 9; Nov. 16–NHL: Canadiens 0, Leafs 3; Nov. 18–Sr. Hockey: Hamilton, Staffords; Nov. 19–Basketball: Cleveland 74, Toronto 72; Nov. 20–Jr. Hockey: Galt 1, St. Michael's 6; Nov. 21–Wrestling: Whipper Billy Watson vs. Sandy O'Donnell; Nov. 22–Basketball: Boston 82, Toronto 83; Nov. 23–Jr. Hockey: Young Rangers 1, St. Michael's 11; Nov. 23–Jr. Hockey: St. Catharines 1, Jr. Marlboros 11; Nov. 23–NHL: Detroit 4, Leafs 2; Nov. 25–Boxing: Dan Webb vs. Arthur King; Nov. 26–Basketball: Washington 78, Toronto 68; Nov. 27–Jr. Hockey: Oshawa 3, St. Michael's 8; Nov. 28–Wrestling: Watson/Christie vs. Wagner/O'Donnell; Nov. 29–Basketball: Cleveland 87, Toronto 68; Nov. 30–Jr. Hockey: Hamilton 2, St. Michael's 12; Nov. 30–Jr. Hockey: Galt 6, Young Rangers 2; Nov. 30–NHL: Chicago 0, Leafs 11; Dec. 2-6: Ice Capades; Dec. 7–Jr. Hockey: St. Michael's 4, Jr. Marlboros 1; Dec. 7–Jr. Hockey: Oshawa 4, Young Rangers 3; Dec. 7–NHL: Boston 1, Leafs 5; Dec. 9–Jr. Hockey: De la Salle 7, St. Michael's "B" 2; Dec. 9–Sr. Hockey: Owen Sound 2, Staffords 5; Dec. 10–Basketball: Philadelphia 85, Toronto 73; Dec. 11–Jr. Hockey: Torraville 2, St. Michael's "B" 14; Dec. 11–NHL: Candiens 3, Leafs 2; Dec. 12–Wrestling: Whipper Billy Watson vs. Bob Wagner; Dec. 13–Basketball: Pittsburgh 62, Toronto 52; Dec. 14–Jr. Hockey: St. Catharines 0, St. Michael's 7; Dec. 14–Jr. Hockey: Young Rangers 1, Jr. Marlboros 3; Dec. 14–NHL: Rangers 2, Leafs 3; Dec. 16–Jr. Hockey: Torraville 0, De la Salle 17; Dec. 16–Sr. Hockey: Stratford 0, Staffords 6; Dec. 19–Jr. Hockey: St. Michael's "B" 2, De la Salle 12; Dec. 19–NHL: Detroit 1, Leafs 3; Dec. 20–Basketball: NY Knicks 70, Toronto 74; Dec. 21–Jr. Hockey: Barrie 1, St. Michael's 8; Dec. 21–Jr. Hockey: Windsor 1, Jr. Marlboros 6; Dec. 21–NHL: Chicago 1, Leafs 3; Dec. 23–Sr. Hockey: Hamilton 2, Staffords 3; Dec. 26–Wrestling: Mike Sharpe vs. Krippler Davis; Dec. 27–Basketball: Chicago 88, Toronto 80; Dec. 28–Jr. Hockey: Windsor 8, Young Rangers 5; Dec. 28–Jr. Hockey: Hamilton 1, Jr. Marlboros 6; Dec. 28–NHL: Boston 3, Leafs 4; Dec. 30–Sr. Hockey: Hamilton 4, Staffords 2; Dec. 31–Basketball: Chicago 76, Toronto 87.

1947 • Jan. 1–NHL: Detroit 1, Leafs 2; Jan. 2–Wrestling: Frank Sexton vs. Vic Christie; Jan. 3–Basketball: Boston 58, Toronto 53; Jan. 4–Jr. Hockey: Jr. Marlboros 3, Young Rangers 2; Jan. 4–Jr. Hockey: Hamilton 0, St. Michael's 10; Jan. 4–NHL: Rangers 2, Leafs 0; Jan. 6–Basketball: Detroit 61, Toronto 76; Jan. 8–Jr. Hockey: Torraville 2, St. Michael's "C" 2; Jan. 8–NHL: Chicago 4, Leafs 10; Jan. 9–Wrestling: Mike Sharpe vs. Bob Wagner; Jan. 10–Hockey: UCC New Boys 5, UCC Old Boys 6; Jan. 10–Jr. Hockey: De la Salle 5, St. Michael's "B" 4; Jan. 11–Jr. Hockey: Windsor 0, St. Michael's 8; Jan. 11–NHL: Boston 3, Leafs 4; Jan. 13–Sr. Hockey: Stratford 3, Staffords 1; Jan. 14–Basketball: Philadelphia 104, Toronto 74; Jan. 15–NHL: Canadiens 1, Leafs 2; Jan. 16–Wrestling: Whipper Billy Watson vs. Paul Boesch; Jan. 17–Basketball: Detroit 74, Toronto 64; Jan. 18–Jr. Hockey: St. Michael's 6, Young Rangers 1; Jan. 18–Jr. Hockey: Jr. Marlboros 6, Galt 5; Jan. 18–NHL: Detroit 4, Leafs 7; Jan. 20–Boxing: Arthur King vs. Cabby Lewis; Jan. 21–Basketball: St. Louis 71, Toronto 72; Jan. 22–Hockey: St. Michael's "B" 5, St. Michael's Old Boys 5; Jan. 22–Jr. Hockey: St. Andrews 4, Upper Canada College 3; Jan. 22–Jr. Hockey: St. Michael's 6, Oshawa 5; Jan. 23–Wrestling: Mike Sharpe vs. Fred Von Schact; Jan. 24–Basketball: York Memorial 31, Etobicoke 32; Jan. 24–Basketball: Providence 96, Toronto 93; Jan. 25–Jr. Hockey: Stratford 3, Young Rangers 1; Jan. 25–Jr. Hockey: St. Michael's 8, Jr. Marlboros 1; Jan. 25–NHL: Rangers 1, Leafs 0; Jan. 27–Basketball: Cleveland 88, Toronto 82; Jan. 29–Jr. Hockey: Pickering 1, Upper Canada College 15; Jan. 29–Sr. Hockey: Hamilton 6, Staffords 5; Jan. 30–Wrestling: Bill Longson vs. Dan O'Mahony; Jan. 31–Basketball: Washington 74, Toronto 83; Feb. 1–Jr. Hockey: Barrie 0, St. Michael's 11; Feb. 1–Jr. Hockey: Oshawa 6, Jr. Marlboros 3; Feb. 1–NHL: Chicago 5, Leafs 4; Feb. 3-7: Ice Follies of 1947; Feb. 8–Jr. Hockey: Stratford 1, St. Michael's 2; Feb. 8–Jr. Hockey: Hamilton 0, Young Rangers 19; Feb. 8–NHL: Boston 2, Leafs 5; Feb. 11–Jr. Hockey: De la Salle 12, St. Michael's "B" 2; Feb. 12–Jr. Hockey: U. of T. Schools 4, Upper Canada College 8; Feb. 13–Wrestling: Whipper Billy Watson vs. Paul Boesch; Feb. 14–Basketball: Pittsburgh 73, Toronto 84; Feb. 15–Jr. Hockey: Galt 4, St. Michael's 5; Feb. 15–NHL: Canadiens 4, Leafs 4; Feb. 17–Boxing: Arthur King vs. Joey Bragnato; Feb. 18–Basketball: Buffalo 17, Toronto Maids 28; Feb. 18–Basketball: St. Louis 57, Toronto 65; Feb. 20–Wrestling: Fred Von Schact vs. Mike Sharpe; Feb. 21–Basketball: Boston 61, Toronto 67; Feb. 22–Jr. Hockey: St. Michael's 8, Oshawa 5; Feb. 22–Jr. Hockey: Jr. Marlboros 4, Barrie 7; Feb. 22–NHL: Rangers 0, Leafs 2; Feb. 24–Comedy: Alex Templeton; Feb. 25–Basketball: York Belting 44, Merriton 30; Feb. 25–Basketball: Providence 60, Toronto 83; Feb. 26–Jr. Hockey: Trinity College 2, Upper Canada College 5; Feb. 26–NHL: Canadiens 1, Leafs 0; Feb. 27–Wrestling: Whipper Billy Watson vs. Sandy O'Donnell; Feb. 28–Basketball: Leaside High 22, Earl Haig High 40; Feb. 28–Basketball: Philadelphia 69, Toronto 77; Mar. 1–Jr. Hockey: Oshawa 4, St. Michael's 9; Mar. 1–NHL: Detroit 5, Leafs 4; Mar. 3–Jr. Hockey: Upper Canada College 5, U. of T. Schools 4; Mar. 5–Jr. Hockey: De la Salle, St. Michael's "B"; Mar. 6–Wrestling: Whipper Billy Watson vs. Bill Longson; Mar. 7–Basketball: Washington 86, Toronto 70; Mar. 8–NHL: Chicago 4, Leafs 12; Mar. 8–Sr. Hockey: Owen Sound 5, Staffords 2; Mar. 10–Jr. Hockey: St. Michael's 8, Galt 1 (OHA "A" Finals); Mar. 11–Basketball: Tip Tops 37, East York 34; Mar. 11–Basketball: St. Louis 71, Toronto 79; Mar. 12–Sr. Hockey: Owen Sound 0, Staffords 2; Mar. 13–Wrestling: Whipper Billy Watson vs. Fred Von Schact; Mar. 14–Jr. Hockey: De la Salle 3, U. of T. Varsity "B" 5; Mar. 15–Jr. Hockey: Galt 3, St. Michael's 9 (OHA "A" Finals); Mar. 15–NHL: Boston 5, Leafs 5; Mar. 17–Jr. Hockey: Hamilton 8, Upper Canada College 2; Mar. 18–Basketball: Pittsburgh 70, Toronto 64; Mar. 19–NHL: Canadiens 4, Leafs 5; Mar. 20–Wrestling: Dusek Brothers vs. Sharpe Brothers; Mar. 21–Basketball: York Belting 44, All-Stars 20; Mar. 21–Basketball: Chicago 99, Toronto 83; Mar. 22–Jr. Hockey: Porcupine 2, St. Michael's 16 (All-Ontario Jr. Finals); Mar. 22–NHL: Rangers 3, Leafs 5; Mar. 23–Variety: Ken Soble's Amateur Show; Mar. 24–Jr. Hockey: De la Salle 9, Corner House 5; Mar. 25–Jr. Hockey: Porcupine 0, St. Michael's 1 (All-Ontario Jr. Finals); Mar. 26–NHL: Detroit 2, Leafs 3; Mar. 27–Wrestling: Whipper Billy Watson vs. Ernie Dusek; Mar. 28–Basketball: Runneymede 43, Western Tech 44; Mar. 28–Basketball: NY Knicks 61, Toronto 71; Mar. 29–Jr. Hockey: De la Salle 6, Corner House 4; Mar. 29–NHL: Detroit 9, Leafs 1; Apr. 1–Boxing: Arthur King vs. Joey Dolan; Apr. 3–Wrestling: Whipper Billy Watson vs. Dusek Brothers; Apr. 5–Jr. Hockey: Montreal 3, St. Michael's 11 (Memorial Cup Eastern Finals); Apr. 5–NHL: Detroit 1, Leafs 6; Apr. 9–Jr. Hockey: Montreal 0, St. Michael's 21 (Memorial Cup Eastern Finals); Apr. 10–Wrestling: Bill Longson vs. Bob Bruns; Apr. 11–Jr. Hockey: East 10, West 4 (Jr. C All-Star Game); Apr. 11–Jr. Hockey: East 4, West 11 (Jr. B All-Star Game); Apr. 12–NHL: Canadiens 2, Leafs 4 (Stanley Cup Finals); Apr. 12–Sr. Hockey: Hamilton 6, Moncton 3; Apr. 14–Sr. Hockey: Hamilton 5, Moncton 4; Apr. 15–NHL: Canadiens 1, Leafs 2 (Stanley Cup Finals); Apr. 16–Jr. Hockey: Hamilton Aerovox 2, De la Salle 8 (OHA "B"Finals"); Apr. 17–Wrestling: Whipper Billy Watson vs. Wee Willie Davis; Apr. 19–NHL: Canadiens 1, Leafs 2 (Stanley Cup-winning game); Apr. 21–Jr. Hockey: Hamilton Aerovox 4, De la Salle 2 (OHA "B"Finals"); Apr. 23–Sr. Hockey: Hamilton 1, Montreal 5 (Allan Cup Eastern Finals); Apr. 24–Wrestling: Primo Carnera vs. John Katan; Apr. 26–Jr. Hockey: Hamilton Aerovox 2, De la Salle 4 (OHA "B"Finals"); Apr. 26–Sr. Hockey: Calgary 3, Montreal 7 (Allan Cup Finals); Apr. 29-30: Ice Revue w/Barbara Ann Scott; May 1–Wrestling: Whipper Billy Watson vs. Wee Willie Davis; May 2–Music: Kiwanas Club Orpheus Male Chorus; May 3–Sr. Hockey: Calgary 3, Montreal 4 (Allan Cup Finals); May 5–Boxing: Bill Goulding vs. Mike Zaduk; May 7–Sr. Hockey: Calgary 1, Montreal 0 (Allan Cup Finals); May 8–Wrestling: Whipper Billy Watson vs. Angel Tillet; May 9–Music: Drummer's Ball; May 10–Sr. Hockey: Calgary 5, Montreal 2 (Allan Cup Finals); May 12–Boxing: Arthur King vs. Jimmy Rizzo; May 15–Wrestling: Whipper Billy Watson vs. Lou Thesz; May 19–Boxing: Al McFater vs. Billy Graham; May 22–Wrestling: Katan/Wagner vs. Sharpe Brothers; May 29–Wrestling: Lou Thesz vs. Whipper Billy Watson; June 23–Boxing: Arthur King vs. Spider Armstrong; Aug. 18-19–Music: The Roman Choir; Sept. 4–Wrestling: Whipper Billy Watson vs. Ken Kenneth; Sept. 11–Wrestling: Whipper Billy Watson vs. Joe Savoldi; Sept. 18–Wrestling: Whipper Billy Watson vs. Primo Carnera; Sept. 23-27: Roller Skating Vanities; Oct. 1–Boxing: Arthur King vs. Joey Bragnato; Oct. 2–Wrestling: Whipper Billy Watson vs. Primo Carnera; Oct. 6-11: Bob Morton's Rameses Shrine Circus; Oct. 13–Hockey: All-Stars 4, Toronto 3 (Schoolboy All-Stars); Oct. 13–NHL: All Stars 4, Leafs 3; Oct. 16–Wrestling: Whipper Billy Watson vs. Lou Thesz; Oct. 18–NHL: Detroit 2, Leafs 2; Oct. 19–Variety: Ken Soble's Amateur Show (Ontario Society for Crippled Children); Oct. 21–Boxing: Joe Brown vs. Arthur King; Oct. 22–NHL: Rangers 1, Leafs 3; Oct. 24–Wrestling: Lee/Masked Marvel vs. Sharpe Brothers; Oct. 25–Jr. Hockey: Young Rangers 1, Marlboros 3; Oct. 25–Jr. Hockey: Barrie 3, St. Michael's 2; Oct. 25–NHL: Chicago 1, Leafs 5; Oct. 27–Boxing: Al McFater vs. Don St. Louis; Oct. 28–Hadassah Bazaar; Oct. 29–NHL: Canadiens 1, Leafs 3; Oct. 30–Wrestling: Lee/Masked Marvel vs. Watson/Flanagan; Oct. 31–Sr. Hockey: Sr. Marlboros 4, Hamilton Tigers 2; Nov. 1–Jr. Hockey: Stratford 5, Young Rangers 3; Nov. 1–Jr. Hockey: St. Catharines 1, Jr. Marlboros 2; Nov. 1–NHL: Boston 1, Leafs 1; Nov. 6–Wrestling: Lou Thesz vs. Hi Lee; Nov. 7–Sr. Hockey: Brantford 1, Sr. Marlboros 12; Nov. 8–Jr. Hockey: St. Michael's 6, Young Rangers 2; Nov. 8–Jr. Hockey: Galt 1, Jr. Marlboros 2; Nov. 8–NHL: Rangers 2, Leafs 7; Nov. 10–Boxing: Arthur King vs. Joe Brown; Nov. 11–Jr. Hockey: St.

Michael's 2, Guelph 1; Nov. 11–Jr. Hockey: Windsor 4, Jr. Marlboros 1; Nov. 12–NHL: Chicago 5, Leafs 4; Nov. 13–Wrestling: Lee/Masked Marvel vs. Watson/Flanagan; Nov. 14–Sr. Hockey: Stratford 3, Sr. Marlboros 3; Nov. 15–Jr. Hockey: St. Michael's 1, Jr. Marlboros 5; Nov. 15–Jr. Hockey: Barrie 11, Young Rangers 2; Nov. 15–NHL: Detroit 3, Leafs 5; Nov. 17-20: Ice Capades; Nov. 22–Jr. Hockey: Oshawa 7, Young Rangers 1; Nov. 22–NHL: Boston 3, Leafs 4; Nov. 24–Boxing: Al McFater vs. Mike Ambedean; Nov. 26–Jr. Hockey: Windsor 9, Young Rangers 1; Nov. 26–Jr. Hockey: Galt 5, Jr. Marlboros 2; Nov. 27–Wrestling: Watson/Flanagan vs. Lee/Masked Marvel; Nov. 28–Sr. Hockey: Kitchener-Waterloo 2, Sr. Marlboros 8; Nov. 29–Jr. Hockey: Jr. Marlboros 3, St. Michael's 1; Nov. 29–Jr. Hockey: Guelph 4, Young Rangers 1; Nov. 29–NHL: Canadiens 1, Leafs 3; Dec. 1–Boxing: Arthur King vs. Terry McGovern; Dec. 3–Jr. Hockey: Stratford 5, Jr. Marlboros 2; Dec. 3–Sr. Hockey: Hamilton Pats 4, Sr. Marlboros 3; Dec. 4–Wrestling: Whipper Billy Watson vs. Lou Thesz; Dec. 5–Sr. Hockey: Owen Sound 1, Sr. Marlboros 5; Dec. 6–Jr. Hockey: Young Rangers 1, St. Michael's 5; Dec. 6–Jr. Hockey: Guelph 1, Jr. Marlboros 3; Dec. 6–NHL: Chicago 5, Leafs 12; Dec. 8–Sr. Hockey: Hamilton Tigers 4, Sr. Marlboros 3; Dec. 10–Jr. Hockey: Jr. Marlboros 3, Young Rangers 5; Dec. 10–Jr. Hockey: Oshawa 5, St. Michael's 2; Dec. 11–Wrestling: Lee/Masked Marvel vs. Watson/Flanagan; Dec. 12–Sr. Hockey: Brantford 0, Sr. Marlboros 11; Dec. 13–Jr. Hockey: Guelph 6, Young Rangers 1; Dec. 13–Jr. Hockey: Galt 4, St. Michael's 1; Dec. 13–NHL: Rangers 4, Leafs 1; Dec. 15–Boxing: Joe Brown vs. Joey Bragnato; Dec. 18–Wrestling: Masked Marvel vs. Jack Clayborne; Dec. 19–Sr. Hockey: Kitchener-Waterloo 1, Sr. Marlboro's 2; Dec. 20–Jr. Hockey: Barrie 2, St. Michael's 0; Dec. 20–Jr. Hockey: St. Catherines 2, Young Rangers 1; Dec. 20–NHL: Detroit 4, Leafs 4; Dec. 25–Hockey: Pittsburgh 7, Sr. Marlboros 3; Dec. 26–Sr. Hockey: Stratford 0, Sr. Marlboros 14; Dec. 27–Jr. Hockey: Galt 11, Young Rangers 2; Dec. 27–Jr. Hockey: Oshawa 2, Jr. Marlboros 1; Dec. 27–NHL: Boston 1, Leafs 2.

1948 • Jan. 1–NHL: Canadiens 1, Leafs 2; Jan. 2–Sr. Hockey: Owen Sound 6, Sr. Marlboros 2; Jan. 3–Jr. Hockey: Windsor 6, Young Rangers 1; Jan. 3–Jr. Hockey: Guelph 3, Jr. Marlboros 6; Jan. 3–NHL: Rangers 5, Leafs 5; Jan. 5–Boxing: Phil Terranova vs. Arthur King; Jan. 7–Jr. Hockey: Torraville, St. Michael's "B"; Jan. 7–Jr. Hockey: Stratford 6, St. Michael's 2; Jan. 8–Wrestling: Masked Marvel vs. The Mummy; Jan. 9–Jr. Hockey: Torraville 1, De la Salle 9; Jan. 9–Sr. Hockey: Hamilton Pats 4, Sr. Marlboros 8; Jan. 10–Jr. Hockey: Stratford 4, Jr. Marlboros 3; Jan. 10–Jr. Hockey: Galt 5, Young Rangers 4; Jan. 10–NHL: Chicago 4, Leafs 6; Jan. 12–Jr. Hockey: U. of T. Schools 0, Upper Canada College 5; Jan. 12–Sr. Hockey: Hamilton Tigers 4, Sr. Marlboros 3; Jan. 14–Jr. Hockey: St. Michael's "B" 3, De la Salle 4; Jan. 14–Jr. Hockey: Windsor 5, St. Michael's 2; Jan. 14–Jr. Hockey: St. Catharines 7, Young Rangers 1; Jan. 15–Wrestling: Masked Marvel vs. Bobby Bruns; Jan. 16–Hockey: UCC New Boys 2, UCC Old Boys 2; Jan. 17–Jr. Hockey: Barrie 3, Jr. Marlboros 5; Jan. 17–Jr. Hockey: Oshawa 6, Young Rangers 1; Jan. 17–NHL: Boston 1, Leafs 4; Jan. 20–Hockey: St. Michael's "B" 1, St. Michael's Old Boys 9; Jan. 20–Jr. Hockey: St. Michael's 3, Oshawa 6; Jan. 21–Music: Toronto Police Association Concert; Jan. 22–Wrestling: Cardiff Giant vs. Hi Lee; Jan. 23–Jr. Hockey: St. Andrews 3, Upper Canada College 12; Jan. 23–Sr. Hockey: Brantford 2, Sr. Marlboros 13; Jan. 24–Jr. Hockey: St. Catharines 1, Jr. Marlboros 4; Jan. 24–Jr. Hockey: Stratford 3, St. Michael's 2; Jan. 24–NHL: Chicago 1, Leafs 2; Jan. 26–Jr. Hockey: St. Michael's "B" 5, De la Salle 4; Jan. 26–Sr. Hockey: Stratford 2, Sr. Marlboros 1; Jan. 28–NHL: Canadiens 3, Leafs 3; Jan. 29–Wrestling: Masked Marvel vs. Cardiff Giant; Jan. 30–Sr. Hockey: Kitchener-Waterloo 4, Sr. Marlboros 2; Jan. 31–Jr. Hockey: St. Catharines 2, St. Michael's 1; Jan. 31–Jr. Hockey: Galt 5, Jr. Marlboros 4; Jan. 31–NHL: Canadiens 3, Leafs 3; Feb. 2-6: Ice Follies of 1948; Feb. 7–Jr. Hockey: Windsor 4, St. Michael's 1; Feb. 7–Jr. Hockey: Stratford 7, Young Rangers 1; Feb. 7–NHL: Rangers 0, Leafs 3; Feb. 9–Boxing: Arthur King vs. Danny Webb; Feb. 11–Jr. Hockey: Barrie 4, Jr. Marlboros 3; Feb. 11–Jr. Hockey: Guelph 1, St. Michael's 4; Feb. 12–Wrestling: Lou Thesz vs. Dr. Ed Meske; Feb. 13–Jr. Hockey: Oshawa 2, Jr. Marlboros 4; Feb. 13–Sr. Hockey: Hamilton Pats 2, Sr. Marlboros 10; Feb. 14–Jr. Hockey: Windsor 2, Jr. Marlboros 0; Feb. 14–Jr. Hockey: Barrie 16, Young Rangers 1; Feb. 14–NHL: Canadiens 2, Leafs 4; Feb. 16–Boxing: John Thompson vs. Ernie Majury; Feb. 17–Sr. Hockey: Owen Sound 1, Sr. Marlboros 12; Feb. 18–Jr. Hockey: Trinity College 2, Upper Canada College 5; Feb. 19–Wrestling: Lou Thesz vs. Whipper Billy Watson; Feb. 20–Jr. Hockey: Pickering 1, Upper Canada College 11; Feb. 20–Sr. Hockey: Hamilton Tigers 1, Sr. Marlboros 3; Feb. 21–Jr. Hockey: St. Michael's "C" 3, De la Salle 6; Feb. 21–NHL: Detroit 2, Leafs 3; Feb. 23–Boxing: Al McFater vs. Mike Garcia; Feb. 25–NHL: Boston 2, Leafs 4; Feb. 26–Wrestling: Whipper Billy Watson vs. Nanjo Singh; Feb. 27–Sr. Hockey: Hamilton Tigers 4, Sr. Marlboros 0; Feb. 28–Jr. Hockey: De la Salle 10, St. Michael's "C" 4; Feb. 28–NHL: Chicago 3, Leafs 4; Mar. 2–Jr. Hockey: St. Michael's "B" 3, De la Salle 2; Mar. 3–NHL: Canadiens 3, Leafs 2; Mar. 4–Wrestling: Whipper Billy Watson vs. Lou Thesz; Mar. 6–Hockey: U. of T. Schools 5, Upper Canada College 6; Mar. 6–NHL: Rangers 1, Leafs 2; Mar. 8–Hockey: Hamilton 4, Toronto Bell AC 9 (Midget Finals); Mar. 8–Hockey: St. Catharines 5, Beaches Lions 0 (Juvenile Finals); Mar. 10–Boxing: Dave Castilloux vs. Simeon Waithe; Mar. 11–Wrestling: Whipper Billy Watson vs. Nanjo Singh; Mar. 13–Jr. Hockey: London 4, Upper Canada College 9; Mar. 13–NHL: Boston 2, Leafs 5; Mar. 15-19–Ice Show: Toronto Skating Carnival; Mar. 20–Jr. Hockey: Kingston 4, Upper Canada College 10; Mar. 20–NHL: Detroit 3, Leafs 5; Mar. 21–Variety: Ken Soble's Amateur Show (Ontario Society for Crippled Children); Mar. 22–Boxing: Clayton Kenny vs. Al McFater; Mar. 24–NHL: Boston 4, Leafs 5; Mar. 25–Wrestling: Whipper Billy Watson vs. Nanjo Singh; Mar. 27–NHL: Boston 3, Leafs 5; Mar. 27–Sr. Hockey: Hamilton Tigers 7, Sault Ste. Marie 3 (All-Ontario Sr. Finals); Mar. 28–Jr. Hockey: Barrie 13, Porcupine 3 (All-Ontario Jr. Finals); Apr. 1–Wrestling: Angel Tillet vs. Wee Willie Davis; Apr. 3–Jr. Hockey: Hamilton Aerovox 7, Upper Canada College 3; Apr. 3–NHL: Boston 2, Leafs 3; Apr. 5–Jr. Hockey: St. Michael's "B" 2, Upper Canada College 4; Apr. 7–NHL: Detroit 3, Leafs 5 (Stanley Cup Finals); Apr. 8–Wrestling: Whipper Billy Watson vs. Cardiff Giant; Apr. 10–Jr. Hockey: Hamilton Aerovox 3, St. Michael's "B" 1 (Ontario "B" Finals); Apr. 10–NHL: Detroit 2, Leafs 4 (Stanley Cup Finals); Apr. 12–Jr. Hockey: Barrie 8, Montreal National 3 (Memorial Cup Eastern Finals); Apr. 14–Sr. Hockey: Hamilton 1, Ottawa 2 (Allan Cup Eastern Finals); Apr. 15–Wrestling: Masked Marvel vs. Angel Tillet; Apr. 19–Boxing: John Thompson vs. Ernie Majury; Apr. 20–Sr. Hockey: Hamilton 2, Ottawa 2 (Allan Cup Eastern Finals); Apr. 21–Jr. Hockey: Lethbridge 1, Port Arthur 11 (Memorial Cup Western Finals); Apr. 22–Wrestling: Whipper Billy Watson vs. Bill Longson; Apr. 24–Jr. Hockey: Barrie 8, Port Arthur 10 (Memorial Cup Finals); Apr. 24–Sr. Hockey: Hamilton 3, Ottawa 4 (Allan Cup Eastern Finals); Apr. 26–Jr. Hockey: Barrie 1, Port Arthur 8 (Memorial Cup Finals); Apr. 27–Boxing: Arthur King vs. Richard Shinn; Apr. 28–Jr. Hockey: Barrie 4, Port Arthur 5 (Memorial Cup Finals); Apr. 29–Wrestling: Nanjo Singh vs. Mike Mazurki; May 1–Jr. Hockey: Barrie 8, Port Arthur 9 (Memorial Cup Finals); May 6-8–Ice Show: Rotary Club Ice Revue; May 10–Basketball: Western Ontario 40, British Columbia 48; May 10–Basketball: Montreal YMHA 47, Vancouver 45; May 11–Basketball: Western Ontario 43, Vancouver 40; May 11–Basketball: Montreal YMHA 34, British Columbia 48; May 13–Wrestling: Nanjo Singh vs. Whipper Billy Watson; May 14-15–Music: Phil Spitalny's All-Girl Orchestra; May 16–Zionist Meeting after declaration of Israeli statehood; May 17–Boxing: Gus Rubicini vs. Martin Gilday; May 20–Wrestling: Gorgeous George vs. Larry Moquin; May 27–Wrestling: Whipper Billy Watson vs. Gorgeous George; June 15-19: Buster Crabbe's Aqua Parade; Sept. 2–Wrestling: Henry/Masked Marvel vs. Watson/Flanagan; Sept. 9–Wrestling: Fred Atkins vs. Nanjo Singh; Sept. 13–Boxing: Al McFater vs. Mickey McFarlane; Sept. 16–Wrestling: Fred Atkins vs. Nanjo Singh; Sept. 20–Boxing: Arthur King vs. Harvey Mathe; Sept. 23–Wrestling: Henry/Masked Marvel vs. Watson/Flanagan; Sept. 30–Wrestling: Henry/Masked Marvel vs. Watson/Flanagan; Oct. 4-9: Bob Morton's Rameses Shrine Circus; Oct. 11–Lacrosse: Toronto Roden AC 1, Port Dalhousie 8 (Pee-Wee Finals); Oct. 11–Lacrosse: New Westminster 11, Hamilton 6 (Mann Cup Finals); Oct. 12–NHL: Whites 5, Blues 2 (Maple Leafs intrasquad game); Oct. 13–Lacrosse: Toronto St. Vincent 9, St. Catharines 17 (Bantam Finals); Oct. 13–Lacrosse: New Westminster 13, Hamilton 11 (Mann Cup Finals); Oct. 14–Wrestling: Bill Longson vs. Whipper Billy Watson; Oct. 15–Lacrosse: New Toronto 4, St. Catharines 7 (Midget Finals); Oct. 15–Lacrosse: New Westminster 7, Hamilton 12 (Mann Cup Finals); Oct. 16–NHL: Boston 4, Leafs 1; Oct. 18–Lacrosse: New Westminster 7, Hamilton 9 (Mann Cup Finals); Oct. 20–Lacrosse: New Westminster 8, Hamilton 12 (Mann Cup Finals); Oct. 21–Wrestling: Whipper Billy Watson vs. Bill Longson; Oct. 22–Music: Simpson's Teen Town Time Dance; Oct. 23–Jr. Hockey: St. Catharines 2, St. Michael's 2; Oct. 23–Jr. Hockey: Guelph 5, Jr. Marlboros 5; Oct. 23–NHL: Chicago 1, Leafs 6; Oct. 25–Boxing: Al McFater vs. Rockey Beau; Oct. 26–Jr. Hockey: Oshawa 3, St. Michael's 1; Oct. 26–Jr. Hockey: Galt 1, Jr. Marlboros 3; Oct. 27–NHL: Canadiens 2, Leafs 3; Oct. 28–Wrestling: Lee/Masked Marvel vs. Watson/Atkins; Oct. 29–Sr. Hockey: Owen Sound 1, Sr. Marlboros 1; Oct. 30–Jr. Hockey: Stratford 3, St. Michael's 6; Oct. 30–Jr. Hockey: Barrie 4, Jr. Marlboros 3; Oct. 30–NHL: Detroit 1, Leafs 2; Nov. 2–Hadassah Bazaar; Nov. 3–Sr. Hockey: Stratford 0, Sr. Marlboros 1; Nov. 4–Wrestling: Lee/Masked Marvel vs. Watson/Atkins; Nov. 5–Sr. Hockey: Kitchener-Waterloo 0, Sr. Marlboros 4; Nov. 6–Jr. Hockey: Guelph 1, St. Michael's 6; Nov. 6–Jr. Hockey: St. Catharines 5, Jr. Marlboros 3; Nov. 6–NHL: Rangers 3, Leafs 3; Nov. 8-12: Ice Capades; Nov. 13–Jr. Hockey: Stratford 3, Jr. Marlboros 2; Nov. 13–NHL: Chicago 6, Leafs 3; Nov. 15–Boxing: Pete Zaduk vs. Harry Hurst; Nov. 17–Sr. Hockey: Hamilton 2, Sr. Marlboros 5; Nov. 18–Wrestling: Lee/Masked Marvel vs. Watson/Atkins; Nov. 19–Sr. Hockey: Owen Sound 4, Sr. Marlboros 6; Nov. 20–Jr. Hockey: Windsor 3, St. Michael's 3; Nov. 20–Jr. Hockey: Guelph 5, Jr. Marlboros 6; Nov. 22–Boxing: Al McFater vs. Chief Davidson; Nov. 23–Jr. Hockey: Galt 1, St. Michael's 3; Nov. 23–Jr. Hockey: Oshawa 0, Jr. Marlboros 2; Nov. 24–NHL: Canadiens 3, Leafs 3; Nov. 25–Wrestling: Fred Atkins vs. Ben Morgan; Nov. 26–Sr. Hockey: Stratford 0, Sr. Marlboros 5; Nov. 27–Jr. Hockey: U. of T. Varsity "B" 8, St. Michael's "B" 4; Nov. 27–Jr. Hockey: Barrie 3, Jr. Marlboros 1; Nov. 27–NHL: Rangers 0, Leafs 3; Nov. 29–Boxing: Al McFater vs. Vincent Tyo; Nov. 29–NHL: Boston 2, Leafs 2; Dec. 1–Sr. Hockey: Kitchener-Waterloo 2, Sr. Marlboros 0; Dec. 2–Wrestling: Fred Atkins vs. Ben Morgan; Dec. 3–Sr. Hockey: Hamilton 3, Sr. Marlboros 5; Dec. 4–Jr. Hockey: St. Michael's "B" 2, Corner Boys 4; Dec. 4–Jr. Hockey: Stratford 2, Jr. Marlboros 2; Dec. 4–NHL: Chicago 6, Leafs 4; Dec. 6–Boxing: Al McFater vs. Norm Thompson; Dec. 7–Jr. Hockey: Windsor 3, Jr. Marlboros 1; Dec. 8–NHL: Detroit 4, Leafs 3; Dec. 9–Wrestling: Six-Man Tag Team Extraveganza; Dec. 10–Sr. Hockey: Owen Sound 1, Sr. Marlboros 6; Dec. 11–Jr. Hockey: Barrie 3, St. Michael's 1; Dec. 11–Jr. Hockey: St. Catharines 2, Jr. Marlboros 3; Dec. 11–NHL: Boston 2, Leafs 3; Dec. 13–Boxing: Al McFater vs. Jerry Shears; Dec. 14–Jr. Hockey: Jr. Marlboros 2, St. Michael's 4; Dec. 15–Sr. Hockey: Stratford 3, Sr. Marlboros 8; Dec. 16–Wrestling: Six-Man Tag Team Extraveganza; Dec. 17–Sr. Hockey: Kitchener-Waterloo 2, Sr. Marlboros 5; Dec. 18–Jr. Hockey: Corner Boys 5, Jr. Marlboros "B" 6; Dec. 18–Jr. Hockey: St. Michael's 1, Jr. Marlboros 2; Dec. 18–NHL: Rangers 3, Leafs 3; Dec. 20–Jr. Hockey: Oshawa 2, St. Michael's 4; Dec. 20–Jr. Hockey: Windsor 3, Jr. Marlboros 2; Dec. 22–Sr. Hockey: Hamilton 1, Sr. Marlboros 4; Dec. 25–NHL: Detroit 1, Leafs 2; Dec. 27–Boxing: George Sinclair vs. Ernie Keleher; Dec. 28–Jr. Hockey: Oshawa 8, Jr. Marlboros 4; Dec. 29–Sr. Hockey: Owen Sound 4, Sr. Marlboros 6.

1949 • Jan. 1–Jr. Hockey: Guelph 4, Jr. Marlboros 9; Jan. 1–NHL: Canadiens 3, Leafs 5; Jan. 2–Boxing: George Sinclair vs. Wily Dube; Jan. 4–Jr. Hockey: Galt 1, Jr. Marlboros 6; Jan. 5–NHL: Boston 0, Leafs 4; Jan. 6–Wrestling: Lou Thesz vs. Masked Marvel; Jan. 7–Sr. Hockey: Kitchener-Waterloo 6, Sr. Marlboros 1; Jan. 8–Jr. Hockey: St. Catharines 2, St. Michael's 1; Jan. 8–Jr. Hockey: Stratford 6, Jr. Marlboros 3; Jan. 8–NHL: Chicago 3, Leafs 3; Jan. 10–Boxing: George Sinclair vs. Fred Harding; Jan. 12–Sr. Hockey: Hamilton 4, Sr. Marlboros 8; Jan. 13–Wrestling: Watson/Atkins vs. Sandy O'Donnell/Lee; Jan. 14–Hockey: UCC New Boys 2, UCC Old Boys 2; Jan. 15–Jr. Hockey: U. of T. Varsity "B" 8, Corner Boys 2; Jan. 15–Jr. Hockey: St. Michael's 2, Jr. Marlboros "B" 4; Jan. 15–NHL: Rangers 1, Leafs 2; Jan. 17–Boxing: Al McFater vs. Simmie Harris; Jan. 18–Jr. Hockey: Galt 0, St. Michael's 1; Jan. 18–Jr. Hockey: Windsor 4, Jr. Marlboros 6; Jan. 19–NHL: Canadiens 4, Leafs 1; Jan. 20–Wrestling: Watson/Atkins vs. Sandy O'Donnell/Lee; Jan. 21–Sr. Hockey: Owen Sound 4, Sr. Marlboros 4; Jan. 22–Jr. Hockey: Stratford 5, St. Michael's 3; Jan. 22–Jr. Hockey: St. Catharines 5, Jr. Marlboros 7; Jan. 22–NHL: Detroit 2, Leafs 2; Jan. 24–Boxing: Al McFater vs. Percy King; Jan. 26–Sr. Hockey: Stratford 0, Sr. Marlboros 8; Jan. 27–Wrestling: Lee/Masked Marvel/O'Donnell vs. Watson/Atkins/McCready; Jan. 28–Jr. Hockey: McMaster, Upper Canada College; Jan. 28–Sr. Hockey: Kitchener-Waterloo 6, Sr. Marlboros 0; Jan. 29–Jr. Hockey: Windsor 6, St. Michael's 5; Jan. 29–Jr. Hockey: Oshawa 2, Jr. Marlboros 4; Jan. 29–NHL: Chicago 4, Leafs 4; Jan. 31–Feb. 4: Ice Follies of 1949; Feb. 5–Jr. Hockey: Jr. Marlboros "B" 2, St. Michael's "B" 7; Feb. 5–Jr. Hockey: Barrie 1, St. Michael's 1; Feb. 5–NHL: Rangers 1, Leafs 1; Feb. 7–Boxing: Carl Zoda vs. Al McFater; Feb. 9–NHL: Canadiens 2, Leafs 2; Feb. 10–Wrestling: Masked Marvel vs. Whipper Billy Watson; Feb. 11–Sr. Hockey: Hamilton 4, Sr. Marlboros 2; Feb. 12–Jr. Hockey: Guelph 3, St. Michael's 5; Feb. 12–Jr. Hockey: Barrie 2, Jr. Marlboros 2; Feb. 12–NHL: Detroit 1, Leafs 3; Feb. 14–Boxing: Al McFater vs. Joe Biausucci; Feb. 15–Hockey: Mills & Hadwin 0, Juvenile Marlboros 3; Feb. 15–Jr. Hockey: Galt 3, Jr. Marlboros 9; Feb. 16–Toronto Police Association Concert; Feb. 17–Wrestling: Whipper Billy Watson vs. Masked Marvel; Feb. 18–Jr. Hockey: U. of T. Schools 2, Upper Canada College 6; Feb. 18–Sr. Hockey: Owen Sound 2, Sr. Marlboros 11; Feb. 19–Jr. Hockey: Jr. Marlboros "B" 8, U. of T. Varsity "B" 4; Feb. 19–Jr. Hockey: St. Michael's 3, Jr. Marlboros 5; Feb. 19–NHL: Boston 2, Leafs 5; Feb. 21–Boxing: Al McFater vs. Angelo Rizzo; Feb. 23–Hockey: Juvenile Marlboros 11, Oshawa 3; Feb. 23–Sr. Hockey: Owen Sound 3, Sr. Marlboros 8; Feb. 24–Wrestling: Whipper Billy Watson vs. Masked Marvel; Feb. 26–Hockey: Brampton 2, Weston 1 (Pee-Wee Finals); Feb.

26–Jr. Hockey: Stratford 3, Jr. Marlboros 4; Feb. 26–NHL: Chicago 2, Leafs 2; Mar. 1–Boxing: John Greco vs. Pete Zaduk; Mar. 2–NHL: Canadiens 2, Leafs 0; Mar. 3–Wrestling: Fred Atkins vs. Whipper Billy Watson; Mar. 4–Sr. Hockey: Kitchener-Waterloo 4, Sr. Marlboros 5 (OHA Sr. Finals); Mar. 5–Jr. Hockey: St. Catharines 2, Jr. Marlboros 4; Mar. 5–NHL: Rangers 1, Leafs 7; Mar. 7–Hockey: Juvenile Marlboros 16, Owen Sound 1; Mar. 10–Wrestling: Fred Atkins vs. Whipper Billy Watson; Mar. 11–Sr. Hockey: Kitchener-Waterloo 1, Sr. Marlboros 3 (OHA Sr. Finals); Mar. 12–Jr. Hockey: Barrie 5, Jr. Marlboros 2 (OHA "A" Finals); Mar. 12–NHL: Boston 2, Leafs 1; Mar. 14-18–Ice Show: Skating Carnival; Mar. 19–NHL: Detroit 5, Leafs 2; Mar. 19–Sr. Hockey: Kitchener-Waterloo 1, Sr. Marlboros 3 (OHA Sr. Finals); Mar. 21–Jr. Hockey: Barrie 8, Jr. Marlboros 4 (OHA "A" Finals); Mar. 22–Jr. Hockey: Belleville 1, Upper Canada College 9; Mar. 23–Sr. Hockey: Sr. Marlboros "B" 1, Sr. Marlboros 10 (OHA Sr. Finals); Mar. 24–Wrestling: Fred Atkins vs. Mike Sharpe; Mar. 26–Jr. Hockey: Barrie 4, Porcupine 0 (All-Ontario Sr. Finals); Mar. 26–NHL: Boston 5, Leafs 4; Mar. 28–Jr. Hockey: Upper Canada College 6, Jr. Marlboros "B" 4; Mar. 29–NHL: Boston 1, Leafs 3; Mar. 30–Sr. Hockey: Sr. Marlboros 1, Sydney 1; Mar. 31–Wrestling: Fred Atkins vs. Whipper Billy Watson; Apr. 1–Hockey: St. Catharines 5, Midget Marlboros 6; Apr. 1–Hockey: St. Catharines 6, Juvenile Marlboros 1; Apr. 2–Jr. Hockey: Upper Canada College 3, Jr. Marlboros "B" 2; Apr. 2–Sr. Hockey: Sr. Marlboros 5, Sydney 3; Apr. 3–Variety: Ken Soble's Amateur Show (Ontario Society for Crippled Children); Apr. 4–Sr. Hockey: Sr. Marlboros 5, Sydney 5; Apr. 6–Sr. Hockey: Sr. Marlboros 4, Sydney 2; Apr. 7–Wrestling: Cardiff Giant vs. Ben Morgan; Apr. 8–Sr. Hockey: Sr. Marlboros 5, Sydney 4; Apr. 9–Jr. Hockey: Barrie 1, Montreal 3 (Memorial Cup Eastern Finals); Apr. 9–Jr. Hockey: Kitchener 6, North Toronto 2; Apr. 11–Jr. Hockey: Kitchener 5, Upper Canada College 3 (OHA "B" Finals); Apr. 13–NHL: Detroit 1, Leafs 3 (Stanley Cup Finals); Apr. 14–Wrestling: Fred Atkins vs. Whipper Billy Watson; Apr. 15–Sr. Hockey: Ottawa 0, Sr. Marlboros 5 (Allan Cup Eastern Finals); Apr. 16–Jr. Hockey: Barrie 4, Montreal 5 (Memorial Cup Eastern Finals); Apr. 16–NHL: Detroit 1, Leafs 3 (Stanley Cup-winning game); Apr. 21–Sr. Hockey: Ottawa 0, Sr. Marlboros 7 (Allan Cup Eastern Finals); Apr. 22–Wrestling: Ray Villmer vs. Fred Atkins; Apr. 23–Sr. Hockey: Ottawa 7, Sr. Marlboros 0 (Allan Cup Eastern Finals); Apr. 25–Boxing: Al McFater vs. Norm Thompson; Apr. 28–Hockey: Port Colborne, Gananoque (OHA Intermediate Finals); Apr. 29–Wrestling: Whipper Billy Watson vs. Ray Villmer; May 2–Boxing: Al McFater vs. Ron Lacelle; May 4–Sr. Hockey: Regina 6, Ottawa 3 (Allan Cup Finals); May 5–Wrestling: Whipper Billy Watson vs. Cardiff Giant; May 10-14: Barbara Ann Scott Ice Revue; May 15–Music: Military Bands; May 16–Boxing: Al McFater vs. Ron Lacelle; May 19–Wrestling: Fred Atkins vs. Whipper Billy Watson; May 26–Wrestling: Atkins/Davis vs. Watson/Szabo; May 30–Boxing: Eugene Mainville vs. George Sinclair; June 14-18: Buster Crabbe's Aqua Parade; June 21–Liberal Party Rally w/Louis St-Laurent; June 24-26: Watch Tower Bible and Tract Society; Aug. 8-11: Order of the Easter Star Shriners Convention; Aug. 18-19–Miss Canada Beauty Pageant; Sept. 1–Wrestling: Wladek Kowalski vs. Hi Lee; Sept. 8–Wrestling: Whipper Billy Watson vs. Fred Atkins; Sept. 15–Wrestling: Whipper Billy Watson vs. Fred Atkins; Sept. 19–Boxing: Ed Zastre vs. Jack Herman; Sept. 22–Wrestling: Atkins/Henry vs. Watson/Flanagan; Sept. 26–Boxing: Al McFater vs. Ron McGillivray; Sept. 29–Wrestling: Watson/Flanagan vs. Atkins/Henry; Oct. 3-8: Bob Morton's Rameses Shrine Circus; Oct. 10–NHL: All-Stars 3, Leafs 1; Oct. 12–Variety: The Bob Hope Show; Oct. 13–Wrestling: Lou Thesz vs. Fred Atkins; Oct. 14–Sr. Hockey: Owen Sound 1, Sr. Marlboros 7; Oct. 15–Jr. Hockey: Barrie 3, St. Michael's 8; Oct. 15–Jr. Hockey: Guelph 1, Jr. Marlboros 4; Oct. 15–NHL: Chicago 4, Leafs 4; Oct. 19–Jr. Hockey: Oshawa 4, St. Michael's 2; Oct. 19–Jr. Hockey: Galt 0, Jr. Marlboros 8; Oct. 19–NHL: Canadiens 3, Leafs 1; Oct. 20–Wrestling: Yvon Robert vs. Seelie Samara; Oct. 21–Sr. Hockey: Kitchener-Waterloo 5, Sr. Marlboros 3; Oct. 22–Jr. Hockey: Windsor 3, St. Michael's 4; Oct. 22–Jr. Hockey: St. Catharines 0, Jr. Marlboros 4; Oct. 22–NHL: Rangers 2, Leafs 2; Oct. 24–Boxing: Ed Zastre vs. Jack Herman; Oct. 26–Sr. Hockey: Hamilton 3, Sr. Marlboros 4; Oct. 27–Wrestling: Yvon Robert vs. Wladek Kowalski; Oct. 28–Sr. Hockey: Owen Sound 5, Sr. Marlboros 3; Oct. 29–Jr. Hockey: St. Catharines 6, St. Michael's 1; Oct. 29–Jr. Hockey: Windsor 3, Jr. Marlboros 5; Oct. 29–NHL: Boston 1, Leafs 8; Oct. 31–Boxing: Al McFater vs. Danny Saunders; Nov. 1–Jr. Hockey: Galt 3, St. Michael's 5; Nov. 1–Jr. Hockey: Oshawa 2, Jr. Marlboros 5; Nov. 2–NHL: Rangers 3, Leafs 3; Nov. 3–Wrestling: Yvon Robert vs. Whipper Billy Watson; Nov. 4–Sr. Hockey: Kitchener-Waterloo 3, Sr. Marlboros 9; Nov. 5–Jr. Hockey: Stratford 0, St. Michael's 3; Nov. 5–Jr. Hockey: Barrie 1, Jr. Marlboros 5; Nov. 5–NHL: Detroit 4, Leafs 3; Nov. 7-11: Ice Capades; Nov. 12–Jr. Hockey: Guelph 3, St. Michael's 4; Nov. 12–Jr. Hockey: Stratford 2, Jr. Marlboros 4; Nov. 12–NHL: Chicago 0, Leafs 4; Nov. 14–Boxing: Al McFater vs. Juan Manuel; Nov. 15–Jr. Hockey: St. Michael's 6, Jr. Marlboros 5; Nov. 16–NHL: Canadiens 0, Leafs 1; Nov. 17–Wrestling: Whipper Billy Watson vs. Yvon Robert; Nov. 18–Sr. Hockey: Hamilton 0, Sr. Marlboros 2; Nov. 19–Jr. Hockey: Barrie 3, St. Michael's 5; Nov. 19–Jr. Hockey: Guelph 2, Jr. Marlboros 4; Nov. 19–NHL: Detroit 5, Leafs 2; Nov. 21–Boxing: Elmer Haskill vs. Glen Dafoe; Nov. 23–Sr. Hockey: Kitchener-Waterloo 2, Sr. Marlboros 6; Nov. 24–Wrestling: Whipper Billy Watson vs. Yvon Robert; Nov. 25–Sr. Hockey: Owen Sound 2, Sr. Marlboros 11; Nov. 26–Jr. Hockey: Windsor 6, St. Michael's 2; Nov. 26–Jr. Hockey: Barrie 0, Jr. Marlboros 4; Nov. 26–NHL: Boston 3, Leafs 3; Nov. 28–Sr. Hockey: Hamilton 3, Sr. Marlboros 5; Nov. 29–Jr. Hockey: St. Michael's 0, Jr. Marlboros 3; Nov. 30–Wrestling: Yukon Eric vs. Hi Lee; Dec. 1–NHL: Detroit 2, Leafs 0; Dec. 2–Sr. Hockey: Kitchener-Waterloo 1, Sr. Marlboros 5; Dec. 3–Jr. Hockey: St. Catharines 6, St. Michael's 3; Dec. 3–Jr. Hockey: Galt 1, Jr. Marlboros 5; Dec. 3–NHL: Rangers 0, Leafs 2; Dec. 5–Boxing: Jean Richard vs. Al McFater; Dec. 7–Sr. Hockey: Hamilton 2, Sr. Marlboros 5; Dec. 8–Wrestling: Fred Atkins vs. Yukon Eric; Dec. 9–Sr. Hockey: Owen Sound 1, Sr. Marlboros 9; Dec. 10–Jr. Hockey: St. Catharines 5, Jr. Marlboros 1; Dec. 10–Jr. Hockey: Guelph 8, St. Michael's 1; Dec. 10–NHL: Boston 1, Leafs 2; Dec. 12–Boxing: Billy Fifield vs. Joey Pyle; Dec. 13–Jr. Hockey: Galt 3, St. Michael's 6; Dec. 13–Jr. Hockey: Oshawa 1, Jr. Marlboros 10; Dec. 14–NHL: Canadiens 2, Leafs 2; Dec. 15–Wrestling: Yukon Eric vs. Fred Atkins; Dec. 16–Sr. Hockey: Owen Sound 1, Sr. Marlboros 7; Dec. 17–Jr. Hockey: Stratford 2, St. Michael's 2; Dec. 17–Jr. Hockey: Windsor 4, Jr. Marlboros 4; Dec. 17–NHL: Chicago 7, Leafs 1; Dec. 21–Sr. Hockey: Hamilton 1, Sr. Marlboros 4; Dec. 23–Sr. Hockey: Kitchener-Waterloo 2, Sr. Marlboros 5; Dec. 24–NHL: Boston 8, Leafs 4; Dec. 28–NHL: Canadiens 1, Leafs 1; Dec. 29–Wrestling: Yukon Eric vs. Mike Sharpe; Dec. 30–Sr. Hockey: Owen Sound 0, Sr. Marlboros 6; Dec. 31–NHL: Detroit 5, Leafs 1.

1950 • Jan. 3–Jr. Hockey: Oshawa 6, St. Michael's 8; Jan. 4–NHL: Chicago 4, Leafs 4; Jan. 5–Wrestling: Nanjo Singh vs. Wladek Kowalski; Jan. 6–Sr. Hockey: Kitchener-Waterloo 3, Sr. Marlboros 8; Jan. 7–Jr. Hockey: St. Michael's 4, Jr. Marlboros 11; Jan. 7–NHL: Chicago 2, Leafs 5; Jan. 11–Sr. Hockey: Hamilton 0, Sr. Marlboros 5; Jan. 12–Wrestling: Whipper Billy Watson vs. Nanjo Singh; Jan. 13–Sr. Hockey: Owen Sound 2, Sr. Marlboros 6; Jan. 14–Jr. Hockey: Barrie 2, St. Michael's 4; Jan. 14–Jr. Hockey: Guelph 4, Jr. Marlboros 3; Jan. 14–NHL: Boston 3, Leafs 4; Jan. 16–Boxing: Billy Fifield vs. Joey Pyle; Jan. 17–Jr. Hockey: St. Michael's 2, Jr. Marlboros 6; Jan. 18–NHL: Canadiens 1, Leafs 0; Jan. 19–Wrestling: Lou Thesz vs. Whipper Billy Watson; Jan. 20–Hockey: UCC New Boys 2, UCC Old Boys 6; Jan. 21–Jr. Hockey: Stratford 1, St. Michael's 3; Jan. 21–Jr. Hockey: St. Catharines 0, Jr. Marlboros 5; Jan. 21–NHL: Rangers 1, Leafs 2; Jan. 23–Boxing: Al McFater vs. Spider Thompson; Jan. 24–Jr. Hockey: St. Michael's 1, Jr. Marlboros 5; Jan. 25–NHL: Rangers 1, Leafs 5; Jan. 26–Wrestling: Whipper Billy Watson vs. Nanjo Singh; Jan. 27–Sr. Hockey: Kitchener-Waterloo 5, Sr. Marlboros 7; Jan. 28–Jr. Hockey: Stratford 4, Jr. Marlboros 8; Jan. 28–Jr. Hockey: Oshawa 3, St. Michael's 6; Jan. 28–NHL: Chicago 1, Leafs 9; Jan. 30–Feb. 3: Ice Follies of 1950; Feb. 4–Jr. Hockey: St. Catharines 2, St. Michael's 3; Feb. 4–Jr. Hockey: Windsor 3, Jr. Marlboros 4; Feb. 4–NHL: Detroit 3, Leafs 3; Feb. 6–Boxing: Al McFater vs. Jean Richard; Feb. 9–Wrestling: Yukon Eric vs. Bob Wagner; Feb. 10–Sr. Hockey: Hamilton 1, Sr. Marlboros 6; Feb. 11–Jr. Hockey: St. Michael's 3, Jr. Marlboros 5; Feb. 11–NHL: Canadiens 0, Leafs 2; Feb. 13–Boxing: Fitzgerald vs. Muir; Males vs. Yonchus; Feb. 14–Jr. Hockey: Oshawa 0, Jr. Marlboros 8; Feb. 14–Jr. Hockey: Galt 2, St. Michael's 1; Feb. 15–Sr. Hockey: Hamilton 1, Sr. Marlboros 7; Feb. 16–Wrestling: Whipper Billy Watson vs. Nanjo Singh; Feb. 17–Sr. Hockey: Kitchener-Waterloo 5, Sr. Marlboros 4; Feb. 18–Jr. Hockey: Barrie 4, Jr. Marlboros 8; Feb. 18–Jr. Hockey: Guelph 2, St. Michael's 5; Feb. 18–NHL: Detroit 2, Leafs 3; Feb. 20–Jr. Hockey: Windsor 5, St. Michael's 5; Feb. 20–Jr. Hockey: Windsor 5, St. Michael's 2; Feb. 21–Toronto Police Association Concert; Feb. 22–NHL: Boston 1, Leafs 3; Feb. 23–Wrestling: Yukon Eric vs. Nanjo Singh; Feb. 24–Sr. Hockey: Hamilton 3, Sr. Marlboros; Feb. 25–Jr. Hockey: Windsor 3, Jr. Marlboros 5; Feb. 25–NHL: Rangers 2, Leafs 4; Feb. 27–Jr. Hockey: Barrie 3, St. Michael's 9; Mar. 1–Jr. Hockey: Barrie 3, St. Michael's 4; Mar. 2–Wrestling: Yukon Eric vs. Nanjo Singh/Bob Wagner; Mar. 3–Sr. Hockey: Kitchener-Waterloo 3, Sr. Marlboros 2 (OHA Sr. Finals); Mar. 4–Jr. Hockey: Windsor 6, Jr. Marlboros 1; Mar. 4–NHL: Detroit 2, Leafs 3; Mar. 7–Boxing: Al McFater vs. Lou Alter; Mar. 8–Sr. Hockey: Kitchener-Waterloo 5, Sr. Marlboros 6 (OHA Sr. Finals); Mar. 9–Wrestling: Whipper Billy Watson vs. Yukon Eric; Mar. 10–Sr. Hockey: Kitchener-Waterloo 0, Sr. Marlboros 4 (OHA Sr. Finals); Mar. 11–NHL: Rangers 0, Leafs 4; Mar. 13-17: Toronto Skating Carnival; Mar. 18–NHL: Chicago 1, Leafs 2; Mar. 18–Sr. Hockey: Kitchener-Waterloo 1, Sr. Marlboros 2 (OHA Sr. Finals); Mar. 20–Boxing: Al McFater vs. Buddy Hayes; Mar. 21–Jr. Hockey: U. of T. Schools 6, Upper Canada College 4; Mar. 22–NHL: Canadiens 2, Leafs 1; Mar. 23–Wrestling: Yukon Eric vs. Whipper Billy Watson; Mar. 25–NHL: Boston 0, Leafs 8; Mar. 25–Sr. Hockey: Sault Ste. Marie 4, Sr. Marlboros 10 (All-Ontario Sr. Finals); Mar. 27–Sr. Hockey: Sault Ste. Marie 0, Sr. Marlboros 11 (All-Ontario Sr. Finals); Mar. 27–Variety: Order of the Eastern Star Fun Parade; Mar. 28–Boxing: Arthur King vs. Humberton Sierra; Mar. 29–Hockey: Juvenile Marlboros 1, St. Catharines 3 (Juvenile Finals); Mar. 30–Wrestling: Lou Thesz vs. Sulie Samarra; Apr. 1–Jr. Hockey: Porcupine 5, Guelph 7 (All-Ontario Jr. Finals); Apr. 1–NHL: Detroit 0, Leafs 2; Apr. 2–Variety: Radio Show of Stars (Ontario Society for Crippled Children); Apr. 3–Sr. Hockey: Cornwall 2, Sr. Marlboros 12; Apr. 4–NHL: Detroit 2, Leafs 1; Apr. 5–Jr. Hockey: Porcupine 3, Guelph 2 (All-Ontario Jr. Finals); Apr. 6–Wrestling: Yukon Eric vs. Whipper Billy Watson; Apr. 7–Sr. Hockey: Cornwall 1, Sr. Marlboros 13; Apr. 8–Jr. Hockey: Porcupine 1, Guelph 3 (All-Ontario Jr. Finals); Apr. 8–NHL: Detroit 4, Leafs 0; Apr. 13–NHL: Detroit 1, Rangers 3 (Stanley Cup game transfered due to circus in Madison Square Garden); Apr. 14–Sr. Hockey: Sherbrooke 1, Sr. Marlboros 3 (Allan Cup Eastern Finals); Apr. 15–Jr. Hockey: Montreal 2, Guelph 7 (Memorial Cup Eastern Finals); Apr. 15–NHL: Detroit 4, Rangers 0 ((Stanley Cup game transfered due to circus in Madison Square Garden); Apr. 17–Sr. Hockey: Sherbrooke 3, Sr. Marlboros 11 (Allan Cup Eastern Finals); Apr. 18–Jr. Hockey: Montreal 4, Guelph 2 (Memorial Cup Eastern Finals); Apr. 20–Wrestling: Yukon Eric vs. Sulie Samarra; Apr. 22–Jr. Hockey: Montreal 5, Guelph 3 (Memorial Cup Eastern Finals); Apr. 24–Boxing: Armand Savoie vs. Al McFater; Apr. 25–Sr. Hockey: Sherbrooke 1, Sr. Marlboros 3 (Allan Cup Eastern Finals); Apr. 27–Wrestling: Yvon Robert vs. Albert Mills; May 2–Jr. Hockey: Regina 1, Montreal 5 (Memorial Cup Finals); May 4–Wrestling: Bill Longson vs. Yukon Eric; May 7–Canadian Slav Committee Concert; May 8–Boxing: Armand Savoie vs. Spider Thompson; May 11–Wrestling: Yukon Eric vs. Bill Longson; May 15–Music: Spike Jones; May 16–Boxing: Arthur King vs. Massimo Sanna; May 18–Wrestling: Yukon Eric vs. Yvon Robert; May 23–Shriners Covention; May 25–Wrestling: Whipper Billy Watson vs. Hi Lee; May 26–Manitoba Flood Relief Fund Rally; May 31–Variety: Jack Benny Show radio broadcast; June 1–Wrestling: Yvon Robert vs. Whipper Billy Watson; June 11–United Church Service; Aug. 14–Canadian Council of Churches Youth Rally; Sept. 18–Boxing: Arthur King vs. Gus Mell; Sept. 19–Wrestling: Geohagen/Watson vs. Henning/Atkins; Sept. 26–Boxing: Davey Mitchell vs. Mickey McKee; Sept. 28–Wrestling: Whipper Billy Watson vs. Fred Atkins; Oct. 1-7: Bob Morton's Rameses Shrine Circus; Oct. 8–Lacrosse: Owen Sound 8, New Westminster 7 (Mann Cup Finals); Oct. 9–NHL: Blues 5, Whites 2 (Maple Leafs intrasquad game); Oct. 11–Lacrosse: Owen Sound 13, New Westminster 6 (Mann Cup Finals); Oct. 12–Wrestling: Whipper Billy Watson vs. Yvon Robert; Oct. 13–Lacrosse: Owen Sound 9, New Westminster 13 (Mann Cup Finals); Oct. 14–Jr. Hockey: Stratford 1, Jr. Marlboros 4; Oct. 14–Jr. Hockey: St. Catharines 1, St. Michael's 1; Oct. 14–NHL: Chicago 2, Leafs 1; Oct. 15–Lacrosse: Owen Sound 5, New Westminster 7 (Mann Cup Finals); Oct. 17–Boxing: Arthur King vs. Bobby Lloyd; Oct. 18–Lacrosse: Owen Sound 8, New Westminster 5 (Mann Cup Finals); Oct. 19–Wrestling: Whipper Billy Watson vs. Yvon Robert; Oct. 20–Lacrosse: Owen Sound 5, New Westminster 6 (Mann Cup Finals); Oct. 21–NHL: Rangers 0, Leafs 5; Oct. 22–Lacrosse: Owen Sound 5, New Westminster 6 (Mann Cup Finals); Oct. 25–NHL: Detroit 0, Leafs 1; Oct. 26–Wrestling: Lou Thesz vs. Timothy Geohagen; Oct. 28–NHL: Boston 2, Leafs 4; Oct. 28–Sr. Hockey: St. Catharines 1, St. Michael's Sr. 5; Oct. 29–Jr. Hockey: St. Catharines 5, Jr. Marlboros 6; Oct. 29–Jr. Hockey: Galt 2, St. Michael's 2; Oct. 30–Boxing: Al McFater vs. Young Junior; Nov. 1–NHL: Canadiens 3, Leafs 5; Nov. 3–Sr. Hockey: Kitchener-Waterloo 2, Sr. Marlboros 4; Nov. 4–NHL: Rangers 2, Leafs 2; Nov. 4–Sr. Hockey: Hamilton 4, St. Michael's Sr. 11; Nov. 5–Jr. Hockey: Windsor 6, St. Michael's 3; Nov. 5–Jr. Hockey: Guelph 2, Jr. Marlboros 4; Nov. 7–Music: Horace Heidt and his Orchestra; Nov. 8–Boxing: Al McFater vs. Tommy Greb; Nov. 9–Wrestling: Yukon Eric vs. Timothy Geohagen; Nov. 10–Sr. Hockey: Hamilton 7, Sr. Marlboros 4; Nov. 11–NHL: Detroit 3, Leafs 1; Nov. 11–Sr. Hockey: Kitchener-Waterloo 3, St. Michael's Sr. 2; Nov. 12–Jr. Hockey: Jr. Marlboros 6, St. Michael's 3; Nov. 13-17: Ice Capades; Nov. 18–NHL: Rangers 4, Leafs 5; Nov. 18–Sr. Hockey: St. Michael's Sr. 6, Sr. Marlboros 5; Nov. 19–Jr. Hockey: Stratford 7, St. Michael's 6; Nov. 19–Jr. Hockey: Oshawa 2, Jr. Marlboros 5; Nov. 21–Jr. Hockey: Barrie 1, Jr. Marlboros 3; Nov. 21–Jr. Hockey: Waterloo 1, St. Michael's 5; Nov. 22–NHL: Chicago 2, Leafs 5; Nov. 24–Sr. Hockey: Kitchener-Waterloo, Sr. Marlboros 2; Nov. 25–NHL: Canadiens 1, Leafs 4; Nov. 26–Jr. Hockey: Windsor 1, Jr. Marlboros 1; Nov. 26–Jr. Hockey: Oshawa 8, St. Michael's 5; Nov. 28–Boxing: Al McFater vs. Tommy McMenamy; Nov. 30–Wrestling: Whipper Billy Watson vs. Yukon Eric; Dec. 1–Sr. Hockey:

Kitchener-Waterloo 4, Sr. Marlboros 5; Dec. 2–NHL: Chicago 0, Leafs 0; Dec. 2–Sr. Hockey: Hamilton 5, St. Michael's Sr. 2; Dec. 3–Jr. Hockey: Jr. Marlboros 6, St. Michael's 3; Dec. 5–Jr. Hockey: Guelph 1, St. Michael's 4; Dec. 5–Jr. Hockey: Waterloo 2, Jr. Marlboros 6; Dec. 6–NHL: Canadiens 1, Leafs 3; Dec. 7–Wrestling: Whipper Billy Watson vs. Yukon Eric; Dec. 8–Sr. Hockey: Hamilton 1, Sr. Marlboros 6; Dec. 9–NHL: Boston 1, Leafs 8; Dec. 9–Sr. Hockey: Kitchener-Waterloo 1, St. Michael's Sr. 9; Dec. 10–Jr. Hockey: Brantford 2, Jr. Marlboros 2; Dec. 10–Jr. Hockey: St. Catharines 4, St. Michael's 2; Dec. 11–Boxing: Arthur King vs. Bobby Lloyd; Dec. 12–Jr. Hockey: Barrie 0, St. Michael's 6; Dec. 12–Jr. Hockey: Oshawa 3, Jr. Marlboros 6; Dec. 13–NHL: Detroit 4, Leafs 3; Dec. 14–Wrestling: Lord Athol Layton vs. Lee Henning; Dec. 15–Sr. Hockey: Kitchener-Waterloo 4, Sr. Marlboros 5; Dec. 16–NHL: Chicago 3, Leafs 2; Dec. 16–Sr. Hockey: Hamilton 1, St. Michael's Sr. 2; Dec. 17–Jr. Hockey: Guelph 6, St. Michael's 6; Dec. 17–Jr. Hockey: Waterloo 0, Jr. Marlboros 8; Dec. 20–NHL: Canadiens 1, Leafs 6; Dec. 22–Sr. Hockey: St. Michael's Sr. 4, Sr. Marlboros 4; Dec. 23–Hockey: Stockyards 6, Downsview 4; Dec. 23–Hockey: Rhodes 2, St. Michael's Meteors 3; Dec. 23–Jr. Hockey: Weston 6, St. Michael's "B" 2; Dec. 23–NHL: Boston 2, Leafs 2; Dec. 28–Wrestling: Whipper Billy Watson vs. The Masked Marvel; Dec. 29–Sr. Hockey: Hamilton 3, Sr. Marlboros 6; Dec. 30–NHL: Detroit 3, Leafs 1; Dec. 30–Sr. Hockey: Kitchener-Waterloo 2, St. Michael's Sr. 6; Dec. 31–Jr. Hockey: St. Catharines 1, Jr. Marlboros 2; Dec. 31–Jr. Hockey: Windsor 3, St. Michael's 1.

1951 • Jan. 3–Boxing: Al McFater vs. Archie Goodbee; Jan. 4–Wrestling: Masked Marvel/Atkins vs. Watson/Flanagan; Jan. 5–Sr. Hockey: Kitchener-Waterloo 5, Sr. Marlboros 4; Jan. 6–NHL: Rangers 4, Leafs 2; Jan. 6–Sr. Hockey: Hamilton 4, St. Michael's Sr. 9; Jan. 7–Jr. Hockey: Jr. Marlboros 4, St. Michael's 1; Jan. 9–Jr. Hockey: Galt 1, St. Michael's 5; Jan. 9–Jr. Hockey: Barrie 3, Jr. Marlboros 3; Jan. 11–Wrestling: Masked Marvel/Atkins vs. Watson/Flanagan; Jan. 12–Sr. Hockey: Kitchener-Waterloo 4, Sr. Marlboros 2; Jan. 13–Jr. Hockey: Unionville, St. Michael's "B"; Jan. 13–NHL: Chicago 3, Leafs 3; Jan. 13–Sr. Hockey: Hamilton 2, St. Michael's Sr. 6; Jan. 14–Jr. Hockey: Guelph 3, Jr. Marlboros 3; Jan. 14–Jr. Hockey: Stratford 4, St. Michael's 4; Jan. 16–Jr. Hockey: Waterloo 5, St. Michael's 2; Jan. 16–Jr. Hockey: Galt 2, Jr. Marlboros 5; Jan. 18–Wrestling: Lord Athol Layton vs. Wee Willie Davis; Jan. 20–Hockey: Rhodes 5, Downsview 0; Jan. 20–Hockey: Stockyards 3, St. Mikes Meteors 2; Jan. 20–Jr. Hockey: Aurora 4, St. Michael's "B" 3; Jan. 20–NHL: Boston 1, Leafs 2; Jan. 21–Jr. Hockey: St. Michael's 6, Jr. Marlboros 4; Jan. 21–Sr. Hockey: St. Michael's 6, Sr. Marlboros 1; Jan. 23–Jr. Hockey: Windsor 2, Jr. Marlboros 4; Jan. 23–Jr. Hockey: Oshawa 3, St. Michael's 4; Jan. 24–NHL: Canadiens 3, Leafs 4; Jan. 25–Wrestling: Watson/Flanagan vs. Masked Marvel/The Manager; Jan. 26–Sr. Hockey: Kitchener-Waterloo 3, Sr. Marlboros 4; Jan. 27–Jr. Hockey: Sr. Marlboros 2, Sr. Marlboros "B" 4; Jan. 27–Jr. Hockey: Hamilton 3, St. Michael's 5; Jan. 27–NHL: Rangers 1, Leafs 2; Jan. 28–Jr. Hockey: Stratford 4, Jr. Marlboros 4; Jan. 28–Jr. Hockey: St. Catharines 5, St. Michael's 2; Jan. 29–Feb. 2: Ice Follies of 1951; Feb. 3–NHL: Chicago 3, Leafs 6; Feb. 4–Jr. Hockey: Jr. Marlboros 2, St. Michael's 2; Feb. 4–Sr. Hockey: Sr. Marlboros 3, St. Michael's Sr. 2; Feb. 5–Amateur Boxing Night; Feb. 6–Jr. Hockey: Barrie 4, St. Michael's 3; Feb. 6–Jr. Hockey: Waterloo 2, Jr. Marlboros 4; Feb. 7–NHL: Canadiens 1, Leafs 3; Feb. 8–Wrestling: Lord Athol Layton vs. Fred Atkins; Feb. 9–Sr. Hockey: Hamilton 2, Sr. Marlboros 4; Feb. 10–Jr. Hockey: Brampton 1, Jr. Marlboros "B" 8; Feb. 10–NHL: Detroit 2, Leafs 1; Feb. 10–Sr. Hockey: Kitchener-Waterloo 3, St. Michael's Sr. 5; Feb. 11–Jr. Hockey: St. Catharines 2, Jr. Marlboros 6; Feb. 11–Jr. Hockey: Guelph 3, St. Michael's 6; Feb. 12–Newsboys International Amateur Boxing Tournament; Feb. 13–Jr. Hockey: Galt 2, Jr. Marlboros 1; Feb. 13–Jr. Hockey: Oshawa 2, St. Michael's 4; Feb. 15–Wrestling: The Masked Marvel vs. Whipper Billy Watson; Feb. 16–Sr. Hockey: Kitchener-Waterloo 3, Sr. Marlboros 8; Feb. 17–NHL: Rangers 0, Leafs 2; Feb. 17–Sr. Hockey: Hamilton 7, St. Michael's Sr. 4; Feb. 18–Jr. Hockey: Windsor 2, St. Michael's 2; Feb. 18–Jr. Hockey: Guelph 2, Jr. Marlboros 2; Feb. 19–Boxing: Kid Flu vs. Alan McFater; Feb. 21–NHL: Detroit 2, Leafs 2; Feb. 22–Wrestling: Whipper Billy Watson vs. The Masked Marvel; Feb. 23–Sr. Hockey: Hamilton 5, Sr. Marlboros 4; Feb. 24–Hockey: St. Catharines Juveniles vs. Marlboro Juveniles; Feb. 24–NHL: Boston 2, Leafs 6; Feb. 24–Sr. Hockey: Kitchener-Waterloo 4, St. Michael's Sr. 5; Feb. 25–Jr. Hockey: Waterloo 2, Jr. Marlboros 6; Feb. 25–Jr. Hockey: Oshawa 4, St. Michael's 3; Feb. 27–Boxing: Armand Savoie vs. Solly Cantor; Feb. 28–Jr. Hockey: St. Michael's 2, Jr. Marlboros 1; Mar. 1–Wrestling: Whipper Billy Watson vs. The Masked Marvel; Mar. 3–NHL: Chicago 0, Leafs 3; Mar. 4–Jr. Hockey: Windsor 0, Jr. Marlboros 5; Mar. 4–Sr. Hockey: St. Michael's Sr. 5, Sr. Marlboros 3; Mar. 6–Jr. Hockey: Galt 0, St. Michael's 6; Mar. 6–Jr. Hockey: Barrie 7, Jr. Marlboros 0; Mar. 7–NHL: Detroit 3, Leafs 0; Mar. 8–Variety: Radio Show of Stars (Ontario Society for Crippled Children); Mar. 8–Wrestling: Yukon Eric vs. Lord Athol Layton; Mar. 9–Sr. Hockey: Hamilton 1, St. Michael's Sr. 3; Mar. 10–Jr. Hockey: Stratford 3, St. Michael's 1; Mar. 10–NHL: Boston 3, Leafs 5; Mar. 10–Sr. Hockey: St. Michael's Sr. 3, Sr. Marlboros 2; Mar. 17–Jr. Hockey: Stratford 4, Jr. Marlboros 6; Mar. 17–NHL: Rangers 1, Leafs 3; Mar. 17–Sr. Hockey: Hamilton 2, St. Michael's Sr. 6 (OHA Sr. Finals); Mar. 20–Jr. Hockey: Stratford 3, Jr. Marlboros 7; Mar. 21–NHL: Canadiens 0, Leafs 2; Mar. 22–Wrestling: Yukon Eric vs. Lord Athol Layton; Mar. 23–Sr. Hockey: Hamilton 3, St. Michael's Sr. 4; Mar. 24–NHL: Boston 1, Leafs 4; Mar. 25–Jr. Hockey: St. Catharines 3, Jr. Marlboros 5; Mar. 26–Boxing: Al McFater vs. Mike Kelly; Mar. 27–Jr. Hockey: St. Catharines 0, Jr. Marlboros 2; Mar. 28–NHL: Boston 2, Leafs 0; Mar. 29–Wrestling: Whipper Billy Watson vs. Chief War Cloud; Mar. 30–Sr. Hockey: Hamilton 0, St. Michael's Sr. 2 (OHA Sr. Finals); Mar. 31–NHL: Boston 1, Leafs 1; Apr. 4–Jr. Hockey: Barrie 4, Jr. Marlboros 7 (OHA "A" Finals); Apr. 5–Wrestling: Whipper Billy Watson vs. Chief War Cloud; Apr. 6–Jr. Hockey: Barrie 2, Jr. Marlboros 5 (OHA "A" Finals); Apr. 7–NHL: Boston 1, Leafs 4; Apr. 9–Boxing: Armand Savoie vs. Al McFater; Apr. 10–Jr. Hockey: Barrie 4, Jr. Marlboros 2 (OHA "A" Finals); Apr. 11–NHL: Canadiens 2, Leafs 3 (Stanley Cup Finals); Apr. 12–Wrestling: The Masked Marvel vs. Timothy Geohagen; Apr. 14–Jr. Hockey: Quebec 2, Barrie 6 (Memorial Cup Eastern Finals); Apr. 14–NHL: Canadiens 3, Leafs 2 (Stanley Cup-winning game); Apr. 18–Sr. Hockey: Saskatoon 2, St. Michael's Sr. 4 (Alexander Cup Semi-Finals); Apr. 19–Wrestling: War Cloud/Watson vs. Masked Marvel/ The Manager; Apr. 20–Sr. Hockey: Saskatoon 3, St. Michael's Sr. 9 (Alexander Cup Semi-Finals); Apr. 21–NHL: Canadiens 2, Leafs 3 (Stanley Cup Finals); Apr. 23–Boxing: Solly Cantor vs. "Sunny" Dave Shade; Apr. 29–Jr. Hockey: Quebec 3, Barrie 8 (Memorial Cup Eastern Finals); Apr. 30–Hockey: CYO Archdiocese Tournament; May 2–Sr. Hockey: Valleyfield 1, St. Michael's Sr. 4 (Alexander Cup Finals); May 3–Wrestling: War Cloud/Watson vs. Masked Marvel/The Manager; May 5–Sr. Hockey: Valleyfield 4, St. Michael's Sr. 4 (Alexander Cup Finals); May 8–Sr. Hockey: Valleyfield 1, St. Michael's Sr. 6 (Alexander Cup Finals); May 10–Wrestling: War Cloud/Watson vs. Masked Marvel/The Manager; May 12–Sr. Hockey: Valleyfield 4, St. Michael's Sr. 1 (Alexander Cup Finals); May 17–Wrestling: Six Man Tag-Team Battle Royale; May 20–Watch Tower Bible and Tract Society; May 21–Boxing: Golden Gloves Tournament; May 25–Wrestling: Six Man Tag-Team Battle Royale; June 1–Wrestling: Great Togo vs. Chief Sun Cloud; June 5–Boxing: Arthur King vs. Armand Savoie; June 30–Variety: Ukrainian Canadian Jubilee Festival; Sept. 6–Wrestling: The Masked Marvel vs. The Zebra; Sept. 10–Boxing: Al McFater vs. Solly Cantor; Sept. 13–Wrestling: The Zebra vs. Tinothy Geohagen; Sept. 20–Wrestling: The Zebra vs. Yukon Eric; Sept. 25–Boxing: Al McFater vs. Freddie Dukes; Sept. 27–Wrestling: Lord Athol Layton vs. Mike Sharpe; Oct. 1-6: Bob Morton's Rameses Shrine Circus; Oct. 9–NHL: 1st All-Star Team 2, 2nd All-Star Team 2; Oct. 10–Music: Duke Ellington/Nat King Cole; Oct. 11–Wrestling: Whipper Billy Watson vs. Wild Bill Longson; Oct. 13–Weston, St. Michael's "B" and Chicago vs. Toronto (exhibitions for Princess Elizabeth and Prince Philip); Oct. 13–NHL: Chicago 3, Leafs 1; Oct. 14–Jr. Hockey: Oshawa 1, Jr. Marlboros 2; Oct. 14–Jr. Hockey: Galt 4, St. Michael's 4; Oct. 15–Boxing: Solly Cantor vs. Al McFater; Oct. 17–NHL: Boston 2, Leafs 4; Oct. 18–Wrestling: The Zebra vs. L'ange Francais; Oct. 20–NHL: Rangers 3, Leafs 2; Oct. 21–Jr. Hockey: St. Catharines 0, Jr. Marlboros 0; Oct. 21–Jr. Hockey: Waterloo 1, St. Michael's 5; Oct. 22–Amateur Boxing Night; Oct. 23–Basketball: Harlem Globetrotters 71, Toledo Mercurys 41; Oct. 24–Jr. Hockey: Barrie 2, Jr. Marlboros 3; Oct. 25–Wrestling: Whipper Billy Watson vs. Lord Athol Layton; Oct. 27–NHL: Detroit 2, Leafs 1; Oct. 28–Jr. Hockey: Windsor 3, St. Michael's 4; Oct. 28–Jr. Hockey: Kitchener 2, Jr. Marlboros 4; Oct. 29–Music: Roy Ward Dickson Show; Oct. 30–Boxing: Al McFater vs. Ron Harper; Oct. 31–NHL: Canadiens 0, Leafs 1; Nov. 1–Wrestling: Whipper Billy Watson vs. Lord Athol Layton; Nov. 3–NHL: Rangers 2, Leafs 1; Nov. 4–Jr. Hockey: Galt 4, Jr. Marlboros 9; Nov. 4–Jr. Hockey: Guelph 3, St. Michael's 3; Nov. 6–Boxing: Armand Savoie vs. Solly Cantor; Nov. 7–NHL: Chicago 0, Leafs 1; Nov. 8–Wrestling: Whipper Billy Watson vs. Lord Athol Layton; Nov. 10–Jr. Hockey: Kitchener 0, St. Michael's 8; Nov. 10–Jr. Hockey: Waterloo 2, Jr. Marlboros 10; Nov. 10–NHL: Detroit 3, Leafs 3; Nov. 12-16: Ice Capades; Nov. 17–Jr. Hockey: Windsor 0, Jr. Marlboros 11; Nov. 17–Jr. Hockey: Oshawa 1, St. Michael's 3; Nov. 17–NHL: Boston 1, Leafs 1; Nov. 19–Boxing: Al McFater vs. Orlando Zulueta; Nov. 21–NHL: Chicago 1, Leafs 5; Nov. 22–Wrestling: Whipper Billy Watson vs. The Zebra; Nov. 23–Jr. Hockey: Jr. Marlboros 3, St. Michael's 1; Nov. 24–NHL: Canadiens 2, Leafs 4; Nov. 25–Jr. Hockey: St. Catharines 3, St. Michael's 7; Nov. 25–Jr. Hockey: Guelph 8, Jr. Marlboros 4; Nov. 28–Jr. Hockey: Barrie 3, St. Michael's 6; Nov. 29–Wrestling: Whipper Billy Watson vs. The Zebra; Dec. 1–NHL: Rangers 2, Leafs 8; Dec. 2–Jr. Hockey: Jr. Marlboros 2, St. Michael's 5; Dec. 3–Boxing: Jack Dempsey Heavyweight Tournament; Dec. 5–NHL: Detroit 2, Leafs 2; Dec. 6–Wrestling: Whipper Billy Watson vs. Lou Thesz; Dec. 8–NHL: Chicago 1, Leafs 3; Dec. 9–Jr. Hockey: Galt 2, St. Michael's 3; Dec. 9–Jr. Hockey: Oshawa 1, Jr. Marlboros 5; Dec. 11–Boxing: Al McFater vs. Snuffy Smith; Dec. 12–Jr. Hockey: Barrie 3, Jr. Marlboros 2; Dec. 12–Jr. Hockey: Waterloo 1, St. Michael's 8; Dec. 13–Wrestling: Layton/Bolias vs. Watson/Geohagen; Dec. 15–NHL: Rangers 1, Leafs 4; Dec. 16–Jr. Hockey: Windsor 3, St. Michael's 7; Dec. 16–Jr. Hockey: St. Catharines 1, Jr. Marlboros 7; Dec. 19–Jr. Hockey: Galt 1, Jr. Marlboros 3; Dec. 19–Jr. Hockey: Guelph 5, St. Michael's 4; Dec. 20–Wrestling: The Great Togo vs. Pat Flanagan; Dec. 22–NHL: Boston 2, Leafs 3; Dec. 23–Jr. Hockey: St. Michael's 6, Jr. Marlboros 3; Dec. 26–NHL: Canadiens 3, Leafs 2; Dec. 27–Wrestling: Layton/Zebra vs. Watson/Geohagen; Dec. 29–NHL: Boston 0, Leafs 4; Dec. 30–Jr. Hockey: Kitchener 2, St. Michael's 6; Dec. 30–Jr. Hockey: Guelph 2, Jr. Marlboros 6.

1952 • Jan. 2–Jr. Hockey: Waterloo 2, Jr. Marlboros 9; Jan. 2–Jr. Hockey: St. Catharines 4, St. Michael's 2; Jan. 3–Wrestling: Yukon/Watson vs. Layton/Zebra; Jan. 5–NHL: Chicago 1, Leafs 2; Jan. 6–Jr. Hockey: Windsor 2, Jr. Marlboros 11; Jan. 6–Jr. Hockey: Oshawa 2, St. Michael's 6; Jan. 8–Boxing: Brian Kelly vs. Dave Shade; Jan. 9–Jr. Hockey: Barrie 2, St. Michael's 3; Jan. 9–Jr. Hockey: Kitchener 2, Jr. Marlboros 5; Jan. 10–Wrestling: Yukon Eric/Watson vs. Layton/Zebra; Jan. 12–NHL: Detroit 3, Leafs 5; Jan. 13–Jr. Hockey: Jr. Marlboros 3, St. Michael's 0; Jan. 14–Amateur Boxing Night; Jan. 16–Jr. Hockey: Barrie 0, Jr. Marlboros 7; Jan. 17–Wrestling: Lou Thesz vs. Hans Hermann; Jan. 18–Hockey: UCC Old Boys 1, UCC New Boys 0; Jan. 19–NHL: Boston 2, Leafs 6; Jan. 20–Jr. Hockey: Oshawa 1, Jr. Marlboros 7; Jan. 20–Jr. Hockey: Galt 5, St. Michael's 3; Jan. 22–Boxing: Arthur King vs. Fitzie Pruden; Jan. 23–NHL: Canadiens 4, Leafs 2; Jan. 24–Wrestling: Hans Hermann vs. Yukon Eric; Jan. 26–NHL: Rangers 3, Leafs 3; Jan. 27–Jr. Hockey: Windsor 3, St. Michael's 8; Jan. 27–Jr. Hockey: St. Catharines 5, Jr. Marlboros 3; Jan. 28–Feb. 2: Ice Follies; Feb. 2–Jr. Hockey: St. Michael's 1, Jr. Marlboros 5; Feb. 2–NHL: Boston 1, Leafs 1; Feb. 5–Boxing: Jimmy Carter vs. Al McFater; Feb. 6–NHL: Rangers, Leafs (Postponed to February 19 due to death of King George VI); Feb. 7–Wrestling: Hans Hermann vs. Whipper Billy Watson; Feb. 9–NHL: Canadiens 2, Leafs 3; Feb. 10–Jr. Hockey: Galt 4, Jr. Marlboros 9; Feb. 10–Jr. Hockey: Waterloo 3, St. Michael's 4; Feb. 11–Newsboys Boxing Show; Feb. 13–NHL: Detroit 3, Leafs 1; Feb. 14–Wrestling: Lord Athol Layton vs. Hans Hermann; Feb. 15–Memorial Service for King George VI; Feb. 16–NHL: Chicago 2, Leafs 2; Feb. 17–Jr. Hockey: Kitchener 4, St. Michael's 5; Feb. 17–Jr. Hockey: Waterloo 2, Jr. Marlboros 3; Feb. 19–NHL: Rangers 3, Leafs 3; Feb. 20–Jr. Hockey: St. Catharines 3, St. Michael's 8; Feb. 21–Wrestling: Lord Athol Layton vs. Hans Hermann; Feb. 23–NHL: Detroit 3, Leafs 1; Feb. 24–Jr. Hockey: Guelph 3, Jr. Marlboros 3; Feb. 24–Jr. Hockey: Oshawa 2, St. Michael's 4; Feb. 27–Jr. Hockey: Windsor 2, Jr. Marlboros 3; Feb. 27–Jr. Hockey: Barrie 9, St. Michael's 5; Feb. 28–Wrestling: Whipper Billy Watson vs. Lord Athol Layton; Mar. 1–NHL: Boston 1, Leafs 1; Mar. 2–Jr. Hockey: Guelph 4, St. Michael's 5; Mar. 2–Jr. Hockey: Kitchener 5, Jr. Marlboros 5; Mar. 3–Music: Fun Parade with the Roy Ward Dickson Show; Mar. 5–NHL: Canadiens 2, Leafs 6; Mar. 6–Wrestling: Yukon Eric vs. Lu Kimm; Mar. 7–Jr. Hockey: Galt 4, St. Michael's 5; Mar. 8–NHL: Detroit 3, Leafs 6; Mar. 9–Jr. Hockey: Guelph 6, Jr. Marlboros 8; Mar. 10-14: Ice Carnival featuring Jacqueline de Bief; Mar. 15–Jr. Hockey: St. Catharines 6, St. Michael's 3; Mar. 15–NHL: Rangers 2, Leafs 5; Mar. 16–Jr. Hockey: Guelph 3, Jr. Marlboros 7; Mar. 17–Boxing: Al McFater vs. Dave Shade; Mar. 18–Jr. Hockey: Guelph 5, Jr. Marlboros 1; Mar. 19–Jr. Hockey: St. Catharines 0, St. Michael's 4; Mar. 19–NHL: Canadiens 3, Leafs 0; Mar. 20–Wrestling: Hans Hermann vs. Lu Kimm; Mar. 22–NHL: Chicago 3, Leafs 2; Mar. 23–Jr. Hockey: St. Catharines 8, St. Michael's 5; Mar. 24–Boxing: Arthur King vs. Fitzie Pruden; Mar. 26–Wrestling: Whipper Billy Watson vs. Hans Hermann; Mar. 29–NHL: Detroit 6, Leafs 2; Apr. 1–NHL: Detroit 3, Leafs 1; Apr. 3–Wrestling: Hans Hermann vs. Bo Bo Brazil; Apr. 6–Variety: Radio Show of Stars (Ontario Society for Crippled Children); Apr. 10–Wrestling: Hans Hermann vs. Bo Bo Brazil; Apr. 13–Jr. Hockey: Guelph 7, Montreal 2 (Memorial Cup Eastern Finals); Apr. 15–Boxing: Baby Face Jones vs. Al McFater; Apr. 17–Wrestling: Yukon Eric vs. Hans Hermann; Apr. 18–Jr. Hockey: Guelph 5, Montreal 2 (Memorial Cup Eastern Finals); Apr. 21–Boxing: Ontario Olympic Finals; Apr. 23-29: Hollywood Ice Revue w/Barbara Ann Scott; Apr. 27–Jr. Hockey: Guelph 4, Regina 2 (Memorial Cup Finals); Apr. 30–Jr. Hockey: Guelph 8, Regina 2 (Memorial Cup Finals); May 1–Wrestling: Lord Athol Layton vs. Bo Bo Brazil; May 2–Jr. Hockey:

Guelph 10, Regina 2 (Memorial Cup Finals); May 6-8: White Shrine Convention; May 9–Wrestling: Bo Bo Brazil vs. Yukon Eric; May 11–Dr. Endicott Peace Rally; May 15–Wrestling: Hans Hermann vs. Whipper Billy Watson; May 22–Wrestling: Whipper Billy Watson vs. Hanjo Singh; May 26–Metropolitan Opera–Aida; May 27–Metropolitan Opera–La Boheme; May 28–Metropolitan Opera–Carmen; May 29–Metropolitan Opera–Rigoletto; June 1–Incorporated Synod of the Diocese of Toronto; June 6–The Cisco Kid and the Western Roundup Rodeo; Aug. 7–Wrestling: Canadian Open Team Championship; Sept. 5–Wrestling: Bo Bo Brazil vs. The Masked Marvel; Sept. 11–Wrestling: Whipper Billy Watson vs. Lord Athol Layton; Sept. 15–Boxing: Al McFater vs. Lem Thomas; Sept. 18–Wrestling: Yukon Eric vs. Hans Hermann; Sept. 20–Music: Nat King Cole, Stan Kenton, Sarah Vaughn; Sept. 25–Wrestling: The Masked Marvel vs. Yukon Jack; Sept. 29–Oct. 4: Bob Morton's Rameses Shrine Circus; Oct. 5–Lacrosse: Vancouver 1, Peterborough 9 (Mann Cup Finals); Oct. 7–Lacrosse: Vancouver 7, Peterborough 8 (Mann Cup Finals); Oct. 9–Wrestling: The Masked Marvel vs. Yukon Jack; Oct. 10–Lacrosse: Vancouver 8, Peterborough 9 (Mann Cup Finals); Oct. 10–Lacrosse: Windsor 13, Brantford 7 (OLA PeeWee Finals); Oct. 11–NHL: Chicago 6, Leafs 2; Oct. 12–Jr. Hockey: Windsor 0, St. Michael's 8; Oct. 12–Jr. Hockey: Oshawa 2, Jr. Marlboros 2; Oct. 13–Lacrosse: Vancouver 6, Peterborough 15 (Mann Cup Finals); Oct. 14–Boxing: Jack Dempsey's Heavyweight Tournament; Oct. 16–Wrestling: Lord Athol Layton vs. The Masked Marvel; Oct. 18–NHL: Rangers 3, Leafs 4; Oct. 19–Jr. Hockey: Galt 3, St. Michael's 3; Oct. 19–Jr. Hockey: St. Catharines 1, Jr. Marlboros 0; Oct. 22–NHL: Detroit 4, Leafs 5; Oct. 23–Wrestling: Lou Thesz vs. Whipper Billy Watson; Oct. 24–Jr. Hockey: St. Michael's 9, Jr. Marlboros 2; Oct. 25–NHL: Boston 4, Leafs 0; Oct. 26–Jr. Hockey: Windsor 2, Jr. Marlboros 4; Oct. 26–Jr. Hockey: Guelph 10, St. Michael's 5; Oct. 27–Music: Fun Parade with the Roy Ward Dickson show; Oct. 28–Variety: Dean Martin and Jerry Lewis; Oct. 29–NHL: Canadiens 5, Leafs 7; Oct. 30–Wrestling: Lou Thesz vs. Whipper Billy Watson; Nov. 1–NHL: Boston 2, Leafs 3; Nov. 2–Jr. Hockey: St. Michael's 6, Kitchener-Waterloo 0; Nov. 2–Jr. Hockey: Galt 1, Jr. Marlboros 5; Nov. 3–Basketball: Harlem Globetrotters 60, Philadelphia 54; Nov. 5–NHL: Rangers 1, Leafs 4; Nov. 6–Wrestling: Watson/Flanagan vs. Marvel/Plummer; Nov. 8–NHL: Detroit 3, Leafs 3; Nov. 9–Jr. Hockey: Guelph 3, Jr. Marlboros 3; Nov. 9–Jr. Hockey: Oshawa 3, St. Michael's 3; Nov. 10-14: Ice Capades; Nov. 15–NHL: Chicago 3, Leafs 1; Nov. 16–Jr. Hockey: Kitchener-Waterloo 1, Jr. Marlboros 4; Nov. 16–Jr. Hockey: Montreal 2, St. Michael's 3; Nov. 17–Boxing: Al McFater vs. Ben Miloud; Nov. 18–Jr. Hockey: St. Michael's 4, Jr. Marlboros 6; Nov. 19–NHL: Boston 2, Leafs 1; Nov. 20–Wrestling: Watson/Flanagan vs. Marvel/Plummer; Nov. 21–Jr. Hockey: Barrie 5, St. Michael's 8; Nov. 21–Jr. Hockey: Montreal 2, Jr. Marlboros 6; Nov. 22–NHL: Canadiens 2, Leafs 2; Nov. 23–Jr. Hockey: Quebec 0, Jr. Marlboros 3; Nov. 23–Jr. Hockey: St. Catharines 2, St. Michael's 3; Nov. 26–Jr. Hockey: Barrie 2, Jr. Marlboros 3; Nov. 26–Jr. Hockey: Quebec 2, St. Michael's 5; Nov. 27–Wrestling: Six-Man Free-for-All; Nov. 29–NHL: Detroit 3, Leafs 1; Nov. 30–Jr. Hockey: Guelph 2, St. Michael's 4; Nov. 30–Jr. Hockey: Oshawa 2, Jr. Marlboros 5; Dec. 1–Boxing: Armand Savoie vs. Al McFater; Dec. 3–Jr. Hockey: Barrie 6, Jr. Marlboros 4; Dec. 4–Wrestling: Six-Man Free-for-All; Dec. 6–NHL: Rangers 2, Leafs 2; Dec. 7–Jr. Hockey: St. Catharines 1, Jr. Marlboros 3; Dec. 7–Jr. Hockey: Galt 3, St. Michael's 2; Dec. 10–NHL: Canadiens 2, Leafs 1; Dec. 11–Wrestling: Raines/Plummer vs. Watson/Flanagan; Dec. 13–NHL: Detroit 3, Leafs 1; Dec. 14–Jr. Hockey: Windsor 1, St. Michael's 2; Dec. 14–Jr. Hockey: Weston 5, St. Michael's "B" 1; Dec. 15–Boxing: John L. Sullivan vs. Gus Rubicini; Dec. 17–Jr. Hockey: St. Michael's 1, Jr. Marlboros 6; Dec. 18–Wrestling: Whipper Billy Watson vs. The Great Togo; Dec. 20–NHL: Chicago 1, Leafs 4; Dec. 21–Jr. Hockey: Guelph 1, Jr. Marlboros 5; Dec. 21–Jr. Hockey: St. Catharines 5, St. Michael's 5; Dec. 24–NHL: Canadiens 0, Leafs 2; Dec. 26–Wrestling: Red Mask vs. The Masked Marvel; Dec. 27–NHL: Boston 0, Leafs 3; Dec. 28–Jr. Hockey: Kitchener-Waterloo 6, St. Michael's 2; Dec. 28–Jr. Hockey: Galt 3, Jr. Marlboros 4.

1953 • Jan. 2–Wrestling: Yukon Eric vs. Red Mask; Jan. 3–NHL: Chicago 1, Leafs 1; Jan. 4–Jr. Hockey: Windsor 0, Jr. Marlboros 2; Jan. 7–Jr. Hockey: Barrie 1, Jr. Marlboros 0; Jan. 8–Wrestling: Gorgeous George vs. Chief Big Heart; Jan. 10–NHL: Boston 1, Leafs 3; Jan. 11–Jr. Hockey: Kitchener 2, Jr. Marlboros 1; Jan. 11–Jr. Hockey: Oshawa 6, St. Michael's 8; Jan. 12–Boxing: Kid Alfonso vs. Gordon Wallace; Jan. 14–NHL: Chicago 0, Leafs 3; Jan. 15–Wrestling: Gorgeous George vs. Chief Big Heart; Jan. 16–Jr. Hockey: Barrie 1, Jr. Marlboros 1; Jan. 16–Jr. Hockey: Trois-Rivieres 1, St. Michael's 4; Jan. 17–NHL: Rangers 0, Leafs 1; Jan. 18–Jr. Hockey: Trois-Rivieres 5, Jr. Marlboros 8; Jan. 18–Jr. Hockey: Windsor 2, St. Michael's 5; Jan. 21–NHL: Canadiens 1, Leafs 0; Jan. 22–Wrestling: Yukon Eric vs. Man Mountain Dean; Jan. 24–NHL: Detroit 0, Leafs 2; Jan. 25–Jr. Hockey: Oshawa 0, Jr. Marlboros 8; Jan. 25–Jr. Hockey: Galt 3, St. Michael's 4; Jan. 27–Tennis: Frank Sedgman vs. Jack Kramer; Jan. 28–Jr. Hockey: St. Michael's 4, Jr. Marlboros 3; Jan. 29–Wrestling: Watson/ Yukon Eric vs. Raines/Plummer; Jan. 31–NHL: Rangers 0, Leafs 4; Feb. 1–Jr. Hockey: Guelph 1, St. Michael's 2; Feb. 1–Jr. Hockey: St. Catharines 1, Jr. Marlboros 2; Feb. 2-6: Ice Follies of 1953; Feb. 7–NHL: Chicago 4, Leafs 2; Feb. 8–Jr. Hockey: Montreal 5, St. Michael's 4; Feb. 8–Jr. Hockey: Windsor 2, Jr. Marlboros 2; Feb. 9–Boxing: Arthur King vs. Al McFater; Feb. 11–Jr. Hockey: Barrie 2, St. Michael's 7; Feb. 11–Jr. Hockey: Galt 4, Jr. Marlboros 6; Feb. 12–Wrestling: Killer Kowalski vs. Bo Bo Brazil; Feb. 13–Variety: The Gene Autry Show; Feb. 14–NHL: Canadiens 2, Leafs 2; Feb. 15–Jr. Hockey: Montreal 4, Jr. Marlboros 2; Feb. 15–Jr. Hockey: Kitchener-Waterloo 2, St. Michael's 1; Feb. 16–Boxing: Newsboys Annual Canada vs. U.S. Tournament; Feb. 18–NHL: Detroit 0, Leafs 2; Feb. 19–Wrestling: Primo Carnera vs. Man Mountain Dean; Feb. 20–Jr. Hockey: St. Michael's 2, Jr. Marlboros 1; Feb. 21–NHL: Boston 2, Leafs 2; Feb. 22–Jr. Hockey: Oshawa 2, St. Michael's 7; Feb. 22–Jr. Hockey: Guelph 2, Jr. Marlboros 1; Feb. 25–NHL: Canadiens 2, Leafs 1; Feb. 26–Wrestling: Killer Kowalski vs. Primo Carnera; Feb. 28–NHL: Rangers 0, Leafs 3; Mar. 1–Jr. Hockey: Kitchener-Waterloo 2, Jr. Marlboros 5; Mar. 1–Jr. Hockey: St. Catharines 2, St. Michael's 2; Mar. 2–Music: The Roy Ward Dickson Show; Mar. 4–Jr. Hockey: St. Catharines 1, St. Michael's 4; Mar. 5–Wrestling: Killer Kowalski vs. Yukon Eric; Mar. 7–Jr. Hockey: Barrie 1, Jr. Marlboros 2; Mar. 7–NHL: Detroit 3, Leafs 0; Mar. 8–Jr. Hockey: St. Catharines 3, St. Michael's 5; Mar. 9-13: Dick Button Ice Show; Mar. 14–Jr. Hockey: Barrie 3, Jr. Marlboros 6; Mar. 14–NHL: Boston 3, Leafs 1; Mar. 15–Jr. Hockey: Galt 4, St. Michael's 6; Mar. 18–NHL: Chicago 3, Leafs 4; Mar. 19–Wrestling: Killer Kowalski vs. Yukon Eric; Mar. 21–Jr. Hockey: Barrie 6, Jr. Marlboros 3; Mar. 21–NHL: Rangers 0, Leafs 5; Mar. 22–Jr. Hockey: Galt 3, St. Michael's 6; Mar. 25–Jr. Hockey: Barrie 6, Jr. Marlboros 3; Mar. 26–Wrestling: Killer Kowalski vs. Whipper Billy Watson; Mar. 29–Jr. Hockey: Barrie 4, St. Michael's 1 (OHA "A" Finals); Mar. 29–Variety: Radio Show of Stars (Ontario Society for Crippled Children); Mar. 30–Basketball: Harlem Globetrotters 79, College All-Stars 68; Apr. 2–Wrestling: Timothy Geohagen vs. Killer Kowalski; Apr. 4–Jr. Hockey: Barrie 4, St. Michael's 6 (OHA "A" Finals); Apr. 8–Jr. Hockey: Barrie 5, St. Michael's 4 (OHA "A" Finals); Apr. 9–Hockey: Little NHL Hockey Tournament; Apr. 9–Wrestling: Timothy Geohagen vs. The Great Togo; Apr. 11–Jr. Hockey: Barrie 4, St. Michael's 2 (OHA "A" Finals); Apr. 12–Hockey: Whites 6, Reds 4 (NHL Old-Timers); Apr. 13–Variety: Horace Heidt Show; Apr. 14–Jr. Hockey: Quebec 2, Barrie 9 (Memorial Cup Eastern Finals); Apr. 15–Tennis: Jack Kramer vs. Pancho Segura; Apr. 16–Wrestling: Togo/Red Mask vs. Raines/Plummer; Apr. 20–Boxing: Arthur King vs. Henry Davis; Apr. 22–Jr. Hockey: Quebec 3, Barrie 7 (Memorial Cup Eastern Finals); Apr. 23–Wrestling: Layton/Blears vs. Geohagen/Flanagan; Apr. 30–Wrestling: Layton/Blears vs. Geohagen/Brazil; May 4–Boxing: U.S. vs. Canada; May 7–Wrestling: Whipper Billy Watson vs. Hans Hermann; May 14–Wrestling: Blears/Layton vs. Watson/Geohagen; May 21–Wrestling: Gorgeous George vs. Timothy Geohagen; May 25–Metropolitan Opera–La Forza del Destino; May 26–Metropolitan Opera–Tosca; May 27–Metropolitan Opera–Lohrengrin; May 28–Metropolitan Opera–Samson et Daliha; Aug. 7–Liberal Party Rally w/Louis St-Laurent; Aug. 21-22–Federated Women's Institutes of Canada Pageant; Sept. 3–Wrestling: Whipper Billy Watson vs. Hans Schmidt; Sept. 10–Wrestling: Hans Schmidt vs. Sky-Hi Lee; Sept. 17–Wrestling: Watson/Robert vs. Layton/Blears; Sept. 18–Music: Guard Republican Band of Paris; Sept. 24–Wrestling: Whipper Billy Watson vs. Killer Kowalski; Sept. 26–Music: Nat King Cole and Sarah Vaughn; Sept. 29–Oct. 3: Bob Morton's Rameses Shrine Circus; Oct. 7–Hockey: Pittsburgh 3, Toronto 1 (benefit game); Oct. 8–Wrestling: Hans Schmidt vs. Yukon Eric; Oct. 10–NHL: Chicago 2, Leafs 6; Oct. 11–Jr. Hockey: Hamilton 1, Jr. Marlboros 5; Oct. 11–Jr. Hockey: Galt 2, St. Michael's 4; Oct. 15–Wrestling: Yukon Eric vs. Hans Schmidt; Oct. 17–NHL: Rangers 1, Leafs 1; Oct. 18–Jr. Hockey: St. Catharines 1, Jr. Marlboros 5; Oct. 18–Jr. Hockey: Kitchener-Waterloo 3, St. Michael's 3; Oct. 21–NHL: Detroit 1, Leafs 1; Oct. 22–Wrestling: Killer Kowalsi vs. Hans Schmidt; Oct. 23–Jr. Hockey: Barrie 1, Jr. Marlboros 6; Oct. 23–Jr. Hockey: Hamilton 5, St. Michael's 3; Oct. 24–NHL: Boston 3, Leafs 2; Oct. 25–Jr. Hockey: Kitchener-Waterloo 0, Jr. Marlboros 5; Oct. 25–Jr. Hockey: Guelph 3, St. Michael's 6; Oct. 27–Sadler's Wells Ballet–Sleeping Beauty; Oct. 28–Sadler's Wells Ballet–Swan Lake; Oct. 29–Sadler's Wells Ballet–Highlights; Oct. 31–NHL: Rangers 1, Leafs 4; Nov. 1–Jr. Hockey: St. Catharines 3, St. Michael's 1; Nov. 1–Jr. Hockey: Galt 2, Jr. Marlboros 1; Nov. 3–Basketball: Harlem Globetrotters 81, Philadelphia 47; Nov. 4–NHL: Chicago 1, Leafs 3; Nov. 5–Wrestling: Lou Thesz vs. Lord Athol Layton; Nov. 6–Jr. Hockey: St. Michael's 6, Jr. Marlboros 4; Nov. 7–NHL: Detroit 2, Leafs 2; Nov. 8–Jr. Hockey: Quebec 2, Jr. Marlboros 4; Nov. 8–Jr. Hockey: Galt 1, St. Michael's 4; Nov. 11–NHL: Canadiens 1, Leafs 4; Nov. 12–Wrestling: Watson/Robert vs. Mills Brothers; Nov. 13–Jr. Hockey: St. Michael's 5, Jr. Marlboros 2; Nov. 14–NHL: Boston 0, Leafs 2; Nov. 15–Jr. Hockey: St. Catharines 1, Jr. Marlboros 8; Nov. 15–Jr. Hockey: Quebec 2, St. Michael's 4; Nov. 16-20: Ice Capades; Nov. 21–NHL: Rangers 0, Leafs 1; Nov. 22–Jr. Hockey: Hamilton 3, St. Michael's 4; Nov. 22–Jr. Hockey: Guelph 3, Jr. Marlboros 6; Nov. 25–Jr. Hockey: Barrie 3, St. Michael's 4; Nov. 26–Wrestling: Mills Brothers vs. Watson/Robert; Nov. 28–NHL: Canadiens 1, Leafs 3; Nov. 29–Jr. Hockey: Kitchener-Waterloo 1, Jr. Marlboros 3; Nov. 29–Jr. Hockey: Guelph 2, St. Michael's 7; Dec. 2–Jr. Hockey: Kitchener-Waterloo 0, St. Michael's 10; Dec. 2–Jr. Hockey: Barrie 1, Jr. Marlboros 3; Dec. 3–Wrestling: Mills Brothers vs. Watson/Montana; Dec. 5–NHL: Detroit 0, Leafs 3; Dec. 6–Jr. Hockey: Quebec 2, St. Michael's 12; Dec. 6–Jr. Hockey: Hamilton 0, Jr. Marlboros 0; Dec. 9–NHL: Canadiens 0, Leafs 3; Dec. 10–Wrestling: Mills Brothers vs. Watson/Hombre Montana; Dec. 11–Jr. Hockey: Barrie 1, St. Michael's 5; Dec. 11–Jr. Hockey: Galt 3, Jr. Marlboros 4; Dec. 12–NHL: Chicago 0, Leafs 2; Dec. 13–Jr. Hockey: Quebec 2, Jr. Marlboros 0; Dec. 13–Jr. Hockey: Guelph 4, St. Michael's 8; Dec. 15–Variety: Israel Bonds Big Show; Dec. 17–Wrestling: Mills Brothers vs. Layton/Atkins; Dec. 19–NHL: Rangers 2, Leafs 3; Dec. 20–Jr. Hockey: Kitchener-Waterloo 2, Jr. Marlboros 2; Dec. 20–Jr. Hockey: St. Catharines 4, St. Michael's 9; Dec. 26–NHL: Detroit 2, Leafs 4; Dec. 27–Jr. Hockey: St. Michael's 4, Jr. Marlboros 6; Dec. 30–NHL: Canadiens 2, Leafs 2; Dec. 31–Wrestling: Mills Brothers vs. Layton/Atkins.

1954 • Jan. 2–NHL: Chicago 0, Leafs 4; Jan. 3–Jr. Hockey: Quebec 1, Jr. Marlboros 2; Jan. 6–Jr. Hockey: Jonquiere 4, Jr. Marlboros 5; Jan. 7–Wrestling: Watson/Montana vs. Mills Brothers; Jan. 9–NHL: Boston 2, Leafs 3; Jan. 10–Jr. Hockey: St. Catharines 1, St. Michael's 5; Jan. 10–Jr. Hockey: Trois-Rivieres 2, Jr. Marlboros 3; Jan. 13–NHL: Chicago 1, Leafs 2; Jan. 14–Wrestling: Watson/Montana vs. Mills Brothers; Jan. 15–Jr. Hockey: St. Michael's 3, Jr. Marlboros 4; Jan. 16–NHL: Rangers 0, Leafs 4; Jan. 17–Jr. Hockey: Guelph 2, Jr. Marlboros 4; Jan. 17–Jr. Hockey: Montreal 2, St. Michael's 7; Jan. 20–Tennis: Frank Sedgman vs. Donald Budge; Jan. 21–Wrestling: Watson/Montana vs. Kowalski/Schmidt; Jan. 23–NHL: Detroit 1, Leafs 4; Jan. 24–Jr. Hockey: Kitchener-Waterloo 0, St. Michael's 3; Jan. 24–Jr. Hockey: Hamilton 0, Jr. Marlboros 0; Jan. 25–Youth for Christ Rally; Jan. 26–Boxing: Tommy Harrison vs. Earl Walls; Jan. 27–NHL: Canadiens 2, Leafs 0; Jan. 28–Wrestling: Mills Brothers vs. Kowalski/Schmidt; Jan. 30–NHL: Boston 2, Leafs 4; Jan. 31–Jr. Hockey: Montreal 5, St. Michael's 2; Feb. 1-5: Ice Follies of 1954; Feb. 6–Jr. Hockey: Barrie 4, Jr. Marlboros 5; Feb. 6–Jr. Hockey: Kitchener-Waterloo 3, St. Michael's 3; Feb. 6–NHL: Chicago 0, Leafs 6; Feb. 7–Jr. Hockey: Montreal 0, Jr. Marlboros 5; Feb. 7–Jr. Hockey: Quebec 1, St. Michael's 5; Feb. 9–Jr. Hockey: Barrie 2, Jr. Marlboros 1; Feb. 9–Jr. Hockey: Jonquiere 2, St. Michael's 4; Feb. 10–NHL: Boston 3, Leafs 2; Feb. 11–Wrestling: Mills Brothers vs. Watson/Montana; Feb. 13–NHL: Canadiens 2, Leafs 2; Feb. 14–Jr. Hockey: Guelph 0, Jr. Marlboros 8; Feb. 14–Jr. Hockey: Trois-Rivieres 1, St. Michael's 7; Feb. 15–Boxing: Newsboys Annual Canada vs. U.S. Tournament; Feb. 16–Jr. Hockey: St. Michael's 9, Jr. Marlboros 3; Feb. 17–NHL: Detroit 0, Leafs 0; Feb. 18–Wrestling: Dusek Riot Squad vs. Watson/Montana; Feb. 20–NHL: Boston 2, Leafs 3; Feb. 21–Jr. Hockey: St. Catharines 0, Jr. Marlboros 0; Feb. 21–Jr. Hockey: Hamilton 3, St. Michael's 2; Feb. 23–Toronto Police Association Concert; Feb. 24–Jr. Hockey: St. Michael's 3, Jr. Marlboros 2; Feb. 25–Wrestling: Mills Brothers vs. Dusek Brothers; Feb. 27–NHL: Chicago 2, Leafs 4; Feb. 28–Jr. Hockey: Montreal 2, Jr. Marlboros 2; Feb. 28–Jr. Hockey: Galt 2, St. Michael's 7; Mar. 1–Music: Fun Parade with the Roy Ward Dickson show; Mar. 3–NHL: Rangers 3, Leafs 3; Mar. 4–Wrestling: Dusek Brothers vs. Mills Brothers; Mar. 6–NHL: Detroit 3, Leafs 1; Mar. 7–Jr. Hockey: Jr. Marlboros 4, St. Michael's 0; Mar. 10–Jr. Hockey: Galt 0, Jr. Marlboros 10; Mar. 10–Jr. Hockey: Barrie 5, St. Michael's 6; Mar. 11–Wrestling: Dusek Brothers vs. Mills Brothers; Mar. 13–NHL: Boston 2, Leafs 1; Mar. 14–Jr. Hockey: Hamilton 4, Jr. Marlboros 1; Mar. 14–Jr. Hockey: St. Catharines 7, St. Michael's 5; Mar. 16–Jr. Hockey: Kitchener-Waterloo 2, Jr. Marlboros 4; Mar. 17–NHL: Canadiens 1, Leafs 3; Mar. 18–Wrestling: Montana/Ursus vs. Mills Brothers; Mar. 20–Jr. Hockey: Kitchener-Waterloo 5, Jr. Marlboros 3; Mar. 20–NHL: Rangers 5, Leafs 2; Mar. 21–Jr. Hockey: St. Catharines 6, St. Michael's 4; Mar. 24–Jr. Hockey: St. Catharines 2, St. Michael's 3; Mar. 25–Wrestling: Montana/Ursus vs. Mills Brothers; Mar. 27–NHL: Detroit 3, Leafs 1; Mar. 28–Jr. Hockey: Kitchener-Waterloo 1, Jr. Marlboros 4;

Mar. 29–Basketball: College All-Stars 94, Harlem Globetrotters 87 (first loss in 263 games); Mar. 30–NHL: Detroit 3, Leafs 1; Mar. 31–Jr. Hockey: St. Catharines 8, St. Michael's 4; Apr. 1–Wrestling: Yukon Eric/Ursus vs. Dusek Brothers; Apr. 2–Jr. Hockey: Hamilton 3, Jr. Marlboros 5; Apr. 4–Jr. Hockey: St. Catharines 5, St. Michael's 4; Apr. 8–Wrestling: Mills Brothers vs. Yukon Eric/Mighty Ursus; Apr. 10–Jr. Hockey: St. Catharines 4, Jr. Marlboros 3 (OHA "A" Finals); Apr. 11–Variety: Radio Show of Stars (Ontario Society for Crippled Children); Apr. 12–Boxing: Earl Walls vs. Tommy Harrison; Apr. 14–Jr. Hockey: St. Catharines 3, Jr. Marlboros 5 (OHA "A" Finals); Apr. 15–Wrestling: Mills Brothers vs. Yukon Eric/Mighty Ursus; Apr. 17–Jr. Hockey: St. Catharines 1, Jr. Marlboros 5 (OHA "A" Finals); Apr. 19–Boxing: City Playgrounds Boxing Championships; Apr. 22–Wrestling: Mills Brothers vs. Tex McKenzie/Mighty Ursus; Apr. 27–May 5: Hollywood Ice Revue w/Barbara Ann Scott; May 6–Wrestling: Mills Brothers vs. Tex McKenzie/Mighty Ursus; May 7–Jr. Hockey: Quebec 2, St. Catharines 4 (Memorial Cup Eastern Finals); May 8–Music: Liberace and Company; May 9–Jr. Hockey: Edmonton 2, St. Catharines 8 (Memorial Cup Finals); May 11–Jr. Hockey: Edmonton 3, St. Catharines 5 (Memorial Cup Finals); May 13–Jr. Hockey: Edmonton 1, St. Catharines 4 (Memorial Cup Finals); May 14–Wrestling: Tex McKenzie/Mighty Ursus vs. Mills Brothers; May 15–Jr. Hockey: Edmonton 2, St. Catharines 6 (Memorial Cup Finals); May 20–Wrestling: Primo Carnera vs. Tiny Mills; May 24–Metropolitan Opera–Luica di Lammermoor; May 25–Metropolitan Opera–Aida; May 26–Metropolitan Opera–The Barber of Seville; May 27–Metropolitan Opera–La Traviata; May 28–Metropolitan Opera–Faust; May 29–Metropolitan Opera–Rigoletto; June 14–Music: Spike Jones; July 22–Wrestling: Whipper Billy Watson vs. Killer Kowalski; Sept. 2–Wrestling: Togo Brothers vs. McKenzie/Watson; Sept. 9–Wrestling: Argentina Rocca vs. Nanjo Singh; Sept. 16–Wrestling: Togo Brothers vs. McKenzie/Watson; Sept. 23–Wrestling: Togo Brothers vs. Dusek Brothers; Sept. 27–Oct. 2: Bob Morton's Rameses Shrine Circus; Oct. 5–Music: Mantovani; Oct. 6–Hockey: Toronto 3, Pittsburgh 2 (benefit game); Oct. 7–Wrestling: Togo Brothers vs. Dusek Brothers; Oct. 9–NHL: Chicago 3, Leafs 3; Oct. 14–Wrestling: Togo Brothers vs. Neilson/Lisowski; Oct. 16–NHL: Rangers 4, Leafs 2; Oct. 18–London's Festival Ballet–La Esmerelda; Oct. 19–London's Festival Ballet–Alice in Wonderland; Oct. 20–London's Festival Ballet–The Nutcracker; Oct. 21–Wrestling: Togo Brothers vs. Neilson/Lisowski; Oct. 23–NHL: Boston 3, Leafs 3; Oct. 24–Jr. Hockey: St. Catharines 2, Jr. Marlboros 7; Oct. 24–Jr. Hockey: Hamilton 0, St. Michael's 5; Oct. 27–NHL: Canadiens 3, Leafs 1; Oct. 28–Wrestling: Claybourne/Lindsey vs. Togo Brothers; Oct. 30–NHL: Rangers 1, Leafs 3; Oct. 31–Jr. Hockey: Galt 2, St. Michael's 3; Oct. 31–Jr. Hockey: Kitchener-Waterloo 0, Jr. Marlboros 7; Nov. 3–NHL: Detroit 1, Leafs 1; Nov. 4–Wrestling: Claybourne/Lindsey vs. Togo Brothers; Nov. 6–NHL: Chicago 2, Leafs 5; Nov. 7–Jr. Hockey: Guelph 5, St. Michael's 1; Nov. 7–Jr. Hockey: Hamilton 0, Jr. Marlboros 4; Nov. 8–Basketball: Harlem Globetrotters 77, Washington 55; Nov. 8–Basketball: Philadelphia 94, NY Knicks 67; Nov. 10–Jr. Hockey: Barrie 0, Jr. Marlboros 8; Nov. 11–Wrestling: Baillargeon/Watson vs. Togo Brothers; Nov. 13–NHL: Detroit 0, Leafs 1; Nov. 14–Jr. Hockey: St. Catharines 3, St. Michael's 7; Nov. 14–Jr. Hockey: Galt 2, Jr. Marlboros 6; Nov. 17–Jr. Hockey: Barrie 4, St. Michael's 8; Nov. 17–NHL: Canadiens 2, Leafs 5; Nov. 18–Wrestling: Baillargeon/Watson vs. Kalmikoff Brothers; Nov. 19–Jr. Hockey: Barrie 3, St. Michael's 6; Nov. 20–NHL: Boston 1, Leafs 0; Nov. 21–Jr. Hockey: Kitchener-Waterloo 1, St. Michael's 6; Nov. 21–Jr. Hockey: Guelph 1, Jr. Marlboros 1; Nov. 22-26: Ice Capades; Nov. 27–NHL: Rangers 1, Leafs 3; Nov. 28–Jr. Hockey: Hamilton 1, St. Michael's 3; Nov. 28–Jr. Hockey: St. Catharines 3, Jr. Marlboros 1; Dec. 1–NHL: Boston 0, Leafs 6; Dec. 2–Wrestling: Baillargeon/Watson vs. McKenzie/Neilson; Dec. 4–NHL: Detroit 0, Leafs 1; Dec. 5–Jr. Hockey: Galt 1, St. Michael's 3; Dec. 5–Jr. Hockey: Kitchener-Waterloo 1, Jr. Marlboros 5; Dec. 7–Jr. Hockey: St. Michael's 5, Jr. Marlboros 4; Dec. 8–NHL: Canadiens 1, Leafs 3; Dec. 9–Wrestling: Kalmikoff Brothers vs. Lindsay/Claybourne; Dec. 10–Jr. Hockey: St. Catharines 6, Jr. Marlboros 3; Dec. 11–NHL: Chicago 2, Leafs 1; Dec. 12–Jr. Hockey: Quebec 4, Jr. Marlboros 4 (Laurier Cup Series); Dec. 12–Jr. Hockey: Guelph 3, St. Michael's 4; Dec. 14-16: London's Old Vic–A Midsummer Night's Dream; Dec. 18–NHL: Rangers 1, Leafs 3; Dec. 19–Jr. Hockey: Galt 2, Jr. Marlboros 4; Dec. 19–Jr. Hockey: St. Catharines 2, St. Michael's 4; Dec. 21–Jr. Hockey: St. Michael's 2, Jr. Marlboros 5; Dec. 23–Wrestling: Kalmikoff Brothers vs. Lindsay/Wright; Dec. 25–NHL: Detroit 3, Leafs 2; Dec. 26–Jr. Hockey: Kitchener-Waterloo 2, St. Michael's 3; Dec. 26–Jr. Hockey: Guelph 4, Jr. Marlboros 2; Dec. 29–NHL: Canadiens 1, Leafs 1; Dec. 30–Wrestling: Baillargeon/Watson vs. Kalmikoff Brothers.

1955 • Jan. 1–Jr. Hockey: Barrie 1, Jr. Marlboros 3; Jan. 1–NHL: Chicago 2, Leafs 2; Jan. 2–Jr. Hockey: St. Michael's 1, Jr. Marlboros 3; Jan. 5–NHL: Boston 2, Leafs 1; Jan. 6–Wrestling: Baillargeon/Watson vs. Kalmikoff Brothers; Jan. 8–NHL: Rangers 0, Leafs 5; Jan. 9–Jr. Hockey: Hamilton 3, St. Michael's 3; Jan. 9–Jr. Hockey: St. Catharines 1, Jr. Marlboros 3; Jan. 12–Jr. Hockey: Barrie 7, St. Michael's 3; Jan. 12–Jr. Hockey: Kitchener-Waterloo 3, Jr. Marlboros 0; Jan. 13–Wrestling: Mills Brothers vs. Watson/Baillargeon; Jan. 15–NHL: Boston 2, Leafs 4; Jan. 16–Jr. Hockey: Galt 4, St. Michael's 3; Jan. 16–Jr. Hockey: Hamilton 3, Jr. Marlboros 4; Jan. 17–Boxing: Earl Walls vs. Jimmy Slade; Jan. 18–Jr. Hockey: St. Michael's 3, Jr. Marlboros 7; Jan. 19–NHL: Chicago 3, Leafs 3; Jan. 20–Wrestling: Mills Brothers vs. Watson/Baillargeon; Jan. 21–Hockey: UCC Old Boys 5, UCC New Boys 0; Jan. 22–NHL: Detroit 1, Leafs 3; Jan. 23–Jr. Hockey: Guelph 3, St. Michael's 2; Jan. 23–Jr. Hockey: Trois-Rivieres 2, Jr. Marlboros 3 (Laurier Cup Series); Jan. 26–NHL: Canadiens 1, Leafs 1; Jan. 27–Wrestling: Kalmikoff Brothers vs. Lee Brothers; Jan. 29–NHL: Rangers 3, Leafs 1; Jan. 30–Jr. Hockey: St. Catharines 4, St. Michael's 4; Jan. 30–Jr. Hockey: Montreal 3, Jr. Marlboros 1 (Laurier Cup Series); Jan. 31–Feb. 4: Ice Follies of 1955; Feb. 5–NHL: Chicago 2, Leafs 2; Feb. 6–Jr. Hockey: Guelph 0, Jr. Marlboros 1; Feb. 6–Jr. Hockey: Kitchener-Waterloo 3, St. Michael's 5; Feb. 8–Jr. Hockey: Galt 5, Jr. Marlboros 1; Feb. 9–NHL: Canadiens 1, Leafs 3; Feb. 10–Wrestling: Mills Brothers vs. Kalmikoff Brothers; Feb. 12–NHL: Detroit 2, Leafs 1; Feb. 13–Jr. Hockey: St. Catharines 2, Jr. Marlboros 7; Feb. 13–Jr. Hockey: Hamilton 1, St. Michael's 1; Feb. 14–Boxing: Teddy Smith vs. George Chuvalo; Feb. 16–Jr. Hockey: Barrie 3, St. Michael's 4; Feb. 16–Jr. Hockey: Hamilton 1, Jr. Marlboros 4; Feb. 17–Wrestling: Mills Brothers vs. Kalmikoff Brothers; Feb. 19–NHL: Boston 1, Leafs 1; Feb. 20–Jr. Hockey: Kitchener-Waterloo 3, Jr. Marlboros 7; Feb. 20–Jr. Hockey: Galt 3, St. Michael's 1; Feb. 22–Toronto Police Association Concert; Feb. 23–Jr. Hockey: St. Michael's 1, Jr. Marlboros 4; Feb. 24–Wrestling: Whipper Billy Watson vs. Argentina Rocca; Feb. 26–Jr. Hockey: Galt 2, Jr. Marlboros 3; Feb. 26–NHL: Detroit 1, Leafs 1; Feb. 27–Jr. Hockey: St. Catharines 2, St. Michael's 3; Mar. 2–NHL: Canadiens 3, Leafs 2; Mar. 3–Wrestling: Whipper Billy Watson vs. Argentina Rocca; Mar. 4–Jr. Hockey: Galt 3, Jr. Marlboros 7; Mar. 5–NHL: Boston 2, Leafs 2; Mar. 6–Jr. Hockey: St. Catharines 5, St. Michael's 5; Mar. 7–Boxing: Earl Walls vs. James J. Parker; Mar. 9–Jr. Hockey: Guelph 3, Jr. Marlboros 4; Mar. 10–Wrestling: Kalmikoff Brothers Vs. Watson/Prince Maiava; Mar. 12–NHL: Rangers 2, Leafs 1; Mar. 17–Wrestling: Kalmikoff Brothers Vs. Watson/Prince Maiava; Mar. 19–NHL: Chicago 0, Leafs 5; Mar. 20–Jr. Hockey: St. Catharines 3, Jr. Marlboros 0 (OHA "A" Finals); Mar. 23–Jr. Hockey: St. Catharines 2, Jr. Marlboros 6 (OHA "A" Finals); Mar. 24–Wrestling: Kalmikoff Brothers vs. Mills Brothers; Mar. 27–Jr. Hockey: St. Catharines 1, Jr. Marlboros 2 (OHA "A" Finals); Mar. 27–NHL: Detroit 3, Leafs 1; Mar. 30–NHL: Detroit 2, Leafs 1; Mar. 31–Wrestling: Kalmikoff Brothers vs. Mills Brothers; Apr. 2–Jr. Hockey: Quebec 4, Jr. Marlboros 1 (Memorial Cup Eastern Finals); Apr. 3–Variety: Timmy's Easter Parade of Stars; Apr. 5–Jr. Hockey: Quebec 1, Jr. Marlboros 4 (Memorial Cup Eastern Finals); Apr. 7–Wrestling: Watson/Prince Maiava vs. Mills Brothers; Apr. 12–Jr. Hockey: Quebec 1, Jr. Marlboros 3 (Memorial Cup Eastern Finals); Apr. 14–Wrestling: Watson/Prince Maiava vs. Mills Brothers; Apr. 21–Wrestling: Argentina Rocca vs. Lord Athol Layton; Apr. 26–Boxing: Al McFater vs. Tony Percy; Apr. 28–Wrestling: Kalmikoff Brothers Vs. Watson/Prince Maiava; May 11–Music: George Formby Variety Show; May 23–Metropolitan Opera–Madam Butterfly; May 24–Metropolitan Opera–Pagliacci; May 25–Metropolitan Opera–La Traviata; May 26–Metropolitan Opera–Tosca; May 27–Metropolitan Opera–Andrea Chenier; May 28–Metropolitan Opera–Carmen; Aug. 16-21: World Convetion of Churches of Christ; Sept. 1–Wrestling: Von Erich/Von Scheber vs. Watson/Layton; Sept. 8–Wrestling: Von Erich/Von Scheber vs. Watson/Hepburn; Sept. 15–Wrestling: Hepburn/Rocca vs. Kalmikof Brothers; Sept. 19–Music: Mantovani; Sept. 22–Wrestling: Hepburn/Rocca vs. Kalmikof Brothers; Sept. 26-30: Bob Morton's Rameses Shrine Circus; Oct. 2–Youth for Christ rally with Billy Graham; Oct. 5–MLG Open House; Oct. 6–Wrestling: Von Erich/Von Scheber vs. Kalmikoff Brothers; Oct. 8–NHL: Detroit 2, Leafs 4; Oct. 11–Music: Queen's Scots Guards Pipe Band; Oct. 13–Wrestling: Von Erich/Von Scheber vs. Kalmikoff Brothers; Oct. 15–NHL: Boston 2, Leafs 2; Oct. 20–Wrestling: Yukon Eric vs. Mighty Ursus; Oct. 22–NHL: Rangers 2, Leafs 3; Oct. 26–NHL: Canadiens 1, Leafs 2; Oct. 27–Wrestling: Yukon Eric vs. Doug Hepburn; Oct. 29–NHL: Chicago 0, Leafs 2; Oct. 30–Jr. Hockey: St. Catharines 2, Jr. Marlboros 1; Oct. 30–Jr. Hockey: Hamilton 3, St. Michael's 3; Oct. 31–Basketball: Harlem Globetrotters 51, NY Celtics 45; Nov. 2–NHL: Detroit 1, Leafs 3; Nov. 3–Wrestling: Von Erich/Von Scheber vs. Watson/Yukon Eric; Nov. 5–NHL: Rangers 3, Leafs 0; Nov. 6–Jr. Hockey: Kitchener-Waterloo 1, Jr. Marlboros 7; Nov. 6–Jr. Hockey: Guelph 2, St. Michael's 4; Nov. 9–Jr. Hockey: St. Michael's 8, Jr. Marlboros 7; Nov. 10–Wrestling: Von Erich/Von Scheber vs. Watson/Hepburn; Nov. 12–NHL: Boston 3, Leafs 2; Nov. 13–Jr. Hockey: Kitchener-Waterloo 5, St. Michael's 3; Nov. 13–Jr. Hockey: Guelph 2, Jr. Marlboros 4; Nov. 16–NHL: Canadiens 3, Leafs 2; Nov. 17–Wrestling: Von Erich/Von Scheber vs. Watson/Hepburn; Nov. 18–Jr. Hockey: St. Michael's 4, Jr. Marlboros 0; Nov. 19–NHL: Boston 2, Leafs 3; Nov. 20–Jr. Hockey: St. Catharines 0, St. Michael's 4; Nov. 20–Jr. Hockey: Barrie 1, Jr. Marlboros 3; Nov. 21-25: Ice Capades; Nov. 26–NHL: Chicago 4, Leafs 7; Nov. 27–Jr. Hockey: Guelph 3, Jr. Marlboros 1; Nov. 27–Jr. Hockey: Barrie 1, St. Michael's 5; Nov. 29–Jr. Hockey: Barrie 2, St. Michael's 4; Nov. 29–Jr. Hockey: Hamilton 1, Jr. Marlboros 3; Nov. 30–NHL: Detroit 3, Leafs 3; Dec. 1–Wrestling: Watson/Yukon Eric vs. Von Erich/Von Scheber; Dec. 3–NHL: Canadiens 3, Leafs 1; Dec. 4–Jr. Hockey: Kitchener-Waterloo 3, St. Michael's 4; Dec. 4–Jr. Hockey: Hamilton 1, Jr. Marlboros 1; Dec. 7–Jr. Hockey: St. Catharines 5, St. Michael's 0; Dec. 7–Jr. Hockey: Barrie 4, Jr. Marlboros 3; Dec. 8–Wrestling: Watson/Yukon Eric vs. Von Erich/Von Scheber; Dec. 10–NHL: Rangers 1, Leafs 6; Dec. 11–Jr. Hockey: Hamilton 1, St. Michael's 3; Dec. 11–Jr. Hockey: St. Catharines 0, Jr. Marlboros 1; Dec. 13–Sadler's Wells Ballet–The Lady and the Fool; Dec. 14–Sadler's Wells Ballet–The Firebird; Dec. 15–Sadler's Wells Ballet–Façade; Dec. 17–NHL: Boston 1, Leafs 5; Dec. 18–Jr. Hockey: Kitchener-Waterloo 4, Jr. Marlboros 7; Dec. 18–Jr. Hockey: Guelph 4, St. Michael's 5; Dec. 22–Wrestling: Von Erich/Von Scheber vs. Watson/Rocca; Dec. 23–Jr. Hockey: St. Michael's 2, Jr. Marlboros 4; Dec. 24–NHL: Chicago 2, Leafs 5; Dec. 25–Jr. Hockey: Kitchener-Waterloo 1, Jr. Marlboros 5; Dec. 25–Jr. Hockey: Montreal 6, St. Michael's 6 (Laurier Cup Series); Dec. 27–Jr. Hockey: Hamilton 1, Jr. Marlboros 3; Dec. 27–Jr. Hockey: Barrie 0, St. Michael's 2; Dec. 28–NHL: Canadiens 0, Leafs 2; Dec. 29–Wrestling: Von Erich/Von Scheber vs. Watson/Yukon Eric; Dec. 31–NHL: Detroit 2, Leafs 2.

1956 • Jan. 1–Jr. Hockey: St. Catharines 5, St. Michael's 4; Jan. 1–Jr. Hockey: Montreal 2, Jr. Marlboros 1 (Laurier Cup Series); Jan. 4–NHL: Chicago 2, Leafs 4; Jan. 5–Wrestling: Von Erich/Von Scheber vs. Watson/Yukon Eric (Joe Louis–Referee); Jan. 7–NHL: Boston 2, Leafs 6; Jan. 8–Jr. Hockey: St. Catharines 4, Jr. Marlboros 2; Jan. 8–Jr. Hockey: Hamilton 5, St. Michael's 1; Jan. 9–Boxing: James J. Parker vs. Johnny Arthur; Jan. 11–Jr. Hockey: St. Michael's 3, Jr. Marlboros 0; Jan. 12–Wrestling: Watson/Yukon Eric vs. Von Erich/Von Scheber; Jan. 14–NHL: Rangers 6, Leafs 5; Jan. 15–Jr. Hockey: Guelph 4, Jr. Marlboros 6; Jan. 15–Jr. Hockey: Kitchener-Waterloo 7, St. Michael's 6; Jan. 18–NHL: Canadiens 3, Leafs 2; Jan. 19–Wrestling: Whipper Billy Watson vs. Hardboiled Haggerty; Jan. 21–NHL: Detroit 2, Leafs 4; Jan. 22–Jr. Hockey: Guelph 7, St. Michael's 3; Jan. 22–Jr. Hockey: Barrie 3, Jr. Marlboros 3; Jan. 25–NHL: Chicago 1, Leafs 3; Jan. 26–Wrestling: Whipper Billy Watson vs. Hardboiled Haggerty; Jan. 28–NHL: Rangers 3, Leafs 1; Jan. 29–Jr. Hockey: Hamilton 2, Jr. Marlboros 3; Jan. 29–Jr. Hockey: Kitchener-Waterloo 2, St. Michael's 5; Jan. 30–Feb. 3: Ice Follies of 1956; Feb. 4–NHL: Chicago 4, Leafs 2; Feb. 5–Jr. Hockey: Guelph 3, St. Michael's 3; Feb. 5–Jr. Hockey: Kitchener-Waterloo 2, Jr. Marlboros 0; Feb. 6–Tennis: Tony Trabert vs. Poncho Gonzales; Feb. 8–NHL: Canadiens 1, Leafs 1; Feb. 9–Wrestling: Smith Brothers vs. Von Erich/Von Scheber; Feb. 10–Jr. Hockey: St. Michael's 4, Jr. Marlboros 6; Feb. 11–NHL: Rangers 0, Leafs 5; Feb. 12–Jr. Hockey: Barrie 2, St. Michael's 1; Feb. 12–Jr. Hockey: Guelph 4, Jr. Marlboros 1; Feb. 15–NHL: Boston 0, Leafs 1; Feb. 16–Wrestling: Von Erich/Von Scheber vs. Smith Brothers; Feb. 18–NHL: Detroit 6, Leafs 1; Feb. 19–Jr. Hockey: Montreal 4, St. Michael's 1 (Laurier Cup Series); Feb. 19–Jr. Hockey: St. Catharines 0, Jr. Marlboros 3; Feb. 22–Jr. Hockey: Barrie 1, Jr. Marlboros 5; Feb. 22–Jr. Hockey: St. Catharines 6, St. Michael's 4; Feb. 23–Wrestling: Pat O'Connor vs. Hardboiled Haggerty; Feb. 25–NHL: Boston 3, Leafs 1; Feb. 26–Jr. Hockey: Montreal 5, Jr. Marlboros 3 (Laurier Cup Series); Feb. 26–Jr. Hockey: Hamilton 1, St. Michael's 6; Feb. 28–Hockey: Marlboro Bantams 3, St. Catharines Bantams 2; Feb. 28–Hockey: Marlboro Midgets 6, St. Catharines Midgets 1; Feb. 29–NHL: Canadiens 1, Leafs 4; Mar. 1–Wrestling: Whipper Billy Watson vs. Lou Thesz; Mar. 3–NHL: Detroit 2, Leafs 2; Mar. 4–Jr. Hockey: St. Catharines 3, Jr. Marlboros 3; Mar. 6-9: Toronto Skating Club Carnival; Mar. 10–NHL: Rangers 2, Leafs 5; Mar. 11–Jr. Hockey: St. Catharines 1, Jr. Marlboros 4; Mar. 12–Boxing: Arthur King vs. Chico Vejar; Mar. 15–Wrestling: Whipper Billy Watson vs. Lou Thesz; Mar. 16–Jr. Hockey: Barrie 2, St. Michael's 6; Mar. 17–NHL: Chicago 1, Leafs 1; Mar. 18–Jr. Hockey: St. Catharines 2, Jr. Marlboros 7; Mar. 20–Jr. Hockey: Barrie 3, St. Michael's 2; Mar. 22–Wrestling: Whipper Billy Watson vs. Gorgeous George; Mar. 24–Jr. Hockey: Barrie 2, St. Michael's 0; Mar. 24–NHL: Detroit 5, Leafs 4; Mar. 25–Variety: Timmy's Easter Parade of Stars; Mar. 26–Jr. Hockey:

Barrie 3, Jr. Marlboros 5 (OHA "A" Finals); Mar. 27–NHL: Detroit 0, Leafs 2; Mar. 29–Wrestling: Whipper Billy Watson vs. Wild Bill Longson; Mar. 31–Jr. Hockey: Barrie 1, Jr. Marlboros 8; Apr. 4–Jr. Hockey: Barrie 3, Jr. Marlboros 5 (OHA "A" Finals); Apr. 5–Wrestling: Tom O'Connor vs. Nanjo Singh; Apr. 8–Jr. Hockey: Montreal 2, Jr. Marlboros 3 (Memorial Cup Eastern Finals); Apr. 12–Wrestling: O'Connor/McClarity vs. Atkins/Haggerty; Apr. 17–Jr. Hockey: Montreal 0, Jr. Marlboros 3 (Memorial Cup Eastern Finals); Apr. 19–Wrestling: Whipper Billy Watson vs. Hans Schmidt; Apr. 22–Jr. Hockey: Montreal 3, Jr. Marlboros 2 (Memorial Cup Eastern Finals); Apr. 23–Boxing: Jack Dempsey's Heavyweight Tournament; Apr. 25–Jr. Hockey: Montreal 0, Jr. Marlboros 2 (Memorial Cup Eastern Finals); Apr. 26–Wrestling: Whipper Billy Watson vs. Hans Schmidt; Apr. 27–Jr. Hockey: Regina 4, Jr. Marlboros 4 (Memorial Cup Finals); Apr. 29–Jr. Hockey: Regina 1, Jr. Marlboros 5 (Memorial Cup Finals); Apr. 30–Music: Bill Haley and his Comets; May 2–Jr. Hockey: Regina 2, Jr. Marlboros 4 (Memorial Cup Finals); May 3–Wrestling: Whipper Billy Watson vs. Hardboiled Haggerty; May 4–Jr. Hockey: Regina 1, Jr. Marlboros 6 (Memorial Cup Finals); May 6–Jr. Hockey: Regina 4, Jr. Marlboros 7 (Memorial Cup Finals); May 10–Wrestling: Von Erich/Von Scheber vs. O'Connor/McClarity; May 17–Wrestling: Von Erich/Von Scheber vs. O'Connor/Maiava; May 24–Wrestling: Killer Kowalski vs. Pat O'Connor; May 28–Metropolitan Opera–Aida; May 29–Metropolitan Opera–Faust; May 30–Metropolitan Opera–Carmen; May 31–Metropolitan Opera–Fledermaus; June 1–Metropolitan Opera–La Boheme; June 2–Metropolitan Opera–Rigoletto; June 11–Boxing: George Chuvalo vs. Johnny Arthur; July 16–Music: Rock and Roll Show; Sept. 6–Wrestling: Brunetti Brothers vs. Von Erich/Von Schober; Sept. 10–Boxing: Joe Micili vs. Arthur King; Sept. 13–Wrestling: Whipper Billy Watson vs. Hardboiled Haggerty; Sept. 16–Lacrosse: Nanaimo 13, Peterborough 13 (Mann Cup Finals); Sept. 19–Lacrosse: Nanaimo 10, Peterborough 9 (Mann Cup Finals); Sept. 20–Wrestling: Haggerty/Hutton vs. Brunetti Brothers; Sept. 23–Lacrosse: Nanaimo 10, Peterborough 8 (Mann Cup Finals); Sept. 23–Incorporated Synod of the Diocese of Toronto; Sept. 26–Lacrosse: Nanaimo 8, Peterborough 7 (Mann Cup Finals); Sept. 27–Wrestling: Haggerty/Hutton vs. Brunetti Brothers; Sept. 29–Music: Rock and Roll Show; Oct. 1-5: Bob Morton's Rameses Shrine Circus; Oct. 11–Wrestling: Whipper Billy Watson vs. Mr. Hito; Oct. 13–NHL: Detroit 4, Leafs 1; Oct. 15-16: Royal Danish Ballet; Oct. 18–Wrestling: Whipper Billy Watson vs. Mr. Hito; Oct. 20–NHL: Boston 2, Leafs 2; Oct. 22–Boxing: Harold King vs. George Chuvalo; Oct. 25–Wrestling: Moto/Mito vs. Brunetti Brothers; Oct. 27–NHL: Chicago 2, Leafs 5; Oct. 28–Jr. Hockey: Hamilton 1, St. Michael's 1; Oct. 28–Jr. Hockey: St. Catharines 3, Jr. Marlboros 7; Oct. 31–NHL: Rangers 2, Leafs 7; Nov. 1–Wrestling: Whipper Billy Watson vs. Mr. Moto; Nov. 3–NHL: Detroit 2, Leafs 1; Nov. 4–Jr. Hockey: Peterborough 1, Jr. Marlboros 4; Nov. 4–Jr. Hockey: Barrie 2, St. Michael's 2; Nov. 6–Basketball: Harlem Globetrotters 79, Washington 60; Nov. 7–NHL: Canadiens 4, Leafs 3; Nov. 8–Wrestling: Whipper Billy Watson vs. Mr. Moto; Nov. 10–NHL: Chicago 1, Leafs 4; Nov. 11–Jr. Hockey: Hamilton 2, Jr. Marlboros 0; Nov. 11–Jr. Hockey: Peterborough 1, St. Michael's 7; Nov. 14–Jr. Hockey: Guelph 5, Jr. Marlboros 3; Nov. 14–Jr. Hockey: St. Catharines 1, St. Michael's 3; Nov. 15–Wrestling: Brunetti Brothers vs. Mito/Moto; Nov. 17–NHL: Chicago 6, Leafs 3; Nov. 18–Jr. Hockey: Guelph 3, Jr. Marlboros 2; Nov. 18–Jr. Hockey: Barrie 0, St. Michael's 2; Nov. 19–Boxing: George Chuvalo vs. Bob Biehler; Nov. 22–Wrestling: Lou Thesz vs. Whipper Billy Watson; Nov. 24–NHL: Boston 3, Leafs 2; Nov. 25–Jr. Hockey: Guelph 1, Jr. Marlboros 3; Nov. 25–Jr. Hockey: St. Catharines 1, St. Michael's 7; Nov. 26-30: Ice Capades; Dec. 1–NHL: Detroit 0, Leafs 4; Dec. 2–Jr. Hockey: St. Catharines 0, Jr. Marlboros 9; Dec. 2–Jr. Hockey: Hamilton 1, St. Michael's 4; Dec. 5–NHL: Canadiens 3, Leafs 1; Dec. 6–Wrestling: Edward Carpentier vs. Hardboiled Haggerty; Dec. 8–NHL: Rangers 0, Leafs 0; Dec. 9–Jr. Hockey: Peterborough 1, St. Michael's 6; Dec. 9–Jr. Hockey: Hamilton 2, Jr. Marlboros 2; Dec. 12–Greater Evangelistic Crusade of Toronto w/Billy Graham; Dec. 13–Wrestling: Mito/Moto vs. Yukon Eric/Managoff; Dec. 15–Jr. Hockey: Barrie 1, Jr. Marlboros 2; Dec. 15–Jr. Hockey: Guelph 5, St. Michael's 2; Dec. 15–NHL: Rangers 1, Leafs 2; Dec. 18–Jr. Hockey: Barrie 2, Jr. Marlboros 5; Dec. 18–Jr. Hockey: Hamilton 4, St. Michael's 2; Dec. 20–Wrestling: Whipper Billy Watson vs. Buddy Rogers; Dec. 22–Jr. Hockey: Peterborough 4, Jr. Marlboros 6; Dec. 22–Jr. Hockey: Barrie 2, St. Michael's 8; Dec. 22–NHL: Boston 3, Leafs 2; Dec. 26–NHL: Canadiens 0, Leafs 1; Dec. 27–Wrestling: Buddy Rogers vs. Whipper Billy Watson; Dec. 29–NHL: Chicago 3, Leafs 6; Dec. 30–Jr. Hockey: St. Catharines 4, St. Michael's 5; Dec. 30–Jr. Hockey: Guelph 0, Jr. Marlboros 1.

1957 • Jan. 2–NHL: Detroit 2, Leafs 0; Jan. 3–Wrestling: Whipper Billy Watson vs. Buddy Rogers; Jan. 5–NHL: Boston 2, Leafs 3; Jan. 6–Jr. Hockey: St. Catharines 1, Jr. Marlboros 3; Jan. 6–Jr. Hockey: Ottawa 4, St. Michael's 4 (Laurier Cup Series); Jan. 10–Wrestling: Watson/O'Connor vs. Rogers/Kiniski; Jan. 12–NHL: Chicago 3, Leafs 4; Jan. 13–Jr. Hockey: Guelph 2, St. Michael's 1; Jan. 13–Jr. Hockey: Barrie 1, Jr. Marlboros 5; Jan. 14–Boxing: George Chuvalo vs. Sid Russell; Jan. 16–NHL: Canadiens 3, Leafs 2; Jan. 17–Wrestling: Whipper Billy Watson vs. Gene Kiniski; Jan. 19–NHL: Boston 1, Leafs 4; Jan. 20–Jr. Hockey: Peterborough 4, St. Michael's 1; Jan. 20–Jr. Hockey: Hamilton 3, Jr. Marlboros 5; Jan. 23–NHL: Rangers 4, Leafs 4; Jan. 24–Wrestling: Whipper Billy Watson vs. Gene Kiniski; Jan. 26–NHL: Detroit 4, Leafs 1; Jan. 27–Jr. Hockey: St. Catharines 1, St. Michael's 9; Jan. 27–Jr. Hockey: Ottawa 0, Jr. Marlboros 4 (Laurier Cup Series); Jan. 28–Feb. 1: Ice Follies of 1957; Feb. 2–NHL: Chicago 3, Leafs 3; Feb. 3–Jr. Hockey: St. Catharines 0, Jr. Marlboros 1; Feb. 3–Jr. Hockey: Hamilton 3, St. Michael's 2; Feb. 6–NHL: Canadiens 1, Leafs 1; Feb. 7–Wrestling: Hutton/Kiniski vs. Watson/Yukon Eric; Feb. 9–NHL: Rangers 4, Leafs 4; Feb. 10–Jr. Hockey: Hamilton 0, Jr. Marlboros 2; Feb. 10–Jr. Hockey: Peterborough 3, St. Michael's 6; Feb. 11–Boxing: Newsboys International Tournament; Feb. 13–NHL: Boston 2, Leafs 2; Feb. 14–Wrestling: Watson/Yukon Eric vs. Miller Brothers; Feb. 16–NHL: Detroit 3, Leafs 1; Feb. 17–Jr. Hockey: Ottawa 0, St. Michael's 0 (Laurier Cup Series); Feb. 17–Jr. Hockey: Peterborough 1, Jr. Marlboros 5; Feb. 18–Music: Rock and Roll Show; Feb. 21–Wrestling: Miller Brothers vs. Watson/Yukon Eric; Feb. 23–NHL: Boston 5, Leafs 2; Feb. 24–Jr. Hockey: St. Catharines 4, St. Michael's 1; Feb. 24–Jr. Hockey: Guelph 2, Jr. Marlboros 2; Feb. 28–Wrestling: Watson/O'Connor vs. Miller Brothers; Mar. 2–NHL: Chicago 4, Leafs 3; Mar. 3–Jr. Hockey: Guelph 4, St. Michael's 1; Mar. 3–Jr. Hockey: Ottawa 0, Jr. Marlboros 0 (Laurier Cup Series); Mar. 4–Boxing: George Chuvalo vs. Walt Hafer; Mar. 5–Jr. Hockey: Hamilton 1, Jr. Marlboros 3; Mar. 6–NHL: Canadiens 1, Leafs 3; Mar. 7–Wrestling: Miller Brothers vs. Haggerty/Hutton; Mar. 9–Jr. Hockey: Hamilton 1, Jr. Marlboros 2; Mar. 9–NHL: Rangers 2, Leafs 1; Mar. 10–Jr. Hockey: Guelph 6, St. Michael's 4; Mar. 13–Jr. Hockey: St. Catharines 3, Jr. Marlboros 9; Mar. 14–Wrestling: Whipper Billy Watson vs. Gene Kiniski; Mar. 16–NHL: Rangers 1, Leafs 14; Mar. 17–Jr. Hockey: Guelph 5, St. Michael's 3; Mar. 18–Toronto Lions Club Boxing Show; Mar. 20–NHL: Canadiens 2, Leafs 1; Mar. 21–Wrestling: Whipper Billy Watson vs. Gene Kiniski; Mar. 23–NHL: Detroit 5, Leafs 3; Mar. 24–Jr. Hockey: St. Catharines 4, Jr. Marlboros 2; Mar. 25–Boxing: George Chuvalo vs. Moses Graham; Mar. 28–Wrestling: Kiniski/Hutton vs. Watson/O'Connor; Mar. 31–Sr. Hockey: Whitby 4, Kitchener-Waterloo 2 (OHA Sr. Finals); Apr. 1–Tennis: Ken Rosewall vs. Pancho Gonzales; Apr. 2–Music: Elvis Presley; Apr. 4–Wrestling: Kiniski/Hutton vs. Watson/O'Connor; Apr. 8–Sr. Hockey: Whitby 4, North Bay 2 (All-Ontario Sr. Finals); Apr. 10–Sr. Hockey: North Bay 7, Whitby 4 (All-Ontario Sr. Finals); Apr. 11–Wrestling: Watson/Farmer Boy vs. Kiniski/Hutton; Apr. 14–Variety: Timmy's Easter Parade of Stars w/Perry Como; Apr. 17–Sr. Hockey: North Bay 5, Whitby 2 (All-Ontario Sr. Finals); Apr. 18–Wrestling: Watson/Farmer Boy vs. Kiniski/Hutton; Apr. 20–Sr. Hockey: Whitby 7, North Bay 5 (All-Ontario Sr. Finals); Apr. 21–Boxing: George Chuvalo vs. Emil Brtko; Apr. 23–Sr. Hockey: Whitby 5, Spokane 2 (Allan Cup Finals); Apr. 25–Wrestling: Pat O'Connor vs. Gene Kiniski; Apr. 26–Sr. Hockey: Whitby 6, Spokane 3 (Allan Cup Finals); Apr. 28–Sr. Hockey: Whitby 7, Spokane 3 (Allan Cup Finals); Apr. 29–Music: Rock and Roll Show; Apr. 30–Sr. Hockey: Whitby 6, Spokane 2 (Allan Cup Finals); May 2–Wrestling: Pat O'Connor vs. Gene Kiniski; May 9–Wrestling: Watson/O'Connor vs. Miller Brothers; May 16–Wrestling: Lou Thesz vs. Gene Kiniski; May 23–Wrestling: Gene Kiniski vs. Whipper Billy Watson; May 25–Music: Pat Boone; May 27–Metropolitan Opera–Le Nozzi di Figaro; May 28–Metropolitan Opera–La Traviata; May 29–Metropolitan Opera–Il Travatore; May 30–Metropolitan Opera–Carmen; May 31–Metropolitan Opera–Tosca; June 1–Metropolitan Opera–La Boheme; June 4–Liberal Party Rally w/Louis St-Laurent; Sept. 3–Wrestling: Kiniski/Von Erich vs. O'Connor/Watson; Sept. 9–Boxing: Bob Baker vs. George Chuvalo; Sept. 10–Wrestling: Kiniski/Von Erich vs. O'Connor/Watson; Sept. 14–Music: Rock and Roll Show; Sept. 17–Wrestling: Kalmikoff Brothers vs. Heffernan/Costello; Sept. 24–Wrestling: Kalmikoff Brothers vs. Heffernan/Costello; Sept. 26–Music: Black Watch Regimental Band; Sept. 30–Oct. 5: Bob Morton's Rameses Shrine Circus; Oct. 10–Wrestling: Watson/O'Connor vs. Kalmikoff Brothers; Oct. 12–NHL: Detroit 5, Leafs 3; Oct. 17–Wrestling: Kalmikoff Brothers vs. Watson/O'Connor; Oct. 19–NHL: Boston 0, Leafs 7; Oct. 24–Wrestling: Kalmikoff Brothers vs. Watson/O'Connor; Oct. 26–NHL: Rangers 0, Leafs 3; Oct. 27–Jr. Hockey: Ottawa 2, Jr. Marlboros 3; Oct. 27–Jr. Hockey: St. Catharines 3, St. Michael's 1; Oct. 28–Basketball: Harlem Globetraotters 86, Washington 57; Oct. 30–NHL: Canadiens 6, Leafs 2; Oct. 31–Wrestling: Von Erich/Kiniski vs. Watson/O'Connor; Nov. 2–NHL: Chicago 3, Leafs 3; Nov. 3–Jr. Hockey: Hamilton 3, Jr. Marlboros 3; Nov. 3–Jr. Hockey: Guelph 1, St. Michael's 1; Nov. 6–NHL: Rangers 4, Leafs 2; Nov. 7–Wrestling: McClarity/Yukon Eric vs. Von Erich/Kiniski; Nov. 9–NHL: Detroit 3, Leafs 3; Nov. 10–Jr. Hockey: Peterborough 3, Jr. Marlboros 1; Nov. 10–Jr. Hockey: Hamilton 2, St. Michael's 5; Nov. 13–NHL: Canadiens 4, Leafs 2; Nov. 14–Wrestling: Dick Hutton vs. Lou Thesz; Nov. 16–NHL: Boston 4, Leafs 2; Nov. 17–Jr. Hockey: St. Catharines 2, Jr. Marlboros 2; Nov. 17–Jr. Hockey: Peterborough 3, St. Michael's 2; Nov. 19–Jr. Hockey: Jr. Marlboros 3, St. Michael's 1; Nov. 19–Jr. Hockey: Weston 7, St. Michael's "B" 2; Nov. 20–NHL: Chicago 1, Leafs 2; Nov. 21–Wrestling: Watson/Yukon Eric vs. Von Erich/Kiniski; Nov. 22–Int'l. Hockey: Moscow Selects 2, Whitby 7; Nov. 23–NHL: Detroit 2, Leafs 1; Nov. 24–Jr. Hockey: Barrie 2, St. Michael's 3; Nov. 24–Jr. Hockey: Hamilton 2, Jr. Marlboros 2; Nov. 25-28: Ice Capades; Nov. 30–Jr. Hockey: Hamilton 2, Jr. Marlboros 4; Nov. 30–Jr. Hockey: Peterborough 6, St. Michael's 0; Nov. 30–NHL: Boston 2, Leafs 3; Dec. 4–NHL: Canadiens 0, Leafs 0; Dec. 5–Wrestling: Dick Hutton vs. Yukon Eric; Dec. 7–NHL: Rangers 3, Leafs 3; Dec. 8–Jr. Hockey: Barrie 6, Jr. Marlboros 0; Dec. 8–Jr. Hockey: Guelph 3, St. Michael's 2; Dec. 9–Boxing: Arthur King vs. Yama Bahama; Dec. 12–Wrestling: Whipper Billy Watson vs. Gene Kiniski (Special Referee–Rocky Marciano); Dec. 14–NHL: Chicago 1, Leafs 4; Dec. 15–Jr. Hockey: St. Catharines 4, Jr. Marlboros 4; Dec. 15–Jr. Hockey: Hamilton 1, St. Michael's 2; Dec. 19–Wrestling: Watson/O'Connor vs. Von Erich/Kiniski; Dec. 21–NHL: Boston 3, Leafs 3; Dec. 22–Jr. Hockey: Guelph 2, Jr. Marlboros 2; Dec. 22–Jr. Hockey: St. Catharines 2, St. Michael's 3; Dec. 25–NHL: Canadiens 4, Leafs 5; Dec. 26–Wrestling: Whipper Billy Watson vs. Hardboiled Haggerty; Dec. 28–NHL: Rangers 1, Leafs 6; Dec. 29–Jr. Hockey: Peterborough 3, Jr. Marlboros 2; Dec. 29–Jr. Hockey: Barrie 2, St. Michael's 4.

1958 • Jan. 2–Wrestling: Watson/O'Connor vs. Miller Brothers; Jan. 4–NHL: Chicago 4, Leafs 2; Jan. 5–Jr. Hockey: Ottawa 4, St. Michael's 4 (Laurier Cup Series); Jan. 5–Jr. Hockey: Guelph 2, Jr. Marlboros 2; Jan. 9–Wrestling: Watson/O'Connor vs. Miller Brothers; Jan. 11–NHL: Boston 2, Leafs 2; Jan. 12–Jr. Hockey: St. Catharines 4, St. Michael's 0; Jan. 12–Jr. Hockey: Barrie 1, Jr. Marlboros 9; Jan. 13–Royal Ballet–Sleeping Beauty; Jan. 14–Royal Ballet–Swan Lake; Jan. 15–Royal Ballet–Petrouchka; Jan. 16–Wrestling: Dick Hutton vs. Whipper Billy Watson; Jan. 18–NHL: Detroit 1, Leafs 2; Jan. 19–Jr. Hockey: Guelph 1, St. Michael's 4; Jan. 19–Jr. Hockey: Peterborough 2, Jr. Marlboros 1; Jan. 20–Music: Rock and Roll Show w/Fats Domino; Jan. 22–NHL: Canadiens 2, Leafs 0; Jan. 23–Wrestling: Argentina Rocca vs. Gene Kiniski; Jan. 24–Hockey: UCC Old Boys 6, UCC New Boys 4; Jan. 25–NHL: Rangers 1, Leafs 7; Jan. 26–Jr. Hockey: Peterborough 3, St. Michael's 3; Jan. 26–Jr. Hockey: Hamilton 4, Jr. Marlboros 4; Jan. 27–Boxing: George Chuvalo vs. Julio Mederos; Jan. 28–Hockey: AP Green 4, Elmira 4; Jan. 28–Jr. Hockey: Jr. Marlboros 3, St. Michael's 2; Jan. 29–NHL: Chicago 4, Leafs 1; Jan. 30–Wrestling: Dick Hutton vs. Whipper Billy Watson; Feb. 1–NHL: Detroit 2, Leafs 9; Feb. 2–Jr. Hockey: Barrie 5, St. Michael's 7; Feb. 2–Jr. Hockey: Ottawa 4, Jr. Marlboros 4 (Laurier Cup Series); Feb. 3-7: Ice Follies of 1958; Feb. 8–NHL: Boston 7, Leafs 3; Feb. 9–Jr. Hockey: Guelph 3, Jr. Marlboros 10; Feb. 9–Jr. Hockey: St. Catharines 0, St. Michael's 2; Feb. 10–Newsboys International Boxing Tournament; Feb. 12–NHL: Canadiens 5, Leafs 2; Feb. 13–Wrestling: Watson/Yukon Eric vs. Von Erich/Kiniski; Feb. 15–NHL: Detroit 6, Leafs 3; Feb. 16–Jr. Hockey: Barrie 8, Jr. Marlboros 4; Feb. 16–Jr. Hockey: Ottawa 4, St. Michael's 2; Feb. 19–Jr. Hockey: St. Catharines 4, Jr. Marlboros 2; Feb. 20–Wrestling: Yukon Eric vs. Fritz Von Erich; Feb. 22–NHL: Chicago 1, Leafs 3; Feb. 23–Jr. Hockey: Barrie 4, Jr. Marlboros 6; Feb. 23–Jr. Hockey: Peterborough 6, St. Michael's 0; Feb. 25–Hockey: Williamson Road 6, Annette 2 (Schoolboy Finals); Feb. 26–Jr. Hockey: Peterborough 2, Jr. Marlboros 6; Feb. 26–Jr. Hockey: Barrie 2, St. Michael's 7; Feb. 27–Wrestling: Watson/O'Connor vs. Miller Brothers; Mar. 1–NHL: Rangers 5, Leafs 4; Mar. 2–Jr. Hockey: St. Catharines 3, Jr. Marlboros 1; Mar. 2–Jr. Hockey: Hamilton 3, St. Michael's 3; Mar. 4–Jr. Hockey: Barrie 4, St. Michael's 2; Mar. 5–NHL: Chicago 2, Leafs 5; Mar. 6–Wrestling: Watson/O'Connor vs. Miller Brothers; Mar. 8–Jr. Hockey: Barrie 3, St. Michael's 10; Mar. 8–NHL: Boston 3, Leafs 3; Mar. 9–Jr. Hockey: St. Catharines 2, Jr. Marlboros 1; Mar. 12–NHL: Canadiens 5, Leafs 3; Mar. 13–Wrestling: Watson/O'Connor vs. Miller Brothers; Mar. 15–NHL: Detroit 3, Leafs 1; Mar. 16–Jr. Hockey: St. Catharines 3, Jr. Marlboros 6; Mar. 17–Jr. Hockey: Hamilton 1, St. Michael's 7; Mar. 19–Jr. Hockey: St. Catharines 4, Jr. Marlboros 6; Mar. 20–Wrestling: Lisowski Brothers vs. Watson/Yukon Eric; Mar. 22–Jr. Hockey: Hamilton 4, St. Michael's 1; Mar. 22–NHL: Rangers 7, Leafs 0; Mar. 23–Jr. Hockey: St. Catharines 3, Jr. Marlboros 11; Mar. 27–Wrestling: Lisowski Brothers vs. Watson/Yukon Eric; Mar. 29–Jr. Hockey: Hamilton 3, Jr. Marlboros 6 (OHA "A" Finals); Mar. 30–Variety: Timmy's Easter Parade of Stars; Apr. 2–Jr.

Hockey: Hamilton 3, Jr. Marlboros 3 (OHA "A" Finals); Apr. 3–Wrestling: Lisowski Brothers vs. Miller Brothers; Apr. 10–Wrestling: Lisowski Brothers vs. Miller Brothers; Apr. 16–Jr. Hockey: Hull-Ottawa 1, Jr. Marlboros 3 (Memorial Cup Eastern Finals); Apr. 17–Wrestling: Watson/Synder vs. Lisowski Brothers; Apr. 20–Jr. Hockey: Hull-Ottawa 4, Jr. Marlboros 3 (Memorial Cup Eastern Finals); Apr. 21–Music: Rock and Roll Show; Apr. 22–Boxing: George Chuvalo vs. Howard King; Apr. 24–Wrestling: Watson/Synder vs. Lisowski Brothers; May 1–Wrestling: Lisowski Brothers vs. Watson/Synder; May 6–Tennis: Pancho Gonzales vs. Tony Trabert; May 8–Wrestling: Lisowski Brothers vs. Watson/Brazil; May 9-10: Moiseyen Dance Company; May 15–Wrestling: Lisowski Brothers vs. Yukon Eric/Synder; May 22–Wrestling: Watson/Brazil vs. Lisowski Brothers; May 26–Metropolitan Opera–Eugene Onegin; May 27–Metropolitan Opera–Madam Butterfly; May 28–Metropolitan Opera–The Barber of Seville; May 29–Metropolitan Opera–Samson and Delila; May 30–Metropolitan Opera–Aida; May 31–Metropolitan Opera–Faust; June 29–Baptist World Youth Conference; Sept. 2–Wrestling: Watson/Vignal vs. Miller Brothers; Sept. 9–Wrestling: Dick Hutton vs. Whipper Billy Watson; Sept. 15–Boxing: George Chuvalo vs. James J. Parker; Sept. 18–Wrestling: Whipper Billy Watson vs. Dara Singh; Sept. 24–Music: Grenadier Guards and Highland Dancers; Sept. 25–Wrestling: Whipper Billy Watson vs. Dara Singh; Sept. 29–Oct. 5: Bob Morton's Rameses Shrine Circus; Oct. 9–Wrestling: Kalmikoff Brothers vs. Watson/Vignal; Oct. 11–NHL: Chicago 3, Leafs 1; Oct. 16–Wrestling: Kalmikoff Brothers vs. Carpentier/Singh; Oct. 18–NHL: Boston 2, Leafs 3; Oct. 19–Jr. Hockey: Peterborough 0, Jr. Marlboros 1; Oct. 19–Jr. Hockey: St. Catharines 7, St. Michael's 5; Oct. 21–Music: Maria Callas; Oct. 23–Wrestling: Whipper Billy Watson vs. Gene Kiniski; Oct. 25–NHL: Detroit 0, Leafs 3; Oct. 26–Jr. Hockey: Guelph 1, St. Michael's 6; Oct. 26–Jr. Hockey: Barrie 0, Jr. Marlboros 2; Oct. 27–Basketball: Harlem Globetrotters 75, Philadelphia 64; Oct. 29–NHL: Canadiens 5, Leafs 0; Oct. 30–Wrestling: Dick Hutton vs. Whipper Billy Watson; Nov. 1–NHL: Rangers 3, Leafs 4; Nov. 2–Jr. Hockey: St. Catharines 5, Jr. Marlboros 1; Nov. 2–Jr. Hockey: Hamilton 1, St. Michael's 1; Nov. 3-7: Ice Capades; Nov. 8–NHL: Boston 3, Leafs 5; Nov. 9–Jr. Hockey: Peterborough 4, St. Michael's 0; Nov. 9–Jr. Hockey: Hamilton 2, Jr. Marlboros 4; Nov. 12–NHL: Canadiens 4, Leafs 1; Nov. 13–Wrestling: Watson/Yukon Eric vs. Kalmikoff Brothers; Nov. 15–NHL: Detroit 4, Leafs 1; Nov. 16–Jr. Hockey: Barrie 3, St. Michael's 7; Nov. 16–Jr. Hockey: St. Catharines 5, Jr. Marlboros 2; Nov. 20–Wrestling: Van Erlich/Hermann vs. Watson/Vignal; Nov. 22–NHL: Rangers 2, Leafs 2; Nov. 23–Jr. Hockey: Guelph 4, Jr. Marlboros 4; Nov. 23–Jr. Hockey: Peterborough 3, St. Michael's 4; Nov. 26–NHL: Detroit 5, Leafs 2; Nov. 27–Wrestling: Dick Hutton vs. Hombre Montana; Nov. 29–NHL: Chicago 2, Leafs 1; Nov. 30–Jr. Hockey: Hamilton 2, Jr. Marlboros 1; Nov. 30–Jr. Hockey: Peterborough 2, St. Michael's 2; Dec. 4–Wrestling: Watson/Yukon Eric vs. Von Erich/Hermann; Dec. 6–NHL: Boston 1, Leafs 4; Dec. 7–Jr. Hockey: Barrie 0, Jr. Marlboros 2; Dec. 7–Jr. Hockey: Hamilton 2, St. Michael's 5; Dec. 11–Wrestling: Kalmikoff Brothers vs. Von Erich/Hermann; Dec. 13–NHL: Rangers 4, Leafs 4; Dec. 14–Jr. Hockey: Peterborough 2, Jr. Marlboros 4; Dec. 14–Jr. Hockey: St. Catharines 2, St. Michael's 1; Dec. 18–Wrestling: Yukon Eric/Dassary vs. Von Erich/Hermann; Dec. 20–NHL: Boston 2, Leafs 2; Dec. 21–Jr. Hockey: Guelph 0, St. Michael's 5; Dec. 21–Jr. Hockey: Barrie 2, Jr. Marlboros 5; Dec. 26–Wrestling: Yukon Eric/Dassary vs. Von Erich/Kiniski; Dec. 27–NHL: Chicago 2, Leafs 2; Dec. 28–Jr. Hockey: Barrie 0, St. Michael's 2; Dec. 28–Jr. Hockey: Guelph 1, Jr. Marlboros 2; Dec. 31–NHL: Canadiens 0, Leafs 2.

1959 • Jan. 1–Wrestling: Kiniski/Von Erich vs. Dassary/Yukon Eric; Jan. 3–NHL: Chicago 2, Leafs 1; Jan. 4–Jr. Hockey: Barrie 3, Jr. Marlboros 2; Jan. 4–Jr. Hockey: Hamilton 2, St. Michael's 2; Jan. 5–Soccer: Hungarians 6, Tridents 3; Jan. 5–Soccer: Eagles 4, Ukrainians 2; Jan. 7–NHL: Detroit 1, Leafs 3; Jan. 8–Wrestling: Kiniski/Von Erich vs. Dassary/Yukon Eric; Jan. 10–NHL: Boston 1, Leafs 4; Jan. 11–Jr. Hockey: St. Catharines 4, St. Michael's 2; Jan. 11–Jr. Hockey: Hamilton 2, Jr. Marlboros 3; Jan. 12–Soccer: Ulster 8, Tridents 4; Jan. 12–Soccer: Hungarians 10, Olympia 1; Jan. 14–NHL: Rangers 3, Leafs 2; Jan. 15–Wrestling: Pat O'Connor vs. Lou Thesz; Jan. 17–NHL: Detroit 1, Leafs 2; Jan. 18–Jr. Hockey: St. Catharines 3, Jr. Marlboros 3; Jan. 18–Jr. Hockey: Guelph 4, St. Michael's 1; Jan. 21–NHL: Canadiens 1, Leafs 3; Jan. 22–Wrestling: Pat O'Connor vs. Lou Thesz; Jan. 24–NHL: Boston 3, Leafs 1; Jan. 25–Jr. Hockey: St. Catharines 4, St. Michael's 2; Jan. 25–Jr. Hockey: Guelph 7, Jr. Marlboros 1; Jan. 26–Music: The Biggest Show of Stars for 1959; Jan. 29–Wrestling: Pat O'Connor vs. Hans Schmidt; Jan. 31–NHL: Rangers 5, Leafs 2; Feb. 1–Jr. Hockey: Peterborough 4, Jr. Marlboros 4; Feb. 1–Jr. Hockey: St. Catharines 4, St. Michael's 2; Feb. 2-6: Ice Follies of 1959; Feb. 7–NHL: Detroit 1, Leafs 4; Feb. 8–Jr. Hockey: Barrie 0, St. Michael's 3; Feb. 8–Jr. Hockey: Hamilton 2, Jr. Marlboros 4; Feb. 11–NHL: Canadiens 5, Leafs 2; Feb. 12–Wrestling: Yukon Eric/Brazil vs. Kiniski/Von Erich; Feb. 14–NHL: Chicago 1, Leafs 5; Feb. 15–Jr. Hockey: St. Catharines 4, Jr. Marlboros 6; Feb. 15–Jr. Hockey: Guelph 2, St. Michael's 5; Feb. 16–Newsboys International Boxing Tournament; Feb. 19–Wrestling: Kiniski/Von Erich vs. Brazil/Wright; Feb. 21–NHL: Rangers 1, Leafs 1; Feb. 22–Jr. Hockey: Peterborough 5, St. Michael's 2; Feb. 22–Jr. Hockey: Hamilton 4, Jr. Marlboros 8; Feb. 25–NHL: Canadiens 2, Leafs 3; Feb. 26–Wrestling: Whipper Billy Watson vs. Gene Kiniski; Feb. 27–Hockey: Malvern 2, Northern 0 (Schoolboy Finals); Feb. 27–Hockey: Sr. Marlboros 2, Oakwood 1 (Schoolboy Finals); Feb. 28–NHL: Detroit 4, Leafs 2; Mar. 1–Jr. Hockey: Guelph 2, Jr. Marlboros 2; Mar. 1–Jr. Hockey: Barrie 3, St. Michael's 2; Mar. 4–NHL: Chicago 2, Leafs 5; Mar. 5–Wrestling: Pat O'Connor vs. Dick Hutton; Mar. 7–NHL: Boston 1, Leafs 4; Mar. 8–Jr. Hockey: St. Catharines 3, St. Michael's 2; Mar. 8–Jr. Hockey: Guelph 5, Jr. Marlboros 3; Mar. 10–Jr. Hockey: Guelph 3, Jr. Marlboros 2; Mar. 11–NHL: Canadiens 6, Leafs 2; Mar. 12–Wrestling: Whipper Billy Watson vs. Gorgeous George; Mar. 14–Jr. Hockey: St. Catharines 3, St. Michael's 5; Mar. 14–NHL: Rangers 0, Leafs 5; Mar. 19–Wrestling: Pat O'Connor vs. Ilio DiPaolo; Mar. 21–Jr. Hockey: St. Catharines 1, St. Michael's 1; Mar. 21–NHL: Chicago 1, Leafs 5; Mar. 22–Variety: Timmy's Easter Parade of Stars; Mar. 26–Wrestling: Whipper Billy Watson vs. Gorgeous George; Mar. 28–NHL: Boston 2, Leafs 3; Mar. 29–Jr. Hockey: Peterborough 1, St. Michael's 4 (OHA "A" Finals); Mar. 31–NHL: Boston 2, Leafs 3; Apr. 1–Jr. Hockey: Peterborough 1, St. Michael's 4 (OHA "A" Finals); Apr. 2–Wrestling: Kiniski/George vs. Watson/Brazil; Apr. 3–Sr. Hockey: Whitby 5, Kitchener-Waterloo 2 (All-Ontario Sr. Finals); Apr. 4–NHL: Boston 5, Leafs 4; Apr. 5–Jr. Hockey: Peterborough 1, St. Michael's 2 (OHA "A" Finals); Apr. 7–Sr. Hockey: Whitby 3, Kitchener-Waterloo 1 (All-Ontario Sr. Finals); Apr. 8–Jr. Hockey: Peterborough 4, St. Michael's 1; Apr. 9–Wrestling: Whipper Billy Watson vs. Gene Kiniski; Apr. 14–NHL: Canadiens 2, Leafs 3 (Stanley Cup Finals); Apr. 16–NHL: Canadiens 3, Leafs 2 (Stanley Cup Finals); Apr. 17–Wrestling: Whipper Billy Watson vs. Gene Kiniski; Apr. 19–Sr. Hockey: Whitby 5, Vernon 2 (Allan Cup Finals); Apr. 20–Tennis: Pancho Gonzales vs. Mal Anderson; Apr. 22–Sr. Hockey: Whitby 5, Vernon 2 (Allan Cup Finals); Apr. 23–Wrestling: Watson/Yukon Eric vs. Kiniski/George; Apr. 24–Sr. Hockey: Whitby 6, Vernon 2 (Allan Cup Finals); Apr. 25–Sr. Hockey: Vernon 3, Whitby 0 (Allan Cup Finals); Apr. 27–Boxing: Pan-American Games Try-Outs; Apr. 28–Music: Benny Goodman and his Orchestra; Apr. 29–Sr. Hockey: Whitby 9, Vernon 3 (Allan Cup Finals); Apr. 30–Wrestling: Whipper Billy Watson vs. Gene Kiniski; May 7–Wrestling: The Great Bobo vs. Whipper Billy Watson; May 14–Wrestling: Whipper Billy Watson vs. Bunny Dunlop; May 21–Wrestling: The Great Bobo vs. Yukon Eric; May 25–Metropolitan Opera–Tosca; May 26–Metropolitan Opera–Carmen; May 27–Metropolitan Opera–Pagliacci; May 28–Metropolitan Opera–Fledermaus; May 29–Metropolitan Opera–Rigoletto; May 30–Metropolitan Opera–Madam Butterfly; June 11–Bolshoi Ballet–Gisele; June 12–Bolshoi Ballet–Highlights; June 13–Bolshoi Ballet–Swan Lake; Aug. 25-27–Variety: Russian Festival of Music and Dance; Sept. 3–Wrestling: Yukon Eric vs. The Great Antonio; Sept. 10–Wrestling: Don Leo Jonathan vs. Edward Carpentier; Sept. 14–Boxing: George Chuvalo vs. Frankie Daniels; Sept. 17–Wrestling: Argentina Rocca vs. Hardboiled Haggerty; Sept. 21–Music: Dick Clark's Caravan of Stars; Sept. 24–Wrestling: Don Leo Jonathan vs. Whipper Billy Watson; Sept. 28–Oct. 3: Bob Morton's Rameses Shrine Circus; Oct. 8–Wrestling: Don Leo Jonathan vs. Whipper Billy Watson; Oct. 10–NHL: Chicago 3, Leafs 6; Oct. 15–Wrestling: Don Leo Jonathan vs. Sam Steamboat; Oct. 17–NHL: Boston 0, Leafs 3; Oct. 22–Wrestling: Don Leo Jonathan vs. Ilio DiPaolo; Oct. 24–NHL: Rangers 1, Leafs 1; Oct. 28–NHL: Canadiens 1, Leafs 1; Oct. 29–Wrestling: Jonathan/Kiniski vs. Watson/Yukon Eric; Oct. 31–NHL: Boston 3, Leafs 4; Nov. 1–Jr. Hockey: Peterborough 2, St. Michael's 4; Nov. 1–Jr. Hockey: Hamilton 1, Jr. Marlboros 5; Nov. 1–Jr. Hockey: Peterborough 2, St. Michael's 4; Nov. 1–Jr. Hockey: Hamilton 1, Jr. Marlboros 5; Nov. 2–Basketball: Harlem Globetrotters 76, San Francisco 60; Nov. 3–Jr. Hockey: St. Michael's 3, Jr. Marlboros 0; Nov. 3–Jr. Hockey: Jr. Marlboros 2, St. Michael's "B" 2; Nov. 3–Jr. Hockey: St. Michael's 3, Jr. Marlboros 0; Nov. 3–Jr. Hockey: St. Michael's "B" 5, Jr. Marlboros "B" 2; Nov. 4–NHL: Rangers 1, Leafs 4; Nov. 5–Wrestling: Jonathan/Kiniski vs. Watson/Thesz; Nov. 6–Jr. Hockey: Dixie 2, Jr. Marlboros "B" 6; Nov. 6–Jr. Hockey: Brampton 2, St. Michael's "B" 4; Nov. 6–Jr. Hockey: Dixie 2, Jr. Marlboros "B" 6; Nov. 6–Jr. Hockey: Brampton 2, St. Michael's "B" 4; Nov. 7–NHL: Detroit 2, Leafs 2; Nov. 8–Jr. Hockey: Guelph 4, Jr. Marlboros 4; Nov. 8–Jr. Hockey: St. Catharines 2, St. Michael's 3; Nov. 8–Jr. Hockey: St. Catharines 2, St. Michael's 3; Nov. 8–Jr. Hockey: Guelph 3, Jr. Marlboros 4; Nov. 9-13: Ice Capades featuring Ronnie "The Blur" Robertson; Nov. 14–NHL: Chicago 3, Leafs 3; Nov. 15–Jr. Hockey: Barrie 3, Jr. Marlboros 4; Nov. 15–Jr. Hockey: Hamilton 0, St. Michael's 3; Nov. 15–Jr. Hockey: Barrie 3, Jr. Marlboros 5; Nov. 15–Jr. Hockey: Hamilton 0, St. Michael's 3; Nov. 16–Jr. Hockey: Peterborough 5, Jr. Marlboros 7; Nov. 16–Jr. Hockey: Peterborough 5, Jr. Marlboros 7; Nov. 17–Boxing: George Chuvalo vs. Yvon Durelle; Nov. 18–NHL: Detroit 2, Leafs 3; Nov. 19–Wrestling: Jonathan/Kiniski vs. Kalmikoff Brothers; Nov. 20–Jr. Hockey: Aurora 2, St. Michael's "B" 5; Nov. 20–Jr. Hockey: St. Michael's 5, Jr. Marlboros 2; Nov. 21–NHL: Canadiens 4, Leafs 1; Nov. 22–Boxing: Floyd Patterson vs. George Chuvalo (closed circuit coverage); Nov. 22–Jr. Hockey: Barrie 3, St. Michael's 3; Nov. 22–Jr. Hockey: St. Catharines 2, Jr. Marlboros 2; Nov. 22–Jr. Hockey: Barrie 3, St. Michael's 3; Nov. 22–Jr. Hockey: St. Catharines 2, Jr. Marlboros 4; Nov. 23–Jr. Hockey: Woodbridge 8, Jr. Marlboros "B" 2; Nov. 23–Jr. Hockey: St. Michael's 2, Jr. Marlboros 9; Nov. 24–Jr. Hockey: Jr. Marlboros 9, St. Michael's 2; Nov. 24–Jr. Hockey: Aurora 3, St. Michael's "B" 5; Nov. 26-27: Polish State Folk Ballet; Nov. 28–NHL: Boston 2, Leafs 2; Nov. 29–Jr. Hockey: Peterborough 1, Jr. Marlboros 7; Nov. 29–Jr. Hockey: Guelph 1, St. Michael's 1; Dec. 1–Jr. Hockey: Guelph 6, Jr. Marlboros 3; Dec. 1–Jr. Hockey: Guelph 6, Jr. Marlboros 3; Dec. 2–NHL: Canadiens 0, Leafs 1; Dec. 3–Wrestling: Jonathan/Kiniski vs. Watson/Yukon Eric; Dec. 4–Jr. Hockey: Unionville 3, St. Michael's "B" 5; Dec. 4–Jr. Hockey: Aurora 5, Jr. Marlboros "B" 5; Dec. 5–Jr. Hockey: Peterborough 3, St. Michael's 4; Dec. 5–Jr. Hockey: Brockville 4, Jr. Marlboros 1; Dec. 5–NHL: Rangers 3, Leafs 6; Dec. 6–Jr. Hockey: Peterborough 1, St. Michael's 4; Dec. 6–Jr. Hockey: Hull-Ottawa 4, Jr. Marlboros 1 (Laurier Cup Series); Dec. 8–Jr. Hockey: Lakeshore 2, St. Michael's "B" 5; Dec. 8–Jr. Hockey: St. Michael's 0, Jr. Marlboros 2; Dec. 8–Jr. Hockey: Jr. Marlboros 2, St. Michael's 0; Dec. 8–Jr. Hockey: Lakeshore 2, St. Michael's "B" 3; Dec. 10–Wrestling: Jonathan/Kiniski vs. Watson/DiPaolo; Dec. 11–Jr. Hockey: Unionville 1, Jr. Marlboros "B" 5; Dec. 11–Jr. Hockey: Dixie 7, St. Michael's "B" 3; Dec. 11–Jr. Hockey: Unionville 3, St. Michael's "B" 8; Dec. 11–Jr. Hockey: Barrie "B" 2, Jr. Marlboros "B" 4; Dec. 12–NHL: Chicago 4, Leafs 2; Dec. 13–Jr. Hockey: Hamilton 1, Jr. Marlboros 5; Dec. 13–Jr. Hockey: Barrie 3, St. Michael's 2; Dec. 13–Jr. Hockey: Hamilton 1, Jr. Marlboros 5; Dec. 13–Jr. Hockey: Barrie 3, St. Michael's 2; Dec. 17–Wrestling: Watson/DiPaolo vs. Jonathan/Kiniski; Dec. 18–Jr. Hockey: Lakeshore 1, Jr. Marlboros "B" 4; Dec. 18–Jr. Hockey: Unionville 3, St. Michael's "B" 5; Dec. 19–NHL: Detroit 2, Leafs 4; Dec. 20–Jr. Hockey: Guelph 3, Jr. Marlboros 8; Dec. 20–Jr. Hockey: St. Catharines 2, St. Michael's 2; Dec. 26–NHL: Rangers 0, Leafs 4; Dec. 27–Jr. Hockey: Hamilton 5, St. Michael's 2; Dec. 27–Jr. Hockey: St. Catharines 5, Jr. Marlboros 2; Dec. 29–Jr. Hockey: Jr. Marlboros "B" 5, St. Michael's "B" 4; Dec. 29–Jr. Hockey: St. Michael's 3, Jr. Marlboros 5; Dec. 30–NHL: Canadiens 3, Leafs 2; Dec. 31–Wrestling: Watson/DiPaolo vs. Jonathan/Kiniski.

1960 • Jan. 2–NHL: Chicago 4, Leafs 2; Jan. 3–Jr. Hockey: Guelph 0, St. Michael's 4; Jan. 3–Jr. Hockey: Peterborough 4, Jr. Marlboros 3; Jan. 6–NHL: Detroit 1, Leafs 3; Jan. 7–Wrestling: Gene Kiniski vs. Ilio DiPaolo; Jan. 9–NHL: Boston 3, Leafs 2; Jan. 10–Jr. Hockey: Barrie 2, Jr. Marlboros 6; Jan. 10–Jr. Hockey: Peterborough 2, St. Michael's 4; Jan. 12–Jr. Hockey: Barrie 5, St. Michael's 0; Jan. 12–Jr. Hockey: Hamilton 1, Jr. Marlboros 5; Jan. 14–Wrestling: Watson/DiPaolo vs. Kiniski/Jonathan; Jan. 16–NHL: Rangers 1, Leafs 3; Jan. 17–Jr. Hockey: Hamilton 0, St. Michael's 3; Jan. 17–Jr. Hockey: Brockville 4, Jr. Marlboros "B" 1; Jan. 18–Jr. Hockey: Jr. Marlboros 4, St. Michael's 4; Jan. 19–Hockey: Whitby 9, Moscow 1; Jan. 21–Wrestling: Watson/DiPaolo vs. Kalmikoff Brothers; Jan. 22–Hockey: UCC Old Boys, UCC New Boys; Jan. 23–NHL: Boston 3, Leafs 3; Jan. 24–Jr. Hockey: Guelph 0, Jr. Marlboros 3; Jan. 24–Jr. Hockey: St. Catharines 3, St. Michael's 0; Jan. 25–Music: The Biggest Show of Stars for 1960; Jan. 26–Jr. Hockey: Jr. Marlboros 5, St. Michael's 3; Jan. 27–NHL: Chicago 1, Leafs 2; Jan. 28–Wrestling: Watson/DiPaolo vs. Von Erich/Jonathan; Jan. 30–NHL: Rangers 2, Leafs 3; Jan. 31–Jr. Hockey: Barrie 0, St. Michael's 4; Jan. 31–Jr. Hockey: St. Catharines 3, Jr. Marlboros 3; Feb. 1-5: Ice Follies of 1960; Feb. 6–NHL: Detroit 4, Leafs 6; Feb. 7–Jr. Hockey: Hamilton 2, Jr. Marlboros 7; Feb. 7–Jr. Hockey: Guelph 2, St. Michael's 4; Feb. 9–Music: Moscow State Symphony; Feb. 10–NHL: Canadiens 4, Leafs 2; Feb. 11–Wrestling: Watson/DiPaolo vs. Kalmikoff Brothers; Feb. 13–NHL: Detroit 1, Leafs 7; Feb. 14–Jr. Hockey: Peterborough 8, St. Michael's 2; Feb. 14–Jr. Hockey: St. Catharines 9, Jr. Marlboros 2; Feb. 15–Tennis: Pancho Gonzales vs. Alex Omedeo; Feb. 17–NHL: Boston 1, Leafs 3; Feb. 18–Wrestling: Watson/DiPaolo vs. Kalmikoff Brothers; Feb. 20–NHL: Chicago 1, Leafs 3; Feb. 21–Jr. Hockey: St. Catharines 0, St. Michael's 5; Feb. 21–Jr. Hockey: Peterborough 2, Jr. Marlboros 7; Feb. 22–Toronto Police Concert; Feb. 23–Music: Fred Waring; Feb. 24–NHL: Canadiens 1, Leafs 3; Feb. 25–Wrestling: Whipper Billy Watson vs. Don Leo Jonathan; Feb. 27–NHL: Detroit 4, Leafs 3; Feb. 28–Jr.

Hockey: Barrie 0, Jr. Marlboros 6; Feb. 28–Jr. Hockey: Guelph 7, St. Michael's 6; Feb. 29–Hockey: Blythwood 3, Kew Beach 2 (Schoolboy Finals); Feb. 29–Hockey: Earl Haig 5, Brock 2 (Schoolboy Finals); Mar. 2–Jr. Hockey: St. Michael's 7, Jr. Marlboros 4; Mar. 3–Wrestling: Watson/DiPaolo vs. Kalmikoff Brothers; Mar. 4–Int'l. Hockey: Czech National Team 2, Whitby 6; Mar. 5–NHL: Boston 5, Leafs 5; Mar. 6–Jr. Hockey: St. Michael's 3, Jr. Marlboros 2; Mar. 9–NHL: Canadiens 9, Leafs 4; Mar. 10–Wrestling: Don Leo Jonathan vs. Lou Thesz; Mar. 11–Jr. Hockey: St. Michael's 3, Jr. Marlboros 2; Mar. 12–NHL: Rangers 4, Leafs 1; Mar. 13–Jr. Hockey: St. Michael's 4, Jr. Marlboros 3; Mar. 16-18–Variety: Timmy's Easter Parade of Stars; Mar. 19–NHL: Chicago 0, Leafs 1; Mar. 23–NHL: Detroit 2, Leafs 1; Mar. 24–Wrestling: Kalmikoff Brothers vs. DiPaolo/Brazil; Mar. 26–NHL: Detroit 2, Leafs 4; Mar. 27–Jr. Hockey: St. Catharines 6, St. Michael's 4 (OHA "A" Finals); Mar. 31–Wrestling: Kalmikoff Brothers vs. Gallagher Brothers; Apr. 2–NHL: Detroit 4, Leafs 5; Apr. 3–Jr. Hockey: St. Catharines 3, St. Michael's 3 (OHA "A" Finals); Apr. 6–Jr. Hockey: St. Catharines 7, St. Michael's 2 (OHA "A" Finals); Apr. 8–Wrestling: Lou Thesz vs. Don Leo Jonathan; Apr. 12–NHL: Canadiens 5, Leafs 2 (Stanley Cup Finals); Apr. 14–NHL: Canadiens 4, Leafs 0 (Stanley Cup-winning game); Apr. 17–Jr. Hockey: Brockville 4, St. Catharines 3 (Memorial Cup Eastern Finals); Apr. 21–Wrestling: Watson/DiPaolo vs. Kalmikoff Brothers; Apr. 22–Jr. Hockey: Brockville 3, St. Catharines 3 (Memorial Cup Eastern Finals); Apr. 28–Wrestling: Whipper Billy Watson vs. Fritz Von Erich; Apr. 29–Jr. Hockey: Edmonton 2, St. Catharines 6 (Memorial Cup Finals); May 1–Jr. Hockey: Edmonton 1, St. Catharines 9 (Memorial Cup Finals); May 2–Boxing: Lions Club Amateur Tournament; May 3–Jr. Hockey: Edmonton 9, St. Catharines 3 (Memorial Cup Finals); May 5–Wrestling: Whipper Billy Watson vs. Frtiz Von Erich; May 6–Jr. Hockey: Edmonton 6, St. Catharines 9 (Memorial Cup Finals); May 8–Jr. Hockey: Edmonton 3, St. Catharines 7 (Memorial Cup Finals); May 13-14: Georgian State Dance Company; May 30–Metropolitan Opera–Il Travatore; May 31–Metropolitan Opera–The Gypsy Baron; June 1–Metropolitan Opera–Andrea Chenier; June 2–Metropolitan Opera–Faust; June 3–Metropolitan Opera–La Traviata; Sept. 19–Music: The Biggest Show of Stars for 1960; Sept. 26–Oct. 1: Hamid-Morton Circus; Oct. 8–NHL: Rangers 5, Leafs 2; Oct. 12–Music: Count Basie and Stan Kenton; Oct. 15–NHL: Boston 1, Leafs 1; Oct. 19–NHL: Canadiens 1, Leafs 3; Oct. 22–NHL: Detroit 2, Leafs 1; Oct. 29–NHL: Chicago 4, Leafs 8; Oct. 30–Jr. Hockey: Niagara Falls 4, Jr. Marlboros 1; Oct. 30–Jr. Hockey: Hamilton 4, St. Michael's 3; Oct. 31–Music: Fabian and Brenda Lee; Nov. 2–Jr. Hockey: St. Michael's, Jr. Marlboros; Nov. 2–NHL: Boston 2, Leafs 2; Nov. 5–NHL: Rangers 3, Leafs 7; Nov. 6–Jr. Hockey: St. Catharines, Jr. Marlboros; Nov. 6–Jr. Hockey: Peterborough, St. Michael's; Nov. 7-11: Ice Capades; Nov. 12–NHL: Chicago 1, Leafs 7; Nov. 13–Jr. Hockey: Hamilton, Jr. Marlboros; Nov. 13–Jr. Hockey: Niagara Falls, St. Michael's; Nov. 16–NHL: Detroit 3, Leafs 3; Nov. 19–NHL: Canadiens 3, Leafs 6; Nov. 20–Jr. Hockey: Guelph, Jr. Marlboros; Nov. 20–Jr. Hockey: St. Catharines, St. Michael's; Nov. 26–NHL: Detroit 3, Leafs 3; Nov. 27–Jr. Hockey: Peterborough 4, Jr. Marlboros 6; Nov. 27–Jr. Hockey: Hamilton, St. Michael's; Dec. 3–NHL: Rangers 2, Leafs 5; Dec. 4–Jr. Hockey: St. Catharines, Jr. Marlboros; Dec. 4–Jr. Hockey: Niagara Falls, St. Michael's; Dec. 7–Jr. Hockey: Guelph, Jr. Marlboros; Dec. 7–NHL: Canadiens 6, Leafs 2; Dec. 10–NHL: Chicago 2, Leafs 5; Dec. 11–Jr. Hockey: Niagara Falls, Jr. Marlboros; Dec. 11–Jr. Hockey: Guelph, St. Michael's; Dec. 16–Jr. Hockey: St. Michael's, Jr. Marlboros; Dec. 17–NHL: Boston 3, Leafs 3; Dec. 18–Jr. Hockey: Hamilton, Jr. Marlboros; Dec. 18–Jr. Hockey: Peterborough, St. Michael's; Dec. 24–NHL: Detroit 4, Leafs 4; Dec. 25–Jr. Hockey: Guelph, Jr. Marlboros; Dec. 25–Jr. Hockey: Niagara Falls, St. Michael's; Dec. 28–NHL: Canadiens 4, Leafs 1; Dec. 30–Jr. Hockey: St. Michael's, Jr. Marlboros; Dec. 31–NHL: Rangers 1, Leafs 2.

1961 • Jan. 1–Jr. Hockey: Peterborough, Jr. Marlboros; Jan. 1–Jr. Hockey: St. Catharines, St. Michael's; Jan. 2-6–Variety: Kiwanis International Show; Jan. 4–NHL: Detroit 4, Leafs 6; Jan. 7–NHL: Boston 1, Leafs 4; Jan. 8–Jr. Hockey: Niagara Falls, Jr. Marlboros; Jan. 8–Jr. Hockey: Hamilton, St. Michael's; Jan. 13–Jr. Hockey: St. Michael's, Jr. Marlboros; Jan. 14–NHL: Chicago 1, Leafs 4; Jan. 15–Jr. Hockey: St. Catharines, Jr. Marlboros; Jan. 15–Jr. Hockey: Guelph, St. Michael's; Jan. 18–Jr. Hockey: St. Michael's, Jr. Marlboros; Jan. 18–NHL: Rangers 4, Leafs 4; Jan. 21–NHL: Boston 3, Leafs 1; Jan. 22–Jr. Hockey: Peterborough, St. Michael's; Jan. 25–NHL: Canadiens 3, Leafs 5; Jan. 28–NHL: Chicago 1, Leafs 2; Jan. 29–Jr. Hockey: Hamilton, Jr. Marlboros; Jan. 29–Jr. Hockey: Niagara Falls, St. Michael's; Jan. 30–Feb. 4: Ice Follies of 1961; Feb. 4–NHL: Detroit 2, Leafs 4; Feb. 5–Jr. Hockey: Peterborough, Jr. Marlboros; Feb. 5–Jr. Hockey: St. Catharines, St. Michael's; Feb. 8–NHL: Rangers 3, Leafs 5; Feb. 11–NHL: Boston 3, Leafs 6; Feb. 12–Jr. Hockey: St. Catharines, Jr. Marlboros; Feb. 12–Jr. Hockey: Hamilton, St. Michael's; Feb. 15–Jr. Hockey: St. Michael's, Jr. Marlboros; Feb. 15–NHL: Canadiens 3, Leafs 1; Feb. 18–NHL: Chicago 2, Leafs 5; Feb. 19–Jr. Hockey: Niagara Falls, Jr. Marlboros; Feb. 19–Jr. Hockey: Peterborough, St. Michael's; Feb. 24–Hockey: Malvern 6, Western 1 (Schoolboy Finals); Feb. 24–Jr. Hockey: St. Michael's, Jr. Marlboros; Feb. 25–NHL: Detroit 1, Leafs 3; Feb. 26–Jr. Hockey: Peterborough 1, Jr. Marlboros 0; Feb. 26–Jr. Hockey: St. Catharines 3, St. Michael's 1; Mar. 1–NHL: Canadiens 1, Leafs 3; Mar. 2–Wrestling: Whipper Billy Watson vs. Lou Thesz; Mar. 4–NHL: Rangers 4, Leafs 5; Mar. 5–Jr. Hockey: Guelph 4, St. Michael's 4; Mar. 5–Jr. Hockey: Hamilton 4, Jr. Marlboros 2; Mar. 8–Jr. Hockey: St. Catharines 3, St. Michael's 1; Mar. 9–Wrestling: Gene Kiniski vs. Primo Carnera; Mar. 11–NHL: Chicago 2, Leafs 2; Mar. 12–Jr. Hockey: St. Catharines 3, St. Michael's 4; Mar. 13–Boxing: Don Ross vs. Joey Durelle w/Patterson vs. Johansson (Live and closed circuit coverage); Mar. 15–Jr. Hockey: St. Catharines 2, St. Michael's 8; Mar. 16–Wrestling: Gene Kiniski vs. Farmer Boy; Mar. 17–Jr. Hockey: St. Catharines 1, St. Michael's 4; Mar. 18–Jr. Hockey: Hamilton 2, St. Michael's 6; Mar. 18–NHL: Boston 2, Leafs 6; Mar. 22–NHL: Detroit 2, Leafs 3; Mar. 23–Wrestling: Gene Kiniski vs. Tom Jones; Mar. 25–Jr. Hockey: Hamilton 1, St. Michael's 5; Mar. 25–NHL: Detroit 4, Leafs 2; Mar. 26-28–Variety: Timmy's Easter Parade of Stars; Mar. 27–Boxing: George Chuvalo vs. Alex Miteff; Mar. 29–Jr. Hockey: Hamilton 3, St. Michael's 3; Mar. 30–Wrestling: Whipper Billy Watson vs. Gorgeous George; Apr. 1–NHL: Detroit 3, Leafs 2; Apr. 2–Jr. Hockey: Hamilton 3, St. Michael's 5; Apr. 6–Wrestling: Whipper Billy Watson vs. Stan Stasiak; Apr. 9–Jr. Hockey: Guelph 3, St. Michael's 6 (OHA "A" Finals); Apr. 11–Jr. Hockey: Guelph 1, St. Michael's 5 (OHA "A" Finals); Apr. 13–Wrestling: Whipper Billy Watson vs. Stan Stasiak; Apr. 16–Jr. Hockey: Guelph 4, St. Michael's 7 (OHA "A" Finals); Apr. 19–Jr. Hockey: Moncton 2, St. Michael's 11 (Memorial Cup Eastern Finals); Apr. 20–Wrestling: Athol Layton vs. Gene Kiniski; Apr. 21–Jr. Hockey: Moncton 2, St. Michael's 6 (Memorial Cup Eastern Finals); Apr. 23–Jr. Hockey: Moncton 2, St. Michael's 11 (Memorial Cup Eastern Finals); Apr. 27–Wrestling: Kalmikoff Brothers vs. Watson/Campbell; Apr. 29–Tennis: Barry MacKay vs. Frank Sedgman; May 4–Wrestling: Whipper Billy Watson vs. Gorgeous George; May 26-27: Moiseyev Dance Company; May 30–June 3: Ringling Brothers/Barnum & Bailey Circus; June 22–Wrestling: Bulldog Brower vs. Man Mountain Campbell; June 27–Boxing: George Chuvalo vs. Willi Besmanoff; July 2-6–Music: Kiwanis International Convention; Aug. 25-31–Variety: Russian Festival of Music and Dance; Sept. 2–Music: Latvian Song Festival; Sept. 7–Wrestling: Bulldog Brower vs. Whipper Billy Watson; Sept. 14–Wrestling: Bulldog Brower vs. Whipper Billy Watson; Sept. 18–Music: The Biggest Show of Stars for 1961; Sept. 21–Wrestling: Bulldog Brower vs. Killer Kowalski; Sept. 28–Wrestling: Bulldog Brower vs. Gene Kiniski; Oct. 2–Boxing: Joe Erskine vs. George Chuvalo; Oct. 5–Wrestling: Bulldog Brower vs. Gene Kiniski; Oct. 8–Music: Dick Clark's Caravan of Stars; Oct. 12–Wrestling: Bulldog Brower vs. Yukon Eric; Oct. 14–NHL: Boston 2, Leafs 3; Oct. 19–Wrestling: Bulldog Brower vs. Stan Stasiak; Oct. 21–NHL: Chicago 1, Leafs 1; Oct. 22-25: Leningrad Kirov Ballet; Oct. 26–Wrestling: Bulldog Brower vs. Whipper Billy Watson; Oct. 28–NHL: Rangers 1, Leafs 5; Nov. 1–NHL: Canadiens 2, Leafs 3; Nov. 2–Wrestling: Brower vs. Yukon Eric; Watson vs. Taro Sakura; Nov. 4–NHL: Chicago 1, Leafs 2; Nov. 5–Jr. Hockey: Whitby 2, Jr. Marlboros 5; Nov. 5–Jr. Hockey: Peterborough 3, St. Michael's 4; Nov. 6-10: Ice Capades; Nov. 11–NHL: Detroit 1, Leafs 5; Nov. 12–Jr. Hockey: Brampton 2, St. Michael's 5; Nov. 12–Jr. Hockey: Niagara Falls 4, Jr. Marlboros 4; Nov. 15–NHL: Canadiens 2, Leafs 3; Nov. 16–Wrestling: Whipper Billy Watson vs. Buddy Rogers; Nov. 18–NHL: Detroit 1, Leafs 6; Nov. 19–Jr. Hockey: Unionville 2, Jr. Marlboros 2; Nov. 19–Jr. Hockey: Hamilton 4, St. Michael's 2; Nov. 23–Wrestling: Bulldog Brower vs. Whipper Billy Watson; Nov. 25–NHL: Rangers 0, Leafs 6; Nov. 26–Jr. Hockey: Whitby 0, St. Michael's 6; Nov. 26–Jr. Hockey: Guelph 3, Jr. Marlboros 2; Nov. 29–NHL: Canadiens 2, Leafs 2; Nov. 30–Wrestling: Bulldog Brower vs. Yukon Eric; Dec. 2–NHL: Chicago 4, Leafs 6; Dec. 3–Jr. Hockey: Brampton 4, Jr. Marlboros 6; Dec. 3–Jr. Hockey: St. Catharines 1, St. Michael's 3; Dec. 4–Boxing: Floyd Patterson vs. Tom McNeeley; Dec. 7–Wrestling: Lord Athol Layton vs. Taro Sakuro; Dec. 9–NHL: Boston 2, Leafs 9; Dec. 10–Jr. Hockey: Unionville 2, St. Michael's 7; Dec. 10–Jr. Hockey: Hamilton 2, Jr. Marlboros 5; Dec. 12-13–Variety: Mazowsze Song and Dance Company; Dec. 14–Wrestling: Brower/Sakuro vs. Watson/Yukon Eric; Dec. 16–NHL: Rangers 2, Leafs 4; Dec. 17–Jr. Hockey: Unionville 0, Jr. Marlboros 5; Dec. 17–Jr. Hockey: Guelph 7, St. Michael's 2; Dec. 23–NHL: Boston 7, Leafs 4; Dec. 24–Jr. Hockey: Brampton 3, St. Michael's 4; Dec. 24–Jr. Hockey: Whitby 1, Jr. Marlboros 1; Dec. 27–NHL: Chicago 0, Leafs 0; Dec. 28–Wrestling: Bulldog Brower vs. Taro Sakuro; Dec. 28–Wrestling: Whipper Billy Watson/Yukon Eric vs. Tolos Brothers; Dec. 30–NHL: Detroit 4, Leafs 6; Dec. 31–Jr. Hockey: Unionville 3, Jr. Marlboros 3; Dec. 31–Jr. Hockey: Montreal 3, St. Michael's 3.

1962 • Jan. 3–NHL: Canadiens 1, Leafs 3; Jan. 4–Wrestling: The Brute vs. Bulldog Brower; Jan. 6–NHL: Chicago 3, Leafs 6; Jan. 7–Jr. Hockey: Brampton 1, St. Michael's 6; Jan. 7–Jr. Hockey: Peterborough 5, Jr. Marlboros 2; Jan. 10–NHL: Boston 5, Leafs 7; Jan. 11–Wrestling: Tolos Brothers vs. Whipper Billy Watson and Yukon Eric; Jan. 13–NHL: Detroit 3, Leafs 4; Jan. 14–Jr. Hockey: Whitby 0, Jr. Marlboros 5; Jan. 14–Jr. Hockey: Niagara Falls 2, St. Michael's 3; Jan. 17–NHL: Rangers 2, Leafs 4; Jan. 18–Wrestling: Whipper Billy Watson and the Brute vs. Tolos Brothers; Jan. 20–NHL: Boston 5, Leafs 4; Jan. 21–Jr. Hockey: Brampton 2, Jr. Marlboros 3; Jan. 21–Jr. Hockey: Whitby 3, St. Michael's 6; Jan. 25–Wrestling: Whipper Billy Watson and the Brute vs. Tolos Brothers; Jan. 27–NHL: Detroit 2, Leafs 4; Jan. 28–Jr. Hockey: Unionville 0, St. Michael's 4; Jan. 28–Jr. Hockey: St. Catharines 4, Jr. Marlboros 2; Jan. 29–Feb. 2: Ice Follies of 1962; Feb. 3–NHL: Rangers 1, Leafs 4; Feb. 4–Jr. Hockey: Whitby 1, St. Michael's 4; Feb. 4–Jr. Hockey: Brampton 3, Jr. Marlboros 3; Feb. 7–NHL: Boston 2, Leafs 2; Feb. 8–Wrestling: Buddy Rogers vs. Bulldog Brower; Feb. 10–NHL: Canadiens 4, Leafs 2; Feb. 11–Jr. Hockey: Unionville 1, St. Michael's 5; Feb. 11–Jr. Hockey: Montreal 5, Jr. Marlboros 3; Feb. 15–Wrestling: Buddy Rogers vs. Bulldog Brower; Feb. 16–Hockey: Malvern 10, Humberside 2 (Schoolboy Finals); Feb. 17–NHL: Rangers 3, Leafs 5; Feb. 18–Jr. Hockey: Brampton 1, St. Michael's 7; Feb. 18–Jr. Hockey: Whitby 1, Jr. Marlboros 6; Feb. 19–Music: Chubby Checker; Feb. 21–NHL: Canadiens 4, Leafs 2; Feb. 22–Wrestling: Bulldog Brower vs. Giant Jim Hady; Feb. 24–NHL: Boston 2, Leafs 7; Feb. 25–Jr. Hockey: Jr. Marlboros 5, St. Michael's 4; Feb. 25–Jr. Hockey: Brampton 3, Unionville 1; Feb. 28–NHL: Chicago 2, Leafs 4; Mar. 1–Wrestling: Buddy Rogers vs. Bulldog Brower; Mar. 3–Hockey: Parks & Rec Hockey Championships; Mar. 3–NHL: Rangers 1, Leafs 3; Mar. 4–Jr. Hockey: Whitby 0, Jr. Marlboros 5; Mar. 4–Jr. Hockey: Unionville 6, St. Michael's 1; Mar. 6–Hockey: Public School Hockey Championships (Schoolboy Finals); Mar. 7–Jr. Hockey: Brampton 1, Jr. Marlboros 4; Mar. 8–Wrestling: Watson/The Brute vs. the Tolos Brothers; Mar. 9–Jr. Hockey: Whitby 2, St. Michael's 8; Mar. 10–NHL: Detroit 0, Leafs 2; Mar. 11–Jr. Hockey: Brampton 3, Jr. Marlboros 9; Mar. 11–Jr. Hockey: Whitby 1, St. Michael's 3; Mar. 14–NHL: Canadiens 2, Leafs 5; Mar. 15–Wrestling: Bulldog Brower vs. Edouard Carpentier; Mar. 17–NHL: Chicago 3, Leafs 1; Mar. 18–Jr. Hockey: Jr. Marlboros 4, St. Michael's 2; Mar. 21–Music: An Evening with Gershwin; Mar. 22–Wrestling: Tolos Brothers vs. Watson/Lyons; Mar. 23–Jr. Hockey: Jr. Marlboros 3, St. Michael's 7; Mar. 24–NHL: Detroit 2, Leafs 2; Mar. 25–Jr. Hockey: Jr. Marlboros 8, St. Michael's 3; Mar. 26–Jr. Hockey: Jr. Marlboros 5, St. Michael's 2; Mar. 27–NHL: Rangers 2, Leafs 4; Mar. 29–NHL: Rangers 1, Leafs 2; Mar. 29–Wrestling: Watson/Lyons vs. Tolos Brothers; Mar. 31–Jr. Hockey: Jr. Marlboros 1, St. Michael's 5; Apr. 1–Jr. Hockey: Jr. Marlboros 2, St. Michael's 5; Apr. 3–Jr. Hockey: Jr. Marlboros 1, St. Michael's 3; Apr. 5–NHL: Rangers 2, Leafs 3; Apr. 5–Wrestling: Siki/Brower vs. Watson/Lyons; Apr. 7–NHL: Rangers 1, Leafs 7; Apr. 8–Jr. Hockey: Hamilton 5, St. Michael's 1; Apr. 10–NHL: Chicago 1, Leafs 4 (Stanley Cup Finals); Apr. 12–NHL: Chicago 2, Leafs 3 (Stanley Cup Finals); Apr. 13–Jr. Hockey: Hamilton 10, St. Michael's 3; Apr. 15–Variety: Timmy's Easter Parade of Stars; Apr. 18–Wrestling: Siki/Brower vs. Watson/Lyons; Apr. 19–NHL: Chicago 4, Leafs 8 (Stanley Cup Finals); Apr. 25-28–Ice Show: Rotary Club Ice Revue of 1962; May 25-26–Music: Ukrainian Dance Company; May 27–Rotary Musical Concert; May 29–June 3: Ringling Brothers/Barnum & Bailey Circus; Sept. 4-14: Moscow Circus; Sept. 25–Boxing: Sonny Liston vs. Floyd Patterson (closed circuit coverage); Oct. 4–Wrestling: Whipper Billy Watson vs. The Beast; Oct. 6–NHL: All-Stars 1, Leafs 4; Oct. 11–Wrestling: Yukon Eric vs. Sweet Daddy Siki/Duke Noble; Oct. 13–NHL: Boston 2, Leafs 2; Oct. 18–Wrestling: Johnny Valentine vs. Enrique Torres; Oct. 20–NHL: Chicago 1, Leafs 3; Oct. 21–Jr. Hockey: Brampton 4, Jr. Marlboros 8; Oct. 21–Jr. Hockey: Oshawa 3, Knob Hill Farms 5; Oct. 25–Wrestling: Watson/Sammartino vs. Brower/Siki; Oct. 26–Jr. Hockey: Oshawa 4, Jr. Marlboros 11; Oct. 26–Jr. Hockey: Knob Hill Farms 2, Neil McNeil 3; Oct. 27–NHL: Rangers 5, Leafs 1; Oct. 28–Jr. Hockey: Brampton 5, Neil McNeil 2; Oct. 28–Jr. Hockey: Whitby 6, Jr. Marlboros 6; Oct. 30–Jr. Hockey: Oshawa 3, Jr. Marlboros 13; Oct. 31–NHL: Canadiens 4, Leafs 3; Nov. 1–Wrestling: Whipper Billy Watson vs. Bulldog Brower; Nov. 2–Jr. Hockey: Jr. Marlboros 5, Knob Hill Farms 7; Nov. 2–Jr. Hockey: Oshawa 2, Neil McNeil 8; Nov. 3–NHL: Detroit 7, Leafs 3; Nov. 4–Jr. Hockey: Knob Hill Farms 5, Oshawa 2; Nov. 4–Jr. Hockey: Whitby 3, Neil McNeil 10; Nov. 5-11: Ice Capades; Nov. 10–NHL: Rangers 3, Leafs 5; Nov. 13–Jr. Hockey: Neil McNeil 3, Knob Hill Farms 3; Nov. 13–Jr. Hockey: Oshawa 2, Brampton 0; Nov. 14–NHL: Canadiens 2, Leafs 4; Nov.

15–Wrestling: Johnny Valentive vs. Bruno Sammartino; Nov. 16–Jr. Hockey: Neil McNeil 5, Oshawa 4; Nov. 16–Jr. Hockey: Jr. Marlboros 2, Knob Hill Farms 3; Nov. 17–NHL: Detroit 2, Leafs 3; Nov. 18–Jr. Hockey: Jr. Marlboros 2, Neil McNeil 4; Nov. 18–Jr. Hockey: Brampton 1, Knob Hill Farms 1; Nov. 20–Music: Royal Scots Guard w/Argyll and Sutherland Highlanders; Nov. 22–Wrestling: Bruno Sammartino vs. Johnny Valentine; Nov. 23–Jr. Hockey: Soviets 6, Metro-BC All-Stars 0; Nov. 24–NHL: Rangers 1, Leafs 4; Nov. 25–Jr. Hockey: Oshawa 3, Knob Hill Farms 2; Nov. 25–Jr. Hockey: Brampton 6, Jr. Marlboros 6; Nov. 28–Basketball: Harlem Globetrotters (with Cab Calloway); Nov. 29–Wrestling: Kiniski/Sammartino vs. Valentine/Brower; Nov. 30–Jr. Hockey: Whitby 2, Oshawa 3; Nov. 30–Jr. Hockey: Knob Hill Farms 2, Jr. Marlboros 4; Dec. 1–NHL: Boston 2, Leafs 8; Dec. 2–Jr. Hockey: Brampton 3, Neil McNeil 2; Dec. 2–Jr. Hockey: Whitby 4, Jr. Marlboros 8; Dec. 5–NHL: Canadiens 1, Leafs 2; Dec. 6–Wrestling: Watson/Sammartino vs. Valentine/Brower; Dec. 7–Jr. Hockey: Knob Hill Farms 5, Jr. Marlboros 3; Dec. 7–Jr. Hockey: Neil McNeil 4, Oshawa 3; Dec. 8–NHL: Chicago 1, Leafs 1; Dec. 10-13: Bolshoi Ballet; Dec. 14–Wrestling: Bruno Sammartino vs. Johnny Valentine; Dec. 15–NHL: Boston 2, Leafs 8; Dec. 16–Jr. Hockey: Knob Hill Farms 3, Jr. Marlboros 1; Dec. 16–Jr. Hockey: Brampton 2, Oshawa 6; Dec. 18–Jr. Hockey: Neil McNeil 1, Knob Hill Farms 1; Dec. 18–Jr. Hockey: Oshawa 0, Jr. Marlboros 3; Dec. 22–Jr. Hockey: Oshawa 0, Neil McNeil 10; Dec. 22–Jr. Hockey: Whitby 5, Knob Hill Farms 2; Dec. 22–NHL: Rangers 2, Leafs 4; Dec. 24–Jr. Hockey: Whitby 9, Oshawa 5; Dec. 24–Jr. Hockey: Neil McNeil 7, Jr. Marlboros 0; Dec. 26–NHL: Detroit 4, Leafs 5; Dec. 27–Wrestling: Johnny Valentine vs. Bruno Sammartino; Dec. 28–Jr. Hockey: Neil McNeil 3, Jr. Marlboros 4; Dec. 28–Jr. Hockey: Brampton 4, Knob Hill Farms 1; Dec. 29–NHL: Chicago 1, Leafs 1; Dec. 30–Jr. Hockey: Brampton 2, Jr. Marlboros 5; Dec. 30–Jr. Hockey: Knob Hill Farms 2, Oshawa 2.

1963 • Jan. 1–Jr. Hockey: Neil McNeil 5, Jr. Marlboros 4; Jan. 3–Wrestling: Johnny Valentine vs. Bruno Sammartino; Jan. 5–Jr. Hockey: Oshawa 6, Jr. Marlboros 6; Jan. 5–Jr. Hockey: Knob Hill Farms 1, Neil McNeil 5; Jan. 5–NHL: Boston 2, Leafs 4; Jan. 7–Jr. Hockey: Whitby 1, Jr. Marlboros 11; Jan. 7–Jr. Hockey: Brampton 1, Neil McNeil 12; Jan. 8–Jr. Hockey: Neil McNeil 6, Jr. Marlboros 4; Jan. 9–NHL: Chicago 3, Leafs 1; Jan. 10–Wrestling: Johnny Valentine vs. Whipper Billy Watson; Jan. 11–Jr. Hockey: Jr. Marlboros 3, Knob Hill Farms 3; Jan. 11–Jr. Hockey: Oshawa 4, Neil McNeil 11; Jan. 12–NHL: Detroit 1, Leafs 2; Jan. 13–Jr. Hockey: Knob Hill Farms 1, Oshawa 4; Jan. 13–Jr. Hockey: Whitby 0, Neil McNeil 8; Jan. 15–Jr. Hockey: Brampton 5, Knob Hill Farms 3; Jan. 17–Wrestling: Watson/Sammartino vs. Brower/Schmidt; Jan. 18–Hockey: UCC New Boys 1, UCC Old Boys 4; Jan. 18–Hockey: Havergal 7, Bishop Strachan 0; Jan. 18–Hockey: UCC Whites 1, UCC Blues 0; Jan. 19–NHL: Chicago 4, Leafs 1; Jan. 20–Jr. Hockey: Neil McNeil 10, Whitby 4; Jan. 20–Jr. Hockey: Oshawa 4, Jr. Marlboros 1; Jan. 22–Jr. Hockey: Neil McNeil 6, Knob Hill Farms 2; Jan. 22–Jr. Hockey: Knob Hill Farms 2, Jr. Marlboros 2; Jan. 23–NHL: Canadiens 1, Leafs 5; Jan. 24–Wrestling: Lou Thesz vs. Buddy Rodgers; Jan. 25–Track and Field: Telegram-Maple Leaf Games; Jan. 26–NHL: Boston 5, Leafs 2; Jan. 27–Jr. Hockey: Brampton 0, Knob Hill Farms 1; Jan. 27–Jr. Hockey: Brampton 2, Jr. Marlboros 5; Jan. 28–Feb. 2: Ice Follies of 1963; Feb. 2–NHL: Rangers 2, Leafs 2; Feb. 3–Jr. Hockey: Oshawa 2, Knob Hill Farms 4; Feb. 3–Jr. Hockey: Brampton 2, Jr. Marlboros 5; Feb. 5–Jr. Hockey: Knob Hill Farms 1, Jr. Marlboros 10; Feb. 7–Wrestling: Lou Thesz vs. Buddy Rogers; Feb. 8–Jr. Hockey: Oshawa 3, Jr. Marlboros 2; Feb. 8–Jr. Hockey: Knob Hill Farms 1, Neil McNeil 7; Feb. 9–NHL: Canadiens 3, Leafs 3; Feb. 10–Jr. Hockey: Whitby 3, Jr. Marlboros 3; Feb. 10–Jr. Hockey: Brampton 2, Neil McNeil 7; Feb. 11–Hockey: Trail 1, Eastern University All-Stars 3; Feb. 12–Jr. Hockey: Hamilton 0, Neil McNeil 3; Feb. 13–NHL: Detroit 2, Leafs 6; Feb. 14–Wrestling: Sammartino/Red Mask vs. Valentine/Brower; Feb. 15–Jr. Hockey: Knob Hill Farms 4, Jr. Marlboros 6; Feb. 16–NHL: Rangers 2, Leafs 4; Feb. 17–Jr. Hockey: Whitby 4, Neil McNeil 11; Feb. 17–Jr. Hockey: Knob Hill Farms 3, Oshawa 1; Feb. 20–NHL: Canadiens 1, Leafs 2; Feb. 21–Wrestling: Watson/Sammartino vs. Valentine/Brower; Feb. 22–Jr. Hockey: Oshawa, Neil McNeil; Feb. 22–Jr. Hockey: Whitby, Knob Hill Farms; Feb. 23–Jr. Hockey: Knob Hill Farms 10, Jr. Marlboros 7; Feb. 23–NHL: Boston 4, Leafs 2; Feb. 24–Jr. Hockey: Brampton 8, Oshawa 3; Feb. 24–Jr. Hockey: Neil McNeil 5, Jr. Marlboros 8; Feb. 25–Tennis: Rod Laver vs. Ken Rosewall; Feb. 26–Hockey: Public School AA Finals; Feb. 26–Jr. Hockey: Neil McNeil 5, Knob Hill Farms 1; Feb. 26–Jr. Hockey: Oshawa 4, Jr. Marlboros 3; Feb. 27–NHL: Chicago 3, Leafs 6; Feb. 28–Wrestling: Valentine/Brower vs. Watson/Sammartino; Mar. 1–Hockey: Malvern 7, Oakwood 3 (Schoolboy Finals); Mar. 1–Hockey: TSSAA All-Stars 4, NHL Oldtimers 8; Mar. 2–NHL: Rangers 3, Leafs 4; Mar. 3–Jr. Hockey: Neil McNeil 7, Jr. Marlboros 7; Mar. 3–Jr. Hockey: Brampton 1, Oshawa 3; Mar. 5–Jr. Hockey: Knob Hill Farms 4, Neil McNeil 6; Mar. 6–NHL: Boston 0, Leafs 4; Mar. 7–Wrestling: Valentine/Brower vs. Watson/Sammartino; Mar. 8–Jr. Hockey: Whitby 8, Jr. Marlboros 13; Mar. 9–NHL: Detroit 3, Leafs 5; Mar. 10–Jr. Hockey: Neil McNeil 10, Knob Hill Farms 1; Mar. 10–Jr. Hockey: Whitby 4, Jr. Marlboros 7; Mar. 13–Jr. Hockey: Neil McNeil 9, Knob Hill Farms 4; Mar. 14–Wrestling: Lou Thesz vs. Bruno Sammartino; Mar. 16–NHL: Chicago 0, Leafs 3; Mar. 17–Jr. Hockey: Whitby 2, Jr. Marlboros 8; Mar. 17–Jr. Hockey: Neil McNeil 5, Knob Hill Farms 2; Mar. 19–Jr. Hockey: Neil McNeil 9, Jr. Marlboros 6; Mar. 20–NHL: Canadiens 3, Leafs 3; Mar. 21–Wrestling: Kiniski/Sammartino vs. Valentine/Brower; Mar. 22–Jr. Hockey: Neil McNeil 8, Jr. Marlboros 3; Mar. 23–NHL: Detroit 2, Leafs 1; Mar. 24–Jr. Hockey: Neil McNeil 2, Jr. Marlboros 8; Mar. 26–NHL: Canadiens 1, Leafs 3; Mar. 27–Jr. Hockey: Neil McNeil 9, Jr. Marlboros 7; Mar. 28–NHL: Canadiens 2, Leafs 3; Mar. 29–NDP Rally; Mar. 31–Jr. Hockey: Neil McNeil 3, Jr. Marlboros 6; Apr. 1–Variety: Timmy's Easter Parade of Stars; Apr. 2–Jr. Hockey: Neil McNeil 6, Jr. Marlboros 2; Apr. 4–NHL: Canadiens 0, Leafs 5; Apr. 7–Jr. Hockey: Niagara Falls 4, Neil McNeil 1; Apr. 9–NHL: Detroit 2, Leafs 4 (Stanley Cup Finals); Apr. 11–NHL: Detroit 2, Leafs 4 (Stanley Cup Finals); Apr. 13–Jr. Hockey: Niagara Falls 1, Neil McNeil 4; Apr. 17–Jr. Hockey: Niagara Falls 5, Neil McNeil 1; Apr. 18–NHL: Detroit 1, Leafs 3 (Stanley Cup-winning game); Apr. 25–Wrestling: Johnny Valentine vs. Bobo Brazil; June 1–Diocesan Eucharistic Day Mass; July 9–Music: Tommy Dorsey's Orchestra; July 19–Music: The Dick Clark Show; July 22–Boxing: Sonny Liston vs. Floyd Patterson (closed circuit coverage); Aug. 13–World Anglican Congress; Aug. 18–Anglican Missionary Service; Aug. 31–Music: Country Music Show; Sept. 17–Music: Black Watch Pipe Band; Sept. 30–Oct. 4: Don Ameche's International Showtime Circus; Oct. 5–NHL: All-Stars 3, Leafs 3; Oct. 10–Wrestling: Lou Thesz vs. Johnny Valentine; Oct. 12–NHL: Boston 1, Leafs 5; Oct. 17–Wrestling: The Beast vs. Johnny Valentine; Oct. 18–Music: Hootenanny; Oct. 19–NHL: Detroit 1, Leafs 2; Oct. 20–Jr. Hockey: Niagara Falls 3, Jr. Marlboros 4; Oct. 24–Wrestling: The Beast vs. Johnny Valentine; Oct. 26–NHL: Rangers 4, Leafs 6; Oct. 27–Jr. Hockey: Oshawa 3, Jr. Marlboros 9; Oct. 30–NHL: Canadiens 3, Leafs 6; Oct. 31–Wrestling: The Beast vs. Johnny Valentine; Nov. 2–NHL: Chicago 2, Leafs 0; Nov. 3–Jr. Hockey: Kitchener 1, Jr. Marlboros 8; Nov. 5-12: Ice Capades; Nov. 9–NHL: Chicago 3, Leafs 3; Nov. 10–Jr. Hockey: Montreal 6, Jr. Marlboros 7; Nov. 14–Wrestling: Lou Thesz vs. Bulldog Brower; Nov. 16–NHL: Rangers 4, Leafs 5; Nov. 17–Jr. Hockey: Oshawa 5, Jr. Marlboros 10; Nov. 20–NHL: Canadiens 3, Leafs 1; Nov. 21-22: Olympic Figure Skating Trials; Nov. 23–NHL: Boston 1, Leafs 4; Nov. 24–Jr. Hockey: St. Catharines 1, Jr. Marlboros 2; Nov. 24-29: Canadian Rodeo Championships; Nov. 30–NHL: Detroit 1, Leafs 1; Dec. 1–Jr. Hockey: Niagara Falls 4, Jr. Marlboros 5; Dec. 4–NHL: Canadiens 0, Leafs 3; Dec. 7–NHL: Chicago 0, Leafs 3; Dec. 8–Jr. Hockey: Hamilton 3, Jr. Marlboros 10; Dec. 11–NHL: Detroit 3, Leafs 1; Dec. 14–NHL: Rangers 3, Leafs 5; Dec. 15–Jr. Hockey: Oshawa 3, Jr. Marlboros 3; Dec. 21–NHL: Detroit 0, Leafs 2; Dec. 22–Jr. Hockey: St. Catharines 2, Jr. Marlboros 3; Dec. 28–NHL: Boston 0, Leafs 2; Dec. 29–Int'l. Hockey: Swedish National Team 3, Canadian National Team 6.

1964 • Jan. 1-4: Tournament of Champions Curling; Jan. 4–NHL: Chicago 0, Leafs 3; Jan. 5–Int'l. Hockey: Czech National Team 8, Swedish National Team 5; Jan. 5–Jr. Hockey: Kitchener 5, Jr. Marlboros 5; Jan. 8–NHL: Canadiens 1, Leafs 6; Jan. 11–NHL: Boston 1, Leafs 3; Jan. 12–Jr. Hockey: Montreal 2, Jr. Marlboros 4; Jan. 15–NHL: Rangers 5, Leafs 4; Jan. 18–NHL: Boston 11, Leafs 0; Jan. 19–Jr. Hockey: Oshawa 6, Jr. Marlboros 9; Jan. 22–NHL: Canadiens 3, Leafs 0; Jan. 24–Track and Field: Telegram-Maple Leaf Games; Jan. 25–NHL: Rangers 1, Leafs 1; Jan. 26–Jr. Hockey: Hamilton 3, Jr. Marlboros 3; Jan. 27–Feb. 2: Ice Follies of 1964; Feb. 1–NHL: Boston 1, Leafs 5; Feb. 2–Jr. Hockey: St. Catharines 5, Jr. Marlboros 2; Feb. 5–NHL: Canadiens 2, Leafs 0; Feb. 8–NHL: Chicago 3, Leafs 3; Feb. 9–Jr. Hockey: Montreal 6, Jr. Marlboros 1; Feb. 15–NHL: Chicago 0, Leafs 4; Feb. 16–Jr. Hockey: Niagara Falls 6, Jr. Marlboros 8; Feb. 19–NHL: Detroit 1, Leafs 1; Feb. 22–NHL: Rangers 2, Leafs 5; Feb. 23–Jr. Hockey: Peterborough 5, Jr. Marlboros 8; Feb. 25–Boxing: Muhammad Ali vs. Sonny Liston (closed circuit coverage); Feb. 29–NHL: Chicago 1, Leafs 4; Mar. 1–Jr. Hockey: Kitchener 0, Jr. Marlboros 12; Mar. 2–Variety: Mazowsze Polish Song and Dance Company; Mar. 4–NHL: Boston 4, Leafs 4; Mar. 5–Wrestling: John Valentine vs. The Beast; Mar. 6–Hockey: Western Tech 1, Malvern 2 (Schoolboy Finals); Mar. 7–Hockey: Playground Hockey Championships; Mar. 7–NHL: Detroit 2, Leafs 4; Mar. 11–NHL: Canadiens 0, Leafs 1; Mar. 12–Wrestling: Whipper Billy Watson vs. The Beast; Mar. 13–Jr. Hockey: St. Michael's "B" 2, Neil McNeil 6; Mar. 14–NHL: Rangers 3, Leafs 7; Mar. 15–Jr. Hockey: Niagara Falls 2, Jr. Marlboros 6; Mar. 16–Variety: Timmy's Easter Parade of Stars; Mar. 19–Wrestling: Sulie Sammara vs. Professor Hiro; Mar. 21–NHL: Detroit 3, Leafs 5; Mar. 23–Jr. Hockey: Niagara Falls 3, Jr. Marlboros 6; Mar. 26–Wrestling: John Valentine vs. Hercules; Mar. 28–Jr. Hockey: Weston 5, Neil McNeil 3; Mar. 31–NHL: Canadiens 3, Leafs 2; Apr. 2–NHL: Canadiens 3, Leafs 5; Apr. 3–Wrestling: Whipper Billy Watson vs. The Beast; Apr. 5–Jr. Hockey: Montreal 5, Jr. Marlboros 5 (OHA "A" Finals); Apr. 7–NHL: Canadiens 0, Leafs 3; Apr. 10–Jr. Hockey: Montreal 3, Jr. Marlboros 6 (OHA "A" Finals); Apr. 11–NHL: Detroit 2, Leafs 3 (Stanley Cup Finals); Apr. 13–Jr. Hockey: Montreal 4, Jr. Marlboros 6 (OHA "A" Finals); Apr. 14–NHL: Detroit 4, Leafs 3 (Stanley Cup Finals); Apr. 19–Jr. Hockey: North Bay 3, Jr. Marlboros 13 (All-Ontario Jr. Finals); Apr. 20–Jr. Hockey: North Bay 4, Jr. Marlboros 11 (All-Ontario Jr. Finals); Apr. 21–NHL: Detroit 2, Leafs 1 (Stanley Cup Finals); Apr. 25–NHL: Detroit 0, Leafs 4 (Stanley Cup-winning game); Apr. 29–Jr. Hockey: Notre Dame de Grace 3, Jr. Marlboros 6 (Memorial Cup Eastern Finals); Apr. 30–Wrestling: Lord Athol Layton vs. Bulldog Brower; May 1–Jr. Hockey: Notre Dame de Grace 3, Jr. Marlboros 11 (Memorial Cup Eastern Finals); May 2–Greek Church Service; May 3–Jr. Hockey: Edmonton 2, Jr. Marlboros 5 (Memorial Cup Finals); May 5–Jr. Hockey: Edmonton 2, Jr. Marlboros 3 (Memorial Cup Finals); May 7–Jr. Hockey: Edmonton 2, Jr. Marlboros 5 (Memorial Cup Finals); May 9–Jr. Hockey: Edmonton 2, Jr. Marlboros 7 (Memorial Cup Finals); May 12-15: Royal Lippizan Stallions; May 16–Variety: Estonian Festival; May 27-31: Ringling Brothers/Barnum & Bailey Circus; June 7-11: Rotary International Convention; July 8-11: Lions Club International Convention; Sept. 7–Music: The Beatles; Sept. 27–Music: Mina and Pargi; Sept. 29–Oct. 4: The Wonderful World of Sports; Oct. 5–Lacrosse: Jim Smith Benefit Night; Oct. 8–Variety: Ireland on Parade; Oct. 10–NHL: All-Stars 3, Leafs 2; Oct. 16–Jr. Hockey: Montreal 2, Jr. Marlboros 4; Oct. 17–NHL: Boston 2, Leafs 7; Oct. 18–Jr. Hockey: Niagara Falls 4, Jr. Marlboros 3; Oct. 24–NHL: Rangers 1, Leafs 1; Oct. 25–Jr. Hockey: Oshawa 9, Jr. Marlboros 6; Oct. 25–Music: Rita Pavone; Oct. 28–NHL: Canadiens 5, Leafs 2; Oct. 29–Music: The Royal Irish Bridage Military Tattoo; Oct. 31–NHL: Chicago 1, Leafs 5; Nov. 1–Jr. Hockey: Kitchener 5, Jr. Marlboros 6; Nov. 1–Music: Gerry and the Pacemakers; Nov. 2–Music: Dave Clark Five; Nov. 6–Jr. Hockey: Montreal 3, Jr. Marlboros 4; Nov. 7–NHL: Rangers 1, Leafs 0; Nov. 8–Jr. Hockey: Peterborough 3, Jr. Marlboros 4; Nov. 11–NHL: Detroit 1, Leafs 3; Nov. 13–Jr. Hockey: Hamilton 3, Jr. Marlboros 6; Nov. 14–NHL: Boston 3, Leafs 1; Nov. 15–Jr. Hockey: Niagara Falls 5, Jr. Marlboros 5; Nov. 18–NHL: Canadiens 1, Leafs 3; Nov. 20–Jr. Hockey: St. Catharines 4, Jr. Marlboros 8; Nov. 21–NHL: Chicago 0, Leafs 1; Nov. 22-27: Canadian Rodeo Championships; Nov. 28–NHL: Rangers 4, Leafs 1; Nov. 29–Jr. Hockey: Niagara Falls 1, Jr. Marlboros 3; Dec. 1-8: Ice Capades; Dec. 5–NHL: Detroit 2, Leafs 10; Dec. 9–NHL: Canadiens 3, Leafs 2; Dec. 12–NHL: Boston 3, Leafs 6; Dec. 13–Int'l. Hockey: Russia 4, Canada 0; Dec. 13–Jr. Hockey: Oshawa 2, Jr. Marlboros 7; Dec. 18–Jr. Hockey: Kitchener 5, Jr. Marlboros 4; Dec. 19–NHL: Rangers 3, Leafs 6; Dec. 20–Jr. Hockey: Peterborough 6, Jr. Marlboros 5; Dec. 26–NHL: Chicago 5, Leafs 3; Dec. 27–Jr. Hockey: St. Catharines 7, Jr. Marlboros 10; Dec. 30–NHL: Canadiens 4, Leafs 3.

1965 • Jan. 1–Jr. Hockey: Hamilton 3, Jr. Marlboros 7; Jan. 2-4: Alcoholics Anonymous Convention; Jan. 2–NHL: Detroit 1, Leafs 3; Jan. 3–Wrestling: Johnny Valentive vs. the Sheik; Jan. 5-8: Tournament of Champions Curling; Jan. 9–Jr. Hockey: Peterborough 6, Jr. Marlboros 6; Jan. 9–NHL: Boston 1, Leafs 2; Jan. 10–Int'l. Hockey: Czechoslovakia 2, Canada 3; Jan. 13–NHL: Chicago 0, Leafs 0; Jan. 16–NHL: Detroit 4, Leafs 2; Jan. 17–Jr. Hockey: Oshawa 4, Jr. Marlboros 6; Jan. 20–NHL: Canadiens 2, Leafs 1; Jan. 22–Jr. Hockey: Kitchener 3, Jr. Marlboros 5; Jan. 23–NHL: Rangers 1, Leafs 1; Jan. 24–Jr. Hockey: Hamilton 3, Jr. Marlboros 3; Jan. 29–Track and Field: Telegram-Maple Leaf Games; Jan. 30–NHL: Boston 1, Leafs 6; Jan. 31–Jr. Hockey: Niagara Falls 4, Jr. Marlboros 4; Feb. 1–Boxing: Floyd Patterson vs. George Chuvalo (closed circuit coverage); Feb. 6–NHL: Chicago 6, Leafs 3; Feb. 10–NHL: Canadiens 2, Leafs 6; Feb. 11–Wrestling: Whipper Billy Watson vs. The Sheik; Feb. 12–Jr. Hockey: St. Catharines 0, Jr. Marlboros 4; Feb. 13–NHL: Detroit 1, Leafs 2; Feb. 14–Jr. Hockey: Montreal 3, Jr. Marlboros 4; Feb. 20–NHL: Chicago 3, Leafs 4; Feb. 21–Jr. Hockey: Peterborough 3, Jr. Marlboros 5; Feb. 24–NHL: Boston 3, Leafs 1; Feb. 26–Jr. Hockey: Montreal 5, Jr. Marlboros 3; Feb. 27–NHL: Rangers 4, Leafs 3; Feb. 28–Hockey: NHL Oldtimers, Canadian National Team; Feb. 28–Jr. Hockey: Oshawa 5, Jr. Marlboros 4; Mar. 2–Hockey: Toronto Public Schools Championships; Mar. 4–Wrestling: John Valentine vs. Bulldog Brower; Mar. 5–Hockey: Malvern 5, North Toronto 4 (Schoolboy Finals); Mar. 6–NHL: Chicago 1, Leafs 4; Mar. 7–Jr. Hockey: Hamilton 6, Jr. Marlboros 5; Mar. 7–Wrestling: Whipper Billy Watson vs. Gene Kiniski;

Mar. 9–Jr. Hockey: Montreal 5, Jr. Marlboros 5; Mar. 10–NHL: Detroit 4, Leafs 2; Mar. 12–World Figure Skating Tour of 1965; Mar. 13–NHL: Boston 2, Leafs 0; Mar. 14–Jr. Hockey: Montreal 5, Jr. Marlboros 3; Mar. 14–Music: Rita Pavone; Mar. 17–Jr. Hockey: Montreal 1, Jr. Marlboros 4; Mar. 18–Music: Claudio Villa; Mar. 18–Wrestling: Johnny Powers vs. Sweet Daddy Siki; Mar. 20–NHL: Rangers 1, Leafs 4; Mar. 21–Jr. Hockey: Montreal 1, Jr. Marlboros 8; Mar. 23–Jr. Hockey: Peterborough 2, Jr. Marlboros 1; Mar. 24–NHL: Canadiens 2, Leafs 3; Mar. 27–NHL: Detroit 4, Leafs 1; Mar. 28–Jr. Hockey: Peterborough 3, Jr. Marlboros 3; Mar. 28–Wrestling: Kiniski/Von Erich vs. Valentine/Watson; Mar. 31–Jr. Hockey: Peterborough 6, Jr. Marlboros 1; Apr. 4–Jr. Hockey: Peterborough 4, Jr. Marlboros 5; Apr. 4–Wrestling: John Valentine vs. The Beast; Apr. 6–NHL: Canadiens 2, Leafs 3; Apr. 7–Jr. Hockey: Niagara Falls 4, Jr. Marlboros 2 (OHA "A" Semi-Finals); Apr. 8–NHL: Canadiens 2, Leafs 4; Apr. 11–Jr. Hockey: Niagara Falls 6, Jr. Marlboros 1 (OHA "A" Semi-Finals); Apr. 11–Wrestling: Watson/Valentine vs. Kiniski/Von Erich; Apr. 13–NHL: Canadiens 4, Leafs 3; Apr. 18–Wrestling: Watson/Calhoun vs. Atkins/Hiro; Apr. 19–Boxing: George Chuvalo vs. Golden Boy Neilson; Apr. 24–Greek Church Service; Apr. 25–Music: The Rolling Stones; Apr. 25–Wrestling: Sulie Sammara vs. Johnny Powers; Apr. 26–Canadian Girls in Training; May 2-7: Six-day Bicycle Race; May 11-14: Moiseyev Ballet; May 16–Music: International Variety Show; May 23–Music: Remo Germani, Nicola di Bari, Narciso Parigi and Roberta Mazzoni; May 25–Boxing: Muhammad Ali vs. Sonny Liston (closed circuit coverage); May 29-30–Music: Latvian Song Festival; June 2-6: Ringling Brothers/Barnum & Bailey Circus; June 8-10: The Royal Ballet w/Rudolf Nureyev; July 2-4: Alcoholics Anonymous Convention; Aug. 17–Music: The Beatles; Sept. 5–Music: The Beach Boys w/Sonny and Cher; Sept. 18-19–Music: Royal Marines Tattoo; Oct. 22–USA vs. USSR volleyball; Oct. 23–NHL: Chicago 4, Leafs 0; Oct. 24–Jr. Hockey: Oshawa 4, Jr. Marlboros 4; Oct. 29–Jr. Hockey: Montreal 6, Jr. Marlboros 8; Oct. 30–NHL: Detroit 3, Leafs 4; Oct. 31–Jr. Hockey: London 8, Jr. Marlboros 6; Oct. 31–Music: The Rolling Stones; Nov. 1–Boxing: Ernie Terrell vs. George Chuvalo; Nov. 4–NDP Rally; Nov. 6–NHL: Rangers 4, Leafs 2; Nov. 7–Jr. Hockey: Peterborough 5, Jr. Marlboros 8; Nov. 10–NHL: Canadiens 3, Leafs 3; Nov. 12–Jr. Hockey: St. Catharines 4, Jr. Marlboros 3; Nov. 13–NHL: Rangers 2, Leafs 5; Nov. 14–Jr. Hockey: Hamilton 7, Jr. Marlboros 3; Nov. 19–Jr. Hockey: Kitchener 2, Jr. Marlboros 2; Nov. 20–NHL: Chicago 1, Leafs 3; Nov. 21–Jr. Hockey: Niagara Falls 1, Jr. Marlboros 3; Nov. 22–Boxing: Muhammad Ali vs. Floyd Patterson (closed circuit coverage); Nov. 24–NHL: Canadiens 2, Leafs 1; Nov. 27–NHL: Boston 2, Leafs 1; Nov. 28–Jr. Hockey: Oshawa 6, Jr. Marlboros 6; Dec. 3–Jr. Hockey: Montreal 2, Jr. Marlboros 4; Dec. 4–NHL: Detroit 5, Leafs 3; Dec. 5–Jr. Hockey: London 4, Jr. Marlboros 4; Dec. 7-12: Ice Capades; Dec. 11–NHL: Boston 3, Leafs 8; Dec. 14–Int'l. Hockey: Russia 4, Jr. Marlboros and All-Stars 3; Dec. 15–NHL: Detroit 3, Leafs 5; Dec. 17–Jr. Hockey: London 2, Jr. Marlboros 2; Dec. 18–NHL: Rangers 4, Leafs 8; Dec. 19–Jr. Hockey: Niagara Falls 4, Jr. Marlboros 4; Dec. 25–NHL: Chicago 3, Leafs 5; Dec. 26–Jr. Hockey: Hamilton 5, Jr. Marlboros 4; Dec. 29–NHL: Canadiens 2, Leafs 3.

1966 • Jan. 1–NHL: Boston 3, Leafs 6; Jan. 2–Jr. Hockey: Kitchener 4, Jr. Marlboros 5; Jan. 5–Int'l. Hockey: Sweden 5, Jr. Marlboros and All-Stars 8; Jan. 8–NHL: Detroit 3, Leafs 1; Jan. 9–Int'l. Hockey: Czechoslovakia 5, Canada 1; Jan. 11-14: Tournament of Champions Curling; Jan. 11–Jr. Hockey: St. Catharines 4, Jr. Marlboros 6; Jan. 13–Jr. Hockey: Montreal 2, Jr. Marlboros 3; Jan. 15–NHL: Boston 1, Leafs 6; Jan. 16–Jr. Hockey: Hamilton 5, Jr. Marlboros 3; Jan. 18–Jr. Hockey: Peterborough 4, Jr. Marlboros 4; Jan. 19–NHL: Rangers 2, Leafs 6; Jan. 22–NHL: Chicago 0, Leafs 4; Jan. 23–Jr. Hockey: Kitchener 4, Jr. Marlboros 5; Jan. 27–Jr. Hockey: Oshawa 1, Jr. Marlboros 6; Jan. 28–Jr. Hockey: St. Catharines 1, Jr. Marlboros 4; Jan. 29–NHL: Boston 3, Leafs 6; Jan. 30–Wrestling: Bruno Sammartino vs. Professor Hiro; Jan. 30–Jr. Hockey: Niagara Falls 2, Jr. Marlboros 4; Feb. 1-6: Ice Follies of 1966; Feb. 5–NHL: Chicago 2, Leafs 5; Feb. 9–NHL: Rangers 0, Leafs 3; Feb. 12–NHL: Detroit 3, Leafs 3; Feb. 16–NHL: Canadiens 1, Leafs 3; Feb. 19–NHL: Rangers 3, Leafs 1; Feb. 20-22–Variety: Hungarian Dance Company; Feb. 23–Toronto Police Association Concert; Feb. 25–Track and Field: Telegram-Maple Leaf Games; Feb. 26–NHL: Boston 2, Leafs 3; Mar. 1–Hockey: Malvern 2, Parkdale 3; Mar. 1–Hockey: Weston 6, North Toronto 2; Mar. 2–NHL: Canadiens 3, Leafs 3; Mar. 5–NHL: Chicago 0, Leafs 5; Mar. 6–AHL Hockey: Hershey 2, Rochester 5; Mar. 6–Jr. Hockey: Peterborough 4, Jr. Marlboros 7; Mar. 9–NHL: Detroit 0, Leafs 1; Mar. 10–Wrestling: Sulie Sammara vs. Professor Hiro; Mar. 11–AHL Hockey: Buffalo 1, Rochester 0; Mar. 12–Jr. Hockey: Peterborough 1, Jr. Marlboros 6; Mar. 12–NHL: Boston 0, Leafs 6; Mar. 13–AHL Hockey: Baltimore 0, Rochester 3; Mar. 13–Jr. Hockey: Peterborough 1, Jr. Marlboros 7; Mar. 16–NHL: Canadiens 7, Leafs 2; Mar. 17–Jr. Hockey: Peterborough 1, Jr. Marlboros 3; Mar. 18–AHL Hockey: Providence 4, Rochester 5; Mar. 19–Hockey: Stratford, Juvenile Marlboros; Mar. 19–NHL: Chicago 2, Leafs 4; Mar. 20–AHL Hockey: Pittsburgh 3, Rochester 4; Mar. 20–Jr. Hockey: Kitchener 1, Jr. Marlboros 6; Mar. 23–Jr. Hockey: Kitchener 2, Jr. Marlboros 4; Mar. 24–Wrestling: Watson/Layton vs. Masked Yankees; Mar. 25–AHL Hockey: Hershey 3, Rochester 6; Mar. 26–NHL: Detroit 1, Leafs 3; Mar. 27–AHL Hockey: Quebec 7, Rochester 4; Mar. 27–Jr. Hockey: Kitchener 5, Jr. Marlboros 3; Mar. 29–Boxing: Muhammad Ali vs. George Chuvalo; Mar. 30–NHL: Canadiens 3, Leafs 1; Mar. 31–Jr. Hockey: Kitchener 4, Jr. Marlboros 2; Apr. 1–AHL Hockey: Springfield 2, Rochester 6; Apr. 2–NHL: Rangers 3, Leafs 3; Apr. 3–AHL Hockey: Baltimore 3, Rochester 4; Apr. 8–Hockey: Windsor 2, Juvenile Marlboros 10 (Ontario Juvenile Finals); Apr. 9–Greek Church Service; Apr. 10–AHL Hockey: Cleveland 3, Rochester 3; Apr. 12–NHL: Canadiens 5, Leafs 2; Apr. 13–AHL Hockey: Quebec 2, Rochester 3; Apr. 14–NHL: Canadiens 4, Leafs 1; Apr. 17–Wrestling: Gene Kiniski vs. Johnny Valentine; Apr. 20–AHL Hockey: Quebec 5, Rochester 3; Apr. 23–AHL Hockey: Quebec 2, Rochester 4; Apr. 24–Wrestling: Masked Yankees vs. Ladd/Powers; Apr. 27–AHL Hockey: Quebec 3, Rochester 6; Apr. 30–AHL Hockey: Cleveland 0, Rochester 4 (Calder Cup Finals); May 1–Wrestling: Masked Yankees vs. Watson/Layton; May 4–Jr. Hockey: Edmonton 7, Oshawa 2 (Memorial Cup Finals); May 6–Jr. Hockey: Edmonton 1, Oshawa 7 (Memorial Cup Finals); May 8–Jr. Hockey: Edmonton 2, Oshawa 6 (Memorial Cup Finals); May 8–Music: Johnny Marandi w/Little Tony and his Group; May 10–AHL Hockey: Cleveland 0, Rochester 7 (Calder Cup Finals); May 11–Jr. Hockey: Edmonton 5, Oshawa 6 (Memorial Cup Finals); May 14–Jr. Hockey: Edmonton 7, Oshawa 4 (Memorial Cup Finals); May 15–Jr. Hockey: Edmonton 2, Oshawa 1 (Memorial Cup Finals); May 30–The Indy 500 (closed circuit coverage); June 29–Music: The Rolling Stones; Aug. 17–Music: The Beatles; Sept. 24–Music: The Toronto Sound; Oct. 1–Poland's Millenium of Christianity Celebration; Oct. 16–Jr. Hockey: Niagara Falls 2, Jr. Marlboros 5; Oct. 22–NHL: Rangers 4, Leafs 4; Oct. 23–Jr. Hockey: Oshawa 1, Jr. Marlboros 2; Oct. 26–NHL: Detroit 2, Leafs 3; Oct. 29–NHL: Boston 3, Leafs 3; Oct. 30–Jr. Hockey: London 4, Jr. Marlboros 2; Nov. 2–NHL: Canadiens 2, Leafs 2; Nov. 5–NHL: Rangers 1, Leafs 3; Nov. 6-7–Variety: Ukrainian Dance Company; Nov. 8-15: Ice Capades; Nov. 14–Boxing: Muhammad Ali vs. Cleveland Williams (closed circuit coverage); Nov. 17–Wrestling: Six-Man Tag-Team Match; Nov. 19–NHL: Canadiens 1, Leafs 5; Nov. 20–Jr. Hockey: Montreal 3, Jr. Marlboros 4; Nov. 20–Music: The Beach Boys; Nov. 23–NHL: Chicago 3, Leafs 6; Nov. 24-25–Music: Royal Highland Fusiliers; Nov. 26–NHL: Boston 2, Leafs 4; Nov. 27–Jr. Hockey: Peterborough 3, Jr. Marlboros 8; Nov. 30–NHL: Canadiens 2, Leafs 3; Dec. 2–Jr. Hockey: St. Catharines 3, Jr. Marlboros 5; Dec. 3–NHL: Detroit 2, Leafs 5; Dec. 4–Jr. Hockey: Hamilton 5, Jr. Marlboros 1; Dec. 10–NHL: Chicago 3, Leafs 5; Dec. 11–Jr. Hockey: Kitchener 8, Jr. Marlboros 5; Dec. 14–NHL: Boston 1, Leafs 2; Dec. 17–NHL: Rangers 3, Leafs 1; Dec. 18–Jr. Hockey: London 6, Jr. Marlboros 6; Dec. 24–NHL: Boston 0, Leafs 3; Dec. 26–Jr. Hockey: Montreal 4, Jr. Marlboros 7; Dec. 28–Hockey: Dominion Stores Open Leafs Practice; Dec. 28–Int'l. Hockey: Czech National Team 4, OHA Jr. "A" All-Stars 2; Dec. 31–NHL: Chicago 5, Leafs 1.

1967 • Jan. 1–Jr. Hockey: Kitchener 2, Jr. Marlboros 3; Jan. 4–NHL: Rangers 1, Leafs 1; Jan. 7–NHL: Boston 2, Leafs 5; Jan. 8–Jr. Hockey: London 6, Jr. Marlboros 4; Jan. 10–Int'l. Hockey: USSR 3, Canada 4; Jan. 13–Jr. Hockey: Peterborough 4, Jr. Marlboros 7; Jan. 14–NHL: Detroit 2, Leafs 5; Jan. 15–Jr. Hockey: Oshawa 3, Jr. Marlboros 7; Jan. 21–NHL: Detroit 5, Leafs 4; Jan. 22–Jr. Hockey: Hamilton 2, Jr. Marlboros 4; Jan. 25–NHL: Canadiens 3, Leafs 1; Jan. 27–Jr. Hockey: Peterborough 6, Jr. Marlboros 5; Jan. 28–NHL: Chicago 5, Leafs 2; Jan. 29–Jr. Hockey: Niagara Falls 4, Jr. Marlboros 6; Jan. 31–Feb. 5: Ice Follies of 1967; Feb. 6–Boxing: Muhammad Ali vs. Ernie Terrell (closed circuit coverage); Feb. 8–NHL: Detroit 5, Leafs 2; Feb. 10–Jr. Hockey: St. Catharines 3, Jr. Marlboros 3; Feb. 11–NHL: Chicago 4, Leafs 4; Feb. 12–Jr. Hockey: Oshawa 6, Jr. Marlboros 6; Feb. 15–NHL: Rangers 0, Leafs 6; Feb. 18–NHL: Boston 3, Leafs 5; Feb. 19–Jr. Hockey: Hamilton 2, Jr. Marlboros 3; Feb. 21–Toronto Police Association Concert; Feb. 22–NHL: Canadiens 2, Leafs 5; Feb. 24–Track and Field: Telegram-Maple Leaf Games; Feb. 25–NHL: Detroit 0, Leafs 4; Feb. 26–Jr. Hockey: Kitchener 3, Jr. Marlboros 3; Mar. 4–NHL: Chicago 0, Leafs 3; Mar. 5–Jr. Hockey: St. Catharines 4, Jr. Marlboros 4; Mar. 8–NHL: Canadiens 4, Leafs 6; Mar. 9–Hockey: Detroit Oldtimers vs. Toronto Oldtimers; Mar. 10–Jr. Hockey: Montreal 1, Jr. Marlboros 8; Mar. 11–NHL: Rangers 2, Leafs 2; Mar. 12–Jr. Hockey: Niagara Falls 8, Jr. Marlboros 6; Mar. 12–Music: Italian Chiama San Remo 1967; Mar. 14–Jr. Hockey: Montreal 5, Jr. Marlboros 4; Mar. 15–NHL: Detroit 4, Leafs 2; Mar. 18–NHL: Chicago 5, Leafs 9; Mar. 19–Jr. Hockey: Montreal 3, Jr. Marlboros 3; Mar. 22–NHL: Canadiens 5, Leafs 3; Mar. 23–Jr. Hockey: Montreal 1, Jr. Marlboros 5; Mar. 25–NHL: Boston 3, Leafs 4; Mar. 28–Jr. Hockey: Kitchener 2, Jr. Marlboros 1 (OHA "A" Semi-Finals); Apr. 1–Jr. Hockey: Kitchener 6, Jr. Marlboros 4 (OHA "A" Semi-Finals); Apr. 1–NHL: Rangers 1, Leafs 5; Apr. 2–Music: The Monkees; Apr. 7–Jr. Hockey: Kitchener 2, Jr. Marlboros 3 (OHA "A" Semi-Finals); Apr. 9–Music: Andy Williams and Henry Mancini; Apr. 11–NHL: Chicago 1, Leafs 3; Apr. 12–Jr. Hockey: Hamilton 2, Jr. Marlboros 6 (OHA "A" Finals); Apr. 13–NHL: Chicago 4, Leafs 3; Apr. 16–Jr. Hockey: Hamilton 2, Jr. Marlboros 3 (OHA "A" Finals); Apr. 18–NHL: Chicago 1, Leafs 3; Apr. 25–NHL: Canadiens 2, Leafs 3 (Stanley Cup Finals); Apr. 27–NHL: Canadiens 6, Leafs 2 (Stanley Cup Finals); Apr. 29–Greek Church Service; Apr. 30–Jr. Hockey: Thetford Mines 1, Jr. Marlboros 9 (Memorial Cup Eastern Finals); May 1–Jr. Hockey: Thetford Mines 2, Jr. Marlboros 5 (Memorial Cup Eastern Finals); May 2–NHL: Canadiens 2, Leafs 3 (Stanley Cup-winning game); May 16–Music: Ontario Folk Arts Festival; May 22–Music: Centennial Cool-Out w/The Guess Who; July 1–Music: The Mamas and the Papas; Aug. 2–Music: Israeli Philharmonic Orchestra; Aug. 9–Music: Herman's Hermits; Aug. 13-19: Bolshoi Ballet; Aug. 20–Music: Herb Alpert and the Tijuana Brass; Sept. 7-9: Progressive Conservative Leadership Convention; Sept. 17–Music: Dominico Modugno; Sept. 19–Variety: Telephone Pioneers of America Stage Show; Sept. 26–Oct. 1: Moscow Circus; Oct. 8–Music: Italian Show w/Nino Tarranto; Oct. 11–Sr. Hockey: Oakville 2, Sr. Marlboros 8; Oct. 13-15–Music: Welsh and Scots Guard Pipe Bands; Oct. 14–NHL: Chicago 1, Leafs 5; Oct. 18–NHL: Detroit 3, Leafs 2; Oct. 20–Sr. Hockey: Orillia 1, Sr. Marlboros 9; Oct. 21–NHL: Rangers 5, Leafs 3; Oct. 22–Jr. Hockey: Kitchener 1, Jr. Marlboros 6; Oct. 25–NHL: Los Angeles 2, Leafs 4; Oct. 26–Sr. Hockey: Galt 4, Sr. Marlboros 2; Oct. 27–United Appeal Gardens Party; Oct. 28–NHL: Oakland 2, Leafs 5; Oct. 29–Jr. Hockey: London 3, Jr. Marlboros 5; Oct. 29–Music: Italian Show w/Little Tony; Nov. 1–NHL: Canadiens 0, Leafs 5; Nov. 4–NHL: Rangers 2, Leafs 4; Nov. 5–Jr. Hockey: Peterborough 4, Jr. Marlboros 8; Nov. 6-12: Ice Capades; Nov. 15–NHL: Boston 2, Leafs 4; Nov. 17–Jr. Hockey: Montreal1, Jr. Marlboros 8; Nov. 18–NHL: Chicago 2, Leafs 2; Nov. 18–Sr. Hockey: Collingwood 3, Sr. Marlboros 4; Nov. 19–Jr. Hockey: Niagara Falls 4, Jr. Marlboros 3; Nov. 19–Music: James Brown; Nov. 22–NHL: Minnesota 0, Leafs 3; Nov. 24–Sr. Hockey: Orillia 2, Sr. Marlboros 5; Nov. 25–NHL: Detroit 2, Leafs 3; Nov. 26–Basketball: Harlem Globetrotters Road Show; Nov. 26–Jr. Hockey: Oshawa 4, Jr. Marlboros 12; Nov. 29–NHL: Canadiens 1, Leafs 2; Dec. 1–Sr. Hockey: Woodstock 5, Sr. Marlboros 3; Dec. 2–NHL: Oakland 0, Leafs 3; Dec. 3–Jr. Hockey: Hamilton 5, Jr. Marlboros 5; Dec. 8–Jr. Hockey: St. Catharines 2, Jr. Marlboros 7; Dec. 9–NHL: Boston 3, Leafs 3; Dec. 9–Sr. Hockey: Belleville 3, Sr. Marlboros 7; Dec. 10–Jr. Hockey: Ottawa 3, Jr. Marlboros 9; Dec. 13–NHL: Pittsburgh 2, Leafs 1; Dec. 15–Jr. Hockey: Oshawa 6, Jr. Marlboros 8; Dec. 16–NHL: Rangers 2, Leafs 4; Dec. 16–Sr. Hockey: Orillia 4, Sr. Marlboros 12; Dec. 17–Jr. Hockey: Kitchener 2, Jr. Marlboros 7; Dec. 22–Sr. Hockey: Oakville 1, Sr. Marlboros 7; Dec. 23–NHL: Detroit 3, Leafs 5; Dec. 26–Jr. Hockey: St. Catharines 4, Jr. Marlboros 3; Dec. 27–NHL: Canadiens 2, Leafs 2; Dec. 29–Sr. Hockey: Collingwood 1, Sr. Marlboros 2; Dec. 30–NHL: St. Louis 1, Leafs 8; Dec. 31–Jr. Hockey: Peterborough 3, Jr. Marlboros 2.

1968 • Jan. 2–Sr. Hockey: Galt 4, Sr. Marlboros 1; Jan. 5–Sr. Hockey: Guelph 2, Sr. Marlboros 6; Jan. 6–NHL: Boston 3, Leafs 3; Jan. 7–Hockey: Italian Nationals vs. Canadian Italians; Jan. 7–Jr. Hockey: London 5, Jr. Marlboros 6; Jan. 10–NHL: Detroit 1, Leafs 2; Jan. 12–Jr. Hockey: Montreal 4, Jr. Marlboros 4; Jan. 13–NHL: Pittsburgh 0, Leafs 7; Jan. 13–Sr. Hockey: Barrie 3, Sr. Marlboros 7; Jan. 14–Jr. Hockey: Niagara Falls 4, Jr. Marlboros 2; Jan. 16–NHL: NHL All-Stars 3, Leafs 4; Jan. 20–NHL: Minnesota 1, Leafs 5; Jan. 20–Sr. Hockey: Belleville 2, Sr. Marlboros 4; Jan. 21–Jr. Hockey: Hamilton 1, Jr. Marlboros 3; Jan. 21–Music: Italian Show w/Caterina Cabelli; Jan. 23–Sr. Hockey: Kingston 5, Sr. Marlboros 6; Jan. 24–NHL: Flyers 2, Leafs 1; Jan. 26–Jr. Hockey: Peterborough 0, Jr. Marlboros 4; Jan. 27–NHL: Chicago 4, Leafs 1; Jan. 27–Sr. Hockey: Guelph 2, Sr. Marlboros 5; Jan. 28–Jr. Hockey: Oshawa 1, Jr. Marlboros 7; Jan. 30–Feb. 11: Ice Capades; Feb. 10–Sr. Hockey: Galt 3, Sr. Marlboros 4; Feb. 13–Sr. Hockey: Oakville 1, Sr. Marlboros 3; Feb. 14–NHL: Canadiens 4, Leafs 2; Feb. 16–Jr. Hockey: St. Catharines 3, Jr. Marlboros 8; Feb. 17–NHL: Rangers 3, Leafs 2; Feb. 17–Sr. Hockey: Woodstock 1, Sr. Marlboros 8; Feb. 18–Jr. Hockey: Ottawa 2, Jr. Marlboros 7; Feb. 21–NHL: St. Louis 5, Leafs 1; Feb. 23–Jr. Hockey: Hamilton 5, Jr. Marlboros 5; Feb. 24–NHL: Boston 0, Leafs 1; Feb. 24–Sr. Hockey: Barrie 3, Sr. Marlboros 7; Feb. 25–Jr. Hockey: Kitchener 5, Jr. Marlboros 2; Feb. 27–Sr. Hockey: Barrie 4, Sr.

Marlboros 7; Feb. 28–NHL: Chicago 1, Leafs 0; Mar. 1–Jr. Hockey: Ottawa, Jr. Marlboros; Mar. 1–Track and Field: Telegram-Maple Leaf Games; Mar. 2–NHL: Los Angeles 2, Leafs 5; Mar. 3–Jr. Hockey: Montreal 4, Jr. Marlboros 6; Mar. 3–Wrestling: Bruno Sammartino vs. Tojo Tahara; Mar. 4–Boxing: Joe Frazier vs. Buster Mathis (closed circuit coverage); Mar. 5–Toronto Police Association Concert; Mar. 6–NHL: Flyers 2, Leafs 7; Mar. 7–NHL: Boston 2, Flyers 1 (Philadelphia home game rescheduled to the Gardens); Mar. 8–Jr. Hockey: London 2, Jr. Marlboros 10; Mar. 9–NHL: Detroit 5, Leafs 7; Mar. 9–Sr. Hockey: Collingwood 7, Sr. Marlboros 2; Mar. 10–Jr. Hockey: Niagara Falls 4, Jr. Marlboros 1; Mar. 10–Music: Italian Show w/Alfred Tucci; Mar. 15–Sr. Hockey: Collingwood 4, Sr. Marlboros 3; Mar. 16–NHL: Boston 0, Leafs 3; Mar. 17–Jr. Hockey: Kitchener 1, Jr. Marlboros 6; Mar. 17–Music: The Greatest All-British Revue; Mar. 19–Sr. Hockey: Collingwood 1, Sr. Marlboros 3; Mar. 21–Jr. Hockey: Kitchener 5, Jr. Marlboros 4; Mar. 23–NHL: Rangers 1, Leafs 3; Mar. 27–NHL: Canadiens 0, Leafs 6; Mar. 30–NHL: Chicago 0, Leafs 3; Mar. 31–Sr. Hockey: Galt 0, Sr. Marlboros 4 (OHA Sr. Finals); Apr. 3–Sr. Hockey: Galt 3, Sr. Marlboros 2 (OHA Sr. Finals); Apr. 7–Music: James Brown; Apr. 7–Sr. Hockey: Galt 1, Sr. Marlboros 3 (OHA Sr. Finals); Apr. 12–Sr. Hockey: Galt 2, Sr. Marlboros 4 (OHA Sr. Finals); Apr. 19–Music: Calypso Festival; Apr. 20–Greek Church Service; Apr. 21–Hockey: Montreal Oldtimers vs. Toronto Oldtimers (for Charlie Conacher Cancer Research Fund); Apr. 21–Sr. Hockey: Victoriaville 4, Sr. Marlboros 1 (Allan Cup Eastern Finals); Apr. 24–Sr. Hockey: Victoriaville 6, Sr. Marlboros 4 (Allan Cup Eastern Finals); May 1-5–Variety: Soviet Navy Ensemble; May 8–Lacrosse: Detroit vs. Toronto; May 11–Variety: Italian Variety Show; June 30–July 3: Kiwanis International Convention; July 14–Wrestling: Bulldog Brower vs. The Assassin; Oct. 4–Music: The Greatest British Variety Show; Oct. 16–NHL: Pittsburgh 2, Leafs 2; Oct. 19–NHL: Chicago 3, Leafs 1; Oct. 20–Jr. Hockey: Kitchener 2, Jr. Marlboros 2; Oct. 23–NHL: St. Louis 4, Leafs 6; Oct. 25–Jr. Hockey: Montreal 5, Jr. Marlboros 6; Oct. 26–NHL: Boston 0, Leafs 2; Oct. 27–Jr. Hockey: London 7, Jr. Marlboros 5; Oct. 27–Music: Italian Show w/Giani Morandi; Oct. 30–NHL: Canadiens 5, Leafs 0; Nov. 1–Music: The Young Rascals and the Union Gap; Nov. 2–NHL: Flyers 3, Leafs 2; Nov. 3–Jr. Hockey: Peterborough 8, Jr. Marlboros 3; Nov. 4-11: Ice Capades; Nov. 13–NHL: Boston 1, Leafs 1; Nov. 15–Music: James Brown; Nov. 16–NHL: Chicago 1, Leafs 3; Nov. 17–Jr. Hockey: Niagara Falls 3, Jr. Marlboros 8; Nov. 19–Watchtower religious meeting; Nov. 20–NHL: Pittsburgh 2, Leafs 5; Nov. 22–Jr. Hockey: St. Catharines 5, Jr. Marlboros 7; Nov. 23–NHL: Detroit 5, Leafs 2; Nov. 24–Jr. Hockey: Ottawa 3, Jr. Marlboros 4; Nov. 30–NHL: Minnesota 3, Leafs 3; Dec. 1–Jr. Hockey: Oshawa 9, Jr. Marlboros 4; Dec. 7–NHL: Rangers 2, Leafs 5; Dec. 8–Jr. Hockey: Ottawa 4, Jr. Marlboros 3; Dec. 11–NHL: Canadiens 4, Leafs 4; Dec. 13–Jr. Hockey: London 6, Jr. Marlboros 5; Dec. 14–NHL: St. Louis 2, Leafs 3; Dec. 15–Jr. Hockey: Hamilton 6, Jr. Marlboros 4; Dec. 18–NHL: Oakland 2, Leafs 5; Dec. 21–NHL: Detroit 3, Leafs 8; Dec. 27–Jr. Hockey: Peterborough 7, Jr. Marlboros 3; Dec. 28–NHL: Los Angeles 4, Leafs 1; Dec. 29–Jr. Hockey: London 6, Jr. Marlboros 4.

1969 • Jan. 1–NHL: Oakland 3, Leafs 7; Jan. 3–Jr. Hockey: Oshawa 6, Jr. Marlboros 4; Jan. 4–NHL: Rangers 3, Leafs 5; Jan. 5–Jr. Hockey: Niagara Falls 2, Jr. Marlboros 7; Jan. 8–NHL: Flyers 4, Leafs 4; Jan. 10–Jr. Hockey: St. Catharines 4, Jr. Marlboros 3; Jan. 11–NHL: Los Angeles 2, Leafs 4; Jan. 12–Jr. Hockey: Kitchener 3, Jr. Marlboros 5; Jan. 15–NHL: Boston 5, Leafs 5; Jan. 18–NHL: Detroit 1, Leafs 1; Jan. 19–Int'l. Hockey: USSR 4, Canada 2; Jan. 19–Jr. Hockey: Ottawa 5, Jr. Marlboros 9; Jan. 21–Feb. 2: Ice Follies of 1969; Feb. 4–Jr. Hockey: Hamilton 5, Jr. Marlboros 2; Feb. 5–NHL: Minnesota 5, Leafs 5; Feb. 7–Jr. Hockey: St. Catharines 4, Jr. Marlboros 4; Feb. 8–NHL: Oakland 4, Leafs 1; Feb. 9–Jr. Hockey: Montreal 3, Jr. Marlboros 4; Feb. 12–NHL: Minnesota 1, Leafs 7; Feb. 14–Track and Field: Telegram-Maple Leaf Games; Feb. 15–NHL: Rangers 2, Leafs 6; Feb. 16–Jr. Hockey: Kitchener, Jr. Marlboros; Feb. 19–NHL: Canadiens 1, Leafs 5; Feb. 22–NHL: Chicago 4, Leafs 2; Feb. 23–Jr. Hockey: Niagara Falls 3, Jr. Marlboros 8; Feb. 26–NHL: St. Louis 2, Leafs 3; Mar. 1–NHL: Pittsburgh 3, Leafs 3; Mar. 2–Jr. Hockey: Peterborough, Jr. Marlboros; Mar. 2–NHL: Chicago 1, Leafs 2; Mar. 5–NHL: Los Agneles 4, Leafs 6; Mar. 8–NHL: Flyers 2, Leafs 2; Mar. 9–Jr. Hockey: Ottawa 6, Jr. Marlboros 4; Mar. 14–Jr. Hockey: St. Catharines 5, Jr. Marlboros 5; Mar. 15–NHL: Boston 4, Leafs 7; Mar. 18–Jr. Hockey: St. Catharines 4, Jr. Marlboros 7; Mar. 21–Jr. Hockey: St. Catharines 6, Jr. Marlboros 2; Mar. 21–Music: The Doors; Mar. 22–NHL: Detroit 1, Leafs 3; Mar. 23–World Figure Skating Exhibition; Mar. 26–NHL: Canadiens 4, Leafs 6; Mar. 28–Music: 48th Highlanders Military Tattoo; Mar. 29–NHL: Rangers 4, Leafs 2; Apr. 5–NHL: Boston 4, Leafs 3; Apr. 6–NHL: Boston 3, Leafs 2; Apr. 12–Greek Church Service; Apr. 27–Music: Paul Mauriat and his Orchestra; May 3–Music: The Jimi Hendrix Experience; May 7-11–Variety: Russian Festival of Song, Dance and Music; June 12-13: International Floor Hockey Tournament (Special Olympics); June 15–Metro Toronto Concert for Timmy; June 20–Music: James Brown; Oct. 2-4–Music: British Tournament and Tattoo; Oct. 6–Boxing: Frank Tunney's Amateur Boxing Night–Canada vs. Italy; Oct. 12–Jr. Hockey: Kitchener 4, Jr. Marlboros 6; Oct. 12–Music: Italian Variety Show w/Rita Pavone; Oct. 15–NHL: Canadiens 2, Leafs 2; Oct. 18–NHL: Chicago 1, Leafs 4; Oct. 19–Jr. Hockey: London 6, Jr. Marlboros 10; Oct. 22–NHL: Flyers 4, Leafs 3; Oct. 24–Jr. Hockey: Montreal 2, Jr. Marlboros 6; Oct. 25–NHL: St. Louis 2, Leafs 4; Oct. 26–Jr. Hockey: Hamilton 4, Jr. Marlboros 5; Oct. 26–Music: Italian Variety Show w/Nino Taranto; Oct. 29–NHL: Boston 2, Leafs 4; Nov. 1–NHL: Rangers 3, Leafs 4; Nov. 2–Jr. Hockey: Peterborough 2, Jr. Marlboros 6; Nov. 3-9: Ice Capades; Nov. 10–Music: Johnny Cash; Nov. 12–NHL: Pittsburgh 3, Leafs 0; Nov. 14–Jr. Hockey: St. Catharines 4, Jr. Marlboros 5; Nov. 15–NHL: Flyers 2, Leafs 4; Nov. 16–Jr. Hockey: Niagara Falls 4, Jr. Marlboros 8; Nov. 19–NHL: Los Angeles 4, Leafs 4; Nov. 22–NHL: Detroit 0, Leafs 4; Nov. 23–Jr. Hockey: Ottawa 4, Jr. Marlboros 6; Nov. 26–NHL: Canadiens 3, Leafs 1; Nov. 28–Music: Englebert Humperdink; Nov. 29–NHL: Minnesota 2, Leafs 5; Dec. 4-7–Music: Osipov Balalaika Orchestra; Dec. 6–NHL: Pittsburgh 0, Leafs 5; Dec. 13–NHL: Detroit 3, Leafs 1; Dec. 14–Jr. Hockey: Hamilton 3, Jr. Marlboros 1; Dec. 20–NHL: Rangers 5, Leafs 2; Dec. 24–NHL: Los Angeles 1, Leafs 8; Dec. 26–Int'l. Hockey: USSR 2, Canada 3; Dec. 26–Jr. Hockey: St. Catharines 5, Jr. Marlboros 3; Dec. 27–NHL: St. Louis 1, Leafs 4; Dec. 30–Jr. Hockey: London 2, Jr. Marlboros 0; Dec. 31–NHL: Oakland 1, Leafs 1.

1970 • Jan. 1–Int'l. Hockey: Czech National Team 4, Canada 0; Jan. 3–NHL: Chicago 2, Leafs 6; Jan. 7–NHL: Minnesota 3, Leafs 3; Jan. 10–NHL: Boston 3, Leafs 4; Jan. 14–Jr. Hockey: Hamilton 3, Jr. Marlboros 1; Jan. 14–NHL: Rangers 7, Leafs 1; Jan. 17–NHL: Pittsburgh 0, Leafs 4; Jan. 20–Feb. 1: Ice Follies of 1970; Jan. 21–Jr. Hockey: Ottawa 3, Jr. Marlboros 5; Jan. 26–Jr. Hockey: St. Catharines 5, Jr. Marlboros 3; Jan. 28–Jr. Hockey: London 2, Jr. Marlboros 0; Feb. 2–Jr. Hockey: Oshawa 4, Jr. Marlboros 4; Feb. 4–Jr. Hockey: Niagara Falls 3, Jr. Marlboros 9; Feb. 4–NHL: St. Louis 0, Leafs 1; Feb. 5–Track and Field: Telegram-Maple Leaf Games; Feb. 7–NHL: Oakland 1, Leafs 5; Feb. 9–Jr. Hockey: Peterborough 4, Jr. Marlboros 4; Feb. 11–Jr. Hockey: Kitchener 6, Jr. Marlboros 7; Feb. 14–NHL: Flyers 3, Leafs 4; Feb. 16–Boxing: Joe Frazier vs. Jimmy Ellis (closed circuit coverage); Feb. 16–Jr. Hockey: Montreal 2, Jr. Marlboros 5; Feb. 18–Jr. Hockey: Ottawa 3, Jr. Marlboros 3; Feb. 18–NHL: Canadiens 3, Leafs 5; Feb. 21–NHL: Detroit 7, Leafs 5; Feb. 25–NHL: Oakland 1, Leafs 4; Feb. 28–NHL: Los Angeles 3, Leafs 3; Mar. 1–Music: Buck Owens and the Buckaroos; Mar. 6–Jr. Hockey: St. Catharines 2, Jr. Marlboros 4; Mar. 6–Toronto Police Association Concert; Mar. 7–NHL: Minnesota 8, Leafs 3; Mar. 8–Jr. Hockey: Montreal 2, Jr. Marlboros 8; Mar. 10–Jr. Hockey: Hamilton 4, Oshawa 5; Mar. 11–NHL: Detroit 3, Leafs 1; Mar. 12–Jr. Hockey: Oshawa 1, Jr. Marlboros 4; Mar. 13–England, Ireland and Scotland in Concert; Mar. 14–NHL: Boston 1, Leafs 2; Mar. 15–Jr. Hockey: Oshawa 4, Jr. Marlboros 7; Mar. 15–NHL: Canadiens 3, Leafs 3; Mar. 18–NHL: Chicago 7, Leafs 4; Mar. 19-30–Ice Show: Disney on Parade; Mar. 28–Jr. Hockey: London 3, Jr. Marlboros 3; Mar. 28–NHL: Chicago 1, Leafs 1; Mar. 31–Jr. Hockey: London 2, Jr. Marlboros 6; Apr. 1–NHL: Rangers 2, Leafs 1; Apr. 3–Music: Delaney, Bonny and Friends; Apr. 4–NHL: Boston 4, Leafs 2; Apr. 7–Jr. Hockey: Montreal 7, Jr. Marlboros 1; Apr. 12–Jr. Hockey: Montreal 7, Jr. Marlboros 2; Apr. 17–Jr. Hockey: Montreal 2, Jr. Marlboros 4; Apr. 25–Greek Church Service; Apr. 26–Wrestling: The Shiek vs. Haystack Calhoun; May 3–Ontario Secondary School Teachers Federation Meeting; May 10–Wrestling: The Sheik vs. Haystack Calhoun; May 15-18: Garden Brothers Circus; June 1-7–Variety: Red Army Singers, Dancers and Musicians; June 11–Music: Tom Jones; June 14–Soccer: World Cup Soccer–Italy vs. Brazil (closed circuit coverage); June 28-30: Moiseyev Dance Company; July 4–Music: Latvian Song Festival; July 31–Variety: Caribana; Aug. 4–Boxing: George Foreman vs. George Chuvalo (closed circuit coverage); Sept. 19–Music: Creedence Clearwater Revival; Sept. 26-27–Music: Coldstream Guards and the Black Watch; Oct. 1–Jr. Hockey: Peterborough 9, Jr. Marlboros 2; Oct. 4–Music: Sly and the Family Stone; Oct. 6-12–Ice Show: Moscow Circus on Ice; Oct. 13–Jr. Hockey: Ottawa 7, Jr. Marlboros 5; Oct. 14–NHL: St. Louis 3, Leafs 7; Oct. 15–Jr. Hockey: Niagara Falls 4, Jr. Marlboros 10; Oct. 16–Music: Blood, Sweat and Tears; Oct. 17–NHL: Rangers 6, Leafs 2; Oct. 20–Jr. Hockey: Montreal 4, Jr. Marlboros 3; Oct. 22–Jr. Hockey: Oshawa 5, Jr. Marlboros 7; Oct. 23–Jr. Hockey: Montreal 4, Jr. Marlboros 3; Oct. 24–NHL: Chicago 1, Leafs 0; Oct. 25–Jr. Hockey: Hamilton 0, Jr. Marlboros 6; Oct. 26–Boxing: Muhammad Ali vs. Jerry Quail (closed circuit coverage); Oct. 28–NHL: Canadiens 2, Leafs 6; Oct. 30–Jr. Hockey: St. Catharines 5, Jr. Marlboros 9; Oct. 31–NHL: Minnesota 3, Leafs 1; Nov. 3-8: Ice Capades; Nov. 11–NHL: Vancouver 4, Leafs 2; Nov. 14–NHL: Boston 2, Leafs 3; Nov. 18–NHL: Buffalo 7, Leafs 2; Nov. 21–NHL: California 3, Leafs 5; Nov. 24–NHL: Pittsburgh 4, Leafs 4; Nov. 26-29: Royal Lippizan Stallions; Nov. 28–NHL: Detroit 4, Leafs 9; Dec. 2–NHL: Los Angeles 0, Leafs 7; Dec. 4–Jr. Hockey: London 0, Jr. Marlboros 4; Dec. 5–NHL: Rangers 1, Leafs 0; Dec. 6–Jr. Hockey: Kitchener 4, Jr. Marlboros 5; Dec. 7–Boxing: Muhammad Ali vs. Oscar Bonavena (closed circuit coverage); Dec. 9–NHL: Canadiens 0, Leafs 4; Dec. 11–Jr. Hockey: St. Catharines 5, Jr. Marlboros 3; Dec. 12–NHL: Chicago 1, Leafs 2; Dec. 13–Jr. Hockey: Peterborough 2, Jr. Marlboros 3; Dec. 18–Jr. Hockey: London 1, Jr. Marlboros 11; Dec. 19–NHL: Buffalo 0, Leafs 2; Dec. 20–Jr. Hockey: Peterborough 2, Jr. Marlboros 12; Dec. 23–NHL: Vancouver 2, Leafs 7; Dec. 26–NHL: Flyers 1, Leafs 9; Dec. 27–Jr. Hockey: Ottawa 4, Jr. Marlboros 4; Dec. 28–Hockey: Canadian University Tournament; Dec. 30–NHL: California 1, Leafs 3.

1971 • Jan. 2–NHL: Detroit 0, Leafs 13; Jan. 3–Jr. Hockey: Niagara Falls 7, Jr. Marlboros 12; Jan. 6–NHL: Minnesota 4, Leafs 4; Jan. 8–Jr. Hockey: Peterborough, Jr. Marlboros; Jan. 9–NHL: Pittsburgh 2, Leafs 5; Jan. 10–Jr. Hockey: Kitchener, Jr. Marlboros; Jan. 13–NHL: California 1, Leafs 1; Jan. 14–Basketball: Lakers 126, Cincinnati 120; Jan. 15–Jr. Hockey: Ottawa 4, Jr. Marlboros 7; Jan. 16–NHL: Los Angeles 1, Leafs 8; Jan. 19-31: Ice Follies of 1971; Feb. 1–Music: Chicago; Feb. 3–NHL: St. Louis 2, Leafs 6; Feb. 5–Track and Field: Telegram-Maple Leaf Games; Feb. 6–Jr. Hockey: London 6, Jr. Marlboros 6; Feb. 6–NHL: Flyers 2, Leafs 4; Feb. 7–Music: Mazowsze Polish Song and Dance Company; Feb. 11-12: Ontario Progressive Conservative Convention; Feb. 12–Jr. Hockey: St. Catharines 9, Jr. Marlboros 4; Feb. 13–NHL: Los Angeles 1, Leafs 8; Feb. 14–Jr. Hockey: Hamilton 2, Jr. Marlboros 8; Feb. 14–NHL: Boston 5, Leafs 1; Feb. 17–NHL: Pittsburgh 3, Leafs 4; Feb. 19–Hockey: Montreal Oldtimers vs. Toronto Oldtimers; Feb. 20–Jr. Hockey: Kitchener 7, Jr. Marlboros 15; Feb. 20–NHL: St. Louis 1, Leafs 3; Feb. 21–Jr. Hockey: Niagara Falls 2, Jr. Marlboros 5; Feb. 25–NHL: Minnesota 1, Leafs 1; Feb. 26–Music: Toronto Police Association concert; Feb. 27–NHL: Buffalo 0, Leafs 2; Feb. 28–Jr. Hockey: Oshawa 4, Jr. Marlboros 8; Mar. 3–Jr. Hockey: Oshawa 1, Jr. Marlboros 16; Mar. 3–NHL: Vancouver 1, Leafs 3; Mar. 6–NHL: Chicago 2, Leafs 2; Mar. 7–Roller Derby: San Francisco Bombers vs. the Midwest Pioneers; Mar. 8–Boxing: Donato Paduno vs. Clyde Gray w/Joe Frazier vs. Muhammad Ali (Live and Closed Circuit); Mar. 10–NHL: Canadiens 1, Leafs 2; Mar. 12–Jr. Hockey: Peterborough 8, Jr. Marlboros 3; Mar. 13–NHL: Flyers 3, Leafs 2; Mar. 14–Jr. Hockey: Ottawa 5, Jr. Marlboros 2; Mar. 19–Jr. Hockey: Montreal 2, Jr. Marlboros 5; Mar. 20–NHL: Rangers 1, Leafs 3; Mar. 21–Jr. Hockey: Oshawa 2, Jr. Marlboros 3; Mar. 31–NHL: Detroit 2, Leafs 2; Apr. 2–Jr. Hockey: Peterborough 2, Jr. Marlboros 5; Apr. 3–NHL: Boston 8, Leafs 3; Apr. 4–Jr. Hockey: Peterborough 1, Jr. Marlboros 6; Apr. 10–NHL: Rangers 1, Leafs 3; Apr. 11–NHL: Rangers 4, Leafs 2; Apr. 14–Jr. Hockey: Ottawa 3, Jr. Marlboros 8; Apr. 15–NHL: Rangers 2, Leafs 1; Apr. 18–Jr. Hockey: Ottawa 2, Jr. Marlboros 6; Apr. 18–Wrestling: The Shiek vs. Tex McKenzie; Apr. 24–Jr. Hockey: St. Catharines 5, Jr. Marlboros 2; May 10–Boxing: Jimmy Ellis vs. George Chuvalo w/Foreman vs. Peralta (Live and Closed Circuit); May 13-16: Garden Brothers Circus; May 21-23–Variety: Georgian State Song and Dance Ensemble; May 28–Music: 48th Highlanders Tattoo; May 29–Music: Tom Jones; May 30–Music: Rock Variety Show; June 4-6: Antique Show and Sale; June 9-10: International Floor Hockey Tournament (Special Olympics); Aug. 7-8: A Canine Extravaganza Dog Show; Sept. 4–Music: Led Zeppelin; Oct. 9–Music: Grand Funk Railroad; Oct. 10–Music: Italian Show w/Nicola De Bari; Oct. 13–NHL: Detroit, Leafs (Postponed to November 1 due to death of Stafford Smythe); Oct. 16–NHL: Rangers 5, Leafs 3; Oct. 20–NHL: Buffalo 7, Leafs 2; Oct. 22–Jr. Hockey: Montreal 7, Jr. Marlboros 8; Oct. 23–NHL: Flyers 3, Leafs 5; Oct. 24–Jr. Hockey: Ottawa 0, Jr. Marlboros 5; Oct. 27–NHL: Vancouver 0, Leafs 0; Oct. 29–Jr. Hockey: Peterborough 5, Jr. Marlboros 3; Oct. 30–NHL: Minnesota 1, Leafs 1; Oct. 31–Jr. Hockey: Hamilton 1, Jr. Marlboros 4; Nov. 1–NHL: Detroit 1, Leafs 6; Nov. 2-7: Ice Capades; Nov. 10–NHL: Canadiens 5, Leafs 2; Nov. 12–Jr. Hockey: Montreal 6, Jr. Marlboros 11; Nov. 13–NHL: Vancouver 2, Leafs 2; Nov. 14–Jr. Hockey: Peterborough 4, Jr. Marlboros 6; Nov. 17–NHL: Los Angeles 1, Leafs 5; Nov. 19–Jr. Hockey: St. Catharines 3, Jr. Marlboros 11; Nov. 20–NHL: California 1, Leafs 5; Nov. 21–Jr. Hockey: Kitchener 4, Jr. Marlboros 8; Nov. 26–Jr. Hockey: Hamilton 1, Jr. Marlboros 5; Nov. 27–NHL: Chicago 3, Leafs 3; Nov. 28–Jr. Hockey: London 3, Jr. Marlboros 4; Dec. 1–NHL: St. Louis 2, Leafs 4; Dec. 2–Basketball: Baltimore 105, Buffalo 109; Dec.

3–Music: Ike and Tina Turner Revue; Dec. 4–NHL: Boston 5, Leafs 3; Dec. 7–Roller Derby: San Francisco Bombers vs. Canadian Chiefs; Dec. 8–NHL: Minnesota 1, Leafs 3; Dec. 9–Music: The Faces w/Rod Stewart; Dec. 11–NHL: Chicago 3, Leafs 1; Dec. 12–Jr. Hockey: Niagara Falls 5, Jr. Marlboros 6; Dec. 15–NHL: Pittsburgh 2, Leafs 3; Dec. 18–Jr. Hockey: Oshawa 1, Jr. Marlboros 5; Dec. 18–NHL: Buffalo 1, Leafs 8; Dec. 19–Jr. Hockey: Niagara Falls 7, Jr. Marlboros 4; Dec. 24–Jr. Hockey: St. Catharines, Jr. Marlboros; Dec. 25–NHL: Detroit 3, Leafs 5; Dec. 26–Jr. Hockey: Kitchener 3, Jr. Marlboros 6; Dec. 29–NHL: St. Louis 6, Leafs 3.

1972 • Jan. 1–Jr. Hockey: Peterborough 3, Jr. Marlboros 5; Jan. 1–NHL: Canadiens 2, Leafs 5; Jan. 5–NHL: Boston 2, Leafs 0; Jan. 7–Jr. Hockey: Oshawa 5, Jr. Marlboros 5; Jan. 8–NHL: Flyers 2, Leafs 2; Jan. 9–Jr. Hockey: Ottawa 3, Jr. Marlboros 5; Jan. 9–Wrestling: The Sheik vs. Bulldog Brower; Jan. 12–NHL: Los Angeles 1, Leafs 1; Jan. 14–Basketball: Indiana vs. Memphis, Kentucky vs. Dallas; Jan. 15–Jr. Hockey: Montreal 4, Jr. Marlboros 9; Jan. 15–NHL: Rangers 3, Leafs 4; Jan. 16–NHL: St. Louis 4, Leafs 3; Jan. 18-30: Ice Follies of 1972; Feb. 2–NHL: Minnesota 2, Leafs 3; Feb. 4–Track and Field: Toronto Star-Maple Leaf Indoor Games; Feb. 5–NHL: Flyers 3, Leafs 1; Feb. 6–Jr. Hockey: Hamilton 5, Jr. Marlboros 7; Feb. 9–NHL: Pittsburgh 4, Leafs 1; Feb. 11–Jr. Hockey: London 4, Jr. Marlboros 5; Feb. 12–NHL: California 0, Leafs 3; Feb. 13–Jr. Hockey: Ottawa 1, Jr. Marlboros 5; Feb. 13–Music: Three Dog Night; Feb. 19–Jr. Hockey: Kitchener 6, Jr. Marlboros 7; Feb. 19–NHL: Buffalo 1, Leafs 4; Feb. 20–Jr. Hockey: London 1, Jr. Marlboros 4; Feb. 23–NHL: Pittsburgh 0, Leafs 2; Feb. 25–Toronto Police Association Concert; Feb. 26–Jr. Hockey: Niagara Falls 3, Jr. Marlboros 8; Feb. 26–NHL: Vancouver 1, Leafs 7; Mar. 3–Jr. Hockey: St. Catharines 3, Jr. Marlboros 14; Mar. 4–NHL: Los Angeles 2, Leafs 3; Mar. 5–Jr. Hockey: Oshawa 5, Jr. Marlboros 12; Mar. 8–NHL: Detroit 1, Leafs 5; Mar. 10–Jr. Hockey: Oshawa 6, Jr. Marlboros 5; Mar. 11–NHL: California 1, Leafs 2; Mar. 12–Jr. Hockey: Niagara Falls 4, Jr. Marlboros 4; Mar. 14–Jr. Hockey: Montreal 4, Jr. Marlboros 5; Mar. 15–NHL: Canadiens 5, Leafs 2; Mar. 17–Jr. Hockey: St. Catharines 2, Jr. Marlboros 9; Mar. 18–Ice Show: Tour of Champions; Mar. 18–NHL: Chicago 2, Leafs 2; Mar. 19–Jr. Hockey: Peterborough 5, Jr. Marlboros 6; Mar. 28–Music: Moody Blues; Mar. 29–NHL: Boston 1, Leafs 4; Mar. 30–Jr. Hockey: Kitchener 5, Jr. Marlboros 9; Apr. 1–NHL: Rangers 1, Leafs 2; Apr. 2–Jr. Hockey: Kitchener 1, Jr. Marlboros 6; Apr. 5–Music: Joe Cocker; Apr. 6–Jr. Hockey: Kitchener 4, Jr. Marlboros 9; Apr. 8–NHL: Boston 2, Leafs 0; Apr. 9–Jr. Hockey: Peterborough 4, Jr. Marlboros 2; Apr. 9–NHL: Boston 5, Leafs 4; Apr. 10–Music: Her Majesty's Scots Guards; Apr. 13–Hockey: Timmy Tyke Tournament; Apr. 14–Jr. Hockey: Peterborough 3, Jr. Marlboros 5; Apr. 16–Wrestling: The Shiek vs. Carlos Rocha; Apr. 17–Jr. Hockey: Peterborough 6, Jr. Marlboros 4; Apr. 19–Soccer: Glasgow Celtic vs. Inter Milan (closed circuit coverage); Apr. 21–Music: Rock and Roll Revival w/Little Richard and Chubby Checker; Apr. 29–Soccer: Italty vs. Belgium; England vs. West Germasny (closed circuit coverage); May 13–Soccer: England vs. West Germany; Belgium vs. Italy (closed circuit coverage); May 31–Soccer: Ajax vs. Inter Milan (closed circuit coverage); June 4–Music: Jethro Tull; June 26–Music: Cheap Thrills w/Edgar Winter and Humble Pie; July 15–Music: Rolling Stones and Stevie Wonder; Aug. 22- Sept. 1–Hockey: Team Canada Training Camp and Intrasquad Games; Sept. 4–Int'l. Hockey: USSR 1, Canada 4 (Game 2 of Summit Series); Sept. 7–Music: The Faces w/Rod Stewart; Sept. 19–United Appeal Gala; Sept. 26–Music: Ten Years After w/Edgar Winter and Peter Frampton; Sept. 28-29–Variety: Ukrainian Dance Company; Oct. 5–Music: Elton John; Oct. 6–Roller Derby: New York State vs. Ontario Royals; Oct. 7–NHL: Chicago 3, Leafs 1; Oct. 8–Jr. Hockey: Sault Ste. Marie 3, Jr. Marlboros 11; Oct. 8–Music: Festival Italiano; Oct. 11–NHL: Canadiens 2, Leafs 2; Oct. 13–Jr. Hockey: Kitchener 2, Jr. Marlboros 7; Oct. 14–NHL: Los Angeles 4, Leafs 6; Oct. 15–Jr. Hockey: London 3, Jr. Marlboros 4; Oct. 17–Liberal Party Rally; Oct. 18–NHL: Pittsburgh 3, Leafs 4; Oct. 20–Jr. Hockey: Sault Ste. Marie 5, Jr. Marlboros 9; Oct. 20–Music: Rock and Roll Revival; Oct. 21–NHL: Detroit 3, Leafs 1; Oct. 22–Jr. Hockey: Peterborough 3, Jr. Marlboros 5; Oct. 27–Roller Derby: Ontario Royals vs. Ohio All Stars; Oct. 28–NHL: Boston 3, Leafs 2; Oct. 29–Jr. Hockey: Oshawa 2, Jr. Marlboros 6; Oct. 31–Music: Yes and The J. Geils Band; Nov. 1–NHL: Buffalo 1, Leafs 7; Nov. 3–Music: Carabinieri – The Continental Band of Rome; Nov. 4–NHL: St. Louis 2, Leafs 4; Nov. 5–Jr. Hockey: Hamilton 2, Jr. Marlboros 6; Nov. 8-13: Ice Capades; Nov. 15–NHL: Atlanta 1, Leafs 2; Nov. 17–Jr. Hockey: Sault Ste. Marie 0, Jr. Marlboros 12; Nov. 18–NHL: Minnesota 4, Leafs 4; Nov. 19–Jr. Hockey: Ottawa 5, Jr. Marlboros 5; Nov. 21–Boxing: Clyde Gray vs. Otho Thyson w/Ali vs. Foster (Live and Closed Circuit); Nov. 24–Jr. Hockey: Peterborough 5, Jr. Marlboros 5; Nov. 25–NHL: California 0, Leafs 11; Nov. 26–Jr. Hockey: Kitchener 3, Jr. Marlboros 6; Dec. 2–NHL: Flyers 2, Leafs 2; Dec. 8–Jr. Hockey: St. Catharines 3, Jr. Marlboros 3; Dec. 9–NHL: Vancouver 5, Leafs 5; Dec. 10–Jr. Hockey: Kitchener 2, Jr. Marlboros 9; Dec. 13–NHL: Rangers 4, Leafs 3; Dec. 15–Jr. Hockey: London 5, Jr. Marlboros 5; Dec. 16–NHL: Detroit 4, Leafs 1; Dec. 17–Jr. Hockey: Hamilton 0, Jr. Marlboros 9; Dec. 23–NHL: Chicago 3, Leafs 5; Dec. 26–Jr. Hockey: St. Catharines 0, Jr. Marlboros 1; Dec. 27–NHL: Pittsburgh 3, Leafs 3; Dec. 29–Int'l. Hockey: Moscow Dynamo 3, Czech National Team 5; Dec. 30–NHL: St. Louis 4, Leafs 5.

1973 • Jan. 3–NHL: Canadiens 8, Leafs 4; Jan. 5–Jr. Hockey: Oshawa 3, Jr. Marlboros 7; Jan. 6–NHL: Los Angeles 2, Leafs 4; Jan. 7–Jr. Hockey: Ottawa 6, Jr. Marlboros 3; Jan. 7–NHL: California 0, Leafs 4; Jan. 10–NHL: Islanders 2, Leafs 4; Jan. 12–Jr. Hockey: Sudbury 7, Jr. Marlboros 14; Jan. 13–NHL: Boston 4, Leafs 1; Jan. 15–Music: Neil Young; Jan. 16-28: Ice Follies of 1973; Jan. 22–Boxing: George Forman vs. Joe Frazier (closed circuit coverage); Jan. 29–Soccer: All Day Soccer Fest (Toronto Indoor Soccer League); Jan. 31–NHL: Islanders 3, Leafs 5; Feb. 2–Track and Field: Toronto Star-Maple Leaf Indoor Games; Feb. 3–NHL: Vancouver 2, Leafs 1; Feb. 4–Jr. Hockey: Kitchener 2, Jr. Marlboros 9; Feb. 5–Soccer: Toronto Canadians vs. Toronto Italia; Toronto British vs. Toronto Canadians; Feb. 7–NHL: California 3, Leafs 5; Feb. 9–Jr. Hockey: Peterborough 1, Jr. Marlboros 11; Feb. 10–NHL: Los Angeles 4, Leafs 2; Feb. 11–Jr. Hockey: Ottawa 2, Jr. Marlboros 11; Feb. 12–Boxing: Clyde Gray vs. Eddie Gray (for Commonwealth Welterweight Title); Feb. 13–Soccer: Portugal vs. Canada; Britain vs. Italy (Toronto Indoor Soccer League); Feb. 14–NHL: Buffalo 3, Leafs 2; Feb. 16–Jr. Hockey: Sault Ste. Marie 1, Jr. Marlboros 15; Feb. 17–NHL: Islanders 2, Leafs 6; Feb. 18–Jr. Hockey: Sudbury 4, Jr. Marlboros 12; Feb. 18–NHL: Canadiens 2, Leafs 1; Feb. 20–Music: Santana; Feb. 21–NHL: Atlanta 2, Leafs 2; Feb. 23–Jr. Hockey: Oshawa 4, Jr. Marlboros 6; Feb. 24–NHL: St. Louis 2, Leafs 4; Feb. 25–Mazowsze Dance Company; Feb. 28–NHL: Vancouver 2, Leafs 7; Mar. 2–Toronto Police Association Concert; Mar. 3–NHL: Chicago 3, Leafs 3; Mar. 4–Jr. Hockey: Hamilton 2, Jr. Marlboros 13; Mar. 9–Jr. Hockey: London 6, Jr. Marlboros 2; Mar. 10–NHL: Minnesota 3, Leafs 4; Mar. 11–Jr. Hockey: Oshawa 0, Jr. Marlboros 2; Mar. 11–Music: Pink Floyd; Mar. 14–NHL: Flyers 1, Leafs 5; Mar. 16–Jr. Hockey: Sudbury, Jr. Marlboros; Mar. 17–NHL: Rangers 5, Leafs 7; Mar. 18–Jr. Hockey: Ottawa 5, Jr. Marlboros 5; Mar. 27–NHL: Detroit 8, Leafs 1; Mar. 28–Jr. Hockey: Kitchener 2, Jr. Marlboros 5; Mar. 30–Music: Liza Minelli w/Desi Arnaz, Jr.; Mar. 31–Jr. Hockey: Kitchener 1, Jr. Marlboros 7; Mar. 31–NHL: Boston 3, Leafs 7; Apr. 1–Music: Festival Italiano w/Gianni Morandi; Apr. 2–Hockey: Timmy Tyke Tournament; Apr. 8–Jr. Hockey: Ottawa 1, Jr. Marlboros 3; Apr. 9–WHA: New England 2, Ottawa 4; Apr. 12–WHA: New England 7, Ottawa 3; Apr. 13–Music: Paul Butterfield Blues Band and Wet Willie; Apr. 14–Jr. Hockey: Ottawa 3, Jr. Marlboros 8; Apr. 15–Jr. Hockey: Ottawa 3, Jr. Marlboros 6; Apr. 23–Jr. Hockey: Peterborough 6, Jr. Marlboros 3; Apr. 27–Jr. Hockey: Peterborough 3, Jr. Marlboros 3; May 2–Jr. Hockey: Peterborough 0, Jr. Marlboros 5; May 4–Music: Frank Zappa and the Mothers of Invention; May 5–Jr. Hockey: Peterborough 5, Jr. Marlboros 5; May 6–Ukrainian Catholic Council; May 11–International Track Association Meet; May 13–Wrestling: The Shiek vs. Bobo Brazil; May 19–Music: Bill Haley and the Comets w/Dion and the Belmonts; May 26–Roller Derby: Canadian All-Stars vs. Boston Bucks; May 30–Music: Jethro Tull; June 8–Music: The Donna Fargo Show w/Hank Williams Jr.; June 24–Wrestling: Harley Race vs. Pat O'Connor; June 28–Music: Herman's Hermits w/Gerry and the Pacemakers; Aug. 29–Music: Santana; Sept. 10–Boxing: Muhammad Ali vs. Ken Norton (closed circuit coverage); Sept. 22–Boxing: Jose Napoles vs. Clyde Gray (World Welterweight Title Fight); Sept. 23–Wrestling: Jack Brisco vs. Eric the Animal; Oct. 5–Roller Derby; Oct. 7–Music: Johnny Lombardi's Italian Festival; Oct. 10–NHL: Buffalo 4, Leafs 7; Oct. 11–Boxing: Ken Buchanan vs. Frankie Otero (Light Heavyweight Championship); Oct. 12–Jr. Hockey: Peterborough 7, Jr. Marlboros 6; Oct. 13–NHL: Los Angeles 3, Leafs 6; Oct. 14–Jr. Hockey: London, Jr. Marlboros; Oct. 19–Jr. Hockey: Sault Ste. Marie 5, Jr. Marlboros 5; Oct. 20–NHL: Rangers 2, Leafs 3; Oct. 21–Jr. Hockey: Oshawa 7, Jr. Marlboros 3; Oct. 21–Roller Derby: Canadian All Stars vs. Brooklyn Bombers; Oct. 23–NHL: Minnesota 2, Leafs 2; Oct. 26–Basketball: Cleveland 97, Buffalo 104; Oct. 27–NHL: Boston 3, Leafs 2; Oct. 28–Jr. Hockey: Ottawa 2, Jr. Marlboros 4; Oct. 30–NHL: Detroit 0, Leafs 7; Nov. 2–Jr. Hockey: St. Catharines, Jr. Marlboros; Nov. 2–Music: The Johnny Cash Show; Nov. 3–NHL: Pittsburgh 0, Leafs 6; Nov. 4–Basketball: Chicago 101, Buffalo 95; Nov. 5–Music: The Edgar Winter Group; Nov. 6–Roller Derby: Canadian All Stars vs. Brooklyn Bombers; Nov. 7–NHL: Canadiens 4, Leafs 1; Nov. 9–Jr. Hockey: Kingston 1, Jr. Marlboros 8; Nov. 10–NHL: Islanders 3, Leafs 3; Nov. 11–Jr. Hockey: Peterborough 4, Jr. Marlboros 4; Nov. 13-18: Ice Capades w/Karen Magnuson; Nov. 22–NHL: Pittsburgh 4, Leafs 2; Nov. 23–Jr. Hockey: Kingston, Jr. Marlboros; Nov. 24–NHL: Chicago 3, Leafs 1; Nov. 29–NHL: St. Louis 1, Leafs 5; Nov. 30–Jr. Hockey: Oshawa 1, Jr. Marlboros 4; Dec. 1–NHL: California 2, Leafs 3; Dec. 2–Jr. Hockey: Kitchener, Jr. Marlboros; Dec. 4–Jr. Hockey: St. Catharines 7, Jr. Marlboros 6; Dec. 5–Roller Derby: Canadian All Stars vs. Chicago Hawks; Dec. 6–Jr. Hockey: Hamilton 3, Jr. Marlboros 6; Dec. 7–Music: Emerson Lake and Palmer; Dec. 8–Jr. Hockey: Sudbury 6, Jr. Marlboros 3; Dec. 8–NHL: Flyers 3, Leafs 1; Dec. 9–Basketball: Boston 118, Buffalo 114; Dec. 9–Jr. Hockey: Sault Ste. Marie 5, Jr. Marlboros 7; Dec. 10–Krasnoiarsk Siberian Dance Ensemble; Dec. 11–Jr. Hockey: Kitchener 2, Jr. Marlboros 4; Dec. 14–Music: Alice Cooper; Dec. 15–NHL: Rangers 2, Leafs 2; Dec. 16–Whipper Billy Watson's Christmas Skate for Timmy; Dec. 19–NHL: California 3, Leafs 5; Dec. 21–Jr. Hockey: Sudbury 3, Jr. Marlboros 5; Dec. 22–NHL: Vancouver 6, Leafs 4; Dec. 23–Basketball: Capital 110, Buffalo 85; Dec. 23–Jr. Hockey: Hamilton 4, Jr. Marlboros 12; Dec. 26–Jr. Hockey: London 4, Jr. Marlboros 3; Dec. 26–NHL: Canadiens 2, Leafs 9; Dec. 27–Hockey: Open Leafs Practice; Dec. 27–Int'l. Hockey: Sweden 2, Jr. Marlboros and All-Stars 4; Dec. 29–NHL: Atlanta 3, Leafs 3; Dec. 30–Jr. Hockey: Ottawa 3, Jr. Marlboros 5; Dec. 31–Music: Seals and Croft w/England Dan and John Ford Colley.

1974 • Jan. 1-8–Int'l. Hockey: CCM International Hockey Tournament`; Jan. 1–Jr. Hockey: St. Catharines, Jr. Marlboros; Jan. 2–NHL: Detroit 3, Leafs 4; Jan. 6–Basketball: Atlanta 109, Buffalo 117; Jan. 6–Jr. Hockey: Kitchener, Jr. Marlboros; Jan. 7–NHL: Atlanta 2, Leafs 6; Jan. 10–Music: Bob Dylan and The Band; Jan. 11–Jr. Hockey: Sudbury 1, Jr. Marlboros 6; Jan. 12–NHL: St. Loius 2, Leafs 4; Jan. 13–Basketball: Houston 121, Buffalo 112; Jan. 13–Jr. Hockey: Peterborough 1, Jr. Marlboros 4; Jan. 15-27: Ice Follies of 1974; Jan. 21–Tae-Kwon-Do Exhibition; Jan. 28–Boxing: Muhammad Ali vs. Joe Frazier (closed circuit coverage); Jan. 31–NHL: Minnesota 1, Leafs 3; Feb. 1–Jr. Hockey: Kingston 4, Jr. Marlboros 6; Feb. 2–NHL: Boston 2, Leafs 6; Feb. 3–Basketball: Israel vs. University of Waterloo; Feb. 3–Basketball: Philadelphia 98, Buffalo 112; Feb. 3–Jr. Hockey: London 2, Jr. Marlboros 6; Feb. 6–NHL: Detroit 2, Leafs 2; Feb. 7–Soccer: North American Soccer League All-Stars vs. Moscow Red Army; Feb. 8–Roller Derby: New York Chiefs vs. Canadian All-Stars; Feb. 9–Jr. Hockey: Ottawa 6, Jr. Marlboros 3; Feb. 9–NHL: Minnesota 1, Leafs 4; Feb. 10–Jr. Hockey: Sault Ste. Marie 3, Jr. Marlboros 4; Feb. 12–Jr. Hockey: Kitchener 2, Jr. Marlboros 5; Feb. 13–NHL: Flyers 3, Leafs 1; Feb. 13–Soccer: Spain vs. Yugoslavia (closed circuit coverage); Feb. 15–Track and Field: Toronto Star-Maple Leaf Indoor Games; Feb. 16–NHL: Atlanta 2, Leafs 7; Feb. 17–Jr. Hockey: Hamilton 4, Jr. Marlboros 2; Feb. 18–Boxing: Clyde Gray vs. Bunny Grant (Commonwealth Welterweight Tilte); Feb. 20–NHL: Buffalo 2, Leafs 4; Feb. 21–Basketball: New York 97, Buffalo 119; Feb. 22–Music: Yes; Feb. 23–NHL: Vancouver 4, Leafs 3; Feb. 24–Jr. Hockey: Ottawa 7, Jr. Marlboros 4; Feb. 24–NHL: Los Angeles 3, Leafs 3; Feb. 26–Int'l. Hockey: Soviet Red Army Midgets 1, Markham Royals 4; Feb. 26–Soccer: West Germany vs. Italy (closed circuit coverage); Feb. 28–Jr. Hockey: Hamilton 3, Jr. Marlboros 7; Mar. 1–Toronto Police Association Concert; Mar. 2–Jr. Hockey: St. Catharines 5, Jr. Marlboros 2; Mar. 2–NHL: Islanders 2, Leafs 5; Mar. 3–Jr. Hockey: Kitchener 3, Jr. Marlboros 2; Mar. 7–NHL: Pittsburgh 2, Leafs 2; Mar. 8–Jr. Hockey: St. Catharines 5, Jr. Marlboros 4; Mar. 9–NHL: Flyers 2, Leafs 1; Mar. 10–Basketball: Portland 112, Buffalo 122; Mar. 10–Jr. Hockey: Kingston 4, Jr. Marlboros 7; Mar. 11–Music: Johnny Winter; Mar. 12–Music: Big Band Cavalcade w/Bob Crosby and Freddy Martin; Mar. 13–International Volleyball Tournament; Mar. 14–NHL: Islanders 1, Leafs 2; Mar. 15–Jr. Hockey: Oshawa 4, Jr. Marlboros 3; Mar. 16–NHL: Boston 5, Leafs 2; Mar. 16–Roller Derby: Baltimore Cats vs. Canadian All-Stars; Mar. 19-24–Ice Show: Peter Pan on Ice; Mar. 26–Boxing: George Foreman vs. Ken Norton (closed circuit coverage); Mar. 27–NHL: Chicago 5, Leafs 3; Mar. 29–Jr. Hockey: London 2, Jr. Marlboros 8; Mar. 30–NHL: Rangers 3, Leafs 7; Mar. 31–Jr. Hockey: London 4, Jr. Marlboros 7; Apr. 2–Jr. Hockey: London 4, Jr. Marlboros 4; Apr. 5–Music: The Guess Who; Apr. 6–NHL: Buffalo 1, Leafs 3; Apr. 7–WHA: Cleveland 0, Toros 4; Apr. 7–Wrestling: The Shiek vs. The Crusader; Apr. 9–WHA: Cleveland 3, Toros 4; Apr. 10–Jr. Hockey: St. Catharines 8, Jr. Marlboros 2; Apr. 13–Jr. Hockey: St. Catharines 6, Jr. Marlboros 5; Apr. 13–NHL: Boston 6, Leafs 3; Apr. 14–NHL: Boston 4, Leafs 3; Apr. 15–WHA: Cleveland 1, Toros 4; Apr. 19–WHA: Chicago 4, Toros 6; Apr. 22–WHA: Chicago 4, Toros 3; May 1–WHA: Chicago 3, Toros 5; May 3-4: Time to Run (movie); May 6–WHA: Chicago 5, Toros 2; May 21–Lacrosse: Toronto Tomahawks vs. Les Quebecois; May 24-25: Ontario Invitational Floor Hockey Tournament (Special Olympics); June 12–Olympic Gymnastic

Tournament–Russia vs. Canada; June 13: World Cup Soccer (closed circuit coverage); June 17–Boxing: Clyde Gray vs. Gil King w/Frazier vs. Quarry (Live and Closed Circuit); June 26–Basketball: International Tournament w/Canada and Italy; July 3: World Cup Soccer (closed circuit coverage); July 19: World Cup Soccer (closed circuit coverage); July 21–Tae-Kwon-Do Exhibition; July 22: World Cup Soccer (closed circuit coverage); July 23: World Cup Soccer (closed circuit coverage); Sept. 8–Evel Knievel's Snake River Canyon Jump (closed circuit coverage); Sept. 10-15–Ice Show: Ukrainian Festival on Ice; Sept. 19–Int'l. Hockey: USSR 1, Team Canada 4 (Game 2 of WHA Summit Series); Sept. 28–Music: Welsh Guards and the Argyll and Sutherland Highlanders; Oct. 2–Music: Eric Clapton; Oct. 7–Music: Rick Wakeman; Oct. 9–NHL: Kansas City 2, Leafs 6; Oct. 12–NHL: Rangers 3, Leafs 7; Oct. 15–WHA: New England 2, Toros 6; Oct. 16–NHL: Los Angeles 1, Leafs 1; Oct. 18–WHA: Indianapolis 1, Toros 3; Oct. 19–NHL: Vancouver 5, Leafs 4; Oct. 20–Jr. Hockey: Ottawa 1, Jr. Marlboros 13; Oct. 20–WHA: Michigan 3, Toros 4; Oct. 21–Music: Van Morrison; Oct. 22–WHA: Minnesota 2, Toros 11; Oct. 23–NHL: Canadiens 3, Leafs 2; Oct. 24–Basketball: New York 91, Buffalo 111; Oct. 25–WHA: Winnipeg 1, Toros 3; Oct. 26–Jr. Hockey: Sault Ste Marie 2, Jr. Marlboros 6; Oct. 26–NHL: Chicago 9, Leafs 3; Oct. 27–Jr. Hockey: Sudbury 3, Jr. Marlboros 5; Oct. 28–WHA: Phoenix 3, Toros 7; Oct. 29–Boxing: Muhammad Ali vs. George Foreman (closed circuit coverage); Oct. 29–NHL: St. Louis, Leafs (Postponed to November 25); Oct. 30–Roller Derby: Canadian All-Stars vs. California Thunderbirds; Nov. 2–Jr. Hockey: Ottawa, Jr. Marlboros; Nov. 2–NHL: Buffalo 6, Leafs 3; Nov. 3–Jr. Hockey: London, Jr. Marlboros; Nov. 4–WHA: Quebec 5, Toros 3; Nov. 5–World Gymnastics Competition; Nov. 6–NHL: Minnesota 4, Leafs 7; Nov. 7-17: Ice Capades; Nov. 18–Music: Elton John; Nov. 20–NHL: Pittsburgh 8, Leafs 5; Nov. 21–Basketball: Philadelphia 95, Buffalo 99; Nov. 22–WHA: Edmonton 8, Toros 2; Nov. 23–NHL: Flyers 6, Leafs 3; Nov. 25–NHL: St. Louis 2, Leafs 2; Nov. 26–WHA: Minnesota 6, Toros 2; Nov. 28–WHA: Vancouver 6, Toros 2; Nov. 30–NHL: Washington 1, Leafs 7; Dec. 1–Jr. Hockey: Hamilton 8, Jr. Marlboros 11; Dec. 3–WHA: Houston 5, Toros 4; Dec. 6–Music: George Harrison with Ravi Shankar; Dec. 7–Jr. Hockey: Sault Ste Marie 4, Jr. Marlboros 17; Dec. 7–NHL: Detroit 3, Leafs 3; Dec. 8–Jr. Hockey: Kitchener 4, Jr. Marlboros 5; Dec. 10–WHA: Minnesota 4, Toros 2; Dec. 11–NHL: Los Angeles 4, Leafs 1; Dec. 12–Basketball: Houston 113, Buffalo 124; Dec. 13–WHA: Cleveland 6, Toros 7; Dec. 14–NHL: Atlanta 2, Leafs 1; Dec. 15–Jr. Hockey: Oshawa 7, Jr. Marlboros 10; Dec. 16–Music: Genesis; Dec. 17–WHA: Winnipeg 4, Toros 1; Dec. 18–NHL: Pittsburgh 4, Leafs 6; Dec. 20–Whipper Billy Watson's Christmas Skate for Timmy; Dec. 21–NHL: Boston 4, Leafs 8; Dec. 22–Jr. Hockey: Sudbury, Jr. Marlboros; Dec. 22–WHA: Chicago 2, Toros 5; Dec. 23–WHA: Cleveland 4, Toros 1; Dec. 26–Int'l. Hockey: Czechoslovakia Jr. Nats 6, Jr. Marlboros 0; Dec. 27–WHA: Chicago 2, Toros 4; Dec. 28–NHL: Islanders 1, Leafs 3; Dec. 29–Jr. Hockey: London, Jr. Marlboros.

1975 • Jan. 1–Jr. Hockey: Kitchener, Jr. Marlboros; Jan. 1–NHL: California 3, Leafs 3; Jan. 2–Int'l. Hockey: Central Red Army 7, Jr. Marlboros 6; Jan. 3–WHA: New England 5, Toros 3; Jan. 4–NHL: Chicago 3, Leafs 6; Jan. 5–Jr. Hockey: Ottawa, Jr. Marlboros; Jan. 7–WHA: Phoenix 3, Toros 2; Jan. 8–NHL: Vancouver 4, Leafs 6; Jan. 9–Basketball: Boston 108, Buffalo 100; Jan. 10–WHA: San Diego 3, Toros 4; Jan. 11–NHL: Los Angeles 7, Leafs 5; Jan. 12–Jr. Hockey: Hamilton 6, Jr. Marlboros 12; Jan. 12–NHL: Islanders 3, Leafs 4; Jan. 14-26: Ice Follies of 1975; Jan. 21–Women's International Volleyball Tournament; Jan. 27–Music: The J. Geils Band; Jan. 28–WHA: Quebec 4, Toros 6; Jan. 29–NHL: California 2, Leafs 4; Jan. 31–WHA: Vancouver 0, Toros 6; Feb. 1–NHL: Boston 2, Leafs 3; Feb. 2–Jr. Hockey: Kingston, Jr. Marlboros; Feb. 6–Music: Marvin Gaye w/Ike and Tina Turner and Tavares; Feb. 7–WHA: Cleveland 1, Toros 4; Feb. 8–NHL: St. Louis 3, Leafs 3; Feb. 9–Int'l. Hockey: Japan 5, Jr. Marlboros 6; Feb. 9–WHA: Indianapolis 5, Toros 7; Feb. 11–WHA: Edmonton 3, Toros 4; Feb. 12–NHL: Canadiens 2, Leafs 2; Feb. 14–Track and Field: Toronto Star-Maple Leaf Indoor Games; Feb. 15–NHL: Pittsburgh 8, Leafs 3; Feb. 16–Jr. Hockey: Peterborough 5, Jr. Marlboros 7; Feb. 18–Basketball: Phoenix 109, Buffalo 124; Feb. 20–WHA: Chicago 4, Toros 3; Feb. 22–NHL: Rangers 2, Leafs 5; Feb. 23–Jr. Hockey: Sudbury 9, Jr. Marlboros 3; Feb. 25–WHA: San Diego 4, Toros 6; Feb. 26–NHL: Kansas City 2, Leafs 4; Feb. 27–Basketball: New Orleans 100, Buffalo 110; Feb. 28–Toronto Police Association Concert; Mar. 1–NHL: Washington 4, Leafs 5; Mar. 2–Jr. Hockey: London, Jr. Marlboros; Mar. 4–WHA: Baltimore 4, Toros 7; Mar. 5–NHL: Detroit 3, Leafs 4; Mar. 7–WHA: Quebec 4, Toros 1; Mar. 8–NHL: Minnesota 3, Leafs 5; Mar. 9–Jr. Hockey: Kingston, Jr. Marlboros; Mar. 9–WHA: Baltimore 2, Toros 8; Mar. 11–WHA: Phoenix 4, Toros 7; Mar. 12–NHL: Canadiens 3, Leafs 3; Mar. 14–WHA: San Diego 6, Toros 4; Mar. 15–Jr. Hockey: Saulte Ste Marie, Jr. Marlboros; Mar. 15–NHL: Flyers 4, Leafs 4; Mar. 16–NHL: Buffalo 11, Leafs 3; Mar. 17–WHA: Houston 4, Toros 5; Mar. 18–Music: Stevie Wonder; Mar. 24–NHL: California 3, Leafs 5; Mar. 25–WHA: Vancouver 4, Toros 8; Mar. 28–WHA: Edmonton 4, Toros 5; Mar. 29–World Figure Skating tour; Mar. 29–NHL: Boston 1, Leafs 1; Mar. 30–Jr. Hockey: Kingston 1, Jr. Marlboros 9; Mar. 30–WHA: New England 4, Toros 3; Mar. 31–Hockey: Timmy Tyke Tournament; Apr. 1–WHA: Indianapolis 1, Toros 7; Apr. 2–NHL: Atlanta 3, Leafs 0; Apr. 3–Music: Johnny Winter; Apr. 4–WHA: Winnipeg 1, Toros 7; Apr. 5–NHL: Buffalo 4, Leafs 2; Apr. 6–Jr. Hockey: Kingston 2, Jr. Marlboros 5; Apr. 6–WHA: Houston 5, Toros 2; Apr. 8–NHL: Los Angeles 3, Maple Leafs 2 (closed circuit coverage); Apr. 9–Jr. Hockey: Sudbury 1, Jr. Marlboros 8; Apr. 10–NHL: Los Angeles 2, Leafs 3; Apr. 11–Jehovah's Witnesses Convention; Apr. 14–WHA: San Diego 2, Toros 5; Apr. 15–Jr. Hockey: Sudbury 6, Jr. Marlboros 8; Apr. 16–WHA: San Diego 5, Toros 6; Apr. 17–Jr. Hockey: Sudbury 2, Jr. Marlboros 3; Apr. 17–NHL: Flyers 2, Leafs 0; Apr. 19–NHL: Flyers 4, Leafs 3; Apr. 20–Jr. Hockey: Hamilton 5, Jr. Marlboros 6 (OHA "A" Finals); Apr. 21–WHA: San Diego 6, Toros 4; Apr. 23–Music: John Denver; Apr. 24–Jr. Hockey: Hamilton 3, Jr. Marlboros 2 (OHA "A" Finals); Apr. 26–Boxing: George Foreman Boxing Exhibition; Apr. 27–Jr. Hockey: Hamilton 3, Jr. Marlboros 5 (OHA "A" Finals); Apr. 27–Wrestling: The Shiek vs. Von Erich/The Mighty Butcher; Apr. 30–Jr. Hockey: Hamilton 3, Jr. Marlboros 8 (OHA "A" Finals); May 2–Music: Alice Cooper; May 10–Music: Frank Sinatra; May 17–The Latamukesh East Indian Concert; June 17-18–Music: The Rolling Stones; June 30–Boxing: Muhammad Ali vs. Joe Bugner (closed circuit coverage); July 19–Music: Yes; July 21–Women's Volleyball featuring Canada, USA, Japan and Russia; Aug. 9–Music: Todd Rundgren; Aug. 17–Boxing: Canadian and Russian Olympic teams; Sept. 1–Music: Jefferson Starship; Sept. 5–Music: The Doobie Brothers; Sept. 27–Ice Show: The Real Thing on Ice w/Toller Cranston; Sept. 29–Music: The Bee Gees; Sept. 30–Boxing: Muhammad Ali vs. Joe Frazier (closed circuit coverage); Oct. 7–Music: Jethro Tull; Oct. 8–Music: Italian Festival w/Claudio Villa; Oct. 11–NHL: Chicago 1, Leafs 2; Oct. 14–WHA: Houston 3, Toros 6; Oct. 15–NHL: Pittsburgh 8, Leafs 4; Oct. 16–Music: Rick Wakeman; Oct. 17–WHA: Edmonton 4, Toros 4; Oct. 18–Jr. Hockey: Kitchener 3, Jr. Marlboros 2; Oct. 18–NHL: Rangers 1, Leafs 4; Oct. 19–Jr. Hockey: Kingston 4, Jr. Marlboros 4; Oct. 22–NHL: Vancouver 2, Leafs 3; Oct. 24–WHA: New England 5, Toros 4; Oct. 25–Jr. Hockey: Sudbury 3, Jr. Marlboros 6; Oct. 25–NHL: California 2, Leafs 2; Oct. 26–Jr. Hockey: Sault Ste. Marie 4, Jr. Marlboros 2; Oct. 27–Music: Rod Stewart and The Faces; Oct. 28–WHA: Quebec 4, Toros 6; Oct. 29–NHL: Buffalo 2, Leafs 3; Nov. 1–NHL: Kansas City 0, Leafs 3; Nov. 2–Jr. Hockey: Hamilton 4, Jr. Marlboros 0; Nov. 4–World Gymnastics Competition; Nov. 5–NHL: Detroit 3, Leafs 7; Nov. 6-16: Ice Capades; Nov. 17–WHA: Indianapolis 6, Toros 2; Nov. 18–NHL: Washington 2, Leafs 4; Nov. 19–Music: Isaac Hayes; Nov. 21–WHA: Cincinnati 7, Toros 8; Nov. 22–Jr. Hockey: Sault Ste. Marie 3, Jr. Marlboros 5; Nov. 22–NHL: Canadiens 4, Leafs 2; Nov. 25–WHA: Cleveland 4, Toros 3; Nov. 28–WHA: Winnipeg 5, Toros 3; Nov. 29–NHL: Flyers 1, Leafs 1; Nov. 30–Jr. Hockey: Ottawa 3, Jr. Marlboros 3; Dec. 5–WHA: Quebec 4, Toros 7; Dec. 6–Jr. Hockey: Sudbury 3, Jr. Marlboros 3; Dec. 6–NHL: Boston 4, Leafs 2; Dec. 7–Jr. Hockey: Peterborough 5, Jr. Marlboros 4; Dec. 9–WHA: Minnesota 5, Toros 3; Dec. 11–Music: The Who; Dec. 12–Music: Rolling Thunder Review w/Bob Dylan and Joan Baez; Dec. 12–WHA: Quebec 4, Toros 6; Dec. 13–NHL: Islanders 5, Leafs 3; Dec. 14–Jr. Hockey: Kitchener 7, Jr. Marlboros 7; Dec. 14–WHA: Calgary 3, Toros 3; Dec. 16–WHA: Winnipeg 4, Toros 3; Dec. 17–NHL: St. Louis 2, Leafs 6; Dec. 18–Int'l. Hockey: Moscow Selects 3, Jr. Marlboros 5; Dec. 19–WHA: Calgary 5, Toros 3; Dec. 20–NHL: Kansas City 1, Leafs 5; Dec. 22–NHL: Los Angeles 3, Leafs 4; Dec. 23–Whipper Billy Watson's Christmas Skate for Timmy; Dec. 26–Jr. Hockey: Ottawa 3, Jr. Marlboros 6; Dec. 26–WHA: Edmonton 5, Toros 8; Dec. 27–Jr. Hockey: Windsor 1, Jr. Marlboros 6; Dec. 27–NHL: Chicago 4, Leafs 1; Dec. 28–WHA: Quebec 6, Toros 1; Dec. 29–NHL: Atlanta 2, Leafs 6; Dec. 30–WHA: Edmonton 4, Toros 6; Dec. 31–NHL: California, Leafs (Postponed to January 1).

1976 • Jan. 1–NHL: California 1, Leafs 5; Jan. 2–WHA: Phoenix 1, Toros 4; Jan. 3–NHL: Detroit 1, Leafs 0; Jan. 4–Jr. Hockey: Peterborough 2, Jr. Marlboros 6; Jan. 6–WHA: San Diego 4, Toros 6; Jan. 7–NHL: Flyers 7, Leafs 3; Jan. 9–Music: ZZ Top; Jan. 10–NHL: Los Angeles 3, Leafs 4; Jan. 13-26: Ice Follies of 1976; Jan. 27–WHA: Edmonton 4, Toros 4; Jan. 28–NHL: Islanders 3, Leafs 2; Jan. 30–WHA: Quebec 3, Toros 3; Jan. 31–Jr. Hockey: London 3, Jr. Marlboros 3; Jan. 31–NHL: Rangers 4, Leafs 6; Feb. 1–WHA: New England 7, Toros 5; Feb. 2–Jr. Hockey: London 3, Jr. Marlboros 6; Feb. 3–Variety: Mazowsze Polish Song and Dance Company; Feb. 4–NHL: Washington 4, Leafs 4; Feb. 6–WHA: Winnipeg 7, Toros 6; Feb. 7–Jr. Hockey: Kingston 7, Jr. Marlboros 4; Feb. 7–NHL: Boston 4, Leafs 11; Feb. 8–Jr. Hockey: Peterborough 3, Jr. Marlboros 5; Feb. 8–NHL: Minnesota 1, Leafs 4; Feb. 13–Track and Field: Toronto Star-Maple Leaf Indoor Games; Feb. 14–Jr. Hockey: London 2, Jr. Marlboros 5; Feb. 14–NHL: Vancouver 4, Leafs 3; Feb. 17–WHA: Minnesota 6, Toros 3; Feb. 18–NHL: Canadiens 7, Leafs 5; Feb. 20–WHA: San Diego 6, Toros 4; Feb. 21–NHL: Buffalo 4, Leafs 6; Feb. 22–Jr. Hockey: Sudbury 8, Jr. Marlboros 4; Feb. 23–NHL: Atlanta 1, Leafs 7; Feb. 24–WHA: Cincinnati 9, Toros 6; Feb. 25–NHL: Detroit 0, Leafs 8; Feb. 27–WHA: Houston 7, Toros 6; Feb. 28–NHL: California 2, Leafs 4; Feb. 29–WHA: Winnipeg 7, Toros 11; Mar. 1–NHL: Minnesota 2, Leafs 4; Mar. 2–WHA: Quebec 2, Toros 5; Mar. 5–Toronto Police Association Concert; Mar. 6–WHA: Calgary 2, Toros 5; Mar. 7–Jr. Hockey: Kitchener 1, Jr. Marlboros 10; Mar. 9–WHA: Winnipeg 5, Toros 2; Mar. 10–NHL: St. Louis 2, Leafs 2; Mar. 12–WHA: Phoenix 5, Toros 2; Mar. 13–NHL: Islanders 2, Leafs 2; Mar. 14–Music: Royal Marines and the Black Watch; Mar. 16–WHA: Cleveland 0, Toros 6; Mar. 19–WHA: Quebec 4, Toros 3; Mar. 20–NHL: Washington 3, Leafs 7; Mar. 21–WHA: Winnipeg 2, Toros 5; Mar. 23–WHA: Calgary 5, Toros 6; Mar. 26–WHA: Edmonton 3, Toros 7; Mar. 27–NHL: Buffalo 4, Leafs 2; Mar. 28–WHA: Calgary 5, Toros 4; Mar. 29–NHL: Pittsburgh 4, Leafs 5; Mar. 30–Hockey: Timmy Tyke Tournament; Apr. 1–Music: Genesis; Apr. 2–WHA: Indianapolis 3, Toros 1; Apr. 4–WHA: Quebec 5, Toros 4; Apr. 6–NHL: Pittsburgh 1, Leafs 4; Apr. 9–NHL: Pittsburgh 0, Leafs 4; Apr. 11–Music: Festival Di Primavera; Apr. 15–NHL: Flyers 4, Leafs 5; Apr. 17–NHL: Flyers 3, Leafs 4; Apr. 18–Music: Bad Company and Styx; Apr. 20–Music: Supertramp; Apr. 22–NHL: Flyers 5, Leafs 8; Apr. 24–Royal Lippizan Stallions; Apr. 26–Music: Kiss; May 1–Music: Frank Sinatra; May 9–Music: Paul McCartney and Wings; May 10–Music: Joe Cocker; May 13–Music: Johnny Winter; May 27–Music: Santana; May 28–Soccer: England vs. Italy (closed circuit coverage); June 11–Olympic Benefit Concert w/Gordon Lightfoot and Sylvia Tyson; June 15–Boxing: George Foreman vs. Joe Frazier (closed circuit coverage); June 25–Boxing: Muhammad Ali vs. Antonio Inoki (closed circuit coverage); July 3-4–Music: Latvian Song Festival; Aug. 8–Wrestling: The Sheik vs. Gene Kiniski; Aug. 11–Music: Bay City Rollers; Aug. 13-14: International Roller Skating Tournament; Aug. 15–Wrestling: Andre the Giants vs. The Sheik; Aug. 18–Music: Loggins and Mussina; Aug. 23-29–Car Show: General Motors New Model Presentation; Sept. 3–Int'l. Hockey: Sweden 5, USA 2 (Canada Cup); Sept. 5–Int'l. Hockey: Czechoslovakia 8, Finland 0 (Canada Cup); Sept. 7–Int'l. Hockey: Sweden 0, Canada 4 (Canada Cup); Sept. 8-10–Car Show: Ford Motor Company New Model Presentation; Sept. 11–Int'l. Hockey: USSR 1, Canada 3 (Canada Cup); Sept. 13–Int'l. Hockey: Czechoslovakia 0, Canada 6 (Canada Cup); Sept. 14–Music: Electric Light Orchestra; Sept. 16–Music: Nazareth and Mahogany Rush; Sept. 23-24: The Ice Show w/Toller Cranston; Sept. 28–Boxing: Muhammad Ali vs. Ken Norton (closed circuit coverage); Oct. 3–Kishore Kumar East Indian Concert; Oct. 5–Music: Jackson Browne; Oct. 9–NHL: Boston 5, Leafs 7; Oct. 10–Music: Italian Festival w/Rita Pavone and Little Tony; Oct. 11–Jr. Hockey: London 3, Jr. Marlboros 1; Oct. 13–NHL: Los Angeles 4, Leafs 4; Oct. 15–Music: Jeff Beck; Oct. 16–NHL: Flyers 5, Leafs 5; Oct. 17–Jr. Hockey: Kitchener 4, Jr. Marlboros 6; Oct. 19–Music: Paul Anka; Oct. 20–NHL: Pittsburgh 4, Leafs 4; Oct. 21–Music: The Who; Oct. 22–Music: Neil Diamond; Oct. 23–Jr. Hockey: Niagara Falls 2, Jr. Marlboros 8; Oct. 23–NHL: Islanders 5, Leafs 2; Oct. 24–Jr. Hockey: Ottawa 2, Jr. Marlboros 5; Oct. 25–Music: Charlie Pride; Oct. 27–NHL: Minnesota 5, Leafs 3; Oct. 30–Jr. Hockey: Kingston 3, Jr. Marlboros 7; Nov. 2–World Gymnastics Exhibition; Nov. 3–NHL: St. Louis 6, Leafs 2; Nov. 4-14: Ice Capades; Nov. 15–Music: The Doobie Brothers; Nov. 16–Music: Frank Zappa; Nov. 17–NHL: Canadiens 0, Leafs 1; Nov. 19–Jr. Hockey: Peterborough 7, Jr. Marlboros 5; Nov. 20–Jr. Hockey: Sudbury 4, Jr. Marlboros 7; Nov. 20–NHL: Minnesota 3, Leafs 8; Nov. 21–Music: Italian Show w/Villa-Cugini; Nov. 24–Toronto Star Maple Leaf Grand Prix Horse Show; Nov. 27–NHL: Boston 2, Leafs 4; Nov. 28–NHL: Cleveland 1, Leafs 5; Nov. 29–Music: The Bee Gees; Nov. 30–Music: Robin Trouer; Dec. 1–NHL: Los Angeles 3, Leafs 6; Dec. 4–NHL: Chicago 2, Leafs 2; Dec. 5–Jr. Hockey: London 1, Jr. Marlboros 4; Dec. 8–NHL: Vancouver 4, Leafs 3; Dec. 10–Music: The Strawbs; Dec. 11–NHL: Rangers 1, Leafs 4; Dec. 12–Jr. Hockey: Sudbury 7, Jr. Marlboros 7; Dec. 15–NHL: St. Louis 1, Leafs 4; Dec. 18–NHL: Rockies 2, Leafs 4; Dec. 20–NHL: Atlanta 2, Leafs 6; Dec. 22–NHL: Pittsburgh 5, Leafs 2; Dec. 29–Whipper Billy Watson's Christmas Skate for Timmy.

1977 • Jan. 1–NHL: Washington 1, Leafs 3; Jan. 2–Jr. Hockey: Peterborough 2, Jr. Marlboros 4; Jan. 2–Music: Rush; Jan. 5–NHL: Rockies 4, Leafs 6; Jan. 8–NHL: Buffalo 4, Leafs 2; Jan. 9–Jr. Hockey: Ottawa 2, Jr. Marlboros 2; Jan. 12–NHL: Los Angeles 2, Leafs 3; Jan. 15–Music: The Beach Boys; Jan. 15–NHL: Chicago 4, Leafs 1; Jan. 18-30: Ice Follies of 1977; Jan. 31–Jr. Hockey: Kingston 2, Jr. Marlboros 6; Feb. 1–Music: Queen; Feb. 2–NHL: Detroit 1, Leafs 9; Feb. 5–Jr. Hockey: Sault Ste. Marie 6, Jr. Marlboros 5; Feb. 5–NHL: Flyers 7, Leafs 5; Feb. 6–Jr. Hockey: Oshawa 2, Jr. Marlboros 7; Feb. 6–Wrestling: Harley Race vs. Terry Funk; Feb. 9–NHL: Atlanta 1, Leafs 5; Feb. 11–Track and Field: Toronto Star-Maple Leaf Indoor Games; Feb. 12–NHL: Washington 0, Leafs 10; Feb. 13–Music: Bruce Springsteen; Feb. 19–NHL: Pittsburgh 6, Leafs 6; Feb. 20–Jr. Hockey: Kitchener 4, Jr. Marlboros 10; Feb. 22–Hockey: Appleby College Seniors vs Lakefield; Feb. 23–NHL: Rangers 5, Leafs 4; Feb. 23–Royal Visit by Prince Andrew; Feb. 25–Jr. Hockey: Sault Ste. Marie 2, Jr. Marlboros 9; Feb. 26–NHL: Buffalo 6, Leafs 5; Feb. 27–Jr. Hockey: St. Catharines 8, Jr. Marlboros 2; Mar. 2–NHL: Cleveland 4, Leafs 1; Mar. 3-4: Adidas Tri-Country Track Meet; Mar. 5–NHL: Vancouver 4, Leafs 4; Mar. 6–Music: Genesis; Mar. 8–Music: Santana; Mar. 9–NHL: Canadiens 2, Leafs 2; Mar. 12–NHL: Detroit 0, Leafs 6; Mar. 13–Jr. Hockey: Sudbury 9, Jr. Marlboros 5; Mar. 19–NHL: Atlanta 4, Leafs 5; Mar. 20–Jr. Hockey: London 5, Jr. Marlboros 4; Mar. 21–NHL: Cleveland 7, Leafs 2; Mar. 22–Music: Peter Gabriel; Mar. 23–NHL: Islanders 1, Leafs 1; Mar. 24–Music: Jethro Tull; Mar. 25–Hockey: Catholic Yough Organization Hockey Tournament; Mar. 26–NHL: Boston 7, Leafs 5; Mar. 27–Jr. Hockey: London 5, Jr. Marlboros 3; Mar. 30–Music: The Eagles; Apr. 1–Jr. Hockey: London 3, Jr. Marlboros 0; Apr. 2–NHL: Buffalo 1, Leafs 1; Apr. 4–Music: Electric Light Orchestra; Apr. 7–NHL: Pittsburgh 6, Leafs 4; Apr. 11–Hockey: Timmy Tyke Tournament; Apr. 15–NHL: Flyers 4, Leafs 3; Apr. 17–NHL: Flyers 6, Leafs 5; Apr. 18–Music: Al Stewart; Apr. 21–NHL: Flyers 4, Leafs 3; Apr. 24–Music: Domenico Modugno Show; Apr. 29–Music: The Kinks; May 1–Music: Boston; May 6-8: Shriners' Circus; June 1-2–Music: Supertramp; June 12–Music: Ted Nugent and Uriah Heep; June 16–Music: Hall and Oates; June 21–Music: Blue Oyster Cult and Todd Rundgren; Aug. 9–Music: Bob Marley; Aug. 15–Music: Peter Frampton; Aug. 27–Ashe Bosle and Group East Indian Concert; Sept. 4-18–Car Show: General Motors New Model Presentation; Sept. 22–The Ice Show with Toller Cranston; Sept. 25–Momahad Rafi and Party East Indian Concert; Sept. 29–Music: Frank Zappa; Sept. 30–Music: Grenadier Guards and Scots Guard bands; Oct. 2–Music: Italian Music Show starring Cocciante; Oct. 5-9: Moscow Circus; Oct. 12–Music: Rod Stewart; Oct. 15–NHL: Buffalo 5, Leafs 2; Oct. 19–NHL: Rockies 4, Leafs 5; Oct. 21–Jr. Hockey: Niagara Falls 6, Jr. Marlboros 2; Oct. 22–Jr. Hockey: Kingston 4, Jr. Marlboros 8; Oct. 22–NHL: Flyers 1, Leafs 6; Oct. 24–Music: Steve Miller; Oct. 26–NHL: Canadiens 2, Leafs 2; Oct. 29–NHL: Detroit 4, Leafs 7; Oct. 30–Music: Italian Show with Franco Franchi; Oct. 31–Music: Chicago; Nov. 1–Ontario Cup International Gymnastics Competition; Nov. 3-13: Ice Capades; Nov. 15–Jr. Hockey: London 5, Jr. Marlboros 1; Nov. 16–NHL: Washington 2, Leafs 5; Nov. 19–Jr. Hockey: Sault Ste. Marie 4, Jr. Marlboros 3; Nov. 19–NHL: Boston 3, Leafs 1; Nov. 21–Music: Queen; Nov. 22–Toronto Star Maple Leaf Grand Prix Horse Show; Nov. 24–Music: Gino Vannelli; Nov. 26–Jr. Hockey: Sudbury 2, Jr. Marlboros 4; Nov. 26–NHL: Washington 4, Leafs 4; Nov. 29–NHL: Cleveland 2, Leafs 3; Nov. 30–Jr. Hockey: Oshawa 5, Jr. Marlboros 5; Dec. 1–Music: Billy Joel; Dec. 2–Jr. Hockey: Peterborough 1, Jr. Marlboros 1; Dec. 3–NHL: Detroit 2, Leafs 4; Dec. 4–Jr. Hockey: Hamilton 4, Jr. Marlboros 0; Dec. 7–NHL: Minnesota 3, Leafs 6; Dec. 10–Music: Aerosmith; Dec. 11–Jr. Hockey: Kingston 2, Jr. Marlboros 7; Dec. 13–Jr. Hockey: Peterborough 4, Jr. Marlboros 2; Dec. 14–NHL: Islanders 2, Leafs 3; Dec. 16–Jr. Hockey: Windsor 5, Jr. Marlboros 4; Dec. 17–NHL: Chicago 1, Leafs 7; Dec. 18–Jr. Hockey: Kitchener 2, Jr. Marlboros 12; Dec. 19–NHL: St. Louis 4, Leafs 4; Dec. 20–Jr. Hockey: Sault Ste. Marie 0, Jr. Marlboros 4; Dec. 21–NHL: Canadiens 3, Leafs 2; Dec. 26–NHL: Pittsburgh 5, Leafs 4; Dec. 28–Christmas Skate for Timmy; Dec. 30–Music: Rush; Dec. 31–NHL: Atlanta 3, Leafs 0.

1978 • Jan. 2–Int'l. Hockey: HC Kladno 8, Leafs 5; Jan. 2–Jr. Hockey: Ottawa 3, Jr. Marlboros 5; Jan. 4–NHL: Rockies 0, Leafs 5; Jan. 5–Variety: Bob Hope and Friends; Jan. 6–Jr. Hockey: Hamilton 0, Jr. Marlboros 4; Jan. 7–NHL: Vancouver 4, Leafs 6; Jan. 8–Jr. Hockey: Oshawa 4, Jr. Marlboros 7; Jan. 9–NHL: Atlanta 5, Leafs 2; Jan. 13–Jr. Hockey: Kingston 2, Jr. Marlboros 3; Jan. 14–NHL: Chicago 3, Leafs 3; Jan. 15–Jr. Hockey: Kitchener 3, Jr. Marlboros 4; Jan. 17-28: Ice Follies of 1978; Jan. 31–Jr. Hockey: Ottawa 6, Jr. Marlboros 7; Feb. 1–NHL: Buffalo 2, Leafs 2; Feb. 2-3–Music: Emerson, Lake and Palmer; Feb. 4–NHL: Detroit 2, Leafs 2; Feb. 5–Jr. Hockey: Windsor 3, Jr. Marlboros 3; Feb. 6–Jr. Hockey: Oshawa 8, Jr. Marlboros 3; Feb. 8–NHL: St. Louis 4, Leafs 5; Feb. 10–Track and Field: Toronto Star-Maple Leaf Indoor Games; Feb. 11–Jr. Hockey: Niagara Falls 5, Jr. Marlboros 1; Feb. 11–NHL: Rangers 2, Leafs 3; Feb. 12–Jr. Hockey: Sudbury 7, Jr. Marlboros 5; Feb. 15–NHL: Boston 4, Leafs 2; Feb. 16–Music: Santana; Feb. 17–Jr. Hockey: Peterborough 8, Jr. Marlboros 2; Feb. 18–NHL: Minnesota 4, Leafs 5; Feb. 19–Jr. Hockey: Kitchener 6, Jr. Marlboros 4; Feb. 22–NHL: Cleveland 3, Leafs 5; Feb. 24–Jr. Hockey: Sudbury 2, Jr. Marlboros 4; Feb. 25–NHL: Washington 0, Leafs 4; Feb. 26–Jr. Hockey: Ottawa 10, Jr. Marlboros 3; Feb. 28–Jr. Hockey: Kitchener 4, Jr. Marlboros 5; Mar. 1–NHL: Flyers 2, Leafs 3; Mar. 2–Jr. Hockey: London 10, Jr. Marlboros 3; Mar. 3–Jr. Hockey: Hamilton 3, Jr. Marlboros 5; Mar. 4–NHL: Vancouver 3, Leafs 4; Mar. 5–Jr. Hockey: Sault Ste. Marie 3, Jr. Marlboros 1; Mar. 7–Jr. Hockey: Niagara Falls 4, Jr. Marlboros 5; Mar. 8–NHL: Los Angeles 5, Leafs 1; Mar. 9–Music: Blue Oyster Cult; Mar. 10–Toronto Police Association Concert w/Tony Bennettt; Mar. 11–NHL: Cleveland 2, Leafs 5; Mar. 12–Jr. Hockey: London 3, Jr. Marlboros 3; Mar. 17–Music: Jimmy Buffett; Mar. 18–Jr. Hockey: Windsor 4, Jr. Marlboros 5; Mar. 18–NHL: Pittsburgh 3, Leafs 2; Mar. 19–World Figure Skating Tour; Mar. 21–Music: Triumph; Mar. 22–NHL: Islanders 6, Leafs 2; Mar. 23–Jr. Hockey: Kitchener 4, Jr. Marlboros 5; Mar. 25–Jr. Hockey: Kitchener 4, Jr. Marlboros 3; Mar. 25–NHL: Rangers 5, Leafs 2; Mar. 26–Hockey: Timmy Tyke Tournament; Mar. 27–NHL: Los Angeles 0, Leafs 3; Apr. 1–NHL: Buffalo 2, Leafs 3; Apr. 2-4: Shriners' Circus; Apr. 5–NHL: Canadiens 6, Leafs 3; Apr. 8–NHL: Boston 3, Leafs 1; Apr. 9–Music: Eric Clapton; Apr. 11–NHL: Los Angeles 3, Leafs 7; Apr. 12–Music: The Tubes; Apr. 21–NHL: Islanders 0, Leafs 2; Apr. 23–NHL: Islanders 1, Leafs 3; Apr. 27–NHL: Islanders 2, Leafs 5; May 1–Music: David Bowie; May 3–Music: Nazareth; May 6–NHL: Canadiens 6, Leafs 1; May 9–NHL: Canadiens 2, Leafs 0; May 20–Music: Bob Seger; June 3-4: Red Foster's Ontario Floor Hockey Games; June 9–Music: Bob Marley and the Wailers; June 11-14: Metro Toronto Billy Graham Crusade; June 17–East Indian Concert w/Noor Jehan; June 19–Music: Ted Nugent; July 2–Music: Lithuanian Song Festival; July 17–Music: Crosby, Stills and Nash; July 25–Music: Leo Sayer; July 30-31–Music: Neil Diamond; Aug. 6–East Indian Concert w/Kishnore Kumar; Aug. 19–Music: Linda Ronstadt; Aug. 21–Music: Boston; Sept. 19-22–Car Show: Ford Motor Company New Model Presentation; Oct. 1–Music: Neil Young; Oct. 3–Music: Frank Zappa; Oct. 5–Music: Billy Joel; Oct. 8–Music: Italian Festival w/Mino Feitano; Oct. 12–Music: Bob Dylan; Oct. 13–Jr. Hockey: Kingston 4, Jr. Marlboros 3; Oct. 14–NHL: Islanders 7, Leafs 10; Oct. 15–Music: Jethro Tull; Oct. 16–Music: Peter Gabriel; Oct. 17–Jr. Hockey: Windsor 1, Jr. Marlboros 9; Oct. 18–NHL: Buffalo 0, Leafs 2; Oct. 20–Music: Donna Summer; Oct. 21–NHL: Flyers 0, Leafs 2; Oct. 24–Jr. Hockey: London 1, Jr. Marlboros 2; Oct. 25–NHL: Canadiens 4, Leafs 4; Oct. 28–NHL: Boston 5, Leafs 3; Oct. 29–Jr. Hockey: Kitchener 3, Jr. Marlboros 7; Oct. 31–Jr. Hockey: Niagara Falls 4, Jr. Marlboros 5; Nov. 1–Music: Al Stewart; Nov. 2-12: Ice Capades; Nov. 13–Grease in Concert; Nov. 14–Ontario Cup International Gymnastics Competition; Nov. 15–NHL: Buffalo 2, Leafs 2; Nov. 16–Jr. Hockey: London 3, Jr. Marlboros 4; Nov. 16–Music: Bruce Springsteen; Nov. 18–NHL: St. Louis 1, Leafs 3; Nov. 19–Jr. Hockey: Ottawa 5, Jr. Marlboros 8; Nov. 21–Jr. Hockey: Oshawa 2, Jr. Marlboros 6; Nov. 25–NHL: Rockies 6, Leafs 3; Nov. 26–NHL: Pittsburgh 2, Leafs 8; Nov. 27–Music: Ten C.C.; Nov. 30–Jr. Hockey: Ottawa 1, Jr. Marlboros 8; Nov. 30–Music: Moody Blues; Dec. 2–NHL: Rangers 2, Leafs 5; Dec. 3–Jr. Hockey: London 2, Jr. Marlboros 8; Dec. 3–Music: Queen; Dec. 5–NHL: Boston 5, Leafs 1; Dec. 8–Jr. Hockey: Peterborough 2, Jr. Marlboros 3; Dec. 8–Music: Bob Seger; Dec. 9–NHL: Islanders 3, Leafs 2; Dec. 10–Jr. Hockey: Windsor 11, Jr. Marlboros 6; Dec. 12–Jr. Hockey: Kitchener 6, Jr. Marlboros 4; Dec. 13–NHL: Vancouver 1, Leafs 5; Dec. 16–NHL: Detroit 2, Leafs 4; Dec. 17–Jr. Hockey: Brantford 4, Jr. Marlboros 8; Dec. 17–Wrestling: Whipper Billy Watson Appreciation Night (Nature Boy Flair vs. Ricky Steamboat; Gene Kiniski vs. Dino Bravo); Dec. 19–Jr. Hockey: Niagara Falls 3, Jr. Marlboros 4; Dec. 20–NHL: Minnesota 2, Leafs 4; Dec. 22–Jr. Hockey: Sault Ste. Marie 9, Jr. Marlboros 10; Dec. 27–NHL: Boston 1, Leafs 1; Dec. 28-29–Music: Rush; Dec. 30–NHL: Washington 5, Leafs 5; Dec. 31–Music: Rush.

1979 • Jan. 3–NHL: Atlanta 4, Leafs 1; Jan. 5–Jr. Hockey: Peterborough 6, Jr. Marlboros 2; Jan. 6–NHL: Chicago 5, Leafs 3; Jan. 7–Jr. Hockey: Brantford 2, Jr. Marlboros 5; Jan. 8–NHL: Vancouver 5, Leafs 1; Jan. 9–Jr. Hockey: Kitchener 7, Jr. Marlboros 6; Jan. 10–NHL: Minnesota 2, Leafs 2; Jan. 11–Jr. Hockey: Niagara Falls 9, Jr. Marlboros 4; Jan. 13–NHL: Rockies 2, Leafs 4; Jan. 14–Jr. Hockey: Sault Ste. Marie 1, Jr. Marlboros 9; Jan. 16-28: Ice Follies of 1979 w/Peggy Fleming; Jan. 31–NHL: St. Louis 1, Leafs 5; Feb. 2–NHL: Canadiens 6, Leafs 3; Feb. 2–Track and Field: Toronto Star-Maple Leaf Indoor Games; Feb. 3–Jr. Hockey: Sudbury 7, Jr. Marlboros 5; Feb. 4–Jr. Hockey: Brantford 3, Jr. Marlboros 6; Feb. 11–Jr. Hockey: Kitchener 10, Jr. Marlboros 0; Feb. 13–Jr. Hockey: Niagara Falls 5, Jr. Marlboros 4; Feb. 14–NHL: Flyers 2, Leafs 2; Feb. 16–Jr. Hockey: Oshawa 5, Jr. Marlboros 7; Feb. 17–NHL: Los Angeles 2, Leafs 5; Feb. 18–Jr. Hockey: Sudbury 3, Jr. Marlboros 4; Feb. 20–Jr. Hockey: London 5, Jr. Marlboros 2; Feb. 23–Jr. Hockey: Brantford 8, Jr. Marlboros 5; Feb. 24–NHL: Rangers 4, Leafs 2; Feb. 25–Jr. Hockey: Windsor 2, Jr. Marlboros 6; Feb. 28–NHL: Atlanta 6, Leafs 4; Mar. 3–NHL: Flyers 3, Leafs 4; Mar. 4–Jr. Hockey: Kingston 4, Jr. Marlboros 1; Mar. 6–Jr. Hockey: Niagara Falls 5, Jr. Marlboros 2; Mar. 7–NHL: Vancouver 0, Leafs 2; Mar. 9–Jr. Hockey: Windsor 5, Jr. Marlboros 9; Mar. 10–NHL: Los Angeles 4, Leafs 9; Mar. 11–Jr. Hockey: Niagara Falls 8, Jr. Marlboros 0; Mar. 11–NHL: Pittsburgh 0, Leafs 4; Mar. 14–NHL: Buffalo 4, Leafs 1; Mar. 17–Jr. Hockey: Kitchener 4, Jr. Marlboros 3; Mar. 17–NHL: Minnesota 4, Leafs 6; Mar. 18–Music: Santana and Eddie Money; Mar. 19–Music: Trooper; Mar. 21–NHL: Detroit 4, Leafs 2; Mar. 24–NHL: Chicago 3, Leafs 3; Mar. 28–NHL: Washington 2, Leafs 6; Mar. 30–Basketball: Harlem Globetrotters; Mar. 31–NHL: Minnesota 2, Leafs 6; Apr. 4–NHL: Boston 3, Leafs 3; Apr. 7–NHL: Buffalo 2, Leafs 6; Apr. 12–NHL: Atlanta 4, Leafs 7; Apr. 13–Hockey: Timmy Tyke Tournament; Apr. 20–Music: Yes; Apr. 21–NHL: Canadiens 4, Leafs 3; Apr. 22–NHL: Canadiens 5, Leafs 4; Apr. 23–Music: Village People; Apr. 25–Music: Gino Vannelli; May 6-7–Music: Rod Stewart; May 9–Liberal Party Rally w/Pierre Trudeau; May 11–Toronto Police Association Concert; May 15–Music: Van Halen; May 25-27: Garden Brothers Circus; June 12–Music: Cheap Trick; June 14–Music: The Cars; June 22–Music: Max Webster; June 28–July 4: Kiwanis International Convention; July 29–Steve Martin Comedy Show; Aug. 4–Music: Kiss; Aug. 25-26: Church of Jesus Christ of Latter Day Saints Conference; Aug. 31–Music: The Bee Gees; Sept. 9–Frank Tunney's Pro Wrestling; Oct. 5–Music: Jethro Tull; Oct. 7–Music: Abba; Oct. 10–NHL: Rangers 6, Leafs 3; Oct. 11–Music: Earth, Wind and Fire; Oct. 12–Music: Little River Band; Oct. 13–NHL: Rockies 1, Leafs 2; Oct. 17–NHL: Minnesota 2, Leafs 6; Oct. 18-19–Music: Styx; Oct. 20–Jr. Hockey: Niagara Falls 2, Jr. Marlboros 11; Oct. 20–NHL: Vancouver 0, Leafs 2; Oct. 23–Jr. Hockey: Brantford 3, Jr. Marlboros 9; Oct. 31–NHL: Hartford 4, Leafs 2; Nov. 1–Music: Bob Marley and the Wailers; Nov. 3–Jr. Hockey: Brantford 6, Jr. Marlboros 3; Nov. 3–NHL: Buffalo 4, Leafs 3; Nov. 4–Jr. Hockey: London 3, Jr. Marlboros 6; Nov. 6-11: Ice Capades; Nov. 14–NHL: St. Louis 2, Leafs 7; Nov. 17–NHL: Boston 2, Leafs 0; Nov. 18–Jr. Hockey: Peterborough 4, Jr. Marlboros 3; Nov. 20–Jr. Hockey: Oshawa 5, Jr. Marlboros 7; Nov. 21–NHL: Edmonton 4, Leafs 4; Nov. 24–NHL: Chicago 2, Leafs 1; Nov. 27–Jr. Hockey: Niagara Falls 4, Jr. Marlboros 5; Nov. 30–Jr. Hockey: Oshawa 7, Jr. Marlboros 6; Dec. 1–NHL: Flyers 4, Leafs 4; Dec. 4–Jr. Hockey: Ottawa 7, Jr. Marlboros 4; Dec. 5–NHL: Canadiens 2, Leafs 3; Dec. 7–NHL: Islanders 6, Leafs 1; Dec. 8–Jr. Hockey: Sault Ste. Marie 3, Jr. Marlboros 5; Dec. 9–Jr. Hockey: Kingston 2, Jr. Marlboros 5; Dec. 11–Jr. Hockey: Windsor 4, Jr. Marlboros 9; Dec. 12–NHL: Rockies 3, Leafs 5; Dec. 14–Jr. Hockey: Oshawa 4, Jr. Marlboros 6; Dec. 15–Jr. Hockey: Sault Ste. Marie 3, Jr. Marlboros 2; Dec. 15–NHL: Atlanta 1, Leafs 8; Dec. 16–Jr. Hockey: Peterborough 3, Jr. Marlboros 0; Dec. 19–NHL: Los Angeles 4, Leafs 4; Dec. 21–Jr. Hockey: Windsor 3, Jr. Marlboros 7; Dec. 22–NHL: Detroit 1, Leafs 2; Dec. 23–Jr. Hockey: Sudbury 2, Jr. Marlboros 8; Dec. 26–NHL: Washington 8, Leafs 2; Dec. 29–Jr. Hockey: Kingston 9, Jr. Marlboros 5; Dec. 29–NHL: Winnipeg 1, Leafs 6.

1980 • Jan. 1–Jr. Hockey: Windsor 6, Jr. Marlboros 11; Jan. 2–NHL: Islanders 3, Leafs 1; Jan. 4–Jr. Hockey: Brantford 6, Jr. Marlboros 5; Jan. 5–NHL: Quebec 7, Leafs 3; Jan. 6–Jr. Hockey: Ottawa 3, Jr. Marlboros 6; Jan. 7–NHL: Pittsburgh 5, Leafs 9; Jan. 8–Jr. Hockey: Kitchener 2, Jr. Marlboros 9; Jan. 9–NHL: Canadiens 5, Leafs 3; Jan. 11–Music: Aerosmith; Jan. 12–NHL: Vancouver 4, Leafs 6; Jan. 13–Jr. Hockey: Peterborough 1, Jr. Marlboros 2; Jan. 16-28: Ice Follies of 1980; Jan. 29–Jr. Hockey: Kingston 4, Jr. Marlboros 4; Jan. 30–NHL: Detroit 4, Leafs 6; Feb. 1–Track and Field: Toronto Star-Maple Leaf Indoor Games; Feb. 2–NHL: Chicago 5, Leafs 4; Feb. 3–Jr. Hockey: Sault Ste. Marie 2, Jr. Marlboros 3; Feb. 8–Jr. Hockey: Niagara Falls 2, Jr. Marlboros 5; Feb. 9–NHL: Los Angeles 7, Leafs 2; Feb. 10–Jr. Hockey: Kitchener 2, Jr. Marlboros 10; Feb. 13–NHL: Pittsburgh 4, Leafs 2; Feb. 16–NHL: Hartford 3, Leafs 5; Feb. 19–Jr. Hockey: Niagara Falls 2, Jr. Marlboros 4; Feb. 22-24: Garden Brothers Circus; Feb. 26–Jr. Hockey: London 5, Jr. Marlboros 8; Mar. 1–NHL: Flyers 3, Toros 3; Mar. 2–Jr. Hockey: Ottawa 5, Jr. Marlboros 4; Mar. 4–Jr. Hockey: Kitchener 3, Jr. Marlboros 11; Mar. 7–Jr. Hockey: Sudbury 4, Jr. Marlboros 1; Mar. 7–NHL: Quebec 2, Leafs 3; Mar. 9–Jr. Hockey: London 4, Jr. Marlboros 7; Mar. 12–NHL: St. Louis 3, Leafs 2; Mar. 15–NHL: Rangers 8, Leafs 4; Mar. 17–NHL: Atlanta 5, Leafs 1; Mar.

18–Jr. Hockey: Brantford 5, Jr. Marlboros 3; Mar. 19–NHL: Winnipeg 1, Leafs 9; Mar. 20–Toronto Police Association Concert; Mar. 21–Music: John Denver; Mar. 22–NHL: Buffalo 5, Leafs 1; Mar. 23–Hockey: Montreal Oldtimers vs. Toronto Oldtimers; Mar. 23–Jr. Hockey: Brantford 5, Jr. Marlboros 4; Mar. 24–NHL: Washington 1, Leafs 6; Mar. 28–Hockey: Toronto Dominion Bank vs. CKEY; Mar. 29–NHL: Edmonton 8, Leafs 5; Apr. 2–NHL: Boston 5, Leafs 2; Apr. 3–Music: ZZ Top; Apr. 5–NHL: Minnesota 1, Leafs 2; Apr. 11–NHL: Minnesota 4, Leafs 3; Apr. 16–Music: April Wine and Johnny Winters; Apr. 23–Tennis: Jimmy Connors vs. Ilie Nastase; Apr. 27–Music: The Beach Boys; May 5-6–Music: The Who; June 3–Music: Nazareth; June 14–Music: Little River Band; June 20–Boxing: Roberto Duran vs. Sugar Ray Leonard (closed circuit coverage); June 21–Music: Prism; June 23-24–Music: Genesis; July 3–Music: Peter Gabriel; July 5-13: The Baptist World Congress featuring Billy Graham; July 17–Music: Joan Armatrading; July 18–Music: Van Halen; July 28–Music: AC/DC and Streetheart; Aug. 6–Music: Kenny Loggins; Aug. 7–Music: Journey; Aug. 9–Music: Cheap Trick; Aug. 29–Music: Yes; Sept. 5–Music: Ted Nugent; Sept. 7–Music: Elton John; Sept. 14–Hockey: Maple Leafs Open House; Sept. 21–East Indian Concert w/Melody Queen, Lata Mangeshkar and Manna Dey; Sept. 26–Music: Triumph; Sept. 28–Music: Paul Simon; Oct. 2–Boxing: Larry Holmes vs. Muhammad Ali (closed circuit coverage); Oct. 11–NHL: Rangers 8, Leafs 3; Oct. 14–Music: Gary Numan; Oct. 15–NHL: Detroit 4, Leafs 6; Oct. 18–NHL: Flyers 2, Leafs 6; Oct. 19–Jr. Hockey: London 3, Jr. Marlboros 6; Oct. 19–Wrestling: Dewey Robertson vs. The Great Hossein Arab; Oct. 21–NHL: Pittsburgh 5, Leafs 8; Oct. 24-26: World Cup Gymnastics; Oct. 28–Jr. Hockey: Brantford 2, Jr. Marlboros 6; Nov. 1–Jr. Hockey: Sudbury 4, Jr. Marlboros 11; Nov. 1–NHL: Rockies 5, Leafs 4; Nov. 2–Jr. Hockey: Sault Ste. Marie 8, Jr. Marlboros 6; Nov. 4-9: Ice Capades; Nov. 11–Music: Frank Zappa; Nov. 12–NHL: Islanders 4, Leafs 2; Nov. 15–NHL: Edmonton 2, Leafs 4; Nov. 16–Jr. Hockey: Niagara Falls 4, Jr. Marlboros 6; Nov. 16–Wrestling: Harley Race vs. Rick "Nature Boy" Flair" (World Title Wrestling Match); Nov. 18–Jr. Hockey: Peterborough 4, Jr. Marlboros 3; Nov. 19–NHL: Canadiens 5, Leafs 4; Nov. 20-21–Music: Barry Manilow; Nov. 22–NHL: Los Angeles 5, Leafs 2; Nov. 23–Jr. Hockey: Ottawa 2, Jr. Marlboros 4; Nov. 25–Boxing: Sugar Ray Leonard vs. Roberto Duran (closed circuit coverage); Nov. 26–NHL: St. Louis 6, Leafs 4; Nov. 27–Soccer: Calgary 4, Blizzard 7; Nov. 29–NHL: Washington 7, Leafs 3; Nov. 30–Jr. Hockey: Kingston 4, Jr. Marlboros 5; Nov. 30–Soccer: Edmonton 10, Blizzard 11; Dec. 2–Jr. Hockey: Niagara Falls 4, Jr. Marlboros 2; Dec. 3–NHL: Pittsburgh 4, Leafs 4; Dec. 5–Jr. Hockey: Kingston 6, Jr. Marlboros 7; Dec. 6–NHL: Quebec 2, Leafs 5; Dec. 7–Jr. Hockey: Sudbury 6, Jr. Marlboros 4; Dec. 9–Jr. Hockey: London 5, Jr. Marlboros 7; Dec. 10–NHL: Vancouver 8, Leafs 5; Dec. 12–Jr. Hockey: Oshawa 4, Jr. Marlboros 7; Dec. 13–NHL: Buffalo 5, Leafs 4; Dec. 14–Jr. Hockey: Kitchener 5, Jr. Marlboros 3; Dec. 14–Soccer: Calgary 4, Blizzard 8; Dec. 16–Jr. Hockey: Niagara Falls 4, Jr. Marlboros 3; Dec. 17–NHL: Minnesota 2, Leafs 4; Dec. 19–Jr. Hockey: Windsor 4, Jr. Marlboros 11; Dec. 20–NHL: Chicago 5, Leafs 2; Dec. 21–Jr. Hockey: Saulte Ste. Marie 3, Jr. Marlboros 4; Dec. 23–NHL: Hartford 7, Leafs 2; Dec. 27–NHL: Boston 6, Leafs 3; Dec. 28–Jr. Hockey: London 3, Jr. Marlboros 4; Dec. 31–Music: Max Webster.

1981 • Jan. 4–Jr. Hockey: Kingston 3, Jr. Marlboros 7; Jan. 4–Soccer: Calgary 5, Blizzard 4; Jan. 7–NHL: Winnipeg 8, Leafs 2; Jan. 8–Soccer: Vancouver 4, Blizzard 3; Jan. 10–NHL: Flyers 4, Leafs 4; Jan. 11–Jr. Hockey: Kitchener 5, Jr. Marlboros 3; Jan. 13–Jr. Hockey: Ottawa 7, Jr. Marlboros 3; Jan. 14–NHL: Edmonton 7, Leafs 4; Jan. 16–Jr. Hockey: Windsor 3, Jr. Marlboros 5; Jan. 17–NHL: Canadiens 5, Leafs 6; Jan. 18–Jr. Hockey: Peterborough 3, Jr. Marlboros 4; Jan. 18–Soccer: Edmonton 4, Blizzard 5; Jan. 20-21–Music: Bruce Springsteen; Jan. 22–Soccer: Vancouver 6, Blizzard 8; Jan. 24–NHL: Hartford 4, Leafs 7; Jan. 25–Jr. Hockey: Ottawa 7, Jr. Marlboros 4; Jan. 26–NHL: Detroit 4, Leafs 2; Jan. 28–NHL: Islanders 6, Leafs 4; Jan. 29–Soccer: Edmonton 4, Blizzard 6; Jan. 31–NHL: Winnipeg 2, Leafs 0; Feb. 1–Jr. Hockey: Sault Ste. Marie 6, Jr. Marlboros 5; Feb. 2-8–Tennis: Molson Challenge; Feb. 9–Music: Elvis Costello; Feb. 13–Track and Field: Toronto Star-Maple Leaf Indoor Games; Feb. 14–Jr. Hockey: Oshawa 4, Jr. Marlboros 5; Feb. 14–NHL: Rangers 3, Leafs 6; Feb. 15–Jr. Hockey: Sudbury 4, Jr. Marlboros 1; Feb. 15–Soccer: Vancouver 6, Blizzard 7; Feb. 17–Jr. Hockey: Brantford 6, Jr. Marlboros 5; Feb. 21–NHL: Minnesota 3, Leafs 5; Feb. 22–Jr. Hockey: Windsor 2, Jr. Marlboros 3; Feb. 25–NHL: Rockies 5, Leafs 9; Mar. 1–Jr. Hockey: Niagara Falls 7, Jr. Marlboros 6; Mar. 2–NHL: Los Angeles 1, Leafs 0; Mar. 3–Jr. Hockey: Brantford 4, Jr. Marlboros 7; Mar. 4–NHL: Vancouver 5, Leafs 2; Mar. 5–Jr. Hockey: Oshawa 1, Jr. Marlboros 5; Mar. 6–Music: Boomtown Rats; Mar. 7–NHL: Calgary 6, Leafs 4; Mar. 8–Jr. Hockey: Kitchener 4, Jr. Marlboros 5; Mar. 11–NHL: Boston 4, Leafs 4; Mar. 13–Jr. Hockey: Peterborough 4, Jr. Marlboros 5; Mar. 14–NHL: Washington 3, Leafs 5; Mar. 17–Music: Ted Nugent; Mar. 18–NHL: St. Louis 2, Leafs 6; Mar. 19–Jr. Hockey: Niagara Falls 4, Jr. Marlboros 7; Mar. 21–NHL: Buffalo 6, Leafs 2; Mar. 22–Jr. Hockey: Niagara Falls 9, Jr. Marlboros 5; Mar. 23-25–Music: Rush; Mar. 28–NHL: Calgary 5, Leafs 9; Apr. 1–NHL: Chicago 2, Leafs 2; Apr. 4–NHL: Quebec 5, Leafs 5; Apr. 11–NHL: Islanders 6, Leafs 1; June 6–Music: Kenny Rogers; June 25–Variety: Astrowars; June 30–Music: Santana; July 17–Music: The Tubes; July 22–Music: Tom Petty; July 28–Music: Ozzy Osbourne; Aug. 4–Music: Van Halen; Aug. 7-8–Music: Styx; Sept. 9–Music: Pat Benatar; Sept. 25–Music: The Kinks; Oct. 10–NHL: Chicago 8, Leafs 9; Oct. 14–NHL: Minnesota 2, Leafs 1; Oct. 17–Jr. Hockey: Sudbury 4, Jr. Marlboros 9; Oct. 18–Jr. Hockey: Sault Ste. Marie 3, Jr. Marlboros 1; Oct. 21–NHL: Rockies 4, Leafs 4; Oct. 23–Music: Nazareth; Oct. 24–NHL: Rangers 5, Leafs 3; Oct. 29–Music: Bob Dylan; Oct. 31–NHL: Winnipeg 6, Leafs 5; Nov. 1–Jr. Hockey: Ottawa 7, Jr. Marlboros 2; Nov. 9–Music: Frank Zappa; Nov. 11–NHL: Islanders 4, Leafs 3; Nov. 13–Music: Foreigner; Nov. 14–Jr. Hockey: Peterborough 2, Jr. Marlboros 6; Nov. 14–NHL: Flyers 0, Leafs 4; Nov. 15–Jr. Hockey: Kingston 4, Jr. Marlboros 11; Nov. 17–Jr. Hockey: Kitchener 1, Jr. Marlboros 4; Nov. 19–Music: Black Sabbath; Nov. 21–NHL: Boston 5, Leafs 3; Nov. 23–Music: Moody Blues; Nov. 24–Music: Alice Cooper; Nov. 28–NHL: Buffalo 4, Leafs 4; Nov. 29–Jr. Hockey: Brantford 4, Jr. Marlboros 6; Dec. 2–NHL: Hartford 5, Leafs 3; Dec. 3–Music: Barry Manilow; Dec. 4–Jr. Hockey: Oshawa 6, Jr. Marlboros 7; Dec. 5–NHL: Washington 4, Leafs 9; Dec. 6-7–Music: Genesis; Dec. 9–NHL: Winnipeg 3, Leafs 3; Dec. 10-11–Music: AC/DC; Dec. 12–Jr. Hockey: Windsor 7, Jr. Marlboros 10; Dec. 12–NHL: Canadiens 6, Leafs 2; Dec. 13–Jr. Hockey: Kitchener 4, Jr. Marlboros 10; Dec. 13–Soccer: Tampa Bay 3, Blizzard 9; Dec. 15–Jr. Hockey: Ottawa 2, Jr. Marlboros 3; Dec. 17–Soccer: New York 2, Blizzard 8; Dec. 18–Jr. Hockey: Oshawa 3, Jr. Marlboros 4; Dec. 20–Jr. Hockey: Sault Ste. Marie 1, Jr. Marlboros 6; Dec. 23–NHL: Pittsburgh 4, Leafs 4; Dec. 26–NHL: Detroit 3, Leafs 8; Dec. 27–Jr. Hockey: London 4, Jr. Marlboros 6; Dec. 29–Jr. Hockey: Cornwall 3, Jr. Marlboros 4; Dec. 30–NHL: St. Louis 6, Leafs 4; Dec. 31–Music: Triumph.

1982 • Jan. 2–NHL: Minnesota 6, Leafs 2; Jan. 3–Jr. Hockey: Peterborough 3, Jr. Marlboros 2; Jan. 3–Soccer: New York 5, Blizzard 6; Jan. 5–Jr. Hockey: Windsor 3, Jr. Marlboros 4; Jan. 6–Soccer: Chicago 6, Blizzard 3; Jan. 8–Jr. Hockey: Belleville 2, Jr. Marlboros 3; Jan. 9–NHL: Los Angeles 3, Leafs 5; Jan. 10–Jr. Hockey: Kingston 4, Jr. Marlboros 5; Jan. 10–Soccer: Tampa Bay 4, Blizzard 2; Jan. 12–Jr. Hockey: London 4, Jr. Marlboros 6; Jan. 13–NHL: Rockies 1, Leafs 2; Jan. 14–Soccer: Tulsa 5, Blizzard 9; Jan. 16–NHL: Edmonton 1, Leafs 7; Jan. 17–Jr. Hockey: Cornwall 3, Jr. Marlboros 9; Jan. 18–NHL: Rangers 2, Leafs 6; Jan. 20–NHL: Calgary 4, Leafs 4; Jan. 21–Soccer: Montreal 4, Blizzard 7; Jan. 24–Jr. Hockey: Ottawa 5, Jr. Marlboros 4; Jan. 24–Soccer: Jacksonville 4, Blizzard 6; Jan. 25–NHL: Minnesota 9, Leafs 2; Jan. 26–Jr. Hockey: Niagara Falls 3, Jr. Marlboros 8; Jan. 27–NHL: Winnipeg 4, Leafs 3; Jan. 29–Track and Field: Toronto Star-Maple Leaf Indoor Games; Jan. 30–NHL: Quebec 2, Leafs 2; Jan. 31–Jr. Hockey: Sudbury 3, Jr. Marlboros 8; Feb. 2-7–Tennis: Molson Challenge; Feb. 9–Jr. Hockey: Belleville 5, Jr. Marlboros 2; Feb. 10–NHL: Vancouver 4, Leafs 1; Feb. 12–Jr. Hockey: Cornwall 8, Jr. Marlboros 5; Feb. 13–NHL: Chicago 6, Leafs 4; Feb. 14–Jr. Hockey: Brantford 6, Jr. Marlboros 7; Feb. 14–Soccer: Montreal 6, Blizzard 5; Feb. 15–NHL: Minnesota 3, Leafs 3; Feb. 17–NHL: Detroit 3, Leafs 3; Feb. 19–Music: Hall & Oates; Feb. 20–Jr. Hockey: Oshawa 1, Jr. Marlboros 6; Feb. 20–NHL: St. Louis 5, Leafs 8; Feb. 21–Jr. Hockey: Belleville 1, Jr. Marlboros 4; Feb. 23–Jr. Hockey: Peterborough 4, Jr. Marlboros 6; Mar. 1–NHL: Islanders 9, Leafs 5; Mar. 2–Jr. Hockey: Niagara Falls 7, Jr. Marlboros 3; Mar. 3–NHL: Los Angeles 4, Leafs 1; Mar. 5–Jr. Hockey: Peterborough 5, Jr. Marlboros 4; Mar. 6–NHL: Canadiens 6, Leafs 1; Mar. 7–Jr. Hockey: Kingston 3, Jr. Marlboros 7; Mar. 10–NHL: Chicago 7, Leafs 6; Mar. 12–Jr. Hockey: Oshawa 2, Jr. Marlboros 4; Mar. 13–NHL: Winnipeg 10, Leafs 1; Mar. 14–Jr. Hockey: Cornwall 5, Jr. Marlboros 9; Mar. 17–NHL: Quebec 3, Leafs 6; Mar. 18–Jr. Hockey: Cornwall 4, Jr. Marlboros 7; Mar. 21–Jr. Hockey: Cornwall 5, Jr. Marlboros 5; Mar. 22–NHL: Chicago 5, Leafs 8; Mar. 24–NHL: St. Louis 3, Leafs 4; Mar. 27–Jr. Hockey: Ottawa 3, Jr. Marlboros 4; Mar. 27–NHL: Detroit 2, Leafs 1; Mar. 28–Music: Rod Stewart; Mar. 30–Jr. Hockey: Ottawa 6, Jr. Marlboros 6; Apr. 3–NHL: Washington 6, Leafs 4; Apr. 17-18–Ice Show: Labatt Pro Skate; Apr. 30–Music: Journey; May 7–Music: Loverboy; May 15–Music: J Geils Band; May 30–Music: John Denver; June 4–Music: Ozzy Osbourne; June 14–Music: The Commodores; July 27–Music: Air Supply; July 29–Music: Elton John; Aug. 23–Music: Jethro Tull; Sept. 2-3–Music: Queen; Sept. 24-25–Music: Neil Diamond; Sept. 28–Music: ZZ Top; Oct. 9–NHL: New Jersey 5, Leafs 5; Oct. 13–NHL: Washington 5, Leafs 3; Oct. 16–NHL: Chicago 3, Leafs 2; Oct. 17–Jr. Hockey: Guelph 5, Jr. Marlboros 9; Oct. 20–NHL: Minnesota 2, Leafs 5; Oct. 23–Jr. Hockey: North Bay 5, Jr. Marlboros 5; Oct. 23–NHL: Calgary 5, Leafs 5; Oct. 24–Jr. Hockey: Ottawa 2, Jr. Marlboros 5; Oct. 26–Music: Van Halen; Oct. 27–NHL: Boston 1, Leafs 4; Oct. 28–Music: Judas Priest; Oct. 30–Jr. Hockey: Sault Ste. Marie 1, Jr. Marlboros 5; Oct. 30–NHL: Buffalo 3, Leafs 3; Oct. 31–Jr. Hockey: Windsor 2, Jr. Marlboros 6; Nov. 8–Music: Peter Gabriel; Nov. 9–Music: Billy Joel; Nov. 10–NHL: Detroit 2, Leafs 8; Nov. 12–Jr. Hockey: Oshawa 6, Jr. Marlboros 3; Nov. 13–Jr. Hockey: North Bay 6, Jr. Marlboros 4; Nov. 13–NHL: Minnesota 3, Leafs 4; Nov. 19–Jr. Hockey: Belleville 4, Jr. Marlboros 3; Nov. 20–NHL: Rangers 6, Leafs 3; Nov. 26–Jr. Hockey: Peterborough 5, Jr. Marlboros 2; Nov. 27–Jr. Hockey: Sudbury 3, Jr. Marlboros 8; Nov. 27–NHL: Winnipeg 6, Leafs 3; Nov. 30–Jr. Hockey: Kitchener 7, Jr. Marlboros 7; Dec. 1–Music: Pat Benatar; Dec. 4–NHL: Islanders 1, Leafs 4; Dec. 5–Music: Kenny Rogers; Dec. 6–Music: Phil Collins; Dec. 8–NHL: Vancouver 7, Leafs 3; Dec. 9–Music: Aerosmith; Dec. 10–Jr. Hockey: Cornwall 5, Jr. Marlboros 7; Dec. 11–Jr. Hockey: Ottawa 5, Jr. Marlboros 5; Dec. 11–NHL: Detroit 6, Leafs 2; Dec. 15–Music: Rush; Dec. 15–NHL: St. Louis 4, Leafs 2; Dec. 16-17–Music: The Who; Dec. 18–Jr. Hockey: Sudbury 4, Jr. Marlboros 8; Dec. 18–NHL: Chicago 8, Leafs 5; Dec. 19–Jr. Hockey: Sault Ste. Marie 6, Jr. Marlboros 3; Dec. 27–Jr. Hockey: Brantford 2, Jr. Marlboros 2; Dec. 29–NHL: Canadiens 5, Leafs 6; Dec. 31–Music: Saga.

1983 • Jan. 1–Jr. Hockey: Kitchener 4, Jr. Marlboros 3; Jan. 1–NHL: Hartford 5, Leafs 7; Jan. 2–Jr. Hockey: Peterborough 5, Jr. Marlboros 1; Jan. 2–NHL: Detroit 3, Leafs 6; Jan. 8–Jr. Hockey: Kingston 3, Jr. Marlboros 9; Jan. 8–NHL: Los Angeles 5, Leafs 7; Jan. 9–Jr. Hockey: Belleville 3, Jr. Marlboros 6; Jan. 12–NHL: Boston 6, Leafs 4; Jan. 14–Music: Kiss; Jan. 15–Jr. Hockey: Ottawa 3, Jr. Marlboros 8; Jan. 16–Jr. Hockey: Kingston 6, Jr. Marlboros 7; Jan. 17–NHL: St. Louis 4, Leafs 4; Jan. 22–Jr. Hockey: Oshawa 2, Jr. Marlboros 4; Jan. 22–NHL: Chicago 3, Leafs 2; Jan. 23–Jr. Hockey: Windsor 3, Jr. Marlboros 5; Jan. 24–NHL: Pittsburgh 2, Leafs 8; Jan. 29–Jr. Hockey: Cornwall 2, Jr. Marlboros 5; Jan. 29–NHL: Buffalo 3, Leafs 5; Jan. 30–Jr. Hockey: Brantford 1, Jr. Marlboros 2; Jan. 31–NHL: Minnesota 4, Leafs 2; Feb. 2–NHL: Hartford 1, Leafs 7; Feb. 3-8–Tennis: Molson Challenge; Feb. 5–Jr. Hockey: London 5, Jr. Marlboros 4; Feb. 5–NHL: Vancouver 4, Leafs 6; Feb. 6–Jr. Hockey: Belleville 4, Jr. Marlboros 5; Feb. 15–Jr. Hockey: London 3, Jr. Marlboros 4; Feb. 16–NHL: St. Louis 3, Leafs 6; Feb. 18–Music: Neil Young; Feb. 19–Jr. Hockey: Kingston 4, Jr. Marlboros 8; Feb. 19–NHL: Calgary 3, Leafs 5; Feb. 21–NHL: Pittsburgh 2, Leafs 4; Feb. 22–Jr. Hockey: Oshawa 5, Jr. Marlboros 3; Mar. 1–Jr. Hockey: Peterborough 3, Jr. Marlboros 6; Mar. 2–NHL: Flyers 2, Leafs 2; Mar. 5–Jr. Hockey: Guelph 6, Jr. Marlboros 8; Mar. 5–NHL: Edmonton 6, Leafs 3; Mar. 7–Music: Hall & Oates; Mar. 9–NHL: St. Louis 2, Leafs 5; Mar. 11–Jr. Hockey: Oshawa 5, Jr. Marlboros 1; Mar. 12–Jr. Hockey: Cornwall 6, Jr. Marlboros 7; Mar. 12–NHL: Chicago 2, Leafs 4; Mar. 15–Jr. Hockey: Cornwall 4, Jr. Marlboros 3; Mar. 16–NHL: Detroit 4, Leafs 3; Mar. 19–Jr. Hockey: Cornwall 4, Jr. Marlboros 4; Mar. 20–Ice Show: Pro Skate; Mar. 21–NHL: Edmonton 4, Leafs 1; Mar. 23–NHL: Minnesota 3, Leafs 6; Mar. 26–NHL: Quebec 1, Leafs 2; Mar. 29–Music: Julio Iglesias; Apr. 2–NHL: Flyers 6, Leafs 3; Apr. 9–NHL: Minnesota 3, Leafs 6; Apr. 10–NHL: Minnesota 5, Leafs 4; Apr. 19–Music: Chris DeBurgh; May 19–Music: Roxy Music; May 25–Music: The Kinks; June 10–Music: Def Leppard and Krokus; Sept. 10–Music: Robert Plant; Sept. 23–Music: Lionel Richie; Oct. 12–NHL: Buffalo 4, Leafs 4; Oct. 15–Jr. Hockey: Cornwall 3, Jr. Marlboros 6; Oct. 15–NHL: Chicago 8, Leafs 10; Oct. 19–NHL: Quebec 8, Leafs 1; Oct. 22–Jr. Hockey: Sault Ste. Marie 3, Jr. Marlboros 5; Oct. 22–NHL: Canadiens 3, Leafs 5; Oct. 23–Jr. Hockey: Sudbury 3, Jr. Marlboros 9; Oct. 25–Music: Black Sabbath; Oct. 26–NHL: Edmonton 3, Leafs 8; Oct. 29–Jr. Hockey: Oshawa 2, Jr. Marlboros 3; Oct. 29–NHL: Los Angeles 5, Leafs 5; Oct. 30–Jr. Hockey: Windsor 3, Jr. Marlboros 6; Nov. 6–United Way Fundraiser; Nov. 9–NHL: New Jersey 1, Leafs 2; Nov. 11–Jr. Hockey: Peterborough 3, Jr. Marlboros 5; Nov. 12–NHL: Flyers 5, Leafs 3; Nov. 18–Jr. Hockey: Kingston 3, Jr. Marlboros 6; Nov. 19–Jr. Hockey: North Bay 0, Jr. Marlboros 12; Nov. 19–NHL: Detroit 4, Leafs 5; Nov. 22-23–Music: Genesis; Nov. 26–Jr. Hockey: Brantford 3, Jr. Marlboros 2; Nov. 26–NHL: Minnesota 7, Leafs 6; Nov. 27–Jr. Hockey: Ottawa 7, Jr. Marlboros 10; Dec. 2–Jr. Hockey: Sudbury 1, Jr. Marlboros 5; Dec. 3–Jr. Hockey: Sault Ste. Marie 6, Jr. Marlboros 6; Dec. 3–NHL: Vancouver 5, Leafs 5; Dec. 7–NHL: St. Louis 4, Leafs 3; Dec. 10–Jr. Hockey: Ottawa 3, Jr. Marlboros 5; Dec. 10–NHL: Calgary 3, Leafs 3; Dec. 11–Jr. Hockey: Peterborough

2, Jr. Marlboros 9; Dec. 14–NHL: Winnipeg 8, Leafs 4; Dec. 15–Music: AC/DC; Dec. 17–Jr. Hockey: Guelph 1, Jr. Marlboros 7; Dec. 17–NHL: Washington 3, Leafs 1; Dec. 18–Jr. Hockey: Kitchener 5, Jr. Marlboros 6; Dec. 18–NHL: Pittsburgh 3, Leafs 3; Dec. 21–NHL: St. Louis 4, Leafs 5; Dec. 26–NHL: Detroit 2, Leafs 6; Dec. 31–NHL: Los Angeles 3, Leafs 5.

1984 • Jan. 1–Jr. Hockey: Oshawa 4, Jr. Marlboros 6; Jan. 7–Jr. Hockey: London 4, Jr. Marlboros 5; Jan. 8–NHL: St. Louis 5, Leafs 2; Jan. 10–Jr. Hockey: Belleville 8, Jr. Marlboros 3; Jan. 11–NHL: Candiens 6, Leafs 4; Jan. 14–Jr. Hockey: Peterborough 5, Jr. Marlboros 4; Jan. 14–NHL: Chicago 2, Leafs 2; Jan. 15–Jr. Hockey: Kingston 6, Jr. Marlboros 9; Jan. 18–NHL: Minnesota 4, Leafs 9; Jan. 20–Jr. Hockey: North Bay 4, Jr. Marlboros 9; Jan. 21–Jr. Hockey: Cornwall 6, Jr. Marlboros 5; Jan. 21–NHL: Rangers 6, Leafs 3; Jan. 23–NHL: Chicago 6, Leafs 2; Jan. 28–Jr. Hockey: Oshawa 3, Jr. Marlboros 4; Jan. 28–NHL: Washington 8, Leafs 0; Jan. 29–Jr. Hockey: Kitchener 8, Jr. Marlboros 6; Feb. 1-5–Tennis: Molson Challenge; Feb. 8–NHL: Boston 4, Leafs 6; Feb. 11–Jr. Hockey: Cornwall 3, Jr. Marlboros 4; Feb. 11–NHL: Quebec 2, Leafs 5; Feb. 12–Jr. Hockey: Windsor 3, Jr. Marlboros 2; Feb. 13–NHL: Islanders 1, Leafs 3; Feb. 15–NHL: Minnesota 3, Leafs 1; Feb. 17–Track and Field: Toronto Star-Maple Leaf Indoor Games; Feb. 18–Jr. Hockey: London 5, Jr. Marlboros 6; Feb. 18–NHL: Hartford 8, Leafs 2; Feb. 19–Jr. Hockey: Belleville 4, Jr. Marlboros 3; Feb. 19–NHL: Detroit 6, Leafs 2; Feb. 29–Jr. Hockey: Belleville 4, Jr. Marlboros 5; Feb. 29–NHL: Rangers 1, Leafs 3; Mar. 2–Music: Saga; Mar. 3–Jr. Hockey: Brantford 7, Jr. Marlboros 8; Mar. 3–NHL: Islanders 11, Leafs 6; Mar. 4-5–Music: Duran Duran; Mar. 7–NHL: New Jersey 4, Leafs 8; Mar. 10–Jr. Hockey: Guelph 6, Jr. Marlboros 4; Mar. 10–NHL: Detroit 3, Leafs 4; Mar. 11–Jr. Hockey: Kingston 4, Jr. Marlboros 10; Mar. 12–NHL: Winnipeg 8, Leafs 7; Mar. 13–Jr. Hockey: Ottawa 3, Jr. Marlboros 1; Mar. 14–NHL: Minnesota 3, Leafs 3; Mar. 15–Music: Kiss; Mar. 18–Jr. Hockey: Peterborough 5, Jr. Marlboros 4; Mar. 24–NHL: Chicago 3, Leafs 7; Mar. 31–Jr. Hockey: Peterborough 4, Jr. Marlboros 7; Mar. 31–NHL: St. Louis 4, Leafs 6; Apr. 2–Music: Judas Priest; Apr. 3–Jr. Hockey: Peterborough 4, Jr. Marlboros 5; Apr. 7–Jr. Hockey: Peterborough 5, Jr. Marlboros 7; Apr. 15–Jr. Hockey: Ottawa 5, Jr. Marlboros 2; Apr. 17–Music: Van Halen; Apr. 19–Jr. Hockey: Ottawa 4, Jr. Marlboros 2; Apr. 25–Music: Ozzy Osbourne; Apr. 30–Music: The Clash; June 7–Music: Air Supply; July 21–Music: Chris DeBurgh; July 28-29–Music: Roger Waters; Sept. 13–Music: Elton John; Sept. 21-22–Music: Rush; Oct. 13–Jr. Hockey: North Bay 4, Jr. Marlboros 8; Oct. 13–NHL: Buffalo 3, Leafs 4; Oct. 17–NHL: Hartford 5, Leafs 3; Oct. 20–Jr. Hockey: Cornwall 2, Jr. Marlboros 4; Oct. 20–NHL: Quebec 12, Leafs 3; Oct. 23–Music: Jethro Tull; Oct. 24–NHL: Detroit 1, Leafs 6; Oct. 27–Jr. Hockey: Sudbury 1, Jr. Marlboros 5; Oct. 27–NHL: Calgary 5, Leafs 3; Nov. 7–NHL: Vancouver 4, Leafs 4; Nov. 10–NHL: Chicago 4, Leafs 4; Nov. 11–NHL: Minnesota 7, Leafs 6; Nov. 12–Music: Cyndi Lauper; Nov. 13–Jr. Hockey: Ottawa 2, Jr. Marlboros 8; Nov. 14–NHL: Los Angeles 4, Leafs 3; Nov. 15–Music: Culture Club; Nov. 17–Jr. Hockey: Hamilton 4, Jr. Marlboros 6; Nov. 17–NHL: Winnipeg 5, Leafs 3; Nov. 23–Jr. Hockey: Windsor 7, Jr. Marlboros 5; Nov. 24–Jr. Hockey: Kingston 6, Jr. Marlboros 13; Nov. 24–NHL: Minnesota 4, Leafs 2; Nov. 27–NHL: Edmonton 7, Leafs 1; Nov. 30–Music: Iron Maiden; Dec. 1–Jr. Hockey: Peterborough 4, Jr. Marlboros 7; Dec. 1–NHL: Rangers 4, Leafs 1; Dec. 2-3–Music: Prince; Dec. 5–NHL: Detroit 4, Leafs 2; Dec. 8–Jr. Hockey: Sault Ste. Marie 7, Jr. Marlboros 4; Dec. 9–Jr. Hockey: Belleville 5, Jr. Marlboros 3; Dec. 12–NHL: Flyers 3, Leafs 6; Dec. 15–Jr. Hockey: Cornwall 5, Jr. Marlboros 7; Dec. 15–NHL: Pittsburgh 5, Leafs 2; Dec. 16–Jr. Hockey: Hamilton 3, Jr. Marlboros 3; Dec. 17–NHL: St. Louis 3, Leafs 2; Dec. 22–Jr. Hockey: Oshawa 2, Jr. Marlboros 6; Dec. 22–NHL: Boston 4, Leafs 6; Dec. 23–Jr. Hockey: Ottawa 4, Jr. Marlboros 4; Dec. 29–NHL: Chicago 5, Leafs 4; Dec. 30–Jr. Hockey: Belleville 6, Jr. Marlboros 8; Dec. 31–Music: Platinum Blonde.

1985 • Jan. 2–NHL: Pittsburgh 2, Leafs 1; Jan. 5–NHL: Vancouver 4, Leafs 1; Jan. 6–Jr. Hockey: Peterborough 2, Jr. Marlboros 5; Jan. 7–NHL: Hartford 7, Leafs 4; Jan. 9–NHL: Boston 5, Leafs 3; Jan. 12–Jr. Hockey: Oshawa 3, Jr. Marlboros 4; Jan. 13–Jr. Hockey: Kitchener 3, Jr. Marlboros 8; Jan. 15–Jr. Hockey: Guelph 5, Jr. Marlboros 4; Jan. 19–Jr. Hockey: Ottawa 4, Jr. Marlboros 7; Jan. 19–NHL: St. Louis 1, Leafs 6; Jan. 20–Jr. Hockey: Kingston 1, Jr. Marlboros 8; Jan. 26–NHL: Chicago 5, Leafs 2; Jan. 27–Jr. Hockey: Peterborough 6, Jr. Marlboros 5; Feb. 1–Track and Field: Toronto Star-Maple Leaf Indoor Games; Feb. 2–Jr. Hockey: London 2, Jr. Marlboros 5; Feb. 2–NHL: Minnesota 5, Leafs 2; Feb. 3–Jr. Hockey: Belleville 5, Jr. Marlboros 3; Feb. 5–NHL: Washington 4, Leafs 1; Feb. 8–Jr. Hockey: Kingston 4, Jr. Marlboros 6; Feb. 10–NHL: Canadiens 2, Leafs 3; Feb. 12–Jr. Hockey: Cornwall 5, Jr. Marlboros 10; Feb. 16–Jr. Hockey: Ottawa 4, Jr. Marlboros 1; Feb. 16–NHL: New Jersey 6, Leafs 3; Feb. 17–Jr. Hockey: Belleville 9, Jr. Marlboros 3; Feb. 19–NHL: Edmonton 9, Leafs 4; Feb. 25–NHL: Chicago 4, Leafs 3; Feb. 26–Jr. Hockey: Oshawa 2, Jr. Marlboros 3; Feb. 27–NHL: Minnesota 1, Leafs 6; Mar. 2–Jr. Hockey: Cornwall 3, Jr. Marlboros 6; Mar. 2–NHL: Islanders 2, Leafs 4; Mar. 3–Jr. Hockey: Peterborough 3, Jr. Marlboros 3; Mar. 6–NHL: Detroit 5, Leafs 3; Mar. 10–Jr. Hockey: Kingston 2, Jr. Marlboros 4; Mar. 13–NHL: Calgary 5, Leafs 3; Mar. 14–Music: Hall & Oates; Mar. 16–Jr. Hockey: Oshawa 5, Jr. Marlboros 2; Mar. 16–NHL: Flyers 6, Leafs 1; Mar. 18–NHL: St. Louis 3, Leafs 4; Mar. 19–Jr. Hockey: Cornwall 4, Jr. Marlboros 3; Mar. 20–Music: The Kinks; Mar. 22–Music: Chicago; Mar. 23–Music: Roger Waters; Mar. 24–Jr. Hockey: Cornwall 6, Jr. Marlboros 5; Mar. 27–NHL: St. Louis 2, Leafs 4; Mar. 28–Jr. Hockey: Cornwall 8, Jr. Marlboros 5; Mar. 28–Music: U2; Mar. 30–NHL: Detroit 9, Leafs 3; Apr. 1–Music: Deep Purple; Apr. 4–Music: Triumph; Apr. 6–NHL: Buffalo 5, Leafs 2; Apr. 11–Music: Triumph; May 23–Music: Madonna; Sept. 23–Music: AC/DC; Oct. 12–Jr. Hockey: Ottawa 6, Jr. Marlboros 4; Oct. 12–NHL: Quebec 4, Leafs 0; Oct. 16–NHL: Washington 6, Leafs 5; Oct. 18–Music: Motley Crue; Oct. 19–Jr. Hockey: North Bay 3, Jr. Marlboros 5; Oct. 19–NHL: Winnipeg 4, Leafs 3; Oct. 20–Jr. Hockey: Cornwall 2, Jr. Marlboros 4; Oct. 21–Music: Paul Young; Oct. 23–NHL: Pittsburgh 5, Leafs 4; Oct. 24–Music: Supertramp; Oct. 26–Jr. Hockey: Oshawa 4, Jr. Marlboros 2; Oct. 26–NHL: Minnesota 7, Leafs 5; Oct. 27–Jr. Hockey: Kingston 9, Jr. Marlboros 4; Nov. 6–NHL: Islanders 5, Leafs 4; Nov. 8–Music: Simple Minds; Nov. 9–Jr. Hockey: Guelph 3, Jr. Marlboros 3; Nov. 9–NHL: St. Louis 2, Leafs 2; Nov. 10–Jr. Hockey: Peterborough 4, Jr. Marlboros 0; Nov. 12–Music: Heart; Nov. 13–Music: Howard Jones; Nov. 14–NHL: Boston 6, Leafs 6; Nov. 16–Jr. Hockey: Hamilton 2, Jr. Marlboros 8; Nov. 16–NHL: Chicago 4, Leafs 6; Nov. 17–Jr. Hockey: Belleville 4, Jr. Marlboros 3; Nov. 18–Music: John Cougar Mellencamp; Nov. 22–Jr. Hockey: Cornwall 8, Jr. Marlboros 7; Nov. 23–Jr. Hockey: Ottawa 4, Jr. Marlboros 7; Nov. 23–NHL: Detroit 3, Leafs 9; Nov. 30–NHL: Buffalo 2, Leafs 3; Dec. 2-3–Music: ZZ Top; Dec. 4–NHL: New Jersey 7, Leafs 10; Dec. 6–Music: Platinum Blonde; Dec. 7–Jr. Hockey: Hamilton 6, Jr. Marlboros 5; Dec. 7–NHL: Canadiens 6, Leafs 3; Dec. 8–Jr. Hockey: Sudbury 8, Jr. Marlboros 7; Dec. 11–NHL: St. Louis 4, Leafs 6; Dec. 17–Jr. Hockey: Oshawa 8, Jr. Marlboros 12; Dec. 21–Jr. Hockey: Windsor 5, Jr. Marlboros 6; Dec. 22–Jr. Hockey: Sault Ste. Marie 2, Jr. Marlboros 7; Dec. 28–NHL: Hartford 6, Leafs 3; Dec. 31–Music: Thompson Twins.

1986 • Jan. 1–NHL: Canadiens 1, Leafs 3; Jan. 4–Jr. Hockey: Ottawa 6, Jr. Marlboros 11; Jan. 4–NHL: Los Angeles 6, Leafs 4; Jan. 5–Jr. Hockey: Kingston 5, Jr. Marlboros 4; Jan. 5–NHL: Detroit 6, Leafs 5; Jan. 8–NHL: Edmonton 9, Leafs 11; Jan. 11–Jr. Hockey: Oshawa 4, Jr. Marlboros 2; Jan. 11–NHL: Quebec 5, Leafs 1; Jan. 12–Jr. Hockey: Peterborough 4, Jr. Marlboros 6; Jan. 13–NHL: Detroit 4, Leafs 7; Jan. 14-15–Ice Show: Torvill & Dean; Jan. 17–Jr. Hockey: London 2, Jr. Marlboros 5; Jan. 18–Jr. Hockey: Kitchener 8, Jr. Marlboros 5; Jan. 18–NHL: Minnesota 5, Leafs 2; Jan. 19–NHL: Calgary 9, Leafs 5; Jan. 22–NHL: Rangers 4, Leafs 2; Jan. 25–Jr. Hockey: Cornwall 7, Jr. Marlboros 6; Jan. 26–Jr. Hockey: Belleville 7, Jr. Marlboros 6; Jan. 29–NHL: Washington 2, Leafs 5; Jan. 31–Track and Field: Toronto Star-Maple Leaf Indoor Games; Feb. 1–NHL: Chicago 7, Leafs 4; Feb. 2–Jr. Hockey: Kingston 6, Jr. Marlboros 3; Feb. 8–Jr. Hockey: Peterborough 5, Jr. Marlboros 4; Feb. 8–NHL: St. Louis 2, Leafs 3; Feb. 9–Jr. Hockey: Belleville 6, Jr. Marlboros 4; Feb. 11–NHL: Minnesota 4, Leafs 2; Feb. 15–Jr. Hockey: Oshawa 5, Jr. Marlboros 6; Feb. 15–NHL: Chicago 3, Leafs 4; Feb. 16–NHL: Vancouver 4, Leafs 4; Feb. 25–NHL: Rangers 3, Leafs 7; Mar. 1–Jr. Hockey: Cornwall 6, Jr. Marlboros 7; Mar. 1–NHL: Detroit 6, Leafs 4; Mar. 2–Jr. Hockey: Peterborough 5, Jr. Marlboros 2; Mar. 3–NHL: Winnipeg 1, Leafs 6; Mar. 6-7–Music: Rush; Mar. 8–Jr. Hockey: Ottawa 4, Jr. Marlboros 4; Mar. 8–NHL: Chicago 3, Leafs 4; Mar. 9–Jr. Hockey: Belleville 5, Jr. Marlboros 3; Mar. 15–NHL: Flyers 6, Leafs 5; Mar. 16–Jr. Hockey: Kingston 5, Jr. Marlboros 4; Mar. 17–NHL: Los Angeles 6, Leafs 7; Mar. 20–NHL: Islanders 7, Leafs 1; Mar. 22–NHL: New Jersey 6, Leafs 3; Mar. 25–Jr. Hockey: Peterborough 3, Jr. Marlboros 1; Mar. 26–NHL: Minnesota 6, Leafs 1; Mar. 28–Jr. Hockey: Peterborough 4, Jr. Marlboros 1; Mar. 29–NHL: St. Louis 1, Leafs 4; Apr. 4–Music: Black Sabbath; Apr. 8–Music: Kiss; Apr. 12–NHL: Chicago 2, Leafs 7; Apr. 22–NHL: St. Louis 2, Leafs 5; Apr. 24–NHL: St. Louis 7, Leafs 4; Apr. 28–NHL: St. Louis 3, Leafs 5; July 16–Comedy: Eddie Murphy; Sept. 12–Ice Show: Torvill & Dean; Oct. 3–Music: Neil Young; Oct. 8–Music: Kenny Rogers and Dolly Parton; Oct. 9–NHL: Canadiens 4, Leafs 7; Oct. 10–Music: Stevie Wonder; Oct. 11–NHL: Buffalo 5, Leafs 5; Oct. 12–Jr. Hockey: Peterborough 3, Jr. Marlboros 4; Oct. 14–NHL: St. Louis 1, Leafs 1; Oct. 18–Jr. Hockey: Ottawa 4, Jr. Marlboros 7; Oct. 18–NHL: Chicago 2, Leafs 3; Oct. 22–NHL: Quebec 7, Leafs 1; Oct. 23-25–Music: Bob Seger; Oct. 26–Jr. Hockey: Hamitlon 3, Jr. Marlboros 4; Oct. 28–NHL: Chicago 1, Leafs 2; Oct. 30–NHL: Hartford 2, Leafs 6; Oct. 31–Music: David Lee Roth; Nov. 1–Jr. Hockey: Oshawa 3, Jr. Marlboros 1; Nov. 1–NHL: Detroit 0, Leafs 2; Nov. 2–Jr. Hockey: Kingston 7, Jr. Marlboros 6; Nov. 5–NHL: St. Louis 4, Leafs 6; Nov. 8–Jr. Hockey: Guelph 3, Jr. Marlboros 2; Nov. 8–NHL: Vancouver 5, Leafs 3; Nov. 9–Jr. Hockey: Cornwall 8, Jr. Marlboros 5; Nov. 11–Music: Orchestral Manoevers In The Dark; Nov. 12-14–Music: Lionel Richie; Nov. 15–Jr. Hockey: London 8, Jr. Marlboros 6; Nov. 15–NHL: Detroit 0, Leafs 6; Nov. 16–Jr. Hockey: Peterborough 2, Jr. Marlboros 3; Nov. 18–Jr. Hockey: Oshawa 6, Jr. Marlboros 3; Nov. 19–NHL: Flyers 2, Leafs 2; Nov. 21–Music: Steve Winwood; Nov. 23–Jr. Hockey: Ottawa 8, Jr. Marlboros 4; Nov. 24–NHL: Boston 3, Leafs 2; Nov. 26-27–Music: Peter Gabriel; Nov. 29–Jr. Hockey: North Bay 10, Jr. Marlboros 4; Nov. 29–NHL: Minnesota 7, Leafs 2; Nov. 30–Jr. Hockey: Belleville 8, Jr. Marlboros 5; Dec. 9–Music: Metallica; Dec. 10–NHL: Washington 2, Leafs 8; Dec. 11–Music: Billy Joel; Dec. 13–NHL: Pittsburgh 2, Leafs 3; Dec. 16–Jr. Hockey: Oshawa 5, Jr. Marlboros 2; Dec. 18–NHL: Minnesota 6, Leafs 5; Dec. 20–Jr. Hockey: Sault Ste. Marie 7, Jr. Marlboros 8; Dec. 20–NHL: Buffalo 4, Leafs 5; Dec. 21–Jr. Hockey: Windsor 1, Jr. Marlboros 4; Dec. 27–NHL: Detroit 5, Leafs 5; Dec. 30–Music: Kim Mitchell; Dec. 31–NHL: Winnipeg 1, Leafs 6.

1987 • Jan. 3–Jr. Hockey: Sudbury 5, Jr. Marlboros 12; Jan. 3–NHL: New Jersey 2, Leafs 7; Jan. 4–Jr. Hockey: Peterborough 1, Jr. Marlboros 4; Jan. 9–Music: Triumph; Jan. 11–Jr. Hockey: Belleville 4, Jr. Marlboros 3; Jan. 14–NHL: Minnesota 3, Leafs 2; Jan. 17–Jr. Hockey: Kitchener 5, Jr. Marlboros 3; Jan. 17–NHL: Edmonton 7, Leafs 4; Jan. 18–Jr. Hockey: Cornwall 4, Jr. Marlboros 5; Jan. 21–NHL: St. Louis 2, Leafs 4; Jan. 24–Jr. Hockey: Kingston 4, Jr. Marlboros 12; Jan. 24–NHL: Hartford 3, Leafs 0; Jan. 25–Jr. Hockey: Hamilton 6, Jr. Marlboros 5; Jan. 26–NHL: Calgary 6, Leafs 5; Jan. 31–Jr. Hockey: Oshawa 3, Jr. Marlboros 1; Jan. 31–NHL: Detroit 4, Leafs 2; Feb. 1–Jr. Hockey: Peterborough 3, Jr. Marlboros 5; Feb. 2–NHL: Flyers 4, Leafs 8; Feb. 3–Jr. Hockey: Kingston 3, Jr. Marlboros 4; Feb. 4–NHL: Los Angeles 4, Leafs 5; Feb. 8–Jr. Hockey: Ottawa 7, Jr. Marlboros 4; Feb. 14–Jr. Hockey: Cornwall 10, Jr. Marlboros 3; Feb. 14–NHL: Boston 5, Leafs 4; Feb. 15–Jr. Hockey: Belleville 6, Jr. Marlboros 4; Feb. 24–Jr. Hockey: Kingston 3, Jr. Marlboros 7; Feb. 25–NHL: Rangers 4, Leafs 2; Feb. 26–Music: Alice Cooper; Feb. 27–Music: Paul Young; Feb. 28–NHL: Vancouver 6, Leafs 8; Mar. 3–NHL: St. Louis 4, Leafs 3; Mar. 5–NHL: Pittsburgh 2, Leafs 7; Mar. 7–Jr. Hockey: Ottawa 9, Jr. Marlboros 10; Mar. 7–NHL: Islanders 2, Leafs 7; Mar. 8–Jr. Hockey: Belleville 3, Jr. Marlboros 8; Mar. 14–Jr. Hockey: Cornwall 9, Jr. Marlboros 5; Mar. 14–NHL: Calgary 4, Leafs 6; Mar. 18–NHL: Chicago 6, Leafs 3; Mar. 19–Music: Pretenders; Mar. 21-22–Music: Iron Maiden; Mar. 25–NHL: Minnesota 6, Leafs 2; Mar. 28–NHL: Edmonton 2, Leafs 4; Mar. 29–Wrestlemania III; Apr. 4–NHL: Chicago 1, Leafs 3; Apr. 6–Boxing: Hagler vs Leonard (closed circuit coverage); Apr. 11–NHL: St. Louis 5, Leafs 3; Apr. 12–NHL: St. Louis 1, Leafs 2; Apr. 16–NHL: St. Louis 0, Leafs 4; Apr. 25–NHL: Detroit 4, Leafs 2; Apr. 27–NHL: Detroit 2, Leafs 3; May 1–NHL: Detroit 4, Leafs 2; May 19–Music: Chris DeBurgh; June 5–Music: Psychedelic Furs; June 23-24–Music: Paul Simon; June 29–Music: Bryan Adams; Sept. 12–Music: Level 42; Sept. 19-21–Music: Neil Diamond; Oct. 10–NHL: New Jersey 2, Leafs 5; Oct. 16–Music: Heart; Oct. 17–Jr. Hockey: Ottawa 2, Jr. Marlboros 5; Oct. 17–NHL: Detroit 4, Leafs 7; Oct. 19–Music: Fleetwood Mac; Oct. 20–Music: Aerosmith; Oct. 21–NHL: Canadiens 10, Leafs 3; Oct. 24–Jr. Hockey: North Bay 4, Jr. Marlboros 8; Oct. 24–NHL: Minnesota 7, Leafs 4; Oct. 25–Music: Motley Crue; Oct. 28–NHL: Islanders 2, Leafs 5; Oct. 31–NHL: Chicago 5, Leafs 6; Nov. 1–Jr. Hockey: Sudbury 4, Jr. Marlboros 5; Nov. 4–NHL: Winnipeg 3, Leafs 7; Nov. 7–Jr. Hockey: London 4, Jr. Marlboros 3; Nov. 7–NHL: St. Louis 4, Leafs 3; Nov. 8–Jr. Hockey: Kingston 7, Jr. Marlboros 8; Nov. 11–NHL: Boston 3, Leafs 2; Nov. 12–Music: The Cars; Nov. 14–Jr. Hockey: Oshawa 7, Jr. Marlboros 6; Nov. 15–Jr. Hockey: Cornwall 7, Jr. Marlboros 4; Nov. 16–Music: John Cougar Mellencamp; Nov. 18–NHL: St. Louis 6, Leafs 3; Nov. 19–Music: Jethro Tull; Nov. 21–Jr. Hockey: Windsor 9, Jr. Marlboros 4; Nov. 21–NHL: Los Angeles 6, Leafs 6; Nov. 22–Jr. Hockey: Peterborough 7, Jr. Marlboros 5; Nov. 28–Jr. Hockey: Kitchener 6, Jr. Marlboros 5; Nov. 28–NHL: Hartford 4, Leafs 2; Nov. 29–Jr. Hockey: Cornwall 8, Jr. Marlboros 3; Dec. 7–NHL: Detroit 4, Leafs 5; Dec. 8–Jr. Hockey: Oshawa 6, Jr. Marlboros 7; Dec. 9–Music: Yes; Dec. 10–Music: Kiss; Dec. 12–Jr. Hockey: Guelph 7, Jr. Marlboros 3; Dec. 12–NHL: Rangers 3, Leafs 4; Dec. 13–Jr. Hockey: Belleville 4, Jr. Marlboros 3; Dec. 14–Music: Depeche Mode; Dec. 15–NHL: Washington 3, Leafs 5; Dec. 19–Jr. Hockey:

Sault Ste. Marie 2, Jr. Marlboros 3; Dec. 19–NHL: Chicago 6, Leafs 2; Dec. 20–Jr. Hockey: Ottawa 7, Jr. Marlboros 3; Dec. 21–NHL: Minnesota 0, Leafs 0; Dec. 26–NHL: Canadiens 4, Leafs 2; Dec. 28–NHL: Washington 4, Leafs 4.

1988 • Jan. 2–Jr. Hockey: Ottawa 7, Jr. Marlboros 5; Jan. 2–NHL: Buffalo 6, Leafs 4; Jan. 3–Jr. Hockey: Peterborough 8, Jr. Marlboros 4; Jan. 4–NHL: Vancouver 7, Leafs 7; Jan. 6–NHL: Minnesota 5, Leafs 5; Jan. 9–Music: Dio; Jan. 10–Jr. Hockey: Belleville 2, Jr. Marlboros 4; Jan. 12–Jr. Hockey: Kingston 6, Jr. Marlboros 4; Jan. 16–NHL: Pittsburgh 4, Leafs 3; Jan. 17–Jr. Hockey: Hamilton 5, Jr. Marlboros 6; Jan. 21–NHL: Quebec 5, Leafs 4; Jan. 23–Jr. Hockey: Oshawa 3, Jr. Marlboros 7; Jan. 23–NHL: Chicago 3, Leafs 2; Jan. 24–Jr. Hockey: Cornwall 6, Jr. Marlboros 7; Jan. 25–NHL: Calgary 11, Leafs 3; Jan. 27–NHL: Los Angeles 2, Leafs 5; Jan. 29–Track and Field: Toronto Sun Miller Lite Challenge; Jan. 30–Jr. Hockey: Ottawa 6, Jr. Marlboros 4; Jan. 30–NHL: Detroit 5, Leafs 5; Jan. 31–Jr. Hockey: Peterborough 7, Jr. Marlboros 3; Feb. 1–NHL: St. Louis 5, Leafs 4; Feb. 9–Jr. Hockey: Kingston 4, Jr. Marlboros 5; Feb. 10–Music: Supertramp; Feb. 11–NHL: Islanders 3, Leafs 4; Feb. 12–Music: Alice Cooper; Feb. 13–NHL: Flyers 4, Leafs 7; Feb. 14–Jr. Hockey: Belleville 5, Jr. Marlboros 4; Feb. 14–NHL: New Jersey 7, Leafs 2; Feb. 15–Music: Sting; Feb. 16–Jr. Hockey: Oshawa 3, Jr. Marlboros 6; Feb. 24–NHL: Minnesota 2, Leafs 4; Feb. 27–NHL: St. Louis 6, Leafs 2; Feb. 28–Jr. Hockey: Kingston 2, Jr. Marlboros 10; Mar. 1–Jr. Hockey: Hamilton 6, Jr. Marlboros 5; Mar. 2–NHL: Quebec 4, Leafs 3; Mar. 5–Jr. Hockey: Cornwall 3, Jr. Marlboros 4; Mar. 5–NHL: Winnipeg 10, Leafs 1; Mar. 6–Jr. Hockey: Belleville 4, Jr. Marlboros 6; Mar. 7-8–Music: Rush; Mar. 12–Jr. Hockey: Peterborough 4, Jr. Marlboros 2; Mar. 12–NHL: Chicago 4, Leafs 6; Mar. 19–NHL: Rangers 4, Leafs 3; Mar. 20–Jr. Hockey: Peterborough 8, Jr. Marlboros 8; Mar. 26–Jr. Hockey: Peterborough 2, Jr. Marlboros 1; Mar. 28–NHL: Edmonton 6, Leafs 4; Apr. 2–NHL: Detroit 3, Leafs 5; Apr. 9–NHL: Detroit 6, Leafs 3; Apr. 10–NHL: Detroit 8, Leafs 0; Apr. 13–Music: David Lee Roth; Apr. 14–NHL: Detroit 5, Leafs 3; May 10–Music: Robert Plant; Sept. 15–Music: Amnesty International w/Sting and Bruce Springsteen; Sept. 19–Music: Scorpions; Sept. 23–Music: Amy Grant; Oct. 2–Jr. Hockey: Kitchener 5, Jr. Marlboros 4; Oct. 5–Music: Prince; Oct. 7–Music: Eric Clapton; Oct. 8–Jr. Hockey: London 8, Jr. Marlboros 4; Oct. 8–NHL: Chicago 4, Leafs 7; Oct. 9–Jr. Hockey: Kingston 3, Jr. Marlboros 4; Oct. 12–NHL: St. Louis 4, Leafs 2; Oct. 13–Music: AC/DC; Oct. 15–Jr. Hockey: North Bay 2, Jr. Marlboros 5; Oct. 15–NHL: Detroit 5, Leafs 3; Oct. 16–Music: Midnight Oil; Oct. 19–NHL: Buffalo 2, Leafs 4; Oct. 22–Jr. Hockey: Niagara Falls 7, Jr. Marlboros 9; Oct. 22–NHL: Calgary 3, Leafs 3; Nov. 1–Jr. Hockey: Belleville 5, Jr. Marlboros 4; Nov. 2–NHL: Boston 7, Leafs 2; Nov. 5–Jr. Hockey: Sudbury 5, Jr. Marlboros 2; Nov. 5–NHL: Los Angeles 6, Leafs 4; Nov. 6–Jr. Hockey: Windsor 5, Jr. Marlboros 2; Nov. 12–Jr. Hockey: Oshawa 3, Jr. Marlboros 6; Nov. 12–NHL: Edmonton 6, Leafs 2; Nov. 14–NHL: Minnesota 5, Leafs 4; Nov. 15–Jr. Hockey: Oshawa 5, Jr. Marlboros 9; Nov. 16–NHL: Pittsburgh 5, Leafs 8; Nov. 18–Music: Sounds United; Nov. 19–Jr. Hockey: Peterborough 6, Jr. Marlboros 7; Nov. 20–Jr. Hockey: Belleville 3, Jr. Marlboros 6; Nov. 21–NHL: St. Louis 0, Leafs 4; Nov. 23–NHL: Chicago 3, Leafs 4; Nov. 24–Music: Rod Stewart; Nov. 26–Jr. Hockey: Cornwall 7, Jr. Marlboros 4; Nov. 26–NHL: Minnesota 6, Leafs 3; Dec. 10–Jr. Hockey: Oshawa 6, Jr. Marlboros 7; Dec. 10–NHL: Detroit 8, Leafs 2; Dec. 11–Jr. Hockey: Belleville 3, Jr. Marlboros 5; Dec. 12–NHL: Calgary 4, Leafs 4; Dec. 13–Jr. Hockey: Peterborough 5, Jr. Marlboros 3; Dec. 14–NHL: Edmonton 8, Leafs 2; Dec. 17–Jr. Hockey: Sault Ste. Marie 2, Jr. Marlboros 3; Dec. 17–NHL: Flyers 7, Leafs 1; Dec. 18–Jr. Hockey: Ottawa 1, Jr. Marlboros 2; Dec. 19–NHL: St. Louis 3, Leafs 4; Dec. 21–NHL: Pittsburgh 6, Leafs 1; Dec. 26–NHL: Islanders 4, Leafs 3; Dec. 31–Jr. Hockey: Cornwall 4, Jr. Marlboros 7; Dec. 31–NHL: Quebec 1, Leafs 6.

1989 • Jan. 7–Jr. Hockey: Kingston 2, Jr. Marlboros 7; Jan. 7–NHL: Buffalo 6, Leafs 1; Jan. 8–Jr. Hockey: Ottawa 2, Jr. Marlboros 5; Jan. 9–NHL: Vancouver 0, Leafs 3; Jan. 11–NHL: Washington 3, Leafs 2; Jan. 14–Jr. Hockey: Ottawa 6, Jr. Marlboros 5; Jan. 14–NHL: Canadiens 5, Leafs 3; Jan. 15–Jr. Hockey: Cornwall 4, Jr. Marlboros 8; Jan. 16–NHL: Hartford 3, Leafs 5; Jan. 17–Jr. Hockey: Guelph 3, Jr. Marlboros 6; Jan. 19–NHL: Minnesota 3, Leafs 3; Jan. 21–Jr. Hockey: Niagara Falls 7, Jr. Marlboros 6; Jan. 22–Jr. Hockey: Peterborough 7, Jr. Marlboros 3; Jan. 25–NHL: Boston 2, Leafs 1; Jan. 28–NHL: Rangers 1, Leafs 1; Feb. 4–Jr. Hockey: Oshawa 5, Jr. Marlboros 9; Feb. 4–NHL: Chicago 3, Leafs 3; Feb. 9-10–Music: Neil Diamond; Feb. 11–NHL: Flyers 3, Leafs 4; Feb. 13–Music: Cheap Trick; Feb. 14–Jr. Hockey: Peterborough 8, Jr. Marlboros 4; Feb. 15–NHL: Hartford 4, Leafs 2; Feb. 17–Music: Tom Cochrane; Feb. 18–NHL: New Jersey 3, Leafs 5; Feb. 19–Jr. Hockey: Ottawa 1, Jr. Marlboros 5; Feb. 21–Jr. Hockey: Kingston 4, Jr. Marlboros 3; Feb. 27–NHL: St. Louis 7, Leafs 5; Feb. 28–Music: Chris DeBurgh; Mar. 3–Music: Sandi Patti; Mar. 4–Jr. Hockey: Cornwall 3, Jr. Marlboros 6; Mar. 4–NHL: Chicago 3, Leafs 3; Mar. 6–Jr. Hockey: Belleville 3, Jr. Marlboros 7; Mar. 11–Jr. Hockey: Kinston 4, Jr. Marlboros 6; Mar. 11–NHL: Detroit 3, Leafs 5; Mar. 18–NHL: Winnipeg 10, Leafs 2; Mar. 19–Jr. Hockey: Cornwall 6, Jr. Marlboros 2; Mar. 20–Jr. Hockey: Cornwall 3, Jr. Marlboros 4; Mar. 22–NHL: Vancouver 3, Leafs 5; Mar. 25–NHL: Detroit 5, Leafs 6; Mar. 26–Jr. Hockey: Cornwall 8, Jr. Marlboros 5; Mar. 29–NHL: Minnesota 1, Leafs 3; Apr. 7–Music: Metallica; Apr. 12–Music: REM; Oct. 11–NHL: Buffalo 7, Leafs 1; Oct. 14–NHL: Winnipeg 5, Leafs 1; Oct. 18–NHL: Vancouver 3, Leafs 4; Oct. 21–NHL: Washington 4, Leafs 8; Oct. 23–NHL: New Jersey 5, Leafs 4; Oct. 28–NHL: Detroit 4, Leafs 6; Nov. 4–NHL: Flyers 7, Leafs 4; Nov. 6–NHL: Minnesota 1, Leafs 2; Nov. 11–NHL: Detroit 2, Leafs 4; Nov. 15–NHL: St. Louis 2, Leafs 5; Nov. 25–NHL: Rangers 4, Leafs 7; Dec. 9–NHL: Canadiens 4, Leafs 7; Dec. 11–NHL: St. Louis 1, Leafs 3; Dec. 16–NHL: Minnesota 4, Leafs 3; Dec. 18–NHL: St. Louis 3, Leafs 6; Dec. 23–NHL: Chicago 7, Leafs 5; Dec. 27–NHL: Detroit 7, Leafs 7; Dec. 30–NHL: Boston 6, Leafs 6.

1990 • Jan. 3–NHL: Quebec 4, Leafs 5; Jan. 6–NHL: Los Angeles 4, Leafs 7; Jan. 8–NHL: Washington 6, Leafs 8; Jan. 10–NHL: Islanders 3, Leafs 1; Jan. 13–NHL: Calgary 5, Leafs 6; Jan. 15–NHL: Chicago 6, Leafs 7; Jan. 24–NHL: Minnesota 3, Leafs 7; Jan. 27–NHL: Canadiens 5, Leafs 3; Feb. 3–NHL: Pittsburgh 4, Leafs 8; Feb. 6–Music: Billy Joel; Feb. 7–NHL: St. Louis 1, Leafs 7; Feb. 11–Music: Tears for Fears; Feb. 12–NHL: Los Angeles 3, Leafs 5; Feb. 14–NHL: Hartford 6, Leafs 6; Feb. 17–NHL: New Jersey 4, Leafs 5; Feb. 28–NHL: Quebec 4, Leafs 5; Mar. 3–NHL: Detroit 5, Leafs 2; Mar. 10–NHL: Edmonton 2, Leafs 3; Mar. 12–NHL: Minnesota 4, Leafs 1; Mar. 14–NHL: Rangers 8, Leafs 2; Mar. 17–NHL: Winnipeg 5, Leafs 4; Mar. 18–Music: New Kids on the Block; Mar. 19–NHL: Chicago 3, Leafs 2; Mar. 28–NHL: Islanders 6, Leafs 3; Mar. 31–NHL: Chicago 4, Leafs 6; Apr. 8–NHL: St. Louis 6, Leafs 5; Apr. 10–NHL: St. Louis 2, Leafs 4; May 16-17–Music: Rush; Oct. 3–Music: Robert Plant; Oct. 10–NHL: Quebec 8, Leafs 5; Oct. 11–Music: ZZ Top; Oct. 13–NHL: Detroit 3, Leafs 3; Oct. 17–NHL: Hartford 3, Leafs 1; Oct. 20–NHL: Chicago 2, Leafs 6; Oct. 22–Music: Judas Priest; Oct. 24–NHL: St. Louis 8, Leafs 5; Oct. 27–NHL: Buffalo 3, Leafs 1; Oct. 30–NHL: Minnesota 4, Leafs 5; Nov. 3–NHL: Calgary 7, Leafs 3; Nov. 4–NHL: Flyers 7, Leafs 1; Nov. 8–NHL: Vancouver 5, Leafs 3; Nov. 10–NHL: Chicago 5, Leafs 1; Nov. 12–NHL: Winnipeg 2, Leafs 5; Nov. 14–NHL: Washington 3, Leafs 5; Nov. 17–NHL: Detroit 8, Leafs 4; Nov. 19–NHL: Boston 5, Leafs 2; Nov. 23–Music: Heart and Cheap Trick; Nov. 24–NHL: Edmonton 4, Leafs 1; Dec. 5–NHL: Minnesota 3, Leafs 2; Dec. 8–NHL: Chicago 2, Leafs 1; Dec. 12–NHL: Canadiens 1, Leafs 4; Dec. 15–NHL: St. Louis 4, Leafs 2; Dec. 27–NHL: St. Louis 4, Leafs 6; Dec. 29–NHL: Pittsburgh 3, Leafs 6.

1991 • Jan. 5–NHL: Los Angeles 4, Leafs 2; Jan. 8–NHL: Calgary 5, Leafs 3; Jan. 12–NHL: Hartford 2, Leafs 2; Jan. 14–NHL: Buffalo 9, Leafs 3; Jan. 16–Music: Iron Maiden; Jan. 17–NHL: Pittsburgh 6, Leafs 5; Jan. 28–NHL: Minnesota 0, Leafs 4; Feb. 2–NHL: Detroit 5, Leafs 2; Feb. 4–NHL: St. Louis 5, Leafs 6; Feb. 9–NHL: Islanders 2, Leafs 3; Feb. 13–NHL: Flyers 6, Leafs 3; Feb. 14–Music: Neil Young; Feb. 16–NHL: Edmonton 2, Leafs 3; Feb. 27–NHL: New Jersey 3, Leafs 7; Mar. 2–NHL: Rangers 5, Leafs 2; Mar. 5–NHL: Boston 3, Leafs 6; Mar. 7–NHL: Vancouver 3, Leafs 3; Mar. 9–Music: INXS; Mar. 16–NHL: Minnesota 3, Leafs 4; Mar. 21–Music: Vanilla Ice; Mar. 23–NHL: Detroit 1, Leafs 4; Mar. 26–NHL: Chicago 2, Leafs 2; Apr. 13–Music: Reba McEntyre; Sept. 14–Music: Gloria Estefan; Sept. 22–Music: Tom Petty & the Heartbreakers; Oct. 3–Music: Garth Brooks; Oct. 5–NHL: Detroit 5, Leafs 8; Oct. 7–NHL: St. Louis 0, Leafs 3; Oct. 9–NHL: Washington 5, Leafs 4; Oct. 12–NHL: Vancouver 2, Leafs 1; Oct. 22–Music: George Michael; Oct. 24–Music: Queensryche; Oct. 26–NHL: Detroit 1, Leafs 6; Oct. 28–NHL: St. Louis 1, Leafs 1; Nov. 2–NHL: Los Angeles 5, Leafs 2; Nov. 4–NHL: San Jose 1, Leafs 4; Nov. 6–NHL: Minnesota 3, Leafs 4; Nov. 9–NHL: Calgary 6, Leafs 1; Nov. 12–Music: Frank Sinatra; Nov. 14-15–Music: Metallica; Nov. 16–NHL: Chicago 2, Leafs 2; Nov. 17–NHL: Hartford 3, Leafs 1; Nov. 28–Music: Allman Brothers and Little Feat; Nov. 30–NHL: Minnesota 4, Leafs 3; Dec. 7–NHL: Vancouver 3, Leafs 6; Dec. 9–NHL: Canadiens 4, Leafs 1; Dec. 11–NHL: Islanders 5, Leafs 4; Dec. 12–Music: Luther Vandross; Dec. 15–Music: Rush; Dec. 18–NHL: Edmonton 7, Leafs 5; Dec. 21–NHL: Buffalo 4, Leafs 1; Dec. 23–NHL: Winnipeg 1, Leafs 3; Dec. 28–NHL: Detroit 5, Leafs 4; Dec. 31–Music: The Cult with Lenny Kravitz.

1992 • Jan. 4–NHL: Chicago 4, Leafs 2; Jan. 6–NHL: St. Louis 2, Leafs 3; Jan. 16–Music: Bryan Adams; Jan. 22–NHL: Boston 5, Leafs 2; Jan. 25–NHL: Flyers 4, Leafs 6; Jan. 29–NHL: Quebec 2, Leafs 5; Feb. 1–NHL: New Jersey 4, Leafs 6; Feb. 5–NHL: Minnesota 2, Leafs 3; Feb. 8–NHL: Canadiens 4, Leafs 6; Feb. 11–NHL: Detroit 3, Leafs 4; Feb. 15–NHL: Winnipeg 3, Leafs 1; Feb. 16–NHL: Edmonton 5, Leafs 7; Feb. 25–NHL: New Jersey 5, Leafs 5; Feb. 29–NHL: Chicago 5, Leafs 6; Mar. 1–NHL: Minnesota 2, Leafs 6; Mar. 3–Music: Roxette; Mar. 14–NHL: Pittsburgh 3, Leafs 6; Mar. 17–NHL: Quebec 3, Leafs 4; Mar. 19-20–Music: Dire Straits; Mar. 21–NHL: Chicago 3, Leafs 1; Mar. 23–NHL: St. Louis 2, Leafs 3; Mar. 24–Music: U2; Apr. 1–NHL: Islanders, Leafs (postponed due to labour dispute); Apr. 4–NHL: Rangers, Leafs (postponed due to labour dispute); Apr. 12–NHL: Islanders 6, Leafs 2 (make-up game for April 1); Apr. 13–NHL: Rangers 2, Leafs 4 (make-up game for April 4); Sept. 15–Music: Morrissey; Oct. 2–Music: Sam Hui Farewell Concert; Oct. 6–NHL: Washington 6, Leafs 5; Oct. 15–NHL: Tampa Bay 3, Leafs 5; Oct. 17–NHL: Chicago 3, Leafs 4; Oct. 18–NHL: Minnesota 5, Leafs 1; Oct. 21–Music: Def Leppard; Oct. 24–NHL: San Jose 1, Leafs 5; Oct. 28–NHL: Buffalo 4, Leafs 4; Oct. 31–NHL: Detroit 1, Leafs 3; Nov. 6–Music: Billy Ray Cyrus; Nov. 7–NHL: Pittsburgh 2, Leafs 4; Nov. 16–NHL: St. Louis 2, Leafs 2; Nov. 24–NHL: Tampa Bay 3, Leafs 2; Nov. 26–NHL: Quebec 5, Leafs 4; Nov. 28–NHL: Los Angeles 2, Leafs 3; Dec. 1–Music: Ministry; Dec. 5–NHL: Chicago 2, Leafs 2; Dec. 9–NHL: Detroit 3, Leafs 5; Dec. 11–NHL: Calgary 6, Leafs 3; Dec. 19–NHL: Ottawa 1, Leafs 5; Dec. 26–NHL: Detroit 5, Leafs 1.

1993 • Jan. 2–NHL: St. Louis 2, Leafs 2; Jan. 6–NHL: Vancouver 5, Leafs 2; Jan. 8–NHL: San Jose 1, Leafs 5; Jan. 11–NHL: Tampa Bay 2, Leafs 4; Jan. 13–NHL: St. Louis 3, Leafs 4; Jan. 16–NHL: Chicago 5, Leafs 3; Jan. 19–Music: Placido Domingo; Jan. 23–NHL: Canadiens 0, Leafs 4; Jan. 26–NHL: Minnesota 2, Leafs 1; Jan. 30–NHL: Rangers 1, Leafs 3; Feb. 3–NHL: Islanders 3, Leafs 2; Feb. 11–NHL: Vancouver 2, Leafs 5; Feb. 13–NHL: Minnesota 1, Leafs 6; Feb. 17–NHL: Calgary 2, Leafs 4; Feb. 19–NHL: Tampa Bay 1, Leafs 4; Feb. 20–NHL: Boston 4, Leafs 4; Feb. 25–Music: Bon Jovi; Mar. 3–NHL: Minnesota 1, Leafs 3; Mar. 6–NHL: Winnipeg 2, Leafs 4; Mar. 10–NHL: Hartford 3, Leafs 5; Mar. 12–NHL: Tampa Bay 2, Leafs 8; Mar. 20–NHL: Edmonton 2, Leafs 4; Mar. 21–Hockey: Acadia 12, University of Toronto 1 (University Cup '93); Mar. 30–Music: Prince; Mar. 31–NHL: Los Angeles 5, Leafs 5; Apr. 3–NHL: New Jersey 0, Leafs 1; Apr. 10–NHL: Flyers 4, Leafs 0; Apr. 13–NHL: St. Louis 1, Leafs 2; Apr. 23–NHL: Detroit 2, Leafs 4; Apr. 24–Music: Van Morrison; Apr. 25–NHL: Detroit 2, Leafs 3; Apr. 29–NHL: Detroit 7, Leafs 3; May 3–NHL: St. Louis 1, Leafs 2; May 5–NHL: St. Louis 2, Leafs 1; May 11–NHL: St. Louis 1, Leafs 5; May 15–NHL: St. Louis 0, Leafs 6; May 17–NHL: Los Angeles 1, Leafs 4 (Stanley Cup Semi-Finals); May 19–NHL: Los Angeles 3, Leafs 2 (Stanley Cup Semi-Finals); May 25–NHL: Los Angeles 2, Leafs 3 (Stanley Cup Semi-Finals); May 29–NHL: Los Angeles 5, Leafs 4 (Stanley Cup Semi-Finals); June 14-16–Music: Neil Diamond; July 11–World Wrestling Federation; Sept. 22–Music: Lenny Kravitz; Oct. 7–NHL: Dallas 3, Leafs 6; Oct. 9–NHL: Chicago 1, Leafs 2; Oct. 10–CHIN Italian Concert featuring Gianni Morandi; Oct. 13–NHL: Washington 1, Leafs 7; Oct. 15–NHL: Detroit 3, Leafs 6; Oct. 16–Royal Lippizan Stallions; Oct. 19–NHL: Hartford 2, Leafs 7; Oct. 20–Music: Luther Vandross; Oct. 31–World Wrestling Federation; Nov. 3–NHL: Florida 3, Leafs 6; Nov. 4–Music: Nirvana; Nov. 6–NHL: Flyers 3, Leafs 5; Nov. 13–NHL: Chicago 3, Leafs 2; Nov. 14–Variety: Macedonian Independance Day Parade; Nov. 15–NHL: Edmonton 5, Leafs 5; Nov. 27–NHL: Boston 2, Leafs 4; Nov. 29–NHL: Buffalo 3, Leafs 0; Dec. 1–NHL: St. Louis 1, Leafs 4; Dec. 4–NHL: Rangers 4, Leafs 3; Dec. 5–Hockey: Toronto Maple Leafs Skills Challenge; Dec. 8–NHL: Winnipeg 5, Leafs 4; Dec. 11–NHL: Calgary 1, Leafs 3; Dec. 15–NHL: Anaheim 1, Leafs 0; Dec. 17–Tennis: Challenge of Champions; Dec. 18–NHL: Los Angeles 1, Leafs 4; Dec. 22–NHL: San Jose 2, Leafs 2; Dec. 26–World Wrestling Federation.

1994 • Jan. 1–NHL: Los Angeles 7, Leafs 4; Jan. 6–NHL: Ottawa 3, Leafs 6; Jan. 8–NHL: Vancouver 3, Leafs 5; Jan. 13–NHL: Dallas 3, Leafs 4; Jan. 18–NHL: Anaheim 3, Leafs 3; Jan. 22–Music: Billy Joel; Jan. 25–Int'l. Hockey: USA 5, Canada 4; Jan. 26–NHL: Islanders 3, Leafs 4; Jan. 29–NHL: Pittsburgh 4, Leafs 4; Feb. 5–NHL: Detroit 4, Leafs 3; Feb. 7–NHL: Tampa Bay 2, Leafs 1; Feb. 10–Music: Tragically Hip; Feb. 15–NHL: Detroit 4, Leafs 5; Feb. 17–NHL: New Jersey 1, Leafs 2; Feb. 19–NHL: Edmonton 2, Leafs 3; Feb. 20–World Wrestling Federation; Feb. 26–NHL: Canadiens 3, Leafs 0; Mar. 2-6: Dorothy Hamill's Ice Capades; Mar. 7–NHL: St. Louis 3, Leafs 2; Mar. 9–NHL: Dallas 2, Leafs 4; Mar. 11–Music: Rock and Roll All-Stars; Mar. 12–NHL: Winnipeg 1, Leafs 3; Mar. 13–Hockey: Lethbridge 5, Guelph 2

(University Cup '94); Mar. 16–NHL: Vancouver 4, Leafs 1; Mar. 18–NHL: St. Louis 2, Leafs 4; Mar. 20–NHL: Calgary 6, Leafs 3; Mar. 24–NHL: San Jose 2, Leafs 1; Mar. 26–NHL: Quebec 3, Leafs 6; Apr. 10–NHL: Winnipeg 0, Leafs 7; Apr. 12–NHL: Chicago 4, Leafs 3; Apr. 15–Stars on Ice; Apr. 18–NHL: Chicago 1, Leafs 5; Apr. 20–NHL: Chicago 0, Leafs 1; Apr. 26–NHL: Chicago 0, Leafs 1; May 2–NHL: San Jose 3, Leafs 2; May 4–NHL: San Jose 1, Leafs 5; May 7–Music: Rush; May 11–Music: Eros Ramazzotti; May 12–NHL: San Jose 2, Leafs 3; May 14–NHL: San Jose 2, Leafs 4; May 16–NHL: Vancouver 2, Leafs 3 (Stanley Cup Semi-Finals); May 18–NHL: Vancouver 3, Leafs 3 (Stanley Cup Semi-Finals); May 21–Music: Star Night '94; May 29–Music: ZZ Top; June 18–Music: Pantera; June 26–World Wrestling Federation; Aug. 4–World Basketball Championship: Puerto Rico 102, Egypt 74; Aug. 4–World Basketball Championship: Greece 68, Germany 58; Aug. 4–World Basketball Championship: Russia 84, Argentina 64; Aug. 4–World Basketball Championship: Canada 83, Angola 52; Aug. 5–World Basketball Championship: Croatia 104, Korea 53; Australia 93, Cuba 87; Russia 94, Angola 57; Canada 91, Argentina 73; Aug. 6–World Basketball Championship: Cuba 92, Korea 79; Croatia 83, Australia 69; Aug. 7–World Basketball Championship: Puerto Rico 72, Greece 74; Germany 78, Egypt 56; Aug. 8–World Basketball Championship: Croatia 105, China 73; Greece 74, Canada 71; Aug. 9–World Basketball Championship: Russia 101, Puerto Rico 85; USA 130, Australia 74; Aug. 10–World Basketball Championship: Russia 103, Australia 76; USA 134, Puerto Rico 83; Aug. 11–World Basketball Championship: Australia 94, Puerto Rico 81; Canada 90, China 58; Aug. 21–World Wrestling Federation; Sept. 11–Music: Megastars '94; Sept. 23–Ice Show: Elvis Tour of Champions; Oct. 5-6–Music: Eric Clapton; Oct. 23–World Wrestling Federation Hart Attack Tour; Oct. 29–MLG Open House; Nov. 23-27: The Great Moscow Circus; Nov. 28–Music: Meat Loaf; Nov. 29–Ice Show: Torvill & Dean; Dec. 1–Music: Nine Inch Nails; Dec. 10–Basketball: Georgetown Hoyas 83, Memphis Tigers 80.

1995 • Jan. 21–Music: Reggae Superfest; Jan. 25–NHL: Vancouver 2, Leafs 6; Jan. 28–NHL: Calgary 1, Leafs 2; Feb. 4–Music: Megadeth; Feb. 6–NHL: San Jose 3, Leafs 7; Feb. 8–NHL: Dallas 3, Leafs 3; Feb. 10–Music: The Tragically Hip; Feb. 11–NHL: Los Angeles 5, Leafs 2; Feb. 12–Hockey: Oldtimers Hockey; Feb. 13–NHL: Chicago 2, Leafs 4; Feb. 15–NHL: Edmonton 4, Leafs 1; Feb. 18–NHL: St. Louis 1, Leafs 3; Feb. 20–NHL: Detroit 4, Leafs 2; Feb. 23–NHL: Anaheim 1, Leafs 3; Feb. 25–NHL: Winnipeg 2, Leafs 5; Mar. 2–NHL: San Jose 4, Leafs 3; Mar. 4–NHL: Calgary 2, Leafs 3; Mar. 8–NHL: Dallas 2, Leafs 3; Mar. 10–Music: Amy Grant; Mar. 11–NHL: Chicago 2, Leafs 2; Mar. 12–Hockey: Moncton 5, Guelph 1 (University Cup '95); Mar. 13–NHL: Los Angeles 4, Leafs 1; Mar. 16–Music: Black Crowes; Mar. 17–Music: Tom Petty and the Heartbreakers; Mar. 18–World Wrestling Federation; Mar. 24–NHL: Winnipeg 2, Leafs 3; Mar. 27–NHL: Edmonton 3, Leafs 4; Apr. 5–NHL: St. Louis 6, Leafs 4; Apr. 7–NHL: Detroit 4, Leafs 2; Apr. 8–NHL: Winnipeg 3, Leafs 4; Apr. 9–Musical Night '95; Apr. 14–NHL: Dallas 1, Leafs 2; Apr. 19–NHL: Anaheim 2, Leafs 3; Apr. 21-22: Stars On Ice; Apr. 26–NHL: Vancouver 2, Leafs 5; May 11–NHL: Chicago 3, Leafs 2; May 13–NHL: Chicago 3, Leafs 1; May 16–Music: Beastie Boys; May 17–NHL: Chicago 4, Leafs 5; May 20–Variety: Bollywood Megastars; June 25–Music: Van Morrison; Aug. 10–Music: Concerto D'Autunno; Sept. 9–Variety: Madhuri Dixit East Indian Show; Sept. 17–Wrestling; Sept. 29–Ice Show: Elvis Tour of Champions; Oct. 1–Toronto Hospital Fundraiser; Oct. 8–Music: Concerto D'Autunno; Oct. 10–NHL: Islanders 3, Leafs 7; Oct. 14–NHL: Rangers 2, Leafs 0; Oct. 17–NHL: San Jose 2, Leafs 7; Oct. 20–NHL: Calgary 3, Leafs 4; Oct. 24–NHL: Florida 6, Leafs 1; Oct. 25–Music: Green Day; Oct. 28–NHL: Los Angeles 2, Leafs 2; Oct. 29–Hockey: Bell Hockey Clinic; Nov. 3–Music: Tim McGraw and Guests; Nov. 7–NHL: Anaheim 3, Leafs 6; Nov. 10–NHL: Washington 1, Leafs 6; Nov. 12–Variety: Dalla Morandi Italian Show; Nov. 18–NHL: Winnipeg 1, Leafs 2; Nov. 21–NHL: St. Louis 2, Leafs 5; Nov. 24–NHL: Hartford 4, Leafs 0; Dec. 2–NHL: Anaheim 4, Leafs 4; Dec. 3–Bobby Orr Skate-a-thon; Dec. 4–Q107 Charity Skate; Dec. 5–NHL: Ottawa 1, Leafs 4; Dec. 9–NHL: Dallas 1, Leafs 3; Dec. 11–NHL: Avalanche 5, Leafs 1; Dec. 17–Royal LePage Charity Skate; Dec. 20–NHL: Chicago 4, Leafs 2; Dec. 23–NHL: Edmonton 1, Leafs 6.

1996 • Jan. 3–NHL: Boston 4, Leafs 4; Jan. 6–NHL: Avalanche 2, Leafs 5; Jan. 7–Hockey: NHL Superskills Competition; Jan. 10–NHL: Los Angeles 4, Leafs 5; Jan. 13–NHL: Vancouver 5, Leafs 2; Jan. 17–NHL: Winnipeg 4, Leafs 2; Jan. 24–NHL: Chicago 2, Leafs 2; Jan. 31–NHL: St. Louis 4, Leafs 0; Feb. 3–NHL: Canadiens 4, Leafs 1; Feb. 6–Music: Lenny Kravitz (originally scheduled for Dec. 30/95); Feb. 10–NHL: Buffalo 2, Leafs 2; Feb. 11–Hockey: Minor Hockey Festival; Feb. 12–NHL: Pittsburgh 1, Leafs 4; Feb. 14–NHL: San Jose 3, Leafs 4; Feb. 15–Jr. Hockey: CHL Chrysler Cup; Feb. 16–Upper Canada College; Feb. 17–Oldtimers Hockey; Feb. 18–NHL: Detroit 3, Leafs 2; Feb. 21–NHL: Tampa Bay 3, Leafs 2; Feb. 24–NHL: Dallas 3, Leafs 2; Mar. 4–Public School Hockey; Mar. 6–NHL: New Jersey 2, Leafs 2; Mar. 8–Music: Bob Seger; Mar. 9–NHL: Calgary 3, Leafs 4; Mar. 10–Hockey: Acadia 3, Waterloo 2 (University Cup '96); Mar. 12–Metro Jr. Blues Hockey; Mar. 13–NHL: Winnipeg 3, Leafs 3; Mar. 15–NHL: Dallas 0, Leafs 3; Mar. 17–NHL: Vancouver 2, Leafs 4; Mar. 18–Music: Melissa Etheridge; Mar. 19–Parks & Recreation Hockey; Mar. 20–NHL: Detroit 3, Leafs 4; Mar. 23–NHL: Flyers 4, Leafs 0; Mar. 31–Hockey: Timmy Tyke Tournament; Apr. 3–NHL: Chicago 5, Leafs 2; Apr. 6–NHL: St. Louis 1, Leafs 5; Apr. 11–Hockey: Separate Schools Hockey; Apr. 13–NHL: Edmonton 3, Leafs 6; Apr. 14–Music: Concerto Di Primavera; Apr. 15–Music: R. Kelly; Apr. 16–NHL: St. Louis 3, Leafs 1; Apr. 18–NHL: St. Louis 4, Leafs 5; Apr. 19-20: Stars On Ice; Apr. 25–NHL: St. Louis 4, Leafs 5; Apr. 28–Rangeele Dilwale Concert; June 29–Variety: Garden Party IV; June 30–MCCT Church Service; Aug. 14–Music: Smashing Pumpkins; Aug. 21–Music: Pearl Jam; Aug. 27–Music: Blue Rodeo; Oct. 5–NHL: Anaheim 1, Leafs 4; Oct. 8–NHL: Edmonton 4, Leafs 2; Oct. 12–NHL: Tampa Bay 7, Leafs 4; Oct. 14–Ice Show: Elvis Tour of Champions; Oct. 15–NHL: Chicago 3, Leafs 1; Oct. 22–NHL: San Jose 3, Leafs 4; Oct. 26–NHL: Phoenix 2, Leafs 5; Oct. 29–NHL: Los Angeles 5, Leafs 2; Nov. 1–Soccer: Toronto Shooting Stars; Nov. 2–NHL: Detroit 2, Leafs 6; Nov. 5–NHL: St. Louis 3, Leafs 6; Nov. 9–NHL: Edmonton 3, Leafs 7; Nov. 19–NHL: Buffalo 3, Leafs 4; Nov. 23–NHL: Canadiens 4, Leafs 3; Nov. 26–NHL: Vancouver 2, Leafs 3; Dec. 3–NHL: St. Louis 0, Leafs 2; Dec. 6–Soccer: Toronto Shooting Stars; Dec. 7–NHL: Rangers 4, Leafs 0; Dec. 8–Soccer: Toronto Shooting Stars; Dec. 10–NHL: New Jersey 5, Leafs 2; Dec. 12-13–Music: The Tragically Hip; Dec. 14–NHL: Phoenix 5, Leafs 3; Dec. 15–Soccer: Toronto Shooting Stars; Dec. 18–Q107 Kids Fund Skating Party; Dec. 22–Soccer: Toronto Shooting Stars; Dec. 23–NHL: Pittsburgh 6, Leafs 5; Dec. 28–NHL: Chicago 4, Leafs 5; Dec. 29–Soccer: Toronto Shooting Stars; Dec. 30–NHL: Islanders 0, Leafs 2.

1997 • Jan. 3–Soccer: Toronto Shooting Stars; Jan. 11–NHL: Avalanche 3, Leafs 2; Jan. 15–NHL: Los Angeles 3, Leafs 2; Jan. 17–Hockey: Upper Canada College; Jan. 18–Soccer: Toronto Shooting Stars; Jan. 18–Soccer Association 3-on-3 Finals; Jan. 19–Soccer: Toronto Shooting Stars; Jan. 19–Soccer Association 3-on-3 Finals; Jan. 22–NHL: Calgary 3, Leafs 5; Jan. 25–NHL: Dallas 5, Leafs 1; Jan. 26–Soccer: Toronto Shooting Stars; Jan. 27–NHL: Avalanche 5, Leafs 2; Jan. 29–NHL: St. Louis 4, Leafs 0; Jan. 31–Soccer: Toronto Shooting Stars; Feb. 1–NHL: Ottawa 2, Leafs 1; Feb. 2–Soccer: Toronto Shooting Stars; Feb. 5–NHL: Anaheim 2, Leafs 4; Feb. 7–Oldtimers Hockey; Feb. 8–NHL: Vancouver 2, Leafs 4; Feb. 9–Hockey: Maple Leafs Superskills Competition; Feb. 12–Jr. Hockey: CHL Chrysler Cup; Feb. 14–Basketball: Milwaukee 106, Raptors 102; Feb. 15–Basketball: Toronto Raptors Open Practice; Feb. 16–Basketball: Detroit 92, Raptors 89; Feb. 21–Soccer: Toronto Shooting Stars; Feb. 26–NHL: Washington 3, Leafs 1; Feb. 27–Hockey: Public School Hockey; Feb. 28–Soccer: Toronto Shooting Stars; Mar. 1–NHL: San Jose 2, Leafs 3; Mar. 3–NHL: Boston 2, Leafs 4; Mar. 5–NHL: Detroit 4, Leafs 4; Mar. 8–NHL: Hartford 1, Leafs 1; Mar. 9–Soccer: Toronto Shooting Stars; Mar. 10–NHL: Dallas 3, Leafs 3; Mar. 12–NHL: Chicago 3, Leafs 2; Mar. 15–Ice Capades; Mar. 17–Hockey: New Brunswick 3, Guelph 4 (University Cup '97); Mar. 18–Basketball: Philadelphia 105, Raptors 117; Mar. 19–NHL: Flyers 6, Leafs 3; Mar. 22–NHL: Phoenix 3, Leafs 0; Mar. 23–Hockey: Timmy Tyke Tournament; Mar. 26–Parks & Recreation Hockey; Mar. 29–Music: Backstreet Boys; Mar. 31–Metro Jr. Blues Hockey; Apr. 1–Separate Schools Hockey; Apr. 2–NHL: Florida 1, Leafs 3; Apr. 5–NHL: Detroit 4, Leafs 2; Apr. 12–NHL: Calgary 1, Leafs 4; Apr. 13–Variety: Punjabi Super Show; Apr. 14–Baycrest Centre Charity Skate; Apr. 17–Music: Bush X; Apr. 18-19: Stars On Ice; May 4-5: Lord of the Dance; May 12–Music: No Doubt; June 1–Mega Stars East Indian Concert; June 7–Hockey: OHL Priority Draft; June 15–Music: Tunes of Glory Militay Tattoo; June 29–MCCT Church Service; Sept. 19–Ice Show: Elvis Tour of Champions; Sept. 28–Hockey: Team Canada '72 Reunion; Oct. 1–NHL: Washington 4, Leafs 1; Oct. 6–Metro All Affiliates Teacher Info Meeting; Oct. 14–NHL: Detroit 3, Leafs 2; Oct. 18–NHL: Dallas 5, Leafs 3; Oct. 19–Jr. Hockey: Ottawa 4, St. MIchael's 0; Oct. 22–NHL: Ottawa 6, Leafs 2; Oct. 25–NHL: Calgary 3, Leafs 4; Oct. 28–NHL: Anaheim 2, Leafs 2; Nov. 1–Hollywoof Dog Show; Nov. 7–Hockey for the Homeless; Nov. 8–NHL: Phoenix 3, Leafs 0; Nov. 9–Music: Andre Rieu; Nov. 11–NHL: Chicago 2, Leafs 5; Nov. 15–NHL: Pittsburgh 5, Leafs 0; Nov. 17–NHL: St. Louis 3, Leafs 2; Nov. 19–NHL: Flyers 1, Leafs 3; Nov. 25–NHL: San Jose 1, Leafs 3; Nov. 29–NHL: Vancouver 4, Leafs 2; Dec. 2–NHL: Anaheim 3, Leafs 3; Dec. 6–NHL: Los Angeles 2, Leafs 7; Dec. 7–Bell/Leafs Easter Seals Skate; Dec. 8–NHL: Dallas 0, Leafs 3; Dec. 10–NHL: Avalanche 2, Leafs 2; Dec. 13–NHL: New Jersey 3, Leafs 0; Dec. 23–NHL: Edmonton 4, Leafs 5; Dec. 27–NHL: Detroit 8, Leafs 1; Dec. 30–Big Brothers Dream Camp; Dec. 31–NHL: Boston 2, Leafs 2.

1998 • Jan. 1-4: The Giant Holiday Circus; Jan. 10–NHL: Chicago 4, Leafs 3; Jan. 14–NHL: Buffalo 4, Leafs 1; Jan. 15–Music: Oasis; Jan. 17–Music: Our Lady Peace; Jan. 18–Jr. Hockey: Guelph 5, St. Michael's 3; Jan. 24–NHL: Tampa Bay 2, Leafs 5; Jan. 31–NHL: Phoenix 5, Leafs 2; Feb. 1–Jr. Hockey: Sault Ste Marie 2, St. Michael's 3; Feb. 2–NHL: Dallas 5, Leafs 1; Feb. 4–NHL: St. Louis 2, Leafs 3; Feb. 7–NHL: Florida 2, Leafs 3; Feb. 8–Hockey: Oldtimers Hockey; Feb. 10–Jr. Hockey: CHL Chrysler Cup; Feb. 13–Music: Bryan Adams; Feb. 20–Jr. Hockey: Barrie 4, St. Michael's 1; Feb. 21–Hockey: Maple Leafs Superskills Competition; Feb. 22–Jr. Hockey: Sarnia 4, St. Michael's 1; Feb. 25–Black Watch and Scots Guard Pipe Bands; Feb. 26–NHL: Rangers 5, Leafs 2; Feb. 28–NHL: Canadiens 0, Leafs 4; Mar. 4–NHL: Avalanche 5, Leafs 3; Mar. 7–NHL: Edmonton 1, Leafs 4; Mar. 14–NHL: Calgary 1, Leafs 2; Mar. 18–NHL: Detroit 5, Leafs 2; Mar. 20–Music: The Shaolin Monks; Mar. 21–NHL: Vancouver 1, Leafs 1; Mar. 28–NHL: Islanders 3, Leafs 4; Mar. 30–NHL: Los Angeles 3, Leafs 2; Mar. 31–Basketball: Los Angeles 114, Raptors 105; Apr. 1–NHL: St. Louis 6, Leafs 4; Apr. 2–Music: Andre Rieu; Apr. 3–Music: Eros Ramazzotti; Apr. 4–NHL: San Jose 5, Leafs 3; Apr. 11–NHL: Carolina 5, Leafs 2; Apr. 12–Music: Radiohead; Apr. 15–NHL: Chicago 2, Leafs 3; Apr. 18–Music: Megastars; Apr. 19–Basketball: Philadelphia 107, Raptors 78; Sept. 6–South Asian Concert; Sept. 24–Jr. Hockey: Ottawa 6, St. Michael's 3; Oct. 2–Jr. Hockey: Owen Sound 9, St. Michael's 4; Oct. 4–Jr. Hockey: Belleville 6, St. Michael's 6; Oct. 8–Jr. Hockey: North Bay 1, St. Michael's 1; Oct. 10–NHL: Detroit 1, Leafs 2 (final visit by the Red Wings and final Leaf home opener in the Gardens); Oct. 11–Jr. Hockey: Kingston 3, St. Michael's 2; Oct. 18–Jr. Hockey: Guelph 4, St. Michael's 3; Oct. 19–NHL: Nashville 2, Leafs 2; Oct. 22–Jr. Hockey: Barrie 6, St. Michael's 2; Oct. 25–Jr. Hockey: Kitchener 4, St. Michael's 3; Oct. 26–NHL: Pittsburgh 2, Leafs 0; Oct. 27–Music: Joni Mitchell and Bob Dylan; Oct. 31–NHL: Buffalo 6, Leafs 3; Nov. 1–Jr. Hockey: Erie 3, St. Michael's 9; Nov. 4–NHL: Avalanche 0, Leafs 3; Nov. 6–Jr. Hockey: Sudbury 6, St. Michael's 6; Nov. 7–NHL: Rangers 6, Leafs 6; Nov. 9–NHL: Islanders 3, Leafs 1; Nov. 11–NHL: Edmonton 2, Leafs 3; Nov. 12–Jr. Hockey: Sault Ste Marie 4, St. Michael's 2; Nov. 14–NHL: Ottawa 1, Leafs 2; Nov. 15–Music: Neil Diamond; Nov. 20–Ice Show: Elvis Tour of Champions; Nov. 21–Jr. Hockey: Mississauga 1, St. Michael's 6; Nov. 21–NHL: Buffalo 1, Leafs 2; Nov. 22–Jr. Hockey: Kingston 3, St. Michael's 6; Nov. 23–NHL: Calgary 2, Leafs 3; Nov. 25–NHL: Vancouver 1, Leafs 5; Nov. 28–Jr. Hockey: Barrie 3, St. Michael's 2; Nov. 28–NHL: Ottawa 2, Leafs 3; Nov. 29–Jr. Hockey: Mississauga 1, St. Michael's 4; Dec. 2–NHL: Los Angeles 1, Leafs 3; Dec. 4–Jr. Hockey: Oshawa 3, St. Michael's 3; Dec. 6–Jr. Hockey: Peterborough 9, St. Michael's 1; Dec. 10–Jr. Hockey: London 8, St. Michael's 5; Dec. 12–NHL: Flyers 3, Leafs 0; Dec. 13–Skate for Easter Seals; Dec. 16–NHL: Phoenix 2, Leafs 5; Dec. 17–Jr. Hockey: Barrie 7, St. Michael's 3; Dec. 19–NHL: Rangers 4, Leafs 7 (final visit by the Rangers and Wayne Gretzky to the Gardens); Dec. 20–Jr. Hockey: Windsor 5, St. Michael's 8; Dec. 21–NHL: Pittsburgh 1, Leafs 7; Dec. 23–NHL: Dallas 5, Leafs 1; Dec. 26–NHL: Canadiens 2, Leafs 1 (final visit by the Canadiens to the Gardens); Dec. 27-28: Giant Holiday Circus; Dec. 30–NHL: Anaheim 1, Leafs 4.

1999 • Jan. 2–NHL: Washington 5, Leafs 2; Jan. 3–Jr. Hockey: Belleville vs. St. Michael's; Jan. 4–NHL: Tampa Bay 4, Leafs 5; Jan. 9–NHL: Boston vs. Leafs (final visit by the Bruins to the Gardens); Jan. 10–Hockey: Maple Leafs Superskills Competition; Jan. 10–Jr. Hockey: Erie vs. St. Michael's; Jan. 15–Jr. Hockey: North Bay vs. St. Michael's; Jan. 17–Jr. Hockey: Peterborough vs. St. Michael's; Jan. 22–Lacrosse: Toronto Rock vs. Buffalo Bandits; Jan. 28–Jr. Hockey: Brampton vs. St. Michael's; Jan. 29–Lacrosse: Toronto Rock vs. Rochester Nighthawks; Jan. 30–NHL: Washington vs. Leafs; Jan. 31–Jr. Hockey: Sudbury vs. St. Michael's; Feb. 6–Public Skate and Open House; Feb. 10–NHL: Carolina vs. Leafs; Feb. 13–NHL: Chicago vs. Leafs (final visit by the Blackhawks and final Leaf game in the Gardens); Feb. 14–Jr. Hockey: Ottawa vs. St. Michael's; Feb. 18–Jr. Hockey: Plymouth vs. St. Michael's; Feb. 19–Lacrosse: Toronto Rock vs. Philadelphia Wings; Feb. 21–Jr. Hockey: Sarnia vs. St. Michael's; Feb. 25–Jr. Hockey: Sudbury vs. St. Michael's; Feb. 26–Lacrosse: Toronto Rock vs. New York Saints; Feb. 28–Jr. Hockey: Mississauga vs. St. Michael's; Mar. 12–Jr. Hockey: North Bay vs. St. Michael's; Mar. 19–Jr. Hockey: Oshawa vs. St. Michael's; Mar. 26–Lacrosse: Toronto Rock vs. Syracuse Smash; Apr. 2–Lacrosse: Toronto Rock vs. Baltimore Thunder.

INDEX

Toronto Skating Club Carnival

ACKNOWLEDGEMENTS

Matt Akler, Maple Leafs Sports & Entertainment Ltd.; Mike Alexander, London, Ontario; Mike Allder, Mississauga, Ontario; Jim Amodeo, Scarborough, Ontario; Dr. John T. Axler, Toronto;

Paul M. Barron, Pickering, Ontario; Ruth-Ann Gilpin Beck, Toronto; Rob Belyea, Ft. McMurray, Alberta; Joe Black, Things & Thoughts Inc.; Joe Blake, Nobleton, Ontario; Jack Blum, Toronto; Alan Boccinfuso, Oshawa, Ontario; Dick Bosher, Ancaster, Ontario; Emily Bradshaw, Toronto; Babe Brown, Oshawa, Ontario; Dave Brown, Toronto; Bob Buchkowsky, Perkinsfield, Ontario;

Gage Campbell, Georgetown, Ontario; Craig Campbell, Hockey Hall of Fame; Debbie Chevarie, Canada's Sports Hall of Fame; Ann Clark, Toronto Maple Leafs; Anna Condra, Scott Library Special Collections; Sharon Corder, Toronto; Darren Cudmore, Toronto; Adolf Curtis Jr., Richmond Hill, Ontario;

Brad Dix, Toronto;

Craig Falkowski, Sherwood Park, Alberta; Sheila Ferber, Toronto; Michael S. Fells, Toronto; Fraser Firth, Toronto; Peter Fleming, Kingston, Ontario; Peter Fillman, St. Michael's Majors; Bob Forsey, St.John's, Newfoundland; Elsa Franklin, Toronto; Norman B. Fraser, North York, Ontario;

Brian Giandomenico, London, Ontario; Sally Gibson, Metro Toronto Archives; Wanda Goodwin, Toronto Sun Syndicate; Barbara Goncalves, Etobicoke, Ontario; Phil Greenwood, Sherwood Park, Alberta; Gary Groleau, Burlington, Ontario; Andrea Guerriero, Toronto;

Jim Hagen, British Columbia Lacrosse Association; Frank Hallarn, Ottawa, Ontario; B. Henderson, Winnipeg, Manitoba; Donna Henderson, Toronto Maple Leafs; Rick Henry, Port Perry, Ontario; Ed Hillier, Peterborough, Ontario; Valerie Hochschild, Toronto; Richard D. Howell, Toronto; David J. Hrynkiw, Vankleek Hill, Ontario; Margaret Hurd, Toronto;

Derek Jackson, Brandon, Manitoba; Les Jones, The Soccer Hall of Fame and Museum; Colin Jose, The Soccer Hall of Fame and Museum;

George Kapasky Whitby, Ontario; Allan Kimpton, Ottawa, Ontario; Terry A. King, Cannifton, Ontario; Jack Kirk, Scarborough, Ontario;

Christine Lombardi, CHIN Radio;

John MacCallum, Toronto; Doug MacLellan, Toronto; Steve MacKinnon, City of Toronto Archives; Lucy Manni, CHIN Radio; Don Manson, Toronto; Ron Marr, Sicamous, B.C.; Clive Marsh, Calgary, Alberta; Bill Masters, Courtice, Ontario; Anne-Marie Maugeri, Willowdale, Ontario; Kyle McCutcheon, Caledon East, Ontario; Don McMullen, Osgoode, Ontario; Gary Meagher,

National Hockey League; Herb Morell, Ontario Hockey League; John Mungham, Woodbridge, Ontario; Paul Myers, San Francisco;

Jim Nichol, Nanaimo, B.C.; Art Nickel, Molson Breweries; Ron Oldridge, Victoria, B.C.;

Paul S. Perantinos, Toronto Maple Leafs; Jay Perera, Niagara Falls, Ontario; Don Peterson, Banff, Alberta; Matt Phillips, New Westminster, B.C.;

Bruce Richards, Oakville, Ontario; Cindy Ross, Toronto Maple Leafs; Stavros Rougas, Brantford, Ontario; Bill Rowell, Cornwall, PEI;

Dan Samoyloff, Oshawa, Ontario; Wayne Scott, Toronto; Peter Skopec, Toronto; Mary Speck, Toronto Maple Leafs; Alan Stewart, Canada's Sports Hall of Fame; Rob Stewart, Brampton, Ontario; Al Stortz, Welland, Ontario;

Ukrainian World Congress;

Alexander Vance, London, Ontario; Casey Vanden Heuvel, Toronto Maple Leafs; Tony Vieira, Toronto;

Judy Watson, Pickering, Ontario; Murray Westgate, Toronto; Brenda Whiteway, Scarborough, Ontario; Paul Wilburn, Surrey, B.C.; Tom and Tiffany Williams, Trenton, Ontario;

James Yee, Toronto.

A special thank you to Stafford Graphics, Toronto, and Transcontinental Printing, Montreal and Toronto.

PHOTO CREDITS

Archives of Ontario – Conn Smythe Collection: 57, 148 (top), 247 (bottom), 248, 263, 267 (top);

Archives of Ontario – LeBourdais Collection: 25, 33, 162 (bottom right);

Athletics Canada: 137, 138, 140, Claus Andersen 144, Allsport/Gray Mortimore 145;

Harold Barkley: 94, 96, 101, 119, 120, 121 (top), 122, 126, 127, 130, 133, 147, 149, 186, 277, 298;

Cathy Bidini: 194, 199, 200;

Bruce Bennett Studios: 209, 325, 334, 335;

Joe Black – Graphic Artists: 28, 35, 42, 43, 68 (top), 69 (bottom), 70, 71, 72 (top inset), 75 (bottom), 95, 114, 118, 128-129, 206, 208, 215, 283, 285, 287, 300, 309;

Michael Burns Photography: 150, 151, 158 (top right);

Canada's Sports Hall of Fame: 6, 7, 18, 24, 104, 110, 113, 141, 234-235, 243, 247 (top), 259;

CANAPRESS: 281, 293;

CHIN Radio Collection: 80, 81;

David Crighton: 195;

Dan Diamond and Associates: 52, 73 (inset), 90, 93, 98, 158 (left), 182, 187-189, 211, 289, 317;

Faculty of Physical Education and Health, University of Toronto: 139;

Dan Hamilton: 214;

Hockey Hall of Fame – File photo: endpapers, viii-1, 2-3, 47, 121 (bottom) 228, 229, 231, 232 (top), 237, 246; Graphic Artists Collection: 23, 123, 124-125, 134, 135, 153, 190, 193, 284, 290, 294-296, 301, 304, 307, 311, 312; Doug MacLellan Collection: 324, 326, 329; O-Pee-Chee Collection: 306; Obodiac Scrapbooks: 233, 245; Frank Prazak Collection: 131, 132, 148 (middle), 313; Program Collection: ii, 13, 14, 19, 22, 31, 32, 36, 38, 46, 48, 53, 54, 56; Dave Sandford Collection: 202, 204-205, 210, 227; Imperial Oil Turofsky Collection: i, 21, 92, 97, 100, 184, 185, 232 (bottom), 250-251, 258, 260, 265, 266, 267 (bottom), 278;

Leo Harrison: 160, 276;

John Hartman: 212;

Bruce Kidd Collection: 136;

Luftspring Family Collection: 242;

Maple Leaf Gardens Archives: 58-63, 84, 152, 156-157, 377;

NK Video and Photography: 332;

Norton Family Collection: 51;

Pro Wrestling Illustrated: 102, 106;

City of Toronto Archives: endpapers, iv, 4, 8, 9, 11, 12, 15, 26, 44, 49, 64-67, 68 (bottom), 78, 79, 82, 83, 88-89, 105, 155, 158 (bottom), 159, 173, 236, 238, 239, 241, 244, 249, 245, 255-257, 270-272, 274; City of Toronto Archives – TTC Collection: vi-vii, 148 (bottom);

Toronto Star: K. Beaty 72 (bottom inset), T. Boch 76 (top); R. Bull 77 (middle right); D. Cooper 39, D. Davies 308; K. Faught 320; file photo 72-73; F. Lennon 74, 142, 143, 315; D. Griffin 314, P. Power 77 (bottom); F. Ross 303; M. Slaughter 77 (middle right); B. Spremo, C.M. 34, 76 (bottom right), M. Stupanyk 75 (top); F. Teskey 69 (top)

Toronto Sun Syndicate: 30, 37, 40, 41, 86, 87, 154, 162 (top left, top right, bottom right), 163 (top right, bottom left, bottom right), 164-169, 172, 173, 175, 177, 180, 181, 197, 230, 240, 252, 273, 279, 288, 292, 302, 310, 316, 318, 319, 321, 322, 323, 327, 328, 330, 331, 333

Toronto Telegram Archives, York University: 16, 17, 29, 55, 76 (bottom left), 77 (top left), 85, 117, 163 (top right), 170-171, 178, 253, 262, 264, 268, 269, 280, 282, 286, 291, 297, 299

Stanley Turner, A.R.C.A., O. S. A.: 375

Peter Wilton: 336-341;

World Wrestling Federation: 103, 107, 109.

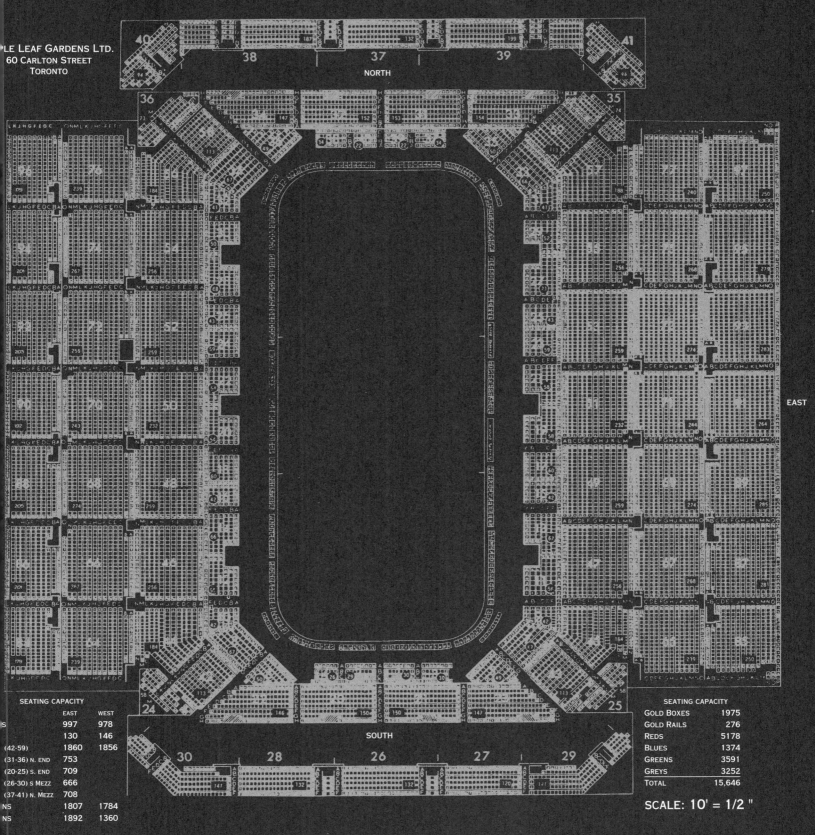

PLE LEAF GARDENS LTD.
60 CARLTON STREET
TORONTO

NORTH

EAST

SOUTH

SEATING CAPACITY		
	EAST	WEST
S	997	978
	130	146
(42-59)	1860	1856
(31-36) N. END	753	
(20-25) S. END	709	
(26-30) S MEZZ	666	
(37-41) N. MEZZ	708	
NS	1807	1784
NS	1892	1360

SEATING CAPACITY	
GOLD BOXES	1975
GOLD RAILS	276
REDS	5178
BLUES	1374
GREENS	3591
GREYS	3252
TOTAL	15,646

SCALE: 10' = 1/2 "

MAPLE LEAF GARDENS SEATING PLAN